Ca... ...*ation*

A Book of Readings

McGRAW-HILL CATHOLIC SERIES IN EDUCATION

Bernard J. Kohlbrenner, Consulting Editor

Catholic
Education

A Book of Readings

Edited by

Walter B. Kolesnik
Professor of Education
University of Detroit

Edward J. Power
Professor of Education
Boston College

McGraw-Hill Book Company
New York   St. Louis   San Francisco
Toronto   London   Sydney

Catholic Education: A Book of Readings

Preface

Well-informed Catholics today are vitally interested in the multiple issues surrounding education. This is indeed fortunate, for there are few, if any, subjects more important to the future of the Church in America and few areas in which the problems are more pressing. These problems are of two types: general educational problems which confront any kind of school or teacher or parent, and particular problems which are of special concern to Catholic schools or parents or teachers. Examples of the general are motivation, discipline, interests, and individual differences in mental ability. Examples of the particular are the teaching of religion; the administration and financing of parochial schools; the weighing of responsibility for education and its subsequent assignment to the Church, the family, and the state; and the rationale for the continuation of a Catholic school system as it is presently constituted.

This book is a compilation of fifty-four selections, each of which reflects *a*—not *the*—Catholic point of view on the kinds of problems identified above. The indefinite article is stressed because in the subjects dealt with there is no single position universally held by all Catholic educators. As a matter of fact, as some of the essays bring out, competent teachers and writers, considering certain problems against the same background of Catholic theology and philosophy, can and often do arrive at sharply different conclusions. The selections are intended to familiarize the reader with some of these conclusions and to facilitate his forming conclusions of his own. This would seem to be a sound way to approach any complex issue on which it is important to have a personal opinion. For dichotomatic purposes and also for alerting the reader to some of the more salient points raised, a series of questions, which might also be used to stimulate individual thinking or group discussions, are posed at the beginnings of the chapters.

The bulk of the selections are taken from professional periodicals or specialized publications which might easily have escaped the attention of the most avid reader. This anthology, then, will enable one to read at his leisure, and without having to search out or carry around scores of bound volumes, articles to which he might not otherwise have ready access. The articles will expose him directly to a diversity of interpretations or recommendations in the words of the original writer, instead of having them filtered through the prose of a commentator. With rare exceptions the selections are reprinted in their entirety. The omissions which do occur are in no instance substantial nor do they in any way modify the author's stated position.

The period from which the articles were drawn covers more than a century; the first article, by Orestes Brownson, was written in 1862 and devotes attention to issues which have a certain freshness about them, issues both persistent and tantalizing. A few were written in 1964 and therefore reflect not only Catholic thinking on contemporary questions in Catholic education but current Catholic thinking. Between these boundary years, 1862 and 1964, Catholic commentators have reflected on and discussed a number of important questions; some of these questions are still being asked and answered. For this reason the first part deals with perennial problems in Catholic education, while the second deals with current problems and criticisms of Catholic education. Not only these two parts but the six which follow try to illustrate some of the metamorphoses in Catholic educational theory. Not everything is new, but neither is everything old. Both educational thought and practice are viable items in human experience. We hope through the choice of articles in this anthology to make this apodictically clear. In view of this broad coverage and the criterion of selection, this anthology may be read with profit by prospective teachers, experienced in-service teachers, school administrators, parents, clergymen, or members of the general public who wish to be informed about recent developments in Catholic educational theory and practice, and who wish to know something of the evolution of these theories and practices which in many quarters today are being so carefully scrutinized and so widely debated.

No one, of course, will be completely satisfied with the judgments made relative to selections for this book. It may even be fair to say that the editors themselves are not completely satisfied. In certain of the chapters some of the articles may be somewhat too technical to interest the general readership we visualize; others may be regarded as too popular for the same clientele. Our hope is that such defects, to the extent that they are real, will cancel out one another and that the majority of selections will serve to inform and stimulate the thinking of those who read them. Hundreds of articles were examined and seriously considered, and among them many fine and perceptive articles had to be excluded either because they dealt with questions outside the ambit of this book, because they restated basic positions already represented by other authors, or simply in order to keep the book portable. Some of the articles not included undoubtedly have merits lacking in some of those selected. There is no necessary implication, then, that the articles included here are in any sense the best, or that in some precise way they contain statements bordering on the definitive, but they do deal with educational questions in such a way as to bring out points on debated, many-sided issues. Despite questions that may be raised concerning the comparative merits of articles, and the unwillingness of the editors to be drawn into any contest of better or best, it is the editors' opinion that a careful reading of any of the articles included will be beneficial for persons genuinely interested in Catholic education.

We should like to acknowledge our indebtedness and gratitude to the authors of the selections included and to *America, Ave Maria, The Catholic Charities Review, The Catholic Counselor, The Catholic Educational Review, The Catholic Educator, The Catholic World, Educational Theory, Fordham Law Review, The Jesuit Educational Quarterly, Journal of Genetic Psychology, Lumen Vitae, National Catholic Education Association Bulletin, National Catholic Education Association Proceedings, Personnel and Guidance Journal, Review of Politics, Social Justice, Social Order, Thought,* The American Catholic Psychological Association, The Catholic University of America Press, and A. C. McClurg & Co., for permission to reprint these selections.

Walter B. Kolesnik
Edward J. Power

Contents

part i

Perennial issues
in Catholic education

QUESTIONS TO GUIDE YOUR READING

*1. Which of Brownson's main points are valid only in their
historical context? Which are relevant to the problems of Catholic
education today?*

*2. How do you think Bishop Spalding would reply to the allegation
commonly being made today that higher education is "wasted" on
wives and mothers who never have a chance to "use" it?*

*3. Explain why you do or do not agree with Cogley that the
four marks of the Church can be used as criteria for evaluating
Catholic schools.*

*4. What changes, if any, do you think Father Shields would make
in his article if he were writing it today?*

*5. What is social pluralism? Why is social pluralism an obstacle
to political and educational freedom? Or is it an obstacle?*

*6. Indicate any assertions Father Weigel makes which, in your
judgment, he does not substantiate. Which, if any, of his remarks do you
disagree with? Which of his points do you consider the most striking?*

*7. Evaluate the various possibilities discussed by Mullaney for
reconciling the rights of the parents and the state in education.*

Catholic schools and education

Orestes A. Brownson

Orestes Brownson, a prominent journalist and controversialist of the nineteenth century, became a Catholic in 1844, and almost at once began to analyze the role of the Church and the stature of Catholics in American life. In the following article he stresses the need for generously distributed educational opportunities for all Americans and examines some of the reasons prompting the American Catholic hierarchy to establish a separate parochial system of education for Catholic children. On the latter point his discussion is two dimensional: What are the fundamental bases of Catholic education? And, why do some Catholics refuse to support Catholic schools when they are established? The article deals with a variety of issues in the theory of Catholic education which are still discussed today.

The importance of education in general needs in no sense to be dwelt on in our country, for no people are or can be more alive to its utility and even necessity than are the American people, especially in the non-Slaveholding States; and no people have, upon the whole, made more liberal provisions for its general diffusion. There would seem to be just as little need of dwelling on the importance and necessity of Catholic schools and Catholic education for our Catholic population. All Catholics feel, or should feel, that education, either under the point of view of religion or of civilization, is useful and desirable no further than it is Catholic. Catholic truth is universal truth, is all truth, and no education not in

Reprinted from *Brownson's Quarterly Review*, 3:66–85, January, 1862.

accordance with it is or can be a true or a useful education, for error is never useful, but always more or less hurtful. Every Catholic, then, indeed every man who loves truth and wishes to conform to it, must be in favor of Catholic schools and Catholic education, if they are Catholic in reality as well as in name.

So believing, our bishops and clergy, supported by various Religious Communities, have lost no time in making the imposing effort to provide under their own direction schools, academies, colleges, and universities for all our Catholic children and youth. They have felt the necessity of giving our children a Catholic education, as the best and surest way of securing their temporal and spiritual welfare, of promoting Catholic interests, and of converting this whole country to the Catholic faith. Yet, strangely enough, they are very far from receiving the hearty and undivided support of our whole Catholic community. Great dissatisfaction has been expressed, and in quarters entitled to respect, with our colleges and female academies, and not a few whose love of Catholicity and devotion to the Church cannot be questioned, refuse to join in the movements for parochial schools, or the establishment of separate schools for our children under the care of our clergy. Whence comes this division of sentiment? Whence comes it that our colleges and conventual schools do not meet the unanimous approbation of Catholic parents and guardians? Whence comes it that so many amongst us prefer the public schools of the country to schools conducted by Catholics? What is the explanation of these facts? How are they to be accounted for? If these schools, whether for the higher or the lower branches of education, are really Catholic, and educate throughout in accordance with Catholic truth, how should it be possible that honest and intelligent Catholics should differ among themselves as to the policy of establishing them, or that any should hesitate to give them their cordial support? These are questions which need and must receive an answer.

There are a great many people, honest people, but not over and above stocked with practical wisdom, who imagine that whatever is done or approved by Catholics in any age or country, in any particular time or locality, must needs be Catholic, and that opposition to it is necessarily opposition to Catholicity itself. These people never doubt that schools and colleges under the patronage and direction of the Bishops, Religious Orders and Congregations, and the Regular and Secular clergy, must necessarily be truly Catholic in character and tendency, and hence they conclude that dissatisfaction with them or opposition to them must indicate a heterodox tendency, or the absence of a thoroughly Catholic disposition. They transfer to the bishops and clergy as individuals the veneration and respect due only to the priesthood and the prelacy, and to the individual members of the Church the infallibility that can be predicted only of the Church as the living body of Christ. But we are permitted neither by Catholic faith nor by Catholic duty to make this transfer, and all experience proves that there is neither wisdom nor justice in making it. It does not necessarily follow that schools and colleges are Catholic because founded and directed by Religious Orders and Congregations approved by the Church, or by bishops and parish priests; and therefore it does not follow that dissatisfaction with the schools and colleges, or even opposition to them, is any indication of a heterodox tendency or of any want of true Catholic faith and devotion. Such schools may themselves fail to educate in a truly Catholic spirit, or to give a truly Catholic character to their pupils, and thus leave it possible that the dissatisfaction or the opposition should arise not from the fact that they are Catholic, but from the fact that they are not catholic, or that, in spite of their name and profession, they are really sectarian and heterodox. The dissatisfaction, in such case, instead of being a reproach to those who feel and express it, would be no mean proof of their Catholic discernment, their strong desire for really Catholic education, and earnest devotion to Catholic interests.

There need be no question as to the purity of motive and honesty of intention on the part of those who are engaged in founding or supporting schools and colleges for imparting a Catholic education, or even of those who will tolerate the expression of no opinion adverse to the system of schools adopted, or to the quality of the education imparted. The bishops and secular clergy, the Religious Orders and Congregations of both sexes engaged in the work of education, are animated, we doubt not, by the most sincere desire to do good, and are doing what they in their best judgment believe the most likely of any thing in their power to promote the interests of our holy religion, and to provide a truly Catholic education for our children. Any hostile criticism which should in any sense impeach their motives or intentions would be manifestly unjust, and should not be tolerated. But the subject of Catholic education itself cannot be prudently withdrawn from discussion, either private or public; nor can its discussion be confined to the prelates and clergy alone. The laity have, to say the least, as deep an interest in it as have ecclesiastics or the Religious, and they have in regard to it the common right of all men to judge for themselves. Parents have certain duties growing out of their relation as parents which they cannot throw upon others, and they must themselves discharge them according to the best of their ability. They are bound by the law of God to give their children, as far as in their power, a truly Catholic education, and they are free to criticize and to refuse to support schools, though professing to be Catholic, in which such education is not and cannot be expected to be given. They are not obliged to patronize schools, because founded or directed by Catholics, any more than they are to support a tailoring or a hatting establishment, because owned by a Catholic who employs Catholic workmen, or because recommended by bishops and parish priests. We protest against the assumption that so-called Catholic schools, collegiate or conventual, parochial or private, because under the control of Catholics, participate in the immunities of the Church, of the priesthood, or of the prelacy, and are sacred from public investigation and public criticism; or that we are necessarily bound by our Catholic faith and Catholic piety to patronize or defend them any farther than we find them Catholic institutions in facts as well as in name.

The first question, then, for us Catholics to settle relates to the catholicity of the education imparted in our so-called Catholic schools. Catholicity, as we have elsewhere shown, is the Idea in its plentitude, and therefore the Catechism tells us that the Church is Catholic, because "she subsists in all ages, teaches all nations, and maintains all truth." She, then, is Catholic (potentially) in space and time, and (actually) in idea,—as she must be, since her life is the life of the Word made flesh, of Him who was at once "perfect God and perfect man,"—and therefore the whole truth living and individuated in both the Divine and human orders in their dialectic union. It is for this reason that the Catechism says she "maintains all truth;" and it is because she maintains all truth, and all truth in its unity and integrity, that she is called the *Catholic* Church; and it is because she is Catholic in idea, that is, embracing in her Ideal all truth, human and Divine, that she is actually or potentially Catholic in space and time.

Catholic would say *universal,* and when predicated of truth means universal truth, all truth, and all truth in and for all ages and nations. They whose views are not universally true, are not applicable to all times and places, and to all subjects, may have truth under some of its aspects, but they are not Catholics. They are heterodox, sectarian, or national. Men cease to be Catholics, in the full sense of the term, by denying the universality of the idea or life the Church is living, the principle she is evolving and actualizing in the life of humanity, and alike whether they deny this universality in relation to space or in relation to time, in relation to the natural, or in relation to the supernatural. They deny Catholicity who deny that it embraces the whole truth in the human order, as they do who deny that it embraces the whole truth in the Divine order. To deny it in relation to the natural order is as much to deny Catholicity, as it is to deny it in relation to the supernatural; and we depart as widely from it in denying its catholicity in time, as we do in denying its catholicity in space. The rule of St. Vincent of Lerins says, *quod* SEMPER, as well as *quod* UBIQUE. Catholic truth is simply truth, all truth in the intelligible order and in the super-intelligible, in religion and civilization, in time and eternity, in God and in his creative act.

Catholic education must recognize the catholicity of truth under all its aspects, and tend to actualize it in all the relations of life, in religion and civilization. Its tendency is to aid the Church in the fulfilment of her mission, which is the continuous evolution and actualization of the Idea, or the life of the Word made flesh, in the life of humanity, or completion in mankind of the Incarnation completed in the individual man assumed by the Word. The completion of this work is the complete union of men, through Christ, with God, the finite with the infinite,—the true term of human progress, or final cause of the Divine creative act. All education, to be Catholic, must tend to this end, the union, without absorption of either, or intermixture or confusion of the two natures, of the human and the Divine, and therefore of civilization and religion. It must be dialectic, and tend to harmonize all opposites, the creature with the Creator, the natural with the supernatural, the individual with the race, social duties with religious duties, order with liberty, authority with freedom, the immutability of the dogma, that is, of the mysteries, with the progress of intelligence, conservatism with reform; for such is the aim of the Church herself, and such the mission given her by the Word made flesh, whose Spouse she is. Fully and completely up to this idea we expect not education in any age or in any nation to come, but this is the type it should aim to realize, and be constantly and, as far as human frailty admits, actually realizing. Such is the character and tendency of what we term Catholic education.

It is with this ideal standard of Catholic education that we have the right to compare our Catholic schools, and we must judge them as they, by the instruction they give, and the influence they exert, tend or do not tend to its realization. We hazard little in saying that our so called Catholic schools, in their actual effect, tend rather to depart from this standard than to approach it. They practically fail to recognize human progress, and thus fail to recognize the continuous and successive evolution of the Idea in the life of humanity. They practically question the universality of the Idea by failing to recognize as Catholic the great principles or ideas natural society is evolving and actualizing in its career through the ages. They do not educate their pupils to be at home and at their ease in their own age and country, or train them to be living, thinking, and energetic men, prepared for the work which actually awaits them in either Church or state. As far as we are able to trace the effect of the most approved Catholic education of our days, whether at home or abroad, it tends to repress rather than to quicken the life of the pupil, to unfit rather than to prepare him for the active and zealous discharge either of his religious or his social duties. They who are educated in our schools seem misplaced and mistimed in the world, as if born and educated for a world that has ceased to exist. They come out ignorant of contemporary ideas, contemporary habits of mind, contemporary intelligence and tendencies, and large numbers of them sink into obscurity, and do nothing for their religion or their country; or, what is worse, abandon their religion, turn their backs on the Church, and waste all their energies in seeking pleasure, or in accumulating worldly wealth. Of the young men educated in our colleges, a certain number have become priests and Religious, and fill the ranks of the clergy and continue the religious orders. Of these we have nothing to say. But, of the others, we would ask: Do we find them up to the level of contemporary civilization, and foremost in all those movements fitted to advance intelligence, morality, and the general well-being of society? Do we find them showing by their superior intelligence, their superior morals, and their loftier aspirations the superiority of their religion and the salutary influence it is fitted to exert on civilization? With very few exceptions, we fear we must answer: This is not the case. Comparatively few of them take their stand as scholars or as men on a level with the graduates of non-Catholic colleges, and those who do take that stand, in most cases, do it by throwing aside nearly all they learned from their Alma Mater, and adopting the ideas and principles, the modes of thought and action they find in the general civilization of the country in which they live.

Whence comes it that such, in general terms, has been thus far in our country the effect of what we proudly call Catholic education? We cannot ascribe it to any innate incompatibility between Catholic truth and the civilization of the country, for that would be to deny the catholicity of the Idea; nor to any re-pugnance between it and modern society, because that would be to deny its catholicity in time. The cause cannot be in Catholicity itself, nor can it be in our American order of civilization, for Catholicity, if catholic, is adapted to all times and to all nations,—as the Catechism tells us, when it says, she "subsists in all ages, and teaches all nations." If we educated in conformity with Catholic truth, those we educate would be fitted for their precise duties in their own time and country, and they would be the active, the living, and the foremost men among their contemporaries and fellow-citizens. When such is not the case, we may be sure that our education fails, in some respect, to be Catholic, and is directed to the restoration of a past severed from the present, and therefore an education that breaks the continuity of life either of the Church or of humanity; and therefore is essentially a schismatic and heterodox education. It repeats substantially the error of the Reformers in the sixteenth century. These Reformers may have had honest and even praiseworthy intentions, for there was then in the Church, or rather amongst Catholics, as there always is, need enough of reform,—deep, thorough, and wide-reaching reform; but they erred fatally in breaking the con-tinuity of the Divine-human life, and in aiming either at reproducing an order of things which had passed away, which they called "primitive Christianity," or in leaping to a future which could have no connection with the past, and be no de-velopment of what it contained in germ,—the law of all true reform, as of all real progress. The cause of the failure of what we term Catholic education is, in our judgment, in the fact that we educate not for the present or the future, but for a past which can never be restored, and therefore in our education are guilty of a gross anachronism.

We do not mean, and must not be understood to say that the dogmas, that is, the mysteries, as defined in the infallible speech of the Church, are not scrupu-lously taught in all our schools and colleges, or that the words of the Catechism are not faithfully preserved and duly insisted upon. We concede this, and that this gives to our so-called Catholic schools a merit which no others have or can have. Without the external Word, the life of the internal expires, and when it is lost or corrupted, there are no means, except by a new supernatural intervention of Almighty God, of renewing the interior Christian life. This fact is of the first importance, and must never be lost sight of or underrated. The man who has not lost his faith, although his faith is inoperative, or, as theologians say, a "dead faith," is always to be preferred to him who has no faith at all; because he has in him a recuperative principle, and it is more easy to quicken it into activity, than it is to beget faith in one who has it not. The education given in our schools, how-ever defective it may be, must always be preferred to that given in schools in which the dogma is rejected or mutilated, and can never be justly censured, save when compared with its own ideal, or with what it should be and would be, were it truly and thoroughly Catholic.

The fault we find with modern Catholic education is not that it does not faithfully preserve the Symbol, that it does not retain all the dogmas or mysteries, so far as sound words go, but that it treats them as isolated or dead facts, not as living principles, and overlooks the fact that the life of the Church consists in their continuous evolution and progressive development and actualization in the life of society and of individuals. They themselves, since they are principles and pertain to the ideal the Church is evolving and actualizing, must be immutable, and the same for all times, places, and men. They are the principles of progress, but not themselves progressive, for the truth was completely expressed and individuated in the Incarnation. The progress is not in them, but in their explication and actualization in the life of humanity. The truth contained in them is always the same, can neither be enlarged nor diminished; but our understanding of them may be more or less adequate, and their explication and application to our own life and to the life of society may be more or less complete. Their evolution is successive, progressive, and continuous. This fact, which lies at the bottom of Dr. Newman's Theory of Development, though not always presented by him in an orthodox sense, is what our Catholic education seems to us to overlook, and practically to deny. It seems to us to proceed as if the work of evolution were finished, and there remained nothing for the Christian to do, but to repeat the past. It aims not at the continuous evolution and realization of the Catholic ideal; but to restore a past age, an order of things which the world has left behind, and which it is neither possible nor desirable to restore, for it could be restored, if at all, only as a second childhood. It is now "behind the times," and unfits rather than prepares the student for taking an active part in the work of his own day and generation. It either gives its subjects no work to do, or a work in which humanity takes no interest and will not work with them,—a work which all the living and onward tendencies of the age obstinately resist, and which, if there is any truth in what we have said, is adverse alike to the present interests of both religion and civilization.

There can be no question that what generally passes for Catholic education, whether in this or any other country, has its ideal of perfection in the past, and that it resists as un-Catholic, irreligious, and opposed to God, the tendencies of modern civilization. The work that it gives its subjects, or prepares them to perform, is not the work of directing and carrying it forward, or of bringing it into dialectic harmony with religion; but that of resisting it, driving it back, anathematizing it as at war with the Gospel, and either of neglecting civilization altogether, and taking refuge in the cloister, in an exclusive or exaggerated asceticism, always bordering on immorality, or of restoring a former order of civilization, no longer a living order, and which humanity has evidently left behind, and is resolved shall never be restored.

This, in our judgment, is its great mistake, a mistake that denies the truth of humanity, and virtually condemns or places in abeyance the human element of Christianity. It virtually denies the human, because it denies that the human evolves in its life Catholic truth, and pronounces its developments false, its tendencies irreligious, and its irrepressible instincts Satanic. We mean that its tendency is in this direction, and hence the manifest and undeniable schism today between the Church and humanity, between religion and modern civilization, which, if we understand it, implies a schism between God and man. It runs to one extreme, as rationalistic education runs to another and an opposite extreme. Extremes meet. Rationalists condemn the Church, because, they say, she is opposed to civilization, and to humanity itself; and many Catholics condemn the civilization humanity in her progress evolves and effects, because, they say, it is opposed to the Church, incompatible with religion and the rightful supremacy of God. Both agree as to the fact and the character of the antagonism, and neither seems disposed to inquire whether a medium of reconciliation, of dialectic union, be or be not possible, so that the Church, which presupposes humanity, and humanity, which cannot attain to its end, or realize its destiny without the Church, may move on in harmony, without any contrariety of will, as there was no contrariety of will between the human and the Divine in Christ, the God-man. If there is any truth in Catholicity, or unless our understanding of it be totally false, there is no necessity for this schism either in the nature of the Church or in the nature of humanity, and it does and must result only from a defective theology on the one hand, and a false philosophy on the other.

These remarks apply to Catholic education not in our own country only, but throughout no small part of Christendom. In scarcely any part of the Christian world can we find Catholics,—we mean men who are earnest Catholics, firm in their faith, and unfaltering in their devotion to the Church,—among the active and influential men of the age. In all, or nearly all countries the Catholic population is the weaker, and the less efficient portion of the population in all that relates to the war of ideas, and the struggle of opinions. Those Catholics who see this and have the courage to place themselves in harmony with the times, are looked upon as, at least, of doubtful orthodoxy, and not unfrequently are held up to clerical denunciation. Even when they are not cried down as heterodox, they are pushed aside as imprudent or unsafe men. It is very widely and, we fear, very generally believed, that true Catholic duty requires us to take our stand for a past civilization, a past order of ideas, and to resist with all our might the undeniable tendencies and instincts of the human race in our day. We are required by the present dominant sentiment of Catholics, to resist progress in every sense and direction, except in the purely ascetic life of individuals, and to content ourselves with the explication and application of the dogmas of the Church, the great and immutable principles of Catholic life, given in past times, and embalmed in the opinions of the theologians of other ages, and the dry, technical, and well-nigh unintelligible formulas of the schools. Hence Catholic education, or rather the education adopted and generally approved by Catholics in our age, especially in our country, fails to produce living men, active, thinking men, great men, men of commanding genius, of generous aims, and high and noble aspirations; and hence it also fails to enable the Church to take possession of humanity, and to inspire and direct its movements.

But the object we urge has a peculiar force and application to Catholic education in our country. Our Catholic population, to a great extent, is practically a foreign body, and brings with it a civilization foreign from the American, and in some respects inferior to it. The great majority of our congregations are of foreign birth, or the children of foreign-born parents, and the greater part of our bishops and clergy, and of our professors and teachers, have been born, or at least educated, abroad, and they all naturally seek to perpetuate the civilization in which they have been brought up. Those even of our clergy and of our professors and teachers who have been born and educated in the country, have been educated in schools founded on a foreign model, and conducted by foreigners, and are, in regard to civilization, more foreign than native. We state the fact as it is. We are not condemning it; we may regret it, but we could hardly expect it to be otherwise. The original settlers of the country were, for the most part, non-Catholic, and but comparatively few of their descendants have been or are Catholics. The very large Catholic population now in the country has not been the growth of the country, but has been chiefly supplied by a foreign and a very recent migration. This is the fact,—a fact which is no fault of the Catholic population, but a fact that must be taken into the account in forming a judgment of the Catholic education in our own country. Catholics from the Old World necessarily bring with them their own civilization, which, whether we speak of France or Italy, Ireland or Germany, is, to say the least, different from ours, and, in some respects, even hostile to it.

But this is not all. The civilization they actually bring with them, and which without intending it they seek to continue, is, we being judges, of a lower order than ours. It may be our national prejudice and our ignorance of other nations, but it is nevertheless our firm conviction, from which we cannot easily be driven, that, regarded in relation to its type, the American civilization is the most advanced civilization the world has yet seen, and comes nearer to the realization of the Catholic Ideal than any which has been heretofore developed and actualized. We speak not of civilization in the sense of simple *civility*, polish of manners, and personal accomplishments, in which we may not compare always favorably with the upper classes of other nations; but of the type or idea we are realizing, our social and political constitution, our arrangements to secure freedom and scope for the development and progress of true manhood. In these respects American civilization is, we say not the term of human progress, but, in our judgment, the farthest point in advance as yet reached by any age or nation. Those who come here from abroad necessarily bring with them, therefore, a civilization more or less inferior to it, and which, in relation to it, is a civilization of the past. If they educate, then, according to their own civilization, as they must do, they necessarily educate for a civilization behind the times and below that of the country.

The fact of this inferiority is conceded or virtually conceded, by our bishops and clergy themselves, in the reason they assign for establishing separate schools for Catholic children. They tell us, and, we must presume, tell us truly, that, if the children of Catholics are educated in the common schools of the country, they will lose their religion and grow up Protestants, or at least non-Catholics. But why so, if the Catholic population represents a civilization not inferior to that represented by the non-Catholic? If Catholic children and Protestant attend the same school, why are the Catholic likely to become Protestant, any more than the Protestant are to become Catholic? The danger alleged could not exist if the Protestant or non-Catholic children did not represent the stronger, and, therefore, the superior civilization. If the Catholic children represented the advancing civilization, the civilization more in accordance with the instincts and tendencies of humanity, and therefore the civilization that has the promise of the future, they would, though inferior in numbers, be the stronger party, and, instead of being themselves perverted, would convert the non-Catholic children, and the opposition to mixed schools would come from non-Catholic, not from Catholic parents and guardians. Why is it that so many of our children, as they grow up and go out into the world, abandon their religion, lose nearly all memory of the Church of their fathers, live, act, and die as Protestants or as infidels? You say, and say truly, that it is owing to the influence of the country; but does not this show that the civilization of the country is stronger, more energetic, and more living than that which you combine, and, to a great extent, insist on combining with the Catholic dogma?

Will you deny our inference, or seek to escape it by attributing the fact to the perversity of human nature, to the seductions of the flesh, and to the temptations and machinations of the Devil? To some extent you may do so; but you must take care lest you forget or deny the Catholicity of the Word, and forget or deny that humanity, in the natural order, even though suffering from the Fall, is living the life of the creative Word. The ideal of humanity which she is realizing in her progress, is true, an element itself of Catholic truth, and, though distinguishable, yet inseparable from the Ideal the Church is herself realizing in her Divine-human life. It will not do, then, to attribute solely to human perversity, to the influence of the flesh, or to the machinations of the Devil, the loss of so many of our children as they grow up; and, therefore, we must maintain that it is in great measure due to the fact that the civilization which Catholics bring with them, and with which they associate their Catholic faith, is inferior, and therefore weaker than the civilization which has been attained to by humanity in our country, and which, unhappily, instead of being associated with orthodoxy, is associated with heterodoxy. The civilization of the country does not owe its superiority to the heterodoxy with which it is associated, any more than the civilization which Catholics bring with them owes its inferiority to the orthodoxy with which it is accidentally associated. The civilization of the country owes its superiority to the truth which it accepts and evolves, and is weakened and prevented from attaining its full development by its association with heterodoxy, as orthodoxy itself is weakened and prevented from gaining the successes it is entitled to, by being associated with an inferior civilization.

The inferiority of the civilization associated in our country with orthodoxy might be inferred *a priori* from the fact that the mass of our Catholic population are from the more uncultivated classes of the Old World, with whom it would be ridiculous to pretend that civilization has reached its highest point of development. Whatever respect we may have for the peasantry of Ireland or Germany, how much soever we may honor them for the firmness with which, under the severest trials and temptations, they have held fast to the orthodox faith, we can by no means take them in respect of civilization as the advance-guard of Humanity. But the facts themselves, facts which nobody can question, sufficiently prove, at least as to our English-speaking Catholics, that their civilization is of an inferior order. Their sympathies are far closer with the slaveholding South than with the free North, and we need not add that the civilization of the free North is far superior to that represented by the slaveholding South. The civilization of the South is based on slavery as its corner-stone, and slavery is the very essence of barbarism. The distinction between barbarism and civilization is precisely the distinction between slavery and liberty. The true American civilization has its type and seat in the Free States, and is best represented by the Puritans and their descendants, who were in fact its chief founders as they are its chief, or, at least, most earnest supporters. Yet, except with a certain number of converts of New England birth and descent, we rarely find a Catholic who does not look upon Puritan New England as the most anti-Catholic portion of the Union, and consider that his best way of promoting Catholic interests is to fight against her.

The great body of our Catholics, no doubt, wish to Americanize, and conform to the civilization of the country, but they have hitherto Americanized, so far as they have Americanized at all, in a Southern rather than in a Northern sense. The type of the Americanism they aim to adopt is in Maryland, not in Massachusetts; Baltimore, not Boston; and nothing can exceed the hostility of the Maryland type, which, properly speaking, is the Virginia type, to the Boston, or New England type. Indeed, it is these two orders of civilization that meet in mortal combat in the civil war which now threatens the integrity of the American nation. The war is a struggle for life and death, a struggle between a civilization based on slavery, represented by the South, and a civilization based on constitutional liberty and the rights of men, represented by the Free States. And, in this struggle, if, as is the fact, the interest and loyalty of Catholics lead them in large numbers to take sides with the North, their sympathies are very generally with the South; and we cannot doubt that, if the South were the loyal party, they would much more readily fight with the South than they now fight with the North. Even, then, where our Catholics aim to be American, it is not American in the sense of the highest, truest, and most advanced Americanism; but in the sense of the lowest, the least advanced, that which is least remote from barbarism, and the farthest removed from that which the Church as well as humanity demands, and never ceases to struggle to obtain.

We are also borne out in our views by the political history of the country. Politically, the Southern leaders have for a long time formed their association with the least intelligent, the least advanced classes in the Free States, and these Southern leaders are those our Catholic population have followed with the most alacrity. This fact proves, on the one hand, that the South represents the lowest order of civilization in the country, and that Catholics are more easily engaged in supporting it than in supporting the superior civilization represented by the Northern States. It is not too much to say that the great influx of the Catholic peasantry of different European States into the country, and the conferring on them, almost on their arrival, of political franchises, have done not a little to corrupt our politics, and to lower the standard of our civilization. Their orthodoxy, as yet, has done less to advance, than their inferior civilization has done to corrupt and lower, our civilization and morals. However humiliating this fact may be to us as Catholics, there is no use in attempting to deny it, or to disguise it. It is a fact which all intelligent Americans see and know, and it is one which we ourselves should dare look in the face. The opposition to us represented by "Native-American," or "Know-Nothing" parties or movements, is not opposition to us as orthodox Catholics, nor, in itself considered, to us as foreigners, but simply representatives of a civilization different from the American, and, in many respects, inferior and opposed to it. We have practically, if not theoretically, insisted that our orthodoxy and our foreign and inferior civilization are inseparable; and the heterodox American people have in this agreed with us, and hence their opposition to us, and ours to them. Heterodoxy, with the heterodox of our country, is no longer a living principle, and is retained only because associated, accidentally associated, with a superior and more advanced civilization. Orthodoxy is opposed not because there is any opposition to it on its own account, but because it is believed to be inseparably wedded to that inferior and less advanced civilization that has come hither with it from the Old World, and which many honest Catholics think, if they ever think at all on the subject, is identical with it.

Now, the objection to Catholic schools, especially those for the people at large, is that they tend, and for a time at least must tend, to perpetuate the association of orthodoxy with this inferior civilization, and thus injure alike the country and the Church. These schools must be taught chiefly by foreigners, or, if not by foreigners, at least by those whose sympathies and connections, tastes and habits are un-American; because what is wanted by their founders and supporters is not simply the preservation of orthodoxy, but the perpetuation of the foreignism hitherto associated with it. Schools which should associate real Americanism with orthodoxy would be hardly less offensive or more acceptable to them than the public schools themselves. They must, therefore, be conducted and taught by men who will keep up the old association, and prevent the association of real Americanism with orthodoxy. Yet it is precisely this latter association which is desirable both for civilization and for religion, and it is only by breaking the old association, and forming the new in good faith, as we are in fact required to do by orthodoxy itself, that Catholics can cease to be in this country an isolated foreign colony, or a band of emigrants encamped for the night, and ready to strike their tents, and take up their line of march on the morrow for some other place.

These are some of the reasons which have led many of our most intelligent, most earnest, and devout Catholics to form their unfavorable judgment of Catholic schools and Catholic education, as they now are, and for some time are likely to be, in the United States. They are solid reasons as far as they go, and fully justify the dissatisfaction with them we began by recognizing. They prove that here and elsewhere, but especially here, Catholc education, or the education given by Catholics, is below the wants of the age and country, and prove that, from the seminary down to the primary school, it stands in need, whether we consult the interest of orthodoxy or that of civilization, of a wide, deep, and thorough reform. Yet, after long reflection and much hesitation, some would say opposition, we must say that we do not regard them as sufficient reasons for abandoning the movement for Catholic schools and education supported by our bishops and clergy. It may be that the movement was premature, and that it would have been better to have used for a longer time the schools of the country, as the early Christians did those of the Empire, before attempting to establish schools of our own, save for the education of the clergy. But it is too late to discuss that question now. The movement has, wisely or unwisely, been set on foot, and gone too far to be arrested, even if it were desirable to arrest it. Our bishops and clergy have decided that the movement shall go on, and the Catholic cause can never be promoted by any anti-hierarchical action. Much good may be done that is not done by or under direction of the hierarchy; but no good end can ever be obtained in opposition to it. This consideration is of itself sufficient to deter us from opposing the movement, and of inducing us to accept it at least as *un fait accompli*, and to make the best we can of it.

That we are to have schools and colleges of our own, under the control of Catholics, we take it is a "fixed fact." Whether the movement for them is premature or not, it is idle, if nothing worse, to war against it. Let us say, then, to those who regard the education actually given by Catholics as we do, and who have not seen their way clear to the support of primary schools under the control of Catholics as a substitute, in the case of Catholic children, for the Common Schools of the country, that we regard it as our duty now to accept the movement, and labor not to arrest it, or to embarrass it, but to reform and render truly Catholic the whole system of Catholic education, from the highest grade to the lowest. Let it be our work not to destroy Catholic education, but to reform and advance it. The first care of all Catholics should be the preservation of orthodoxy, and, in the actual state of our Catholic population, it may be that orthodoxy will be better preserved by schools under Catholic direction that it can be by sending our children to the public schools. The objections we have set forth are, after all, only temporary and accidental. They grow out of the present and past state of our Catholic population, and must disappear under the slow but effectual operation of time and causes already in operation amongst us. We might gain something under the point of view of civilization by adopting the schools of the country; but, as our prelates and clergy are strongly opposed to them, and have done much to bring them into disrepute with Catholics, we should probably lose, under the point of view of orthodoxy, more than would thus be gained. Schools under the control of Catholics will, at least, teach the Catechism, and though they may in fact teach it as a dead letter, rather than as a quickening spirit, it is better that it should be taught as a dead letter than not be taught at all. It is only by preserving the dogma intact that we do or can preserve the Christian Ideal, or have the slightest chance of securing our final destiny. The hopes of the world for time and eternity are dependent on the preservation of the orthodox faith.

The reform in our schools and in education will go on just in proportion as it goes on in our Catholic community itself, and perhaps even much faster. The dissatisfaction we hear expressed with our collegiate education for boys, and with that of our conventual schools for girls, is an encouraging symptom; it proves that there is, after all, a growing Americanization of our Catholic population, and that the need of an education less European and more truly American is daily becoming more widely and more deeply felt. It will be more widely and more deeply felt still as time goes on, and as Catholics become more generally naturalized in habit, feeling, and association, as well as in law. It indicates also the revival of Catholic life in our population, that Catholics are becoming more earnest and living men, and unwilling that their orthodoxy should be wrapped up in a clean napkin and buried in the earth. In proportion as their Catholic life revives and grows more active, they will demand an education more in accordance with Catholic truth in all its branches, than is that now given. The demand will create a supply. And when the present civil strife is over, the integrity of the nation reestablished, and American civilization has proved itself capable of subduing the barbarism of the South, and of marching onward and upward with humanity, in her career of progress to union with the infinite, we trust Catholics will find and feel themselves real Americans, differing from other Americans only in the respect that orthodoxy differs from heterodoxy, truth from error, life from death. Then our schools will assume their true character and position, and exert a truly Catholic influence. They will preserve orthodoxy not as a dead letter, not as isolated and inoperative dogmas, but as a quickening spirit, as living and operative truth. Then, under the point of view of civilization, instead of tending to recall a dead past, they will accept the living present, and associate the living civilization of the day with the orthodox faith,—reunite in a living and productive whole the scattered members of the torn and bleeding body of truth, and aid both the Church and the nation in carrying forward our civilization to the last term of its progress. Then our schools will send out living men, live with the love of God and of man,—men of large minds, of liberal studies, and generous aims,—men inspired by faith and genius, who will take the command of their age, breathe their whole souls into it, inform it with their own love of truth, and raise it to the level of their own high and noble aspirations. Let us console ourselves for what Catholic education now is with what it may become, and with what we may by well-directed effort aid it in becoming. This is the conclusion to which we ourselves have come, and if we are not satisfied with Catholic schools and education as they are, we are satisfied with their capabilities, and shall henceforth content ourselves with doing what in us lies to bring them under the great law of progress, which we have insisted on, and which is the law of all life, even of the Divine life, —as is proved in the eternal Generation of the Word, and the Procession of the Holy Ghost, or in the assertion of theologians that "God is most pure act," *actus purissimus*.

Women and the higher education

Bishop John Lancaster Spalding

*John Lancaster Spalding, Bishop of Peoria, Illinois,
was the principal advocate in the Third Plenary
Council, 1884, for founding the Catholic University
of America. From the time of its founding to his
death, Bishop Spalding was a constant supporter of
the university and higher learning. His conception
of higher studies was somewhat broader than that
of his episcopal colleagues, for he argued for a
"real" university while they were usually content
with what was called a "high school" of theology.
In this selection the Bishop turns his considerable
literary skill to the issue of higher education for
women, lays a philosophical and theological
foundation for it, and gives his full support to
Trinity College, a Catholic women's college
associated with the Catholic University of America.*

As we look back to the beginning of the nineteenth century, the achievements
with which it has been crowded thrill us with a sense of gratitude and wonder.
In its hundred years man has made greater progress than in any preceding thousand. His control of nature seems now first to have begun. Steam and electricity
have placed him in a new world where time and space lose half their tyrannous
power. With utmost speed he flies over oceans and continents, delivering his
precious wares in every part of the earth; the electric current writes his thought
at the distance of thousands of miles; he holds conversation from city to city; his
streets and houses are as luminous almost by night as by day. Photography places
before the eyes of all whatever is worth seeing in any part of the world. Spectrum

Reprinted with permission from *Opportunity and Other Essays and Addresses,*
A. C. McClurg & Co., Chicago, 1900, pp. 45–67.

analysis reveals the relative heat and chemical constitution of the stars; the Roentgen rays make the opaque transparent, while the use of anesthetics and antiseptics renders the most difficult surgical operations painless and free from risk. The eighteenth century has not a single discovery or invention which may be compared with any one of these. In the seventeenth we have the telescope and some rude beginning of the steam engine; in the sixteenth nothing of the first importance; in the fifteenth, the printing press, and in the twelfth the mariner's compass, which made possible the discovery of America. To find another invention of world-wide import we must go back to the mythical time when the alphabet and the Arabic numerals were first introduced and became the great instruments for the increase, diffusion, and preservation of knowledge, or to a still remoter period when man first began to understand the uses of fire or the power of culture to cause wild grasses and shrubs to bear nutritious grain and delicious fruits.

But the progress of the nineteenth century has not been solely or chiefly material and practical. The advance in theoretical knowledge has been great enough to change the point of view from which we contemplate the heavens and the earth. The principle of conservation of energy, of definite and multiple proportions in chemistry, and the theory of organic evolution have given us deeper insight into the laws which govern the universe. The discovery of the function of the cell in all vital processes, and of the part germs play in zymotic infections, has given us a truer knowledge of the conditions of health and of the means of prevention and cure of disease. Geology has rewritten the history of the earth; physiology has reconstructed the human body; philology has thrown light on the origin and growth of language; and sociology has explained the principles by which human aggregates are upbuilt and destroyed.

But it is especially in the matter of education that the superiority of our age over all others is most manifest. In the past, knowledge was the privilege of the few, and the masses were ignorant; and hence the State was monarchical or aristocratic, even when the form of government was called democratic. By the beginning of the present century, however, a gradual movement, which has been in progress from the beginning of our era, whose origin, impulse, and abiding force were Christian, had brought the multitude to a perception of their rights and powers, and in consequence had sharpened the sense of the need of popular education. All, it was felt, should be taught, since all have duties to perform and rights to defend. The public opinion which demanded that education should be made universal was led by a logical necessity to ask that it be made free, and therefore that the schools be maintained by a system of taxation imposed by the State. The result is that illiteracy has almost disappeared from the great Christian nations, and that the average intelligence of the world has become much higher than it has hitherto ever been. The theory that the citizen needs instruction that he may properly fulfil his functions as a member of a free State is now merging into the wider view that man must be educated to be made rightly human; and thus the ideal of good citizenship is giving way to that of perfect manhood. Having built schools for all, we feel that our chief business now is to improve them until they become nurseries of a richer, nobler, and more Godlike life.

In considering this question, another superiority of our century—its chief glory perhaps—a splendor which falls on our own country more than on any other, is revealed—the position and the opportunities it has given to woman. The indelible stain on the page of history is the world's treatment of woman. Through the ages man had been unjust to man, cruel even, but woman seemed to be almost beyond the pale of humanity. She was his drudge, his slave, his chattel. She was a thing to be bought and sold, to be played with in idle hours, and for the rest to be immured in the twofold darkness of ignorance and confining walls.

The savage went wife-hunting as he hunted beasts of prey; the barbarian also captured his woman in war, or he bought her; the civilized pagan was a polygamist, or looked on himself as wholly free from obligations of marital fidelity. Woman was the great outcast of the human race, and it would seem that only the coming of a god could have given her courage to hope for a better fate.

"She is an impudent animal," says Seneca, "and unless she has advanced in philosophical knowledge and in various learning, she is cruel and incontinent." "Neither in woes nor in welcome prosperity," says Aeschylus, "may I be associated with womankind." In the Hebrew Scriptures we have indeed a nobler view of woman's worth; it is, however, but a partial light. It was Christianity that gave the first impulse to the recognition of her dignity and mission. The Virgin Mother of Jesus was lifted up before the eyes of the world as an ideal; women were the Master's most devoted disciples; they were among the first and most enthusiastic converts the Apostolic preaching made; and as martyrs for the faith they met death with a constancy and heroism unsurpassed by their husbands and sons.

"What women these Christians have!" exclaimed Libanius, the friend of Julian. It is on the womanly virtues that Christ seems to lay chief stress, as it is in propagating them that His religion has been most successful. Love, chastity, enthusiasm, devotion, self-surrender, and self-consecration to the highest aims, are woman's strength and glory, and in the exercise of these heavenly powers she has shown herself superior to man. The great renunciation, the supreme act whereby one turns from the superficial and animal self to the real self, whose world in unseen and permanent, the condition on which alone one can enter Christ's Kingdom, is easier for woman than for man. Unlike the philosophers, the divine Master appeals to the heart rather than to the head, and to such appeal woman more readily than man yields glad and spontaneous assent. What He asks first and last is that we be drawn to Him, that we love Him with a personal love, stronger than all earthly ties, and of such love woman is more capable than man. He first understood the heart of woman and the divine words He spoke to her who dried with her hair the feet she had bathed in tears, lifted the whole sex to a higher and wider plane of life. Woman, who followed Him in life, who stood beneath His cross, who watched by His grave till she saw Him rise immortal, has ministered to Him with an undying devotion through all the centuries even until now, when at last she stands side by side with man, as mother, wife, and friend; his equal, his counsellor, his inspirer, his guide and best defence.

The transformation has indeed been slow, as the whole upward movement of the race has been slow, but the force that has wrought the change is not machinery or trade or philosophy or science, but the Christian religion which consecrated purity and deified love.

The custom of ages, become a second nature, which led man to look upon woman as inferior because she had less muscular strength, was not easily overthrown, nay, it has not yet been wholly done away with; but the enlightened opinion of the world is no longer guided by physical standards in its estimate of human worth, and woman's delicacy of bodily structure, in ceasing to be a disgrace, has become the vesture and symbol of her spiritual excellence.

The Christian ideal is moral rather than intellectual. The followers of Christ find themselves in a school of religion and virtue, not in a school of philosophy. A pure and loving heart, yearning for peace and righteousness, is to be preferred to a mind curious for knowledge and busy with speculation about what is beyond man's reach. The childlike enter the kingdom of heaven. It is the home of the meek and humble. The world of the senses is transitory, is largely an unreal world; the soul's abiding dwelling is in the unseen, which is permanent and infinite, toward which it stretches the arms of faith, hope, and love. The rest is illusion of the senses, is vanity. The farthest vision of the mind can but show us that God loves the good. Do right and fear him—this is the whole of life.

It is but natural, then, that the Christian world should have turned its first thought and devoted its prime energy to moral culture. Nay, it is forever true that knowledge without virtue is worthless, that the science which does not make man better is as though it were nescience.

Let us therefore be patient as we watch the slow progress of the world in the things of the mind. In the end, few of us can know much, and all of us are called on to do much. Little learning is needed when the heart is right, and great learning will profit nothing if it be wrong.

Nevertheless, reason is man's highest attribute—it is what makes him man; it is the power which gives meaning and value to all he hopes or loves or does. It is the immediate revelation of God in each soul; the arbiter of conscience, the master-light of all our seeing, the fulcrum on which we rest to move the universe in the direction of divine and eternal purposes.

It is not the privilege of a few; but all, if they be rightly educated, may be made capable of judging truly and discerning wisely; and the public opinion which recognizes this principle in theory impels more and more to its actualization. In the primary and secondary schools throughout Christendom girls and boys are taught the same things, by the same methods, and with equal success; but the inveterate prejudice which held woman to be mentally as well as physically inferior to man has not yet altogether or everywhere been overcome when there is question of the highest intellectual culture. The old sophisms have not wholly lost their persuasiveness, despite the marvellous progress in education made by woman, especially during the latter half of the present century.

It is still asserted that woman is incapable of serious mental training, and that the habits she forms in attempting to acquire the best education make her discontented with her proper work, unfit her to become wife and mother, take from her something of the sweetness, purity, and moral beauty which constitute her greatest charm, and on which the welfare of the race so largely depends. A learned woman still appears to some of us to be an abnormal being. We do not, of course, agree with Fenelon when he says that contact with learning would be almost as fatal to womanly delicacy as contact with vice; nor with Lessing in the opinion that the woman who thinks is as ridiculous as the man who puts on rouge; but there are still many serious minds who are not without grave misgivings as to the result of the higher education of women. In reply to whatever doubts and objections of this kind, it is enough to say that the adversaries of the highest intellectual culture for women either do not understand what education is or do not believe in its divine efficacy. Education is simply the process whereby the powers which constitute a human being are strengthened, developed, and brought into act. If these endowments are good, education is good; and the best is best, whether for man or woman. What interests the one must interest the other; what benefits the one must benefit the other. Women not less than men need strong and open minds, the capacity to form definite ideas and sound judgments, to deduce conclusions logically from premises, to weigh evidence and to estimate the value of proof. They, more than men even, may be helped if they are permitted to live in the high and serene worlds which the study of philosophy, poetry, history, and science will throw open to them; for they, probably more than men, dwell in the present, are too much dominated by the senses; and a better education, by enabling them to live more in the past and the future, will tranquillize, deepen, and purify their whole being.

What shall women learn? Whatever experience and the insight of the wisest have shown to have most efficacy in opening, strengthening, and supplying the mind, whether literature or science or metaphysics or history. Is not such superficial acquaintance with these branches of knowledge as may be made in our academies and other similar schools for girls sufficient for them? It is sufficient for those who cannot or will not take up the work of intellectual culture in a serious spirit and with earnest purpose, and these unfortunately are the many, whether there be question of women or of men. A few only are urged by the impulse to grow ceaselessly in mental power, as but a few hunger and thirst for righteousness. They are the best; their value is greater than that of numbers, because their life is of a higher quality and potency. It is they who uplift the ideals in whose light the multitude walk; it is they who open ways to undiscovered worlds; it is they who show to the crowd what right-hoping and right-daring human souls may achieve. Were it not for them the whole people would sink to lower planes of thought and aspiration.

Now, these chosen ones, whom God bids grow unceasingly, are not found in one sex alone.

The eternal womanly, which the poet says draws us up and onward, leads woman herself to yearn for the infinite best. Who shall hope by futile argument to stay her feet in the way in which the inner voice bids her ascend? Her average intelligence is not less than that of man, and if hitherto no one of her sex has been able to enter the small circle of supreme achievement, it is permitted to believe that this may be due to the force of custom, habit, opinion, and law, and not to inferiority of mental endowment. If a few women of exceptional gifts and attainments have seemed to lose something of feminine virtue and refinement, this, it is lawful to think, is to be ascribed to the accidents of individual character or to the environment into which they have been thrown. The best intellectual culture can have no tendency to make man or woman coarse or flippant or irreverent. On the contrary, it is favorable to the virtues and graces which go to the making of a gentleman or a lady. An open, flexible, and enlightened mind wins its way to all companies more surely than the charm that lies in mere accomplishments or in tricks of dress and behavior. Beauty itself, to which a very real value belongs —beauty of feature, and above all beauty of expression, the luminous mind suffusing the countenance with a spiritual glow and radiance, is heightened by intellectual culture.

The more we learn to live in the serene air of delightful studies the longer do we retain the freshness and charm of youth. The more adaptable also do we become, the more capable of high and ennobling companionship. In marriage, as in friendship, as in whatever sphere of life, human relations are chiefly spiritual, and the more thoroughly educated a woman is the more able is she to fulfil in a noble way the duties of wife and mother. The primary aim, however, is not to make a good wife and mother, any more than it is to make a good husband and father. The educational ideal is human perfection, perfect manhood, and perfect womanhood. Given the right kind of man or woman, and whatever duties are to be performed, whatever functions are to be fulfilled, will be well performed and well fulfilled. Woman's sphere lies wherever she can live nobly and do useful work. The career open to ability applies to her not less than to man. We may not put legal or social restrictions on the spiritual growth of the one or the other. It is good to have a strong and enlightened mind; therefore it is good for woman to have such a mind. It is always good to know a thing; therefore, it is good for woman to know whatever she is capable of knowing. To be a human being, many-sided and well-rounded, is to be like God; therefore, it is good that woman be developed on many sides in harmony and completeness.

Since the close of our civil war America has entered on the work of providing for the higher education of women, with an energy and a generosity unequalled by any other country. With us women have access to all kinds of schools, and to nearly all the professions. They are no longer accustomed to look to marriage as to their one aim in life. They are brought up to trust to their own intelligence and industry to maintain themselves in the world. Their success in study is equal to that of men, and their eagerness to improve themselves seems to be greater. The number of women who, in the various institutions, are receiving the higher intellectual culture is large, and it is rapidly increasing. These institutions are of three kinds: In the first, men and women are educated together, as at Oberlin and most of the Western universities; in the second—Vassar, Wellesley, Smith, and Bryn Mawr—women alone are received; and then there is a third type—Radcliffe, Barnard, and Evelyn—in which education is given exclusively to women by Professors of Harvard, Columbia, and Princeton.

These higher schools for women, to whichever type they belong, are not all equally good, and in some of them doubtless grave defects are found; but the best of them afford facilities for thorough intellectual training or special research not existing in similar institutions elsewhere, even in Europe, and certainly not in our Catholic academies for young ladies. Our Catholic schools have grown to be a fact of national significance. In them we are already instructing more than a million pupils, and, while the number is constantly increasing, we are making strenuous efforts to improve the efficiency of the teaching. Our Sisterhoods have made this work possible, and their spirit of self-sacrifice, their courage, their eagerness to follow in the way of pedagogical progress are our chief ground for having confidence in the continuance and development of our system of religious schools.

Of the education they give to girls it is not necessary to speak in praise. Their success in cultivating the virtues which are woman's glory—lacking which no degree of mental culture can make her beneficent and delightful—pure-mindedness, modesty, patience, piety, reverence, gentleness, amiability, and helpfulness —is conceded by friend and foe. On this foundation must we build if we would raise woman's mind to the ethereal heights of intellectual truth and splendor, without risking the loss of her heart of goodness and love. It is from this foundation that Trinity College shall rise. It is the logical result of our secondary schools or academies for girls, as the university stands as the natural development of our system of secondary schools or colleges for boys. A woman's heart founded the University, and women will upbuild and maintain Trinity College. Here shall they stand side by side, a light and encouragement, each to other, twins of learning, to scatter over the land the blessings of religion and knowledge. The graduates of our academies, who feel the impulse to mental progress urgent as the growth of wings, will flock here as to a central home of learned men and wise women.

The genuinely great are seldom to be met with. How rare is a great poet, artist, historian, orator, general, physician, or lawyer. So rare also are great teachers. Nay, rarest of all, it may be, since it is not the intellect or the imagination or the heart alone that educates, but the whole man. Agassiz held that a student gains more by being brought into contact even for a brief time with a man of profound knowledge on whatever subject, than a professor who knows little more than he attempts to teach could give him in many months. As we become capable of deeper insight, the clearer shall we see that only the greatest men and women can educate. The rest are repeaters and trainers. Take from any nation the hundred minds who are first in all the spheres of human activity, and the national life is lowered.

This is also true of the Church, for in the supernatural as in the natural, God works through agents; and the radical blunder is to imagine that He will do immediately what He has made us capable of doing for ourselves. Indeed, there is nothing which Catholics more need to learn, in whatever part of the world they may live, than that it is vain and superstitious to hope that God in some miraculous way will come to save them from the perils into which blindness, sloth, and indifference may have thrown them. Human endowments remain latent unless self-activity bring them into play. We are not born men, nor do we become men through a process of spontaneous development. We make ourselves men by long study and labor, by observation and reflection, by holding the mind steadfastly to the light of reason and the will to obedience to the stern voice of duty. True manhood is the result of severe and constant discipline, and the merely natural man is little more than animal.

But culture, like religion, is propagated; it is a light transmitted by luminous minds and ardent souls. It is a torch carried in the hands of genius, or in the hands of those whom deep yearning for truth and beauty makes twin brothers of genius, and whoever would catch a spark from the heavenly flame must draw near to these light-bearers. Since the propagators of culture are few, is it not wise to gather them in centres to which all who seek illumination may repair? It is idle to hope that we shall find genuine teachers in many places. Such teachers are not many, and to have their proper influence they require the right environment.

What we most need in America to-day is concentration, not expansion. The depth, not the tumult of the soul, is pleasing to the gods. It is easier to found a hundred schools than to create one which shall radiate enthusiasm, courage, and enlightenment. For us the Catholic University is the one institution which it is possible to make a centre of intellectual life for the Church in America. Of the urgent demand for such a centre it is scarcely necessary to speak. To those who cry, Wait! echo will answer, Too late. On all sides there is a vast and eager movement toward higher culture of mind. The material aids, both the State and the generosity of individuals provide with a lavishness which in other ages would have seemed fabulous. The progress America is making in university education, if not the most striking, is one of the most real and potent influences in shaping our national character and destiny.

The relatively higher intelligence of the masses makes thorough mental discipline indispensable in the few. Not only are the multitude more intelligent than they have ever been, but the best knowledge on all subjects is now within the reach of many readers, so that in every community, in every audience, there are some at least who will not tolerate that the accredited public teachers should give evidence of ignorance or of the lack of the best training. In former centuries there have been men of superior genius, as well as individual minds of wide knowledge, but never has there been an age so enlightened as our own. In the presence of all this it were blindness in Catholics to rest content with what they have done or are doing. The life that is not growing is decaying. The self-complacent are, at the best, futile beings—as leaders and educators of men they are wholly incompetent. We are striving to help the abandoned, the fallen, the old who have none to care for them. Let us do more to bring into play the endowments of the strong, quick to recognize and appreciate talent in man or woman, and ready to offer opportunities for its development.

Let us not be so dull as to ignore the gifts of woman. Let us not be of those who still doubt whether it is not better that she should be a simpleton; who think that only superficially educated women can make good wives and mothers. If, as Goethe says, it is a frightful thing to see ignorance at work, is it not most frightful when the work is that which woman is called to do in the home and in the school? In all companionship the lower tends to pull the higher down, for it is easy to sink and hard to rise. Hence, an ignorant wife and mother will dull the minds of her husband and children, while one who is intelligent and appreciative will be for them a strong stimulus to self-activity. It is the nature of an enlightened mind to diffuse light, of a generous soul to make love prevail, of a noble character to build character. American education, whether given by the State or by the various religious denominations, is now largely and increasingly in the hands of women, and if progress is to be made, they must themselves receive a more thorough mental culture. If to demand the higher education for women still seems absurd to some, let us recall that for ages it was deemed preposterous to give her any education at all. If in the past she has been mentally inferior, is it not because the incentives, means, and opportunities of intellectual growth were denied her? If her capacity has seemed to be chiefly that of a domestic, is it not because she was refused admission to wider fields?

To discourage is to enfeeble; to destroy self-confidence is to blunt the spur to noble action; and yet it has been held wise and by many is still thought proper to take a deprecatory tone whenever there is question of conceding to women the opportunities of education and work which are given to men. Let us assume their capacity; let us help them to believe that they are able, and they will be able. Above all, let us applaud and assist every effort made by women themselves to uplift, strengthen, and enlighten woman.

It is the privilege and the glory of the English-speaking peoples, with the noise of whose deeds the world is filled to-day, to have been the first to understand woman's right to the highest education, and to provide for her the opportunities.

We Catholics who are part of the life of the English-speaking race; we, whose ancestors in the faith first uplifted to the eyes of the world the Ideal Woman, who have ever been the foremost in proclaiming the infinite worth of chastity, the mother-virtue of womanhood, we surely must feel a thrill of joy when we behold the open door inviting women to enter the institutions where highest wisdom is taught. Is this not a favorable omen for the Church, since the lack of religion among such numbers of men in France, and in other countries, is doubtless due, in no small degree, to the very imperfect mental culture of their mothers and wives? Were it not enough if we could only hope that the man who is to be shall be parted as by a gulf from him who has been and still is? And may we not find some ground for such hope in the ascent of women to wider and nobler life? That which draws us on is the thing that is to be. To this the all-hoping human heart turns ever from the world of facts, since what has become is fixed and limited, and we are dwellers in a boundless universe. It is this that gives the bud a charm denied the full-blown flower. It is this that bends the race in glad service to the dawn of promise that lies in childhood's eyes; it is this that makes right life a ceaseless effort to attain what is for evermore about to be; it is this that makes us the bond-servants of noble thoughts and high aims, willing, if thus led, to perish rather than to succeed in the bare world of what is merely matter.

Ah! hasten then the day when Trinity College shall stand beside the Catholic University, twin stars, to lure and illumine the all-generous souls who are drawn to God by the love of truth and goodness and beauty.

Catholic education: the basis of true Americanization

Rev. Thomas Edward Shields

Father Thomas Shields was a pioneer in professionalizing Catholic education; both as a professor at the Catholic University of America and in his books and articles he exerted an important and lasting influence on Catholic educational thought. In the following article he deals with a vital issue facing all schools—but especially Catholic schools—during the early years of the twentieth century: the problem of Americanization. What was the school's role, and how was it to be fulfilled, in preparing foreign-born children for life in American society? Father Shields maintained that the Catholic school had certain advantages over public schools, for in addition to its acceptance of citizenship as an appropriate objective it could pay allegiance to spiritually oriented objectives. One of the intangible bonuses of Catholic education, according to this author, was to be found in the superior motivation of Catholic teachers.

The tide of immigration, pouring into our country for many decades in ever increasing volume, was interrupted briefly during the years of the European War, but is now resumed in increased volume which is limited only by the carrying

Reprinted with permission from *The Catholic Educational Review*, 19:3–19, January, 1921.

capacity of the ships that pass between European ports and our own. This tide of immigration presents many unsolved problems. We need much more labor than has been available during the past few years unless we are to drop back into an elementary condition in which we export our raw materials and import our necessary manufactures. On the other hand, an abundant supply of labor is likely to reduce the wages of the working man and to lower his standard of living. The adjustment of these opposing factors must be undertaken by the national government. But this is not the only problem nor indeed the chief problem which the situation presents. Our experience of the past few years has taught all who are willing to learn that we have failed in large measure to deal with many vital issues that are involved. As a result we hear on every side the demand for the Americanization of the foreigner and the public is looking to the school to take its part in this work.

It will be convenient to consider Americanization of the foreigner as two distinct tasks: The Americanization of the adult foreigner and the Americanization of the foreign child, born here or abroad. The latter task has always been assigned to the school and we are now attempting to enlarge the function of the school so as to include the former. Evidently the school may render assistance in Americanizing the adult but it will be necessary to draw upon other social forces to cooperate in the work and the school will be able to lend effective help in proportion as it has learned to deal effectively with its own peculiar problem, namely, the Americanization of the foreign child.

The state public school and the Catholic public school have both endeavored, each in its own way, to Americanize the children of the foreigner who has come to dwell in our midst. In fact it is the boast of many an advocate of the state school system that our state school is a melting pot in which the foreigner is transformed into an American citizen. Obviously the state school has functioned as a melting pot for these children, a melting pot in which national customs and national traits of all sorts were lost, but it takes more than a melting pot to make a citizen and the destruction or removal with undue haste of national traits and national customs from the foreign-born child leaves him so weak and debilitated that it will be difficult to build him up into a worthy citizen. Overzeal in this direction has not produced commendable results. It will be admitted readily that it would have been difficult for the state school to avoid these results, desired or otherwise. When the children of a dozen different nationalities meet in the same school we are likely to find Paddy laughing at Dutchy, both of them ridiculing Polack and all three jeering at Frenchy, with the result that all of the children lose reverence and respect for their own parents and for family traditions which for countless generations have served to inspire and support the moral and patriotic nature of the child, and when this destruction has taken place it will be scarcely possible to give the child reverence for America or for American institutions and customs. Moreover, these children are likely to represent various religions, and the result is similar in this respect. The Methodist jeers at the Baptist, and both of them show little respect for the Lutheran or the Episcopalian. The Catholic mistrusts the Protestant and the Protestant returns the distrust to which is often added hatred or contempt. The result is too often a disgust for all religion and for all churches, and the child grows into a man or a woman who feels it to be the right thing to disown all religious affiliations and to be so broad minded as to believe that one religion is as good as another. This process has, in fact, emptied our Protestant churches. The policy has continued from the days of Horace Mann;— the result, a nation that has lost its religion. In a rapidly increasing population denominational churches are obliged to resort to all manner of social attractions in order to secure an attendance.

The Catholic Church has consistently adopted another policy. She built her own school system so that her children might grow up in reverence for the Church and for its teachings and in obedience to its laws, but she also dealt with the problem of the foreign child in a manner consistent with her policy. As far as her means would allow she organized congregations and parochial schools for the Catholics of each nation who were pouring into our country. Thus you will find in the cities in which this tide of immigration settled Catholic schools known as Polish schools, French schools, German schools, etc. In these schools the children's reverence for their own parents and for the traditions of their native country is preserved and they grow up in this country gradually imbibing its spirit and adopting its customs in a spirit of reverence and love and they come to forget all too soon the traditions and customs of the land of their forefathers. In two or three generations these children are found to be more thoroughly American than the Americans themselves.

Obviously we should endeavor to form a clear concept of just what it is that goes to the formation of an American citizen before we can adopt intelligent means for the achievement of our aims, and we may be permitted to begin with enumerating a few things that, in spite of ill-considered statements to the contrary, do not enter into the making of an American citizen. It is not necessary, for instance, that an American citizen should know only one language and that he should be familiar with the history of no other country than the United States. An added language is always an added asset of no mean value. When the committee of nine appointed to draw up a suitable curriculum for the public high schools of the United States made their report it recommended that two of the prescribed units should be in some foreign language. It is, indeed, plain to all students in the matter that we can never know our own language thoroughly until we have learned some other language sufficiently to serve purposes of contrast and comparison. Where can one find the wisdom to justify us in leading the foreign child to forget his native tongue during the years that he is receiving an elementary education. Surely no intelligent man would claim that this was necessary in order to Americanize a child. Will any intelligent man maintain that anyone will understand American institutions better or love them more through remaining in ignorance of the history and institutions of England or of France. It is an unwise policy to destroy this knowledge in a child, or to neglect to cultivate it under the most favorable of circumstances on the pretext of making a good American citizen.

Even if every nation in Europe were our avowed enemy it would still be a short sighted policy to cultivate in our citizens ignorance of the ideals and resources of these countries. In the past we have had to import skilled workmen, trained in European schools to take charge of our manufacturing processes. We failed to make a satisfactory microscope in this country until workmen, trained in Europe, were imported from Jena. And the same is true in many another line of industry. Does anybody suppose that the skill these workmen brought to this country was a thing to be despised and rejected, or a thing militating against good citizenship? In like manner the habits of reverence for parents and for social institutions, no matter in what country these habits are formed, must be looked upon as an asset in every immigrant that seeks residence within the limits of our country. It is perfectly true that these things by themselves are not sufficient for worthy citizenship in this country. The foreign child and the foreign adult alike must learn the language of the country in order to understand its laws and to cooperate intelligently in the social and economic life of the country. The point we wish to make here is that what the foreigner brings to us may be of very great value and should be dealt with accordingly. If he brings with him an attitude of hostility to our form of government, or to our institutions, then it is time that we look into the matter and see that he is kept out of the country; for while we are perfectly willing to welcome those who come to us with good intentions, willing to put on the mantle of our citizenship, and to cooperate in sustaining our traditions and our institutions, we are not, and we should not be, willing to admit to the privilege of citizenship those who come only to tear down and to destroy.

It is the obvious duty of every school in this country to put forth every reasonable effort to develop the children entrusted to its care into worthy citizens but this is a constructive policy and continuity must be its first principle. We can engraft upon the root of a wild crabapple tree a branch of a pear or a peach and the fruit resulting will not be wild crab but pears or peaches. If, however, we fail to secure a flow of sap from the native root into the engrafted branch there will be no fruit and no life in the branch and the same is true of a child. Whatever qualities we would engraft upon a child so that he may grow into a worthy citizen of this free country, must draw their nourishment and support, not only from the individual life of the child, but from his social life which comes to us as the organized instincts of a people under the form of social customs and family and national traditions. We must guide the native impulse into proper channels but be exceedingly careful to lose out nothing that is of value in the native root. The policy that would seek to prevent the flow of sap from the wild root into the engrafted branch in the fear that wild fruitage might replace or injure the cultivated fruit would be no more fatuous than that which expresses itself in a school policy that tends to belittle or destroy the individual or social life of the foreign pupil lest he should grow into an American citizen with a tainted or foreign attitude.

Much is being said and written these days on the subject of Americanization. Some of it is not worthy of a lasting place in our literature. It is high time that all those that are interested in this work should consider carefully what it is that makes an American citizen. What are the qualities that are indispensable in a man or woman who benefits by our institutions and takes an active part in their support and in their betterment?

I would divide these into two categories, in one of which I would place the obvious and immediate training for citizenship that should be given to all who do not already possess it, whether it be child or adult, foreigner or native born. If our government was conducted by a few individuals of a favored class who made our laws, administered and enforced them, the duty of the citizen might be reduced to that of simple obedience to the command of his superiors. But this country is built on a totally different foundation. The state in a democracy must operate unceasingly for the interest, not of the majority, but of the whole people, and the welfare of the whole people demands the highest possible education of the few who must control our public policies. In a government such as ours the tendency to shape public action in the interest of the majority leads toward the jungle and the beastial struggle for existence, and the survival of the strong. We cannot overemphasize the statement that it is the duty of the state in a democracy to maintain the interest of the whole people: although the majority governs, the right of the minority must not be ignored. Action for the greatest good of the greatest number is a pernicious fallacy. The greatest good of the minority may at times be identified with the greatest good of the whole state; whereas the greatest good of the majority may work deep and lasting injury if it is made the norm and rule of state action. This truth may be illustrated in a variety of ways. The state, for example, needs a small group of men with the highest possible education to enact its laws and to administer them wisely. A public policy that would be shaped by the intelligence of the majority of voters in a country like the United States would lead rapidly to demoralization and to arrest of the forces making for civilization. Respect for vested rights, for equity, and justice must curb the will of the majority, otherwise the country will suffer from strife, contention of class with class, strikes and reprisals and shut-outs, to the great detriment of the whole people. Obviously native-born Americans need to be Americanized in this respect quite as much as some of the strangers who have come from Europe to make their home with us. Our problem might well be stated the Americanizing of all children, native-born as well as foreign-born, or those born of foreign parents. Overemphasis is being laid just now on the Americanization of the foreign child. Again, in order to serve the country the school should aid at imparting such skill to each boy and girl as will enable the men and women, not only to support themselves, but to contribute their share to the support and education of the children of the nation, of the aged and infirm, and of the dependent classes generally. If the school fails in this it fails to make worthy citizens. This necessary skill may be along mechanical lines or it may lead in a direction demanding long and arduous years of training to fit the individual to render valuable professional service as a teacher, as a physician, or as one competent to frame our laws and take part in the administration of justice. A democracy, more than any other country demands inequality in the education given to its members. Those who are especially gifted by nature, must, for the public good, receive such training as will fit them for leadership, and this training is neither possible nor necessary for the rank and file of voters whose duty it is to second the efforts of the leaders whom they conscientiously select from the ranks of those who, by training and virtue, are available for leadership.

Over and above the skill which the individual should possess in order to discharge effectively the duties of his vocation, the welfare of the state demands that he maintains a right attitude towards our government and towards the institutions of our country, and that he possess certain moral qualities among which the following six are conspicuous:

1. The faith of man in his fellow man lies at the foundation of a democracy. Without it our social institutions and the state itself must cease to exist. The son who has no belief in his mother's virtue beyond that which might be established by evidence that would convince an indifferent or hostile jury, is unworthy to bear the title of son. The husband who has no belief in his wife, and the wife who has no belief in her husband, beyond that determined in a similar way renders marriage futile and home impossible. The success among the people of any movement for freedom or uplift depends in last analysis upon the faith of the people in their chosen leaders. Our courts of justice, our property rights, and even our lives, rest upon public faith in the truthfulness of witnesses and in the integrity of judges and jurors. Destroy public confidence in our merchants and in our bankers, in our social and religious leaders and in our public officials, and all the institutions of a democracy will collapse. Moreover, it is the child's faith in his teacher which makes it possible for him to accept without question the wisdom of the ages as his guide in the building up of his own character, and in the formation of his attitude towards his fellow man and the institutions of civil life. Without this faith in the child the state would be unable to perpetuate itself.

2. Hope is scarcely less necessary to the citizen than faith. Through faith he is put into possession of the treasures accumulated by the generations that have passed away. Through hope he anticipates the harvests of the future. Faith broadens his view and clears his understanding while hope supplies the reason for putting forth his energy and spending himself. A man marries and founds a home in the assured hope of its permanence. He plants his crops in the hope of reaping the harvest. He builds railroads, develops commerce and establishes factories in the hope of reaping the legitimate rewards of his investment. Faith in the permanence of the social order is the source from which hope springs, and hope is the effective force that carries the past and the present over into the

future. Take away from man hope and not only will his own life become vain and empty but all progress of the race comes to an end, and all that has been achieved by civilization in the past will disappear. It is the hope of what the future may bring that moves every wheel and presses every spring of action in human life. By hope the parents live in anticipation the lives of their children and rejoice in their joy. They are carried out of the sordidness of the present with its selfishness and greed and, by living through hope in an ideal world, are purified and ennobled. But to produce this salutary effect hope must not only spring from faith but it must be accompanied and controlled by love.

3. Man's love for his fellow man is, in fact, the fundamental principle on which Christian civilization rests. The Christian state is bound together in solidarity by the internal bonds of faith and hope and charity instead of by coercion of armed forces. In Christian civilization all social institutions are built upon the intelligence, the emotions, and the will of the individuals. The home which is created by the faith and hope and love of one man for one woman and of one woman for one man is the foundation upon which the welfare of the whole social body rests. The Christian home is indispensable for the maintenance and proper upbringing of children. The close contact of the child with the daily manifestation by Christian parents of self-oblation and self sacrifice is required to build in the child's soul the unshakable foundations of faith and hope and love. These virtues implanted in the home must be broadened by the school until they embrace the entire nation. In the Christian state the citizen must believe in his fellow man; he must labor for his interests and for the interests of the generations to come after him. If police force is required the necessity arises from the failure of education to form all the children into worthy citizens and force must be invoked to accomplish what should have been achieved in a far higher degree by the fundamental virtues which should characterize the citizens.

The state in educating for citizenship may not proceed effectively with the work of broadening the faith, hope, and charity of the individual beyond national limits, unless indeed the League of Nations should achieve in some measure this most desirable end. The Church, however, knows no boundaries, not even of color, of race or creed. She aims at lifting into the consciousness of each individual an effective recognition of the Fatherhood of God and the Brotherhood of Man. Cooperation secured by the Church among the children of men may be likened to the cooperation of the divers form of life, whereas the cooperation called for to perpetuate the nation may be likened to the cooperation among the members of the same species.

Competition, or the struggle of individual with individual, or of group with group, moves under the banner of selfishness and greed which are always near the surface. Christianity, on the contrary, drawing to itself the finer elements of human nature and the choice souls among the children of men, seeks unceasingly to supplant competition by cooperation. The love of the parent for the child, acting through the child's instinctive tendency to imitate, shifts the centre of gravity from the child's self to the group. It teaches them to strive for the good of the larger self. Upon the success of the parent in this important educative function, reinforced by the school and the Church, rests the welfare of the home, the city, the nation, the Church, and humanity itself. It is for this reason that thoughtful people will hesitate before dealing with the foreign child in such a way as to lessen the influence of parents and of home upon the formation of his character, and we are in grave danger of weakening this influence by our overzeal for hasty transformations in the child, which ignore the roots of his moral being that have struck deep into the customs and traditions of the land of his forefathers.

The element of progress contained in cooperation as opposed to competition is manifesting itself in art and literature, in medicine, in scientific research, in public libraries and museums, in public parks and public highways, and the principle is just now receiving a most striking illustration in the economic and industrial revolution which is carrying us from a tool to a machine civilization.

Faith, hope and charity—these three virtues constitute the foundation of Christian character and they must always remain the foundation of citizenship in a democracy. No one of them may be dispensed with without disaster. To produce these virtues in the children and to cultivate and develop them to a high degree of efficiency must therefore be included in all education for citizenship, but in effective education for citizenship the fundamental virtues should be supplemented by at least three additional virtues: disinterestedness, reverence for law, and self-control.

4. The worthy citizen must ever hold public good above all private gain. The good which he shares with his fellow man must appeal to him more strongly than the good which ministers to his own individual need. He must realize that what he does for others goes out in ever widening circles and is likely to flow onward to enrich future generations, whereas the good directed toward self is likely to end there. This principle holds good even in material matters but it finds its fullest fruition in the things of the mind, which, like the quality of mercy, blesses him that gives and him that takes.

Were this virtue of disinterestedness properly developed in our men in public life and in public office bribery, fraud, and graft would be unknown in our midst. As it is, men may readily be found who are willing to die for their country but even through years of training we find it difficult to produce men who will live for it. The sudden awakening of the martial spirit or a wave of popular sentiment may sweep men from their fireside to the battle front, but education of our citizens must do more than this; it must give the individual the power to live for his country and to exert himself in its behalf day by day. He must learn to labor unceasingly for the public welfare without the aid that comes from a tide of public feeling. The native impulse, with its note of self-oblation and self sacrifice which leads to parentage, must be converted by education for citizenship into a permanent, constantly operative principle of conduct, and here again we see the great danger that lurks in the rash intrusion of overzealous Americanizers into the sanctity of the homes of our foreign born citizens. We may readily destroy the delicate, vital bonds that are destined by nature to pass over from the parents

to children, transforming the latter from selfish, greedy, little beasts into generous, self-forgetting citizens who will labor for the common good. It has been
questioned, and it is still open to question after the nation-wide experiment which
has been made in our midst during the past seventy-five years, whether this result
may be achieved without invoking God and a belief in supernatural sanction in
which alone the individual may find himself and the public brought into unity,
but whatever results may be expected to reward the endeavor, schools of every
character must strive to lead their pupils toward this ideal.

5. The quality of obedience to law sufficed for the masses where government
was conducted by the aristocracy, but in a country like ours where the government is "of the people, for the people, and by the people" the citizen must be
educated in a threefold capacity to support law. He must be trained to take his
due share in the enactment of just and wise legislation. He must lend his support
and cooperation to the judiciary and the executive branches of the government,
and he must obey loyally and help to secure the obedience of others to the existing laws. Education for citizenship must, therefore, include among its aims the
development in each individual of qualities which will enable him to vote intelligently and induce him to vote conscientiously for men and measures that
seem calculated to promote the public good. The school must also aim at producing men and women of fine ability to fill public offices, men and women who will
loyally support the educational efforts calculated to secure the greatest freedom
of selection and the greatest efficiency in educating public servants.

6. Finally, the citizen must be trained to curb his own appetites and to sub-
jugate his own desires so that he may labor for the public good and work no
injury to his fellow man, nor interfere with any right or privilege possessed by
another. Each individual must learn to govern himself and the kingdom of his
own passions before he is fit for citizenship, and before he may safely be entrusted to participate in the government of others.

Americanization, or educating for citizenship, should therefore mean much
more than equipping the individual for economic efficiency or the developing in
him of those qualities which may minister to his selfish pleasures and aggrandise-
ment. It means chiefly the production and development in the children of the six
virtues which we have just enumerated. With this brief consideration of the problem which confronts us in our attempts to Americanize foreign born children and
the children of foreign born parents we may be permitted to examine and contrast the state public schools with the Catholic public schools with a view of
ascertaining how each of these institutions operate to secure the desired result. If
we contrast the two schools it is with no wish to belittle the achievements of our
state schools but with the legitimate desire to bring home to ourselves and to our
fellow citizens the splendid work in this direction which has been done, and is
being done, by our Catholic schools.

The State supports its schools to the end that the children may grow up into
self-supporting, self-respecting and efficient members of society, into men and
women who, instead of becoming a public burden, will contribute their share to

the public welfare, into men and women who, instead of demanding armed force to prevent them from indulging in acts of dishonesty, will promote public morals by the integrity of their own lives, into patriotic citizens who will be ever solicitous for the public welfare, and who will always place public good above all private gain. In a word, the ultimate aim in state education is, and must always remain, to educate for citizenship. As far as the state is concerned, all other educational aims are either indifferent or secondary, but she must insist upon education for citizenship, not only in her own schools but in all other schools which undertake to train her future citizens. The realization of this aim demands the cultivation in the pupil of the fundamental virtues and qualities set forth above, among which disinterestedness occupies a prominent place. Nevertheless the state is obliged to use self-interest as the main motive in attracting her teachers and in keeping them in her service. The Church, on the contrary, requires of each individual who seeks a place in any one of her teaching communities that he first relinquish all ownership of property, and all claims to monetary compensation for his future labors. By a vow of poverty he frees himself once for all from the control of the financial motive and is enabled to devote his life and his services unreservedly to the children who may come under his care, without thought of personal gain or benefit in return. He does not marry and consequently has no children depending upon him, and if parents or other members of the family necessarily depend upon him for support he will be denied admittance to the community. The force of this example, acting on the children day by day, is more potent in its socializing influence and in the production of disinterested citizenship than any formal teaching of morality could be. In this respect our religious teachers imitate, as far as human fragility will permit, the example of the Master, who spoke of Himself as the Good Shepherd who lay down His life for His flock, and who said to His disciples: "My little children, love one another as I also have loved you."

The primary aim of the Church is, of course, salvation of souls, and in her educational work her unceasing purpose is the cultivation of supernatural virtues, but in this field she does not meet the state. In the production of supernatural virtues, however, she cultivates and strengthens the natural virtues with which alone the state is directly concerned and it is this aspect of the question with which we are concerned at the present moment.

The Church is not content with selecting for her teaching force men and women whose social consciousness is so highly developed that they joyfully renounce all earthly possessions in order to devote their energies throughout the rest of their lives to the service of others, irrespective of race or creed or country. In the noviciate the candidate is not only given time to make sure that his call to the religious life is permanent, but he is exercised in the practice of the six great fundamental virtues for two or more years before he is allowed to take his place with the active teaching force. Moreover, this training follows him through life as he is constantly called upon to practice the virtues in question.

In the Catholic school system the supply of teachers is secured through the operation of principles which eliminate all but the chosen souls who possess in a high degree the qualities discussed above as pertaining to good citizenship. Not content with these qualities as they appear in the young men and the young women of the world, it carefully trains them with a view to the further development of these qualities and takes every means to preserve and continue the development of these same virtues throughout the lives of her teachers. There is no other society in the world that operates so effectively to produce in its membership the great fundamental virtues of human faith and hope and brotherly love, of disinterestedness, self-control and loyalty to law as the religious communities in the Catholic Church. The candidate not only gives up earthly possessions, but is called upon to renounce the high privilege of parentage, of home and of independence. He must obey, not only the commandments and the fundamental laws, but also the Gospel counsels of perfection. His love must not only be purified of self, but of family and of nationality; it must be broadened until it embraces all mankind, strengthened until it supplies sufficient motive for any sacrifice, and lifted up from earth until it is transfigured by the love of God. The Catholic school supplied with teachers of this character should prove incalculably more efficient than the state school in promoting worthy citizenship, nevertheless, the Church has never accepted education for citizenship as the goal of educational process and she never can accept it as the ultimate aim of the education given to her children. The Church recognizes in each child a future citizen, but she also recognizes in him a child of Heaven who must grow to maturity and live out a brief span with his fellows in the industrial, social and civic environments of his day and country.

There is another noteworthy difference to be observed in contrasting the state school with the Catholic school. The state, through her educational system, seeks to transmit to the rising generation the institutions and spiritual treasures built up by the present and the past while all advance of society is to be looked for in the activities of the adult population. In the Catholic system, on the contrary, the deliberate purpose is to lift adult society to a higher level through the school. This purpose the Church seeks to accomplish through her teaching communities. The secular teacher brings with him into the school daily the atmosphere of the world in which he lives; the women who form such an overwhelming majority of the teachers in the state system are an integral part of the social and economic world of their day and they share its spirit and its progress. The teacher, however, is seldom in the forefront of social or economic progress; her professional duties withdraw her during her working hours from the actual strife, hence she cannot transmit the latest achievements of society, the things that are actually growing where the struggle is intense, and no other source of inspiration and guidance is provided for her. The religious teacher, on the contrary, is withdrawn from the world and lifted above its strife and turmoil. Through daily religious exercises and the practice of the rules of the community and the virtues enjoined thereby, she brings the redeeming influence of Jesus Christ and of his saving teachings to bear upon the children who come under her influence, thus implanting high ideals and thus shaping their lives to standards that far outrun the highest achievements of the world.

The Catholic Church, both through her organic teaching and through her schools, has ever continued her work of redeeming society. She is not, and she cannot be, content to transmit the achievements of one generation to another. She has a treasure to impart that is not produced by men, a civilizing and socializing influence to wield which has its source in Jesus Christ. The Church finds that her educational aims are best achieved through the organization of her teachers into religious communities which are governed by the counsels of perfection, and it is hard to see how she could have achieved her results in any other way. The world, left to itself, soon loses the spirit of sacrifices and abnegation. It condemns humility and erects individual aggressiveness into an ideal. It makes no provision for creating and sustaining a body of teachers that can afford to be wholly disinterested in its motive. In fact it must keep the financial motive in the foreground in the selection, improvement, and retention of its teaching force.

Mr. Pritchard, former President of the Carnegie Foundation, in a public address delivered in North Carolina some years ago, emphasized this aspect of the situation when he declared that "outside of the schools conducted by the religious communities of the Catholic Church teaching was strictly an economic function."

State school systems, here and elsewhere, in spite of the authority and the funds at their disposal, have absolutely failed to call into existence a force of professional teachers whose motives in teaching are lifted above personal and financial gain. Nor need this surprise anyone for the state schools are limited in their scope to the teaching of secular branches and in their aims to temporal and economic success. The teachers are obliged to look out for their individual support and for the support of those depending upon them, and, like other human beings, they must make provision for a rainy day, for sickness and old age. All the forces playing upon them in fact lift the financial motive into the central place. It is to be hoped, however, that altruistic and social motives are added and stimulated as far as possible, but in such a system these motives must remain subordinate to the main issue which is measured in terms of dollars and cents.

In the great task before us of Americanizing the children of the nation, particularly the foreign born and the children of foreign born parents, the Catholic school has many advantages which the state schools do not share and the Catholic schools should, therefore, be proportionately more effective in performing this patriotic service. The Catholic school need abate not one jot or tittle of its own peculiar work, or forego one inspiration of its own spirit in order to emphasize the proper formation of citizenship in its pupils and any neglect on the part of the school to perform this service in a worthy manner must inevitably react unfavorably upon the Catholic Church and the Catholic school system as a whole. It is necessary, therefore, that all those who are vested with authority in the matter will see to it that every legitimate demand of the state in this respect is fully complied with.

Freedom and education: the pluralist background

Charles Donahue

This article poses a fundamental question relevant to both political and educational theory. How is it possible to achieve social unity in a country where theoretical differences on the meaning of the democratic charter are so acute? Perhaps the solution—not altogether acceptable but workable nevertheless—is to operate from a base of practical necessity: We support the democratic charter because we have found it to be an effective way of living together. The author illustrates the dilemmas of public and independent schools vis-à-vis unity and divisiveness, and deplores the unenviable and often defensive postures independent schools must assume. He concludes that public education may be a fitting symbol of our need for secular unity, but he argues against being content with secular unity.

"Divisive" has come to be a favorite word among those who believe that all American education, at least for the first twelve years, should be tax-supported, secular, and entirely under public control. A second favorite word is "sectarian," and recently a third has become popular, "spiritual values." The public schools will teach and practice spiritual values, but, of course, they will not be sectarian, because sects are divisive. When nearly all are compelled by economic pressure— the decision in the Oregon school case forbids other pressures—to attend public schools such as our present public school, the nation will continue to benefit from

Reprinted with permission from *Thought*, 27:542–560, Winter, 1952.

the spiritual values of the Judaeo-Christian tradition, so the theory has it, while divisive sectarian rage, confined to the churches on Sunday, will abate.

The case for a monistic and secular public education has a certain plausibility. Religious denominations can be divisive, and the potential danger of such division has been frightfully demonstrated in our own generation by the use made of the fact that some Germans were denominated "Christians" and some, "Jews." The recognition of a civic need for the spiritual values of the Judaeo-Christian tradition makes the case still more appealing, and the implied promise that the public schools can keep these values alive without the divisive inconvenience of the world religions that generated them does not seem strange to the large number of Americans who follow the Liberal Protestant tendency to regard conduct rather than belief as the central religious fact.

To the American religionist not of the Liberal Protestant persuasion, the conservative religionist, whether Catholic, Protestant, or Jew, the program is less plausible. In the first place, the proposition that the spiritual values of the Judaeo-Christian tradition can be kept vigorous when torn out of their religious context seems to him, purely from the point of view of cultural history as well as on doctrinal grounds, extremely dubious. Further, he is likely to resent the purely utilitarian attitude toward spiritual values that the program implies. Religion generates socially useful conduct, but from the religionist's point of view this conduct is not an end in itself; it is only a by-product of that right relation between the rational creature and his Creator which is the end of religion and the supreme human value. Further, for such a religionist, freedom of religion means the right to work out that relation in terms of the doctrines of his own faith and the right to pass those doctrines on, as the most valuable part of his culture, to his children without interference by the civil power. Now, the conviction that man's relation to God is an intellectually simple matter is another Liberal Protestant conviction. The Catholic—and, I believe, many other conservative religionists—tends rather to regard the faith as something proportioned to the needs of the individual. It is simple in the simple; complex in the complex. As the personality, through education, becomes more complex, there must be a corresponding development in the breadth and profundity of the individual's hold on religious doctrine. Otherwise, the resultant attempt to lead the life of an educated adult with a child's intellectual grasp of religious doctrine will ultimately result in a kind of ideological schizophrenia. But simultaneous development of the religious and secular aspects of education is impossible if the child is compelled to devote a large portion of the energy he has available for education to the curriculum of a purely secular school. The secularist school program, then, seems to the conservative religionist a blow directed at the most sensitive point in his scheme of values, exactly that point where his religious convictions and his relation to his children intersect; it seems incompatible with any generous notion of religious liberty.

Perhaps the conservative religionist is merely being whimsical when, at times, he can see only a verbal difference between a public educational system such as some educators envisage and a Liberal Protestant (or secularist) State Church. In any case, he is extremely unhappy about the present relation between the tax-supported schools and the religious convictions of the nation those schools serve. Often, he is reluctant to speak out too strongly because he does not wish to give the false impression that he is an enemy of public education or that he is truculently attempting to make the already difficult task of the public-school authorities still more difficult. The majority of Americans are either Liberal Protestants or non-churchgoers who live by a vaguely theistic or perhaps agnostic humanitarian ethos descended from Liberal Protestantism. This majority probably can, if it wishes, force its concept of what tax-supported education should be on the rest of the community. The following remarks are offered in the hope that it will not insist upon doing so if a different approach to the problem of religious and moral values in the school can preserve the present benefits of public education and, at the same time, win for that education wider and more enthusiastic public support.

I. PLURALISM

At the outset, the school problem must be posed in terms of the solution our society has in fact arrived at to the dilemma raised by our fundamental theoretical disagreements on the one hand and our practical necessity for acting corporately as a nation on the other. This solution I call pluralism. It is intended not as a name for a new theory as to how we ought to act but simply as a convenient term for what we are in fact doing. It is hoped that, once we become more generally conscious of what we are doing, we may have the basis for a more fruitful and less acrimonious discussion of such problems as that of freedom and the schools.

Perhaps the best way to arrive at that clearer consciousness is by a few general considerations on the climate of opinion at the time the United States was formed.

From the point of view of the historian of ideas (and of sensibility) the American Constitution would seem to have been written and the American experiment launched in a period of calm interregnum between two civil pomposities. The grandiose Renaissance State with its sacral king had been trimmed down even in England. Its pomps had no appeal whatever to the colonial imagination (as they still had to England's) nor its ideas to the colonial intellect. That equally grandiose construction, the metaphysically committed state of the Jacobins, ruled by the elected representatives of the General Will, had not yet arrived. Although it was dimly discernible on the intellectual horizon, it was clearly not wanted here. The American Constitution launched a state which was neither metaphysically nor religiously committed. We cannot call it an uncommitted state, for act implies commitment and the state must act. An uncommitted state would be no state at all. It can be called, however, a state of limited commitment. The First Amendment is the first of a series of thou-shalt-not's addressed to the state. Its effect was to remove man's search for and convictions about ultimate values from the state's competence. What it offered was a machinery of government and—more important—a few convictions regarding the spirit in which that machinery was to be operated. These convictions were partly implicit in the machinery itself, partly stated or implied in the Preamble and the first ten Amendments to the Constitution, and partly left for granted among citizens formed by English common law and Enlightenment Whiggery. They included the conviction of inalienable human rights and the conviction that the necessary coercive power of the state was a potential danger to these rights.

Part of the importance of these attitudes and convictions is that they do not constitute a complete and satisfactory pattern of conviction for the conduct of the whole of human life. Because it is limited, the state offers elements which, to be effective, must be integrated in more complete and adequate total patterns of conviction. The other elements in that total pattern of conviction the citizen must seek elsewhere. The state has nothing to offer. The necessity that the citizen must look beyond the data of the state's traditions for his convictions—a necessity imposed by the limited conviction of the state—is and doubtless was intended to be a most important means of assuring to the citizen and his posterity "the blessings of liberty."

The move was a bold and original one because the success of the state obviously depends upon the total character and total formation of its citizens. The American state left this formation to a plurality of forces which it placed beyond its control—confining itself to the political level of the human personality and consciously leaving the sacral elements of the national life to be worked out pluralistically by the moral and spiritual traditions freely operating among the people. Events, so far, have justified the move. The system of permitting to the citizen development of character according to patterns of conviction freely arrived at and freely held has, so far, developed characters of sufficient strength and sufficient devotion to our national convictions to enable the state to meet the limited objectives it has set for itself.

While the material concerns of the state have, on the whole, developed favorably, the free moral forces motivating that development have become more numerous and more diverse. In the early Republic, the moral forces were primarily varieties of Protestantism. Deism of the mild English variety was also a real force. Catholics and Jews were not numerous. The essentially pluralistic character of the nation was maintained by the Constitution, by the diversities of Protestantism, and by the tendency to fragmentation characteristic of nineteenth-century Protestantism. The full possibilities of the civilization we are developing by means of the limited state in the pluralistic nation could not be apparent so long as Americans were, in fact, overwhelmingly Protestant. The test of the limited state is its power to hold together in civil peace diverse and potentially antagonistic moral forces, to permit free development of these forces, and to employ the human characters formed by these forces in the common interest. The large influx of Catholic immigration which began before the middle of the nineteenth century provided a decisive test of the sincerity of American pluralism.

There seems to have been a widespread idea that most of the immigrants would eventually assimilate themselves to one or another of the prevailing Protestant patterns. It was only after it became clear that the Catholics were using the essentially pluralistic idea behind the American Constitution to establish a freely developing and increasingly conscious Catholicism as a moral force operating side by side with the older moral forces that there was alarm, and with the alarm some unpleasantness. The unpleasantness is unimportant today. What is important is that the Protestant majority abided by our constitutional pluralism and permitted it to come into complete act. It was a generous move and an indication that most Protestant patterns of conviction had successfully incorporated the basic political assumptions underlying the state of limited commitment. Whatever convictions regarding Church-State relationships Protestants had brought with them to the colonies had been changed by the American atmosphere.

The pluralistic character of the American nation became even more apparent with the immigration, a little later than the first wave of Catholic immigration, of a considerable number of Jews. Like the Catholics, the Jews brought with them a religious pattern of conviction of great age, great complexity, and great flexibility. Like Catholicism, Judaism is a culture as well as a religion, and, to an even greater extent than Catholicism, a culture developed independently of national cultural patterns. The arrival of Jews in significant numbers brought into the pluralistic family the third great Western spiritual tradition. And here Judaism has found at last something better than tolerance. In a pluralistic nation, it has an opportunity for full and free development of its impressive spiritual and cultural resources as a partner in the common task of forming the character of American citizens.

II. THE ANTI–PLURALISTIC DELUSION

It is perhaps typical of our national habits of thought and action—habits that are basically traditionalist, pragmatic, anti-intellectual, Anglo-Saxon—that we should have lived our way into a magnificent arrangement, lived by that arrangement during crucial years, and failed to be clearly and generally conscious of the fact that it is an arrangement and that it is magnificent. But in this case more than a dislike of theory stood in the way of an immediate recognition of precisely what we are doing. The very character of the arrangement tended to obscure the forces that were at work. In the first place, our system confronts the individual citizen directly with the state, and the state asks only that the individual be a good citizen—law-abiding, reasonably energetic for the commonweal, informed according to his capacities for his decisions at the polls. The state asks no questions about the total pattern of conviction in which the individual citizen's character is based. The moral forces operating in our public affairs, consequently, are not on the center of the civic stage. They are behind stage and work through the citizens they have formed. Their importance can be overlooked by an observer not trained to see them or by one who has conscious or unconscious motives for not wanting to see them.

Further, these forces, particularly in so far as they are directly and consciously religious, are obscured by social conventions which forbid anything but the most abstract discussion of religious conviction. A Jewish religionist who, as a citizen, works and votes for increased social security is not going to say publicly that his action is motivated by a conviction that God commanded the children of Israel to show mercy to the widow and the orphan. If he did so he would be regarded as a poseur, a fanatic, and probably a hypocrite. The affairs of the limited state are secular affairs and we discuss them in secular terms. But this convention is harmful if it blinds us to the real sources of the moral dynamism behind our conduct of secular affairs.

Finally, the state of limited commitment not only permits full and free development to organized moral forces within the nation. It permits dissent against any or all of them, free change of commitment from one to another, and noncommitment to any of them. A considerable number of Americans have no formal connection with any organized moral force. Some disapprove of the very idea of an organized moral force. Most of these people are good citizens, and those who are have more or less consciously held patterns of conviction on which they act. When these patterns of conviction are examined, it is usually quite clear, particularly to an historian of ideas, that they are eclectic structures built up from elements taken, often not at first hand and not consciously, from the Western religious traditions.

It is not our purpose to discuss here the comparative value of patterns of conviction nor whether or not it is better to ally oneself organically with one of the great traditions or to remain outside all traditions and to construct eclectically a personally satisfying and civilly useful pattern of conviction. The state of limited commitment leaves the choice up to the citizen. It is to be noted, however, that in either case, directly in the first and indirectly in the second, the state relies on the traditional organized moral forces for the character of its citizens. It is to be noted too that the person formed by organic connection with one of the traditions and the person formed outside any of them by means of more or less individual pattern of conviction are identical as they face the state as citizens. Both have full civic rights and both will be regarded by the state as good or bad according to their actions in forwarding the purely secular and mostly material concerns of the limited state. This last is an obvious fact, a truism, but failure to apprehend its full significance has resulted in a popular delusion—sometimes even a learned delusion—which has obscured our full consciousness of the pluralist society we have brought into being. This delusion—it is hardly articulate enough to be called a theory—consists in a more or less vague feeling that some sort of "nonsectarian" and possibly religiously agnostic ethos is or should be the ethos of the nation and that it should enjoy state favor while other patterns of conviction, because they are religiously committed, will be tolerated but deprived of all state favor because of the First Amendment.

The delusion arises partly from the uniqueness of our accomplishment. We worked out our state of limited commitment in a world where such a state was unknown. The colonies were religiously committed statelets and some had even tried to be sacral statelets on the Geneva model. The great states of Europe were religiously committed, and shortly after we launched our experiment France abandoned its religious commitment and began its experiments with the meta-physically committed state. The antipluralist delusion begins in an inability to grasp the full significance of the state of limited conviction, a refusal to believe that our uncommitted state is really uncommitted, and in a consequent groping for some pattern of conviction which would be more "American," which would give its holder a more complete sense of "belonging," and which would be more worthy of state support than other patterns of conviction. This groping can take place only among the diverse patterns of conviction found in the pluralist nation, and there one finds the great variety of patterns developed within the Western spiritual traditions and a still greater variety eclectically constructed by the dis-associated. The next maneuver is to make the very noncommitted and limited character of the state a criterion for choice between patterns. The state is limited mainly to secular concerns. The state is uncommitted to any particular religious tradition. That pattern of conviction, therefore, which is secular and uncommitted is, consequently, felt to be most appropriate in a nation governed by such a state as ours.

By the same reasoning it could be shown that the best horse is the one that looks most like the cart, but, of course, we are not dealing with a reasoned con-viction. This antipluralist delusion is a vague popular feeling, an inarticulate yearning for something that does not exist, a standard national ethos—whether one calls it a religion or a philosophy is indifferent—supported and propagated by state power, a measure of all other patterns of conviction which, if they diverge too much, will be viewed as abnormal and eccentric, "tolerated" but not wel-comed. The prevalence of the antipluralist delusion is, in short, an indication that many Americans are still haunted by the ghost of the committed state. If the antipluralist delusion were embodied in our institutions, the effect would be reactionary and we would be led back from pluralism to the religiously com-mitted state or, more likely, to a secularized variant of the committed state.

It is, however, not very likely that the antipluralist delusion will result in a widespread conscious demand such as could, under our system, change the char-acter of the state by the lawful use of means provided by the state. Those who have caught the pluralist vision incline to believe that once these inarticulate yearnings have become articulate and conscious they will tend to disappear. Meanwhile, they are with us, and tend to becloud issues. As we shall see, they becloud educational issues so seriously as to prevent even an adequate posing of the problems involved. Their prevalence betrays itself in popular speech. Such "tolerant" expressions as "an American who happens to be a Methodist"—or "a Jew" or "a Catholic"—are signs of befuddlement about our real situation. They imply the existence of a national norm which may be but need not be supplemented by adherence to a "sect." If we see the thing from a pluralist point of view, we do not look first to the citizen, for in our system the "citizen" is an abstraction. The actual existent is a concrete human person, and the concrete human person is never just a "citizen." If he were, it would mean that the state was concerned with the whole of human life. He is always a citizen and something else: *idem civis et Judaeus, idem civis et Methodistes, idem civis et Catholicus,* and the moral drive for his citizenship always comes from that something else. The Methodist attains his civic character through his Methodism; the Jew, through his Judaism. The Methodism of the one and the Judaism of the other are not mere augments to something already existing and capable of independent existence, "the citizen."

Here a purely semantic trap is ready for us. What has been said about the Methodist citizen and the Jewish citizen is true of every other citizen whatever including those for whose "something else" there is no name. Ryan is a Catholic. That means that an organic connection with a well-defined and named group is part of Ryan's pattern of conviction. He derives the ultimate moral values which motivate his civic character as a member of the group. He is *idem civis et Catholicus,* and would cheerfully admit it. Smith, on the other hand, is an earnest non-churchgoer. He is sincerely convinced that "organized religion" is an impediment to the good life, to free personal development. But he has convictions, more or less conscious, which motivate his character. He may or may not be aware that these convictions are derived, sometimes at more than one remove, from "organized religion." They are certainly not derived from the state, because the state, in America, although it uses ultimate moral values, is not a source of such values. Ryan's pattern of conviction has a name. He is a Catholic. Smith's other neighbors go to churches that have names. But there is no name for Smith's pattern of conviction, and that linguistic accident makes it possible for Smith to think in such terms as this: "Ryan is a decent fellow who happens to be a Catholic; Jones is a decent fellow who happens to be a Methodist; Bernstein is a decent fellow who happens to be a Jew; but I, Smith, am just a decent fellow, a plain American and nothing else." Give Smith's pattern of conviction a name, say Smithianism, and it becomes clear that Smith is *idem civis et Smithianus.* His relation to the state and the nation is exactly the same as his neighbors'. Admirable fellow that he is, Smith will be blind to the pluralist vision until his semantic difficulties are cleared up. Until that time, he will be particularly vulnerable to secularist propaganda which will tell him that "sects" are "divisive" and ought to be discouraged for the sake of a unified America. His views on public affairs such as education will be notably lacking in pluralistic subtlety.

When a new arrangement such as ours is arrived at by a process of development, it will invariably leave in its wake a series of semantic problems. Consciousness demands semantic clarification. One such case has been considered. Another case is the current use of the words "sect" and "sectarian" as pejorative terms. "Sects" are something we tolerate but don't welcome. But, from the point of view of national pluralism, the term "sect" is completely meaningless, a semantic ghost.

"Sect," something cut off, is meaningful only in a context where some entity is regarded as central, normal. From an Anglican point of view, the Methodists are a sect; from a Catholic point of view, all Protestants are sectarians; from a conservative Jewish point of view, I suppose, all Christians are sectarians. But from the point of view of the state of limited commitment, no pattern of conviction is regarded as standard or normal. As a general rule, the state takes no cognizance of patterns of convictions *as such*. It sees only persons in their aspect as citizens. From the point of view of the state of limited commitment or of the pluralistic nation, therefore, there are no such things as sects or sectarians. The very use of the word in a civil context is an indication of failure to grasp fully the pluralistic vision; for, given a civil context and a pluralistic nation, either all are sectarians or none is. In short, the word is meaningless and can only serve as an emotional tag for propaganda purposes.

Some people now object to the word "tolerance" and this objection is a sign of at least a dawning pluralist consciousness; for, like "sect," the word "tolerance" implies the existence of a norm from which divergences are permitted but not welcomed. In the case of religiously committed states, such as England still is, at least in theory, the word has a meaning. In an English civic context, one can say that Catholicism is tolerated. But in an American civic context, the statement would obviously be nonsense, as would the statement that Methodism, Judaism, or Smithianism are tolerated. Unlike the English state, which has the English Church, the American state has nothing of its own with which to replace Catholicism, Methodism, Smithianism, or any other pattern of conviction. It has abolished tolerance by transcending it.

III. PLURALISM AND DISCRIMINATION

Now it may be objected that such a statement is mere semantic razzle-dazzle, that, in our daily lives as citizens, we have not only not transcended tolerance, we have notably failed to attain it. It is indubitably true that our idea of a civic brotherhood that transcends tolerance is very far from complete actualization. Discrimination, ranging from the snub by the lifted eyebrow to the grossest cruelty and injustice, is one of our national problems. It is, in part, an economic problem. In part, it may be a psychiatric problem. Here, in our ventilation of ideas, we can consider it only in so far as it is a problem in ideas and ideals. On this level, it can be said that—however our practice may lag—we have an ideal of civic brotherhood and some progress has been made in actualizing it. Now, discrimination ordinarily has one or both of two grounds—ostensibly at least. It is either racial or ideological. At present, racial discrimination is far crueler than religious discrimination and represents, from the point of view of the ideas involved far different, and simpler, problems. But behind both racial and religious discrimination is, I believe, the antipluralist delusion we have been discussing, the delusion that there is some national norm and that divergences from it are less national, less "truly American" and may, therefore, be subject either to tolerance or discrimination. The stereotype, "This is a white man's country" lies behind much anti-Negro prejudice, just as behind antisemitism there is the stereotype "This is a gentile country," and behind anti-Catholic prejudice the stereotype, "This is a Protestant country." The growth of a pluralist consciousness, which means the decay of the antipluralist delusion, will necessarily eliminate these stereotypes. They are, in the main, atavistic survivals of the committed state. Such a growth should, therefore, be of considerable help in meeting the problem of discrimination.

The pluralist solution to the problem of discrimination has, in addition, the great advantage that it leaves in free and effective operation the moral forces, especially organized religion, that have been in the past our most potent weapons against the grosser cruelties of racial discrimination and are becoming equally potent weapons against discrimination itself. The alternative solutions to the problem of discrimination (on the level of ideas, not on that of economic or psychic therapy) seem to be based on the notion that a weakening of religious ideas and loyalties would lead to an increased civic fraternity. It is difficult to see how such weakening could do otherwise than exacerbate our gravest problem of discrimination, which is a racial not a religious problem.

Even in the case of religious discrimination where the alternative solution— the secularist solution—has a certain plausibility, it is very doubtful that a general religious relaxation would be accompanied by an increase in civic fraternity. The reasons for this are profoundly embedded in the doctrine and spirit of the Judaeo-Christian tradition. But here we can content ourselves with the empirical observation that, even in our present society, pluralist in structure but not wholly in consciousness, it is not ordinarily the deeply committed religionist, well-informed and spiritually developed within his own tradition, who practices or countenances religious discrimination in his civic life. He is repelled by it. It is rather among weakly committed, relatively uninformed, and often merely nominal religionists that one finds a tendency toward religious discrimination, and behind this tendency there is usually hidden the antipluralist delusion. Denuded of its religious content, the religious commitment has become simply the badge of belonging to something more normal, more "typically American," than something else and consequently an excuse for discrimination against the less normal, less typical outsider. Hence arises the nonsense of "the Protestant neighborhood" and "the Christian neighborhood." It is needless to say that this is not religion; it is a use of the external trappings of religion for secular purposes. The suburban dwellers in "Protestant neighborhoods" know nothing and care nothing about Luther or Wesley, Barth or Niebuhr. Those who seek out "Christian neighborhoods" are not seeking there for Christ. Such offenses against civic brotherhood cannot be cured by secularism. Those who commit them are secularists already. A growth of pluralist consciousness, on the other hand, may do some good.

In general, however, religious differences are not a basis for the more odious form of discrimination. In most cases, anti-Catholic feeling is at least vaguely associated with some kind of racial prejudice. The problem of antisemitism is a special problem and a very complex one. It is neither a problem of religious nor of racial discrimination. Judaism is a religion, and a religion which generates a culture of its own. Both the religion and the culture were maintained with stubborn courage during long centuries while Christianity was absorbing with only partial success the vast mass of northern barbarism it had taken into the fold at the fall of the Roman Empire. During those centuries, the Jew, in the midst of that barbarism half-tamed by Christianity, was the Other, the Different. The barbarian impulse against the Other was always directed against him. Whether the rationalizations by which that impulse sought to justify itself were directed at the religion or the culture of the Jew is really not important.

The most recent and perhaps the cruelest outburst of antisemitism showed the pattern in a particularly stark form. Hitler's persecution was directed against the Jew solely as the Other. The racial myth served to emphasize the Jew's otherness and indeed to force him to remain the Other. The objection was not to the Jew's religion, since change of religious affiliation in no way changed his status. It was not to the particular culture of the Jew, since completely assimilated Jews were also persecuted. One might almost say that the persecution was directed against the idea of otherness, and that anyone who, for any reason, could have the word "Jew" attached to him was forced to incarnate this idea. The rest of the German nation, on the other hand, were compelled to incarnate Us-ness. To accomplish this they were encouraged to slough off Christianity and consider themselves as pure barbarians. Rosenberg and Cardinal Faulhaber agreed at least on this, that Christians are spiritually Semites. Christianity was therefore—to Rosenberg an unwelcome link between the Us and the Other. It had to be got rid of before the unalloyed Us could confront the completely Other, and the idea of persecution be actualized in its purest form.

Now, it is clear that the reason for the Jew's suffering in the West has been his insistence on living pluralistically. He steadfastly refused to confront the state as a typical member of the national mass formed only by the national culture. The price he has paid for this refusal in a society not yet ready for pluralism has ranged from the milder pressures and discriminations of the better periods to outbursts of sadistic cruelty of which our own generation has witnessed perhaps the worst. He was always there to be the Other when pathological impulses demanded an Other. He was always there, too, to be tolerated when Western barbarism under the impulse of the better forces working within it—and these forces were, directly or indirectly, Christian—was ready for a move toward tolerance. He is here now, an expert in pluralist living, and the one best qualified by his traditions to cooperate in the advance from tolerance to pluralism.

IV. MONISM OR PLURALISM?

Even Hitler's ghost is an antipluralistic force. Pluralism is based on a free development of differences, and German National Socialism abused the very idea of difference in setting the Us against the Other. The demonstration of the terrible possibilities of such abuse has led to a widespread feeling, particularly among people whose own patterns of conviction do not include direct commitment to any religious tradition, that differences are a source of danger and should be discouraged. The Us cannot be set against the Other if there is no Other. It would be better if we could pool our differences and move toward some kind of monistic civilization rather than toward a more fully developed pluralism. This widespread feeling that differences are dangerous is, of course, a powerful ally of the antipluralist delusion. It is unfortunately a feeling, not a theory propounded with full consciousness. Were it so propounded, its latent possibilities for tyranny would become apparent. What do those who are constantly warning against "divisiveness" really want? Do they really want to return to a monistic nation and a committed state? Is the ideal solution for us really one where each individual citizen faces the state as a monad, as nearly as possible like every other monad, either unformed or formed only by forces operating alike throughout the entire nation? Yet surely that is going to be the goal if we think of our ideological and cultural problems only in terms of national uniformity.

Once the feeling against divisiveness has been clearly brought to the level of a conscious theory and put in the form of a question, the answer is almost automatically supplied. The monistic alternative simply could not be attained without a sacrifice of intellectual and spiritual freedom, for, surely, freedom means the right to be convinced as well as the right to abandon conviction; it means the right to work out one's life in association with a group as well as individually. The reasons ought to be very good before we abandon a course which has brought both freedom and unity.

The only real reason for shifting to a monistic course is Hitler's demonstration that modern Western man is by no means as civilized as he thought he was. As long as there is an Other, he is capable of being led into a barbarian attack upon it. But Hitler showed more than that. He laid bare the essential nature of barbarian persecution, and thus proved that—at least in the West with its Judaeo-Christian tradition—neither theological nor cultural differences are, in themselves, causes of persecution. The mere name of Jew was enough to subject a man to persecution. And the persecutors were men anxious enough to slough off the name of Christians. Hitler showed, in short, that a monism will have to be very monistic indeed if it alone is going to save us from outbreaks of barbarism against the Other. Only when the very name of Jew is forgotten, apparently, is the danger of antisemitism over, and the same is true of any other minority that might conceivably be called upon to incarnate the Other, for it is not specifically what the other represents that is attacked; it is the idea of otherness.

It is obvious that we could not pass peaceably and rapidly from our present pluralist condition to so thoroughgoing a monism that no group could be distinguished and named and thus become the other. If it were to be a peaceful process, it would have to be drawn out over a long period of time. During this time the direct moral force of the great Western religious traditions, Judaism, Catholicism, and the various Protestantisms, would presumably decline and these forces would be subjected to increasingly vigorous propaganda attacks as "divisive" influences. Meanwhile, the new national ethos, the new Us-ness in which we would sink our differences, would emerge and begin to function as the pattern of conviction which would supply ultimate values and character to all. This ethos would presumably be some vague form of secular humanitarianism, probably with permitted variations, theist, agnostic, and atheist. During the long period of transition, before the very name of Jew, Catholic, and Protestant had been abolished, there is no reason whatever to believe that secular humanitarianism would be more effective in taming the barbarian in us than the traditional religious forces. The danger of barbarian outbursts might very well increase.

And when the process had reached its term, when everybody was ideologically like everybody else and, except within narrow limits, there was no freedom because there was no choice, the danger of persecution would still not be over. Clear proof of that has been recently offered by the Russian experiment. The USSR is a good example of a thoroughgoing monistic society produced and controlled by a metaphysically committed state. The citizen faces the state as an empty monad, a vessel into which the state pours its ideology. Here, surely, persecution should be impossible, for the Other has been wholly abolished. But Stalin has shown that even in the most thoroughgoing monistic society, it is always possible for the demagogue to produce an Other if he has any reason to bring the barbarian forces of persecution into play. All that is required is a slight twitch of the party line, and the most scrupulous walkers of the line can be suddenly and without any act on their part turned into an Other. That sort of thing can go on as long as there is hate and demagogues who are willing to use hate. The most thoroughgoing monism is no protection against it.

As for the problem with which we started, the problem of discrimination and particularly—since Hitler showed its dangers so vividly—of antisemitism, monistic thinking offers no real solution. It holds up a distant goal which could be arrived at only by a dangerous path, and at the end of the path it offers the Jew nothing except complete assimilation, the very thing he has refused for centuries, although, except under special and pathological conditions such as those of Hitler's Germany, the way was always more or less open. Even under present conditions, pluralism offers something better than that. It offers the individual Jew, as every other citizen, the right to determine his own relation to the traditions he has inherited. He is free to adopt them in any form he chooses or to reject them if he chooses. The pluralist solution is the best and most decent solution attainable at the present time. If something better is to come, it can come only through the growth of a more completely pluralist consciousness, for pluralism will leave free and active those forces which, however slowly and with however many twists, reversions, and abuses, have brought us thus far up on the way from barbarism.

Faced squarely with the choice, Americans certainly will not choose to abolish antisemitism by abolishing Judaism and to end hard feelings between Catholics and Protestants by abolishing both Catholicism and Protestantism. We can best meet our problems by clarifying the pluralist consciousness and approaching them in pluralist terms. Up to the present, our pluralism has been a lived thing rather than a theory. But, once the mists of the antipluralist delusion are dispersed, the basic structure of our national life is clear enough. A pluralist attitude is not indifferentism, and is not expressed by such clichés as "It matters not the way" or "One man's opinion is as good as another's." Pluralism is a way to civil peace without reducing the intellectual and spiritual life of the nation to a formless pulp. It recognizes the absolute character of religious conviction and, consequently, the sharpness of doctrinal distinctions. It recognizes, too, the importance of the sacral aspect of the national life. On the other hand, our pluralistic tradition has insisted that "everybody ought to get along together." Our way of life has not been favorable to the extension of sacral institutions as such into secular life (though they penetrate the latter through the order of mind and conscience). We have, and want to have, a true society on the secular level, not a system of contingent ghettos. We prefer mixed neighborhoods, mixed labor unions, mixed business and industrial establishments. In our system, the sacral interpenetrates the secular not through these institutions as such but as incorporated in persons who are cooperating fraternally and precisely as persons in secular affairs. The basic structure of our national life can, then, be seen through a metaphor of two intersecting planes, the plane of the secular and the plane of the sacral. The person, *idem civis et Christianus* (or *Judeaus* or *Smithianus*), is the line of intersection, oriented toward the absolute on the sacral plane, toward the common affairs of his fellow citizens on the secular plane.

This basic structure of our national life is necessarily the first datum in any consideration of the relation between freedom, spiritual values, and the education of the young, for education is concerned not only with the citizen and not only with the sacrally oriented individual but with the person who is both of these at once. A second datum is our present educational system. The central fact of that system is the tax-supported school, a state institution limited as the state is limited in its orientation toward the sacral. The sacral aspects of education are left to the family either alone or aided by a church of its choice. An alternative, possible in most communities, is the religious school with its primarily but not exclusively sacral orientation. Most American families are satisfied with the first alternative. As long as they are satisfied, the public school will continue to be the central fact in American primary and secondary education. Neither the importance nor the continued existence of these schools is in question. Every sane person wishes them well. But religious schools are under attack and on the defensive. Ordinarily, the argument for an exclusively public education comes down to the single point already mentioned, that independent schools, particularly religious schools, are "divisive." In the light of everything that has been said about pluralism one can admit that this is a weighty consideration. There is no doubt that a firm fraternal unity on the secular plane is essential for maintaining such a society as ours. It is all the more necessary because we have only a limited basis for unity grounded in the sacral. Perhaps the public school is a fitting symbol of our need for secular unity. But, unless one misconceives the basic structure of our attitudes and loyalties, one cannot stop with secular unity. The freedom and the importance of the sacral are equally parts of our way of life, and it is these equally American values that are symbolized by the independent religious school.

The school question, then, is an acute case of a necessarily recurrent American tension between our desire and need for unity on the one hand and our desire and need for freedom on the other. Our treatment of the question must necessarily keep hold of both terms. If we look at our educational structure in the light of the metaphor of the two planes, the actual complexities of that structure and of the problems it raises become apparent. Any satisfactory development of American education must necessarily keep these complexities in view. We cannot abolish tension by brutal suppression of one of its terms. We may alleviate it and perhaps transcend it by an approach which starts out by admitting that there is a problem and that the problem is not simple. Once the problem is posed, it can be attacked in a spirit of good will and understanding. It will not be exorcised by the incantation of such words as "sectarian" and "divisive."

The four marks

John Cogley

*The Church is one, holy, catholic, and apostolic.
Does it follow, therefore, that Catholic education
should be characterized by the same marks? Mr.
Cogley, a former editor of* Commonweal *magazine,
thinks that it does. In an address to the National
Catholic Education Association convention in 1961,
he set forth his criteria for excellence in Catholic
education, using the marks of the Church as his
guideposts. The major portion of that address
constitutes the next article.*

What are the criteria for Catholic education? This is the first question I asked
myself. And the first word that came to me was that it should be Catholic, both
with a small "c" and a large one. I was reminded then that almost a quarter of a
century ago Robert Maynard Hutchins, at that time the young President of the
University of Chicago, who is now older and mellower but no less searching—
and who is, incidentally, my present boss at the Center for the Study of Democratic Institutions in Santa Barbara—addressed himself to this subject at an
NCEA meeting. At that time Dr. Hutchins told the Catholic educators who came
to hear him that the trouble with their schools was that they were not Catholic
enough. He said that because so many of them were imitating the worst in secular
education and slighting much of the best in the long Catholic tradition of Christian humanism, they were guilty of professional sins of omission and commission. I do not think that the same charge could be made so tellingly today. It
seems to me that Catholic schools have improved on both scores. But I do think
that in stressing the ideal of catholicity, Dr. Hutchins put the emphasis where it
belongs in any discussion of education carried out under the auspices of the
Church.

Abridged and reprinted with permission from the *National Catholic Education
Association Bulletin,* 58:304–312, August, 1961.

Furthermore, might it not be that the other three marks of the Church—oneness, holiness, and apostolicity—could be applied to a consideration of excellence in Catholic education? Could not these words, lower-cased to distinguish them from the same qualities applied to the Church itself, mark the outlines of the abiding challenge to Catholic educators? In any case, that is how I intend to go at it.

Let us look, first of all, to the first of the four words, *one*. We say the Church is one, and the word is sometimes taken in a misleading way. In Latin, it is *una,* rather than *sola.* The theologians' emphasis is on the corporateness and unity of the Church, not as an impossible ideal but as a God-given fact. Of course, it follows from basic Catholic ecclesiology that there is only one Christian Church with full claim to that title. But the original emphasis was not so much on *sola* exclusivness as on *una* unity. The *one* told us something about the glory of the Church; the essential emphasis was not on the challenge to the Church's competitors. In applying the word analogically to the ideal of Christian education, that is how I would like you to think of it—as an eminently positive idea.

It seems to me that there is much in that word *one* that applies to the role of the Catholic educator. First of all, there is the simple proposition developed by Saint Thomas that the truth is one—that God is the Author of all truth—that every truth proceeds from the Holy Spirit. This, I would say, should be the first characteristic of the Catholic school in our society. Almost alone in the total educational enterprise, it is the Catholic school that relates the life of learning to the life of the spirit. At its best, Catholic education can form minds and shape attitudes that see distinctions, very necessary distinctions, between the truths of reason and those of Revelation. But it can also stress the fact that there is no impregnable wall of separation between religion and life, the world of the City and the world of the Church, the truths of science and the truths of theology, the life of nature and the life of grace. It can accent the relevance of Christianity to the life men lead in the world and, *mutatis mutandis,* the relevance of the common culture and the problems of the world to the life of the Christian.

Now this is easily said; it is not so easily done. For as you know better than I, the relationship between the Christian and the world is sown with paradox. On the one hand, we live in a world that God loved so much that He gave His Only Begotten Son to redeem it. It is a world that we too should love because it came to us from the Hand of God. On the other hand, we are constantly warned in the Scriptures to beware of worldliness. We are told to despise the things of the world. I take it that the two positions can be reconciled. I take it that what we are warned against is a kind of perverse one-worldism, against thinking and acting as if this were the only world. We are warned against loving it at the expense of loving its Maker. In the ancient formula, we are told to be *in* the world but not *of* it, for it is in the world that we are to work out our salvation; and it is by becoming totally creatures of the world that we can accomplish our damnation.

Perhaps this is going to sound too much as you would expect one to sound whose vocation is to be in the thick of things. Nevertheless, I will state a position in flat terms. I would like to see Catholic education put more emphasis on the positive attitude toward the world, for it seems to me that we need to get back to the idea that the world is good, that God loves it even if we do not seem to. We need to emphasize that the Christian has a proper and genuine interest in the world's prosperity, that the Christian has a duty to help solve the world's problems, and an obligation to see to it that it is handed down intact to the generations yet to come.

Perhaps this too will sound paradoxical, but it seems to me that the problem of worldly men is not that they love the world too much but that they do not love it enough. At the one extreme are people like the French existentialists and the American beatniks who seem to have turned their backs on creation as a meaningless muddle, a Big Joke, or a nauseous cosmic horror. At the other are the hardy abstractionists who can talk almost casually about blowing the world to smithereens in the pursuit of a victorious Justice, Liberty or Freedom which may survive in some Platonic heaven but certainly will not survive on this earth if the earth itself is turned to ashes.

The Christian truth must lie somewhere between these extremes. I would say that the Christian truth is that the world is worth keeping, despite the fact that for the first time we know how to destroy it. I would say that the Christian truth is that we are obliged to use all our natural gifts, our skills, our wit, our political intelligence, our cumulative knowledge of whatever kind, first, to keep the world intact, and, second, to make it a better place to live in, not only for ourselves but for our children and their children. The world is not ours to destroy as we see fit, no more than our lives are. It is for its proper Sovereign to say when it will be brought to an end. If I may paraphrase President Kennedy's inaugural address: "Do not ask what the world can do for you; ask what you can do for the world."

Here, then, is the first challenge—the challenge of oneness. It is for Catholic education to establish in the minds of the next generation—if there is going to be a next generation—that the world and the peace of the world are worth their time and effort. This world is worth their time, effort and loving care for precisely the same reason that the next world is, because it is God's world. Politics, though it requires compromise, disappointment, frequent defeat, and rubbing up against some of the less lovely aspects of life, is worth their time because politics is the way to get things done in the communities of men. The man who is too pure for politics is too pure for humanity. Science, whether biological, physical or social science, is worthy because science is the way to understand the truths about the world. The arts of civilization are worth cultivating because creation is good, order is heaven's and should be earth's first law, and the genuine work of art is a mirror through which men can see the beauty of God Himself.

Now I know it would be easy here to be taken as saying something I have no wish to be taken as saying. I am not arguing for a theological imperialism in the schools. I am holding that science should be taught on its own terms, as should all the other disciplines. I am holding, with Saint Thomas I trust, that philosophy or natural truth has to be sharply distinguished from theology or the truths of

Revelation. I am insisting that the scientific method is proper to science, as the theological method is proper to theology. I am not claiming that all art should be in the service of the Church or that the natural beauty around us is unworthy of the artist's devotion.

The oneness I am holding out for is to be found in the educated person, who in the mysterious core of his being relates and unifies his knowledge while yet respecting the autonomy of each branch of learning. This, I take it, is the definition of the wise man. And the process by which he becomes wise begins back in his earliest days in school when he is first introduced to the idea that separate truths, though they may impel him to think—to take on the burden of putting the jigsaw puzzle together—cannot pull him apart if they are really true.

In religious circles these past years, we have heard a great deal about secularism. It has been denounced furiously from the pulpit and from the Catholic press. I am afraid that we have sometimes been shooting at the wrong target, for in my wanderings I am sure that I have run across many more people who mistook the secular for the sacred than those who mistook the sacred for the secular.

Perhaps the time has come then for Catholics to insist that there is a sense in which we too are "secularist." We believe in the world. We respect its essential goodness. We think it is worth working for. We think the effort put into making a better place for the City of Man is neither mistaken nor misplaced. We are ashamed that we have not done more to make of the world a better place than it is. We admire the efforts of those outside our body who have. We acknowledge gratefully that we have benefited from the labors of those who have done what we should have done to improve the lot of mankind. And we can go further than this. We can regret the fact that what was accomplished by men who did not have our faith in God was sometimes impeded and obstructed by believers like ourselves who, because of laziness or greed or fear of change or self-satisfaction or some other human shortcoming, failed to relate religion to life.

What I see as the problem today is not so much a false secularism as a false "sacralism"—if I can make up a word to cover the fashioning of false gods. All you have to do is to look around and you find a great deal of idealism, vast efforts of heart and mind, and impressive devotion being given to unworthy little deities. The problem is not so much a rampant atheism as it is a creeping idolatry—the secular turned into the sacred, men worshipping at the shrine of Man, or at the shrine of Progress, or the shrine of Affluence. We are becoming a people of idolaters—and if the beatniks and rebels among us have lost their faith, it is often an idolatrous faith that they have lost—faith in the god of Money, Comfort, Conformity, de-Christianized Christianity—faith in the goddess of Success.

Perhaps, then, the biggest challenge facing Catholic education is to restore the worship of the true God both by de-sacralizing the things of this world and by giving them their proper value and significance. Perhaps the challenge is to raise up a generation that will not despise the world with its problems but love it for what it is and at the same time relate the truths of this world to the truths of the next in their own person.

I never met the late Dr. Tom Dooley, but from what I know of his life it seems to me that he may be a worthy example of what I have in mind—a man who worked tirelessly for his fellow man and was vitally interested in human progress but who also bent his knee only before the one true God. This kind of man is the type I would like to see the Catholic schools turning out. The unity of nature and grace, science and religion, humaneness and other-worldliness that Tom Dooley achieved in his short life is the kind of oneness the world needs. Catholic education should look upon imparting it to the upcoming generation as an abiding challenge.

I turn now to the word *holy*. What I have to say here is very intimately connected with what has gone before. Of course, in Catholic education the word *holy* has primary emphasis in what you do to make Christian men and women out of your students. In most cases, your whole lives are dedicated to that work, and I will not offend you by telling you what it is.

Rather, I am interested in the challenge to education that might be put under the category of *holiness*. Again, can't we say that Catholic education at its best is almost alone in giving pupils that which so many modern men miserably lack—a sense of their own holiness, or sacredness, which I take to be a sense of their worthiness in the sight of God?

On all sides, man is being told that he is nothing as an individual, that his only worth derives from his membership in the group or collective body or humanity or some other abstraction. From the Organization Man of the current sociological studies to the Collective Man of Communism, the emphasis has been taken away from the individual and focused exclusively on the social unit. One thing Catholic education can do for the world, then, is to insist that man himself, the individual person, is a *res sacra*—best translated as a "sacredness." He is a "sacredness"—a holy creature—because he is worthy in the sight of God.

This often is, but should not be, a religious cliché, for it is really a startling idea that the most miserable wretch on Skid Row is worthy of respect; that the most monstrous brute in a totalitarian prison camp is worthy of love. It is so startling that we cannot often bear to think about it. But today when everywhere individual men are being diminished, whether by totalitarian governments, the tyranny of technology or the calculated use of mass media, we have to think about it. When propaganda of one kind or another is belittling man—treating him with cruelty and indifference, or harassing him with shouts and demands that he conform, conform, conform to the image of mass man—in this day, it is absolutely imperative that somebody speak up for man, and for the sacredness that man is.

If we do, we will get a hearing. We will get a hearing by insisting on our doctrine of the human person and the individuality and essential equality of every baby born into the world, and the right of every man and woman to be treated with respect. We will get more of a hearing this way than we can expect when we play the mass-man game ourselves by relying on the power of boycotts, picketlines and massive protests to do our work in the world. When Arthur Miller wrote *The Death of a Salesman,* a bitter protest against using men as a means to an end, the world listened. But how much more attentive it would be if the great Catholic body in the United States, by word and example, gave its own testimony to the Church's teaching about the sacredness of the individual person.

Somehow this idea has to be brought alive for the generation now in the parochial schools and impressed deeply on their consciousness, for the temptation to be mass men will probably be even greater as the bigness of American life overwhelms us. We need practice in being treated as individuals with minds and hearts and wills of our own. We need assurances that our individual lives, individual choices and decisions are meaningful in the sight of God and should be significant in our own eyes.

During the recent presidential campaign a storm was blown up about whether Catholicism and the free society of the United States were compatible. Some of the talk was uninformed at best; some of it represented genuine concern. But whatever doubt we might have had about its quality, the experience should spur American Catholics, not least of all educators, to show just how at the most profound level these two, the Church and the democratic society, come together most intimately. And isn't this in the emphasis each puts on individual worth?

It is significant that neither the theologians nor the American political theorist characteristically speak of the "masses." The "mass," as distinguished from the "people," is a national body swayed by its leaders now this way, now the other. What place is there in mass society for individual judgment or conscientious decision? The unit is more likely to be the cell or the cadre than the individual taking separate thought and acting on his own initiative. The individual is swallowed up in the whole. He lives and breathes and has his being in the organization.

It is precisely at this point that the conformity between the Catholic idea of the free person and the American idea of a democratic society made up of free persons is most evident. Through the ages the Church has insisted on the importance and centrality of individual destiny. As Maritain insists, it was originally the preaching of the Gospel that turned men's thoughts to the infinite importance of individual men. Even the best Greek philosophers of democracy were stuck with the idea that there were such people as natural slaves. Certainly it took long generations to give the Christian impulse full political expression. But could it not be that in the idea of the free society that is America's we have reached a new level of Christian maturity?

I would hope, then, that in the effort to make good Americans in the parochial schools, anything that smacks of jingoism or tribalism or mindless conformity would be avoided. I would hope that the rock-bottom basis of the democratic idea—the idea that individual men are worthy of respect and capable of self-government and should not be led like a flock of stupid sheep through the political byways of history—would be stressed.

Today, even our democratic society is threatened by impersonalism. It is a problem in the arts, in politics, in labor, business, communications. The trend toward impersonalism is probably even in your schools, for it is pervasive every-

where. Somehow, someway, something has to be done about it. The authentic
Catholic tradition needs a more dramatic expression than it has been given in
this age of bigness. Certainly we cannot think of the "holiness" of the Catholic
educational enterprise in the United States without putting tremendous stress on
the fact that it is central to our tradition that man himself is a sacredness, a *res
sacra*.

What about the word *Catholic*? I will not try to elaborate on the implications
of that word for the kind of religious and cultural education the parochial schools
have to offer. It would not be fitting for me, a layman, to speak about such a
matter to so many devoted priests and religious. I will, rather, take the word in
its small "c" sense and proceed from there.

The word, of course, comes from two Greek terms which together mean
according to the whole. One story about its first use goes this way. It was said that
when heresy appeared among the early Christians those who accepted the full
doctrine of the Church, who took it all, described themselves as Catholics, believers of the whole truth. I cannot vouch for that story, but it illustrates what the
word can mean to us.

It can mean, and should mean, as the famous French Jesuit Père DeLubac
once put it, that the Catholic is obsessed with the unity or wholeness of the
human family. It should mean that we are not true to our tradition when we are
narrow nationalists uninterested in the plight of others or when we draw color
lines in the classroom or chapel. It should have for us all the implications that the
last three Popes* have been tirelessly pointing out in their encyclical letters on
race, social reform, and the establishment of world peace. I have no right to pose
as an interpreter of those papal letters. You have all read them and know what
they say. But if they add up to anti-integration, anti-foreign aid, anti-United
Nations—and I take it that some of my journalistic conferees interpret them that
way—then I will eat my shirt. But this is an old argument. I will not revive it
here any more than I already have.

I take it that the word *catholic* implies that there is nothing narrow or sectarian about the authentic Catholic tradition. When we lapse into clubbiness, as
we sometimes do, we have failed somewhere. I take it that there is no place in
the Catholic approach for thinking of the "our own kind" type. I take it that when
the Church is looked upon as the particular property of one race or nationality or
class of people, we are betraying the catholic spirit. I take it that when we vote for
a candidate merely because he is a Catholic; when we give awards to Hollywood
actresses not because they are good actresses but because they are Catholics, even
if not especially good ones; when we pray our heads off that Notre Dame will beat
Southern Methodist; when we strain history to try to prove that the Founding
Fathers were secret converts; when our history texts overemphasize the arrival
of the first Ursuline nun in the United States and deemphasize the landing of the
Pilgrim Fathers; when the colorful story of the California missions takes up more

* [Pius XI, Pius XII, and John XXIII.]

space than the history of New England; when third graders are taught how to abbreviate "Monsignor" before they know how to abbreviate "Street" or "Avenue"; when the vices of the villains of Catholic history are exaggerated all out of proportion and the heroes of that history are turned into plaster saints; when students are left with the impression that several shaky Catholic poets are the real if unrecognized giants of English literature; when pupils leave school with the idea that the only real issue of the Reformation was whether or not Martin Luther could marry a nun—when we do things like this, I take it we are not only being foolish but being untrue to the authentic Catholic mind. If we really take that word *catholic* seriously as an abiding challenge to Catholic education, our lower-case catholicity will be manifested in a hundred different ways—in poise of mind; in calm acceptance of the human frailty to be found within the Church and the heroic virtue to be found outside it; in welcome acceptance of the good, the true and the beautiful wherever they are found. It will be given expression in everything that is the opposite of pettiness of concern, narrowness of view, smallness of mind or intolerance of spirit.

The point I am belaboring, I suppose, is that the word *catholic* implies a fullness of truth, not cut short by any silly sectarian loyalty, nationalistic bias, or sorority house clubbiness. It means that there is nothing of truth or goodness or beauty in other traditions, whether they be political, cultural, or religious, that the Catholic cannot wholeheartedly admire and take for his own. It means that the Catholic educational task is never finished because, as new truths arc discovered, they bear some relationship to the old truths. It means, for instance, that Natural Law is not a closed book or discovering its specifications a task finished in the remote past, because the more we learn about man and the world he lives in, the more of the Natural Law that is discoverable. It means that literature and the arts, with their special insights, have a particular contribution to make to the Catholic's understanding of his spiritual life.

In a word, what I am saying is that the Catholic need never be intellectually bored because his tradition is not static; it is open-ended.

Each generation is called upon to add to its richness and to purify it of its previous errors of fact or of emphasis. We in America, enriched beyond others by our experience with political freedom, have a particularly exciting task here—to add our experience and the wisdom learned from it to the total tradition that stretches back to the first Christians. Some progress on this has been made. We do have our Father Murray, Father Ong, Jacques Maritain, Msgr. Ellis, Thomas Merton. But the most productive work will be done by the pupils now in your schools. That is why I stress the need for a catholic, a well as Catholic attitude.

We come now to the last of the four marks—*apostolicity*. Again, I am going to pass over the theological aspects as much as I can and speak about the idea of the *apostolic* as it applies to the specific task of the schools. I will take it for granted we are all convinced of the need for lay participation in the work of the Church, in accordance with the wishes and mandates of ecclesiastical authorities. The question it would be proper to ask here is what specific challenge to Catholic education is found in that word *apostolic*. How does the work of education as such contribute to the apostolate?

Perhaps the first thing to be said is that the school can make its greatest contribution to the over-all apostolic effort by being above all a good school. The school will make its greatest claim on the respect of the world by being a model of what it is, a school, and the Catholic teacher will fulfill the first requirement of his or her vocation by striving for professional excellence.

It is not for me to tell you what a good school is. I am sure you could all answer that question with more competence and assurance than I can summon. I can only repeat something else that you all know—a reminder that an apostolic motive is no substitute for professional excellence. A faculty of saints ill equipped to do the professional job of instructing its students might remain a model of sanctity but would not be fulfilling the task it had set out to do. I suspect, therefore, either that such a group of saints would not undertake a teaching assignment, or if for some reason they did, would soon equip themselves to do it well. Unlike some people I know well, they would stick with their dreary Tests and Measurements courses, not just to prove their virtue but to prepare themselves for what they had undertaken to do.

Let us say, then, that the first application of *apostolic* to the challenge we are talking about is to produce schools as good as any in the United States, or better.

The parochial school is the most evident and dramatic of all the public efforts the American Catholic community undertakes to fulfill its mission in the world. It should be associated in the public mind with excellence. That association has not always been made, and with some justice. But our failures have been understandable and wholly forgivable. The task the founders of the parochial school system took on was so gigantic, their resources so slim, the venture so daring, that as Dr. Johnson said about the dog walking on his hind legs, the surprise was not that it was done badly but that it was done at all.

But the time for satisfaction with less than the best is forever gone. As the nation's political leaders have insisted, second-rate education is not good enough for the American generation that will have to face the problems of the decades ahead. If the United States is to fulfill its role in history and meet its obligations while yet maintaining a free society and self-government, we are going to require the greatest educational effort any people in history has ever made. Most of that effort will have to come from those who bear responsibility for public education. But because Catholic schools are privately maintained, they have no less obligation to the common good. They are obliged to turn out their full share of leaders of thought and men of accomplishment.

And if the nation's need for educational excellence is great, the Church's need is no less. The sorry fact is that up till now Catholic education has not been producing its share of national leaders. I have no intention of reviving the controversy about this that Msgr. Ellis' findings provoked a few years ago. That controversy inevitably provoked a measure of defensiveness but the good thing about it was that it also provoked a great deal of self-criticism and resolution to do better. There may be such a thing as excessive self-criticism, but even in excess self-criticism is preferable to self-satisfaction. Whatever may be said of its abuse, candid confession is often required before the firm purpose of amendment becomes meaningful.

In any case, thanks in part to Msgr. Ellis' forthrightness, it is no longer necessary to stress the need for excellence. We all know that the situation of America in the world and of the Church in America requires it. Moreover, it is required by the very notion of the apostolic.

In the nineteenth century, as the Popes of that time warned, the Church stood in danger of losing the working people of Europe. Meeting that problem, even to this day, has required heroic efforts on the part of those whose lives are given to the service of the Church. You are familiar with that story. I do not have to detail it for you.

In this country there never was such a break. The Catholic workers of America, by and large, stayed close to the Church and indeed, more than any other group, built it from its poor beginning to its present eminence. The problem for us is that the Church may lose some of the sons and daughters of this generation, young men and women who have benefited from the class mobility of our society and are now destined to be the intellectual leaders of the country. If a sense of alienation grows up in them between the Catholic tradition they received from their families and the intellectual currents of modern American culture, the results could be as tragic as the loss of the working class in Abbé Michonneau's France.

This problem is not met by denouncing intellectualism, or by making snide reference in the diocesan press to "eggheads," or by speaking contemptuously of the life of learning in the pulpit or, God help us, in the classroom itself. Heaven knows that sort of thing is easy enough to do and some of our writers, preachers and even teachers do it extremely well. But in doing it, they only reinforce the image of the Church as an intellectually stifling institution, illiberal in spirit and repressive of genuine curiosity or intellectual concern. They drive out; they do not invite in. Doors are closed; they are not opened.

There is a long Catholic history of respect for the intellect and the work of the mind. It is neither an accident nor an unwitting accomplishment that the Church in its long history has been not only the mother of saints but the mother of great philosophers and artists too. And, incidentally, some of the saints were themselves philosophers and artists: they saw no contradiction between their vocation as Christians and their vocation as intellectuals.

It seems to me that the foremost apostolic task of American Catholicism today is to restore that tradition, to enrich it and add to it. We have a kind of double challenge here, one, to show that Christianity has something to say to modern man that will give meaning and focus and purpose to his life; and, two, to receive into the cumulative treasury of the Catholic intellectual tradition what modern knowledge can contribute to its perennial vitality. Here is a job for the theologian, the philosopher, the man of parts—but not least of all it is a challenge to you who teach the young in the parochial schools, for it is in the classroom that lifelong attitudes are first shaped, the seeds for future growth are sown.

There is a sense, then, in which the Catholic educator is a bridge between the Church and the world. The teacher in the classroom is the link between the two societies that his students are destined to live in. It is for the teacher to make clear that there is no fixed gulf between the two societies that his students are destined to live in. It is for the teacher to make clear that there is no chasm between these two worlds, no contradiction between the claims of grace and the claims of nature, the pursuits of the soul and the pursuits of the mind, the truths of reason and those of Revelation. Yours is indeed a high vocation—and one who does not share it with you can well envy you for the meaning that it gives to your lives. You do what the poet Gerard Manley Hopkins asked us all to—Give beauty back, beauty, beauty, beauty, back to God, beauty's self and beauty's giver.

American Catholic intellectualism: a theologian's reflections

Gustave Weigel, S.J.

In recent years a symposium—some would say a controversy—has been carried on by speakers and writers who deplored the low level of intellectualism among American Catholics. One of the most prominent voices heard in these discussions was that of the late Gustave Weigel, S.J. In this article he illuminates many of the facets of this interesting and profitable discussion.

The intellectual life is neither committed to Christianity nor does it antecedently reject it. That it is not committed to Christianity is clear enough from history. Plato, Aristotle, Archimedes, Moses Maimonides, Ibn Sina and Einstein were not Christians but no one would deny that they were scholars. That the Christian can be a scholar is just as plain. Abelard, Aquinas, Copernicus, Galileo, Erasmus, Newton and Newman were Christians and no one would deny that they were creative intellectuals.

This very simple truth is often ignored by Catholic apologetes. Some give the impression that Christian faith inclines to make every Christian an intellectual; that scholarship is an inevitable byproduct of Christian commitment. This is hardly true. In the long history of the Church we note a double tendency, and both tendencies are dynamic in every period. There are those who, with Kempis, would rather feel compunction than be able to define it. There are others like Aquinas who believe that the disinterested contemplation of truth is the highest form of Christian life. The presence of these two tendencies produces a tension for the Catholic who wishes to be an intellectual. He finds many Christian thinkers urging him on in his work of scholarship, but there are others who look on him with suspicion as a fifth columnist. Galileo certainly met with ecclesiastical op-

Reprinted with permission from *The Review of Politics*, 19:275–307, July, 1957.

position and even Aquinas was faced with the hostility which always confronts an innovator.

To put it quite simply, faith by its own inner essence does not produce scholars. On the other hand it does not exclude them from its community. The call to scholarship is independent of the call to faith. However, if the Christian is a scholar, his intellectual life will be in function of his faith. What is the place of the intellectual in the Church? That is one of the questions we wish to discuss.

I

Father Antonin Sertillanges, O.P., wrote a book earlier in the present century called *The Intellectual Life*. It is a "pep-talk" for Catholics with ambition to the life of scholarship. It was a valuable work and even today many of the things Sertillanges said are still relevant. However, the French Dominican only gave instructions how to lead the intellectual life from the standpoint of the Christian principles of behavior. He did not try to give us the meaning of scholarship in the theoretic world-vision of Catholicism.

Instead of working out a theory from general Catholic sources, perhaps we can see how certain significant Catholic intellectuals looked on their own work. In the earliest days of the Church, Origen was certainly the greatest of the Christian intellectuals. Beside him, Justin and Clement are smaller figures.

Origen was from childhood bright. He became what we would call today a high school teacher at the age of seventeen. At eighteen the Bishop of Alexandria gave him the task of instructing the catechumens of the city, and in the course of this work, Origen developed into a Christian intellectual, opening his own philosophical school where learning was pursued and given a Christian orientation.

The case of Origen is important. During his entire career in Alexandria, he was a layman. In spite of the fact that there were Christian intellectuals before him, Justin, Pantaenus and Clement for example, yet it is in Origen that we find the first Christian attempt to confront reflexly the question of secular science in its relation to Christian belief and practice. The earlier Christians, by and large, were uneducated men and it need not be surprising that they showed no great concern for the secular learning of their day. The only group which manifested familiarity with the thought-schemes of the time were the Gnostics and they were sectarians not accepted by orthodox Christians.

In this atmosphere Origen developed his own vision of learning. He was in many respects like the Christian educators who later followed him in time. He approached the problem of learning from a strictly pragmatical standpoint. He was not initially interested in the formation of young men in secular learning for its own sake. He was more anxious to form true Christians. However, he saw that it could not be done solidly unless they were versed in the natural sciences of their contemporaries and predecessors. Origen therefore taught "holy mathematics:

unambiguous geometry, so dear to all, and heaven-roving astronomy." [1] In the formation of the perfect Christian, Origen wanted the Christian prepared by all the knowledge that mankind had achieved, with or without the aid of revelation. His enthusiastic student, Gregory Thaumaturgus, says

> Nothing was undiscussed, nothing was kept secret, nothing inaccessible. We were allowed to study any doctrine; Greek or alien, eternal or secular, divine or human. In all freedom we could wander among them all, examine them all, and so enjoy the good things of the soul . . . Briefly, for us it was like a park, a replica of God's great Paradise. [2]

For Origen, then, the intellectual life was the true preparation for Christian wisdom. The Christian intellectual would not stop with the nuggets of knowledge found outside of revelation. He would take these and build them into the vision produced immediately by revelation.

What limits Origen in his theory of the intellectual life is his own understanding of it. For him, the intellectual life perfects the individual and its purpose is to produce the perfect man. He did not envisage the intellectual life as the development of an objective discipline. He had a polymathic conception of science. The true scientist was the man who formed in himself a vision of wisdom which drew from all the disciplines. He was not to dedicate himself to the exclusive pursuit of one. Origen would not oppose a predilection for one discipline over the others, but even with this predilection the others must also be known in order to culminate in the total vision. Hence, the pursuer of a fragment of science cannot stop there. He must ultimately get into theology as the last and highest source of universal synthesis.

In Origen, knowledge is pursued for the individual. It is the individual in whom the vision is produced. Origen has no concept of science as a communal achievement. His ultimate justification of the intellectual life is that, in its total amplitude, it is identical with the highest form of Christian existence. There is no pure love of scientific investigation. Science enriches the life of the scientist and, since it necessarily needs revelation for its own completeness, the intellectual life culminates in Christian sainthood. In a word, for Origen, science is a function of perfect Christian living but not a justifiable enterprise if unrelated to the Christian absorption of it into something different. It is not a limited career which the Christian can adopt, though it is a necessary phase of Christian evolution. Science ultimately is always Christian. Origen has no concept of a science which can stand alone. Any single science is a part of a whole, and that whole is the true science, and it will always be Christian.

---

[1] Trans. from the Greek of St. Gregory Thaumaturgus, *Panegyric on Origen*, c. 8, MG 10, 1077 c.

[2] Trans. from the Greek of St. Gregory Thaumaturgus, *op. cit.*, c. 15, MG 10, 1096 a-b.

Needless to say, this is not the contemporary view of science. Consequently Origen cannot solve our problems directly. He does, however, give us lights to solve our own question.

It would be well worthwhile to study Augustine's attitude to the intellectual life. However, he was too unsystematic in his own pronouncements on the intellectual life to permit us a well-defined view. He was certainly a contemplative of things intellectual. He certainly believed that it could be a career for a Christian, since he never felt the need of making apologies for having been a professor of rhetoric. He had also studied the philosophies of his day and commented on them. However, he believed that the knowledge proper to a Christian was more mystical than logical. He did not quarrel with logical knowledge and favored its cultivation. But he was not interested in it except in as far as it prepared and stimulated the Christian to meet God with something like immediacy in the depths of the individual's own soul. He could understand a Christian being a professor of any discipline, because the disciplines formed a part of the social structure of his universe. What he did not seem to understand was that Christian contemplation could be anything else than divine contemplation. Except for theology culminating in mysticism, Augustine's attitude to the disciplines was one of pragmatic tolerance. The Christian could engage in them but they would not be his specific Christian activity whereby he was sanctified and brought to God. There was good in scientific lore, but it was ancillary, propaedeutic, apologetic, and not self-justifying. There is a parallel between Augustine's attitude to secular learning and Augustine's attitude to marriage. Marriage was not bad but hardly the best thing. Given the weakness of men, it is better that they marry than sin through incontinence. So too in the realm of the spirit, the pursuit of secular knowledge was a good far better than ignorance and barbarism, but yet it should lead and cede to divine contemplation.

The mind of the monks of the desert is clear enough. They saw no value in secular knowledge and ignored it altogether. As monasticism became cenobitic, secular learning was cultivated in the monasteries, especially in the West, where the monasteries for centuries were the only centers of learning and education. Yet monastic science was not secular science, nor did it pretend to be so. The first step toward a chemistry, other than a prosaic pharmacy, was alchemy and it was looked upon with suspicion though there were monks and religious who pursued it.

The thirteenth century saw the rise of the universities. The monasteries and the cathedral schools lost their dominion over things intellectual. Superficially, one would say that science had now become secular, for of the four university faculties, three were explicitly of this world: arts, medicine and law. It is undoubtedly true that in these three faculties the laymen were kings. This was especially true in medicine, and only less true for arts and law. Yet theology was the queen of the faculties and the ultimate norm for all. Not only that, the universities were clerical institutions with charters from the Church, and under Church control they were exempt from the jurisdiction of the civil government. The Philosophy of the Middle Ages, which has maintained its significance in our time, is not the product of the faculties of arts, but the philosophy which can be derived from the theology of St. Thomas. The mediaeval intellectual was in a broad sense clerical, even though not necessarily a cleric with tonsure and orders. The great intellectual names of the period are, with few exceptions, men of the clergy.

Yet, in this time, there is a break with the tradition of Augustine, though not a revolutionary break. In the *Summa* Aquinas makes many references to the sciences. In one place[3] he teaches that studiousness is a virtue. Moreover, he says, that the study of philosophy for itself is licit and praiseworthy.[4] He gives a theological reason for this position by stating that the laudability of such study comes from its search for the truth which God revealed to the philosophers through the works of creation.

Moreover, St. Thomas defends the right of a religious order to dedicate its members to study.[5] His treatment of the theme is interesting. In one of the objections to his position he proposes the difficulty that the religious is a professor of Christian perfection. The Gentiles had professors of philosophy and Aquinas adds that even in his own time there were some seculars who called themselves professors of the sciences. However, the religious cannot follow the example of Gentiles or seculars.

Against such difficulties St. Thomas justifies the study of letters with three arguments. He supposes that divine contemplation is the true work of the religious. However, intellectual pursuits prepare the religious for such contemplation and prevent him from making errors in it. Then, too, the religious who include preaching in their work must study in order to preach adequately. Finally, there is an ascetical value in the study of the sciences, for they steer man away from the disorderliness of the flesh.

In this defense of science Aquinas clearly considers it as a means to contemplative piety and valid preaching. Science is a means for the religious; definitely not his end. Given the context of the discussion this is as it should be, for the religious by definition is pursuing a goal which is not the natural good of scientific study. As St. Thomas says, philosophers as such, remain within the secular limits of philosophy. If the religious pursues the same study, he must restrict himself to the themes which are religiously relevant. He himself was a perfect example of this doctrine. He never was a pure philosopher, for he philosophized in function of his theology or in defense of the faith.

Hence, for Thomas, the high light of mediaeval Christianity, the pursuit of the intellectual life as a secular commitment is licit and laudable. Such a com-

---

[3] *Summa Theologica*, II, II, q. 166.
[4] *Summa Theologica*, II, II, 167, 1, ad 3.
[5] *Summa Theologica*, II, II, 188, 5.

mitment is not proper to religious, but they too can study letters as a means toward their religious goals, contemplation and preaching.

In St. Thomas, the Christian justification of a secular dedication to learning comes from the fact that knowledge is a human good. All truth is from God, and in the achievement of any truth, man achieves God at least partially. Even the knowledge derived from the observation of creation is divine in its source because creation is itself a divine revelation according to the Epistle to the Romans. Hence, the study even of the natural sciences is an indirect encounter with God, man's true end.

In St. Thomas, we find secular intellectual life given full citizenship in the city of God. What Aquinas did was a lasting achievement, for never since has it been seriously challenged.

Yet the doctrine of the great doctor is not complete for our time, though the substantial elements are already there. The Middle Age related secular learning very closely to theology and piety. The effort at neutrality, so typical of intellectual activity today, is completely missing in mediaeval thought. It is indeed true that Aquinas and others of that time clearly distinguished the methods and limits of theology and non-theological sciences. It was primarily St. Thomas who made two different intellectual areas of contemplation, reason and faith, thus enabling later secular science to develop as it has. But if Aquinas distinguished, he did not wish to separate. Faith and reason for him were distinct, each with its own rights and privileges, but true wisdom can come only from their collaboration; not from their separate activities in unconcerned isolation. Aristotelian physics illuminated the presence of Christ in the Eucharist and that presence gave a new light to Aristotelian physics. But there is the rub. Aristotle would certainly have been glad that his physical theories were helpful in Christian theology, but he probably would have resented the Thomist assumption that Christian faith could give to Aristotle's doctrine new data, valid correctives or limitations.

This difficulty was already confusedly felt in the Middle Ages. Siger of Brabant is always associated with the "double-truth" theory, though he was less interested in it than others of his contemporaries. It can be questioned if there ever was a serious faith in double truth. What actually was being defended was the autonomy of philosophy and the non-theological sciences. In following their methods these sciences, according to Siger, should be free to come to any conclusion validly derived from the methods and assumptions of the disciplines, no matter what theology thought about it. Men like Siger and Boethius of Dacia were not opposed to reconciling philosophical and theological findings. Siger certainly made efforts to do so. However, the legitimacy and liceity of following secular learning according to the laws of its own structure was being upheld, though few of the men involved in the controversy were fully aware of it.

Certainly Thomas, Albert the Great, and Bonaventure rejected the position of Siger. No matter what Aristotle said, if it went contrary to the faith, it had to be expurged or reinterpreted. Theology was the norm of valid teaching even in the disciplines beyond theology.

II

This position became the working first principle for Catholics from then onwards. The clearest proof on record is the Galileo case. His physical doctrines were condemned *qua* physical doctrines not because of the methodological invalidity of his physical arguments, but because of the supposed incompatibility of Galileo's theses with theological findings.

The Galileo incident was unfortunate for Catholic intellectualism. Galileo was condemned by the Roman Inquisition but upheld by the new culture forming in the west. As a result the new science simply cut itself off from the supervision of theology and faith. This did not mean that the practitioners of the new learning necessarily dropped faith. Most of them did not. But they worked in their own way, nor did they submit the assumptions or findings of their disciplines to the judgment of theologians. As time went on, it became difficult to see how this could have been done even if the scientists had been willing to do it. The language and objectives of science and the language and preoccupations of theology became so different that effective communication between the two was very difficult.

For a Catholic engaged in intellectual life this situation could be trying. The principle of St. Thomas that theology had the power of veto in all the other sciences was not analyzed to see precisely what it meant. It became for churchmen an absolute principle with unlimited applicability. The result was that ecclesiastical intellectualism, based on the widest interpretation of the Thomistic principle, became isolated from the intellectual life of the surrounding world. In its isolation, the Baroque version of the mediaeval category-system was retained, although these categories were gradually becoming quite meaningless to the world at large. The old questions were still discussed; the old points of departure were still accepted. A serious attempt to understand just what the new science tried to be or do was not made and it was always assumed that its problematic and methodic were basically identical with those of the Catholic philosophers and theologians. If the chemist spoke of substance, then obviously he was to be judged in the light of Aristotle's doctrine on substance. If the psychologist spoke of unconscious thought-processes, this must be labeled nonsense; in scholastic philosophy thought is conscious by definition and unconscious knowledge is an absurdity. In the late nineteenth century, in spite of the impact of Hegel on German thought, the majority of German Catholic seminarians never read a world of him, nor were they ever told what he was getting at. He was simply labeled as an adversary to a Baroque or mediaeval thesis which was discussed by the seminarians and their professors in its Baroque or mediaeval purity.

Catholic ecclesiastical intellectualism was energetic enough. Brilliant men were industriously active in it. However, it was not the intellectualism of the world at large. There it was unknown as the secular intellectualism was unknown to it.

The Church, however, can never be a closed-in preserve. It is God's presence in the whole world. Its children live in the world, open to the world's action. There were Catholics working in the intellectual life as constructed by the world. Catholic theologians were suspicious of them but were glad that some of our people were in contact with the "enemies of faith." Some Catholic scientists were churchmen, and they accepted the principle that theology has veto-power over the sciences. Such churchmen divided into two groups: one group concretely preoccupied with the apparent opposition of their science to the theology they sincerely admitted; the other group abstractly admitting the veto of theology, but existentially oblivious of it.

But it was the Catholic layman in the secular intellectual world who was in an anomalous position. He knew no theology and found the ways of the new science satisfactory. He felt no need to reconcile his science with a theology of which he knew little or nothing. When this man talked, the theologians held their peace until he touched some point they considered vital to their theology. Then they discreetly attacked him by appealing, of course, to their theology, an appeal the scientist did not understand. Nor could he understand why his case should be tried beyond the jurisdiction of his own field.

It seems safe to say that the Catholic community did not have too many representatives in the world of the new learning. When Galileo was condemned by the Church, the new science almost literally left the Church. Kepler, Newton, Farraday, Rumford, Maxwell, Kelvin, Planck, Einstein, Darwin, Huxley, Marx, Durkheim, Von Ranke, Mommsen, Freud, Adler, Jung were outside of the community of the Church. Many of the Catholics who do loom importantly in the story of the new learning like Pasteur, Volta, Ampere and Fermi were not close to the Catholicism to which they were still attached in varying degrees.

There will be no one who will deny that science and learning are today secularized. One exception, of course, is theology, but even in this discipline the theologian of our day is forced to recognize the relevance of sciences which have developed without his assistance and perhaps even against his protest.

Ever since the First World War, a new temper is to be found both in the world of the sciences and in the Church. The intellectuals of today do not quarrel with religion and many modern Catholics, clerical and lay, have entered into secular intellectual life with enthusiasm. So many of these men are deeply religious and patently devoted to the Church. Some feel no tension in their two devotions. Pope after Pope has repeated the Thomistic doctrine that there can be no conflict between natural knowledge and the knowledge of faith. With this principle, many Catholic intellectuals are quite content. They resent any insinuation coming from Catholic or non-Catholic that their faith is in any way an obstacle to their faithful pursuit of sciences, which nevertheless on formal principle, deny any veto-power to theology. There are others who vaguely feel some division in their souls because of their double allegiance to faith and secular learning. They are even trying to overcome the division so that the two allegiances will fuse. Our moment is propitious to such endeavors because science is giving a new importance to religion and the Church is blessing Catholic scientists over and over again. The Pontifical Academy of Sciences includes not only Catholics but non-Catholics as well.

III

What is the theological attitude to the present situation? I would say that it is confused. To date, no theology of the intellectual life, as we know it, has appeared. Sertillanges's little book is far too exhortatory and too antiquated to be called a theological analysis of current intellectualism. The pontifical pronouncements, though many, have not yet been gathered into a corpus of doctrine. Hence, different Catholic theologians approach the question from different points of view. Let us see some of these attitudes as concretized on the American scene where the weak presence of Catholics in national scholarship is a Catholic problem.

In this country there are theologians who consider the problem an apologetic one. It is a fact that in the United States, where the Catholics form something between a fifth to a third of the population, the proportion of Catholics in American scholarship is nowhere near the overall figure. The Catholic Commission on Intellectual and Cultural Affairs, for example, has a membership of fewer than three hundred persons. The Commission has anxiously kept its eyes open to enlist all distinguished Catholic scholars. There are distinguished Catholic intellectuals in the land who are not members of the organization, but even if they were in its company, its numbers would not be spectacularly swelled.

It has been my fortune to visit many of the large universities of the country. On these campuses there are thousands of students and hundreds of professors. On the student level, I have come to expect a Catholic population of at least a fifth of the total in the average eastern university, but on the faculties there are rarely enough to make up a twentieth of the whole. Of course, the situation is different in our Catholic institutions where both faculty and students are well over ninety per cent Catholic. Yet, more than fifty, perhaps as much as seventy-five per cent of the Catholic college and university student population are not in these Catholic centers, and consequently they study where the Catholic scholar is not numerically conspicuous.

How does the American Catholic theologian apologize for this indisputable lack of Catholic intellectuals? Some initially try to deny that there is a lack, but the more attention they give to the statistics relevant to the situation, the less they are inclined to insist on this approach. Some point to a supposedly large number of invisible scholars, but since these are invisible there is so little you can say about them. They certainly cannot be numbered. When pressed for concrete instances, the apologetes of the invisible intellectuals point to many studious Catholics. But intellectualism means more than studiousness; it means scholarship. In Thomistic terms, studiousness is a habit but it is distinct from the habit of science.

There are other theologian apologetes who analyze the situation with a more subtle tactic. They admit that a paucity of Catholic intellectuals in secular disciplines is a fact and they admit that it can be regretted. However, the regret need not be a wail. There is a sufficiency of Catholic scholarship in theology and it is most productive. To take the acceptance of secular society as a norm for valid Catholic scholarship is, for these apologetes, an error. Scholarship is a medium for the attainment of truth. But truth is identical with the genuine teaching of the Catholic Church. We can point to many who are giving this teaching clearly and logically. Their exact number is unimportant. American Catholic scholarship from this point of view has not failed. It has been eminently successful.

This position rests on tacit assumptions; some dubious, others irrelevant. From the standpoint of faith, the simplest Baltimore Catechism gives the truth. Yet no one would call it a monument of theological scholarship. In the approach of the apologetes of truth, truth always means ultimate credal truth. But with the exception of theology, the intellectual disciplines are not constructed to arrive at such truth. Even in theology, the mere repetition of particular truths of faith is not enough. Theology is a scholarship no less than other sciences. If the truths of theology are not meditated in the context of their sources, Scripture and tradition, if they are not correlated with other truths in and out of the field and with the concerns of contemporary man, the enterprise is not truly theological, not scholarly. Besides, the problem of the scarcity of Catholics in intellectual life is not primarily a question of theology. The intellectual life spreads over a wide field of interests. Wherever there are Catholics there will be some kind of theology. But even for it, its orthodoxy is no proof of its scholarly worth. If all that can be said for the American Catholics is that they have spokesmen of orthodoxy, then indeed is it admitted that we are not engaged in scholarship.

There is a third type of theologian who does not consider American Catholic weakness in scholarship a theological problem at all. Such theologians point out that in France, in the German-speaking lands, and in Italy, many Catholics are engaged in every phase of the intellectual life. There is nothing in Catholicism which is an obstacle to scholarly dedication in any field. The American Catholic problem is a sociological one, not theological. The peculiar situation of a Church, whose historical roots are a non-intellectual proletariat, gathered from all over Europe and only recently rising to economic conditions requisite for scholarly dedication, is the cause of our poor intellectual showing. Let therefore the sociologists examine the phenomenon and guide us to something better.

Basically these theologians are right. However, there is one point which they must consider before they make the problem the exclusive concern of the sociologists. The problem is indeed sociological but one dimension of it is specifically religious.

The intellectual is an explorer into the yet unfamiliar areas of truth. Because the areas are unfamiliar, the scholar is in great part on his own. His only staff is the method of scholarship, something not understood or appreciated by society at large. Society exists in terms of set structures erected by the past to meet problems of the past. Society and those who direct it are attached to these structures. They have become accustomed to take them for granted and have adjusted their lives to such a degree that they seem to be the structures of life itself. To question the structure or to criticize it, is for them equivalently an invitation to suicide. Change is hazardous and always entails the acquisition of new habits of existence and operation—a laborious and irritating process. Only when the existing structure collapses into complete inefficiency is there a willingness to reconstruct. Before that time, society and directories are loath to make changes.

In Catholicism this is perhaps truer than in other societies. The Church must, by divine mission, guard the deposit of faith. Any novelty, even when it is only renovation rather than innovation, is suspected. It seems that, to keep the deposit of faith, it is safest to keep all of its expressions not only formally but even materially as we received them from the past.

This is clearly seen in liturgy. The ankle-length tunic was a quotidian dress of the Romans. The priest today still wears it as an alb, though the tunic, as a garment, has long gone out of use. The later Romans wore an overcoat which, like the Spanish-American poncho, covered the whole man. In most parts of the West this article of clothing has totally disappeared but the priest still wears it in the stylized form of the chasuble. Actions which once were meaningful from their immediate physical circumstances are retained though the circumstances are completely changed. Since the old meaning can no longer explain, a symbolism is found to justify something originally quite unsymbolic. Thus the priest still washes his hands in a strictly symbolic washing at the point of the Mass where the ancient priest, having handled food and drink, washed his hands of necessity.

In liturgy this hardening of ancient usage is no defect but a virtue. The ancient, merely by being ancient, has a solemnity and venerability recommending it to religious rite. The nature of liturgy is symbolism and through symbolism ancient actions can be given meanings they did not have in their origins.

But not all of religion is liturgical. Most of it is a form of living to be exercised beyond liturgy. Yet even here, there will be a spontaneous tendency to keep the older way until it just can no longer be kept alive. The same conservatism of the Church carries with it a tendency to be conservative of things not essential to its being.

To this tendency the scholar is a threat. He studies phenomena and tries to get at their meaning according to the categories his discipline of scholarship currently employs. To study is to judge. To judge is to criticize. But criticism makes the criticized thing a defendant at the bar rather than the judge. When this is done the phenomenon under study loses its inviolability. Hence, it is that the mere act of criticism of anything accepted is an act of *lèse majesté* for those who consider that that which obtains is normative and privileged. You cannot judge the king by the law because the king is above the law; the king can do no wrong.

This explains the suspicion people have against the intellectual. The cold, calm, ivory-tower contemplative is potentially subversive. He seems to live in isolation and on a plane far removed from pedestrian life. Yet he threatens the structure of man's work-a-day world. The highly abstract studies of Einstein and the theoretical physicists produced the atom bomb which quite literally can render the whole earth uninhabitable.

There is a paradoxical quality in this suspicion of the intellectual. Every people has respect for knowledge. The professional knower, with us, the scientist, is not without honor in his community. The people do not want him extirpated. He is useful not only in a crassly pragmatic sense, but in a higher way, for learning is a superior human good. The collectivity wants it.

This produces conflict for the directors of society. They simultaneously want and do not want the intellectual. The solution adopted by and large is to isolate him in a controlled quarantine. In some sense he must exist for the good of the society, but his subversive power must be carefully neutralized. What the intellectuals do within their own quarantined confines bothers the directors not at all. But what leaks out of the intellectual precinct must be carefully dammed and filtered lest it swamp the general community. For their own purposes the directors will use as much of what they want in the intellectual reservoirs. The rest must not be circulated freely in the commonwealth. The perfect situation from the director's point of view is to have the intellectual say on his authority what the director wants him to say, and no more. Unfortunately the intellectual cannot do this indefinitely, for it denaturalizes him. When scholarship is restricted to the activity of a bureau for the defense of government through public relations, it dies.

When the survival of a community is at stake, intellectualism goes to sleep. *Primum est vivere; deinde philosophare.* When Russia was invaded by the Germans, the ideologues in government shelved their ideology. They made the most elemental appeal to the people. They went back to a notion irreconcilable with their ideas, and called the people to defend holy Russia. The people were called upon to defend their Russian existence, not Marxian scientism.

American Catholicism, until very recently, has always had the feeling of being a beleagured community. An ubiquitous, formidable enemy was threatening its very existence. Loyal defense was needed, not a divisive effort of criticism. Everything that was, took on a holy aspect; to be loved and died for. Such an atmosphere was not propitious to American Catholic intellectualism. Yet the increased social power of the Catholic group and its greater economic independence have gradually diminished our sensation of siege. The very fact that the Catholic Commission on Intellectual and Cultural Affairs can now honestly recognize and publicly discuss the dearth of Catholic intellectuals shows that our Catholic body is no longer exclusively concerned with mere survival. Our young Catholics are not worried about defense. They want to expand Catholic life as a life. Intellectualism therefore must assume greater proportions in our collectivity. With no intentions of being revolutionary, many Catholics are advocating an intellectualistic change in our own existence.

This, however, is a dangerous position. The new voices are exposing themselves to the hostility of some of our own people. Some of them, because of an immature need for security, insist that we have no shortcomings, and become resentful when anyone points out quite plain inadequacies in our collective being. Others, fearful of what evils may come from a greater number of intellectuals in our midst, look with alarm at the mere discussion of the problem. Intellectuals are perforce critical and those who command them must commend their commands with something more than an *ipse dixit*.

The prospect of more intellectuals in the Catholic community may also disturb some of the clergy. They by the essential structure of the Church are in positions of command. They have also achieved some degree of intellectual formation, if only the training of the seminary. That the seminary is not the locus of high scholarly endeavor some will candidly recognize and others unwillingly suspect, even if incapable of admitting it explicitly. Hence, many of these truly excellent men are ill at ease in the company of scholars. They cannot enter confidently into the dialogue because they do not even know the language. So many of them went through a course of learning where the points of departure and the categories employed were totally alien and irrelevant to the scholarly discourse of the time we live in. Willingly or unwillingly caught in situations of challenge, they may try either haughtily or angrily to bluster their way through an encounter with scholars, but they come out of it knowing that the impression left was not good. The result is an uncomfortable feeling of frustrating inadequacy producing a reluctance to re-enter such situations, and a strong resentment for those who put them ill at ease. This resentment occasions a relatively bitter campaign against the intellectual fraternity through sneers, innuendoes and accusations, calculated to make the scholars suspect in the general Catholic community. Such members of the clergy will be the foes of intellectualism and the stout champions of democratic "common sense."

And they are in command. Sincerely they will feel an obligation to use the resources of authority to repress the scholars. Sincerely and with the best of intentions they will try to strait-jacket the intellectuals by setting up arbitrarily their own rules and their own supervised centers for intellectualism—a domesticated intellectualism incapable of being a threat.

I am not referring to the supervision which the Church must by its mission exercise over its own schools. This we expect and respect. The *magisterium* must teach Christ's revelation and keep its eye on those who teach it in her name. I am thinking rather of those areas of intellectual research where the *magisterium* itself gives amplest freedom. Here some churchmen can feel the temptation to curtail the liberty granted by the Church herself.

It is at this point of strictly sociological situation that theology enters in. Why do some churchmen insist that they can tell the intellectual what he has to find and say even in the fields of unrevealed truth? It is because of the principle always honored in the Church that theology is the norm to which all the disciplines must conform and theology in its turn must always conform to the doctrine of the *magisterium*. Why did churchmen of the past reject as valid the findings of palaeontologists who gave us vast numbers for the years of the history of the world? Not on palaeontological grounds, for the ecclesiastics were utterly innocent of any palaeontological training. Their rejection derived from their theology—a poor theology, as we know today. The principle that theology has veto-power over all the arts and sciences was taken absolutely and without restriction. Some even took it in the sense that any theologian could correct and criticize the work of a scientist without the theologian himself being an adept in the science under consideration.

Such use of the principle has proved embarassing to Catholics in recent times. Brashly some individual theologian will declare a certain scientific statement to be false, and yet as the years go on the statement is accepted by all men, Catholics included. Until the statement has been socially validated by universal consenus, the people at large and the Catholic scientist in particular suffer needlessly from internal conflict. They do not wish to go counter to their faith nor yet can they fly in the face of propositions validly achieved in the sciences. Such validity is measured not by a norm outside of the science but only by the principles and methods intrinsic to the science itself.

What is the meaning of the principle that theology is the norm of all the sciences? It certainly cannot mean that the scientist must constantly submit his work to the theologians. Such a submission would be quite senseless because the theologian *qua* theologian does not know the formal significations attached by scientists to their symbols, even when those symbols are words which are used by men in general. Substance in chemistry does not mean what substance means in philosophy. It certainly has a more precise meaning than the word has in common usage, where it can mean anything or everything. The problem of the transposition of a statement of one science into a valid statement meaningful in another science is complex. It is not only a problem of linguistics but of inter-disciplinary semantics. It certainly cannot be done on a common-sense basis because the propositions at stake are not common-sense statements. Scientific affirmations cannot be reduced to common-sense. The tacitly assumed postulate of so many non-intellectuals that they can, is false and vicious.

St. Thomas was keenly aware that each science had its own methodology and principles. According to him the first principles of a particular science are not necessarily to be proved in that science. They can be derived from some other science, metaphysics ultimately. In the days of St. Thomas the sciences were much more homogeneous in method than they are today. Aristotelian physics is philosophical physics. Today physics is empirical and mathematical. In the thirteenth century a philosopher could discuss a physical statement because it was formally a philosophical affirmation. That is not true today. Much of the philosophic cosmology found in our Catholic schools today suffers from the ignoring of this basic truth.

A scientific judgment is valid if it conforms to the principles and methodology of its own science. The truth of the statement is not guaranteed by its validity. For centuries the scholastics have taught with Aristotle that a good conclusion is not necessarily a true one, nor is a true conclusion necessarily a good one. Logic teaches us how to infer correctly, but logic itself cannot discover new truth; it only gives rationally valid transpositions of the old. Right inference is what we demand of the scientist. We justifiably hope that the result will be truth. Nor are the inferential techniques exactly the same in the different sciences. The logic sufficient for philosophical work is insufficient for work in mathematics, and it would be presumptuous to criticize the mathematician in the exclusive light of Aristotle's meager *Organon*. The old text-books notwithstanding, not every inference can be reduced to a syllogism in the mode and figure of *barbara*.

The principle that theology is the norm for all sciences, metaphysics included, cannot mean that the theologian can deny or affirm the rightness of the conclusion of a non-theological scientific inferential process. Theology is the discipline of ultimate truth and it is not formally concerned with truths which are less than ultimate. If a particular science makes an ultimate affirmation, that science is acting theologically, and the theologian then has every right to deal with the proposition. He can show by theological method that the proposition in question is badly derived theologically and thus merits no theological respect. The theologian can also call it false in the light of the data which certainly base theology as a discipline. When this happens, theology is not exercising some singular privilege bestowed on it from without. It is functioning in accord with its own inner structure. It is not discussing a physical statement made by a physicist but a theological statement proffered by a physicist. Theology has no jurisdiction over the physicist but it has full jurisdiction over a theological proposition, and physics has none. If theology has jurisdiction, *a fortiori* the *magisterium* has it, for the theologian operates in function of the *magisterium* on which he totally depends for his data.

The veto-power of theology is the veto-power of the ultimate over the proximate. As long as the proximate science deals with the proximate, the ultimate discipline is not involved. When the proximate discipline makes an ultimate statement, that statement is either invalid or if conceivably valid, in harmony with the findings of the science of the ultimates. This is not some arbitrary pronouncement of the theologians or the Church, but the obvious meaning of proximate and ultimate. If a scientist says there is no ultimate science, he is making an ultimate statement.

The principle that theology is the negative norm and in some sense a positive norm for all the disciplines can only refer to the realm of the ultimate statements. It never meant that theology is competent to criticize the work of the proximate sciences. The theologian knows no physics even though he has the right to judge any ultimate statement made by a physicist. As long as the physicist gives answers to the problems of the area of proximate human concern the theologian has no competence and no authority to criticize the physicist and his theses.

Therefore, the relationship of theology to the other disciplines offers no difficulty in the abstract. In the concrete it does. A proposition of faith is necessarily expressed in some language, at some point in the history of that language. An historical moment of language supposes the world-image which that moment has for the group which uses the language. Statements are effective communication to the degree that they can adjust to such an image. The proposition denotes its own sense which may be timeless but connotes a cultural corpus of postulates whose sole substance as a corpus is purely temporal. The dogma may have no intention of asserting the connotation at all, but it is difficult to separate by analysis the denotation and the connotation for they fuse in the statement. Hence, theologians face the risk of reading connoted mythology into denoted truth. This certainly happened in the Galileo case. The theologians thought that the revelation of God's creation of the world included the cosmic-image of the people who expressed that revelation in language. Theology in its later advance clearly rejected the cultural image surrounding the revelational communication as irrelevant to the dogmatic truth. The modern believer has no quarrel with Galileo.

But cannot the theologians of today make the same generic mistake of their predecessors in the days of Galileo? What is more, are they not prone to do so? I do not think that the danger today is as great as then. The one and perhaps only good which resulted from the Galileo incident was the chastening of the theologians. Today more than ever, the rationale and meaning of the sciences is understood. The propositions of the proximate sciences wish only to be proximate, no matter what they sound like to the man on the street. The theologian knows this now and he is not so inclined to see theological meaning in scientific assertions nor scientific content in theological statements. Because the inclination is in favor of the non-theological interpretation of scientific formulae, the theologian is much calmer in the presence of expressions which formerly would have driven him to arms. Sigmund Freud did not believe in theism's God, but that does not mean that the Freudian scientific theory of psychiatry is in any sense theological or atheological. The religious intranquilities rising from Freudian approaches to the psyche were relatively shortlived and dynamic psychology did not have to wait as long as the new physics to receive the Church's blessing.

There are at least two pronouncements of the present Pope * which confirm these observations. Speaking to the Fifth International Congress of Psychotherapy and Psychology on April 13, 1955, he said:

> We certainly should not find fault with Depth-psychology because it takes as its own the content of religious psychic processes; because it makes every effort to analyze them and reduce them to a scientific system, even though this type of research be new and its terminology unknown in the past. We raise this last point because it is so easy to come to misunderstandings, for psychology gives a completely new meaning to already existing expressions. In and out of psychiatry we look for prudence and discretion in order to avoid false interpretations and to render possible mutual understanding.
>
> It is the proper function of your science to shed light on the questions of the existence, structure and operational modes of psychic dynamics. If the results of your endeavor prove positive, there is no need to declare them irreconcilable with reason for faith.[6]

* [Pius XII.]
[6] Trans. from the French, *Acta Apostolicae Sedis* (Vatican City), 45 (1953), 284.

The second affirmation of the Pontiff is no less pertinent. It is taken from the allocution to the Richelieu Center of Sorbonne Students, April 9, 1953.

> In your studies and scientific research rest assured that no contradiction is possible between the certain truths of faith and established scientific facts. Nature, no less than revelation, proceeds from God, and God cannot contradict Himself. Do not be dismayed even if you hear the contrary affirmed insistently, even though research may have to wait for centuries to find the solution of the apparent opposition between science and faith.[7]

In both of these statements and in the context which surrounds them, we find an affirmation that theology is the norm of the other disciplines. But it is evident from the Pope's words that he does not understand the principle as a despotic domination of theologians over non-theological disciplines. Both citations make it clear that the valid statements of a science need not be rejected just because theology has valid statements which seem to go contrary to the scientific propositions. The seeming impasse only calls for renewed research in both disciplines. To use the words of the Pontiff, "the certain truths of faith" and "established scientific facts" never cancel each other out. In the totality of being they harmonize. The theologian will investigate to see to what degree and in what sense he has certainly achieved a truth of faith and the scientist will see to what degree and in what sense the scientific fact is established.

It seems that in basic theological theory our time has overcome any possible conflict between the proximate sciences and theology. Ultimate propositions, no matter where they come from, belong to the jurisdiction of theology, the science of the ultimate. That is the meaning of the principle that theology is the ultimate norm of all sciences. Statements of less than ultimate concern are controlled by the several non-theological sciences themselves. Such propositions demand from the theologian his respectful hearing; they do not tolerate his criticism.

However, the problem created by the numerical smallness of American Catholic intellectuals will not be solved merely by clarifying the meaning of the primacy of theology. As we have seen, the problem is essentially sociological with theological positions involved.

IV

There is a quasi-theological preoccupation which can attempt to play a part in the solution of the problem. The sociological need of Catholics in the diverse intellectual fields is so obvious that it is widely seen. Some Catholic masters in secondary and college schools feel that Catholic absenteeism in scholarship is harmful to the Catholic society, but this feeling is based on the supposition that the harm derives from the fact that current secular science does not teach the

[7] Trans. from the French, *Acta Apostolicae Sedis* (Vatican City), 45 (1953), 277.

lessons of the Church. Hence, they urge their students to enter into intellectual life to be apostles, as they say.

Now this counsel, noble in its intentions, is actually perverse. Behind it stands the American folk-dictum: if you can't lick 'em join 'em. The counselors seem to conceive the Catholic scholar's task to be double. First of all he should use scholarly methods to introduce into sciences Catholic teachings which are really derived outside of them, and negatively he should refute, in scholarly fashion, the work done by those whose findings apparently are hostile to the faith. There is secondly a more human task. The Catholic scholar should try to become respected and liked by the other members of his fraternity, so that as a result, they will either become Catholics or at least be friendly to Catholicism.

The root sin of this conception of the role of the Catholic scholar is that it is once more an attempt to domesticate science and knowledge. If we cannot control science by an appeal to the normative power of theology, we shall bore from within so that, because of our representatives, future science will admit what the present intellectuals will not.

For St. Thomas and Catholic thinkers in general, contemplation is the highest activity of man. The highest form of contemplation is divine, but the contemplation of the finite is still contemplation and superior to external activity. In this light the apostolate of the intellectual is not to defend theological positions but to be a contemplative of finite truth. Any apologetic or missionary byproduct of such work is not of the essence; cannot be the teleology urging the scholar in his work. What is more, to propose this as the motive for Catholic participation in American scholarship is self-defeating. Once the intellectuals become aware of such dynamism in Catholic scholarly work, they will ignore it and ignore the men producing it. The fifth columnist betrays himself and he need not be surprised if he is then treated as a traitor.

The intended apostolate of the intellectual can be only one—the rational contemplation of truth, finite or infinite. This is a high human endeavor, worthy and justified in itself. The scholar looks for truth as framed by his discipline. That is why he is a scholar. Since scholarship is not solipsistic, the scholar extends the vision of truth not only in himself but also in society. The Catholic scholar's apostolate is therefore to contemplate, to dedicate himself zealously and wholeheartedly to the investigations of his discipline. This will sanctify him and sanctify society through him. Any other apostolic good which sprouts as a side-issue from his scholarly work will be incidental, even if highly desirable. Even if the incidental offshoots are not forthcoming, the scholar is justified by his scholarly pursuit.

However, this missionary preoccupation of some Catholic recruiting agents for the intellectual life is more a sociological, than theological aspect in our Catholic community. It shows that a significant part of the community does not really know the true good of scholarship and therefore tries to attract young people to it with a good which is not its proper object. This is disorientation, not genuine guidance.

V

This missionary preoccupation manifests clearly the sociological character of the problem of American Catholic intellectualism. It seems that the basic fact is that scholarship is not widely esteemed in our Catholic community, and this lack of esteem comes from a widespread ignorance of what the thing really is. No one will say that intellectualism in the abstract is anywhere suppressed in our Catholic circles. We are all convinced that it is a good and our tradition has always favored it. Catholics at large expect at least their priests to be learned and we have always made much of those Catholics, clerical or lay, who have distinguished themselves in science. Yet, with all this in favor of scholarship, the number of Catholics who take it up in America is small. It is not for me to deal with the sociological problem. Others properly equipped must do that, but I would like to point out certain non-theological but yet religious elements in the sociological phenomenon. I have already tried to show what are the theological considerations which affect the issue.

I make a postulate to explain our situation. The postulate has already been stated. The general Catholic community in America does not know what scholarship is. Instead of a true concept, false conceptions are prevalent.

One common persuasion among us is that intellectual is the same as intelligent. The boy or girl who does well at school, in the sense that with ease he wins high marks, is considered by many to be a scholar, not a professional scholar, of course, for he is too young for that, but substantially the same as the adult scholar with only an age differential against him. Yet it should be very plain to all that not all intellectuals are markedly intelligent and most intelligent men are not intellectuals.

Others consider a studious temperament to be scholarship. A sincere affection for reading and acquiring knowledge would thus be the essence of intellectualism. But studiousness is not scholarship, even though the scholar must to some degree be studious. The dedicated reader of works of history does not by that fact become an historian. The dilettante who reads widely in all fields or even in one field is not a scholar. An effective desire to know what is going on does not make an intellectual. For all these men the Spaniards have a word. They are intellectualoids. Yet in vast areas of our American Catholic community, the intellectualoid is given the place of the intellectual.

Another common persuasion among our people is that smart boys should go into the priesthood. Those students who distinguish themselves in high school are always asked if they intend to study for the priesthood. Actually the seminaries get a good percentage of them. What is not recognized, often not even by the priests, is that priestly formation need not be scholarly nor is scholarship its true aim. There can be no doubt that many of those who do enter seminaries have the basic equipment for intellectual achievement, but their studies will not necessarily canalize these powers into scholarship. The seminary wants to train ministers of the Church. It *hopes* that some of them will become scholars but it does not consider it its function to make them so.

Another source of disorientation is the manner of teaching philosophy in our Catholic colleges. Rightly Catholic colleges make much of their philosophy course. It is undoubtedly one of the richest of the liberal arts. In Catholic institutions it is held up as a high point of scholarship, all other secular disciplines being inferior to it.

But what many a student experiences in these courses makes him vilipend philosophy and consequently scholarship which is supposed to be identical with it. Much stress is placed on the use of reason, but the student is discouraged from using it originally. His problems and the precise problems of his time are not considered. Instead, a scheme of questions carried over from the past is proposed to him. The questions are treated mathematically; to each word in the question a definition is given *a priori*. The definitions are then analyzed and compared. Finally a synthetic residue of all the definitions is given as an answer to the question. The process is so mechanical that there is no doubt that an IBM machine could give the right answers. It is not without reason that many text-books of philosophy in Catholic colleges are bare schematisms. A verbalized scheme is offered and to this philosophy is often reduced. The search for meaning and the exhilarating spiritual experience of intellectual discovery have no place in such courses. In their place, verbal formulas are previously constructed as answers to questions the student did not raise and whose historical significance he does not know. The questions of his time are not ventilated; they are dismissed by the easy declaration that the corollaries of answers to ancient questions will solve them. The thought of thinkers nearer to our time is presented in strangling epitomes, constructed through a logical reduction, made in the light of principles the thinker himself was unaware of or explicitly refused to use. All the insights and enriching pointers involved in the original thinker's work are leached out in the reductive presentation of his thought. It is hardly surprising that he comes out of the process looking slightly silly.

This is not creative philosophy, not valid scholarship. If this is intellectualism, the average student is quite right in wanting no part of it. Yet, if in his innocence he asks for something different, although he knows not what, the look of scandalized horror on the teacher's face prevents him from making the petition again. Subtly he is given the impression that he has just denied his faith, which is the last thing the student wants to do. With a sigh, he goes back to memorize the text-book's definition of the terms of his thesis and construct out of them a syllogism winding up in a foregone conclusion, for the definitions were originally so made that this and only this conclusion could be reached. If the student asks how this definition came into being, he is told that it represents what the author means by the word. Now who can quarrel with that?

Usually the teacher also has a strong apologetic drive in him. He is always preparing the student for a debate with the adversaries of faith. In fact, much of the problematic selected for philosophical consideration is taken from the field of religious or ethical polemic. It would seem that for not a few teachers of philosophy the objective of the courses is to supply the logical refutations for all possible objections to the tenets of the Church. These the student is to file away and extract from his files when the opportunity calls for it. It is not too extreme to say that in many cases the classes of philosophy are used to form defending debaters of Catholic positions. Philosophy is not envisaged as a personal quest for truth but rather as a predigested apologetic of religious belief. Young men, firm in their faith and lovers of debate, esteem this highly, but they escape the encounter with scholarship.

Some of these apologetic preoccupations flow over into the other subjects of college instruction, though they are not so conspicuous there because the fields are in the main theologically neutral. However, because of the general defense-mentality of the teachers for all problems, there is a marked preference for solutions given in the past. This is often labeled as conservatism, but it really is not. It is tutiorism. Older solutions have proved to be perfectly consonant with theological thinking. A new solution has no such guarantee, even though on the face of it it seems neutral enough. But one never knows. Better to stick to the answer we know is existentially innocuous. If this stand were merely conservative, there would be nothing objectionable in it. Any conservative quite rightly refuses to make changes until the new unquestionably shows its superiority over the old. But the tutiorist is not considering the proposed problem in itself. He always looks at the possible repercussion of a concrete solution on the field of theological controversy. The concrete solution in his proper field might satisfy the principles of the discipline beautifully and the teacher sees this readily enough. But one must be so careful; it might have implicit relevance to questions the theologians wrestle with. Hence he feels safer if he does not accept the new solution. If the years prove that it is theologically innocent, there will be time enough to accept it. Of course, by that time the solution is commonplace, and the problem no longer vital.

Tutiorism is a real danger in Catholic teaching circles. It produces a palpable tendency to eliminate movement and fluidity from the questions of the disciplines. There is a strong urge to make questions timeless with timeless answers. New questions are preferably reduced to old ones and hence they need not be answered anew, because the old answer is already there. This deep-freeze technique gives the students the impression that there really are no new questions. Contemporary men only rediscover in their time the eternal questions already eternally answered in the past.

It is interesting to see the reaction of not a few Catholic students to a discussion in which they are engaged. They hear some man's thought being expressed, and with joy they come to a gradual recognition. The man is a materialist! Now there is perfect serenity in the young man's soul because the thinker has been reduced to a timeless verbalism, and that was taken care of in the classroom treatment of the spirituality of the soul. The students have been trained immediately to stick any thought into pigeonholes constructed for them in college. Once the idea is in its pigeonhole, it can be ignored. It has already and forever been examined. Such students simply do not enter into the living thought of the living thinker. Rather, they substitute for it a lifeless abstraction which was included in a once-and-for-all given dictionary of definitions. In this unabridged and un-revisable dictionary there are bad words and good words. As soon as the diction-ary word is applied to a phenomenon, the phenomenon is *eo ipso* judged. If the man is a materialist, he is no good and his doctrine is absurd. There is no schol-arly task to be done now. It was done long ago.

But as Kant said quoting a French Abbé, there is no such thing as philosophy. There are only philosophers. Materialism does not historically show up as ever the same thing. There are Aristotelian materialism, Epicurean materialism, Stoic materialism, Feuerbachian materialism, Marxian materialism and a Patristic materialism. These various visions cannot be reduced to a common affirmation. It is not at all explanatory to call an idea materialism. Unless you tell me whose materialism is under consideration, I simply do not know what you are talking about. The materialism of the monk Faustus of Riez in the fifth century has noth-ing in common with the mechanistic materialism taught by some nineteenth century thinkers. To this kind of observation, the bright student impatiently replies that everyone knows that the essence of materialism is the denial of the spiritual. But if the eager student reads the thoughts of men labeled as material-ists, he will find that not one denied the existence of the spiritual. All that the bright student can answer to that is that they did not rightly use the word spiritual, which on ultimate analysis means that they did not use the dictionary he was given in his college days. By that dictionary he judges all things.

VI

In our American Catholic body as a sociological phenomenon we find a religious influence in its outlooks on scholarship. In as far as theology itself affects the problem, there is no reason to account for the small number of American Catholic intellectuals. In the constant theological tradition there is an enthusiastic approval and justification of intellectualism. The principle that theology is the norm for all the disciplines has been clarified especially by the present Pope so that the principle does not interfere with the scholar's unhampered work in a non-theological field of study.

If theology has no part in causing a lack of American Catholic scholars, yet certain religious preoccupations in our Catholic community do have a part. These religious elements do not totally explain the phenomenon under consideration. There are other factors which are not religious and these should be examined by those who are competent for such analysis.

The religious though not theological factors at work in preventing greater numbers of scholars are principally two. The first is a vague widespread persua-sion that young people with manifest capacity for scholarship should be directed to the priestly or religious life. This persuasion does not favor the swelling of

Catholic scholarly ranks because it is not in general the function of priestly and religious training to produce scholars. Secondly, it overlooks the secular dimensions of current scholarship, distracting the attention of youngsters away from the appeal of the secular disciplines.

The more important feature of our American Catholic body is its obsession with the apologetic defense of Catholic positions, ever looking to verbal debate with opponents who are only projections of subjective fear. This defense mentality produces insecurity in the general body. Orthodoxy is a constant preoccupation, producing an abiding compulsion to make this orthodoxy capable of overcoming unrecognized deviations within the group and critical attacks from without.

In consequence of this obsession philosophy and the disciplines are often used not as opportunities for the calm contemplation of truth but rather as occasions to defend theological orthodoxy. The disciplines can thus become denaturalized and tutiorism may become common. A debating defender of Catholic causes is produced rather than a novice in scholarship.

The insecurity animating the apologetic spirit of Catholic teachers makes them prone to undermine the real work of intellectualism. They wish to prevent the students from meeting thought which has not yet been apologetically sterilized. Instead of making the disciplines an intellectual encounter with the real as it swims into our experience, they prefer to petrify it by reducing it to a logical scheme of abstract verbalisms. The student is habituated not to consider the existent real with its confusions, effervescence and rich variety. He is taught to look spontaneously for a given atemporal scheme of terminological coordinates which he can superimpose on reality, concentrating on the scheme and ignoring the reality. The schemes are a heritage from an unexamined past where they were made under the pressures of that moment but not necessarily relevant to our day. The student in consequence feels an unreality in his vision of the real. Memorization has been valued over direct investigation. A contemporary thought must not be analyzed for what it contains but quickly categorized so that it will fall into a place in the prefabricated scheme. Once in its place, it can be ignored, because knowing is reduced to categorizing, and the categories were justified once and for all.

This kind of training leads away from scholarship. The postulate of all scholarly investigation is the nagging existence of mystery. The training of not a few young Catholics makes them believe that there is no mystery. It is all objectively clear and the category schemes of the past can make it manifest. If that is so, there is nothing more to be done. It has been done already and why waste time doing it over again? Better to dedicate one's life to something more rewarding.

VII

The practical question is what are we to do about it. I can see no easy, quick and certain answers. It may be presumed that we are mature enough not to expect

that all can be changed by appropriate legislation. It would certainly be imprudent, if not impudent, for some few intellectuals representing no one but themselves to approach the bishops with a demand that they decree reforms. The
ordinaries are vexed with so many immediate problems of urgency that a blurry
thing like a program for fomenting scholarship can hardly loom large among their
worries. Besides you cannot produce scholars by fiat nor can you get rid of the
spiritual deficiencies inherent in a sociological situation by laws.

Even manifestos directed to the heads of Catholic educational agencies are
of dubious efficiency. Since they can be interpreted as censures of their own institutions, they may even irritate the people in power and render them hostile to
any appeal for help.

A few voices can rarely change the mental attitudes of an indefinite group if
it is not already psychologically near to the message carried by those voices. It is
hard to see how a man obsessed with apologetic concerns for orthodoxy can
overcome his obsession just because some one points out to him that his preoccupation is needless and harmful. Rather, he will consider the pointers as
unorthodox and with angry attack attempt to repel them.

Perhaps the only thing that can be done and the only thing that need be done
is to draw attention to the inadequacy of our intellectual situation in the present.
This must be stressed in season and out. What is required is a general awareness
of what we need and an awareness that the need is not being filled. The more we
become aware of it, the nearer we shall be to the moment when the situation will
be better. Our moment is more propitious than we think. The young people studying in the universities vaguely feel that something is not right and that feeling is
conducive to discovering what is right. Our hope is in the youth, not in the generation actually in possession of the field. The older generation cannot give us too
much because most of them were not properly stimulated nor effectively orientated. Yet among them there are many who want something better and they will
do all in their power that the new generation get what they needed and did not
receive.

Esteem for scholarship will not be produced by legislation or even construc-
tions of programs. It is a matter of creative love. To love you must be acquainted.
To look for new acquaintances, there must be dissatisfaction with what is at hand.
If the small band of Catholic scholars persistently testifies to what it sees, these
two necessary conditions for a more widespread acceptance of the life of scholarship will be realized. At the moment we can dangle no attractive rewards to entice
the new generation. We can however appeal to the generosity and spirit of adventure which are abundantly churning in young people.

But one error we must avoid. There must be no urging of youth to a life of
scholarship with the whip of the Church's need. If this is the motive we propose,
we shall not produce the scholars we want. It is essential to woo young men and
women to this vocation because it is good in itself. It must not be sought because
of a good extrinsic to it.

There is no need to propose the good of secular contemplation as a merely natural good. Our long Christian tradition shows that it is a laudable Christian career. It is a true Christian vocation and an effective means of sanctification. Not only is it licit but highly praiseworthy, for next to the contemplation of God, the contemplation of God's creation is the noblest action of man.

This we must preach. This our youth must hear. Hearing they will be attracted, and from then on the attraction does what no plan can do. Above all we must avoid quarrels and controversies. Our message must be serene and our disinterestedness transparent. If others wish to quarrel, let them see to it. We shall not do so.

We are all in the hands of God. If the Lord wants a more dynamic scholarly group in the American Church, He will raise it up and no man can get in His way. If He does not want it, no man will be able to produce it. It is not arrogance to believe that the interest already aroused for this cause is already a manifestation of God's action among us. Let Him bring to term what He has begun.

The natural law, the family and education

James V. Mullaney

In this article the author discusses the natural law and relates it to education with emphasis on the rights of the family, the student, the teacher and the state. He concludes by considering some alternatives for harmonizing these rights with particular respect to the problem of religious education.

I. DEFINITIONS

A. The Natural Law

1. Natural Law Considered in Itself. a. Each type, each species of natural thing has its determinate essence or nature which distinguishes it from each other species. That determinate essence or nature gives rise to characteristic ways of operating, of functioning. A frog croaks, a bird sings, a lion roars.

Now natural law is merely this normalcy of functioning this correspondence between a determinate essence and its determinate way of operating.

b. Like all natural beings man has a determinate essence or nature, including determinate powers or faculties like intellect, will, emotion, imagination and speech. Each of these powers has its determinate mode of operation. Such normalcy of functioning is man's natural law. Man's natural law, then, is the use of his various powers according to their inner structure and resultant dynamism. Take the power of speech: its normal function, its natural law, is to communicate man's thoughts. Man's natural law could be phrased abruptly: use your powers according to their nature.

c. In man, natural law takes on a complication not found in infrahuman things: a complication which arises from man's freedom.

Reprinted with permission from the *Fordham Law Review*, 24:102–116, Spring, 1955.

This complication can be expressed in various ways. We might say that the operative verb in the vocabulary of natural law changes, in the case of man, from *must* to *should*. Perhaps the most direct way of expressing the complication is this: for man, natural law is violable; for all infrahuman things, it is inviolable.

This means that man may, through the intervention of his freedom, use the powers of his nature in an *abnormal* functioning: he may use nature against nature. He may, for example, use his power of speech to deceive his auditors rather than to communicate his thinking. He may use his intellect, not to discover and submit to the truth, but to ingeniously build up a sophistical justification for what he knows to be false. He can use a power contrary to the nature of that power. There are numerous instances of such perversions in human behavior.

d. In man, then, we find natural law, but we find freedom too. But to use freedom *against* law rather than *under* it is a swollen freedom, an insolent freedom. For in the case of man the right relationship between law and freedom is always law first, and freedom under the law. The reason for this relationship— and this is the pivotal point—is that man's free will is itself bound by natural law: the law of seeking what is genuinely and objectively good and right, rather than what is apparently good or subjectively satisfying. Given freedom which freely wills law itself there is no complication; there is only freedom's submission to law.

2. *Man's Knowledge of the Natural Law.* a. Man's nature, I have said, is determinate: and since natural law arises from man's nature, being its normal way of functioning, natural law is also determinate. It is fixed, not progressive.

Many of our contemporaries experience a genuine intellectual difficulty at this point. The idea of a fixed, immutable, final law seems not only irksome but unenlightened, obscurantist, an arresting of man at one stage of his evolutionary development.

b. Intellectual justice must be done both to the traditionalist who insists on the fixity of natural law and to the progressivist who insists on the fluidity of the human situation. To achieve this justice it is imperative that we draw a distinction between natural law on the one hand, and the human knowledge of natural law on the other hand.

Natural law, considered in itself, is neither more nor less changeable than human nature itself, because it is only the normalcy of functioning of that nature. But the human knowledge of natural law *is* progressive, *is* subject to development even, presumably, to indefinite development over the whole course of human history. Thus primitive man was, in the matter of sexual ethics, aware at least that sexual union between humans should not be as completely casual as it is in the case of many animals. But only men of the Judeo-Christian West are aware that natural law itself requires that this non-casualness should take the specific form of a monogamous and life-long marriage; and not even all of them live out this awareness.

c. An interesting corollary follows from this view that although natural law is not progressive or developmental, still man's knowledge of it is. That corollary is this: man is not bound, at a given point in time, by those portions of the natural law of which the species is, at that time, invincibly ignorant. For one element in a binding law is that it be promulgated. Now the only way in which the unwritten natural law can be promulgated is by being discovered by human insight into the implications of manhood. Undiscovered natural law is non-binding natural law.

3. *Law and Rights.* The word "rights" appears nowhere in the title of the present paper, yet I must examine it. For I wish to speak of various natural rights in the field of education.

a. The English term "right" is almost as rich as the related Latin term *"jus."* We speak, on the one hand, of *"the* right" in the sense of the righteous as opposed to the evil. So we say that man is obligated to do the right as he sees it. In this sense "right" means the morally sound, the morally correct and obligatory.

b. But we speak also of *"a* right" as "a right to life," "a right to reputation" and so on. Now what is the connection between these rights and *the* right?

c. Every "a right" is simply a claim to pursue "the right." I have, for example, a right to worship God according to my conscience because that worship is *the* right, the righteous thing to do, relatively to God.

d. How does *the* right give rise to *a* right? Through law. The function of natural law is to make *the* right obligatory, binding on the human person. Now when law commands some phase of *the* right, it gives rise to a duty in the persons so commanded. And duty in turn gives rise to *a* right, a moral claim to the means necessary to fulfill the duty. The sequence is as follows: (1) *the* right (2) is made obligatory by law (3) which gives rise to a duty in those bound by the law (4) which postulates in those so bound *a* right to the means necessary to fulfill that duty. *The* right, law, duty, *a* right: such is the sequence. My rights, then, spring proximately from my duties, intermediately from law, and ultimately from the claims of righteousness, *the* right, the moral universe, upon me.

e. Since rights spring intermediately from law, there are different kinds of rights as there are different kinds of law. Natural rights spring from natural law, and man-made rights spring from man-made law.

B. Education

1. *Definition.* a. The term "education" is used in three distinct, though related, senses. In one sense it means the sum total of all those processes through which a human person is led toward fulfillment of any and every kind. It is in this sense that it is correctly said that education is life-long, and that one's school days are the least part of one's education. "Education" so understood is co-extensive with human life, if not synonymous with it, and is too vast for discussion this afternoon.

b. "Education" is used less extensively to mean every type of formation which adults undertake with regard to young people. In this sense the term includes intellectual, moral, emotional, religious, physical, esthetic, social, cultural, political, military and every other kind of formation. So understood "education" is co-extensive with childhood, adolescence, and young maturity, if not identical with them. Significant discussion of so vast a topic is impossible within this paper.

c. Finally—and it is in this final sense that I use the term—education means the specific task of intellectual formation undertaken by elementary and secondary schools, and by colleges and universities. In the restricted sense "education" is the name of the function of the school, as "sanctification" is the name of the function of the Church.

d. I said that the school undertakes *intellectual* formation. For as the family is especially responsible for the child's emotional and moral formation, and the Church for his religious or supernatural development, so the school is especially charged with his intellectual growth. Confusion on this point is almost universal in our time. The simple fact that schools, colleges and universities exist to train not the heart, not the will, not the taste, not the body, but the *intellect* has been lost sight of. No one agency can do all of these things: that is why the family invented the school to carry part of the load—the intellectual part.

2. *Aims of Education.* a. The *direct* aim of education is intellectual excellence. Its indirect aims are (1) the formation of moral character; (2) preparation for a profession or job; and (3) preparation for coöperative friendship and for membership in numerous societies, including especially that society which is the State.

b. By "direct aim" I mean what education intends first, last and always; its specific job. By "indirect aim" I mean goods which education actively seeks, but seeks through achieving its direct aim. Thus a trial lawyer has, I assume, as his direct aim, the winning of a judgment for his client. But he has at least two indirect aims: (1) to serve the common good through helping to establish the rule of justice; and (2) the support of his family. Obviously he can do this last only through winning his cases: for the lawyer who loses every case he tries won't support his family long. But he can also help establish the rule of justice only through winning his cases, for it is part of justice itself that any litigant has a right to the most excellent counsel he can obtain. Directly, then, the lawyer intends to win; but indirectly, that is through winning, he intends to serve the common good and to take care of his family.

Similarly the teacher intends, by every legitimate means, to refine, to purify, to bring to the highest possible pitch of development, the intellect of each of his students. Through this intellectual development he intends also to help form the moral character of the student. How? By leading, through intellectual means, the student to see the majesty of the moral realm, so that he may freely choose to live according to it. Through the same intellectual development the teacher intends to prepare the student for his professional life. How? By leading the student to see that the sons of Adam are not made for aristocratic leisure, but for the doing of a job, for the love of excellence in work, and for the perception that every form of work is a service to one's brother, and therefore a fulfillment of the commandment to love one's neighbor. Finally, the teacher intends, through intellectual excellence, to lead the student to social coöperativeness by perceiving that every person is as important as he himself is, and that the common good always transcends the individual good in the same order. Thus intellectual development may lead to the formation of a devoted friend, collegue, citizen.

But all these aims—moral excellence, professional excellence, social and civic excellence—the school can seek not directly, but only indirectly through seeking that intellectual excellence which will enable the student to perceive the reasons for devotion in all these other spheres.

c. We must take no mean view of this intellectual excellence which is the direct aim of the school. For this excellence is the pure passion for truth. And truth in turn is being as knowable. Intellectual excellence then is the conquest of being, the progressive realization of the significance of knowledge already attained, and the progressive attainment of new knowledge. Intellectual excellence is the humble placing of oneself in the infinitely rich context of what is, of the universe of reality, and the reverent examination of all that is. It is man's entry into his predestined place: that of being the one inhabitant of the universe who can, through knowledge, perceive the complexity but also the connectedness of what is, and through that perception transform the teeming realm of brute fact into spiritual significance. He conquers the universe to utter it in a new way, the way of spiritual re-creation, the way of knowledge.

d. I have said, then, that education has only one direct aim, which is intellectual excellence, the pure passion for truth, the personal conquest of being. But it has three indirect aims: moral character, professional competence and social coöperativeness. Corresponding to these four aims are four dispositions to be fostered in the student.

i) If the student is to pursue intellectual excellence then there must be kindled in him the simple love of knowing the truth. This means openness of soul in the face of the whole of reality, a rejoicing in existence—his own existence, of course, but also in the existence of God and of the universe; a welcoming into his being of the whole of being; a saying "yes" to all that is.

ii) If moral character is to be formed, then there must wax strong in the student a love or righteousness and even a special love of the heroic to which unspoiled young people respond so generously.

iii) If education is to care, even indirectly, for professional competence, then it must instill a respect for work well done; a sense of responsibility for the task at hand; a knowledge that success or failure *does* matter, *does* make a difference; that today's job is to be done today because tomorrow's job will take up all of tomorrow. One must begin to learn in youth that the shorter one's life is, the more it hurries away, the more important it is to get done all that one sees it is his to do. This pure love of work is rare in our dissatisfied society, and we are the poorer for its absence. Perhaps we can rekindle it in our young people.

iv) If coöperativeness, love of others and consideration for them is to be an aim of education, then the spirit of group activity must be fostered. Through group activity the student learns early the most valuable of all practical lessons—

the spirit of legitimate compromise over means in order to attain valued ends; the hard, precious lesson that half a loaf is better than no bread at all. He learns how to do his horse trading without sacrificing his good humor or his good morals.

II. THE RIGHTS OF THE FAMILY IN EDUCATION

A. *Rights of the Parents*

1. The family does not exist merely to generate children—promiscuity would achieve that. The family exists to beget *human* beings: to give children not life, merely, but a specifically human life, a civilized life—intellectual, moral, spiritual, emotional, esthetic, social; life having depth, breadth and restraint.

Put the matter another way. Those who are responsible for the *being* of the child are responsible also for his *well-being*. This includes his intellectual well-being, his command of those arts and sciences which are the common patrimony, the common wealth, of civilized men; and his command too, over those specialized techniques necessary for his life's work.

2. In the discharge of these crushing obligations parents call upon other agencies; and for his intellectual well-being they call upon the school. The parent has the fundamental duty, and therefore the fundamental right to educate his children. Hence the school acts as the *agent* of the parent. So long as the child is indeed a child, the teacher stands in the place of the parent having such authority as the parent delegated to him.

This conviction that the fundamental right to educate pertains to the parents was given classical formulation by the Supreme Court of the United States, when it spoke as follows, through Mr. Justice McReynolds, in the *Oregon* case: "The child is not the mere creature of the State; those who nurture him and direct his destiny have the right, coupled with the high duty, to recognize and prepare him for additional obligations." These words are enshrined not only in the history and the practice of our country, but also in one of the most official pronouncements of the Roman Catholic Church, for Pope Pius XI made them his own in his encyclical letter *"On the Christian Education of Youth."*

3. But it must be noted that to say that parents have the fundamental right to educate does not deny the existence of surrounding and limiting rights on the part of others: indeed the phrase "fundamental right" implies others have rights which may be less fundamental but no less real. A *fundamental* right is not an absolute, unconditional and unlimited right.

4. As a necessary means to implementing their educational rights, parents have also a right to such amounts of property as will enable them to exercise decent freedom in the selection of the school. This is, of course, only one of the several grounds which make it clear that property is the guardian of freedom, at least when the ownership of property is so widespread that each family has modest, unostentatious resources.

B. Rights of the Student

1. The very first right of the student is to be treated by his teacher as a human person, not as an automaton. This means the student has the right to expect that appeals be made to his reason and his good will, and not to his fears and his passions. It means, too, that he has a right to expect, gradually and according to his years and his capacity, to be trained to do his own thinking. Docility, teachableness, so highly prized by the teacher, easily degenerates into passivity, suggestibility, parroting. He who is willing, in his early years, to parrot his lessons without asking any whys will be willing in adulthood to sop up uncritically the message of any imposing propaganda movement. The student has a right to be trained in critical reflectiveness, in intellectual self-reliance. Not subservience to teacher's opinions, but independence of mind, tractable to and humble before evidence, but healthily reserved in the face of opinion—this is the right of the student and the protection of every society against imposing subverters. For even a child is a *rational* animal, and rationality is the root of decent self-reliance.

2. But rationality is, of itself, a mere capacity, and like any other capacity it must be fed. On what shall it be fed except on the products of human reason itself? And what are these products of reason? The collective name for them is civilization, culture. This word, civilization, is the name of the life of reason as realized in history. It is not self-evident, then, that every person has, simply by virtue of his rationality, a natural right—it is the student's second right in education—to share in the fullest measure his capacities permit, in the fruits of civilization? Each generation stands on the shoulders of its predecessor. Hence the life of reason, in each of our young people, must be quickened and nourished by being fed on the achievements of that social reason which is civilization.

The most efficacious means of achieving personal possession and appropriation of the intellectual treasures of civilization is collegiate training in the liberal arts. From which it follows that each young person has a natural right to such training before entering upon vocational or professional studies, provided, of course, that he has both the desire and the capacity for it.

3. Naturally there are those who dispute the existence of the right here alleged. Liberal collegiate education they hold is the exclusive privilege of some élite, which usually turns out in practice to mean the members of a given economic group. But every right, newly discovered is contested; and I remind you that man's knowledge of the natural law, and therefore of natural rights, is progressive or developmental, and that this right of all to liberal education is one of the most recently realized natural rights. The right of working men to unionize, of the people to select their own government, of slaves to be free men—all these rights were bitterly contested and won with difficulty. But they were, and are, genuine rights. So man's right to knowledge, to civilization, to the liberal arts is a genuine, though newly recognized right.

4. But to recognize the right is not to deny the difficulties which accompany its implementation. One should not press too hard, too quickly for the imple-

mentation of this right. To do so at this time would jeopardize higher goods; for the great problem is the financial one. At this moment in history much of the common funds of our society must go to survival which surely has a priority over genuine rights of a less elemental kind. We have recognized the right to such education and we are moving towards its achievement by all. The day has by no means passed when finances present no barrier to capable young people who wish such education; but it is slowly passing. We have taken to heart the recognition that because liberal education is the sort that enables each man to think as well as his abilities permit, that it is therefore appropriate to each young person who is both capable of and willing to undertake it.

5. I cannot pass over this right to liberal education without brief reference to its social and political implications. Specialization not grounded on general intelligence is the specific mark of the beast. Only an animal is the perfect specialist, totally concentrated on the single task peculiar to the species: dam-building in the case of the beaver, honey-gathering for the bee. Technical specialization unaccompanied by liberal knowledge is a brutalization of man; and that is one reason why the totalitarianisms of our time are so keen on it. Such specialists are a profound threat to any democracy. For democracy is a daring act of faith in the general intelligence and good will of the persons who compose it. It affirms their ability not merely to perform a specific operation or technique but to pass rational judgment on that which concerns the general welfare, the common good. Democracy rests squarely on the intelligence and the virtue of its citizens, on the spiritual, enlightened freedom of man. The unenlightened technician, the illiberal specialist is, potentially at least, the totalitarian man. There can be "government of the people, by the people, for the people" only where the people are capable of governing. And the people are capable of governing only if the intellect has been developed, strengthened, liberated from prejudice, stupidity and superstition through that liberal education which is the recapitulation in the life of each of the historical civilizing of the species. Democracy withholds man's natural right to liberal learning at a dreadful risk to itself.

6. It is, I trust, unnecessary to add that criticism of the illiberal specialist is no defense of the sophist, the dilettante, or the esthete who sometimes parade themselves as liberal artsmen. These delicate fellows who have never soiled their hands with technology nor their minds with practical obligations to other human beings are the parasites of our society, as the illiberal specialists are its unconscious subverters. What is needed is a man who can use his head to think, his heart to love, and his hands to work—an arrangement which seems to approximate what the Creator had in mind.

C. Rights of the Teacher

1. The teacher, we have agreed, is the agent of the parent, having authority to teach this student by way of delegation from the parent: that is why I include his rights under the rights of the family. For the teacher has been delegated the right and the authority to spark and to direct the intellectual life of his students.

He must have therefore the means necessary to exercise this right; namely, that professional freedom which every professional man must jealously guard; a freedom arising from his professional competence, his special experience and his personal endowments. Legitimate parental concern as expressed by interest in the personnel and the policies of school boards, by participation in P.T.A., by conferences with the teacher, is admirable and necessary. But there is an area, the specific area which is the cultivation of the intellectual life, which is specially reserved to the teacher. His efforts are sterilized by parents who fail to respect the authority they themselves have delegated to him.

2. The first right of the teacher, the right to determine how to implant and foster intellectual excellence in the student, implies a further right of the teacher: the right to lead an adult intellectual life himself. The teacher is society's custodian of the intellectual life, as the doctor is society's custodian of health. Now no one can give what he hasn't got. If the teacher is to lead the student to the intellectual life, then he must live it himself. If there is no flame of intellectuality in the teacher, there will be none anywhere: our society shall have ceased to be intellectual, and therefore human.

3. This means that the teacher must be free to pursue the truth, to investigate ideas. The first qualification for the teacher is, as Whitehead used to say of philosophers, to be genial, to be even-tempered, in the face of any idea no matter how foreign, false, or outrageous. He must be left free to live out his simple enchantment with ideas as such. It is an addiction which he can no more explain than "whodunit" enthusiasts can explain the strange hold of detective fiction over them. The teacher simply experiences an enduring fascination with the little vestige of truth in every human thought: that is what makes him tick. Other people may, should they choose, live in a black and white world where every human idea is either true or false. But the teacher must be left free to locate exactly, and to treasure the little fragment of truth in the blackest of errors; and to see and reject the little blot of error in the truest of human judgments.

4. Our society has become suspicious of this preoccupation with ideas. It has become impatient of the intelligence which is critical as well as creative—as though intelligence could ever be uncritical. It is indeed true as one famous American had drily phrased it: "*Via ovicipitum dura est*" (the way of the egghead is hard).

One of the common slogans by which it is sought to limit the intellectual freedom of teachers is this: "Error has no rights." The trouble with this particular dictum is that it proves too much. Why has error no rights? Because error is a quality of a judgment and no judgment or quality of a judgment ever has rights: only persons have. But is not truth also a quality of a judgment? It is. Has it then any rights? None whatever, if error has no rights. But persons *have* rights including, paradoxically, the right to be wrong.

This right to be wrong exists on two levels. Morally, and in the natural order, one has the duty and therefore the right to hold as true what conscientious research and reflection suggest as true, even though subsequent study show it to be objectively false. So astronomers had the moral right to teach that the sun moves around the earth until the researches of Copernicus established that the earth moves around the sun.

Civilly, one has a more extensive right to be wrong, however silly it may be to exercise it. For the state has no competence to decide theoretical issues, and therefore any citizen has, from the point of view of the state, as much right to hold scientific or philosophic errors as to hold scientific or philosophic truths.

5. Speaking just a year ago to a group of Italian jurists, one great religious leader, Pope Pius XII, expressed this point by emphasizing that there is often a civic duty to tolerate error, even religious and moral error, for the sake of the public peace. Often, he pointed out, we have neither the duty nor the right to impede or repress what is clearly erroneous and false. Every group must be prepared to put up with a large margin of error in every other group. If it happens to be blessed with modesty, each group may also safely assume that a healthy percentage of error enters into its own natural thinking.

6. The teacher's right to investigate ideas, to search out the truth, is, of course, limited by the virtue of prudence. No man should give his mind to an area of investigation which he knows to be morally dangerous to himself. One should not, for example, study alcoholism in such a way that one becomes an alcoholic himself. Yet I must add that we should not be too ready, in this matter, to legislate for each other. What is dangerous for one person due to his personal weaknesses, may be quite innocuous for another.

7. I have defended the right of the teacher to intellectual freedom on the ground that unless the light of intellectuality burn brightly, and therefore freely, in his mind, it cannot be communicated to the mind of the student. But freedom to investigate ideas is not the same as unrestricted freedom to teach. However noble intellectual values are, still there are higher values. To the degree that teaching a given subject matter might reasonably be expected to upset these higher values, that subject matter should not be taught. "Never dig a ditch that you can't fill up" was a dictum of Aquinas. It is a warning against being a sophist instead of a teacher. But it is a warning too against reporting to the young disturbing research which has not yet been harmonized with established knowledge. Thus the Kinsey Reports seem to me valuable sociological research, however problematic may be the statistical theory employed. But the indiscriminate distribution of these reports is indefensible. Teaching, like every art, is selective. We are not obligated to teach everything we know, and at times we are obligated by the virtue of prudence not to teach something we know.

III. THE RIGHTS OF THE STATE IN EDUCATION

A. General Rights of the State

1. The rights of the family in education are, we have agreed, primary, but not absolute or unlimited. Like all human things they are limited. Specifically they

are limited by the rights of others, notably of the state. For the state has a high stake in education, and particularly the democratic state.

2. The state exists to promote the general welfare, to provide for the common good; the good not of some, nor of most, nor of all collectively, but of *each*. By virtue of this commitment to the common good the state is committed first to insuring, to fostering, the educational rights of the family and of those groups which are the agents of the family in education. For it pertains to the common good to secure the legitimate rights of each person and each society within the state. This is the primary, but indirect, role of the state in education.

3. More directly the state has the duty and the right to do in education whatever the family and its agents cannot do. Hence the state normally, in our time, institutes a public school system by drawing through taxation on the resources of all citizens, whether or not they have children to be educated in these schools. The specific form which such a school system takes legitimately varies from country to country.

4. In addition to providing a public school system the state also has the duty and the right to set minimum standards for all schools, public and private, secular and religious. It pertains to the common good, which is the province of the state, to see that its citizens achieve a certain minimum cultural level. This minimum level must be much higher in a democracy than is necessary in an authoritarian or totalitarian state, for the democracy must insure the competence of the citizenry to reflectively decide their collective destiny. Finally, the state has a clear right to establish a monopoly in certain areas of training, such as the military.

5. The state must be aware that its rights are no more absolute than those of the family and its agents, whose rights are prior to and limiting of the rights of the state. The very first task of the state is to reaffirm the rights of the family even against the state itself, and to continue respecting those prior rights in its subsequent tasks, such as establishing a public school system. This means that the reasonable wishes of the parents must be respected by the public authorities in determining the character of the public school.

B. The Problem of Religious Education

1. That last sentence—that the state must respect the reasonable wishes of the parents in determining the character of the public schools—leads us to one of the bitter controversies of our time, the problem of religious diversities and the public schools. Unhappily the controversy has generated passion on both sides, and slogans have replaced sober thought.These factors—emotion and slogans—embitter and lengthen the debate.

Now it is unlikely that you and I shall bring any significantly calming oil to these troubled waters, but we can at least make the effort to conceive the problem in a cool and generous spirit.

2. In a religiously diversified political society like our own there are funda-

mentally only two alternatives for the state in establishing a public school system: to provide a religiously neutral school system, or to provide a religiously plural-istic school system; that is, a Protestant school system, a Catholic school system, a Jewish school system and, for those of no religious convictions, a neutral or secular school system. America has chosen the former solution; England, Scot-land, the Netherlands, and the province of Quebec in Canada have chosen the latter. What would be intolerable in a religiously diversified country would be public schools of one denomination only.

3. Now the first alternative—a religiously neutral public school system—has the obvious merit of giving preferential treatment to no religious group. In this precise sense of avoiding preferential treatment it can be said to be in the spirit of the first amendment to our federal constitution. Yet it has the obvious demerit of being a clear case of injustice. For the citizens in general provide the means for the public school system; and the parents have the right to determine the character of the education of their children in that public school system. Parents of no religious conviction have every right to expect a religiously neutral educa-tion for their children. But religious-minded parents have an equal right to ex-pect a religious education for *their* children, Protestant, Catholic, Jewish as the case may be.

4. The second alternative—a religiously pluralistic public school system—would provide schools of every character: Protestant, Catholic, Jewish, secular or neutral. In theory, this should be ideal. At least it has the obvious merit of be-ing just, of respecting the prior rights of the parents. But mere justice is insuf-ficient for any practical program: that program must also be expedient, workable. It happens that the pluralistic system, which operates satisfactorily elsewhere, has been found highly unsatisfactory in this country, to officials of both state and church.

5. Americans are insufficiently aware of the degree to which this experiment of secular and religious public schools has been tried in the United States. There is scarcely one of the forty-eight states which has not at one time or another experimented with it, usually on a small scale and without too much publicity. The reaction has almost invariably been the same: citizens object on the ground that public funds are being used for private religious purposes, and churchmen object on the ground that they have lost control of religious schools to public officials. Both groups are discontented. Religious discontent with religious public schools in America was symbolized about sixty years ago when the Holy See, in the person of Pope Leo XIII, determined that in America parochial schools should be pushed, and that Catholic action for religious public schools should be dropped. It would, therefore, seem that the atmosphere of the present debate might be clarified if Catholics at least would publicly acknowledge that while they find one fundamental solution unjust, they find the only other fundamental solution inexpedient, since they will not yield control of Catholic schools.

6. When basic solutions are both ruled out, one naturally turns to compro-mises. There would seem to be two theoretically possible compromises. The first

would be the establishment, as at present, of a religiously neutral school system, but complemented by a system of state subsidies to religiously controlled religious school systems. This compromise, however, would seem impossible on two grounds. First, if citizens generally find publicly financed, publicly controlled, religious schools unacceptable, much more would they find unacceptable publicly financed and privately controlled religious schools. Second, even though religious minded parents would gain financially, they would probably themselves object that public funds should not subsidize private aims. There would seem to be a lurking injustice here.

7. The only remaining compromise would seem to be the establishment of a religiously neutral school system, as at present, plus a system of subsidies, not to private school systems, but to the child whose parents cannot conscientiously enroll him in the public schools. This subsidy would, of course, go to the school of the parents' choice, but it would be a subsidy of the child. It was in this way that the Veterans Administration subsidized the education of veterans after World War II. Educational equality is given to all, yet the prior rights of the parent are respected; direct subsidies to any private group are avoided; the child, and not the system, is the center of attention. All this is as it should be. Whether actual experimentation would reveal flaws not now discernible I do not know.

8. If even this compromise proved unworkable and religious-minded Americans continue to find their legitimate wishes unjustly frustrated, then for the sake of public peace it would be well for religious-minded parents to concentrate not on the manifest injustice of the present arrangement, but on its many sound features.

a. Religious school systems here operate largely in freedom, and without undue interference from the state or the public school system. Only the lunatic fringe, and not the American people generally, agitate for the dissolution of all religious and private schools. There is freedom for religious education; and that fact is more important than the further fact that the price is very high.

b. The control of the religious school systems is where it belongs, in the hands of religious, not public, authorities.

c. With the exception until last year of California, all property of religious schools is tax exempt. This is an indirect subsidy of religious education on the part of the American people generally, the non-religious as well as the religious.

d. It is the mark of adults to be happy in choosing, not the ideally best, but simply the lesser evil. To be the victim of injustice is certainly a lesser evil than to disturb the public peace by untimely demands. We knew well enough that the majority is often wrong when we agreed to live by majority rule. But it is less often wrong than any other type of rule. We must, with tolerance and good humor, live out the implications of our commitment to this democracy even when it pinches.

part **ii**

Contemporary problems
and criticisms
of Catholic education

QUESTIONS TO GUIDE YOUR READING

*1. After reading Dr. McGarry's article, what do you predict the
status of Catholic education will be ten years from now?*

*2. Explain why you do or do not agree with Father McCluskey's
likening of Catholic education to dinosaurs.*

*3. What objections, if any, do you find in Sister Ann Virginia's
proposals? Are you more inclined to agree or disagree with her? Why?*

*4. Which of Father Drinan's points do you think would be most
convincing to a well-educated non-Catholic? Why do you think his
interpretations are not generally accepted in the United States—
or are they?*

*5. Suppose that public funds, in large amounts, were granted to
Catholic schools tomorrow. Which of the problems discussed in these
articles would be solved, which of the criticisms of Catholic schools would
remain, and which new problems might emerge?*

*6. Do you find Father Johnson's review of progressive education
acceptable? Has progressive education changed since the article was*

written? Have Catholic attitudes toward progressive education changed in the past twenty-five years?

7. What is your studied reaction to Father Cunningham's bases for general education. Do you think a distinction ought to be made between general and liberal education?

8. For reopening lines of communication between Catholic and non-Catholic philosophers and educators, Father Phelan suggests that consideration be given to certain emphases and distinctions. List and explain these emphases and distinctions.

The crisis in education: will Christian schools survive?

Daniel D. McGarry

The term "crisis" has a certain shock value and sense of urgency about it, but it has come to be so widely and loosely used that it may be coming to have no more meaning than the boy's cry of "Wolf!" The crisis of which Dr. McGarry writes in the following article cannot, however, be lightly dismissed for it pertains to the very existence of Catholic and other independent schools. Dr. McGarry's answer to the question which constitutes the subtitle of his article is neither overly optimistic nor pessimistic, but it sets a background for examining the future of Christian schools.

The noted Catholic intellectual, Christopher Dawson, currently teaching at Harvard, in his recent book, *The Crisis of Western Education,* observes:

> It is the function of education to open up the mind to an appreciation of the spiritual as well as the scientific and humanistic inheritance of culture. If . . . the spiritual vacuum in modern Western culture is a danger to its existence, it is the duty of the educationalist to point this out and to show how this vacuum has been filled in other ages and other cultures.

The "spiritual vacuum" of which Dawson speaks is dramatically pointed up by the recent decision of our Supreme Court outlawing even the recitation of a simple, non-denominational prayer in the public schools of New York State. Yet,

Reprinted with permission from *Social Justice Review,* 55:188–191, October, 1962.

the current crisis in education is *not* the secularization of our public education: that is perhaps inevitable and has been long accepted.

Parishes without Schools

The *real* crisis in education is the question as to the survival of Christian education outside the public schools, a question which may very well involve the survival of Christianity itself. To put it simply, secularistic public education is constantly spreading, and by virtue of a tax-monopoly and a resultant economic compulsion, it is forcing private education out of existence.

Thus, despite the fact that it is incumbent upon Catholics by the law of their Church—and is independently desired by most Catholics—to send their children to Catholic schools, only forty-five per cent of Catholic school children in this country attend Catholic schools. In many areas—and, I am told, even in the highly solvent Archdiocese of St. Louis, no new Catholic elementary schools are being constructed. New parishes are being established without schools, contrary to the old custom, whereby the school preceded the church, church services being held in the school hall until a church also could be constructed. Kindergarten is being regularly abandoned, and there is talk all over the country of giving up the primary grades, perhaps all grades on the elementary level in our schools. Yet, those who have children realize that these are perhaps a child's most impressionable years. If elementary education is surrendered, what will eventually become of secondary education, which has always been more expensive and more difficult to provide? Will not the same problems and the same principles, in increased magnitude, maintain here?

"Signs of the times" are seen in the growing difficulty of maintaining the traditionally high quality of our schools. Mainly for financial reasons, and because we are allowed no share in our educational tax-dollars, our school buildings are often overcrowded, our classes twice as large as those in neighboring public schools, our laboratory equipment scanty. Despite these difficulties, our devoted and hard-working teachers, lay and religious, are doing a remarkable job and educating the whole child in a way that prepares him for eternal as well as temporal life, and in a way for which we are willing to make the greatest sacrifices. But how long can this continue?

Religious Education Necessary

There are many of us who believe, with our forefathers, that religion must be an integral and continuing part of education. If education is the process whereby we transmit what is best and most valuable in our culture from generation to generation, how can we afford to omit from it the most precious part of all: Christianity? For Christianity is like a fragile plant, the most beautiful flower of our civilization, requiring the most painstaking and continuous care, precisely because it is supernatural.

What can we substitute for Christianity if it is lost from our civilization? What could replace this "pearl of great price?" Attention given to religion in the education of children should take second place to no other subject. What educator would think of teaching the English language—including reading, writing, spelling, and literature—on other than a day-to-day basis? What educator would consent to relegate this important aspect of education to forty-five fleeting minutes on Sunday or a "catch-as-catch-can" basis?

We should not nourish the delusion that religious training is merely "catechetical." It includes catechetics, but it is much more. The inculcation of a religious way of life and outlook, a habitual religious pattern of thought and action, is a difficult, day-to-day process. Because of the stakes involved, we cannot afford to take any chances in this matter. In the best interests of our children, coming generations, and society at large, we must insure the success of religious education. We are here concerned with true happiness and eternal welfare.

If we were to omit mathematics and science from our day-to-day education, the latter would be rightly judged anti-mathematical and anti-scientific. If we were to omit literature and history, it would be rightly judged anti-humanistic and anti-social—whatever our protestations and excuses. If we omit religion from regular education, that education becomes secularistic or worldly and non-moral. Not only do we create the impression that religion and morality are unimportant, but we are liable to turn out a product that lacks a firm grounding in religion and morality while we run the risk of producing irreligious and immoral generations.

Origins of the Crisis

The ancient Greeks and classical Romans, the early Christians and men of the Middle Ages and Renaissance, and modern men up to about a century or so ago— considered religion and morality essential and integral parts of any scheme of true education. But recent trends in modern society have tended to obscure the realization of this principle and to eradicate religion from education. Many leaders and observers, Catholic, Lutheran, Christian Reformed, Jewish, etc., have looked with alarm upon this turn—or shall I say "twist?" Religion has been excluded from public schools because of a diversity of religious beliefs and unbeliefs. All inclusion of religion in education, even in independent, parent-controlled schools, is now seriously endangered.

The present threat to independent education in the United States is financial, and arises from an unfortunate conjunction of factors. Included are soaring costs of education, ever increasing taxes, and ignorance or apathy. Especially hostile is the growing concept of a socialized welfare-state in conjunction with an inhibition against allowing a share in educational tax benefits to students who attend other than public schools.

We are all familiar with soaring inflation. Yet costs of education have risen much more than most things. Thus the average cost per pupil in the public schools of Missouri at the close of World War II in 1945 was $128 per year; to-day, only seventeen years later, it is $515.

Taxation and Schools

It is estimated that over a third of our national income is now taken by taxes, and the end is not in sight. The greater part of our local and state taxes go for education, and the federal government is increasingly assuming a share of the burden. It is estimated that the public in the state of Missouri, one of the more conservative states in this respect, now spends something like $7,000 for each student who graduates from high school and $12,000 for every student who graduates from college in the public system. I have been told that this amounted to about $35,000 for students who have obtained doctorates of medicine in recent years. In the whole United States, the estimated cost of public education has risen 600 per cent in the last two decades. And yet those students whose parents send them to independent schools because of religious and moral convictions or other reasons obtain no share in these billions and billions of dollars which they help to provide in taxes.

One reason for the current crisis is the growing vogue of the socialized welfare-state in which we provide for more and more of our needs in a public rather than a private manner. The state is becoming like a great funnel, which increasingly sucks in all available funds and then redistributes them according to public purposes and individual needs. One of the first fields in which this procedure has been asserted is education. Here the principle of universal education at public expense has been first extended on the elementary level, then to secondary education, and now to college. We have no bones to pick with this, as long as it does not exclude from general tax-benefits education which includes religion along with secular subjects.

Taxation and Personal Freedom in Education

We have allowed the accretion in this country of an unreasonable inhibition against allowing any portion of educational tax-funds to students who attend schools which are not completely under the control of the state. This despite the fact that we admit that the primary right to direct the education of children belongs to their parents, as was declared by our Supreme Court in the *Pierce* or *Oregon case* (1925). How serious is this inhibition is emphasized by three recent decisions of state supreme courts. Last year (1961) the Vermont Supreme Court rejected tuition grants for high school students applicable in the school of their choice provided by the South Burlington School District which had no high school of its own. Also last year, the Oregon Supreme Court declared unconstitutional public provision of free textbooks for students in private and church-connected schools. And only recently this year (1962), the Wisconsin Supreme

Court threw out a state law which would have allowed free bus transportation for private school students to the public school they would otherwise attend.

We do not have this inhibition against allowing freedom of choice and private enterprise in other fields of public welfare and works. We do not maintain it in such things as old age and unemployment benefits, hospitalization, relief, construction of roads, bridges, public buildings, etc. The excuse alleged in education is that allowance of free choice and private enterprise here might indirectly aid religious instruction. It would be more accurate to say that such would help prevent further involuntary omission of religious instruction. For the direct effect of continuing to refuse a share of tax aid to those children who attend church-related schools will be to curtail and eventually eliminate such schools and instruction.

Religious diversity and acceptance of the principle of separation of church and state have not prevented aid to children who attend other than government controlled schools in our sister democracies, such as England, Scotland, Canada, France, Holland, Belgium, West Germany, and the Scandinavian countries. In such countries all students who attend accredited schools are allowed some share in public funds for the general support of education.

A terrifying ultimate possibility presents itself. If the state continues to take more and more of our money, yet maintains that it cannot contribute to anything that even indirectly aids religion, such as allowing individual and family choice in the matter of schools attended, what will happen when the state takes most of our money? How could we maintain not only church-related schools and their teachers, but even churches and ministers of religion, if the all-powerful state would refuse any money to individuals which they might apply to activities having a relationship with religion? To retain any freedom would not the quasi-socialized state have to admit allowances which individuals could apply at their own discretion?

Facing the Crisis

A crisis exists. And we are lucky that it is still a "crisis" that we can do something about, rather than a "funeral" where all is over. *What can we do* about this crisis? In the first place, we cannot simply ignore it. The stakes are too important; the issue too serious. Nor can we expect it to cure itself. The crisis has been developing for too long a time, and has been getting constantly worse, rather than better. In fact, the situation has reached the point where we cannot even "Let Joe do it." Every possible "good Joe" is needed to work for the survival of independent education.

In the second place, we should not abandon our heritage. We must keep Christian education both alive and healthy as long as we can, even at the cost of great sacrifice, and even without any share in tax-funds. Our forefathers, often poor and struggling immigrants, made great sacrifices to establish our schools;

we must make similar ones to keep them in existence. If our costs are greater, so are our resources. Where they often sacrificed virtual necessities, we have only to forego certain luxuries.

Nor should we jeopardize or attenuate our children's education. We must not short-change our children from a secular and temporal point of view any more than from a spiritual and religious point of view. It may be necessary notably to increase the ante on our educational expenditures and contributions. We should probably distribute the burden of cost more over the whole religious community, instead of reserving so much of it for young parents whose expenses are often greater and their income smaller. We may even have to defer purchasing a new car or house, new clothing or furniture, but it will be worth it.

Another way in which we can help to ease the problem is by encouraging religious vocations, male and female. We are told that vocations are falling off. But whose fault is it? Is the clerical and religious life any less beautiful and noble, any less meritorious and rewarding? Are we adequately explaining the opportunity and needs to our younger generation? Are not young people volunteering in droves to serve in the Peace Corps: what about the service of the "King of Peace?"

Still another way we can help keep Christian education alive and healthy is by enlisting the full cooperation of the laity. I refer not only to the use of reasonable pious lay persons as coadjutors in the work of teaching, but also to greater use of the laity, especially parents, on parochial and diocesan school boards and the like. Who are more vitally interested in the continuation of Christian schools, who have the eternal as well as the temporal welfare of their children more at heart, than parents? Whose is the primary educational responsibility? The clergy are neglecting a vast untapped well as long as they do not invite the fullest possible cooperation of the laity in the preservation of our Christian schools. It has also been observed by persons who should know that greater lay representation on school boards of church schools would make it easier to obtain government aid.

A final way is by restrained political action. While keeping our schools alive and healthy, we must work and pray to obtain some "fair share" in educational tax benefits for those children who attend independent schools. It is indubitable, in my estimation, that this will eventually be necessary for survival. Let us not be deterred by the difficulty of the task; but let us address ourselves to it with courage and vigor. What must be done, must be done. God will give us grace to find a way to accomplish our purpose. Each generation must solve its own crises and surmount its own difficulties. First we must inform ourselves, and then we must inform others. We must explain, not only to our co-religionists, but also to the public at large, that there is no question of trying to obtain a "free ride," but one of the survival of personal rights and independent education, with which the very futures of democracy and the free world may be inextricably connected. Finally, we must organize and work cooperatively as well as prayerfully and perseveringly and must continue, despite reverses and criticism, to take "the long term rather than the short term view" in education.

The dinosaur and the Catholic school

Neil G. McCluskey, S.J.

One reason for the dinosaur's having become extinct
was his inability to adapt to new conditions. If
Catholic education is to escape the fate of the
dinosaur it must, according to Father McCluskey,
make at least three major adaptations. These along
with four great challenges to Catholic education
which make the modifications necessary are
discussed in the following article. Father
McCluskey, formerly an associate editor of America,
is the author of Catholic Viewpoint on Education
and is a member of the Gonzaga University faculty
in Spokane.

Since 1940, American Catholic school enrollment has increased 147 per cent, so that today our elementary and secondary schools enroll slightly more than five million pupils. This is truly a remarkable achievement. There is little time, however, for the kind of preening or mutual admiration that induces euphoria. You superintendents are already well aware that the sixties bid fair to be the most challenging decade in the history of American Catholic education.

There is always a temptation to look upon bigness as a guarantee of security and survival. It is not. Back in the good old days of the Mesozoic Era, nothing more grand and fearful strode the earth than the mighty brontosaurs and tyrannosaurs and stegosaurs. Yet these fierce monsters with their tiny brains and huge bodies, along with the rest of the dinosaur family, suddenly disappeared. Paleontologists generally agreed that one reason these unwieldy giants became extinct is that they were unable to adapt to new conditions imposed by climatic

An address to the Conference of Diocesan School Superintendents, National Catholic Education Association, Chicago, Ill., April 21, 1960. Reprinted with permission of Father McCluskey from Catholic Mind, 58:323–331, July–August, 1960.

upheavals. There may not be an ice age ahead for us, but if Catholic education is to continue to flourish in the decades ahead, those responsible for leadership must be keenly aware of present challenges and make required adaptations.

In this year of the decennial census, we can identify four new factors in the educational scene which present critical challenges to Catholic education. They are: (1) the growth in population; (2) the beginning of extensive Federal aid to public education; (3) the demand for excellence; (4) the changing attitude of the American community toward things Catholic.

Population Growth

Suppose we approach the first challenge by looking at some figures. During the sixties, the projected population of the United States will rise from 180 million to 207 million, representing a gain of 15 per cent. Total school enrollment will increase by 25 per cent with the high-school part of the school population doubling. Now if Catholic school enrollment simply follows the national prediction, by 1970 you will have between six and seven million children in your Catholic schools. (We shall later return to the dark side of this situation: the six or seven million Catholic youngsters of elementary and secondary school age that will not—as things are going now—be provided for in Catholic schools.)

This year some 2.6 million young people are celebrating their 18th birthday, but in five years that number will rise to nearly four million. There will be a 57 per cent increase in the total of Americans aged 18-21, and better than one-half of them will be heading for college. "We are approaching the time," Arthur S. Adams, president of the American Council on Education, wrote recently, "when two years of college, either to develop a vocational skill or to prepare for further collegiate education, will be as necessary and commonplace as graduation from high school is today."

By 1970, it is predicted, today's college population will nearly double, reaching 6.4 million, but some prophets estimate that the total will be closer to 9 million. Precise figures are lacking, but we do know that the current Catholic college population of 303,000 is more than surpassed in numbers by the Catholics who attend non-Catholic colleges and universities. Come 1970 and perhaps three out of four Catholic students will be enrolled in non-Catholic collegiate institutions.

Federal Aid

The second challenge introduces a delicate subject. Any mention of a financial "challenge" or competition from public education to Catholic schools exposes one to the risk of having his words twisted into an attack on what many people consider the sacred foundation of the American Republic. As citizens and taxpayers, however, we do share in the gratification over the broader community support for and significant improvement in our public schools. The American public has an increased awareness of its schools. In many parts of the country impressive strides are being made to improve the academic tone in the common schools, to strengthen the curriculum—particularly in languages, science and mathematics— to better provide for the gifted student, to attract and prepare a better class of teacher to articulate a sound philosophy of education.

American taxpayers are presently paying enough to get good schools. The public school bill for 1959–1960 is an estimated $15.5 billion—an increase of nearly ten per cent over the preceding year and a sum representing 3.8 per cent of the nation's total income. (Ten years ago our public school bill took 2.7 per cent of the national income and 15 years ago 1.6 per cent.) Officials of the National Education Association say the figure will be $20 billion in 1965 and $30 billion by 1975.

What is more relevant here is the changing pattern of support over the past 20 years. Local revenue dropped from 69 to 55 per cent of the total; State support increased from 29 to 41 per cent; and Federal sources of support increased from 1 to 4 per cent (*School Life*, Feb. 1960). Moreover, the hour of Federal aid is about to strike. Twelve years of massive propaganda have conditioned the public to the absolute necessity of large-scale Federal expenditure to solve our national school problems. The first bill to come out of the hopper—will it be this year or next?—is only going to be a modest forerunner of what may in time become a $5–10 billion annual appropriation. How will Federal aid for public school salaries and construction affect nonpublic schools? Evidently, the recruitment and retention of qualified lay teachers will become a formidable problem. The Federal boost for public school construction will be a lesser problem.

Demand for Excellence

The subject of increased financial support for public education is not unrelated to the next challenge, that of excellence, about which we have heard so much during this convention. As the world grows older in the complexities of the space age, American society is growing more insistent on quality, thoroughness and efficiency in the schools. The Catholic schools in almost all dioceses compare very favorably, frequently excel, the publicly supported school systems in the same areas. Where they do not, their difficulties often flow from the straitened financial circumstances under which they are forced to operate.

This audience is thoroughly aware of the energetic and successful efforts being made to achieve the highest academic excellence in Catholic schools. There is small complacency in the Catholic educational world despite the fact that the customers seem inordinately well-satisfied and come back in ever-increasing numbers. It would be less than honest, however, to open this topic without repeating the warnings that have already run through the convention hall about the danger of deterioration in the traditional excellence of our Catholic schools.

The post-war expansion has forced some schools in some dioceses to fall back on measures of desperation, notably overcrowding of classrooms and the utilization of substandard teachers. We can smile at gangs of college sophomores vying to see how many human beings can squeeze into a telephone booth, but there is nothing funny about using a classroom for the same purpose.

You are the people who must put your foot down to prevent well-intentioned pastors or principals from piling 50, 60 and 70 youngsters into a classroom. Pastors and others must be made to see the hard cold fact that there is a point of diminishing educational returns in such a practice. Overcrowding is not fair to the children who are deprived of that close individual relationship to the teacher. It is not fair to the sister or lay teacher whose stamina and morale are frequently sacrificed on the cross of that "extra row of seats along the window aisle." It is not fair to parents who are no longer as unknowing or uncritical of obviously poor pedagogical practices. It is not even fair to those parents whose importuning forced the pastor to open the door for one more child but who later will not blame themselves for the child's faulty foundation. The day may come, indeed, when with perfect right the State will step in and by legislative decree end serious overcrowding in classrooms everywhere. Our own vigilance and sense of responsibility will be the surety that such an intrusion will not take place.

Again, enrollment pressures and inadequate finance have forced some Catholic schools to have recourse to substandard teaching personnel. The good intentions of the pastor who resurrected her, and the generosity of dear arthritic Mrs. O'Leary who left her retirement to cope with a roomful of squirming sixth-graders at St. Mary's school, are to be praised, for sure. But Catholic schools are subject to the same laws that govern excellence in any school, and St. Mary's cannot be built on the Mrs. O'Learys. The truism that a school is not better than its faculty applies inexorably to our own schools. Teacher certification standards must be at least as high in Catholic schools as those in public schools.

Other questions about quality can be raised. How conspicuous have Catholic schools generally been in educational leadership? How commonly have our schools pioneered and perfected the new techniques in early teaching of foreign languages? How universally have we modernized our approaches to the teaching of mathematics and the sciences? How much have we made our students at home in the library and given them a passion for reading? Have we been really successful in making our young people alive to the grave social and political issues at home and abroad? Have we inspired widely a love for Christ and the Church and souls? These questions are part of the continual examination of conscience for leaders of Catholic education which must be made if Catholic education is to lead.

Non-Catholic Attitudes

The fourth factor presenting both challenge and opportunity is the new widespread interest by non-Catholic Americans in Catholic life. We can leave the full explanation of this to sociologists and analysts of our culture. The phenomenon, however, is indisputably real—and I am not referring here simply to the public following of the political fortunes of Senator John Fitzgerald Kennedy. The

Church in the United States may be feared, hated, admired, or respected but it is noticed. The nation is aware as never before of the Catholic presence—and of Catholic schools.

We have an admirable philosophy of education rooted in the Judeo-Christian tradition from which America has always derived its moral strength. The contributions of our schools to the intellectual and cultural riches of the nation yearly grow more impressive. Why is it then that there is so little public recognition of the current pressures upon Catholic schools, and why is there almost no discussion in public of how to help them solve these problems? How can a community, a quarter or one-half of whose school children attend Catholic schools, remain so indifferent to Catholic school needs?

And yet an awareness is growing that the sheer dimensions of the Catholic school system make its needs and interests more than the concern of the Catholic community. The social realities of 1960 are not those of 1928, nor of 1860 nor of 1828. If American society however is ever to find a way of translating its appreciation of the religious school into a corresponding pattern of appropriate support, we must do a better job of taking our case to the public. A strong claim can be made that it is in the best interests of the American nation that the church-related schools, which have assumed a generous share of the nation's educational burden, receive appropriate recognition and support. For only in this way can the constitutional guarantee of freedom of religion be effectively safeguarded, and only in this way can the nation's youthful talent be fully realized. The fact that a majority of the States still do not provide the constitutionally approved child-welfare benefits, e.g., bus transportation, eloquently underscores our failure in community relations.

Perhaps greater interest on our part in the corresponding problems of public education is one step toward improving them. Instead of giving an impression of aloofness or hostility, we could join more enthusiastically with those forces in public education that are striving for higher standards in school safety, classroom instruction, teacher certification, and working to preserve a high moral and spiritual tone in the schools. In any event, today's great concern or curiosity or simply interest in things Catholic presents us with a challenge and an opportunity.

The challenges under discussion require some basic retooling in contemporary Catholic education. The three major modifications that I am going to boldly suggest will concern *administration, finance,* and *emphasis.*

Administration

The parochial school as an independent, parish-controlled and parish-financed operation is an anachronism. For the greater good all parochial schools should become diocesan schools. This will mean of course that pastors will have to yield control over their schools. We speak loosely of a Catholic school "system," but only a few dioceses approach education systematically. Close your eyes for a moment and visualize what the difference would be (including the change in your own work-load!) if all the parish schools were welded into a single diocesan system.

Take the planning of schools. A central planning board would allocate schools and priorities in building, would pass on additions, consolidations and suppressions of schools. Special schools would be located at strategic points in the diocese. In these schools the exceptional children would at long last get their full due. There would be special schools and staffs for the mentally retarded and physically handicapped. There would be a special diocesan transportation provision for the handicapped who attend regular schools. College preparatory schools, terminal schools, pre-professional and technical schools would likewise be centrally located for patronage by youngsters of the entire area or diocese.

We may wince at the charge, but unhappily there is a basis for the accusation that Catholic schools, especially our high schools, make a practice of using the public schools as a "dumping ground" for "problem" children and difficult learners. Until we reorganize our schools systematically, this charge will not down.

Let us turn to the teacher. Under this plan all teacher contracts would be arranged by the diocesan office. Salary scales, assignments, transfers, replacements, promotions would be handled on a diocesan level by a central office. Health benefits, tenure, retirement, sick leave and pensions would be provided for in the same way.

Curriculum planning and experimentation, teacher accreditation, standards for promotion, advanced placement, selection of textbooks, enforcement of library standards, etc.—all these important items would now come under a diocesan central office. Should ten schools in the diocese offer Russian language courses in the sixth grade? Can Latin or French be started in this particular school at the fourth-grade level? Is there profit in accepting a long-term loan for science equipment under provisions of the National Defense Education Act? These would all become routine matters for the diocesan superintendent's office. The diocesan superintendent will be assisted by an active school board, equally composed of clerical and lay members, which meets regularly and works closely with him in evolving policy and practice for the diocese. In sum, the office of the diocesan superintendent of schools becomes a position of authority over and leadership of the Catholic school *system*.

Finance

Finance comes next. Tuition is now abolished. In its place there is a school tax levied on every wage-earning family in the diocese, a plan which in some dioceses is partially in operation. The present system of financing Catholic school education is unbelievably archaic, obsolete and inefficient. In this matter we are a good one hundred years behind the public schools whose architects long ago argued successfully that the burden of support for the commonly used public schools was a total community responsibility. The token tuition collected by the parochial school today is usually supplemented by an occasional "throw-it-in-the-Sunday-basket" appeal to parish generosity. How much fairer and more practical to share the tax burden and to concentrate during certain periods of the year on whatever all-diocesan drives for supplementary funds prove necessary. Henceforth, let the education of the youngsters in the rich suburban parish and the declining down-town parish be paid for out of the same central fund. And if private schools di-rected by religious orders want to be supported in this way, it is only proper that they become an integral part of the diocesan system.

Once a central control comes over the parish schools, intelligent planning for expansion can take place. Economy can become the keynote. Facilities can be shared as much as possible. Several neighboring schools can make use of expen-sive facilities like auditoriums, gymnasiums, high-school home economics depart-ments and industrial arts wings. If needed, school buses can be made use of to bring pupils to these centrally located facilities.

Emphasis

The third step is emphasis. There is an ideal of Catholic education, sometimes summed up in the phrase, "Every Catholic child in a Catholic school." Yet, para-doxically, the greater our Catholic school population grows, the farther we seem to be from this ideal. Better than five million of today's Catholic children—at least two-thirds of those of high-school age and more than 40 per cent of those of elementary-school age—are not in a Catholic school. As things stand now, they are not going to get even a partial Catholic schooling, and the number of the un-accommodated each year will be larger. A blunter way of stating this point is that in effect we are turning our backs on one-half of our Catholic children as far as their formal schooling goes. Does this not indicate the imperative need for re-thinking the present pattern of Catholic education?

In those areas where the Church cannot educate all of our young people all the time, is it not the part of wisdom to concentrate our human and fiscal resources so that we can provide some years of Catholic schooling for all and on the more influential levels of schooling? The school, which in 1884 the Third Plenary Coun-cil of Baltimore decreed was to be erected near each church "within two years," was an elementary school—in those days the kind of school wherein were satis-fied the educational needs and ambitions of most Americans. Seventy-six years later we are still preoccupied with putting up elementary schools while the focal point in the pattern of American education has moved up the ladder. The high school has long since replaced the grammar school as the focus of loyalties and educational influences for the average American. But even this is changing.

The normal pattern of American publicly supported education is beginning to cover a 13th and 14th year or junior college. In 1959 one of every four college students began higher education in a junior college. Within a very few years, at least one-half of the beginning college class in many States will be in junior col-leges. Moreover, as entrance requirements for the four year colleges tighten and as tuition continues to rise, there are excellent reasons why more and more of our college students should pass through the two-year program which would be sufficient for a high proportion of them.

If we are forced to abandon a section of formal Catholic schooling, it ought to be the first six grades. To achieve maximum results Catholic education should start with the 7th grade or junior high school, continue through senior high school and include the 13th and 14th grades or junior college. A network of junior colleges under diocesan and religious-order direction would mean that many tens of thousands of Catholic young men and women, at a critical stage of intellectual maturation, would have at least some access to what few of them will ever discover elsewhere, the philosophical and theological treasures of Christian humanism as well as the great documents of Catholic social thought.

The thought of dropping some of the elementary grades distresses many people who feel that this is abandoning Catholic children during their early formative years. But what alternative do they propose to provide *some* formal Catholic schooling for 1970's six or seven million Catholic youngsters of elementary and high-school age and the million young people of college age who are destined to be left out?

Perhaps these people also underestimate the capability of our parishes and Catholic families to adjust to a new challenge. There is no valid reason why priests and parents could not make more than adequate provisions for the religious training and influence of our children. Let's bring them to the Catholic school building every day following their school day. Let's step up our CYO, Girl Scouts, Boy Scouts, Brownies and Cub programs. Let's draw them in closely to the parishes' liturgical and social life. Let them get acquainted with the priests and sisters and lay youth leaders in these programs. And let them be eager for the day when they will be able to slip into that privileged place—the Catholic school. This plan is frankly an alternative which falls below the ideal. Yet it comes to grips with the realities, among them, the limitation on the resources of the American Catholic people. This is not "pessimism," or "defeatism," or "disloyalty." To speak this way is simply realism.

It would be far more in keeping with the spirit of the Council of Baltimore to study the objectives the bishops had in mind in legislating for separate schools, and then determine whether these goals are being achieved through our concentration on elementary rather than high school and college education. Are objectives like the strengthening of the faith and the development of lay leadership in society and the multiplication of vocations best realized by clinging to the educational pattern of 1884, or rather do the times demand some basic reorganization?

Imagination and courage have marked the growth of Catholic education in the United States. May the Holy Spirit insure a sufficiency of these commodities during the next decades, so that we can make the right adaptations for the survival and growth of Catholic education.

Can public funds be constitutionally granted to private schools?

Robert F. Drinan, S.J.

No one has seriously suggested that all the problems of Catholic education are basically financial, but it is generally agreed that many of them could be solved and others at least alleviated if more money were available. Although the United States Constitution, as interpreted by the Supreme Court, seems to preclude such assistance, many Catholic parents and educators maintain that their schools are both legally and morally entitled to Federal aid. In this article, the Dean of the Boston College Law School reviews pertinent Supreme Court decisions and shows why and how public funds can be granted to private schools within the framework of the Constitution.

It would be an easy answer to the question discussed in this article if we could simply state that no public funds should ever be expended for private purposes. With regard to schools, however, the fact is that no nonpublic school can be private in every sense of that term. American law recognized in *Pierce* v. *Society of Sisters* [1] the right of the private school to exist and has thereby given to it a juridical status. This status, however ambiguous, has rendered the private school a quasi-public, or if you will, a para-public institution.

The fundamental issue, therefore, in the controversy over public funds for

[1] 268 U. S. 510 (1925). The *Pierce* case, also known as the Oregon School case, held a state law requiring children to attend only schools operated by the state to be unconstitutional as a deprivation of liberty guaranteed by the Fourteenth Amendment.

Reprinted with permission from *Social Order*, 13:18 ff., March, 1963.

private schools arises out of the fact that private schools are public schools for the purpose of compulsory attendance laws but have not been designated as public schools capable of being the beneficiaries of public funds. The anomalous juridical status of the private school in America has no parallel or precedent in any other phase of our law.

Those who seek to retain *Pierce* and yet reverse *Everson* v. *Board of Education* [2] do not appreciate the implications of the juridical position conferred on the private school by *Pierce*. Those who seek to retain *Pierce* and who would accept *Everson* as containing the ultimate concessions which can be made to the private school likewise do not appreciate the logical implications of the holding in *Pierce*.

THE PUBLIC DIMENSIONS OF PRIVATE SCHOOLS

Let us start then with *Pierce* and see if from this decision there can be developed a line of reasoning by which the private school can claim to be an institution charged with a public responsibility and hence eligible for some public funds.

As is well known, *Pierce* was decided a few days before the guarantees of the First Amendment were for the first time transferred to the states via the Fourteenth Amendment. Consequently, *Pierce* decided nothing about First Amendment freedoms in relation to the existence of the private school. But the spirit of the *Pierce* decision clearly affirmed that no institutionalized dissent from educational orthodoxy could be constitutionally suppressed. The brief opinion in *Pierce*, however, left almost totally unsolved the extent to which a private school, legally recognized as a permissible substitute for the public school, could on this basis claim a right to be supported by public funds.

A plausible argument can be made for the proposition that the *Pierce* decision elevated the private school to the status of a publicly recognized institution which cannot logically and fairly be granted state accreditation and denied state subsidization. Even if, however, everyone agreed with this conclusion, the real issue confronting the nation today and the thorny problem to be discussed in this paper would not be resolved. That issue is, of course, not the private school as private but the church-related school, and more particularly, the Catholic school.

In order, therefore, to give reality to the discussion, it is proposed to write here, not in a conceptualistic way about public money and private schools, but in a realistic way about Federal aid and Catholic educational institutions. At the same time it must be recognized that no satisfactory resolution of the controversy over subsidy to church-related schools, which is in issue in connection with Fed-

---

[2] 330 U. S. 1 (1947). In the *Everson* decision the Supreme Court upheld the constitutionality of the New Jersey law of transportation of children to parochial schools. The opinion of the majority of the Court was that the transportation is a welfare benefit of the state and that the incidental benefit to religion is not unconstitutional as an "establishment of religion."

eral aid, can be reached without attaining some agreement on the function and juridical nature of the private school in America.

What then is the claim being made by Catholic parents and Catholic officials? The claim is a very small one: the Catholic contention is that, *if* Federal aid is to be enacted, *some* recognition should be given to Catholic schools. This Catholic request is grounded on several factors among which are the following:

1. About 92% of all children attending private schools in America today are enrolled in Catholic elementary and secondary schools.

2. Some six million students—or every eighth child in America—attend a Catholic school. Any program designed to elevate the nation's standards of educational excellence which ignores the 12% of the nation's school children enrolled in nonpublic schools is neglecting in a serious manner a significant element in the population.

3. The first program of massive Federal aid to education must in the nature of things be designed either to help public schools alone or to elevate the educational excellence of *all* schools. Consequently, an important public policy decision must be made before Federal aid can become a reality.

Even this telescoped version of the Catholic case for a share in the distribution of Federal aid to education will indicate that the controversy over this issue involves profound questions of public policy. These questions can be resolved in a speculative way by peering into the interstices of the half-dozen church-state opinions which the Supreme Court has written from the *Everson* case to *Engel* v. *Vitale*.[3] But even the most resourceful and convinced advocate or opponent of Federal aid for Catholic schools must confess that the most careful reading of all Supreme Court decisions and dicta leads only to the feeling that the real questions have not yet been asked, much less resolved, in Supreme Court jurisprudence.

Some few "absolutes," however, with regard to religion and education have emerged from the *Everson* to *Engel* line of cases. The following principles seem to have a secure place in church-state law:

I. The benefits of public-welfare legislation may not be granted or denied to citizens because of their religious faith or their lack of it.

II. If the state, in the pursuit of a legitimate public purpose, selects means to achieve an incidental effect of assisting religion, such means are not thereby unconstitutional—especially if no alternate means are as easily available.

III. No sectarian teaching or religious practice may be constitutionally permitted on the premises of a tax-supported school—even if student and teacher participation is on a truly voluntary basis.

---

[3] 370 U. S. 421 (1962). The Supreme Court ruled in *Engel* that a New York school district could not require the recitation of an officially composed prayer at the beginning of the school day.

Analyzing in turn each of these three broad principles, what can one conclude about the constitutionality of a grant of public money to a Catholic school?

I. Public-welfare Legislation

If there was one thing that Mr. Justice Black sought to make clear in *Everson*, it was the finding that the challenged statute authorizing reimbursement to Catholic parents for school-bus transportation for their children was public-welfare legislation. Mr. Justice Black assumed or asserted several conclusions which formed the following line of reasoning:

1. Public-welfare legislation is ordinarily identifiable as a particular type of law and should not be nullified by the courts except for the gravest reasons.

2. Such public-welfare legislation is not unconstitutional even if it facilitates attendance at church-related schools.

3. Such legislation does not offend against the wall of separation between church and state provided that (1) any aid given to religion is incidental to the main purpose of the law and (2) a denial of such aid would be discrimination against persons or groups because of their faith or lack of it.

It may be that someone would challenge the foregoing summary of *Everson* as inadequate and even misleading. Such a person could indeed cite respectable authority for his position, because the fact is that several state courts have been confused about the meaning and thrust of *Everson*. The opinion of Mr. Justice Black is more encouraging to the advocate of Federal aid for Catholic schools than are the several interpretations placed on the opinion by the four dissenting justices in *Everson*. Equally discouraging are the interpretations given to *Everson* by the Supreme Courts of the states of Washington, New Mexico, Oregon, Wisconsin, and Alaska. All these tribunals have given lip service to *Everson* but have declared laws granting bus transportation or other benefits to Catholic school children to be unconstitutional even though these laws were concededly written and enacted as public-welfare legislation. In other words, state courts have *not* accepted the idea that public-welfare legislation is constitutionally permissible if it only grants to children in Catholic schools those benefits which are also granted to pupils in public schools. The basic rationale of *Everson* have either been misunderstood, misinterpreted, or rejected. Only the Supreme Courts of Connecticut and Maine have accepted and followed *Everson* as meaning that bus-transportation statutes can be framed as public-welfare legislation in such a manner as to be constitutionally unassailable.

The confusion over the meaning of *Everson* has not been lessened by the fact that the Supreme Court has since 1951 refused to review decisions based on *Everson* from the states of Washington, Connecticut, Oregon, and Alaska. One can argue, therefore, either that *Everson* is properly interpreted by the highest court of Connecticut, which sustained the constitutionality of a law authorizing bus transportation to private schools, or on the other hand, that *Everson* has almost no relevance or meaning at the state level—as the highest courts of Washington, Wisconsin, and Alaska have declared.

It will be seen, therefore, that the history of *Everson* does not encourage one to employ it as a firm foundation for a case for Federal aid to Catholic schools. At the same time, the literal wording of Mr. Justice Black's opinion in *Everson* supplies a solid basis for a line of argument that would support the case which Catholics and others are making on behalf of the constitutionality of Federal aid for private schools. The fact is that *Everson* v. *Board of Education* reaffirmed *Cochran* v. *Louisiana State Board of Education* [4] and the child-benefit theory and that *Everson* is still good law—despite *McCollum*,[5] *Torcaso*[6] and *Engel*. Mr. Leo Pfeffer highlights the consequences of Mr. Justice Black's opinion in this comment:

> When the *Everson* decision is coupled with the *Cochran* decision they lead logically to the conclusion that the state may, notwithstanding the First Amendment, finance practically every aspect of parochial education, with the exception of such comparatively minor items as the proportionate salaries of teachers while they teach the catechism (*Church, State and Freedom*, p. 476).

One could add a dimension to Mr. Pfeffer's reading of the *Cochran-Everson* rule by urging that in the ultimate analysis *Everson* follows from *Pierce*: public money, in other words, cannot logically be withheld from the private school if it is publicly accredited as an institution where children may fulfill their legal duty to attend school.

The many ambiguities in the *Pierce-Cochran-Everson* line of cases arises from the enigma which lies behind the institution to which has been assigned the non-descriptive and unenlightening name of the nonpublic or private school. Schools of this kind have an equivocal juridical status in America, and until that status is clarified, the entire controversy over the financing of such schools will be carried on in language and with concepts which do not really express the realities which they seek to describe.

The terminology of *private* and *public* schools becomes even less useful when the private school in issue turns out to be a church-related school. The thorny issues involved in this area lead us to a discussion of the second "absolute" in the

---

[4] 281 U. S. 370 (1930). The Court held in *Cochran* that the use of state funds to provide textbooks for children in parochial as well as public schools was an expenditure for a public purpose. Consequently, the expenditure of tax funds was not an unconstitutional taking of the taxpayer's property for private purposes.

[5] *McCollum* v. *Board of Education*, 333 U. S. 203 (1948), held unconstitutional the released-time program of the Champaign, Illinois, School District which permitted religious organizations to conduct classes in religion for their adherents on public-school premises during the school hours.

[6] In *Torcaso* v. *Watkins*, 367 U. S. 488 (1961), the members of the Court were unanimously agreed that Maryland could not require a public official (a notary public) to declare his belief in the existence of God. Such a law was said to prohibit the free exercise of religion.

Everson to *Engel* line of cases—namely, the proposition that the state may con-stitutionally achieve a legitimate public purpose in such a way that an unintended incidental benefit comes to religion.

II. State Programs Which Give Incidental Aid to Religion

The various Supreme Court opinions in the Sunday-law cases [7] made it very clear that the requirement of separation between church and state does not mean that the state, in carrying out a legitimate secular purpose, must do so in a way which gives no aid to religion. It is significant to note that Mr. Justice Black, who wrote the rigorously separationist language in *Everson* and *McCollum,* sees no problem involving establishment or free exercise of religion in Sunday laws which, what-ever their present purpose may be said to be, clearly aid the Christian religion by fixing Sunday as a day of universal rest.

It is the *secular* purpose behind Sunday laws which, in the mind of the Su-preme Court, renders them constitutional. As Mr. Justice Frankfurter put it in his concurring opinion in the Sunday-law cases: ". . . not every regulation, some of whose practical effects may facilitate the observance of a religion by its ad-herents, affronts the requirement of church-state separation."

Employing this reasoning, the majority of the Supreme Court held that the incidental aid which Sunday laws give to the Christian religion does not make them unconstitutional. Nor are these laws contrary to the First Amendment be-cause of the "indirect burden on religions observance" which they impose on Sab-batarians. There is, however, a qualification on the power of the state to impose such a burden. As Chief Justice Warren put it:

> If the state regulates conduct by enacting a general law within its power, the purpose and effect of which is to advance the state's secular goals, the statute is valid despite its indirect burden on religious observance *unless a state may accomplish its purpose by means which do not impose such a burden.* (Em-phasis supplied.)

Is it arguable from this principal that the state in carrying out its "secular goals" in the field of education has some obligation to do so, if possible, in a man-ner which does not impose even an "indirect burden on religious observance"? If Catholics could demonstrate that the denial of aid to their schools imposed a burden on their religious observance, would such a law be subject to the qualifica-tion which Chief Justice Warren attached to Sunday laws?

---

[7] *McGowan* v. *Maryland,* 366 U. S. 420; *Gallagher* v. *Crown Kosher Super Market,* 366 U. S. 617; *Two Guys from Harrison-Allentown* v. *McGinley,* 366 U. S. 582; and *Braunfeld* v. *Brown,* 366 U. S. 599, all decided in 1961. These cases sustained the con-stitutionality of state Sunday-closing laws.

Whatever one might answer to that question, it is clear that the establishment clause has *not* been interpreted by the Supreme Court to mean that the secular aims of the state must be achieved in a manner deliberately designed to preclude any incidental aid to religion. In view of this position then, what policy can the state adopt with regard to the distribution of funds for the purpose of raising the nation's standards of excellence in education?

The advocates of Federal aid for Catholic schools ground their plea on the principle that the state, in carrying out its secular goals in the field of education, can comply with the First Amendment if it makes available funds for strictly secular purposes in *all* schools. Under such an arrangement no aid is intended for religion and whatever benefits students in church-related schools may receive are exclusively of a secular nature.

The two most fundamental objections to this line of reasoning are the following:

1. Even if public money were given to a Catholic school for strictly secular objectives, these objectives would be carried forward in an atmosphere permeated by a Catholic orientation.

2. Even if this permeation can be prevented the grant of public money to a Catholic school makes available to this school funds which would otherwise be committed to the teaching of secular subjects.

Let us try to analyze, and if possible, bring some clarification to these two issues.

Reflections on Permeation. The permeation argument against aid to Catholic schools does not contend that the legitimate secular purpose which the state seeks to fulfill in giving aid for education in secular subjects is thwarted or frustrated in Catholic schools. The secular purpose is concededly carried out in Catholic schools, but it is permeated—and somehow constitutionally contaminated—by a sectarian atmosphere. The argument against aid to church-related schools because of the permeation of sacred or sectarian values into the teaching of secular subjects must assume for its validity the viewpoint that the state is constitutionally required to seek ways to carry out its secular objectives which will not give even incidental aid to religion. No such constitutional requirement can be found in the decisions from *Everson* to *Engel* and indeed the opinions in the Sunday-law cases expressly deny the existence of any such constitutional requirement.

The opponents of Federal aid for Catholic schools who place great reliance on the permeation argument must logically say that the secular or silent attitude with regard to religion in the public schools is the only official orthodoxy which the state is allowed to promote in the pursuance of its public-welfare objectives. This may be a philosophy of education subscribed to by a majority of the American people, but it is not good constitutional law or, it is submitted, sound public policy.

Some recent writings on the permeation issue have focused attention on some graphic examples of the intermingling or rather the intrusion of sectarian teaching into textbooks on secular subjects used in Catholic schools. Two comments on this matter seem appropriate:

A. No scientific study has ever been done on the question of the extent of the permeation of sectarian teaching in the instruction in secular subjects in Catholic schools. Concrete examples of such permeation in textbooks can be cited, but an important distinction should be made between the factitious and indefensible insertion of sectarian symbols or teaching into secular subjects and the conclusions or judgments based on religious values which are properly found in texts in the area of the social sciences. The latter type of permeation is much more significant than the former and is, moreover, a justifiable exercise of academic freedom by social scientists writing from a particular point of view.

B. Although there undoubtedly exist some unjustifiable examples of permeation in secular textbooks used in Catholic schools, little work has been done on the extent to which ultranationalistic or secularistic symbols and teachings have permeated the textbooks used in the public schools of America. Studies have shown, however, that the beliefs of minority groups, religious influences in American history, and the religions of lands different from America have received very inadequate treatment in the textbooks which enjoy widespread use in the nation's public schools. Many of these texts can be fairly and properly criticized as being permeated with an excessive emphasis on the secular with a resulting failure to give adequate treatment to the sacred, the sectarian, or the spiritual elements in the life of man and of society.

Permeation is, therefore, a factor in every textbook, since values are omnipresent. If the state, therefore, cannot constitutionally give public money for instruction in secular subjects because religious values are commingled in the instruction, the state is equally disabled from financing instruction in secular subjects where the orientation of the instruction is, by silence or by implication, permeated with a secularistic outlook.

Those who argue against Federal aid for Catholic schools because there exists in these schools some permeation of secular subjects with sacred values must be prepared to accept the major premise of their argument—the assumption that the orientation or secular humanism is the only type of educational orthodoxy which the state can subsidize.

Even if permeation of secular instruction with sectarian teaching can be prevented, however, the additional argument is made that the granting of public money to a nonpublic school for instruction in secular subjects relieves this school from a financial obligation which it would otherwise have. Hence, a church-related school would have more funds available to it and such funds could be used for sectarian purposes.

The logical thrust of this argument leads to the conclusion that any church-related school must be placed, not in the category of a school, but of a church. To deny public funds to nonpublic schools for secular instruction because such a grant would bring to the church-related school a freeing of otherwise committed funds is to state that the fully accredited school which is affiliated to a church thereby loses its right to any public funds even for exclusively secular purposes. Such a conclusion is specifically contrary to the *Everson* decision where Mr. Justice Black in effect conceded that the public money granted to parents for bus transportation of their children to a Catholic school would make available to the parents and to the school more money for other purposes.

The contention that the state should refuse public funds for the attainment of a secular purpose unrelated to the religious function of a church-related school simply because such a grant would free the funds of this school for a religious purpose leads logically to the conclusion that no church-related institution may be entrusted with the implementation of any of the secular objectives of the state. Such a conclusion runs contrary to the basic traditions and the widespread contemporary practice of the state assisting church-related social-welfare agencies in caring for the sick, the aged, and those in need of social sciences.

It should be remembered that *Everson* sustained the constitutionality of a law which granted the benefits of public-welfare legislation to individuals even though such benefits helped them to get to a church-related school. This result was reached in an opinion in which Mr. Justice Black stated:

> No tax in any amount, large or small, can be levied to support any religious activities or institutions, whatever they may be called, or whatever form they may adopt, to teach or practice religion.

This famous sentence proscribes tax support *only* for "*religious* activities or institutions" in whatever form they may adopt "to teach or practice *religion.*" (Emphasis supplied.) It does *not* proscribe public funds for instruction in secular subjects even though such instruction may be conducted under the auspicies of a religious institution. Far less does it forbid the granting of public funds to a church-related institution for the accomplishment of a secular purpose simply because such a grant might liberate other funds of this institution for a religious purpose.

Aid to religion as such is clearly forbidden by all the decisions from *Everson* to *Engel.* But state aid for the improvement of secular education need not be distributed only under circumstances where not even any incidental aid to religion may occur. The broadening of the concept of separation of church and state to this point must necessarily assume the validity of the theory that America is a completely secular state. Such a viewpoint makes it difficult, if not impossible, to reconcile the mandate of the establishment clause with the guarantee of the free-exercise-of-religion clause.

It must be noted, however, that Supreme Court opinions from *Everson* to *Engel* are ambiguous at best with regard to the central question of whether America is a completely secular state. No decision has repudiated Mr. Justice Douglas' assertion in *Zorach* that "We are a religious people whose institutions presuppose a Supreme Being," but in the very same opinion Mr. Justice Douglas wrote that "Government may not . . . blend secular and sectarian education." The Court has seemingly supported a theistic basis for America's legal institutions but has simultaneously insisted that the public school may not blend any "sectarian education" into its program. This apparent paradox leads us to a consideration of our third "absolute" in church-state law—the unconstitutionality of religious teaching or practices in the public schools, even when they are conducted on a truly voluntary basis.

III. The Secular Orientation of the Public School

Mr. Justice Rutledge, dissenting in *Everson*, gave as a reason for the *Pierce* decision his conviction that children should not be required to attend public schools because "their atmosphere is *wholly secular*." (Emphasis supplied.) While it would be difficult to prove or disprove that the Supreme Court has agreed that the public school must have an "atmosphere" that is "wholly secular," the Court would seem to be pointing in that direction.

If the Supreme Court in its present term declares the reading of the Bible and the recitation of the Lord's Prayer to be unconstitutional in a public school, the secularization of the public school will be, at least in popular opinion, considerably extended. In a certain sense, however, the reasoning of the Court in the Bible-reading case will be more important than the result reached. The Court can develop a line of reasoning employed in the past and forbid Bible-reading as contrary to the establishment clause—even if no infringement of religious liberty is found to be present. The Court seems to have followed this reasoning in the *Engel* decision, although the fact of state authorship of the prayer involved in that case made the Court's decision unique.

Very few scholars and no group of religionists have sought to explore the implications of the Supreme Court's recently developed interpretation of the establishment clause as constituting a source of rights independently of the free-exercise-of-religion clause. The theory that the establishment clause is merely instrumental to the implementation of the free-exercise clause has been rejected by the Court. And by this rejection the Court has opened up the following possible arguments on behalf of the constitutionality of aid for private schools:

1. Can religionists claim that the secularized public school violates the establishment clause because it prefers irreligion over religion?

2. Can religionists claim further that the state by assisting only the secularized school subscribes to and promotes an orthodoxy which is imposed on all students to whom by law the state has given a pledge of a free education unaffected by any officially established indoctrination?

Let us search through these ideas in the light of the recent Supreme Court interpretation of the establishment clause.

1. *Secularized Schools and the Establishment Clause.* The theory advanced

by Mr. Justice Black in *Torcaso, McGowan* [8] and *Engel* that the establishment clause can be violated without a violation of the free-exercise-of-religion clause may now have become an accepted part of Supreme Court jurisprudence. Under this interpretation of the First Amendment, can it be argued that the secularization of the public school amounts to a violation of the establishment clause, since a particular form of religion (or irreligion) is given a preferential status? If such a violation of the establishment clause can be shown, Catholics or others can enjoin it even though there is no infringement of anyone's religious freedom.

Aside from the question of standing to sue, can religious parents prove a violation of the establishment clause if the state gives financial assistance only to the school where education is deliberately divorced from religion? Preferential treatment to irreligion would seem to be as constitutionally objectionable as any preference given to religion.

Some Catholics have asserted that attendance at a public school by their children violates or restricts the religious freedom of both children and parents. The assertion is made that Catholics have a right to be treated like conscientious objectors or like Jehovah's Witnesses who have been granted an exemption from laws requiring a flag salute in a public school.

Mr. Justice Frankfurter saw the force of this analogy when, dissenting in *West Virginia State Board of Education* v. *Barnette,* [9] he voted against granting an exemption from the flag salute to children conscientiously opposed to the practice. Mr. Justice Frankfurter saw the consequences of the Court's bowing to the religious scruples of a minority and raised this question:

> What of the claims of equality of treatment of those parents who, because of *religious scruples, cannot* send their children to public schools? (Emphasis supplied.)

This potential argument of the Catholic or other parent has not been developed or litigated. To be able to show that religious parents "because of religious scruples cannot send their children to public schools" (to use Mr. Justice Frankfurter's language) would seem to require more proof of an antireligious bias in the public school than would appear to be now provable.

It is not now necessary, however, to have such proof before one can claim rights by reason of the First Amendment. Under the interpretation of the establishment clause adopted in recent years by the Supreme Court, any preferential treatment granted by the state to religion or irreligion constitutes a violation of constitutional rights. The allegation that is difficult to prove is, of course, the assertion that the secularized public school gives preferential treatment to irreligion. The widespread and deeply held conviction persists that silence about

---

[8] The Sunday-closing-law case.

[9] 319 U. S. 624 (1943). The *Barnette* opinion concluded that the state could not constitutionally force a schoolchild to salute the American flag if such an act violated the child's religious belief.

religion in the public school is the same as neutrality or impartiality. On this basic conception is built the whole thesis that the public school can be fair to believers and non-believers by assuming that their differences for the purposes of education are without significance. It is this basic assumption of the public school which, it is submitted, violates the letter and the spirit of the establishment clause.

The secularized public school meets and treats its students only as future citizens. Their religious or spiritual beliefs are to be regarded as irrelevant and hence unimportant with respect to the entire educational process. It is this basic disregard of the great ideas and religious aspirations in the lives of the students in a public school which is the burden of the religionist's complaint. To the believer—at least to many believers—the silent assumption by the public school that religion in any meaningful sense is irrelevant to the educational process amounts to an official establishment of secular values.

2. *Secularized Schools and the Ideal of a Free Education.* Two of the greatest ideas underlying American democracy were born in the mid-nineteenth century: They are the pledge of the state to give a *free* education to every child and in an atmosphere not affected by a sectarian orientation. When these twin ideals emerged more than a century ago, their fulfillment was relatively easy in a pan-Protestant nation. Today, however, in a religiously pluralistic society these ideals have become more difficult to realize because the nondenominational pan-Protestant environment of the common school has been largely displaced by a secularistic orientation. The tendency of the law from *Everson* to *Engel* has been to make mandatory the secularization of the public school without at the same time providing for a *free* education in a school without a secularistic orientation.

The denial of public funds to church-related schools means in effect that the ideal of a *free* education in an atmosphere apart from any officially fixed indoctrination has been compromised. The important thing here to prove, of course, is that there is a secularistic indoctrination which accompanies an education in the public school. This is the most important and the most difficult point of dispute in the entire controversy over public funds for private schools. But in a nation whose law knows no heresy and whose legal institutions support no orthodoxy, how is it possible to reject the contention made by a substantial minority of citizens that the tax-supported school by its silent disregard of religion thereby promotes irreligion? This, of course, is the essence of the Catholic parent's case and no satisfactory answer seems to have been given.

It is uncertain what American law would say if tomorrow all the Catholics of the nation withdrew all their children from the public schools because of their conviction that the secularistic orientation of these schools was destructive of the faith of their children. American courts could compel the children to return to the public schools or could give financing for schools consistent with the consciences of Catholics.

American law today confronts the situation where about half of all the Catholic children of the nation have withdrawn from the public school because of a profound disagreement with the approach to education and to life which that institution has adopted. American society and American law do not seem concerned that these children, who for compelling religious reasons have forfeited the education offered to them, must be thereby deprived of their right to share in the commitment of the state to provide a free education for very future citizen.

SUMMARY AND CONCLUSIONS

It seems clear that many converging forces have precipitated the national debate about the advisability of parochial schools sharing in some part of Federal aid to education if such assistance is authorized by the Congress. The debate is filled with anomalies, the most curious of which is the fact that no controversy exists at the state level over parochial schools, since at that level the question was resolved in the last century when virtually all states enacted laws prohibiting the distribution of public funds to sectarian schools. In the Federal-aid controversy, Catholic spokesmen are in effect asserting that this policy embraced in the last century by the states is not a wise or fair one for the Federal Government to follow.

Cogent arguments exist to support the Catholic contention. Among them are the following:

1. The fully accredited private school has important public dimensions in that it carries out the secular goals of the state. Because of this semipublic status conferred on the private school, this institution has some claim to share in the public funds set aside by the state for the education of all of its future citizens.

2. Public-welfare benefits surely include secular education, and by the rulings in *Cochran* and *Everson* the benefits extended by the state to all citizens may not be denied to anyone because of his religious faith or lack of it.

3. In the distribution of these public-welfare benefits no Supreme Court opinion has held that the only constitutional formula is one which prevents even some incidental aid to religion. The Sunday-law decisions, in fact, expressly hold that the state is not precluded from implementing its secular goals in a way which bestows some collateral benefits on religion.

4. In view of clear Supreme Court rulings precluding sectarian teaching and religious practices in public schools, it can be persuasively argued that the granting of funds only to the public school is a violation of the establishment clause because such a policy endorses and prefers one educational and philosophical orthodoxy over all others. This is the very essence of the Catholic case.

It seems fair to conclude that neither the Congress nor the Supreme Court of the United States has confronted the claim which is being made by parents who are dissenters from the orthodoxy which the public school represents. No quotation seems more appropriate to express their sentiments and to affirm the spirit

with which the entire controversy over church-related schools should be discussed
than the ringing words of Mr. Justice Jackson in the *Barnette* decision:

> If there is any fixed star in our constitutional constellation, it is that no official,
> high or petty, can prescribe what shall be orthodox in politics, nationalism,
> religion, or other matters of opinion or force citizens to confess by word or act
> their faith therein.

The cruel choice facing Catholic education

Sister Ann Virginia, I.H.M.

The acuteness of Catholic education's financial and personnel problems has led to the proposal that Catholic educators concentrate exclusively on either elementary or secondary schooling. This proposal has given rise to a continuing debate over the question of which level to maintain and strengthen, and which to drop. As the title of Sister Ann Virginia's article states, the choice is a cruel one for those who may be called upon to help decide. Sister Ann Virginia explains and defends the forced choice she would make.

The ideal for Catholic education in the United States was spelled out in clear, bold language at the Third Plenary Council in Baltimore in 1884—"Every Catholic child in a Catholic school." Some Catholic educators seem to be whittling down this daring goal to "Some Catholic children in Catholic schools," but we sisters want to go on record that we have not substituted and will not substitute any other. We hold firmly, moreover, that this ultimate goal of "Every Catholic child in a Catholic school" should extend from nursery through graduate school. Some way or other, with or without federal aid, but with a trust in the continued support of Catholic parents and with a strong conviction that the power of the Spirit will bring to a practical fruition the mandate of Christ to teach all nations, we will some day achieve that ultimate goal.

So emphatic a pledge of ourselves to such an ideal makes it obvious that we are not arguing against Catholic elementary schools. We are FOR Catholic ele-

Reprinted with permission from *The Catholic World*, 195:343–349, September, 1962.

mentary schools, FOR Catholic secondary schools, FOR Catholic colleges and universities. But, the existing, concrete situation in Catholic education in this country today forces the question of priorities if we are to bridge the gap between where we are and where we are determined to go. The assets are many: steadily increasing numbers of students in Catholic schools, continued sacrifice of Catholic parents that make Catholic schools possible, growing numbers of religious vocations to teaching communities, heroic efforts of teaching communities to improve professional status of teachers, and the ever increasing number of qualified and dedicated lay teachers on Catholic school teaching staffs. These strengths are tremendous.

At this point in educational history, however, it is on the debit side of the picture that attention is centered: the inadequate facilities which bar approximately one half the elementary and secondary Catholic school population from Catholic schools and make the building of junior colleges almost impossible; the overcrowded classrooms; the overworked sister-teachers; the underpaid and/or submarginally qualified lay teachers; the scant provisions for exceptional children; the increasing demands of accrediting agencies; the acute sister shortage; the growing dissatisfaction of parents with the unavailability of Catholic education; and the burden of financing.

These adverse conditions, threatening to grow worse, leave us far from the goal of the Council of 1884. One thing is clear, however. These concrete realities force us to make choices. If the ideal is to be reached, we must set up some intermediate, short-range objectives drawn from the exigencies of the present situation, accomplishment of which may set us securely on the road to our determined destination. If the objectives are accepted, the question of priorities may be easier to handle. I propose five.

The first objective has to do with parents. We must, at all cost, keep the good will of parents, first, by working out a fair admissions policy, acceptable to them and productive of the common good of the entire Catholic educational system. We must keep their good will also on the score of quality. Catholic parents have sacrificed in the past because they believed in Catholic education; they will continue to sacrifice as long as the end product bears the stamp of excellence.

Quality has to be considered in the preparation of teachers, the calibre of administrators, the curricula—all oriented toward the development of excellence in our students. In the national examen on quality education, we are asked to investigate whether our schools are really comprehensive, liberal, goal-centered, challenging and integrated. Parents desire just such investigation to be assured that we are thinking seriously regarding the quality of each individual school. Only this assurance will urge them to make Catholic schools possible.

I propose, as a second objective, that we offer the high level of religious education necessary to prepare parents to teach religion effectively. Religious teachers cannot now and will not in the foreseeable future be able to reach all Catholic children; some lay persons, then, must be prepared to teach religion. If, in some areas, decisions are made to build secondary schools, children in the first eight grades will attend public schools. Parents and lay catechists will have to provide for their religious education. Only men and women with mature religious training will be equipped for such educational responsibilities. The decision to build Catholic secondary schools will make provision for such training. On the other hand, if decisions are made to build elementary schools, then Catholic high school students will attend public secondary schools. Parents will take over the job of carrying on religious education where elementary teachers leave off. Can we envision the sort of religious education parents will give if they themselves terminated their religious education at eighth grade? Without mature religious education, what will they have to transmit to their own teen-agers?

I propose a third objective—that we keep intellectual respect for Catholic education and guard carefully against any action which will lower that respect by having Catholic education associated exclusively with elementary level. No educational system—and certainly not ours—can scorn prestige. We flinch when a national publication repeats the judgment made twenty years ago by D. W. Brogan, "In no Western society is the intellectual prestige of Catholicism lower than in the country where in such respects as wealth, numbers, and strength of organization, it is so powerful." (*Time*, LXXIX, February 9, 1962, p. 48.) If we have not proportionate representation in American intellectual achievements, will the situation improve if we go all out for elementary education? It is ironic that the Catholic attitude toward scholarship should need defense when through the ages the Church has always championed the cause of learning and truth; we have to admit, however, that we are being asked for evidence of a high respect for intellectual values.

Any series of objectives that omits the vocation situation is unrealistic. I propose, then, as a fourth objective, a study of the sources of vocations and action taken to enlarge the most promising sources.

Studies indicate that many candidates to religious life give serious thought to vocations on the grade school level. A significant study, however, of four thousand religious shows that 9% of them *decided* to enter religion at the age of twelve; 31% between the ages of thirteen and fifteen; 41% between sixteen and twenty; 16% after twenty. Should we not concern ourselves much more with decisions about vocations, with those ultimate practical judgments which move girls to packing suitcases for novitiates rather than with intermediate practical judgments that seventh graders might make?

Several studies indicate that the educational environment most productive of religious vocations is the all-girl or all-boy Catholic secondary school. Easy as it is to find fault with statistics, the figures are so generally overwhelming—one national study estimates the figure at 75%—to set us quite clearly on the path to the most fruitful source of vocations. Might we also ask what is being done to widen this source when figures in the *1961 Official Catholic Directory* indicate that the majority of sisters are engaged in teaching in schools producing the least number of vocations. (The Directory reports 564,000 students in diocesan and parish co-educational high schools as contrasted with 340,000 in private all-girl or all-boy schools.) Further studies show that vocations to communities of teaching brothers are increasing much more rapidly than vocations to communities of teaching sisters—some 31% of their total number as contrasted with 16% for sisters in the same ten-year period. Brothers are concentrated in secondary schools where the greatest number of vocations are drawn.

If the vocation dearth comes close to being the Church's number one problem, it seems obvious that we must soon take practical steps to increase the number of students at the level most productive of religious vocations.

The fifth objective straddles both short and long-range planning. We must provide education for life, all of life. We are not speaking here of comparative values; not whether elementary education is important or not, nor whether secondary education is important. The question is—in a time of crisis when decisions are forced upon us, at what level can we insure the fullest Catholic education to the necessarily limited number of students we will have for a limited period of time?

The keyword here is *fullness*. We have heard Catholic education equated with religious education, even with CCD education. Catholic education is religious education; it is also intellectual education, social education, education which touches man at every point—religious, academic, psychological, social, cultural, physical. We have not time to consider all these aspects, but we need to pose a few questions to throw light on the priorities we are considering in this discussion.

If we consider religious education for all of life, we ask: does a grade school child have sufficient power of abstraction to understand the rational foundation of his faith? Will not a public high school student need to justify his beliefs on a higher level than grade school religious education can give him? Are the habits, attitudes, virtues of a thirteen-year-old so solidly rooted and so sufficiently formed that they can survive the secularistic atmosphere of the public school? No matter what our elementary schools can produce through excellent religious training, be it angels, are eighth graders ready to cope with the amorality, the immorality of teen-age society today? Is the elementary school the place to talk about birth control, abortion, sanctity of marriage?

Psychology books tell us that a child's character is formed some time between the ages of four and eight, that if we can have the child during his earliest years, anyone can take him after that and we need have no fear. Moving from the psychology books into the realm of experience, we seriously question whether the faith of the grade school children now in Catholic schools will survive and mature, their vision be clarified and enlarged, their interest in the things of God be kept alive if their religious education is not kept at the level of their secular education. Will elementary religious education suffice to stave off what one author calls "a slow growing cancer of a spiritual vacuum"? (James E. Noonan, O.M.I., "Collectivism via Approved Textbooks," *Homiletic and Pastoral Review*, LIX, Jan. 1959, p. 330.)

And what of intellectual education? We want to insure integration of the truths of revelation on the same intellectual level as other knowledges: science, literature, social studies. We want our children to make use of experimental and scientific methods and to see the limitations of such methods. We want them to grasp intellectually the revealed and philosophical principles which form the bases of Christian living. Can elementary education insure these things?

When we consider social education, we ask if a grade school child can understand the Christian social principles, grasp the ramifications of social justice, social prudence, social charity? Where do we tell him about business ethics? the population explosion? world responsibility? Where and under whose direction does he read the *Rerum Novarum? Mater et Magistra?*

Need we question *ad infinitum?* Suffice it to ask: where can we best insure education for all of life? That answer we want.

Here, then, are five short-range objectives necessary, I believe, for the preservation of the whole system of Catholic education. We must consider more than the needs of the individual student. The Catholic system of education does not exist for the individual *per se*. It exists for society and for the Church. Each of the five objectives has a social, a Mystical Body dimension; each is concerned not only with *a* Catholic child today, but with the continuation and growth of the Church tomorrow, and this consideration is basic to my proposal.

My proposal is twofold: first, that at some level we take all Catholic students who ask for admission; secondly, that the level we choose be the terminal level, whatever the terminal level may be in Diocese X or Community Y.

Universal admission at some educational level may help keep the good will of parents. In 1959 Bishop Lawrence J. Shehan proposed experimentation along this line. He stated, "At least we would have nothing to lose and perhaps much to gain if carefully planned and observed experiments were tried where the full course of Catholic education cannot be offered to all children at the present time." ("Christian Education: Our Commitments and Resources," *NCEA Bulletin,* LVI, August, 1959, p. 40.) I suggest that in areas where choices have to be made we accept all students who apply at the terminal level and extend admission downward, as far as administration of any individual school can afford to do so. National planning is not possible. Resources differ, and Catholic education should be offered whenever and wherever we can offer it. Such planning as I propose would be done diocese by diocese, city by city, parish by parish.

A pastor in diocese X would assess his resources, determine the number of classrooms, the size of the staff he could maintain, and as long as terminal level is secondary level, begin by offering Catholic education to all twelfth graders who apply, extending registration down as far as resources permit. Affluent circumstances would permit Catholic education from twelfth through nursery school in some areas; limited resources might cut off registration at sixth or ninth grade level in other areas.

Now, why terminal education? Why begin with twelfth grade instead of with first? When we speak of terminal education, we speak in terms of another NOW. Terminal education for the vast majority now is secondary education; nothing in the educational scene suggests a regression. Any change in this country seems more likely to be in the direction of a higher level. Realistically, then, terminal education means mature education, mature powers, mature content. It is only on the mature level that here and now the five short-range objectives we have enumerated can be reached.

Can quality education, encompassing the natural and supernatural ends of man as well as the natural and supernatural means to attain that end, be secured at any level by a staff of administrators and teachers, whose own formal religious education terminated at eighth grade level? In an age when Fulbright and National Merit Scholarships, Advanced Placement, CEEB scores are common parlance, would parents who have poured money into maintaining a parochial school system be content to face their neighbors, the nation, to point to a thirteen year old and say, "This is the end product of Catholic quality education. This is the final return for our investment"? Would we teachers be content never to say, "This painstaking research scholar, this keen debater, this intuitive creative writer is a product of our educational system"? Yet, if we settle for elementary education, won't we have to content ourselves to see others claim the finished product?

Reasons for proposing terminal education as the best and perhaps only immediate practical means of attaining the other objectives have been suggested in the explanation of those objectives. To prepare parents to teach religion effectively, we have to prepare them on an adult level; to keep respect for Catholic education, we must keep Catholic education at the terminal level. Factually, this level of education already has status. The bill for federal aid to higher education is now before a conference committee. The motives of the federal government for moving into the educational field were to raise the level of educational excellence. The fact that the bill has been quite favorably received indicates a mental climate; it indicates that higher education, including Catholic higher education, has status. This should help us to determine choices. The conclusion to start at terminal level is implicit, too, in the objective regarding vocations. If vocations are more plentiful at the terminal level, then we want more boys and girls on that level.

Education for all of life is impossible short of mature level. We cannot speak of fullness of life where it does not exist. Only at the mature level can full intellectual powers be developed, full social consciousness be instilled, religious education be rounded out, and a Catholic be equipped, ready to give, to assume responsibilities of strengthening, increasing and glorifying the Church.

We may shrink from the responsible action acceptance of such a proposal entails. Why? Is it perhaps easier to justify the *status quo?* Could any slight *ego* involvement in a present secure position make us unwilling to accept the sacrifice change would demand? We might argue that grade school teachers are not prepared to teach high school. That may be true, but this is the day of the Sister Formation Movement. Religious communities have been making an all-out effort to meet future as well as present needs. The Sister Formation program has set a standard in the education of sisters. If it is still true that the majority of elementary teachers are inadequately prepared to teach on higher levels, the situation proposes a real hazard to the future of Catholic education, but might it not be a greater hazard in this moment of history to cling to the *status quo?*

If terminal education moves up to include the junior college, I propose that we begin by accepting all Catholic children in Grade 14 and hope that we have sufficient resources to include all grades down through the nursery school.

The bishops at the Third Plenary Council of Baltimore in 1884 set an ideal; some eighty years later I propose that, wherever and whenever we are forced to make choices, we concentrate on terminal level education in order to approach in the future the realization of the dream of those far-seeing bishops who convened in Baltimore and declared in council: "Every Catholic child in a Catholic school."

Progressive education

Rt. Rev. Msgr. George Johnson

*Progressive education may not have measured up to
the standards imposed by a theory of Christian
education, but this should not be taken to mean
that everything in Progressive education must be
condemned. Monsignor Johnson admonishes
Christian educators to take a close look at their
instructional practices to ascertain whether or not
they might be renewed. He does not counsel
borrowing from the progressives, and he does not
want to embrace the phrase* progressive education,
*but he does believe the valuable techniques of
progressives, notably techniques involving self-
activity of learners, should be exploited to the
objective of higher quality learning. After all, he
maintains, Christian education is essentially
progressive.*

"It has been truly said," writes E. I. Watkin in the stimulating book which he has called "The Catholic Center," "that every heresy is the revenge of a forgotten truth." This is, of course, another way of saying that there is a grain of truth in every error, but a more arresting way. It emphasizes the fact that, in the hurly-burly of controversy and in its effort to meet the error on a shifting front, Catholic apologetic may easily enough overlook certain truths that are implicit in its own position or at least fail to appreciate their full importance. This is particularly the fact when the truths in question have been distorted to fit into some un-Christian philosophical thesis or caricatured by being applied in ways that contradict the principles of sound reason. It is always a difficult thing to winnow the wheat from

Reprinted with permission from *The Catholic Education Review*, 38:257–264,
May, 1940.

the chaff, and it requires no little patience to sit watchfully by until the harvest, when it will be possible to destroy the cockle without injuring the growth that is sound and wholesome.

A case in point is this thing called Progressive Education. Obviously the theory of it, as expounded by its prophets, is a heresy. It is theological heresy because it denies the whole concept of the supernatural and is based on a false naturalism that knows nothing about Redemption, or Grace, or Original Sin. From the point of view of Christian philosophy, it is philosophical heresy because it takes no stock in ultimate principles of truth and morality and makes its act of faith in Pragmatism and Instrumentalism. It is pedagogical heresy because it shrinks from scientific evaluation and flies in the face of experience and common sense. Yet not a bit of attention would it receive and no progress would it make were it not for the fact there lurks in it a truth concerning the educative process that has been largely forgotten, a truth which has been protesting, vainly for the most part, against the regimentation, the standardization, the routine and the artificiality that have been the concomitants of our effort to provide and administer an education that would reach all the children of all the people.

By means of Progressive Education, this truth is taking its revenge. It has been overlooked, and now it is stealing the limelight; it has been sinned against, and now it is doing some sinning of its own; it has not been understood, and now it is assuming forms past understanding.

It strikes me that the best way to meet the challenge of Progressive Education and preventing it from doing too much harm is to understand the truth that it masks and to put that truth to work. The way to silence it is to steal its thunder. We have Divine Authority for the statement that the children of this world are often wiser when it comes to achieving their purposes than the children of light. If those who know not Christ stumble upon something that has possibilities in the way of improving education, those who know Him cannot afford to sulk.

What is this vengeful truth that is getting even by means of Progressivism? It is a simple truth, rather obvious, as a matter of fact. It is generally respected in the field of informal education. It is accepted as a matter of course in family life, in ordinary social relations, wherever men and women and children learn from one another out of school. Dr. Shields gave expression to it when he wrote, "The temptation of the teacher is to ignore the fact that the temple of life and mind can be built by none other than the inward dweller."

The teacher ignores this fact when he puts a premium on pupil passivity and loses sight of the fact that personal experience is the only sound basis for learning. It is not enough for them to be hearers of the word, they have to be doers also; in the degree that they do, what they hear becomes intelligible to them. Progressive Education has done a service by emphasizing this truth. St. Paul tells the Ephesians that it is by "doing the Truth in charity that we grow up in all things to Him Who is the Head." Action, activity, living, doing, are the condition necessary for learning. In the degree in which we live our religion, for instance, we penetrate into its deeper meanings; as long as we are content to carry some information about it along in our memories and fail to express it in our daily behavior, we are just sounding brass and tinkling cymbals. This holds for every other aspect of life, be it cultural, social, economic, or civic. That man is truly wise who shares his knowledge, puts it to work in his daily life, for by putting it to work he masters it, assimilates it, makes it part and parcel of him.

Emphasizing this truth, Progressive Education has done us all a service; it has done us a disservice by overemphasizing it, or by interpreting it too narrowly. It interprets it too narrowly when it gives the impression that only overt, physical activity is worth while; it overemphasizes it when it leaves no room at all for passive acquiescence. There will always be things that children, because they are children, will have to take on faith; truths they must learn that they cannot here and now put to the test of experience. The Church prays the Lord to give us a "docile heart"; we save ourselves much loss of time and much grief by learning to bear the yoke from our youth. Yet even obedience, though often classed as a "passive" virtue, requires activity on the part of the will and is best developed in an atmosphere of cooperation and mutual understanding; it is seldom the fruit of compulsion.

The principal of self-activity, of learning by doing, involves, of course, a much greater measure of freedom for the learner than is usual in the conventional classroom. On this score the jokesmiths on the pedagogical Right have their field day at the expense of the Progressives. It may well be that some progressive practices are as wild as the current anecdotes would have us believe; if some progressive theories were carried to their logical conclusions, they would be. Divine Revelation is not necessary to prove to us that all human beings, including children, need to be restrained. One does not have to live very long to discover that discipline has its blessed uses and that happiness is born of curbing impulses. Revelation tells us about the Fall of man and its effects on each and every one of us. The Progressives may assume a superior air about that Doctrine, but no amount of prating on their part about the innate goodness of human nature can gainsay the fact that the average child, if left to his own devices and the dictates of his own whims, will degenerate into a first class brat.

However, belief in the Doctrine of Original Sin is no justification for despotism in the classroom; it gives no license for harsh regimentation and the rule of fear. It does not prescribe that children should be anchored to their seats and never speak unless spoken to by the teacher. According to the teaching of the Church, human nature, though fallen, is in no manner essentially vitiated. As a matter of fact, we are born with the capacity for that holy newness which comes to us in baptism. The Creator trusts children enough to endow them with a free will; teachers ought to be able to trust them enough to exercise that freedom. If youngsters are never allowed to direct themselves, how are they to acquire habits of self-direction? He commits a crime against children who leaves them to their own devices and allows them to do what they want to do; but he also sins who never affords them an opportunity to do freely the things they ought to do.

The Progressives follow up their insistence on activity and freedom with the demand for a curriculum that will answer the needs of the learner. They inveigh against the imposition of subject-matter that is remote from the interests of childhood and want only those things taught which the child can use here and now. They maintain that on no other basis can learning be truly purposeful. Some of them would even make their curriculum from day to day, depending on what happens to be uppermost in the children's minds.

Here we come upon our truth again, squirming and fighting and getting even with a routine school practice that makes a fetich out of organized subject-matter, regards it as an end in itself, never modifies it, refuses to try to see it in relation to the learner's needs and abilities, gives lessons only to hear them and then give more lessons, that stores up information in the memory as against some future day when it may be utilized, and forgets all the while that children are living here and now.

But children are living here and now, and the tree of their later lives will be inclined in the direction that the twig of their immaturity is bent. What we want them to know, what we want them to do, what we want them to be, as adults, we best guarantee by directing them as to knowledge, and action and character in their daily lives as children. The habits that are involved in keeping physically fit, economically productive, socially cooperative, culturally fine, and morally virtuous can all be practiced on every level of development, and, unless they are so practiced, they will be found wanting when manhood or womanhood is finally attained. It is by understanding the truth as it applies to him and living the truth from day to day that the child advances from stage to stage in his education, and, unless he has so advanced, the mere remembering of some things that he learned about life while he was at school will be of small avail to him when he faces the realities of existence.

The Progressives go too far, too ridiculously far, when in the name of activity they overstimulate children on the physical side and exalt activity for activity's sake. The Progressives go too far, too tragically far, when in the name of freedom they emancipate children from all restraint and make them suspicious of all adult standards. The Progressives go too far, too foolishly far, when they throw overboard all organized subject-matter, underestimate the value of drill, and treat with disdain the accumulated wisdom of the ages. However, it is in no measure condoning their excesses to admit that organized education, in its smugness, its zeal for routine and standardization, in its failure to take account of social change or to profit by the findings of educational science, has all too frequently lost sight of the child and his needs and made of itself an end rather than a means.

The fetich of the conventional school has been subject-matter, all neatly organized and wrapped up, ready to be stored up in the mind and labeled, "Not to be opened until you grow up." In presenting this subject-matter to the learner it overstressed teacher activity and demanded of the child passive receptivity and acquiescence. The degree of the teacher's addiction to Calvinism or Jansenism determined the amount of unpleasantness that pervaded the situation. Because the reason for everything was so remote from the child's day by day experience, it was necessary to either scare him or bribe him into behaving himself. Of course, he could not be allowed much freedom, because he would not know what to do with it.

The daily program never changed. The curriculum consisted of formal subject-matter, logically arranged and determined by convention. No matter what the abilities of the children, their attitudes or needs, lesson plans were made and followed mechanically, with the main view of covering the assignment. In the offing always loomed the examination which all the children, regardless of individual differences, had to take, success in which depended on giving back to the teacher, as intact as possible, the information which she and the textbook had conveyed. Little attention was paid to the "inward dweller" or to what was really happening in the way of building the temple of life and mind.

Perhaps it was never quite as bad as this, but at any rate it was bad enough to cause the Progressive revolt which proclaimed adult standards a snare and a delusion and which made the child, his whims and caprices the measure of all things. It grovelled before the young and, with an abject *mea culpa*, begged their forgiveness for having made a mess of the world and society and begged them to lead us out of the house of grown-up bondage into the joyous freedom of babyhood. It feared to impose restraints lest it destroy the mental hygiene and create complexes that might result in future compensations at the expense of society. Each day was to be a glad adventure in pursuit of will-o'-the wisp of childish whimsy. And the philosophers of the movement discovered new, brave words to describe it all, vague words, indefinable words, words as a matter of fact that gloried in being indefinable, for definitions inhibit, make things static, are mediaeval.

Our obligation as Catholics, as I see it, is to rescue "the forgotten truth" from the hands of the Progressives and reestablish it in the central place where it logically belongs. The term "Progressive Education" should not be used by us, not because it is not an honorable word in itself, but because it has been keeping questionable company and has come to mean many things to which we cannot subscribe. Nothing in history is or has ever been as progressive as Christianity. It is a leaven working in society and gradually transforming the face of the earth. Our term then should be "Christian education," because that means an education which is based on a true and valid concept of human nature and human destiny. Christian education is not synonymous with conventional education, for Christianity always opposes the killing influence of the letter with the life-giving power of the spirit. There are many things in so-called Progressive Education which are based on reason and common sense, and of course these will naturally be utilized by the Christian teacher. We should never raise our eyebrows at methods and devices simply because they are new, for the true scribe "brings out of his treasure new things and old." Pope Pius XI advised his priests to be "healthily modern" and reminded them that the Church is never afraid of progress, especially not scientific progress, as long as it is truly scientific.

We always have to avoid the temptation of taking it for granted that, because we have the Truth, we know how to make the Truth work. Pedagogically we shall always have a lot to learn and educational science will always have a lot to teach us.

There is no profit in dreaming of the "golden, olden days." They are gone forever, and there is reason for some suspicion that they might not have been so golden after all. The tempo of social change has been much accelerated in the last quarter of a century. We are living in a different world, a technical world, a motorized world, a radio world, a cinema world, a world in which the wildest dreams of yesterday are commonplaces. Cities are different, neighborhoods are different, homes are different and, as a consequence, children are different. We cannot, even if we would wish to do so, fit them into the straitjacket of things that used to be.

The Gospel is a dynamic document. Christ is a divine energy that seeks outlet through our lives and actions. It is not enough for our children to come to know some few facts about the Saviour and His teachings; they must learn how to live and move and have their being in Him. It is only thus that their faith can withstand the onslaughts of modern paganism and their morals be immunized against the contagion of the things of the world.

In our schools our aim should be to guide them in the direction of Christian living and, though we are thinking of their future as adults, we should miss no opportunity to make it possible for them to express the principles they are learning in their daily life here and now. We want them to develop the knowledge, the habits, the skills, the abilities, the attitudes and the interests that are implied in the concept of Christian character.

The Catholic classroom should be a happy place in which teacher and pupils work together at a common task. The teacher, of course, represents authority and must insist that that authority be respected. It will be respected if it is respectable; that is to say, if the children are taken into confidence and come to understand the ultimate motives for obedience. Freedom there will be, but not license. As much as is humanly possible, the source of restraint will be an inward one. The love that is of the very essence of things Christian will cast out fear.

Of course, there will be definite time allotments for the skill subjects and plenty of opportunity for drill. Yet the daily program will be flexible, planned in advance by the teacher, and so administered as to make capital of the emerging interests and needs of the children.

There will be a definite and balanced curriculum, recognizing the values that are inherent in organized subject-matter, but adaptable to circumstances and times. Correlation there will be throughout in content subjects and such integration as is rational. Any form of integration which is forced and artificial will not be attempted, even with religion as its basis.

The emphasis in method will be upon pupil activity, physical and manual activity when such activity promises results in terms of real learning, intellectual activity in all circumstances. Children learn through their eyes and their ears, but they also learn through their hands. Every means of expression, manual, vocal, dramatic, constructive, musical, should be utilized to make the truth a living, dynamic thing in the heart of the child.

Of course, there will be tests and examinations to keep a constant check on progress and to reveal to pupil and teacher alike not only defects in learning but the reasons for such defects. All of the while, however, the teacher will realize that there are certain educational outcomes which are of tremendous importance but for which no test has ever been devised. Our mission is "to cooperate with divine grace in forming Christ" in these children. It will profit the child little, and be of no avail as far as the Catholic school is concerned, if he masters his reading, his spelling, his arithmetic, his geography, but exhibits attitudes and appreciation and points of view that contradict the spirit of Jesus Christ.

I conclude with the plea for more of the creative, more of the dynamic, more of the artistic, more of forthright vital Christianity in Catholic schools. This we can have without sacrificing one iota of thoroughness, order and discipline. We know fairly well what is wrong with other people's kind of education. Do we know practically enough and courageously enough what is right with our own?

General education
in high school and college

William F. Cunningham, C.S.C.

*The late Father Cunningham, for several years a
Professor of Education at the University of Notre
Dame, gained with sincerity, tolerance, patience,
and a perceptive mind the respect and admiration
of education philosophers throughout the United
States. He is remembered as the "dean" of Catholic
educational theorists. In this article he builds a
foundation for a curriculum of general (liberal)
education in high school and college. This
foundation is the human abilities of thought and
expression: a Christian and humanistic
interpretation of man's nature leading to
educational programs committed to the goals of
social transmission and individual development.*

My understanding is that I am to introduce this topic of general education in high
school and college. It will not take long to do this. The best way, I believe, is to
place in your hands the diagram you now have before you and comment briefly
upon it. In column three in this diagram you have what I like to call the "Great
Fields of Knowledge." This diagram is not in any sense a curriculum but it is, I
believe, the basis from which is drawn any curriculum dealing with general education on any level whether in the elementary school, high school or college. It is
a logical classification of the different knowledges which man has acccumulated

**Reprinted with permission from the *National Catholic Education Association
Proceedings*, 46:193–198, August, 1949.**

through the centuries, what we commonly call the "social inheritance." My suggestion is that any branch of human knowledge falls logically into one of the six fields into which the diagram is divided.

The philosophical basis for general education

The two human abilities	Man's worlds and man's works	The great fields of knowledge	Butler's spiritual inheritance	Academic divisions
Thought about (the sciences)	The physical world	Natural sciences	Scientific	Math. and nat. science
	The human world	Humanistic sciences	Institutional	History and soc. science
	The spiritual world	Philosophical sciences	Religious	Theology and philosophy
Expression of (the arts)	The True	Liberal arts	Literary	Language and literature
	The Beautiful	Fine arts		
	The Good	Applied arts	Aesthetic	Music and visual arts
	(for something, i.e., the useful)			Vocational and professional training

We begin by contrasting the first column "The Two Human Abilities" with those that follow. This brings out that education is a dual process: first, *social transmission,* that is, passing on to each rising generation the accumulated knowledge of the race; and second, *individual development,* the development of the powers of each individual pupil as he carries on this process of assimilating the inheritance of the race. These two processes are not conflicting; rather, they are complementary. One cannot go on without the other. If both go on in any adequate degrees, we can say that the pupil is in process of receiving a general education in the proper meaning of the phrase. We begin by analysing the human abilities. We see that man as a rational animal has two abilities distinctly human which mark him off from the lower orders of the animal kingdom, the power of thought and the power of expression. Man, in the exercise of these two powers, through the ages has accumulated what we call the social inheritance. It is well for the school to say that its primary task is to train the pupil in thinking, and in the expression of thought. But the only way to train the pupil in thinking is to bring him in contact with the best that has been thought by man, and is left to us in the written record, the literature of the ages. In fact, this is Matthew Arnold's definition of culture: "pursuit of our total perfection by means of getting to know, on all matters which most concern us, the best which has been said in the world." [1]

---

[1] Matthew Arnold, *Culture and Anarchy,* preface.

I. The Power of Thought

What are the fields into which the thought of man logically divides itself? Or, in other words, what are the fields of knowledge with which we wish through the curriculum to bring the pupil in continued contact? We submit that there are three worlds in which man lives, and one phase of the process of education consists in becoming acquainted with these three worlds. There is first of all the material world, that is, the physical universe. Antithetical to this we have the world of spirit, which, in the Christian concept, means the world of God, the Eternal Spirit. Intermediate between these we have that combination of matter and spirit, which is man, the human world. These three worlds, then, the material world, the spiritual world, and the human world, are the worlds with which the educated man must become acquainted. We repeat again that in the act of becoming acquainted with these three worlds he will be developing his power of thought as well as his power of expression. Now the bodies of knowledge which represent man's thought about these three worlds are the sciences. We have first of all the natural sciences dealing with the world of nature, which may be divided into the physical sciences, physics, chemistry, etc., and the biological sciences dealing with living matter. On the other extreme we have what we may call the philosophical sciences, philosophy and theology. Philosophy deals with God, and with man and the physical universe, relating them to God for their origin, but it is studied through the unaided light of human reason. Theology, on the other hand, as commonly understood, deals with God as made known to us through revelation and man's relations to God, again studied through the light of revelation. In the third place, we have that group of sciences dealing specifically with the world of man, commonly called the "social sciences." A much better label for this group is the "humanistic sciences," since it includes general psychology, dealing with man as an individual, as well as social psychology, sociology, economics, politics, and history, the latter tracing man's thought and action in all these fields through the ages. Here then are three bodies of knowledge which must be handed over to the pupil by the teacher through the curriculum. They are constantly growing, and from this point of view, we must expect that the curriculum will constantly be undergoing change. Less than a century ago, one of the subjects in the curriculum of general education was natural philosophy. Looking into the content of one of those old texts carrying that title, we see that it was made up of the knowledge man then had of what we now call physics and chemistry. But today we no longer teach "natural philosophy," so-called. We teach the science, physics and chemistry, since the knowledge which has grown up in these fields is so great that they have justified their right to separate themselves off from the house of philosophy and set up housekeeping for themselves.

Similarly, we are now confronted with the same situation in the humanistic sciences. The problems of private property, of marriage, and of government were once taught only as part of social ethics. But now, with the great increase in knowledge in these three fields, we have the three separate sciences, economics, sociology, and politics. In the realm of the philosophical sciences, that is, theology and philosophy, a change, too, is continually going on, since, although the principles formulating these sciences are permanent, the application of these principles to the business of living is subject to constant change. Usury was one problem during the Middle Ages, but today interest as a problem under justice and right finds itself in an entirely different setting in the greatly complex economic, social, and political situation in which we are living.

II. The Power of Expression

The second human ability which makes man man is the power of expression. Expression occurs most commonly through language, oral and written, but it is not confined to this. Expression includes all those ways which man has invented to register his thought in some concrete embodiment for his own satisfaction or for the satisfaction of others, which means the communication of his thought to others. All the arts are means of expression, but it is the linguistic arts which are pre-eminent in serving this function, expression through words as symbols, that is, words serving as labels for ideas. Here we repeat that language is not merely a means of communication; it is also a tool for thinking. This is no place to discuss whether thought is possible without words. Our affective life, the feelings and emotions, is often at a loss for words to express itself adequately. But this does not deny the fact that we search for words and other means by which to give expression in some form to our deepest feelings. The poet is one who has special facility in this art, and that very power of expressing emotional life in words with rhythmic cadence is what makes him a poet. With words as labels for ideas we can hold ideas in the mind and compare them one with another, seeking out relationships. Such perception of relationship is thinking in the higher reaches of the intellectual life. This twofold function of language, that is, as a means of communication and as a tool for thought is so important in the development of the pupil that we can say without fear of disagreement by anyone who has given careful consideration to the problem, that language must always be part of the core of the curriculum on all levels of general education. It may be taught formally in language classes or informally through use in the study of other subjects, but taught it must be, if the pupil is to come into his intellectual heritage in all its richness without loss of time and effectiveness.

Language, however, is not the only medium for the expression of thought. Words are not the only symbols in which man registers his mental life and communicates it to others. On the contrary, all the arts are means of expression. The fine arts in particular have their place in the life of man for the development of his intellectual and emotional life while the applied arts, on the other hand, aim specifically toward making this world of ours a more comfortable place to live in. Since we are now speaking of general education in contrast with vocational education, we leave this question and turn our attention to the place of the fine arts as a medium for the expression of man's mental life in symbolic representation or through imitation.

To understand the place of the fine arts in general education for all students on all levels of the educational ladder, it is necessary to determine the function of art in the life of man as contrasted for example with the sciences; and, with this determined, to distinguish the different ways in which that function may be performed for various groups of individuals. Again we lay down the principle that what makes man man is his mental life. He is a rational animal. In the operation of his reason the intellect has for its object truth, and the sciences in all fields of knowledge are the repository of the accumulations of the intellect of man throughout history. The means for their preservation and improvement are the intellectual virtues. The object of the emotions is the beautiful and the means for its realization in the life of man, if we may coin a phrase, are the "emotional virtues." We mean by this certain attitudes of appreciation or taste, the power of discerning order, symmetry, proportion, and beauty and finding pleasure in these perceptions.

In the arts this quality of appreciation functions on three different levels. We will illustrate from music. There is at the top the creative artist. He has the ability, the genius, we are inclined to say, not merely to enjoy, i.e., to appreciate, the works of the masters which have been preserved for us, but to add to this store of treasures through his own creations. On the second level we have what may be called the reproductive artist. He may not have the ability to create anything of lasting worth, but he does have the ability of performance, and through skillful performance not only gives expression to the artistic urge within himself, thereby enriching his own emotional life, but in addition he enriches the lives of those who are privileged to enjoy his skillful performance. This last situation brings us to the third level of appreciation without the ability either of creation or performance. On this third level all are called to be artists in the sense that taste should be cultivated so that a love for music will manifest itself in domestic life, civic life, religious life, and leisure life in general. The phonograph and the radio are great aids to the school in this task of elevating the taste of pupils and through them reaching back into the homes to improve the taste of the generation that was denied this experience during their school days.

But there are other ways besides words and musical sounds through which man expresses his mental life. The pictorial and plastic arts have design and color, shape and form, giving us the arts of drawing, painting, sculpture, and architecture and the lesser arts like ceramics, etc. Another type is through motion in the dance. Perhaps no art has been so neglected by the school as this one. Yet if we could develop in the minds of youth an understanding of the principles directive of the expression of beauty through motion, perhaps no influence would be so helpful in elevating the tone of social dancing which plays so conspicuous a role in the activities of students outside the classroom.

Any distinction between the literary and the fine arts is evidently quite arbitrary. This is well illustrated by poetry. We may say it is "the finest of the fine arts" meaning by that, that it offers the best medium for the expression of the emotional life of man at its deepest. It is a combination of sound and word symbol. To a certain extent all literature partakes of this characteristic as illustrated through the cadence of beautiful prose. Literature is the written record of the race, the story of the part that truth, beauty, and goodness have played and are playing in the life of man, and of their opposites—the false, the ugly, and the evil. This is one of the fine arts which has won a respectable position in the curriculum.

Before passing on to the sixth field of knowledge I give to you the famous quotation from Nicholas Murray Butler in which he speaks of the "spiritual inheritance."

> If education cannot be identified with mere instruction, what is it? What does the term mean? I answer, it must mean a gradual adjustment of the spiritual possessions of the race, with a view to realizing one's own potentialities and to assisting in carrying forward that complex of ideas, acts, and institutions which we call civilization. Those spiritual possessions may be variously classified, but they certainly are at least fivefold. The child is entitled to his scientific inheritance, to his literary inheritance, to his aesthetic inheritance, to his institutional inheritance, and to his religious inheritance. Without them all he cannot become a truly educated or a truly cultivated man.[2]

It is interesting to note that this division of the spiritual inheritance is only fivefold. There is no mention of what in the diagram we are calling the "applied arts," i.e., the arts employed for the making of something useful. In the Catholic school, since what I am calling the "philosophical sciences," i.e., theology or religion and philosophy, are the very core of the curriculum, this question of whether the applied arts have any place in the curriculum of general education is perhaps the only place in which controversy arises. But this controversy is perhaps more acute in secular schools. We have the followers of Dewey on the one hand demanding that pupils have contact with the applied arts so that they may deepen their understanding of the civilization in which they are living and in which these arts play such an important part—on the other hand, the followers of President Hutchins of Chicago University, who even goes so far as to say that training in them should not take away any of the time needed for general education. Even in vocational education specific skills have little part to play since they change so rapidly. In his opinion, they must be learned on the job. If learned in school they may be a positive hindrance to advancement in a vocation and will have to be unlearned when the worker is put before the new machines continually being brought forward as improvements over the old ones as production becomes more mechanized. The middle ground here seems to be the most reasonable, namely, that there are certain general skills that should be learned in school since they can be carried over to advantage in almost any employment as well as applied in life itself in

[2] Nicholas Murray Butler, *The Meaning of Education*, (rev. 1915) pp. 25–6.

ordinary household activities. For the Catholic school, however, since the equipment of shops is so expensive the financial burden involved has been the great deterrent in keeping us from siding with those who say that the applied arts are entitled to a place in general education. Without doubt more has been done here for the girls than for the boys with the introduction of the household arts. It is easy to justify the position, in the light of what has happened to the modern home, that household arts should be a part of the general education of girls, the home builders of tomorrow.

This brief review of the two intellectual abilities that make man man and of the great fields of knowledge will furnish an adequate basis I believe for the discussion of this problem of general education on both the high school and the college level. Knowledge has grown so great that today the most pressing problem is that of integration. How can we present to the pupil today this social inheritance so that his experience with it will be an integrated whole? No one has yet found the solution to this question and its presence here on our program is evidence that we all realize this. I am convinced that it will remain one of our most pressing problems for years to come. But this combined meeting of the Secondary School and the College and University Departments gives us some hope that both will work towards a solution of this problem cooperatively, and that at least is an encouraging sign that we are making some advance.

The problems of communication between Catholic and non-Catholic educators and philosophers

Rev. Gerald B. Phelan

This problem, according to Father Phelan, is not speculative but practical; the issue is primarily one not of agreement but of understanding. It is important for Catholics to understand and appreciate the positions taken in philosophy and education by non-Catholics; and it is imperative that Catholics make their positions clear to those who do not share their views. He argues for a spirit of goodwill basic to such communication, and he insists upon fair-minded, honest, frank, and, above all, competent, expert, and well-informed discussion. The starting point for Catholics in such dialogues, he writes, is the encyclical letter of Pius XI, Christian Education of Youth.

The problem of communication between Catholic and non-Catholic educators and philosophers presents a practical, not a speculative, issue. It concerns the task of achieving a mutual understanding, if not a common agreement, between persons who differ widely in their views and convictions.

Catholic philosophers and Catholic educators differ notably among themselves on many important points. We are not proposing to direct our present inquiry to such divergencies of opinion. No Catholic educator or philosopher,

Reprinted with permission from *The National Catholic Education Association Bulletin,* 54:135–141, August, 1957.

however, whatever his attitude towards particular issues, either speculative or practical, would question the truth and validity of teaching of the Church on matters educational and philosophical or her authority to pronounce upon them. Papal encyclicals, such as those on *Christian Philosophy* of Pope Leo XIII and on the *Christian Education of Youth* of Pope Pius XI, are authoritative documents for all Catholics. It is this common allegiance to definite principles that justifies the grouping together of educators and philosophers, among whom many differences of opinion may prevail, under the general rubric of Catholic educators and Catholic philosophers.

Non-Catholic educators and philosophers likewise differ among themselves and even more widely and deeply than their Catholic colleagues. On the other hand, they are *not* united by the common acceptance of any positive principles which all regard as universally valid for any and every educational or philosophical theory or system. Their basic views and convictions regarding education and philosophy may vary from very close approximation to what Catholic educators and philosophers hold, to utter incompatibility and unqualified repudiation of what Catholics stand for. The sole justification for regarding them as a single group is that none of them fully agree with the Catholic attitude towards education and philosophy.

In the light of these facts, the general problem of communication between these two groups raises two distinct questions: first, what can we do to understand and appreciate, though we cannot agree with, the views and attitudes on education and philosophy which non-Catholics entertain; second, what can we do to facilitate an understanding and appreciation by our non-Catholic colleagues of the Catholic position of these questions, the principles upon which it rests and the strength, depth and sincerity of the convictions it represents?

Innumerable problems arise when it is a question of dealing with particular aspects of that general problem, such as those which depend upon the extent to which some common ground of agreement exists and a friendly attitude prevails, or upon the almost complete absence of understanding and sympathy. Here, as in every situation where human relations and personal intercourse play an important role, prudence and charity must be coupled with wisdom and knowledge if mutual understanding, appreciation and respect are to result. Sympathetic agreement may, else, dull critical perception and lead to undesirable compromise, while strenuous opposition, especially when coupled with either bitterness or ridicule, may arouse undue indignation, anger or resentment. The wrath of the polemicist is unbecoming among educators and philosophers—"*In tantae coelestibus mentibus irae!*"—and should not be allowed to disturb the polite, though firm, expression of opinion in courteous controversy and discussion. Yet, it should be ever borne in mind that a frank and honest disagreement is of far more value than an ignoble and hypocritical compromise.

While it is true that courtesy, consideration and the decent amenities of normal human relations should prevail in all our conversations and discussions with non-Catholic educators and philosophers, there is a difference to be observed in our mental attitude where matters of speculative philosophy are concerned and where the subject under discussion impinges upon the practical order—I do not mean simply ways and means of arriving at an acceptable *modus vivendi,* "getting along" with people who do not share our outlook and convictions. I mean rather, and indeed, principally, discussions in which principles of practical knowledge, principles of the practical intellect, govern the solution of the problems at issue.

The speculative philosopher is confronted with an order of things already established in the universe, an order which his reason has not set up, and about which his thinking can do nothing but learn what it is like, how it works, what makes it go, who started it going and what is its purpose. In other words, the speculative philosopher is curious to understand the essence, nature, power and operations of existing things in order, ultimately, to grasp the very being in which all things share. His intellect is faced by an order which he has not made and which he can only observe and contemplate. His will plays no part in determining that order of things. When he examines it, reflects upon it and sizes it up, he can come up with a series of propositions about it, all of them couched in terms like, "That is what things are like," "That is the way they work," "That is what really is." When what he says and what actually is correspond to one another, he has got at the truth.

The practical philosopher is in a very different situation. The order of things with which he is concerned is not all set up for him. He has to make that order himself. By reflection and mature consideration, he has to decide, not, *"That is the way things are,"* but, *"This is the way things ought to be."* This is the moral order. It does not stand there ready made, as the order of nature does, but it is for us to make it. Here it is not the "nature" of things that provides the principle of judgment, but their "end." The truth of the judgment which the practical philosopher makes is not verifiable by reference to existing reality, but by reference to the rectitude of his will; the straight line, so to speak, which joins the will to the ultimate end of man is the rule—the "straight-edge," as the Englishman would say—which determines whether the practical judgment conforms to, or deviates from, truth. That ultimate end of man, the Beatific Vision, cannot be known except by revelation and faith. Consequently, an adequate practical philosophy of morality is intrinsically involved in revelation and theology, both in its principles and in its conclusions.

Such is not the case, as we have noted, for speculative philosophy. Consequently, one's mental attitude in discussing speculative and practical problems of philosophy, respectively, will differ considerably. In this connection, incidentally, it is important to recall the words of Pope Pius XI in his encyclical on the *Christian Education of Youth:* "It is therefore as important to make no mistake in education, as it is to make no mistake in the pursuit of the last end, with which the whole work of education is intimately and necessarily connected." Since education essentially consists, as the same Holy Father so aptly put it, in forming man to be and to do what he must be and do in this life in order to attain the end for which he was created, the philosophy of education to which every Catholic educator is committed implies the acceptance of revealed truth regarding the end of man and the theological teaching of the Church in respect to its attainment.

In trying to establish communication between Catholic and non-Catholic educators and philosophers, it appears to me that our consideration should be directed to four different aspects of the case, and due distinctions made in respect to each.

First, there is the question of communication between Catholic *philosophers* and non-Catholic philosophers on problems of speculative philosophy—philosophy of nature, mathematical philosophy, metaphysics, theory of knowledge, logic and so forth—from the point of view of understanding what non-Catholic philosophers regard as properly philosophical methods, arguments and procedures in these matters.

Second, there is the question of communication among *philosophers* on these same speculative matters, from the point of view of making known to our non-Catholic colleagues how Catholic philosophers regard the whole philosophical enterprise and why they think that certain methods and procedures are authentically philosophical while others are not.

Third, there is the question of communication between *educators* from the point of view of understanding what non-Catholic educators regard as the basic aims and purposes of education, the theories of education upon which their contentions are based and the best means to attain them.

Fourth, there is the question of communication between *educators* from the point of view of achieving an understanding, on the part of our non-Catholic colleagues, of the stand which Catholic educators take in respect to these problems.

The spirit of all such efforts should be neither polemical nor defensive, neither apologetical nor missionary, neither disputations nor antagonistic, but fair-minded, honest, frank and, above all, competent, expert and well-informed. Their purpose is to serve freedom: the freedom of every human person to withhold his assent to any proposition until he sees (by reason or by faith) that it is true and the freedom of the Church, and of those who are her agents in the education of youth, to perform their appointed task without let or hindrance.

The first two aspects of the problem are of less interest to this gathering than the latter two. It is important, however, to realize that the majority of non-Catholic philosophers regard the whole philosophical enterprise in an entirely different light from the way in which Catholic philosophers envisage the task of the philosopher. To put it briefly, for the Catholic philosopher, philosophy is *knowledge of reality,* specifically, natural wisdom, that is, knowledge of the highest causes of *what is.* For the non-Catholic philosopher, generally, philosophy is *not knowledge of reality,* but a more or less adequate system of concepts constructed in view of explaining experience. The failure of many attempts adequately to construct such a system along idealistic lines was the occasion for the rise of various types of philosophical inquiry in which reason was held in suspicion (voluntarisms, intui-

tionisms, existentialisms, relativisms) and of positivistic types of empiricism, culminating in systems of pure logic (symbolic logic, logical positivism, semantics,
analytical procedures of the type so popular in England today).

The course of modern philosophical thinking was roughly charted from the
time of René Descartes. Once it became established in the minds of men that to
accept the evidence of the senses was to be philosophically naive and that the
only course open to a philosopher worthy of the name was to proceed from the
evidence of thought, the outcome was inevitable. Gilson's lectures on *The Unity
of Philosophical Experience* have clearly established the inner necessity of the
ideas which brought about the proliferation of modern systems from the moment
it became generally accepted that the existence of the external world needed to
be demonstrated.

To understand what our contemporary non-Catholic philosophers regard as
truly philosophical questions, one has to make a valiant effort to place oneself in
a world of thought entirely foreign to our habitual outlook. It requires an almost
heroic effort to strip one's mind, provisionally, of cognitions which, to us, are
obvious deliverances of ordinary common sense, and to maintain constant vigilance lest they intrude at any point to prejudice our understanding of the particular system of thought which the person (or persons) with whom we are trying
to communicate advocates. It is a difficult but rewarding task. The mere fact that
one has succeeded in understanding the problem and following the process of
reasoning, even in the absence of any personal acceptance either of the problem
or of its solution, establishes a basis upon which communication is possible.

I am personally convinced that in order to achieve any appreciable measure
of success in such an undertaking, a determined, persistent and unflagging study
of the history of philosophy, pursued in the most impartial fashion of which one
is capable, is an indispensable requisite. There was never a great philosopher but
had his vision of truth, never a great mind but strove to communicate his vision
to others. To share that striving with each, in turn, of the thinkers who have
shaped the history of philosophical reflection, to rejoice in and applaud their
successes, to regret and deplore their failures and to live in sympathy with their
yearnings for light—all that prepares the mind and heart to bend one's best efforts
to understand, appreciate and respect our colleagues and contemporaries in their
present-day philosophical undertakings.

Knowledge of the history of philosophy will likewise facilitate the task of
communicating, to those who do not accept the outlook of the Catholic philosopher, a better understanding of what we regard as the object of philosophy and
a clearer appreciation of what we conceive to be properly philosophical problems.
Philosophy is not an orderly arrangement of abstract principles, propositions, demonstrations and conclusions. It is a very concrete quality of the human mind.
It lives only in the minds of men. History is its very life. Its problems have all
arisen in historical circumstances. Its vocabulary and the formulae in which its
findings are technically expressed all stem from history—and they are lifeless,
arid and, not seldom, meaningless, when divorced from the historical situations to

which they owe their origin. If we wish to communicate to our non-Catholic colleagues some appreciation of the relevance and value of the philosophical questions we regard as of crucial importance, we must divest them of their abstract, intemporal, almost ethereal, character and disclose them being hammered out, and their solutions forged, in the workshop of history. Definitions conned by rote, "proofs" learned by heart, pat formulae borrowed from textbooks mean nothing to men who have spent their lives in seeking in the history of thought for living ideas to vitalize their own philosophy.

Much of the teaching and learning of Catholic philosophy is oriented towards providing an arsenal of arguments for the defense of traditional "scholastic" positions. This is, of course, regrettable in itself, since the study of philosophy should, by its very nature, be cultivated above all for the enrichment of the mind by the wisdom of the past and the equipment of the human person to face up to the life and problems of his own day with the confidence and assurance that comes of mature knowledge and reflection. But it is also most regrettable from the point of view of our present concern, namely, communication. One who feels that he is always obliged to defend a position or to marshall arguments to prove a point— albeit a true position or a valid point—will find it all the more difficult to state or explain his philosophical outlook to one whose intellectual formation is radically different from his own. Simply to set forth as clearly as one can just what one holds and the reasons for holding it, and then to leave it at that, is generally more efficacious in establishing a basis for communication than the most brilliant efforts to refute or to convince.

Non-Catholic philosophers may differ widely and radically from Catholic philosophers on practically every issue but, generally speaking, there is one thing they almost instinctively respect, and that is complete scholarship. A Catholic philosopher who is at home in the literature of his subject, who can discuss intelligently movements and currents of philosophical thought, who is as conversant, let us say, with the writings of Hume or Kant or Bergson, or James or Santayana or Dewey, as are his non-Catholic colleagues, who can present his own views in a like critical and scholarly spirit, such person invariably gains the respect of his non-Catholic associates and gets a sympathetic hearing in any gathering of philosophers.

It is never necessary to surrender any position or to water down one's views in order to establish communication with others who do not share these views; but it *is* necessary, however, to preserve an unflagging objectivity, an unimpeachable intellectual honesty, a profound mental humility and a constant imperturbability in the face of misunderstanding and incomprehension. All this demands enormous goodwill; but it also demands self-discipline and arduous intellectual labour, until one feels at home in the company of men whose intellectual outlook is utterly foreign to one's own and is welcome among them.

One final remark with respect to communication between Catholic and non-Catholic philosophers. In philosophy, especially in the order of speculative knowledge, the Catholic philosopher, like any other philosopher, bows only to the evidence of the subject as unaided reason is capable of grasping it. Consequently, the knowledge which he may have by faith in divine revelation does not bear upon the validity of his philosophical convictions. Like any of his non-Catholic colleagues, he is "on his own" where philosophical questions are at issue. It would be an unfortunate mistake to leave the impression that the teachings of the Church are involved where purely philosophical problems are under discussion. It would be still more unfortunate if any particular solution of a philosophical problem— were it even St. Thomas'—should be propounded as Catholic doctrine. There are not a few Catholic philosophers with whose views I, personally, have little sympathy and which *I* could not readily reconcile with revealed truth. That does not alter the fact that we are one in a common faith and all of us believe unquestioningly whatever Christ revealed and the Holy Catholic Church believes and teaches. But it does make communication with some of my Catholic colleagues in philosophy almost, if not quite, as difficult as communication with non-Catholic philosophers.

With regard to the third and fourth aspects of the question of communication which I have mentioned above there is no need, it seems to me, to distinguish the particular problems which confront Catholic educators from those which confront the Catholic philosopher. Educators, to be sure, have their own problems—questions of organization, administration, finance and so forth, on every level of instruction; questions of discipline, teaching methods, pedagogical procedures, examinations, credits and a host of others involving the techniques of the profession—but these matters involve no special problem of communication with non-Catholic educators, except in so far as they impinge upon the aims and ends of education itself and the differences which divide non-Catholic theories of education from the teaching of the Church.

Catholic educators and philosophers in our day find less difficulty in understanding what their non-Catholic colleagues regard as of primary importance in matters educational than is the case in philosophy. There are, of course, many shades and varieties of educational theory among non-Catholic educators but it is possible, I think, to distinguish two broad and general categories: those, namely, upheld by educators who profess some definite religious beliefs and are affiliated with some religious denomination, on the one hand, and those whose educational outlook is naturalistic and secularist.

In regard to the former, their views and opinions will be understandably coloured by the particular religious convictions they embrace, and their conception of the aims and purposes of education will be to make their pupils or students good Protestants, Jews, Moslems or Hindoos, as the case may be. The Catholic educator will find little difficulty in understanding such an attitude, however much he may regret that the fullness of the truth of the true religion of Christ is not their inspiration. He will find, moreover, agreement in principle on certain points. He may, on occasion, be edified by the courage, sincerity and zeal of many such educators in sticking to their principles even at the cost of not inconsiderable sacrifices and be inspired to like zeal and loyalty to his own convictions.

The naturalistic or secularist attitude, however, is so completely foreign to the mentality of a Catholic that he will find it difficult to understand how any reasonable human being could sincerely adopt it. Experience shows, nevertheless that —apart from the conscienceless racketeers, who exploit education for their own selfish purposes—there are many purely secular-minded persons in our civilization to whom the Catholic view of education is nothing but a throwback to an obsolete and superstitious culture from which the progress of modern thought has, forsooth, delivered us. Difficult as it is to enter into the minds of such men, the effort must be made. Placing ourselves in their position and asking ourselves the question, "Suppose that I had never received the gift of faith and could not understand what religious educators are really talking about, what would be my attitude towards the problems of education?" would no doubt help us to grasp the difficulties these secularists have to face and, perhaps, to find means of sowing seeds of doubt in their minds regarding the validity of their thinking. At all events, no communication can be established, even in view of any fruitful discussion, unless some such method of learning to appreciate that heresy and unbelief have so poisoned and weakened the minds of otherwise decent folk that they have nothing left but a pagan naturalism bereft even of the polytheistic beliefs of the pagan cultures of antiquity.

When it is question of our own efforts to communicate some understanding of the stand of Catholics on the problem of education to non-Catholic educators, it behooves us to take full advantage of the present widespread dissatisfaction with the godless and irreligious education that has prevailed for so long among us. It can be pointed out that each new protest against the exclusion of religious teaching from the schools, each new effort to find a way to restore some sort of religious instruction in the secular colleges and universities of the land, each new declaration of the need to provide our youth with a spiritual outlook that will give meaning to their lives, are all vindications of the unwavering attitude of the Church towards the question of religion in education at every level.

Fair-minded non-Catholic educators can, and many do, understand that for Catholics the sort of undogmatic religious teaching, presumably acceptable to all religious groups because it does not ruffle the sensibilities of any, which not a few of our fellow citizens advocate for all schools, would be quite unsatisfactory from the Catholic point of view. And it should not be too difficult to get them to appreciate that the impression given by the attempt to provide instruction by Catholic, Protestant and Jewish persons, alternately, namely that the Catholic Church is one denomination among many and it is up to the individual student to make his choice, is definitely Protestant in principle and utterly inacceptable to Catholics. Progress will indeed be made in the matter of communication when non-Catholics begin to understand and appreciate the reasons why Catholics would rather suffer that type of injustice and persecution which compels them to pay taxes for educational purposes and compels them, if they want to reap any benefit from their taxes, to accept a type of education from which religion is excluded, than to abandon their Catholic principles. Those reasons have been clearly and authoritatively stated by the late Holy Father Pope Pius XI in his encyclical letter on the *Christian Education of Youth* (December 31, 1929).

Indeed, if we wish to establish communication with our non-Catholic colleagues, there is no better method, in my opinion, than to read and discuss with them that great encyclical paragraph by paragraph. There they will find what the Church truly stands for and we would not be honest or fair to them to gloss over or sugar-coat any of the forthright statements which it contains. Nothing is gained —on the contrary, only misunderstanding can result—from failure to point out how utterly antithetical to the Catholic teaching on education is the whole spirit of that liberalist and secularist philosophy which is reflected in our public education. The non-Catholic who reads that: "Every form of pedagogic naturalism which in any way excludes or weakens supernatural Christian formation in the teaching of youth is false," and: "Every method of education founded, wholly or in part, on the denial or forgetfulness of original sin and grace, and relying on the sole powers of human nature is unsound," will, doubtless not agree, but he will be under no misapprehension as to what the Catholic Church teaches about education. When he knows where we stand and why, communication becomes possible and until he does we shall be talking at cross purposes. Incidentally, while reading that same encyclical with our non-Catholic colleagues, we ourselves may come to realize that our own understanding and appreciation of what the Church really stands for in matters educational may well benefit from more serious study of what Peter has said.

part iii

The psychology of teaching and learning

QUESTIONS TO GUIDE YOUR READING

1. Is it possible to learn without thinking? Is it possible to think without learning? Explain and defend your answer.

2. After reading Father Robertson's article, which of the scientific theories of learning do you find most compatible with Catholic and Scholastic thought? Which of the theories do you think the typical Catholic school is based upon?

3. With which of the four major forms of thinking described by Dr. Kolesnik do you think the Catholic schools are doing the best job? The worst? Give your reasons.

4. Evaluate Father Lanvin's suggestions. Do you consider them practical and down to earth or rather idealistic? Why?

5. In the light of Dr. Kelly's article explain why you do or do not agree that a course in educational psychology should be required of every prospective teacher.

6. Father McAvoy's article deals primarily with college teaching. Do you agree or disagree that talk about great teaching and great teachers has a strong flavor of the myth about it? How would your reaction to his article differ if he were discussing elementary or high school teachers?

7. According to Dr. Schneiders, what is the teacher's responsibility for students' mental health and emotional adjustment?

8. Of the various aspects of motivation discussed by Father McDowell, select the two that seem most significant to you and justify your choices.

163

Psychology in educational practice

William A. Kelly

In the following article, Dr. Kelly emphasizes the
important progress made in psychology in the
twentieth century and underscores particularly the
relevance of applied psychology to classroom
teaching and learning. One branch of applied
psychology—educational psychology—focuses on
the learner and the learning process. Especially in
the areas of retention and motivation, Dr. Kelly
states, has educational psychology made important
contributions to pedagogy. Finally, he calls
attention to the priority educational psychology
ought to have among Catholic psychologists and
educators.

In the long view of history, the first half of the twentieth century will be epochal
in the effect that the advance of science has exercised upon man's knowledge and
understanding of himself. Especially in America, psychology as the scientific
study of man has developed so extensively during the past five decades, that it
may well emerge as the decisive science of the century.[1] Describing this extensive
development in psychology from his vantage point of forty-five years of active
participation in the profession, Dr. John F. Dashiell in an address at the Knox
Conference on the Relation of Psychology to General Education (1954), stated:

[1] G. W. Allport, *The Individual and His Religion: A Psychological Interpretation*
(New York: Macmillan Co., 1954), p. v.

Reprinted with permission from *The Catholic Educational Review*, 54:596–608,
December, 1956.

American psychology is like a vigorous plant whose fronds are spreading in many directions . . . however, these spreading fronds grow from a common stalk and retain their vigor only so long as they remain attached to it.[2]

At the present time a dominant feature in this development is the emphasis placed upon the applied aspects of psychology. Not only have technological advances opened vast new opportunities for application, especially in the clinical and counseling phases, but also industry, government, and military services have recognized new areas in which psychological applications may be utilized advantageously. Actually anything which concerns man has a psychological aspect and so all human endeavors and activities can be approached psychologically. This emphasis upon application is not at all strange, for other sciences, notably chemistry and physics, and mathematics as well, have experienced a similar history.

The insights which scientific psychology has provided through research resources constitute a framework of concepts, facts, principles, and values concerning human nature which endeavor to explain man's mental life, behavior, and personality, as well as his relations to his fellowmen and to his environment. The problem now confronting psychology is not one of comprehension but rather of application of these insights. The significance of modern psychology is dependent not alone upon research carried on and results produced in experimental laboratories, for, research is not wholly complete when reported, data do not speak for themselves, facts gathered are not meaningful per se. The technical knowledge which research and investigation represent, must be interpreted, translated into utility and made widely available.

Relationship of Psychology to Education

The major field for applying psychological knowledge has always been education. In fact, the first branch of psychology definitely to have flourished in America was educational psychology, involving both understanding and methods of psychology in their applications to the learning-teaching process, with focus upon and emphasis directed toward the classroom situation. Men who played important roles in the development of psychology in America were interested in its application to education and contributed directly to the basic research which constitutes the foundation upon which much of modern educational theory and practice rests.[3] Pioneers in applying the scientific methods of psychology to education were

[2] R. S. Harper, "The Knox Conference on the Relation of Psychology to General Education," *The American Psychologist*, IX (December, 1954), 804.

[3] E. G. Boring, *History of Experimental Psychology* (rev. ed.; New York: Appleton-Century-Crofts, Inc., 1950), p. 569; E. A. Haggard, "The Proper Concern of Educational Psychologists," *The American Psychologist*, IX (September, 1954), 539–543; A. A. Roback, *History of American Psychology* (New York: Library Publishers, 1952), pp. 377–379.

Thorndike, Judd, and Terman. In addition Cattell, G. Stanley Hall, and William James also contributed much to the work which has given educational psychology its basis as an applied field. It is noteworthy that each of these men served as president of the American Psychological Association. Moreover, during the early decades of the century psychologists whose interest was fundamentally educational led in the development of the areas of learning, individual differences, the developmental processes, personality, emotions, and measurements.

Educational psychology derives its meaning, its purposes and its functions from two disciplines—psychology and education. In straddling these two disciplines, however, it seems to have developed peripheral associations with both without actually becoming an integral part of either. The result has been that the many contributions which educational psychology has made to both fields have lacked the recognition and prestige which they have merited. Several groups within the two fields recently have made efforts to clarify in a definite and explicit fashion the relationship of psychology to education. Among the psychological groups which have been seriously concerned with this task are several committees of Division 15 of the American Psychological Association, the Division of Educational Psychology. In fact at the most recent meeting of A.P.A., in September, 1956, the Committee on Relations between Psychology and Education (Division 15) held an open meeting at which a panel of seven educational psychologists discussed the situation. The most active consideration given to this problem in the field of education is the report by the Executive Committee of the National Society of College Teachers of Education, entitled *Educational Psychology in Teacher Education*.[4] There has been a noteworthy agreement expressed in the reports issued by the groups in both fields that more than a nebulous relationship exists between psychology and education. In fact, each group recognized that since all educational practices are deeply rooted in psychological foundations, educational psychology is essentially and fundamentally an area of applied psychology and the educational psychologist is primarily a psychologist whose field of application is the school.

The concern of the various committees within both fields has been primarily with the organization and co-ordination of the services which psychology can render both to implementing educational practices and likewise to the professional preparation of teachers and other educational specialists. This concern has led to the consideration of very practical aspects, that is, to the making of recommendations concerning the place of educational psychology in the training of the teacher, the professional preparation of the educational psychologist, the contents of textbooks in the field, and the treatment of various areas of the subject matter contained in these texts. Undoubtedly these aspects are significant but it seems that the various committees, in limiting their concern to these phases, have overlooked an issue which is much more basic. This issue involves the development

[4] W. W. Cook and W. C. Trow, *et al.*, *Educational Psychology in Teacher Education*, National Society of College Teachers of Education, Monograph No. 3 (1953).

of an understanding of the strategic position which educational psychology occupies as the foundation science upon which all educational practice rests. It involves an appreciation of the opportunities which educational psychology affords for expanding the knowledge of human behavior through systematic research programs pertaining to learning, problem solving, maturation, personality development and adjustment, and other key problems involved in the educational process.

The problems to which educational psychology is devoted are genuinely important, and involve some of the most significant with which man has to deal. They concern vitally the activities of the individual pupil in the school situation together with the effects and changes which are produced in mental, social, emotional and moral development. Since the educative process is concerned with the whole individual, with his abilities, attitudes, needs, interests, values, ideals, and outlook on life, educational psychology has the responsibility for providing the psychological principles governing growth, development, and maturation; individual differences, particularly the provisions for gifted and retarded; personal and social adjustment; character formation; guidance and counseling; and most fundamental of all, the motivation, direction, transfer, measurement, and evaluation of learning.

Roughly then educational psychology is concerned with two large areas: the study of the learner and of the learning process. This encompasses a great deal of content and implies contributions from many phases of psychology. It involves through a process of integration and correlation, the merging of materials derived from the social and clinical phases with the most relevant experimental research on learning. It has aptly been said that educational psychology is the meeting place of all of the studies concerned with the individual.[5] Hence, all developments in psychology require examination for educational implications. For example, modern research in social psychology and in child study has yielded valuable information regarding the learning of attitudes and values, social adjustments, conduct traits, loyalties, and ideals. The utilization of such materials will be of aid in the effective study of some of the central problems involved in the educative process.

Translating Psychological Findings into Education

There is need, therefore, for exploring, co-ordinating, systematizing and integrating the relevant psychological materials which can be translated into educational practice and, it might be added, as an aid in overcoming the artificial dichotomy between research and the technology of application. There is need also to interest psychologists who are not working in schools or with problems of education but who are engaged in general, clinical, developmental and social areas, in recogniz-

[5] Haggard, *op. cit.,* 539.

ing the educational implications of their research and theories. As Snygg has so
well stated:

> All psychologists have a personal stake in educational psychology. In the
> first place, the status and prestige of psychology as a profession depend to an
> uncomfortable degree on its effectiveness in the field of education. Almost all
> candidates for teaching certificates are required to take at least one course in
> educational psychology and a large percentage of them take no other psychol-
> ogy courses. To most members of this large and influential group, psychology
> means the educational psychology course they took in college and their atti-
> tudes toward psychology and toward psychologists will depend upon the
> effectiveness or ineffectiveness of this course. . . .
>
> In the second place educational psychology is important to psychology as
> a proving ground for theory and as a source of new concepts. The educational
> psychologist who fulfills his function by actually working on educational prob-
> lems is required to deal with problems which can be ignored or postponed in
> the laboratory. The need for the educational psychologist to deal with a wider
> range of phenomena has always tended to make him more receptive to new
> concepts and has caused theorists in educational psychology to anticipate the
> concepts of the experimental laboratories.[6]

Educational psychology involves a scientific approach to an understanding of
the learner, of the learning process, of the teaching process, and of the ways in
which the outcomes of the learning and teaching processes may be appraised and
evaluated. While it has the responsibility for selecting, organizing, and interpreting the facts, principles, materials, and techniques derived from the various
aspects of psychology which have a practical and functional bearing upon educational practice, nevertheless, it does not serve merely as a sort of "middle man"
between psychology and education, extrapolating from laboratory data and
providing teachers with "rule of thumb" procedures. The material and data from
the various areas of psychology will become useful only if and when the range and
possibility of educational meaning and application have been explored adequately
and critically. This involves the task of verifying for educational application the
validity of research findings in the various areas of psychology.

The implications of psychological theory in educational practice must be particularly explicit in the area of learning, because of its fundamental importance
in the understanding and control of human behavior. Since all complex human
behavior involves learning its pervasiveness in the life of man is recognized generally. Likewise, since it is obvious that education is possible only because human
beings can learn, it is evident that learning is the basic phenomenon and the key

[6] D. Snygg, "Special Review: Some Recent Texts in Educational Psychology,"
Psychological Bulletin, LVIII (November, 1955), 511.

aspect in the educative process. The main business of the school is learning, and extension of knowledge concerning learning will have a direct and profound effect upon educational practice. Accordingly, the scientific study of learning constitutes the central theme and is the proper concern of educational psychology. An understanding of how the pupil learns and of the conditions under which he learns best is the first and major contribution which psychology can make to educational practice. Actually how well the pupil in school will learn depends upon the extent to which the classroom teacher understands and applies what is known regarding the process of learning, for teaching is the applied psychology of learning.

Scientific Study of Learning

The scientific study of learning not only gives promise of providing solutions to many complex problems, but also has an important bearing upon the methodology employed in, the aims set for, and the objectives sought by the educative process. This scientific study of learning will involve any phase of psychology which will add to the understanding of the learning process. Moreover, all of the materials considered within the domain of educational psychology have meaning fundamentally as they relate to learning. Thus, measurement to ascertain capacity to learn and appraisal of progress attained and guidance and counseling to provide for efficient learning and to determine the sources of learning difficulties serve to provide knowledge regarding the conditions regulating the process of learning. In order to be effective in influencing educational practice, psychology must provide scientifically correct information concerning how learning takes place, what should be learned and the specific ways in which pupils learn definite types of materials. In addition, it must also provide accurate information regarding the thought processes in relation to classroom learning, the means to be employed to re-enforce learning, the satisfaction attained through interest in and attitudes toward the materials learned, the levels of maturation at which pupils learn best materials of various degrees of difficulty, the types of motivation which will function successfully in classroom situations with pupils who are bright and also those which will work with pupils who are slow in learning.

Proper appreciation of available evidence concerning learning, derived from experimental psychology should exercise a significant influence upon educational practice. In fact, experimental research particularly in the area of retention and some aspects of motivation has provided facts and information which have led to insights which are valuable in educational application. However, educational psychology must do its own research in order to ascertain the relevance of these findings for educational practice. Experimental results are useful only insofar as they relate to actual purposes and conditions in the school. Before there can be assurance that experimental findings are useful, these findings must be tested in a school situation in order to verify their application in practice, and also to complement and extend them in ways serviceable to the teacher. Moreover, in order to aid in the solution of the problems of children's learning in school situations, it is essential to test experimental findings at the level at which application is to be made. Educational psychology must be extremely cautious about making too hasty a translation of experimental findings to the classroom, since learning has a much broader denotation in the classroom than in the laboratory. The situations in school learning are much more complex, involving the interaction of many factors and so do not follow the simple model of the laboratory experiment. Likewise, conditions in the classroom cannot be controlled with the preciseness commanded in the laboratory. While it is well nigh impossible to carry experimental findings across to the school room in exact detail and with full value, nevertheless experimental findings do furnish leads worth testing in practice.

Providing information and facts without a background of theory in terms of which to interpret and point up the implications of these facts and information lessens the effectiveness of their influence upon educational practice. Theory lies close to the heart of practice and lack of clarity concerning theory leads to a corresponding lack of clarity in practice. There exists a definite need for a close integration of theory with practice and "it is to be hoped that an increasing number of psychologists will find this task attractive."[7] However, there is general acknowledgment that because a satisfactory systematic treatment of the aspects and phenomena of learning has not been achieved, considerable confusion surrounds current professional thinking concerning the nature of learning. Within the field of educational psychology it has long been recognized that it is essential to determine a theoretical structure to facilitate the organization and application of the knowledge regarding learning, a structure upon which may be built a sound and reasonable pattern of educational practice. The competing theories developed in co-operation with programs of experimental research have not been very useful to educational psychology in its endeavors to deal with the complexities of learning in the classroom. The need persists for a meaningful, comprehensive, systematic, testable theory to explain how and in what ways learning takes place, a theory which will encompass the kinds of learning in which man engages and which will really influence the work of the teacher in the school situation.

Educational psychology is the most likely source for the development of an adequate theory of learning. It occupies a strategic position to achieve the clarification of differences, the synthesis of the common factors, the reconciliation of the valuable elements of conflicting interpretations together with the formulation of clearly defined principles in terms particularly of a development and cognitive nature which can be verified by psychometric and experimental research to determine their relevance for educational practice.

Shortcomings of Current Learning Theories

A theory of learning which is meaningful and comprehensive must be based upon an adequate and correct understanding of the nature of man and of his mind. It

---

[7] E. R. Hilgard, *Theories of Learning* (2d ed.; New York: Appleton-Century-Crofts, Inc., 1956), p. 488.

is necessary to know what man is before it is possible to study effectively what man does. Most of the current theories of learning consider man as a "physical-istic machine."[8] However, the nature of man as a being in whom reason is dom-inant indicates that human learning is rational, and accordingly the aspect which must be stressed in a comprehensive theory of learning, is the cognitive factor. That education is concerned with concept formation, with problem solving, with critical and reflective thinking, with discovering and expanding meaning, with deepening understanding points the direction for the formulation of a theory of learning to guide the educative process in achieving these purposes. Educational psychology could well base the formulation of learning theory upon Arnold's definition of learning as, "setting up a new goal of knowing and doing and finding rationally approved means to achieve it. This definition implies that human learn-ing is rational, based upon recognition of means-ends relations and deliberate choice of means and ends." [9]

A serious limitation in the development of an adequate theory of learning is the fact that much of current theory has been elaborated from evidence furnished almost exclusively by studies of animal behavior. Melton has described the situa-tion in this way:

> One obvious criticism of what has happened in the last 25 years is the domination of theories of learning by the rat. . . .[10]
> I predict that there will be a social revaluation among students of learning wherein man establishes his dominance over the rat. . . .[11]

Granted that animal studies offer certain advantages in the way of simplifica-tion and control, nevertheless, experiments with animals, which lack symbolic and verbal capabilities, cannot provide adequate information regarding how children comprehend the meaning of fractions or grasp the significance of the printed word. Results of animal studies cannot be used by analogy to direct learn-ing practices with children in school, and animal experiments have made little, if any, contribution to the theory and techniques of classroom learning. Accord-ingly, in its endeavors to formulate a learning theory, educational psychology is obligated to conduct intensive and extensive experimental research in the class-room situation utilizing children as subjects and on an ideational and problem-solving level. This trend is substantiated by Melton who has stated:

> There will be a sharp upturn in the interest of psychologists in the use of human subjects as the focus of research and theory shifts to the learning of organisms capable of symbolic and verbal activities of the highest order. In

[8] Haggard, *op. cit.*, 541.
[9] M. B. Arnold and J. A. Gasson, *The Human Person* (New York: Ronald Press Co., 1954), p. 337.
[10] A. W. Melton, "Present Accomplishment and Future Trends in Problem Solving and Learning Theory," *The American Psychologist*, XI (June, 1956), 279.
[11] *Ibid.*, 280.

particular . . . children of all ages will become the preferred subjects of theory and experiment in learning and problem solving. . . .[12]

Another shortcoming in current learning theory is the fact that even when human subjects have been utilized, a large proportion of the investigations have been concerned with meaningless, rote, piecemeal, segmental materials which involve artificial verbal responses rather than with learning which is meaningful to the child and related to his activities. The findings of such studies do not constitute a proper basis for making recommendations to the school and surely could not appeal to the solution of problems or the development of initiative. Educational psychology is committed to the basic principle that learning is most effective when the learner is aware of and understands meaningful relations between and among the elements of the matter to be learned and is aware of the goal which he strives purposefully to achieve.

Hilgard in the new edition of his *Theories of Learning*, in discussing the improvement of the contributions of psychology to the practical understanding and control of learning, advocated:

> Psychologists should lean more heavily on studies of problem solving and creativity than on studies of rote learning. . . . Of far more practical importance is the ability to make relevant use of past experience in facing new problems, of maintaining motivation until a difficult task is completed and a baffling problem solved, . . . of learning how to diagnose a problem; how to fill gaps in necessary knowledge . . . how to use information in relation to presented problems. . . .[13]

Finally, since all educational efforts aim primarily at efficiency in learning, first, as it is applicable in school and then as applied to life situations, so in a comprehensive theory of learning which is to exert influence upon educational practice, the pivotal issue must be the crucial problem of transfer of learning, involving generalization and the development of intellectual habits. The essential test of learning is its transfer value. In fact, "that which does not transfer is educationally worthless if indeed not a positive encumbrance." [14] All programs of education are considered preparations either for further learning or for life situations. Education necessarily implies transfer for it is an activity which never becomes exhausted but which grows always broader and wider affecting everything one does. It is not mere possession of knowledge, but ability to reflect on one's knowledge and to translate life's values into concrete acts. Transfer can be achieved only by promoting understanding; by generalizing insights, by making

[12] F. J. Kobler, "Contemporary Learning Theory and Human Learning." *The Human Person*, ed. M. B. Arnold and J. A. Gasson (New York: Ronald Press Co., 1954), pp. 314-329.

[13] Hilgard, *op. cit.*, 488.

[14] J. B. Stroud, "Experiments in Learning in School Situation," *Psychological Bulletin*, XXXVII (December, 1940), 777-807.

relationships meaningful in order that learning may be applied to a wide range of situations.

Catholic Psychologists and Catholic Education

There seems to be a particularly compelling reason for Catholic psychologists to be interested in the implications of psychology in educational practice. The Church has developed and maintains a complete system of education which encompasses the whole aggregate of human life. This system which includes all scholastic levels from the kindergarten through the graduate and professional schools of the university is designed to accomplish the complete formation of man. It involves necessarily the learning-teaching situation and, consequently, is confronted by all of the complexities inherent in that situation as well as by the countless problems which grow out of it. Technical psychological knowledge interpreted properly, made available generally, and applied adequately offers help in understanding these inherent complexities and aid in the solution of the resulting problems. Catholic psychologists have much to contribute toward accomplishing the integration of modern scientific psychology with education. However disparate their interests in various aspects of psychology, nevertheless, they are in agreement concerning the nature of man, the ultimate meaning of life and the Universe which provides a common starting point and a frame of reference for practical collaboration with education. This would seem to be in accord with the basic purposes for which The American Catholic Psychological Association was founded, namely, to interpret to Catholics the meaning of modern psychology, to advance its acceptance in Catholic circles, and, above all, to work toward the integration of psychology with Catholic thought and practice.[15]

[15] W. C. Bier, "The Place and Function of the Department of Psychology in the Liberal Arts College," *Bulletin of the National Catholic Educational Association,* L (August, 1953), p. 193-198.

Psychologists on learning: help or hindrance?

Rev. Lloyd J. Robertson

The student's job as a student is to learn; the teacher's job is to direct the learning process. But what is learning? How does it take place? What happens when a person learns, and how can the process be facilitated? For answers to questions such as these the teacher turns to the psychologist. But the psychologist does not have any simple, definitive, universally accepted answers to give. All that he can offer are theories to explain learning. In the following article, Father Robertson compares and evaluates the major groups of learning theories against a background of Thomistic philosophy.

It would be wonderful if, in treating this topic, one could set forth the convictions of some six or seven major schools of psychology and say: "Now there you have it. All that is to be said on this matter is there before you—cut and dried. All modern thinkers hold one or the other of these theories. Which one do you prefer?" Things just aren't that simple. They could not be, for as Hilgard points out: "Discipleship in one or another of the major schools is not characteristic of most psychologists working in the field of learning." [1] Even though "some may lean toward one school and some toward another . . . on the whole the psychologists of the present time are proceeding on their way in the middle of the road." [2] Even within a school, there are apt to be discordant notes. But, schools there are.

While some writers, surveying the present-day psychological scene, like to write in terms of two major families into which learning theories fall, namely

Reprinted with permission from *The Catholic Educator*, 31:476 ff., February, 1961.

stimulus-response theories and cognitive theories, most authors prefer to discuss learning theories under the three main headings: "Connectionism," "Conditioned Response (or simply "Conditioning" or Behavioristic) Theory," and "Field (or Gestalt) Theory." In practice the authors are writing about the same theories—we have only a difference in viewpoint.

In this article we shall follow the second manner of procedure, realizing as do the various writers that, while there are other theories of learning, the three already mentioned are representative and at the same time are by far the most outstanding and widespread. However, we add a fourth theory which we consider as modern as man himself, a theory which we shall refer to as "The Traditional Theory" (though Thomistic is perhaps more proper).

MODERN THEORIES OF LEARNING

In these pages we cannot hope to give more than a thumb-nail sketch of each basic theory. Certainly, no exhaustive attempt will be made to detail major differences among schools or among psychologists within the same school.

1. *Connectionism.* According to the "Connectionist" theory learning consists in the formation of, or in the strengthening of, a *connection* or bond between a specific *situation* or *stimulus* and a specific *response.* These "connections," said Peter Sandiford, "presumably have their physical basis in the nervous system, where the connections between neuron and neuron start learning." [3] This has led some to call connectionism the synaptic theory of learning. It would seem obvious from this description of learning that the more opportunity a person has to form such associations the more he will learn. This led Sandiford to state quite blandly that "a person's intellect is the sum total of the bonds he has formed. The greater the number of bonds he has formed, the higher is his intelligence." [4] Although other Connectionists (Arthur I. Gates, for example) seem rather shocked by some of Sandiford's statements, and rightly so, his words just quoted appear to express a fair and logical conclusion from connectionist theory.

Washburne points out that this view of learning fits in with many of life's situations, and then goes on to indicate, in these words, the importance of trial and error learning in education:

> To gain efficiency in trial and error learning is to gain efficiency in reasoning, in independently attacking novel problems.
>
> Certain school subjects afford the greatest opportunity for training in trial and error learning. These are the "reasoning subjects," science, mathematics, social science, and so forth. But they are valuable in this respect only if they are taught by trial and error procedures, where problems *but not methods of solution* are presented, where objectives are clear and means of gaining them are obscure, where the learner does not follow a laboratory manual of procedures or a mathematical formula, but makes his trials and errors in his own way and evaluates his own methods. [5]

Conditioned Reflexes

2. *Conditioned Response (Behaviorist) Theory.* "Behaviorism maintains that the conditioned response with its power of substituting one stimulus for the other is the basis of all learning." [6] Conditioned reflexes must be formed, either singly or in series; if in series we have what is called "telescoping." Thus involuntary anticipatory adjustments will be acquired.

> The importance of anticipatory adjustment is great. It is the involuntary foundation of all voluntary behavior, it is the active desire which sets the goal toward which the organism strives in trial and error learning. It determines the "mind set," or organic pattern of readiness and inhibitions. Without control of anticipatory adjustment, learning itself cannot be controlled.[7]

The present writer, after considering the tenets of these theorists, finds it hard to understand how there is much place left for either control or voluntary behavior.

Washburne tells us how conditioned response learning has application:

> Those in which conditioned reflex learning predominates are the habit subjects such as reading, writing, spelling, and language.
>
> In these subjects automatic, uniform responses to cues are of chief importance. Therefore, in teaching them, trial and error methods are inappropriate. Thus, experiments have shown that reasoning about spelling, or language usage, that attempting through trial and error to apply correctly rules of spelling and grammar, results in less efficient learning than does being quickly supplied with the proper phrase or spelling at the moment when the response to the typical stimulus calling for their use is active.[7]

> With this automatization of behavior it would seem that the power of reasoning becomes a superfluous capacity.

Field Theory

3. *Field (Gestalt) Theory.* The central notion of this theory, as the name implies, is that of a field within which events occur and which gives meaning to the items or parts included within it. All perception, therefore, is through configuration, the whole being more than a mere composite of its parts. Consequently, the best learning occurs when there is "insight," when the situation is grasped as a whole. This insight arises from attempts to solve problems; it does not wait on the solution itself. Initial insight is instinctive and automatic and should have been attained before there is any effort made at piecemeal or trial and error learning.

"From the Gestalt viewpoint a pattern is destroyed when it is broken up into its constituent parts." [8] This has led some to claim that field theorists have no use for analysis in the learning process. To this charge Lewin answers:

> It has been said frequently that field theory and Gestalt theory are against analysis. Nothing could be more erroneous. . . . What is important in field theory is the way the analysis proceeds.[9]

The implications of this theory for educational practices are rather obvious.

Traditional Theory

4. *Traditional Theory.* William A. Kelly gives a quite comprehensive description of learning and knowledge in these words:

> Learning may be defined as the mental activity by means of which knowledge and skill are acquired, resulting in the modification of behavior and in the gaining of an appreciation of and a control over the values of life.
> Knowledge in which this learning process results . . . may be described as the mental consciousness of any object, fact, or principle within the mental, physical, or meta-physical order which it is possible to attain in any manner by the cognitive faculties, namely, by the external senses, by the internal senses, by the intellect.[10]

According to this view it is evident that learning in man occurs insofar as he is man, that is, has a soul and body. The learning process is confined neither to the physical capacities, powers, and potentialities of man on the one hand, nor to the mental on the other, but embraces both. A human being learns as a unit.

Though the major factor in learning is the intellect ("Truth is the adequation of the *intellect* with the thing perceived, *not of the sense organ* with the object sensed" [11]), it, alone, cannot provide man with knowledge. Other factors must enter in. The external senses use the cerebro-spinal nervous system as a medium to make known the existence and properties of particular objects. The imagination provides the sensory representations upon which the intellect can act. The memory can retain these representations, can recall them for recognition when the external objects are absent; it can retain, recall, and recognize as past experiences previous mental acts and states of consciousness. As Kelly remarks, even "the feelings and the emotions are an essential factor in the assimilation of knowledge since they constitute the motive forces of life." [12]

Such a theory of learning as this requires the teacher to guide and direct pupils toward making the best use of all that they possess for learning—their will, reason, imagination, memory, their five external senses. The good teacher will not despise as materialistic, but rather will eagerly seize as valuable aids, such principles as those of similarity, contrast, and contiguity, so important to the formation of logical associations. Likewise a trial and error method will be recognized as a basis for sensorimotor learning. In short, this theory of learning requires a teacher to explore every possible avenue, to employ every possible means, ancient and modern, that is of assistance in helping children learn.

HOW HELPFUL ARE VARIOUS THEORIES?

Which, if any, of these various theories are well-founded and comprehensive? We might begin by accepting as a fact that not one of the four schools or theories provides all the answers. Even proponents of traditional psychology must admit that, while their theory gives a comprehensive and realistic view of the learning process, it still leaves many questions open to investigation.

However, we need not subscribe to Hilgard's opinion when he states: "There are no laws of learning which can be taught with confidence." [13] That seems a little pessimistic, even when you consider strictly modern theories alone, that is, those developed over the first half of this century. Nor need we accept Heidbreder's view that "there is not enough fact in the whole science of psychology to make a single solid system." [14] This may be readily admissible if you restrict your notion of science to the modern concept of a natural science. If, however, you consider the term *science* in its full meaning, then the traditional theory, outlined above, can be accepted as a single, comprehensive, well-founded explanation of the learning process in the science of psychology.

Weakness of the Modern Systems

Because the strictly modern theories of learning (Connectionists, Conditioned Response, Field) have been nurtured in a soil deprived of the richness and reality of philosophic truth, as well as in an atmosphere of naturalism in religious convictions, we can expect to, and do, find them materialistic and incomplete. The tragedy is that the theorists do not seem to realize that the incomplete state of their systems springs in large measure from the materialistic threads with which they are woven. So, while they lament their failure to arrive at a satisfying and complete theory, these psychologists seem happy enough with their materialism. Heidbreder, admirable writer on psychology that she is, takes pride in the fact that present-day psychologists can look "upon the most intimate and intricate thoughts and feelings, however they may be named, as parts of the same natural order as tides and planets and muscular contractions." [15] This, she says, is a result of "a notable agreement among psychologists that the rational and cognitive sides of human nature have been enormously overemphasized in the past." [16] Hilgard quotes Hull as saying: "The natural science theory of behavior being developed by the present author and his associates assumes that all behavior of the individuals of a given species and that of all species of mammals, including man, occurs according to the same set of primary laws." [17] Even the Gestalt school did not shake off the bonds of materialism: "If we wish, as the Gestalt psychologists do wish, to fit the world of behavior and direct experience into the physiochemical world of natural processes, we must look for fields and patterns in the physical world." [18]

While we may, perhaps, recognize the above views as rising out of an innocent (but not innocuous) materialism, we are somewhat shocked by the blatant materialism of some in the field. Sandiford, for example, asserts:

> Connectionism has also some affinities with Watsonian behaviorism in that it stresses the mechanistic aspects of behavior. Neither one finds it necessary to evoke a soul in order to explain behavior. . . . According to connectionism those things we call intellect and intelligence are quantitative rather than qualitative affairs. [19]

Boring, as quoted by Moore, writes in somewhat the same vein:

> The existence of intelligence is another moot point, and perhaps also of emotions. It may be that both concepts, resisting rigorous definition, are now on the way to join the limbo to which will has been consigned, and whither thought, as a concept independent of learning, is bound. [20]

Origin of This Weakness. What has contributed to this present state of psychology? Fundamentally, a lack of sound philosophy coupled with a tendency to naturalism in religion. This has led one observer to write:

> Fifty years of subjectivism have destroyed the foundations, both philosophical and religious, on which our traditions were founded. Fifty years of pragmatism have done away with the common standards that we had for morality and values. We are harvesting today in our education the inevitable outcomes of this destruction. [21]

The same writer goes on to report that for ten years the Philosophy of Education Society had been striving to outline the content of elementary course in the philosophy of education and had failed. Similarly, the American Philosophical Association met with failure when in its deliberations it tried to reach agreement on the meaning of philosophy.

However, we should not conclude that this plight of modern psychologists is a disease of only recent origin. It goes back at least to Descartes. As Phelan points out:

> Once it became established in the minds of men that to accept the evidence of the senses was to be philosophically naive and that the only course open to a

philosopher worthy of the name was to proceed from the evidence of thought, the outcome was inevitable. Gilson's lectures on *The Unity of Philosophical Experience* have clearly established the inner necessity of the ideas which brought about the proliferation of modern systems from the moment it became generally accepted that the existence of the external world needed to be demonstrated.[22]

If common sense was to abdicate its throne, it might be expected that, for some philosophers, non-sense would be legitimate successor to the crown, not that these philosophers were or are to be considered insincere in their proposals of philosophic theories. Most are simply reaping a harvest, the seeds of which were planted generations ago. Pertinent are Moore's remarks concerning Titchener:

> Titchener's thought remained to the last dominated by the English philosophy he had learned in his youth. It was English philosophy and not the limitation of experimental technique which narrowed his psychological horizon to such an extent that he could see in the mind of man nothing more than sensations, images, and affections.[23]

Yet, Major Contributions Have Been Made

We cannot hope, then, to receive a complete and adequate theory of learning from the hands of strictly modern psychologists whose hands have been tied by materialism and naturalism. However, it would be foolhardy to overlook the major contributions these men and women have made to education. Much of learning is on the sensory level, a fact which some caught up with their love for the intellect, have tended to put in the background. Their insistence on the soul has lessened their recognition of the body. Then, too, there have been traditionalists who, resting on the laurels of St. Thomas Aquinas and forgetting what he taught, have treated the child as merely a miniature adult and have failed to realize in practice that the efficient cause of learning is the learner. So, then we value the many investigations into such factors in the learning process as association, insight, conditioned response, readiness, motivation, reward and punishment, drill, review, trial and error, practice, learner activity, recall and transfer of training. As many authors point out, though psychologists on the theoretical level are very insistent, almost belligerent, in proposing their own theories of learning and opposing those of others, on the practical level they are willing to accept many of each other's suggestions for the guidance of learning in actual educational situations. This has led to improvement in both teaching and learning methods. The great danger, as Melton notes, lies in "the too hasty translation of principles of learning from the laboratory to the classroom." [24]

WHAT OF THE FUTURE?

As has been already stated, none of the three modern theories presented in this paper have provided educators with a complete and adequate view of the learning process. Nor do their proponents suggest that they have. The traditional theory gives a complete picture of the process but, nevertheless, leaves many of its aspects open to investigation.

Now, the moderns recognize their current position. They see in their various theories many points of differences and agreement. Some are brave enough to label what they behold as confusion, but a confusion which to them has a goodly measure of health in it because it shows growth and vitality in the young science. Heidbreder is of this opinion.[25] While we do not agree with this version of the signs of health, we can accept with the theorists that in practice their educational consequences and implications are not set off in such sharp antithesis as the theories themselves.

Strictly Moderns Seek a Synthesis

Various authors of the modern schools express the hope that a unified system of psychology will be formulated in the future. Heidbreder looks for a unifying victory of some type for psychology—a scientific breakthrough as it were.[26] Woodworth hints that unity could already be found within the bounds of functional psychology.[27] His idea of unity, however, must be very elastic, for he seems to feel that merely by including all modern systems under the all-embracing arms of functional psychology oneness has been achieved. Washburne, speaking of the learning process in particular, advances a "genetic viewpoint of learning," which regards the development of learning in seven principal stages of overlapping activities.[28] This viewpoint he offers as a possible unifying theory of learning.

Where Can We Look for Unity

Of course, there can be no unifying victory or synthesis that will satisfy until the underlying causes of disunity are removed, that is, until the need is felt of rising out of materialistic chaos.

An adequate synthesis of the several theories of learning can only be built within the framework of the traditional theory. Psychologists cannot hope to arrive at truth in this matter while they refuse to recognize man for what he is— a being consisting of a soul and a body, the two being co-principles of operation in a single human nature. Their restricted notion of man makes it impossible for such men to reach anything but an inadequate theory of learning. Hilgard has not yet arrived, but at least is on the right track when, in discussing how some psychologists equate the learning of lower animals and men, he writes:

> It is strange that the opposite point of view is not more often made explicit—that at the human level there have emerged capacities for retaining, re-organizing and foreseeing experiences which are not approached by the lower animals, including the other primates. . . . It is quite probable that these different kinds of learning follow different laws, and it is foolhardy to allow our desire for parsimony to cause us to overlook persisting differences.[29]

Melton worries about the same problem: "The great majority of research in learning at the present time is accomplished with the white rat—where perceptive and cognitive functions are presumably limited or with human subjects under conditions designed to restrict and ignore the cognitive processes." [30] Now these utterances do not indicate that the men responsible for them are out of the woods, but certainly show that they realize they are in them and need to get out.

Traditionalists Can Help; Errors to Avoid

Here is where believers in the traditional theory can assist. Hilgard's statement, in particular, suggests that we have been remiss. This is only partly true, for there have been men such as Moore and Maritain, who have been vociferous, but who have been greeted by their contemporaries like voices crying in the wilderness. The soil has not been ready for their seed. And so there remains confusion, for as Moore says: "Empiricism without the guidance of the goals and principles of philosophy ultimately ends in chaos." [31]

In striving to reach a synthesis, Catholics and non-Catholics alike must be careful to avoid making a religious and theological issue out of an educational and philosophical discussion. For Catholics "it would be an unfortunate mistake to leave the impression that the teachings of the Church are involved where purely philosophical problems are involved." [32] For non-Catholics there must be an honest examination of their own ideas to see whether, perhaps, their reluctance to bring a soul, an intellect, supra-sensuous knowledge, and the principles of learning formulated by Saint Thomas Aquinas, into the scope of psychological investigations springs from an implicit fear of capitulating to the Catholic Church, or from a confusion between the natural and supernatural. Such fear and such confusion are not grounded in present-day reality, but in the errors of a bygone age.

Similarly to be avoided is the attempt to confine psychology to the narrowed range of the commonly accepted concept of a natural science. Let psychology be simply *a* science, and let it use *every* possible and helpful means to arrive at scientific truth. Heidbreder betrays the mistake made by many modern psychologists when, in order to fit the subject studied—man—into their restricted notion of science, they restricted their concept of man: "Every one of the systems studied, in so far as it has dealt with the mind-body problems at all, has adopted a formulation which has made possible the treatment of its chosen subject matter as part of the natural world, and which has made that subject matter amenable to the regular procedures of science."[33]

There is here an unexpressed but underlying conviction that traditional psychologists or philosophers treated of "mind-body problems" on other than a natural plane. It would seem that if one talks as though there were three levels of life—namely, vegetative, sentient and rational—one is beyond the pale of scientific procedure, one has failed in "the attainment of the scientific attitude." which "habit psychology is now acquiring."[34]

Human behavior cannot be *completely* explained or understood by an appeal to principles which are strictly those of natural science. We have an inner mental life and while:

> It may be difficult to study our inner mental life . . . it is undoubtedly a field of investigation, and a field of investigation which has long been termed psychology. This inner mental life is of interest to many investigators, and they have every right historically to term this science of our mental life psychology. It is impossible to investigate everything in our mental life by objective method, for this inner experience is far richer than its manifestations by actions or reactions that can be the objects of an external observer's experience.[35]

Let psychology, then, be *a* science. Let it use experiments, observations, introspection, in fact, anything which will enable psychologists to obtain insight into the mental life of men—how they react to life as they face it.

CONCLUSION—KEEP THE DOORS OPEN

Psychology in general and the learning process in particular are so important and so vast as fields of investigation that all should try to work together towards a common goal—a better understanding of men and their mental processes as they really are. This will be truly possible only if psychologists can agree on essentials, on basic philosophic principles, on a complete and true concept of the nature of man.

We cannot expect this kind of unity overnight. There is too much involved. The situation as we have it has been too long and painful in the formation. But we can, and should, work sensibly towards this unity.

We who are Catholics, who hold the Thomistic and traditional view of learning (incidentally, we are not alone in holding it), can begin by trying to understand the position of our non-Catholic friends. Only in this way can we hope to open an avenue of approach to them. So admirably does Phelan write on this point that probably we do best in quoting his remarks in full:

> The naturalistic or secularist attitude, however, is so completely foreign to the mentality of a Catholic that he will find it difficult to understand how any reasonable human being could sincerely adopt it. Experience shows, nevertheless that—apart from the conscienceless racketeers who exploit education for their own selfish purposes—there are many purely secular-minded persons in our civilization to whom the Catholic view of education is nothing but a throwback to an obsolete and superstitious culture from which the progress of modern thought has, forsooth, delivered us. Difficult as it is to enter into the minds of such men, the effort must be made. Placing ourselves in their position and asking ourselves the question, "Suppose that I had never received the gift of faith and could not understand what religious educators are really talking about, what would be my attitude towards the problems of education?" would no doubt help us to grasp the difficulties these secularists have to face and, perhaps, to find means of sowing seeds of doubt in their minds regarding the validity of their thinking. At all events, no communication can be established, even in view of any fruitful discussion, unless some such method of learning to appreciate that heresy and unbelief have so poisoned and weakened the minds of otherwise decent folk that they have nothing left but a pagan naturalism bereft even of the polytheistic beliefs of the pagan cultures of antiquity.[36]

By beginning in this way we can hope to gain their good will, and by means of that good will obtain a hearing for our words. However, we must know what we are talking about, we must be scholarly and lucid. We must be above sarcasm, ridicule, and haughty disdain. We must realize, as McKeough well says, that "the persons with whom we are dealing are generally sincere and intelligent men and women who will be impressed by well expressed reasoning." [37] Traditional philosophy and psychology are not like Gray's flower "born to blush unseen" but, vibrant with perennial youth and rooted in objective truth, are destined in their beauty to enlighten man concerning himself and all that surrounds him.

NOTES

1. Ernest R. Hilgard, *Theories of Learning* (2nd ed.: New York: Appleton-Century-Crofts, Inc., 1956), p. 457.
2. Robert S. Woodworth, *Contemporary Schools of Psychology* (Rev. Ed.; New York: The Ronald Press Co., 1948), p. 254.
3. Peter Sandiford, "Connectionism: Its Origin and Major Features," *Psychology of Learning*, N.S.S.E. 41st Yearbook, Part II (Chicago: University of Chicago Press, 1942) p. 98.
4. *Ibid.*, p. 99.

5. John N. Washburne, "Viewpoints in Learning," *Educational Psychology,* ed. Charles E. Skinner (Rev. ed.; New York: Prentice-Hall, Inc., 1945) pp. 305-306.
6. W. A. Kelly, *Educational Psychology* (3rd ed., Milwaukee: The Bruce Publishing Co., 1946), pp. 271-272.
7. Washburne, pp. 306-308.
8. *Ibid.,* p. 313.
9. Kurt Lewin, "Field Theory and Learning," *Psychology Learning,* N.S.S.E. 41st Yearbook, Part II, p. 217.
10. Kelly, pp. 255-256.
11. T. V. Moore, *The Driving Forces of Human Nature* (New York: Grune and Stratton, 1948), p. 43.
12. Kelly, p. 262.
13. Hilgard, p. 457.
14. Edna Heidbreder, *Seven Psychologies* (New York: D. Appleton-Century Co., Inc., 1933), p. 3.
15. *Ibid.,* p. 421.
16. *Ibid.,* p. 418.
17. Hilgard, pp. 460-461.
18. Woodworth, p. 134.
19. Sandiford, pp. 98-99.
20. Moore, pp. 16-17.
21. M. J. McKeough, "Education's Need for Philosophy," *Planning for Our Educational Needs,* NCEA Bulletin, August 1954 (Washington, D.C.: National Catholic Educational Association), p. 308.
22. Gerald B. Phelan, "The Problem of Communication Between Catholic and Non-Catholic Educators and Philosophers," *Education and Communication,* NCEA Bulletin, August 1957, pp. 137-138.
23. Moore, p. 29.
24. Arthur W. Melton, "Learning," *Encyclopedia of Educational Research,* ed. Walter S. Monroe, rev. ed., 1950, p. 685.
25. Heidbreder, pp. 16-17.
26. *Ibid.,* p. 422.
27. Woodworth, p. 255.
28. Washburne, pp. 318-320.
29. Hilgard, pp. 460-461.
30. Melton, p. 685.
31. Moore, p. 28.
32. Phelan, p. 139.
33. Heidbreder, p. 421.
34. *Ibid.*
35. Moore, p. 5.
36. Phelan, p. 140.
37. McKeough, p. 311.

The myth of the great teacher

Thomas T. McAvoy, C.S.C.

*One of the favorite themes among "old grads"
during homecoming week is the memorable teachers
who started them down the road to success. Father
McAvoy challenges the dogmatic assumption that
the professor who is remembered—often for his
skill in relating anecdotes or for his idiosyncrasies
of dress or manner—is necessarily a great teacher.
He suggests that the qualities of the teacher which
make him remembered are too often qualities which
are really obstacles to learning. This insightful
discussion should lead us to inquire further into the
fundamentals of the teaching art.*

American education has suffered from many unfriendly traditions. For generations, especially on the frontier, the notion was broadcast that book learning was a handicap to manly accomplishment. In the pre-depression days of the nineteen-twenties when college education was associated with football stadia and raccoon skin coats, the heresy was passed along that higher education was 98 per cent association and 2 per cent studies. In recent years, I have heard some educational theorists talk about the need of great teachers, thereby creating new difficulties for the ordinary teacher with the daily task.

Magical Books and Magical Teachers

Probably because I do not consider myself a great teacher, I have been bothered by the persistent notion among many Catholic educators that the essence of great education is a great teacher. Likewise I have also been disturbed about much of

Reprinted with permission from *The Catholic Educational Review*, 56:361–367,
September, 1958.

the talk about great books as a tool for education for the simple reason that books, no matter how great, do not teach themselves. The fact of the matter is that neither a great teacher nor a great book alone constitutes great or superior education. Furthermore, I have an opinion based on evidence that the stories about the great teacher and the great book have been concocted by students and administrators who are afraid of the humdrum work of real education. Education is not the work of the teacher but of the student, and there is no magical book or teacher who can change the dullard or slothful youth into a wise and learned youth. I would like to make an earnest protest against this myth of the great teacher and, in a sense, of great books as the secret of successful education. I regret this myth—however well used occasionally—as a product of modern soft living.

The argument about great books is hard to down because no one should ordinarily read a second-rate book when he can read a masterpiece on the same subject. Why read Cajetan when one can read Aquinas? Yet there is an answer. We do not learn books, we learn ideas, principles, and facts; and no one book has been written that gives us these matters perfectly. To be able to quote extensively from great authors gives erudition but it does not give wisdom, understanding, or virtue. So also we must remember that in education a teacher, no matter how distinguished he may be, may fail to convey the needed truth or discipline to his student, while the tyro or the simple teacher can be the most successful.

No one denies that there have been unusual teachers. By experience I have found that I dare not criticize to alumni even the poorer teachers I have known because frequently the teacher whom I regard as, at best, mediocre was a great inspirer for one or another old student. There is also, on nearly every campus, the tradition of one notable person who seems to violate all the general rules of education, especially the hard ones, yet of whom everyone says he is a "great teacher." He may be a great teacher, but usually his teaching ability is a myth, a goblin worked up by clever students, or bad administrators to scare away the tough teacher who believes too much in the subject and content of his class.

There are, of course, many things taught in a class besides the subject matter. I have been in a classroom where the teacher, while scarcely saying anything about religion, made it understood that formal religion, especially Catholicism, was something discarded by intelligent men. Sometimes such a teacher is a good teacher and therefore effective not only in his subject but perhaps even more effective in conveying his prejudices to his students. At least one teacher under whom I studied was so little respected by his students that they were likely to accept as probably good any teaching or personal faith that he attacked. But, of course, this man was not a good teacher, even though I have met a former student of his who admired him deeply.

Appraisal by Incidentals

Much confusion over who is or who is not a great teacher depends not on what he teaches formally but on what he says, as it were, accidentally in a class. At

Columbia University someone suggested that I get up front in one class because the noted teacher occasionally told a good joke which I might not hear if I sat in the back of the room. I also recalled a student survey of teachers at the University of California in which the famous Professor Herbert Bolton was voted a very dull teacher. I heard also of a layman history teacher in a girls' college who was remembered chiefly because he spoke so understandingly of the problems in his home. There is another teacher whom students admire because he does such a good job of picking flaws in the other teachers, particularly those in authority. Such a critical "know-all" spirit in the classroom added to high marks for the student and a few departures from normal procedure seldom fail to impress the adolescent mind. And then there is the flatterer who makes all his students feel so proud to be his students—a rare one, but one found in schools as well as in public relations offices.

This myth of the great teacher has been especially influential for evil in Catholic schools because religious institutions tend to place great emphasis on ideals and to play down the factual content of the class. Yet high ideals are not the subject of any class. Some administrators are always ready to challenge this statement. For several years I argued this point with a history teacher and insisted that the subject of his history class was history and not citizenship. I was surprised by the tenacity with which he opposed my dictum. Finally, he told me that he always insisted that his pupils be high class citizens and gentlemen and he could not understand why I objected to this practice. Then, for the first time, we found that we were actually in full agreement, because he was not really teaching these ideals as the subject of the class. I also insisted that he taught a good class in history in which his students learned the facts of the past, the historical movements, and their relations to each other. I am convinced this Brother is a good teacher because I have had experience with his students and have found that they were not only gentlemen but that they knew their history to a high degree. He is a good teacher not because of what he implied or thought about citizenship but because he attained the purpose of his teaching—the production of the well-instructed student. But he also was a good disciplinarian and a good example in those things that pervade every classroom. Was he a great teacher? Not in the traditional sense, because he never drew attention to himself.

Some teachers are considered great merely because they make an impression on our memories. Some former teachers whom we remember best were usually a bit queer in appearance, manner, or methods. Thus, I have a special recollection of the lady who taught us the multiplication tables to the tune of a yardstick, supplemented by a buggy whip. But the class did learn the multiplication tables backward and forward, and no one was ever punished for anything except failure to learn. Then there was that calm, sharp-eyed lay teacher of high-school physics who seemed always so much in command that everyone worked hard at least when he was in charge of the class. Also, he could explain the subject of the class. I remember also a high-school teacher who seemed so very far above the small town in which she taught; at least she was conscious of the world of literature and expressed constantly the desire that we should be leaders in our community if not in national and world affairs. Yet, I think her greater skill was in imparting not only knowledge but a desire for knowledge and a desire to be someone of importance. In college I remember one priest-teacher of economics who was really an expert teacher in explaining his subject matter, but not a successful teacher of creative work. The clarity of his explanations was almost perfect and his skill in argumentation was almost superhuman. His classes were too large to provide personal contact between himself and the individual student and probably many of them were unimpressed. In recollection I feel that he had a way of quietly illustrating the lessons with concrete fact and such a genial humor that only obstinacy kept the capable student from learning.

Inspiration without Good Works

Having become a teacher myself and a director of teachers—even a trainer of teachers—I have had many occasions to try to evaluate the myth of the great teacher. I have learned to measure the teacher by his success in imparting knowledge, in bringing the student to learn to read and to write. According to his proper ability, I am accustomed to hear personal criticism of the teacher who marks severely and the teacher who insists on hard work. The complaints usually have a basis in some known fact about the teacher. He is frequently a bit too young and inexperienced, does not speak very loudly, has a notable accent, does not dress well, or does not know his subject well enough to leave his notes behind. I have found the ordinary student very tolerant of these same faults if the teacher gives high marks and yields to student excuses.

Against this hard working teacher I see offered the notion of the great teacher, who probably has grown a bit careless about his notes and consequently makes many slips in matters of detail but who does not wish to bore the student or himself with tests, or to correct papers, or to read many themes. How many times have I heard administrators or unlearned business men extol the greatness of this man who inspires his students without boring them with details. Usually his lectures are a bit thin, punctuated, however, with good stories; but after all he is a "great" teacher and therefore can do no wrong. It is true that the experienced teacher is frequently a great scholar, but if he is a scholar he ordinarily wants to talk to scholars, except for recreation. I have been impressed with excellent teachers who, at the end of their career, were just as careful about following their notes, and about the reading of tests and examinations and term papers as when they began teaching. I have also noted that their better students tended to become scholars also. I also found that the only students who could enjoy the lectures of real scholars had to come with their minds already prepared by their own study.

When I went to graduate school I was impressed by the number of prominent lecturers whose fame as scholars was nationwide. The basic reason for their fame was some book or books which had changed the accepted history of some event or period. They were often abominable public lecturers. But since this was higher education the students were on their own and what they learned was dependent not so much on the teacher as on the student effort. I also soon learned that the real power of these men lay in the teaching of their seminars with small groups which they successfully directed these students from apprenticeship to mastery. These teachers probably deserved their reputations as great teachers not because of some word of worldly wisdom or oratory but because under their direction and discipline their students learned likewise to read and to write and of course to do the thinking that accompanies both. Thus the "great" teacher who is superior to all these humdrum rules of the profession is a myth.

Harm to American Education

This myth of the great teacher has been a very harmful one for American education. On it I place much of the blame for the American lack of appreciation of the teaching profession. There is scarcely a successful businessman or politician who does not think he could do a better job in the classroom than the plodder he remembers or sees in the classroom today. These orators have a wrong concept of the teacher. Teaching is an art and it is a principle of artistry that in artistic production the agent and the tools cease to exist as agent and tools and become embodiments of thought. I admit that it is difficult for a human being to disappear as a human being and become an idea, especially when performing under the watchful eyes of a roomful of youngsters. Yet in teaching, that is the perfection of teaching—when the teacher disappears and leaves the students with only the ideas and ideals for which they have come to class.

But you ask me why I regard this myth of the great teacher as a particular handicap to Catholic education in this country. The principal damage of the myth arises from the authoritarian nature of so much of the Catholic religious teaching. Almost all early education depends upon the authority of the teacher and the books they read. Now the distinguishing characteristic of Catholic schools must be the teaching of religion and religion is something we learn by the authority of the teacher. Accidentally this notion of dependence on the teacher has pervaded all Catholic teaching and one defect of this leaning so much on authority, outside of the field of religion, has been the neglect of the sciences and especially of social sciences where learning is not so much from authority as from observation. There is a tendency here to depend upon the teacher not only for information but for guidance and propulsion. All children like to blame the teacher for their failures, but children in religious schools have more than their share of this tendency to blame and praise the teacher.

All this dependence on the teacher is not bad. Thus Catholic schools have avoided the opposite error of the "Progressive" educators who, with their students, accept nothing on authority. But one need not go as far as the "Progressive" educator to avoid the evil of too much dependence on the teacher. Virtue here as in all matters lies in balance. I think this balance in American Catholic schools and colleges has been weighted too much to the praise and the blame of the teacher and an underevaluation of the student. This is a serious defect because, after all, learning is the aim of teaching and learning can be done only by the pupil.

Best Teachers for the Gifted

Probably the best example of this problem can be seen in the handling of the specially gifted student. No one now is afraid of intellectual snobbery in Catholic schools. Even in times past there was less danger of this than of an adoration of the athlete. But now that the country is aware that it needs scientists and youngsters capable of deep and sustained thought various schemes have been proposed to find and encourage the gifted youth. To those who are laboring under the notion that the teacher is the essence of education, this gifted youth must be taken away from the ordinary teacher and given to the guidance of a great mind. But if learning is the work of the student the great mind can be only a difficulty to the gifted student. The better solution is to give the student a chance to start first on his own level of study and then advance to the care of the scholar. Granted competency in the teacher, that teacher will be best who best aids and directs the student to educate himself on the level the student happens to be at that time.

I have called the tradition of the great teacher a myth and I have described some of the most renowned teachers I know. Actually I have described them as notable not because their students have advanced in learning under them but because by their idiosyncrasies or peculiarities they have caused their students to remember them. I do not feel I am exaggerating when I say that I remember them for those things that distracted from the learning process of their students. By way of exception, there are some whose idiosyncrasies can be ignored. I insist that the best teacher is he who disappears in the process of making the student learn. It is time that we give due honor and pay properly the real teacher—the one who keeps the student at work and who enables the student to learn and to grow in wisdom and in knowledge. This may sound like a strange theory but the successful students will prove its validity.

There will always be stories of fabulous teachers whose stories or mannerisms or tantrums distinguished them from their colleagues who bore the brunt of the work of teaching. Actually I think there is room for the clown and the orator on most college campuses, less room for one in the high school and practically none for one in the grade schools; and there will always be orators whose inspiration is greater than their knowledge.

Creative learning

Edward J. Lanvin, S.J.

The preceding articles in this chapter deal with learning, thinking, creativity, and teaching. The following article, in effect, interrelates the four concepts by focusing on the creative aspect of the learning process. Father Lanvin describes and defends a problem-solving method of teaching and learning which duplicates what he calls "the electric quality and the intensity of the creative situation." He maintains that the greatest advances in learning take place when such a method is employed.

Creativity is fast arriving at the dubious status of a fad. There are creativity terms, and creative kits, and even creative luncheons. Nevertheless, creativity is no joke. In their own silent way the intricate space-trails of the Sputniks and Luniks are constantly reminding us of this. This paper is an attempt to show the close connection of the problem of creativity with the very old problem of understanding. For the educator these analogous problems present themselves as an investigation of the best means of setting up a learning situation where understanding and creativity can take place. The complexities of these problems about the learning process are enormous since their solution presupposes some answers to the spiny problems of communication and knowledge. Obviously there are no simple solutions to these kind of things and progress in their understanding will have to be an amalgam of many insights drawn from many different kinds of experiences. It is my hope that this article can contribute something to this gradual progress of understanding.

From my reading of the lives and letters of the great artists, from discussion

Abridged and reprinted with permission from *The Jesuit Educational Quarterly,* 21:205–219, March, 1960.

with present day artists, and from reflection on my own creative experiences, I have formulated a rough working idea of the conditions which are essential to the creative process. This list of conditions, like an anatomy chart, is only a remote proximation of the beautiful and delicate reality, but it has been a useful thing. Its first usefulness became apparent to me when I realized that it was also the chart of the conditions which were inevitably present in the good learning situations of my experience. The mild astonishment that this caused was perhaps naive since I should have realized that the situations would be the same. Nevertheless, this second realization has also proved very useful. It is this relationship between the creative act and the act of understanding that I wish to explore in this article. The investigation of the learning process through its relation to the creative process will reexamine some generally trite educational principles, and will make clear some general principles of methodology.

I

Before I begin with the analysis, I feel that it is necessary for the sake of completeness to mention some of the presuppositions of the argument. Some of these are obvious, some not so obvious; all of them should be discussed, but not, I'm afraid, within the limits of this paper.

A. I presuppose that the question of real understanding is a real and vital problem for the teacher. Moreover that he sees that the non-creative and non-understanding situation is really an anti-creative and anti-understanding situation. It is possible to multiply horrible examples of this, but I do not think that this is necessary.

B. Understanding is an organic thing, a growth by assimilation. If the human personality is conceived of in a mechanical way, as a receptor-organizer-transmitter, then the only function of an educator is to present the machine with new and clearer facts, to improve the organizing functions (by logic for instance), and to improve the means of communication. This electronic brain sort of thing is certainly a part of education but it most certainly is not the totality. The analogue of the human personality is not the machine, but the tree and it is clear that you don't stuff a tree; rather you encourage its intrinsic growth.

C. Creativity is a fundamental drive of all men. Each human person is responsible for the creation of the final image of his soul. His material, the developing personality, is most subtle and powerful, and most capable of beautiful expression. This impulse for self-fulfillment gives stimulus in every area of a man's life. In this process of self-fulfillment, the teacher is the supreme artist, for his function, though indirect, is crucial. He provides the direction and at times the stimulus for this creative development and his touch must be as delicate and as sure as Rembrandt's.

D. There is a close relationship between the creative act and the act of understanding. This is not very surprising since they are both acts of the mind. But besides this generic similarity, it may be possible to show an even closer connection between them by making a simple distinction between newness and originality. The artist produces something new. This is a newness that has a social dimension, since the artist's product is new not only to himself but also to the rest of man. This added circumstance, the social dimension, adds the idea of originality to the idea of newness. This is what St. Thomas and Raphael did. They gave to the world an entirely new vision, something that no one had ever seen before. Perhaps it is because of this social dimension that these people feel such a violent need to communicate.

On the other hand, the act of understanding also produces something new to the human person. The revelation that comes to a boy when he sees the coherence of a geometry theorem is certainly not very original but it is certainly new to him. It is the newness of growth, of understanding. Thus newness is common to understanding and to creativity and because of this community it may be possible to say that creativity is merely understanding with an added dimension. They are essentially the same act.

Fortunately the proof of the relationship between these two acts does not rest entirely on this slim theoretical base. A much more convincing evidence of their relationship comes from the clear similarity of the psychological state that accompanies each of them. Thus the urgency and especially the personal involvement which accompany the creative act are also abundantly clear in a student at the time of real insight. At this moment, Beethoven and the student of geometry are brothers, or at least cousins. The intensity of this moment of enlightenment is one of the real rewards of teaching. I must emphasize this idea of personal involvement, since it is basic to all that I have to say. It will appear again and again in the pages that follow.

The connection between the creative act and the act of understanding is most fundamental because my method will be a series of jumps from the necessities of the creative process to the analogous necessities of the learning situation. And so the analysis itself will be the best proof of the relationship since these necessities are perfectly obvious in both cases and the similarity of the methodologies of both processes will be a most evident proof of their relationship.

II

It will soon be clear that much of what I am to say is not new. The newness of my presentation will be in the fact that I wish to unify all these elements into a single integrated approach. It is important to realize that I am not talking about individual points of method, but about a spirit of approach. The monolithic character of the presentation will sometimes make it appear to be a bit lyrical in the face of practical and institutional exigencies. This is most evident to me and I will try to correct this fault in my conclusions. Since what I am trying to describe is a spirit rather than any particular activity, it is difficult to categorize, but for practical reasons I have divided what I must say into three parts. The first deals with the process of learning itself and this includes four parts: (1) some preconditions, (2) the problem, (3) the solution, and (4) the critique. The second section deals with the atmosphere which is necessary for this process to develop. They are: (1) freedom, (2) integrity, (3) seriousness, and (4) quality. The final section will present some conclusions.

III. THE PROCESS OF LEARNING

The pivotal insight of the whole discussion is that every creative act is the solution to a problem. Whether or not this statement could be shown to be theoretically true of the act of understanding also is not too important. It is sufficient to say that most frequently the act of understanding takes place in the matrix of a problem. In the diagram below I am attempting to present what I conceive to be the process. It should be noted that I am not trying to present an essential definition but only a spatial temporal description of external circumstances.

Preconditions	The problem	The solution
a. search	(The alignment	(The resolution
b. sensibility	of the elements)	of the elements)
c. technique		The creation
d. information		The understanding
(The acquisition of the		
elements of knowledge)		

The critique
(Reexamination and reevaluation)

In the sections that follow I will try to describe each of these stages and try to point out their application to class room procedure and methodology.

A. Some Preconditions

The mind of a creative person is an incredibly vital thing. In its restless activity it is like a bird; it is constantly probing and searching; it quivers with excitement and expectation; it is far-ranging and yet sensitive. Indeed, so overwhelming is this desire for knowledge and fulfillment that it sometimes becomes an insupportable burden. The tragic life of Vincent Van Gogh is eloquent testimony of this.

The presence of this vitality of the human spirit is obvious enough when it is present, but precisely because it is a spirit it is a difficult thing to classify. Greatly oversimplified, it seems to include at least four things; (1) The most basic thing is the desire to know, the spirit of *search*. There are two modalities of this search; (2) *sensitivity*, the way in which this knowledge is received, a lack of grossness in man's experiential functions; (3) *technical equipment*, or the way in which the knowledge is used. This would include logic, mathematical or scientific or communication techniques, in fact, whatever techniques the man will need in his field; (4) finally, a certain minimum number of necessary facts and bits of *information*.

That these qualities are present in the very great artists is quite clear. Technique is very obvious, but search and sensibility are equally obvious, and perhaps much more important.

The technique of the masters is beautifully apparent. Some of them have been so sensitive that ugliness and falsity have been almost a physical pain. The whole life of people like Michelangelo and El Greco and Picasso can be focussed down to the single point of search.

A simple reflection makes it plain that these qualities are also present in the man of understanding. Not less evident is the fact that they are not the prerogatives of the great, but are present, or at least possible in all of us. These simple observations make it profitable to examine the learning situation for these signs of vitality. Clearly we will not find the intense activity of the great minds but an analogous, less intense and broader vitality could be expected.

It is unfortunately true that much education contents itself with the two most inert phases of these preconditions, that is, technique and information. These two elements are necessary, perhaps the most necessary in the practical order, but a total or near total emphasis on them will surely misdirect or block the other two elements, the search and sensibility. Thus we have the common phenomenon of the boy who has a really consuming interest in electric trains, or rock and roll, or stamps. He is searching but he has been blocked or misdirected. The lack of sensibility manifests itself in many ways. A common example of it is the liturgist's problem of the presentation of symbols. Because the emphasis in education is on discursive reason (even in the teaching of poetry), the students have great difficulty in experiencing the full meaning of the delicate symbolism of the sacraments or of poetry. This important part of their development is now filled by the sledge-hammer symbols of advertising, TV, and the movies. The business men are today's poets.

It seems evident that no one will argue against vitality and awareness, but since it is difficult to achieve these things, it might be profitable to discuss their necessity. Besides the general principle which was already given, that a lack of this spirit is a positive impeding force for its development, there are other important considerations. The data of experience must somehow come to the learner. This can happen in two ways. The matter, the cognitive bits, can be presented to the student. When this is done, these normally charged things become more or less inert. They don't move or combine or grow; they become stagnant. But if these data come to the student as a result of his own search, then the dimension of personal involvement is added to them and they are charged with their own vitality and with the vitality of involvement. In a word, what a student discovers himself is more meaningful to him. This is indeed a trite principle but a radical one. For unless the data of experience are meaningful to the student he will not be able to achieve true understanding. Can the data be meaningful except through personal discovery? A simple question like this can overturn many ivory towers of methodology.

Again, if the spirit of inquiry is never developed, education can have very little influence in the total life of the student. Indeed it must cease with the end of his formal training. This is in fact what most frequently happens. And so teaching becomes not a training of the developing human spirit but an expensive kind of lion taming. The inert spirit can learn facts but it does not develop.

I fully realize that the difficulty in this matter is that these kinds of things can not be taught in the strict sense. Rather they must be fostered in a very explicit way. This makes the difficulty a regressus ad infinitum, because the teacher is the key. If the teacher lacks the spirit it can hardly be communicated to the class, and frequently the reason the teacher doesn't have the spirit is that he has never been exposed to it, and so on. It is the most vicious of circles.

There are simple exercises which can be of some help. One example is an exercise that is used in an Art course but which could also be used with great profit for English and science. For twenty minutes the student studies a very simple thing, like a leaf, or a twig, or a piece of bread. Then he writes twenty things about the object, using no comparisons; then twenty things using only comparisons. Simple exercises in observation like this could be very valuable, as also are meaningful problems in research.

These kinds of things are important but they are merely manifestations of the spirit of the teacher and will be used naturally by a vital teacher. On the other hand, the inert and unaware teacher can never generate and preserve the spirit. His methodology is informed by his attitude. Indeed to the non-seeker, the seeker usually appears mad, or impertinent, or at least unintelligible. The real solution to this problem is most difficult. The only certainty that I have is that the problem must be exposed very clearly and explicitly and that we must never presume that either the spirit or the realization of its importance will take place naturally. Each teacher will have to try to foster vitality and awareness in his own way but it must be a very explicit effort.

This section has dealt with some of the preconditions of knowledge: search, sensibility, technique, and information. It is by means of these that the data of experience are acquired, more or less personally. If these data, which are all the intentional elements necessary for the act of understanding, are acquired in the proper way, then they become charged; they have hooks; they want to grow and combine. They must be aligned for this combination and the alignment of them is the next step in the creative process, the problem.

B. The Problem

When Michelangelo created the ceiling of the Sistine Chapel, what he was really doing was solving a problem. In like manner the creations of Einstein and Mozart are essentially the solutions to problems. So also the sophomore solves a problem when he reduces the elements of the character of Brutus into some kind of an insight about this complex personality. The acts of creation and understanding are very like small atomic explosions. The elements, uranium or whatever, must be brought into proper contact with each other before they can react. In the same way, the intentional elements which are necessary for any given act of creation or understanding must be brought into meaningful contact with each other. It is the problem which brings these elements into the proper alignment and tension. It also provides the necessary charge for their inter-reaction. When this reaction occurs and they are reduced to some kind of union, we have the act of understanding or creation.

Whether this analogy be apt or not, the word *problem* is a good one to describe this stage in the creative act. It means, in general, the tension of diverse elements which must be reduced to unity.

In addition to this, it carries with it the added dimension of personal involvement, the quality which is so characteristic of creativity. It also gives us a clue to the methodology which is essential to the acts of creation and understanding. Malraux says that the central problem for the artist is to personalize the tradition, that is, he must break away somewhat from the tradition, or better, he must inject his personality into the tradition. In this way, the whole life of an artist becomes an attempt to solve a very real problem. Whether this be true or not, the artist is faced with problems on several levels. Cézanne's avowed problem was to find the way to show forth God's glory which is manifested in His creation. To do this he had to reduce the various visual elements, the trees and stones, through the distillation of his own personality and to join them with his central problem. Then he had to combine this derived solution with the elements of his technique, the brush, canvas, and paints. The final work was the beautiful solution to these problems. The same kind of process is described very clearly by the mathematician Poincaré in the book, the *Creative Process.*

Is it true to say that understanding also always occurs as a solution to a real problem? On the practical level I have chosen, it is possible to bypass this theoretical question and state simply, as a matter of common experience, that understanding most frequently takes place in the matrix of problem and involvement. In practice there are four kinds of learning situations which correspond to the four kinds of teachers, the stuffer, the pusher, the leader and the steerer.

a. The *stuffer* gives his students answers. In this method there is no real understanding unless the student has the spiritual vigor to work back from the answer to the problem. This kind of inversion is really too much to expect from the average student. There is a good deal of this kind of teaching. "In this play the character of Marc Anthony is . . ."

b. The *pusher* presents the problem to the students and then gives them the answer. This is really not much better than the first method because it never gets into the interior processes of the student. "See how Marc Anthony acts in this situation. This means that he . . ."

c. The *leader* presents the students with the problem and allows them to work it out for themselves. This is a vast improvement over the first two methods. "Why does Marc Anthony act in this way?"

d. The *steerer* is the teacher who presents his matter in such a way that the problem arises from the student himself. The problem is not then induced but rises immanently. "Would you vote for Marc Anthony if he were running for mayor?"

There may not seem to be much difference between the last two methods but the class reaction to them can be enormously different. The reason for the difference in the results and reactions to these four methods is that they represent four degrees of problems, and thus four degrees of personal involvement. And it is involvement which is the mark of real understanding because it indicates that the growth of the personality is immanent, that it is real growth. From this it is evident that the problem must be intrinsic. There can be an engagement with knowledge on an extrinsic level. Many students are really involved in the acquisition of knowledge but only for passing examinations. This kind of extrinsic problem can never lead to real understanding because understanding must be the result of inner growth.

In practice this question can be asked. Is the better teacher the man with real problems or the man with answers? Of course this is a false dichotomy since the teacher must be both, just as he must employ all four of the methods I mentioned above. Nevertheless the question is useful for examining the controlling attitude of the teacher. Which method does he prefer to use? How often does he try to bring out a real problem?

If it is true that the problem is more or less necessary for real understanding, then the question of methodology arises. It does not seem that the change in methodology would be too difficult for an experienced teacher if he thought of this in an explicit manner as a desirable or even necessary thing. The whole of the *Rime of the Ancient Mariner* could be handled around the central problem of punishment. The student of physics could be asked not only to do the experiment but to work out for himself what the experiment must be like. While it is not too difficult, this method does require a certain amount of imagination and intensity and so can be easily forgotten. On the level of the personality of the teacher the problem is much more difficult and complex. You can not do too much with the man who has all the answers.

C. The Solution

If the data have been gathered in a meaningful way and have been properly aligned in the dynamism of the problem, the solution will follow. This solution is the creative act or the act of understanding. It is true that this does not always happen since these things operate in their own mysterious way. One of Poincaré's solutions came to him as he was stepping on a bus and Mozart composed a whole symphony as he was riding in a carriage. We know from our own experience that understandings come in utterly unexpected times and manners. But if we are teaching some that do have coherence and meaning and if we have set up the proper conditions for understanding, in most instances understanding will take place. To be practical we should admit that if the answer does not come, it will have to be given. But this is an expedient and should not be the normal situation.

D. The Critique

A human person is naturally in love with his own solutions, and like most people in love is not very objective. Thus the student must be trained to examine his understandings. The critical faculty is as necessary as the spirit of inquiry and like any habit it must be trained. Does his solution really answer the problem; is it true to the data; is it logical; is it true to experience; how does it relate to other truths? These and similar questions must always be asked.

The critical faculty extends and must be trained in two directions. We must examine our own solutions and those of others. The first of these is rarely developed, first, because there are so few personal understandings, and second, because we tend to take this critique for granted, whereas it must be done explicitly. There is normally a fair amount of the second kind of criticism but it is usually an extrinsic kind of thing and then it becomes carping. Trying to examine another man's insights without entering his problem is as futile and much less honorable than tilting with windmills.

Besides the obvious motive of integrity there is another reason for the development of the critical faculty. The inspection and examination of solutions leads inevitably to further problems and thus the process starts all over again. This is why each understanding is like a seed and why the truly learned man never stops learning.

IV. CONDITIONS OF UNDERSTANDING

The previous section was an attempt to describe the normal process of the act of creation and the act of understanding. It is now necessary to mention briefly some of the qualities which are usually present in this process. These qualities are the atmosphere of learning. They are the light and air of intellectual growth.

A. Freedom

Beethoven wrote the following words on the top of his manuscript of *The Great Fugue*, "The Great Fugue, sometimes free, sometimes careful." This is the way it is with all great art. Creativity is always a tension, a balance of freedom and restriction. The artist is restricted by his technique, his materials and the tradition. He is free to the degree that he produces newness, originality. These two forces, restriction and freedom, must stretch against each other until the tension of beauty is reached. In different ages the proportion of each is different. In Byzantine art, the restrictive predominates; today freedom is much more noticeable, but each is beautiful in its own way. The proportion depends upon many things, the state of the tradition, the spirit of the times, the techniques available, etc., but whatever the proportions, both elements must be present.

The freedom of understanding is analogous to the freedom of creation. Creativity must be free to the degree that it is original because originality means a break and an advance in the tradition. The artist is free not only in what he creates but in the way that he creates it. The act of understanding is not free to this degree, since there are limits to the meaning of the thing understood, as the meaning of a poem or the construction of a theorem. The freedom of understanding must be present in the process, in the acquisition of the data and in the structure of the problem. In other words, wherever possible the student should be able to seek his own data, to ask his own questions, and at times to hold his own solutions.

It is fairy obvious that a certain amount of freedom in the learning process is desirable. The reason for this is also quite clear. It is again the necessity for personal involvement. Given the ethos of the American student, the fact that in some ways he is more independent at an earlier age than any other child in civilized history, complete restriction in any area will be deadly. It is trite but true that we are a free people.

There is indeed a paradox in this whole matter. We are surely a free people but we are not less surely a people who are addicted to conformity. The result of this is that an individual will rebel if his freedom is restricted from the outside and yet if he is left to himself he will restrict his own freedom to a remarkable degree. There are multiple examples of this kind of behaviour in any class room, or living room or bar room. This means that freedom in education is a delicate thing; there is a silent, even unconscious revolt when the areas of knowledge are completely restrictive and yet when a certain amount of freedom is allowed to the learner, he may have to be pushed into using it for it requires great courage. However delicate, a certain amount of freedom is necessary and especially for Catholics since we do have a little bit of our much discussed tendency to be sheeplike.

Obviously I am not talking about discipline or an unreal type of permissiveness. I am talking about freedom within set areas of curricula and methodology. This is not as dangerous as it sounds. If the subject has its own truth and coherence and the wise teacher is able to steer the process in the proper direction, the student should come to the point of understanding that the teacher thinks important. Indeed it may be true to say that if the student cannot come to this point himself, the point is not really important. Even though there are an infinite number of questions which can be asked about Lady Macbeth, there are only a certain number that can and should be asked by a seventeen year old boy. It is much more important that the student have answers which are meaningful to him and a basis for future development than that he have an answer which is a kind of meaningless intellectual subway token.

The balance of freedom and restriction may be somewhat difficult to control because it will be an exercise in human relationships. But no matter how difficult or delicate, it must never be abandoned. Our emphasis should always be on the greatest, not the least profitable degree of freedom.

V

The next three qualities are important but very obvious and it is not necessary to say much about them. They are important because they act as a guidance system for this whole method. They prevent the process from becoming precious and overly clever.

B. *Integrity*

Georges Rouault once destroyed hundreds of his paintings because he thought that they did not measure up to his vision. This kind of vigor and ruthlessness is just as necessary in education. It means complete honesty in the face of one's work and understanding. This application of this spirit to the learning situation is manifold and it is not necessary to develop it. Obviously no one is against intellectual honesty but it is sometimes avoided on the grounds of practicality. This can be the cancer of intellectual development.

C. *Seriousness*

Art and understanding can be exhilarating but they are not a game. The creative man is deadly earnest about his work. This spirit must also be in the learner. He must realize that he is engaged in a serious business. Not that learning is somber; it can be fun at times but it is a job, serious work in a very real sense.

D. *Quality*

To inject a note of toughness and stiffness into a thing that might become too lyrical, it is necessary to insist on quality work. This is part of the balance of freedom and a function of integrity. The student who has a really silly and meaningless answer must be told so. The difficulties in this area, the different degrees of quality and the problem of testing real understanding, have been much discussed and there is no need to go into them here.

VI. CONCLUSION AND PRACTICE

Even at the very uncomfortable risk of being tedious, it was necessary to list and briefly explain these more or less obvious things about the learning situation. First, because it happens frequently enough that these qualities are omitted in practice, even though they are commonly recognized as valuable. Second, it was necessary to show the very close similarities between the creative situation and the learning situation. Third, there was a real need to make very clear what was meant by this process and its qualities since I wish to do something a little unusual with them.

The central purpose of this whole article is to try to demonstrate a practical method which will duplicate in the learning situation the electric quality and the intensity of the creative situation. I do this because my experience in learning and teaching has convinced me that the greatest advances in learning take place when these conditions are present.

The method is really quite simple. In its extreme form it consists in the explicit and *exclusive* use of the process and qualities I outlined. Imagine, if you can, a teacher who never presented anything which was not a real problem to him. This would result in a learning situation where the relationship between the teacher and the student would be a partnership in discovery, where each would help the other to advance. This would be the method of creative dialogue, an existential problem method.

Luckily this little Platonic dream admits of stages and degrees. One step below this somewhat fanciful situation is the one where the teacher prepares his course in such a way that it revolves around things which are or can be made into real problems for the students. A fair amount of freedom would have to be permitted to the student at this stage. One more step below this is the situation of the teacher who is aware of the method and consistently tries to use it as often as he can. This stage is the one which is the most practical and the one which I am trying to present. For once you get below this level you come down by varying degress to more and more inert levels until you come to the dead bottom, the memory of information.

To speak very plainly, I must confess that I think that too much of our teaching is of the more or less inert quality. The reason for this is that we never make *explicit* to ourselves the creative possibilities of the process I have presented. Too often we allow nature to take its course in these things and it is much too important for this. The statement that personality is 75% of teaching is this kind of facile evasion. The result of all of this is that the process is frequently not present at all and teaching becomes too tight. Sometimes our students are like those beautiful little Japanese trees, perfect in every detail, but only the tiniest fraction of the size of the true tree. Sometimes even, these little trees become distorted. The learning situation must be loosened up a bit to allow for growth.

To be practical some things must be said. First, I fully realize that there are many difficulties in this, especially in the areas of time and freedom. Self-development like any growth takes time. And so it seems inevitable that there will be conflicts between freedom and the text book and the syllabus. These latter are certainly very essential but truth usually lies somewhere in the middle of extremes. The syllabus and the text book can be just as dangerous as too much freedom. Second, some courses are obviously more open to this kind of thing than others. A course in English or creative writing or art appreciation is clearly a wonderful opportunity for this. A more restrictive course, like grammar, is less open but even here there will be opportunities. Third, this method might be dangerous in the hands of a young teacher who is still trying to find his classroom personality and his discipline and presentational techniques. Yet this young teacher will be more inclined to use it, while the older, more experienced, teacher who could handle the method most effectively would be less likely to use it. Fourth, it will be very necessary to find the degree of freedom proper to each stage of the student's development. Naturally the graduate student has to be freer than the high school freshman. Yet psychologists say that the most dangerous age for the loss of the spirit of creativity is between the ages of 10 and 13. Therefore in some measure or other this method must be used at all levels of education. Creativity and understanding are a matter of steady growth.

Granting these practical and institutional necessities, we can still make a general principle. The method of the free real problem should be explicitly used as often and to as great an extent as possible. The method will be limited as necessary by the exigencies of the text book, syllabus, student ability and teacher ability. This principle puts the emphasis of attitude in the proper place.

Of course information must be given and memorized. But from this stage each teacher will be able, and sometimes even obliged to rise up through the various stages I mentioned, even, at select times, to the high stage of creative dialogue. There would have to be small beginnings and careful experiments. For instance, it might be a very valuable experiment to take a second year English class and try this method for about two weeks. You could start with a problem which is especially acute at that time, like discipline, or punishment, or responsibility, or self-revelation. You could then select material which would give some kind of a start to the process and add more material to exemplify the direction the discussion took. I think that the results would be startling.

If most of what I have said is theoretically obvious, it is not so obvious in practice and this is, after all, the important thing. If some were to disagree with me totally, even this would be a very good thing because my statements will then have caused a certain awareness, a reexamination of the bases of teaching, a problem, and the beginning of a creative-learning process.

Of mice and men: a study of motivation

Rev. John B. McDowell

*In this article the author reviews some of the
investigations that have been made into the
phenomenon of motivation. He leaves the reader
with the impression that he is not always
enthusiastic about some of the results of research on
motivation because men are not mice and the
transfer of conclusions arrived at through animal
research to man's motives is hardly ever legitimate.
He prefers to alert the reader to the role of the will,
the effects of competition, and the importance of
information in forming motives. The significance of
motive is not questioned but endorsed when he
admonishes teachers to be concerned not only with
the work children do, but to be heedful also of
their motives for working.*

An examination of psychology texts, bibliographies, and summaries of research reveals that a vast amount of experimental work has been undertaken in the field of motivation. Before attempting a discussion of the nature of motivation it will be helpful to review briefly some of the typical investigations that have been made.

Studies of Animal Motivation

The majority of authors writing on the subject of motivation draw heavily upon experimental work done with animals. Young, for example, lists many studies of

Reprinted with permission from *The Catholic Educational Review,* 50:24–32 and 89–101, January, February, 1952.

this nature, and it is apparent that much of the theory is based on the conclusions derived from them.[1]

In 1921, Maupin summarized the studies regarding the acquisition of behavior for animals.[2] He listed seventeen investigations in which various kinds of "motives" were employed, such as food, hunger, escape, punishment, society, shade, and nesting. Commenting on these and other similar studies, Young writes: ". . . the first essential in all animal experimentation, whether it be upon learning, discrimination, delayed reaction, thinking, or other psychological problems, is to supple adequate motivation." [3] Since there is a typical pattern followed in all these so-called motivational studies it will suffice to cite one example.

In 1908 Yerkes and Dodson formulated the law which bears their names.[4] According to this law, the strength of that stimulus which is most favorable to habit formation approaches the threshold as the difficultness of discrimination is increased. The law was the result of the following experiment. Mice were placed in a discrimination box. They were to select one of two entrances on the basis of brightness. Making the wrong choice resulted in an electric shock while the right choice led to the nest box. The criterion of learning was three successive runs without error. It was discovered that the brightness of the entrances was related to the ease of learning: the greater the difference in brightness, the easier of learning. As the difference decreased, the difficulty increased. As the electric shock increased, the learning rate increased to a certain point after which no improvement was evident. All this was expressed in the law cited above.

This is an experiment in "motivation" according to many of the psychologists who write on the topic. Such studies could be multiplied many times but all of them follow generally the pattern indicated above.

Cognitive Motivational Studies

Among the countless studies classified as "motivational" one finds some having a decided cognitive element. For example, Arps reported a study where the subjects were given different degrees of information and their achievement was then compared with those having no information. The conclusion was that the quantity and rate of the work improved in proportion to the knowledge imparted.[5]

Ross worked with three groups. The first was known as the complete knowledge group and the subjects were given exact information on the results of their work. The second group received partial information of the results: they were

[1] P. T. Young, *Motivation of Behavior.* New York: J. Wiley and Sons, Inc., 1936.

[2] O. Maupin, "Habit Formation in Animals," *Psychological Bulletin*, XVIII (November, 1921), 573-620.

[3] Young, *op. cit.*, p. 170.

[4] R. M. Yerkes and J. D. Dodson, "The Relation of Strength of Stimulus to Rapidity of Habit Formation," *Journal of Comparative Neurology*, XVIII (November, 1908), 459-482.

[5] G. F. Arps, "A Preliminary Report on 'Work with Knowledge versus Work without Knowledge,'" *Psychological Review*, XXIV (November, 1924), 449-455.

told that the work was good or bad. The last group received no information. The results indicated a positive relation between the amount of information and success with the task.[6]

Many of Thorndike's studies will fall within the animal or the cognitive category. In one study, he presented two hundred rare English words to subjects who were to indicate which of five alternates was the correct meaning. If the selection was correct the experimenter called: Right. If the student erred, he called: Wrong. The results were calculated in order to determine the effect of calling right or wrong on the subsequent choices of the subjects. Thorndike concludes that ". . . right produces a substantial strengthening but the wrong does not raise the frequency of responses other than that particular wrong above what chance would give."[7]

It was studies of this nature which led Thorndike to the formulation and subsequent reformulation of his law of effect. Many authors include these studies under the general heading of "motivation." Subsequently it will be pointed out that these experiments may involve a motivational element although it can never be the controlled factor.

Concept of Motivation

The concept and definition of motivation is not a simple one. Young defines motivation as the why of all activity. "Broadly conceived," he writes, "the study of motivation is an attempt to explain all actions whether human or animal, in terms of their causes or conditions. . . . It deals with the why of behavior."[8] Everytime there is an exercise of power in the animal or man there must be some motivation according to this theory, for it is an attempt "to explain all actions whether human or animal."[9] This concept of motivation is rather generally accepted and it may have implications which are not apparent at first sight. It may be helpful, then, to re-examine certain fundamental facts.

There are four types of activity which may be predicated of man; three of these are predicable of animals. The types of activity are movement, growth, sensing, and interpreting. The theory indicated above would imply that the reason for all movement, growth, sensing, and interpreting is the flow of energy released by some motive or stimulus. This would involve a rather unique concept of human and animal life. When, for example, the organism unfolds and develops, when the glands secrete, or the nerves react, there is something which evokes this activity.

It is true that there is some reason for these activities, and as one begins to

---

[6] C. C. Ross, "An Experiment in Motivation," *Journal of Educational Psychology,* XVIII (May, 1927), 337-346.

[7] E. L. Thorndike, *The Fundamentals of Learning,* p. 280. New York: Columbia University Press, 1932. Chapter xi (pp. 276-313) contains a number of similar experiments conducted by Thorndike and his students.

[8] P. T. Young, "Motivation," *Encyclopediae of Educational Research,* p. 755. New York: Macmillan Co., 1950.

[9] *Ibid.*

appraise the situation it becomes apparent that an ancient controversy is revived. The answer to this question clearly illustrates the difference between two schools of thought: the mechanist and the vitalist. According to the mechanist, man is a mere automaton made up of so many levers and operating in virtue of some chemical or electric substrate. Something starts the machine going and it merely reacts; man is a passive receptor. But for the vitalist, man is not a passive machine but rather he is a living, thinking organism capable of immanent activity. He reacts, to be sure, but he also acts and this activity has its source in his very nature. Not every one who calls himself a vitalist will go as far as this, and consequently it is not easy to determine how many so-called vitalists really differ from the avowed mechanists.

Because of their fundamental concept the mechanists cannot explain any activity in terms of the intrinsic endowments of the organism. To be consistent all activity is explained in terms of factors extrinsic to the fundamental nature. The countless laws of association have always been the refuge of those who follow this way of thinking. Man learns, they say, because he is ready to learn; because he repeats things over and over; because pathways are hewed out in the neural system; because of certain things which precede or follow the reaction. It should be clear that such explanations are not only concerned with the learning process as they understand it but are, in fact, concerned with the definition of man. That is one reason why the true vitalist cannot reduce all learning to mere association. The living organism as a vital agent is not merely a passive receptor.

Careful research within recent years has clearly shown that man has so many fundamental powers.[10] The research on reminiscence, retroactive inhibition, and their higher thought processes not only gives considerable information on these phenomena but also indicates that the mind is an active and not a passive thing. These studies point clearly to the fact that man has so many abilities or powers and that these powers are vital or dynamic. To be sure, most psychologists do not pursue these facts to their ultimate conclusion, but honest investigation would demand acceptance of these elementary facts.

Furthermore, each of these powers has a specific object. Once this object is presented the power may go into action. In this sense there is a why for every activity, but this involves a dynamic concept of the organism. Since each power has its own object one can say that each is goal-oriented. The flower is drawn toward light; its roots stretch out toward water. The animals seeks food when it is hungry; it flees when in danger. But this propensity is not in itself the result of motivation nor does it necessarily involve motivation. Growth does not involve motivation, nor does thinking, in itself, involve motivation. These are, fundamentally, actions of living things.

It is difficult to understand what certain psychologists mean when they write about motives and motivation. For example, in Chapter I of Section I of the

10 E. A. Monaghan, *Major Factors in Cognition*. Washington, D.C.: Catholic University Press, 1935.
T. V. Moore, *Cognitive Psychology*, p. 593. Philadelphia: J. B. Lippincott Co., 1939.

Forty-Ninth Yearbook of the National Society for the Study of Education, entitled *Learning and Instruction,* Anderson and Gates state: "Motivation is assumed to be an inner state of need and is a necessary condition if the learner is to engage in learning activity." [11] This would seem to imply that motives are part of the native endowment. However, in Chapter II of Section I of the same yearbook, Hilgard and Russell giving a definition of motivation write: "*Motivation:* A very general term for describing need-satisfying and goal-seeking behavior. It includes physiological drives, unconscious motives, clearly formulated purposes, ideals, etc." [12] Moreover, hunger is considered by Hilgard and Russell as a primary need,[13] while other psychologists frequently use the example of hunger as a motive and food as an incentive to show a distinction between the concepts of motive and incentive.

Young explains in detail the concept of motivation which is rather generally accepted:

> What motivates a man? . . . In considering this question from the physical point of view the following points are important: first, the immediate energy source of behavior and of all muscular work is certain chemical substances stored in the body. Second, stimuli, both environmental and internal, release this energy which is stored within. And third, in the energy transformation, heat and work are produced. Finally, energy expenditure is regulated and directed so as to produce certain results in behavior.[14]

Again he writes:

> In the last analysis the energy with which we are concerned . . . is physical and the conditions called motivating are those which release this physical energy and regulate direction of its expenditure. Physiologically the energy is derived immediately from the chemical reactions within the muscle cells and other cells of the body.[15]

And all this leads to the conclusion: "Drive is Energy." [16]

Young, therefore, admits a certain fundamental power in the organism which he calls energy. It is this energy which underlies every activity and which is controlled by those stimuli acting on the organism. These stimuli he calls motives. What arouses these motives? The answer to this, of course, is the incentive. There

[11] G. L. Anderson and A. I. Gates, "The General Nature of Learning," *Learning and Instruction,* p. 16. Forty-Ninth Yearbook of the National Society for the Study of Education, Part I, ed. by Nelson B. Henry. Chicago: University of Chicago Press, 1950.

[12] E. R. Hilgard and D. H. Russell, "Motivation in School Learning," *ibid.,* p. 38.

[13] *Ibid.,* p. 40.

[14] P. T. Young, *Motivation of Behavior,* p. 70. New York: J. Wiley and Sons, Inc., 1936.

[15] *Ibid.,* p. 77.

[16] *Ibid.,* p. 78.

are three elements to be considered: the drive or the fundamental power; the incentive and the motive. These elements may be considered from another point of view.

What Young calls drive or energy may correspond to the fundamental and dynamic powers with which the vitalist is concerned. For Young this power is reducible to physical energy. The true vitalist cannot accept this, not merely because it is contrary to his philosophical convictions but also because it has never been experimentally verified. Vital activity is reducible to some vital principle or entelechia which prevades the organism and constitutes it as dynamic. The incentive of which the author speaks might correspond with the specific object of the basic vital powers of the organism. How, then, does motivation fit into this picture?

To understand the proper place of motivation it is necessary to consider the following distinction. One must accept the distinction between the end of the task and the end of the agent. Any particular activity may be viewed from two aspects: the action itself has some natural termination and the person acting has some goal. Eating is the natural objective of hunger; seeing is the natural end of the capacity to see; thinking is the natural end of intellectual activity. Beyond this there is a goal which may be set up by the agent; there is some purpose which the agent has in undertaking this task. In the first instance one may speak of a general goal-oriented behavior. Every activity of every living thing has some goal in this sense. In the second instance the goal is one established by the agent and it may or may not be the same as the natural termination of the task itself. Furthermore, it may or may not be present and it may or may not be conscious.

No psychologist has ever been able to prove that the mouse can have its own formulated goal. The mouse does not say that "I shall seek the food because it will keep me alive," or "I shall run the maze so that my experimenter can get his Ph.D." The burden of proof would be upon those psychologists who would imply or maintain such a notion. The human subject, however, can do precisely this. He may establish his own goal. For example, the end of the task in the problem, "What is 2 times 2?" is the correct answer, "4." But the end of the agent performing this task can be one or many things. It may be "4"; it may be the good will of the instructor; it may be avoidance of punishment; it may be some form of recognition or satisfaction. It may be any goal which the human agent is capable of establishing. This *why* of the agent is properly and strictly the motive. Depending on this motive the exertion of the fundamental power is affected to a greater or lesser extent, but the power is not made *vital* by the motive nor is it necessarily *activated* by the motive. The motive could actually inhibit the activity. The fact is that the power is already dynamic; its activity, then, may be explained by its own nature, or by its object, or by the motive.

Students of animal behavior can offer absolutely no information on the nature of behavior under motivational conditions. The rodent that avoids the charged entrance and seeks the food through the shockless door cannot have a motive. One does not need motivation in order to explain this activity and according to

Morgan's canon, which presumably every psychologist accepts, one should not explain in terms of higher processes what is explicable in terms of lower processes. In the typical situation the rodent is hungry; it is presumably aware of its hunger. It can also sense food. Likewise, it feels the electric shock. One does not need to resort to any other elements except sensory memory and sensory discrimination to explain the associations which are eventually made. As long as the hunger persists the association may be formed by mere repetition. The only motives that can possibly be measured in a situation like this are those of the experimenter who works patiently with these animals.

In a similar situation a man would act quite differently. Because he can bring insight to bear on the situation the learning is much easier and more rapid. But more important, he is capable of very different behavior than an animal. He may refuse to run the maze. The whole of experimental work on animals is based on the fact that if hungry they will invariably seek the food. Unlike the animal, man may say: "I shall seek the food in order to remain alive," or "I will seek the food in order that the experimenter may learn more about behavior," or even, "I shall not seek the food despite the fact that I am quite hungry." He can, then, set up his own goal and thereby establish a motive for an activity which is already explicable in terms of his dynamic nature.

Man alone is capable of formulating motives and these are clearly distinct from the fundamental abilities or "energies" which they may affect. Ultimately, motivation comes down to an act of the will, an intention which the agent has in undertaking some activity. There are several interesting experiments in the literature which will shed more light on this matter and help in formulating a clearer understanding of a concept that has, for such a long time, been a source of tremendous confusion.

Role of the Will in Learning

There are several interesting studies in the literature concerned with the intention to learn. Woodworth, for example, reports the following study. He prepared a list of twenty pairs of unrelated words. Adults were instructed to learn the list so that they might give the second term when the first was called. In 74 per cent of the cases, the recall was made after the first terms was indicated by the experimenter. Without further instruction, the second term was presented and the subjects were asked to give the first term. In only 7 per cent of the cases was any response made.[17]

Poppelreuter conducted the following experiment. Giving a list of nonsense syllables to several groups he instructed some to read them and others to learn them. Those who were told to read them could not give a perfect recitation although they had the same opportunity to learn them as the second group. He

[17] R. S. Woodworth, "Revision of Imageless Thought," *Psychological Review,* XXII (January, 1915), 18.

reports that in his own case he was unable to give a perfect recitation after fifty readings but when he determined to learn them twelve readings sufficed.[18]

It would be foolish to say that there is no learning without some act of the will. This would be contrary to the evidence gained not only from experimental work with animals but also from a great many studies made with human subjects. One's own experience would contradict this for many things are remembered when there is no intention to learn and even when there is a deliberate intention not to learn. Nevertheless the intention to learn is important in learning and the amount of learning is usually in direct proportion to the intention of the learner.

All things being equal man learns to the degree that he intends to learn. But when a man intends to learn there must be some reason for it. This reason, as previously explained, is the motive. The motive, however, is important not only because it is directly related to the learning but also because the reasons which a person has when he acts are of fundamental importance. Before considering the importance of the motives in themselves it will be helpful to see how they affect learning. Certain studies give the information needed.

Experimental Studies in Motivation

The studies made by Hurlock in this area have long been accepted as outstanding. Three of her works are of special interest and they will be reviewed here for the information which they give on the problem at hand.

One of Hurlock's earliest studies was based on an examination of children's performances on intelligence tests under various motivational conditions.[19] Two forms of the same test were used. After the first test the students were equated and grouped. The following tabulation reveals the results of the second testing in terms of per cent gained or lost under the conditions indicated:

Group	Per cent gained	Per cent same	Per cent losing
Control	49.5	10.9	39.6
Praised	79.1	3.3	17.6
Reproved	79.1	6.6	14.3

As one examines the data cited several factors apparently call for consideration. First, it may be assumed that the two forms of the test employed were actually equivalent and if not, no particular group enjoyed any special advantage. Moreover, practice does not account for all the improvement as can be seen by comparing the controlled and experimental groups. There is no question of

[18] W. Poppelreuter, "Nachweiss der Unzwechmassigkeit die gebrauchlichen Assoziationsexperimente mit sinnlosen Silben nach dem Erlernungs—und Trefferverfahren zur exakten Gewinnung elementarer Reproduktionsgesetze zu verwerden," *Zeitschrift fur Psychologie*, LXI (January, 1912), 14.

[19] E. B. Hurlock, "The Effects of Incentives upon the Constancy of the I.Q.," *Pedagogical Seminary*, XXXII (September, 1925), 422-435.

adaptation to testing, special techniques, nor instructional methods involved. The instructional and motivational value of a single reproof or a single commendation is apparently about the same, although it will be pointed out subsequently that frequent reproof has quite a different effect. Both the praised and the reproved groups make the same marked improvement. There is, then, something happening within the framework of reproving and praising that stimulates the student to greater effort.

Another of Hurlock's studies, frequently quoted in the literature on motivation, gives even better opportunity to examine the improvement due to certain motivating conditions. Presented below are the means achieved by the four groups participating in the study after each of five testings: [20]

Group	Means				
	Test 1	Test 2	Test 3	Test 4	Test 5
I Control	11.81	12.34	11.65	10.50	11.35
II Praised	11.81	16.59	18.85	18.81	20.22
III Reproved	11.85	16.59	14.30	13.25	14.19
IV Ignored	11.84	14.19	13.30	12.92	12.38

After equating all groups, the control group was separated from the others. The three remaining groups were placed in the same classroom. In the presence of their classmates some were reproved while others were praised. The third group was merely ignored although they witnessed both the reproof and the praise of their classmates. The results of the five tests were then calculated and are indicated above. Hurlock pointed out certain specific trends. Older children, for example were more responsive to all forms of stimulation; boys made greater improvement than girls when ignored or praised; praise seemed more effective with those of lower ability while the bright responded more to reproof. Generally the brighter students showed greater improvement than the slower students.

It will be noted that the control group shows slight improvement only on the second test after which the mean remains steady. The results indicated are not due to mere practice and obviously the motivating conditions employed are the important and decisive factor.

It is interesting to note that at the second testing the praised and reproved groups are identical. This situation was noted on the previous study cited. Subsequently, however, the two groups become clearly distinct and this fact suggests that continual reproof has a negative effect on learning. The reason for this is not immediately apparent. The studies made by Child and Adelsheim [21] as well at

[20] E. B. Hurlock, "An Evaluation of Certain Incentives Used in School Work," *Journal of Educational Psychology*, XVI (March, 1925), 145-159.
[21] E. L. Child, and E. Adelsheim, "Motivational Value of Barriers for Children," *Journal of Genetic Psychology*, LXV (September, 1944), 97-111.

that of Zander [22] suggest that continual reproof causes frustration. Human nature demands success and continual reproof militates against this basic need. Although reproof may be effective in some instances the use of continual reproof defeats the very purpose for which it is intended.

The ignored group shows some improvement at the second testing although it is not as marked as that reported for the praised and reproved groups. From that point, however, there is a continual drop in the means of the ignored group. Continued disinterest leaves its mark. It should be obvious that the children in this group were not doing the work which they were capable of doing.

Generally, then, praise is the most effective of those conditions used in this study. Reproof has some value but if used continually the effect is negative. Likewise, ignored children do not work up to their capacity and show only slight improvement over the control group.

It should be noted that these conclusions are based on group data and that they do not always obtain in cases of certain personality types. For example, Hunnicutt and Thompson demonstrated that introverts who were praised did better than introverts who were reproved.[23] Likewise, extroverts who were reproved did much better than extroverts who were praised or introverts who were reproved. Moreover, individual differences must be considered in this area of school work as in all others and "there is no known formula or infallible set of procedures to motivate all pupils all the time," [24] or all pupils in the same way.

Competition as a Motivating Condition

Hurlock has also used group rivalry as a means of motivating children. In one particular study, the experimental group was subdivided into various competitive sub-groups.[25] Each was given its own score as well as the scores of competing groups and was told that everyone had the same chance to win. At the end of the experiment, all the scores of the sub-groups were combined and compared with those of the sub-groups of the control group.

The investigator concluded that students of low ability showed greater improvement under competitive conditions than did those of high ability. Likewise, the sub-group scoring lowest on the first day never surpassed those having initial success. Girls responded more favorably to this form of motivation than boys. Certainly the data derived from this experiment clearly indicate that competition is an effective form of motivation.

[22] A. F. Zander, "A Study of Experimental Frustration," *Psychological Monograph,* LVI, No. 3, 1-38. Evanston, Ill.: American Psychological Association, 1944.

[23] G. G. Thompson and C. W. Hunnicutt, "Effect of Repeated Praise or Blame on the Work Achievement of Introverts and Extroverts," *Journal of Educational Psychology,* XXXV (May, 1944), 257-266.

[24] E. R. Hilgard and D. H. Russell, "Motivation in School Learning," *Learning and Instruction,* p. 37. Forty-Ninth Yearbook of the National Society for the Study of Education, Part I. Edited by Nelson B. Henry. Chicago: University of Chicago Press, 1950.

[25] E. B. Hurlock, "The Use of Group Rivalry as an Incentive," *Journal of Abnormal and Social Psychology,* XXII (October, 1927), 278-290.

Sim's report on the effects of competition in three equated groups gives another interesting insight into this technique.[26] The control group made only slight progress. The second group was subdivided into competing sections. Each was told its own scores as well as those of the competing section. The improvement made was significantly better than that of the control group. In the last group the subjects were paired and each informed of his own and his partner's progress. Here the percentage of improvement was considerably greater than that reported for the first and second groups.

Competition is an effective technique to motivate children as the research indicates. Individual competition is more effective than group competition but some authors suggest that it be used cautiously. It can, they warn, give rise to undesirable behavior and attitudes and cannot be universally applied. A form of self-competition or self-appraisal is free of these disadvantages. A child can always do better than his past record and a system of self-appraisal can be easily employed in any area. Such a system would also be more in accord with the fact of individual differences.

These motivating conditions that have been studied by experimentalists do affect the learning. Praise, reproof, and competition gives the student some reason for exerting himself and to use, to a greater extent, the abilities which he possesses. The important question that remains to be considered is this: why is it that such conditions do affect the learning in this way? The answer seems to be that a motive may have a two-fold role: first, it may be informational, and secondly it has a peculiar relation to the human subject.

The Informational Role of Motives

There can be no doubt that motives have a profound influence on the learner. The studies indicated above clearly show that under certain motivational conditions marked improvement is evident in the work of students who under ordinary conditions simply do not improve significantly. In each study the groups are equated and therefore have the same potentialities. The control group shows little or no progress while those working under various motivating conditions show marked improvement. No doubt studies of this sort have given rise to the axiom that "motivation is the basis of all learning." The statement as it stands cannot be accepted. It ignores certain other fundamental conditions involved in the learning process and also clouds the proper nature of the motive itself. In the same way, Young's statement that "the study of motivation is an attempt to explain all actions" [27] and the remark in the Forty-Ninth Yearbook of the National Society for the Study of Education that "motivation is an inner state of need

[26] V. M. Sims, "The Relative Influence of Two Types of Motivation on Improvement," *Journal of Educational Psychology*, XIX (October, 1928), 480-484.

[27] P. T. Young, "Motivation," *Encyclopedia of Educational Research*, p. 755. New York: Macmillan Co., 1950.

and is a necessary condition if the learner is to engage in learning activity" [28] confuse the meaning of motivation.

The motivating conditions that have been cited affect learning in two ways. Usually, the motives employed give definite information which is just as important for progress in learning as the motive itself. There is, so to speak, a heads and tails in most of the conditions that have been employed in research work. Reward or praise, reproof or punishment, are not only motivating but also give information which the child needs if he is to improve. When the child is praised he knows that what he has done is correct. This assurance is equivalent to telling him that he should repeat the performance which he just gave. Telling him that he is wrong has a similar effect. The information which he gains from reproof is not as helpful as that which comes from praise. It tells him that what he did was wrong and that he should attempt something else. In each instance, however, it gives some information which directs to a greater or lesser degree his subsequent attempts. This information is quite distinct from the purpose of the motive itself. In other words, most of the motives employed in the studies cited are actually fulfilling a dual role: they give the child some reason for acting and also give information which he needs in order to succeed. The two are not convertible. A motive may or may not give information, but in the strict definition of the term it does not have to give information. Likewise, information may or may not motivate.

Research workers have not always understood this fact; there are many studies cited in the literature on motivation which show that this confusion exists. For example, Trowbridge and Cason repeated one of Thorndike's line drawing experiments.[29] They used four groups which may be identified by the different degrees of information which each received. The groups and the results in terms of percentage of average error are as follows:

Group	Average error
Control (merely drew line; no information given)	. . . .6.45
Nonsense (after each performance the experimenter called some nonsense syllable)	. . . .8.62
Right-Wrong (after each performance the subject was told whether he was right or wrong)	. . . .5.51
Exact Information (subject was told that he was right or wrong and if wrong the precise information on the direction of the error was given)	. . . .1.32

[28] G. L. Anderson and A. I. Gates, "The General Nature of Learning," *Learning and Instruction,* p. 16. Forty-Ninth Yearbook of the National Society for the Study of Education, Part I. Edited by Nelson B. Henry. Chicago: University of Chicago Press, 1950.

[29] M. H. Trowbridge and H. Cason, "An Experimental Study of Thorndike's Theory of Learning," *Journal of General Psychology,* VII (October, 1932), 245-258.

Hamilton,[30] and Book and Norvell [31] report similar studies. In all such studies the dominating and decisive factor is the informational one. No doubt there is some motivation at work but it is a variable which has not been controlled. The experimenters have made an unwarranted assumption that information and motivation are convertible. Nevertheless, an examination of such studies throws considerable light on the learning process and the role of the motive in learning.

There are several factors that must be considered. Doubtlessly, in the learning situation, the fundamental factor is the ability of the student as it is conditioned by his background of experience. Beyond this, however, the student must know what to do. The experiment cited above clearly indicates that there is a direct relation between the degree of information given and progress in the task. Furthermore, there is the motive, the reason for undertaking the task, and this is another condition of learning. It is difficult to distinguish the net contribution of these elements in practice for these are all interwoven in an intricate network in the learning situation. Man, after all, is a unit and in the learning situation brings to bear all his abilities upon the task at hand. He must be able to perform the task; he must know how to do it, and he must want to do it. Certain motivating conditions may give a reason for undertaking the task and also give the student the information he needs to proceed successfully, but these elements are clearly distinct.

The motive, then, is not the basis of all learning. It is certainly an important factor in learning and there is a marked relation between the motive and improvement, other factors being present. Considered from this point of view, that is, insofar as it gives the student a reason for acting, it is of great importance. But there is another viewpoint. The aim of the school should not be improvement at any price as if the motive itself were relatively unimportant except as it contributes to success. On the contrary, the motive itself is of basic importance. It is important to know why students act and it is important that they act with the best of motives. This may be best understood by recalling certain fundamental philosophic concepts. In this way the nature of the motive will be more clearly understood and its implication more easily determined.

Why the Motive Works

All nature is ordered toward that which is good. This is true of the animate and the inanimate world. The sun, earth, and stars work together in indescribable exactness and with a precision that amazes the greatest students of the universe. All things truly work together for good. So it is in the animate world. The plant grows, flowers, and bears fruit according to the imponderable laws of nature. In the higher forms, the sentient beings, this propensity toward the good appears in another way: the sensitive appetite. This is an organic power which animals have

[30] H. C. Hamilton, "The Effects of Incentives on Accuracy of Discrimination Measured on the Galton Bar," *Archives of Psychology*, XVI (March, 1929), 1-73.
[31] W. F. Book and L. Norvell, "The Will to Learn," *Pedagogical Seminary*, XXIV (December, 1922), 305-362.

to seek the good as it is apprehended by the senses. The brute seeks food when hungry and flees when in danger. It always seeks that which is good. In man, a higher form of this propensity is found. Beyond the sensitive appetite there is in man an intellectual appetite or the power of seeking the known good. This power is the will. Man cannot and will not seek anything except the good. And this voluntary pursuit of the good, the act of wanting what is good and acting because of it, is characteristic of intelligent creatures. It is the good perceived in the object that moves the will and constitutes the motive.

The child may do his problems because he wants to get out of school on time, or because he wants to be recognized or praised, or to show up his fellow students, or simply because he likes problems. Whatever the immediate reason may be, and despite the fact that these may be classified as attitudes or sets or interests, the basic reason is that these are goods and therefore the child strives after them.

All things in reality are good as they come from God and as they participate to some degree in the infinite essence of God. At the culmination of all these goods in reality is the ultimate and complete source of all goodness: God Himself. This the child must appreciate and so the problem of developing within him the habit of seeking the good is of paramount importance. This habit of seeking the good is known in Catholic terminology as a moral virtue. It is a habit of prime importance especially in those schools whose philosophy accepts God as the ultimate good and whose pledged purpose is to cultivate the moral virtues.

Consequently, the reason why a child acts is as important as the act itself when considered from this viewpoint. The whole area of motives must be understood in this broader sense if this lofty aim is to be accomplished. And although the aim is lofty it is by no means impossible. If it is to be attained certain facts must be kept in mind.

The will is an appetite which follows the action of the intellect. The good which the will seeks is that which is known. Before it can be expected that the child will seek a good he must first understand it. It is clearly the province of the school, along with other educational agencies, to communicate such understanding. For unless he understands the good he will not seek it. The objection that is usually raised at this point is: why does the child prefer to stay in bed when he could be at Mass? or why does he play when he should be studying? There are several facts which must be considered in answering this question.

St. Thomas tells us that if any object is perceived as totally good from every aspect, the will necessarily strives after it. But any object which may be perceived as evil under any aspect is not necessarily desired.[32] The simple fact is that the will is free. That is why the habit of eliciting the good must be developed. The moral virtue is this persistent tendency to select the good. It is not enough that the child knows the good, although this is of fundamental importance, but the good known must be accepted by the will as a good, and, further, the will must be habituated toward the selection of the right goods. Since it is true, then, that it is the child who wills, and freely wills, it follows that the moral virtues cannot

[32] St. Thomas Aquinas, *Summa Theologiae*, I-II, 10, 2, resp.

be taught directly. There are, however, certain things which can and should be done.

The first thing which the school must do is to give the child an intellectual understanding of the good. This it accomplishes through its curriculum. He must be shown that certain objects are always good and others are always bad. Further, he must understand that there is a hierarchy of goods. In the example given above, sleeping, Mass, studying, and play are all goods but of different orders. Sleeping and playing are goods of the physical order; studying is a good of the intellectual order; Mass is a good of the supernatural order. The child must be brought to an understanding that the physical is to be subordinated to the intellectual as the latter is to be subordinated to the supernatural. All this is within the province of the school.

But it does not follow that simply because the child knows the good or even the hierarchy of goods that he will necessarily choose what he should. It is not merely a question of intellectual understanding although this is an indispensable phase in the whole process of cultivating the moral virtue. There must be an acceptance by the will of the known good and the known hierarchy of goods as there must be a habituation of the will to strive after these goods. After all, one can know what he is to do and still not do it. The problem, therefore, is to present the good motive and induce the child, by understanding, example, urgings, and the like, to act in the presence of such motives. In attaining this objective, certain psychological facts will be helpful.

Those principles which are basic to human learning are to be observed here. The child cannot go from nothing to the most perfect and complete motive in one bold leap. Therefore, he must not be asked to begin with the most complete motive of all. Just as in arithmetic one does not begin with the number concepts but deals with concrete objects and sets the framework within which the concepts may develop, so also with motives the first step must be with the particular and the concrete. It must not stop here. Gradually more general motives should replace the specific motives until the most complete and universal of all is attained.

It may be that there is a tendency to leap too far too soon. Motives must be developed gradually and with due respect for the nature and experiential background of the child. If the will is to accept something as good, then it must be something that is meaningful to the child: he must be able to understand it. It may be that some have not developed the habit of eliciting the really good, not because they were not told what it is, nor because they were not urged to embrace it, but because they were told it before they could understand and appreciate it.

So while it is true that the moral virtues cannot be taught directly, it is equally true that they cannot emerge accidentally. What the school can do is quite clear. It can communicate an understanding of the good and of the hierarchy of goods which exists. Furthermore, it can set before the child the correct motives for acting and urge him to act in the presence of such motives. And this it can do best by considering the experiential background of the child and by planning a framework wherein this can be accomplished. Certainly this should receive as much consideration in the curriculum as other phases of the program.

The motive may not be the basis of all learning but it is certainly a very important factor in learning both as a means to improvement and as an outcome. It is important to be concerned with the work children do but it is equally important to be heedful of the motives they have in working. It is a tremendous task which the Catholic teacher has undertaken but it has been made all the more feasible through God's grace which works through the teacher and the child.

Throughout, nothing has been said of the moral virtues from a supernatural viewpoint. Such was not intended to leave the impression that this phase is unimportant. Obviously it is the most important aspect. But the moral virtues have been considered at the natural level with a view to considering the psychological and philosophical implications. It is hoped that this information will be of some help to the classroom teacher, especially at the elementary level, where the process of developing proper motives must begin.

Mental hygiene in the classroom

Alexander A. Schneiders

Dr. Schneiders builds his discussion around the premise that teachers contribute most to mental hygiene when they do their principal work well. Confusion of roles on the teacher's part may not only affect his own mental health—it may also have a detrimental influence on students. In other words, the teacher is an instructor, not a moral master or a therapist. Yet the primacy of responsibility should not obscure the fact that schools and teachers must be educational agencies and agents in the complete sense and not mere dispensers of intellectual culture. But even as dispensers of intellectual culture, the author insists, teachers can and do exert powerful influences on students' mental health.

Some Basic Concepts

As every educator knows, there has existed for many years a strong tendency, in secondary schools as well as colleges and universities, to integrate mental hygiene principles with classroom procedures. This tendency is due to several things, but especially to the growth of mental hygiene in the past 50 years, the increasing emphasis on adjustment that goes far beyond the traditional concepts of intellectual and moral development, and to the dubious ambition of some educators to convert the classroom into a counseling or even a therapeutic situation.

Needless to say, this projection of the principles and practices of mental health and adjustment into the teaching situation has been regarded with con-

Reprinted with permission from *The Catholic Counselor*, 4:96–103, September, 1960.

siderable skepticism and outright opposition by many educators who feel that the essential purpose of education is to develop the person intellectually, and perhaps morally, with small regard for other aspects of development. As Jacques Barzun says in his brilliant essay, *The House of Intellect*, "Thus the school is not to teach, but to cure; body and mind are not to use for self-forgetful ends but to dwell with narcissus' adoring anxiety; the arts not to give joy and light, but to be scanned for a 'diagnosis' of some trouble, a solution of some 'problem,' or else exploited for the common good in occupational therapy; . . . ." (23–24) In this brief comment Barzun epitomizes with striking clarity the distaste of many educators for the indiscriminate mingling of the teaching art with the art of healing. Because of these differences in viewpoint, we need to clarify our terms very carefully and see exactly how the principles of mental hygiene can fit into the classroom situation without doing violence to the business of teaching.

First of all, let me clarify my own position in regard to the relationship between teaching, mental hygiene, and counseling. Personally, I do not at all subscribe to the idea that the classroom can be converted into a counseling or therapeutic situation. The primary and essential business of a college or university is to teach, and therefore to promote intellectual growth. Through this growth, the individual should mature spiritually, morally, and socially. If he also matures emotionally, so much the better; but it is not the business of higher education to utilize the classroom situation for the purpose of emotional development. The classroom and the clinic, the couch and the lectern are distinct entities whose purposes and functions belong to different aspects of human service. For much the same reason, I do not subscribe to the blunt and unqualified introduction of mental hygiene into college teaching.

However, there is some justification for the use of certain principles of mental hygiene in classroom instruction, without doing violence to the essential purpose of the teaching art. In the development of this thesis, let me first of all define what I mean by mental health and mental hygiene. Unfortunately, mental health is often regarded from a negative viewpoint. Writers in the field are prone to say that mental health is the absence of symptoms of disabling behavior, of behavior that brings the individual into conflict with society, with morality, or with other standards of behavior. In this view, mental health means that the person is not beset with doubts, uncertainties, inferiority, hostility, insecurity, and the like. This, obviously, is a very negative approach.

Let us try to develop a more positive approach. If any one of us were asked "What is physical health?", I think that we could give a pretty good definition of what physical health is. I do not think that we would say that it's the absence of pneumonia, the reduction of fatigue, or the absence of brain pathology. We would instead give it a positive connotation. The concept of mental health can be presented in the same way. Essentially, it is a quality of the individual human organism by which he is able to organize his mental life, his behavior, and his feelings in such a way as to be, or become, a productive human being. Mental health generates organization, efficiency, productivity, creativity, and a host of other qualities such as security and self-confidence, that leave little or no room for disabling symptoms, crippling feelings, or personality disorganization.

Here at least we see a close relationship between mental health and learning in the college situation. If a student does not possess mental health, if he is mentally disturbed or emotionally unbalanced, the teacher will soon find it out. The student often acts in an unusual or bizarre fashion so as to disturb the classroom situation. His attitude toward the teacher often indicates that there is something basically wrong. Such a student finds it hard to concentrate and to study, and therefore he cannot learn efficiently. All such contingencies interfere with productive and efficient student effort. In this type of situation we encounter a very tangible reason why mental hygiene should be brought into, and in some way integrated with, the college situation. We know from broad experience that the lack of mental health often interferes with student performance, and the best antidote to mental disturbance is mental hygiene.

Mental Health versus Adjustment

One distinction that is important here is that between mental health and adjustment. In recent years there has been considerable objection raised to the intrusion of the concept of adjustment into the teaching situation. Writers of books and articles who are critical of contemporary educational procedures insist that students are not getting the education they require or that the students in other countries are getting, because we have forsaken the intrinsic goals of education and have worshipped too long at the shrine of Professor Dewey for whom the adjustment of the child was the all-important task of education.

Many persons are critical of this adjustment-oriented education; and while I personally do not agree that adjustment is a bad concept, I do think that we have to examine our concepts and our procedures regarding education very carefully in the light of recent objections. Certainly, if we were to organize our educational process in such a way that the ideal of adjustment would replace the idea of sound intellectual growth, we would have taken a perilous step backward into the dark ages of education. Whether the Catholic educational system is as much a victim of this philosophy of education as are non-Catholic schools is doubtful. The Catholic school is more bound to tradition and does not accede readily to the progressive, modern point of view just because it is progressive and modern. The Church-related school moves much more slowly, and may therefore bounce back much more quickly with a better program of education when this becomes necessary to the common welfare.

The difficulty with injecting adjustment into the educational process is not necessarily characteristic of mental hygiene, because mental health and adjustment are not the same thing. Mental hygiene is the application of sound psychological principles in a way to promote mental health. It is basically prophylactic rather than corrective or therapeutic. And in a number of ways it is possible to utilize hygiene principles without getting involved with the problem of adjustment. Mental hygiene in the classroom means simply the direct or indirect application of principles of mental health to the student and to student relationships in a way to preclude the development of undesirable and inefficient methods of thinking, feeling, or behaving. And, as we shall see, there are many ways in which these principles can be used without in any way interfering with the proper aims of education, and often in a way to promote these aims. These possibilities we will explore in the following pages.

The Primary Role of the Teacher

The first task that we must confront directly is the role of the teacher in college. What is he supposed to do? Is it his job to acquaint himself with and utilize concepts of mental hygiene in his work? Obviously, if the role of the teacher precludes the use of mental hygiene principles, then the issue is settled, since we should not inject anything into the teaching process that would undermine or disrupt this role. This role confusion is exactly what happens to many teachers and even to parents. They begin as teachers and end up as counselors or therapists. Fathers often undermine their role by trying to play different parts, and not doing any one of them very successfully. Many persons fail as fathers and mothers because they do not know what their proper role is, or they refuse to accept it, and thus disrupt proper relationships with the children.

The primary role of the teacher is as a custodian of truth and a purveyor of knowledge. If a teacher fails to fulfill this role, he is not a real teacher. And this role has little to do, at least directly, with mental health. A second aspect of teaching comes closer to mental hygiene principles. Beyond communication of knowledge, the teacher acts as a stimulant to his students and as a source of inspiration for total development. In this instance, a teacher's effort goes beyond the student's intellect and moves toward his will, and also toward his emotions, his social life and other aspects of development. This type of teacher is the one classically referred to as "inspiring," one who has always been held up as a model and an ideal for other teachers to emulate. Certainly the teacher should, by his behavior in class, by his principles and ideals, and by his relationships with others, inspire the students with whom he comes into contact, and thus contribute importantly toward the total development of the student. In enacting this role, the teacher is using mental hygiene principles of the highest order.

Thirdly, whether he likes it or not, the teacher functions *in loco parentis*. And this role is very important from the mental hygiene point of view. The teacher is a male figure with whom the student can identify, and often he is a father figure to the student. In some instances, he even spends more time with the student than does the boy's real father. If, in addition to teaching, he engages in faculty advising or counseling, he may develop a much more intimate, basic relationship with the student than do the parents themselves.

Relationships of this sort often begin in the classroom, and are developed further as the student reaches toward an authority figure with whom he can identify and to whom he can take his conflicts and difficulties. Through the medium of such relationships, the teacher lays the groundwork for promoting personality growth and character development. No teacher sets out with a clear-cut, definitive goal aimed at character-formation. He does not start out with the proposition that "These boys need character and I am going to see that they get it," but willy-nilly he is a molder of character. Character is intimately related to will, to the emotions, and to the intellect; and in some respects the teacher is concerned with all these facets of personality. Thus, as the custodian of truth, and the purveyor of knowledge, the teacher often develops in the classroom certain basic principles that underlie the social, moral, and theological virtues, and in that way clearly affects the shaping of individual character.

Finally, the teacher often becomes an ideal for the student, and this has important implications for mental hygiene. This does not mean that the student should emulate the teacher vocationally, but rather that he may emulate the teacher as a person; and there are countless students whose lives have been enriched and perfected in degree by reason of the teachers with whom they have come in contact. This influence of the teacher-ideal is mental hygiene of the best kind. It is immeasurably better than defining or repeating ethical principles, reading a text book on mental health, or listening to a lecture on how to be mentally healthy. The teacher who functions as a worthwhile ideal for the student will unconsciously and indeliberately promote mental health without ever intending to do so.

The Teacher and Mental Hygiene

This brief description of the teacher's role brings us to the point at issue regarding the teacher and mental hygiene. As a mental hygiene person, the teacher can serve as a model of wholesome adjustment, of self-discipline, and of respect for the integrity and dignity of others. If the teacher is a well-adjusted person in the best sense of this term, his performance in the classroom is stable and well-organized, he isn't excitable, he doesn't go to pieces over student rebellion or misbehavior; and he isn't fighting with the dean or with other faculty members. The well-adjusted person likes his work, he derives personal satisfaction from teaching, and he gets along with the students. As a discipline person, he knows how to play his role effectively as a teacher, and how to develop healthy interpersonal relationships. In this way the teacher can exert a great deal of influence on his students and help to promote their mental health.

Farnsworth expresses this same idea when he says that learning to conduct oneself with credit, satisfaction, and effectiveness, is enormously complicated, but

> Exposure to and identification with persons who are emotionally mature is probably the most effective method of hastening one's own acquisition of mature attitudes. Hence, if a college takes seriously the task of teaching its students about emotions in such a way as to promote their own maturity, the

faculty members will have as much or more influence because of what they are than because of what they know. A program for a proper understanding of the emotions is not one which affects the students alone, but instead concerns every person involved in the educational institution. (Farnsworth, 1957, 191)

Here, then, we have a clear-cut definition of the way in which a teacher can play a definite role in implementing mental hygiene, even though he has never read a book on the subject, and may not know what you are talking about when you discuss mental hygiene in the classroom. In fact, he may not even be particularly interested, and yet promote the mental health of students by being this kind of a person.

Looking for a moment at the negative side of this picture, we can get a clearer perspective on the mental hygiene attitude. Everyone is acquainted with the teacher who exemplifies in his behavior and his attitudes the reverse of mental health. They run the gamut from hostility to prejudice, from favoritism to suspiciousness, and from lack of self-confidence to chronic dissatisfaction. Their classroom behavior and their out-of-class relationships replete with anger and blaming, unfairness, inferiority, disdain for the teaching profession and for authority, chronic frustration, racial biases, anti-clerical attitudes, lack of organization, lack of humor, or projection of personal inadequacies. All of us have seen teachers who exemplify one or another or a combination of these characteristics. Such a teacher will destroy the possibility of mental hygiene in the classroom. Such qualities stand out most sharply in the teacher who actively dislikes young people, or is ashamed of or disdainful of his own profession. In their dealings with youngsters they are impatient, hostile, sarcastic, and intolerant of any interference with established routine. In such instances, it is obvious that the teacher cannot play the role of a healthy, well-adjusted, self-disciplined authority person.

From counseling theory and practice, we learn how important it is to be accepting and permissive with other persons; to create a warm, healthy atmosphere in which learning can take place most effectively; to act in such a way as to foster healthy interpersonal relationships. These principles need not be limited to the counseling situation, but can be carried over into the classroom in order to stimulate the kind of learning and growth for which the classroom is primarily intended.

Here would be a good place to mention also the mental hygiene value of discipline. A good teacher maintains sound, healthy discipline in the classroom, and here we see a direct relationship to mental hygiene since discipline is essential to mental health. In order to define this relationship adequately, we have to think of discipline in the right way. We must not confuse discipline with techniques of discipline. This confusion is the reason why many persons think of discipline in terms of punishment. But punishment and other techniques for the control or modification of behavior must be carefully distinguished from discipline itself.

Essentially, discipline is the *establishment of order*. For the person it is the ordering of his life, and in the classroom it is bringing order into what could easily be a chaotic situation. Here we see why the *method* of discipline can be directly opposed to discipline itself. If one punishes a child or a student in class harshly, because of hostility, anxiety, or inferiority, etc., with little regard for justice, he is not achieving order, and therefore is not achieving discipline. If, because of the method used, the student quits school, hurts or injures someones in his rage, or fails in his subjects, discipline fails completely. Thus the methods of discipline, so-called, are often opposed to discipline itself since they fail to bring order into a person's life.

This is one thing that the teacher can do for students—to teach them discipline and order whenever opportunity arises. Order in the classroom, in submitting assignments, in the writing of assignments, in relation with others in the classroom, and in their thinking, are all facets of a healthy, logical development; and this is discipline of a high type. Discipline conceived in this way is an essential part of mental hygiene. As a disciplinarian, therefore, but not in any sense as a punitive person, a teacher can play a basic role in furthering mental hygiene. What is more, he does so naturally, without particular regard for textbooks in the field, special treatises on mental hygiene, etc. And all the time promoting the total development and mental health of the student. It is for this reason that tardiness, excessive absences, failure to hand in assignments on time, talking in class, and similar behaviors should not be tolerated. They are clear signs of immaturity, and immaturity is diametrically opposed to discipline.

A third way in which mental hygiene concepts and principles can be brought into the classroom without any formal effort is for the teacher to act and to function as a model of achievement and of competence, especially for the superior students. The good teacher, by reason of his knowledge, his personal achievement, his competence as a teacher, and his enthusiasm for his subject matter, for his profession, and for the acquisition and development of truth, can inspire the better student to higher and higher levels of achievement and personal growth. Moreover, the teacher can help the student to define and crystallize important goals and to make positive decisions in line with those goals. This type of influence is mental hygiene in the fullest sense of the term. Every psychologist and counselor knows that mental health and good adjustment are directly dependent upon the ability to achieve, to realize personal potentialities, to actualize oneself, and to establish and work for realizable goals. Whenever a teacher helps students in this way, he is practicing mental hygiene without doing anything more than fulfilling his role as a good teacher.

This basic attitude can be carried further by the dedicated teacher who functions as a confidant or counselor to the student who is not superior, who has trouble of one kind or another, whether this be in the realm of academic effort, disciplinary matters, or emotions that are interfering with self-discipline and performance. Here he can, and often does, bring mental hygiene directly into the classroom situation or into his relationship to his students. The teacher can also develop an alertness to the relationship between personality factors and achievement, regardless of what he does with respect to mental hygine. He should learn to "size up" different students, for example, the chronically tardy student, the aggressive student, the bored student, the absentee student, the argumentative student, the day-dreaming student, etc. All of these factors are related to performance, and the alert teacher should be aware of these things and what they mean.

Finally, the alert teacher can promote the aims of mental hygiene by the use of referral of students to the right counselor. The teacher in the classroom can be alert to signs of trouble, and can often nip a problem in the bud by referring the student to some person on the faculty or on the counseling staff who is particularly skilled in dealing with the kind of problem that the student manifests. When all of these attitudes and procedures are added together, we have a total mental hygiene program for the classroom, that in no way interferes with the primary business of teaching, namely, the intellectual and personal development of the student.

REFERENCES

Farnsworth, D. L. *Mental Health in College and University.* Cambridge, Mass.: Harvard University Press, 1957.

The nature and improvement of students' thinking

Walter B. Kolesnik

**Learning is more than the acquisition of
information. In a fuller sense, it involves the
reorganization of information and the development
of the person's ability to think. The following article
describes the major forms or modes of thinking and
offers some general suggestions for improving the
thought processes. It also touches upon the charge
that Catholic schools are not doing as good a job as
they should in fostering independent thinking in
their students.**

Ask the first 100 teachers you meet if they agree that "teaching students how to think" is one of the most important objectives of the school at any grade level and the chances are that they will all respond in the affirmative. But ask them what thinking is or how the quality of their students' thinking can best be improved and you will probably get 100 different answers, many of them incomplete and some of them contradictory. The purpose of this article is not to provide the final and complete answers to these questions, but to summarize and integrate the views of psychologists and experienced educators on the matter.

First of all, what do we mean by the word *think?* The verb *to think* is popularly employed to designate a variety of mental activities: to recall, to predict, to guess, to believe, to imagine, to associate, to decide or to hope, among others. Thus conceived, *thinking* refers to the stream of images or the sequence of ideas which pass through consciousness rather unsystematically in a manner which is sometimes beyond our control and maybe even against our will. For example,

Reprinted with permission from *The Catholic Educational Review*, 62:231–240, April, 1964.

when I hear the strains of "Adeste Fidelis" I cannot help "thinking" of a complex of events which directly or indirectly are related to Christmas—even though, at the moment, these thoughts may be distracting and I would prefer not to have them.

We shall be using the term in a more restricted sense. For our purposes, thinking may be defined as the deliberate ordering of ideas toward a conclusion; the process of drawing inferences or of discovering concealed relationships; the systematic rearrangement of concepts.

Before proceeding with an analysis of the thinking process and an elaboration on these definitions, let us pause to note that thinking has to do with the ordering or rearrangement of ideas or concepts. But what is an idea or a concept? These two terms may be used interchangeably with either referring to an understanding of what a thing is. One who has a concept of a horse, of justice, of democracy or of God knows what these are. The concept is the fundamental unit of all thought. It is through the process of concept formation, the simplest act of the intellect, that one generalizes and differentiates his experiences and comes to recognize the essential features of objects or situations. These essential features are his concepts.

Concepts emerge from a group or pattern of sensory experiences. One who perceives and remembers a number of objects eventually comes to recognize that they are in some ways alike and in other ways different from one another. Concepts are formed through a process of abstracting these similarities and differences. Accidental qualities and unnecessary details are stripped away, leaving only the essential features of the object. Thus the concept "horse" applies to every creature of a certain type, regardless of size, color, breed or other specific characteristics. A concept, in short, is a universal idea which applies to all objects of a particular class and distinguishes the object from those in other classes. Before one can begin to think about horses—or democracy or carburetors or chromosomes—he must know what these are.

Every concept is abstract in the sense that it is abstracted from sensory experience. But some ideas are of situations or qualities which never have been and never can be directly present to the senses. These are referred to as abstract ideas to distinguish them from those which are palpable, but they are formed in essentially the same manner as concrete ideas. For example, from a number of situations in which people have been seen to act in a certain way, the common element in their behavior is abstracted and given a name, such as justice or courtesy or independence.

Concepts are arranged or structured or ordered in different ways for different purposes. Thus, it is possible to distinguish among different forms or modes of thinking. Although there is considerable overlapping among them and they are not separate and distinct or mutually exclusive processes, we shall consider three of the main forms: reasoning, critical thinking and problem-solving.

Reasoning is the basic form of thinking in which concepts are reorganized in such a way that a new meaning or understanding emerges from previously established knowledge. The term *inference* is often used to designate this process—or, more accurately, these processes, for there are two main forms of reasoning. Deduction is reasoning from the general to the particular; induction, from the particular to the general. It is by means of induction that laws or rules or generalizations are established; by deduction these generalizations are applied to particular instances.

Deductive reasoning is syllogistic. In the syllogism three concepts, such as *birds, Dickie* and *the ability to fly* are arranged in such a way that a conclusion which had been previously hidden or implicit is made explicit:

> All birds can fly.
> Dickie is a bird.
> Therefore, Dickie can fly.

The truth or the validity of the conclusion of a syllogism depends upon the truth of the first two statements or premises. If the premises are both true and the form of the syllogism is correct, the conclusion necessary follows. In the example given, the first statement or major premise is, of course, untrue, so that even if Dickie is a bird, it does not follow that he can fly.

The science of logic is concerned with the study of correct forms of syllogisms. We cannot go into the technicalities of this science here, but we can recommend that every teacher who is genuinely interested in working to improve the quality of her students' thinking familarize herself with the subject sufficiently to point out common syllogistic errors when they arise in her class.

The validity of major premises, as has been suggested, is established through the reasoning process of induction. A distinction can be made between two kinds of inductive procedures: those involving complete enumeration and those using samples or incomplete enumeration. With complete enumeration it is necessary to examine each and every individual case in a particular situation. For example, it can be induced that all members of the United States Senate are American citizens or that no woman is a member of the College of Cardinals. More often than not it is impossible to study each and every case. In such instances, conclusions or generalizations are based on samples or representative cases. By means of incomplete enumeration it has been induced, for example, that children tend to resemble their parents in physical characteristics. This second type of induction is usually based on observation, experimentation, statistical techniques and sometimes analogy. It is much more subject to error than is the first type since there are always such dangers as hasty generalizations or the drawing of conclusions from atypical experiences. As a minimum in this regard, teachers should encourage their students to use sparingly such universals as *all, none, always* or *never*, substituting instead such qualifiers as *apparently, probably, some, many, most, usually* or *sometimes*.

Critical thinking is the reorganization of concepts so as to evaluate some object or proposition. This is the form of mental activity that is usually implied by such expressions as "thinking for oneself" or "making up one's own mind." Critical thinking might be classed as a special form of reasoning—one involving a judgement which asserts or denies or compares the merit or value of something. It assumes the existence of some standard or criteria for making value judgments and a comparison of some specific case or cases with these criteria. For example, through the process of induction one might generalize that A, B and C are the essential qualities in a good novel. For purposes of this example, let A, B and C stand for whatever you wish; but if a novel has these qualities, it is a good one. If it lacks them, it is not. Our major premise, then, is: A, B and C are the character- istics of a good novel. For our minor premise, we must examine the particular novel or novels under consideration to judge whether or not they "measure up." We might judge that *Silas Marner* has A, B and C. The conclusion follows, there- fore, that *Silas Marner* is a good novel. Perhaps *Silas Marner* has only a little A, a great deal of B, and a very small amount of C, while *Moby Dick* has consider- ably more A and C, and at least as much B. Therefore, we might conclude, *Moby Dick* is superior to *Silas Marner*.

One difficulty in critical thinking centers around the establishment of criteria. In the final analysis, it is often a matter of taste or opinion, rather than absolute certitude, that A, B and C, rather than D and E are the most valid hallmarks, as is evidenced by the fact that literary critics—to say nothing of advertisers, news- paper editorialists, political candidates and others involved with controversial issues—so often disagree with one another as to which criteria are most pertinent in a given situation. The second difficulty is that of estimating whether this or that novel—or political platform, or pair of shoes, or set of religious beliefs— more closely fits the criteria.

As a minimum here, teachers might acquaint their students with different points of view and encourage them to adopt or adapt or formulate one of their own which they are able to defend. It goes without saying that in any given area such as literary criticism, economics, politics or religion, one point of view is not necessarily as good as another, and that the more information a person has about the area, the more valid his criteria are likely to be.

Just as critical thinking involves reasoning, so does our third major mode of thinking—problem solving—involve critical thinking. Problem solving is the reorganization of concepts or the restructuring of experience so as to overcome an obstacle and attain a goal. It is a conscious, deliberate striving for an answer which a person feels he needs in order to relieve some tension or improve his ex- isting condition. Problems arise when a person finds it impossible to attain his goal quickly and directly, when previously-used solutions do not work in the present situation, when established principles are apparently not applicable.

The heart of the problem solving process is the formulation and verification of hypotheses. A hypothesis is a tentative solution based on available knowledge, or an "educated guess" as to what one should do. It is usually stated, at least by implication, in *if-then* terms: If I do this, then that will happen. If I do the other thing, then something else will result. Then comes critical thinking or the making of a value judgment: I would rather have "that" happen than "something else." Therefore, I shall do "this" rather than "the other thing."

Problem solving, then, is largely a matter of acting with an end in view or attempting to foresee the consequences of one's acts or beliefs. A bridge player, for example, on the basis of information he has acquired during the bidding and previous play hypothesizes that he should lead a certain card in order to win the trick. Similarly, the scientist hypothesizes that if he does such-and-such, then so-and-so will occur. The procedures of the bridge player and the scientist are essentially the same as those we might use in solving our day-to-day problems, or those that high government officials might employ in attempting to solve theirs. Once a card is played or some other move is made, it is too late to think about what should have been done (although one can, of course, learn through his mistakes). Before making the move, then, the efficient problem solver tests his responses mentally or symbolically. Cross-table discussions may be frowned upon by bridge players, but not so in the class room, for well-conducted discussions are perhaps the most effective means of helping a person perceive the implications and anticipate the consequences of his proceeding in a particular manner.

Any of these three forms of thinking occurs when and only when at least two conditions are met: something is known and something is unknown. These conditions suggest the two-fold function of the teacher in improving the quality of her students' thinking. First, the student must know something about the subject area in which he is expected to think. Quite obviously, one cannot reason or think critically or solve problems about economic or political or social or scientific or religious matters unless he has some knowledge about them. The more concepts in a given field that he has, the more effectively he will be able to think in that field. Thus, one of the teacher's main tasks is to guide the student toward a systematic grasp of organized bodies of fundamental knowledge. Since this knowledge is an indispensible prerequisite for thinking, no teacher need ever apologize for teaching "facts" and demanding that her students learn them well. To expect students to learn to think effectively without having a store of concepts to reorganize—or information to think about—is to expect them to achieve an end without having the necessary means. Knowledge of subject matter, then, is a *necessary* condition of good thinking—but alone it is not a *sufficient* condition.

The second necessary condition is something unknown. One who does not have, or does not recognize that he has, problems—that is, difficulties, doubts, perplexities, uncertainties—does not, because he cannot, engage in productive thinking. The second function of the teacher, then, is to guide students toward an awareness of problems; to create doubts and uncertainties in their minds; to challenge their existing views; to show them that their opinions are inconsistent or contradictory; to whet their curiosity; to induce them to feel dissatisfied with their existing store of knowledge and beliefs as they are presently organized; in short, to motivate and challenge them to want to find out and think for themselves. Instead of always giving them the answers, providing them with the solutions, or getting them out of their intellectual difficulties herself, she should give them the opportunities, and require them, to do so on their own.

Toward the improvement of students' thinking, the teacher at any grade level in any subject area should be on the alert for effective means of developing such basic attitudes and skills as intellectual curiosity, sensitivity to and awareness of problems; intellectual humility, or a readiness to recognize one's ignorance and admit his mistakes; intellectual honesty, a willingness to follow the evidence wherever it might lead; the acceptance of responsibility for one's own decisions or conclusions; freedom from prejudice; openmindedness or the suspension of judgment, the consideration of many points of view and all of the available evidence before forming a conclusion; flexibility or the ability to change one's procedures when such seems to be warranted; orderliness in arranging data and persistence in the face of difficulty; the acceptance of cause and effect relationships and the rejection of superstition; decisiveness and the courage to maintain one's convictions when one is as certain as possible that they are true.

Toward the attainment of such convictions, the student needs to learn, and the teacher's job is to help him learn, how to check the adequacy and consistency of data; to determine whether the facts warrant or support a conclusion; to generalize or make inferences or see implications; to apply generalizations to new situations; to recognize errors in his own thinking and in that of others; to recognize and identify the central, critical issue in an argument or a problem; to distinguish the essential from the incidental, the relevant from the irrelevant; to recognize and make explicit the underlying assumptions in arguments he encounters; to distinguish emotional from intellectual appeal; to consider the qualifications and motives of persons who are trying to influence his thinking; and to make proper use of authority.

Making proper use of authority poses a problem for educators in general and for Catholic teachers in particular. In general, most people find thinking to be hard work, something to be avoided if possible. It is much easier to accept the conclusions of others than it is to arrive at them through one's own efforts. This is why we tend to rely on teachers, public speakers, news commentators, writers and others to do our thinking for us; to tell us what to think, or believe, or value or do. At times, of course, everyone must rely on some authority. Since we cannot always have first-hand experience with a matter, we have no choice but to rely on the experience of others. Since we cannot always prove or verify a point ourselves, we must accept the testimony of those who are qualified to do so. In matters which are relatively non-controversial, and on which the experts are themselves in agreement, this reliance on their authority constitutes no difficulty.

But in other situations, where the point at issue is controversial, where the authorities disagree among themselves, when there are two or more defensible positions, when the problem is in the practical order involving something the individual should do, each person has a responsibility to do his own thinking and reach his own conclusion.

In recent years the charge has been made that Catholic schools are not doing as good a job as they could and should be doing in developing their students' abilities to do independent thinking because of their over-reliance on authority. This charge has been levelled, not so much by enemies of the Church who might be primarily concerned with destroying Catholic education, but by members of the clergy and hierarchy and by dedicated laymen whose genuine interest is the improvement of Catholic education. Their argument goes something like this:

Catholics are taught that in matters of faith and morals, they may—indeed, they must—regard the teaching of the Church as the final word, to be accepted uncritically even though it might not be fully understood. They are also taught that their Catholicism, their faith and morality, should permeate all aspects of their lives. Finally, they are taught that their bishops and priests, as well as the Sisters and the lay teachers in their schools, participate in the teaching authority of the Church. From these premises, our students often apparently infer that they can and should accept unquestioningly the word of any Catholic teacher on practically any question as the Truth (with a capital T) which they are bound to accept, perhaps even under the pain of sin. By extension, they come to rely on "Catholic" books and magazines (whatever these might be), as well as Catholic teachers (or more accurately, perhaps, teachers in Catholic schools) to do their thinking for them. As any Catholic parent knows, the infallibility of the Pope is as nothing compared with what "Sister says" in the mind of the parochial school child. This child all too often grows up with the idea that "Father knows best" in all areas.

One kind of evidence to support this charge is the quest that so many Catholics engage in for "the" Catholic position on political, economic, social, scientific, educational, artistic and other practical matters. What they fail to recognize is that in these areas there is no one Catholic position; rather there are several defensible Catholic positions. Certainly there are principles which might be regarded as Catholic underlying the problems in these areas, but these principles must be applied to concrete cases, and they can be and have been applied in various ways. Thus, one can be totally consistent with the teaching of the Church and still be for or against federal aid to education, government-financed medical care, corporal punishment in the schools, secondary boycotts in labor-management disputes, "modern art" or Mass in the vernacular.

To what extent the above-mentioned criticism of Catholic education is justified is, of course, debatable—and it has been debated. Undoubtedly, the situation varies from school to school, and from classroom to classroom within a school. But Catholic teachers can never afford to become complacent in their work with respect to the matter under discussion. They, perhaps more than public school teachers, must make a special effort to guide their students toward a clear understanding of the distinction between proper and improper, legitimate and illegitimate, healthy and intellectually-deadening reliance on authority.

There are several classroom procedures which can be expected to contribute to the development of attitudes and abilities such as those which were mentioned earlier. The specifics of these procedures will vary, of course, with the subject being taught and the maturational level of the students. But first and perhaps most important, every teacher—in any kind of school at every grade level—should encourage and reward independent thinking. An exhortation on the bulletin board to "Think!" is hardly enough. As has been noted, the student must be stimulated with a problem to think about—a problem in which he is genuinely interested, one which he feels a need to solve. So-called "problems" in many text-books do not fit the bill since they are actually little more than drill exercises. Not that there is anything wrong with drill exercises; they undoubtedly serve a useful purpose—but not the purpose which is presently under discussion. The teacher should strive to give assignments—as homework as well as classwork—which emphasize the *way* or the *how*, rather than simply the *who, what, when* or *where*, assignments which require students to compare, contrast, explain, analyze, synthesize, evalute, decide or otherwise employ their higher mental processes, and not just repeat the factual information to which they have been exposed.

Thus motivated to begin, students should be praised, especially in the early stages, for making the effort to think independently even if the quality of their product leaves much to be desired. Many teachers, unfortunately, pay lip service to the fostering of independent thinking, but they scold or otherwise penalize their students for expressing interpretations different from those of the textbook, and reward conformity and the reproduction of the teacher's own views. Students should not only be permitted, but should be encouraged, to express their dis-beliefs in what they may read or be told. They should be invited to demon-strate honest doubt and healthy skepticism, to demand proof and to refuse to accept everything on faith alone. They should never fear to advance their own opinions, but must be made to understand that it is their responsibility to defend these views against the objections of the teacher or other students.

The teacher should both expect and accept errors in students' thinking. Thinking necessarily involves the making of mistakes. To a great extent, it is a matter of symbolic trial and error, a process characterized by false starts, re-visions, digressions, back-tracking, new beginnings, periods of dormancy, mo-ments of futility, and hopefully flashes of insight which at last lead to tenable conclusions. But before such conclusions are achieved, the student is bound to make mistakes. His mistakes must, of course, be corrected. Preferably, he should be guided by the teacher's skillful questioning to detect and correct his own errors. He should certainly not be ridiculed or chastised for them, lest he become discouraged, withdraw from the situation, hesitate or refuse to try again, and content himself with giving the tried and true "safe" answers when he is called upon the next time.

There are many other suggestions that could be given, and many detailed refinements which could be made of those suggestions which have been offered. But there are dangers in being too specific. In the final analysis, it is up to each and every teacher to work out her own procedures—appropriate to the subject she is teaching and the age of her students—whereby she can contribute to the actualization and improvement of their most precious and distinctively human gift, the ability to think.

part iv

Individual differences
in mental ability

1. Do you find any reason for supposing that Professor Nordberg's views on intelligence are novel? How would you evaluate his views?

2. What do you regard as the principal uses and limitations of testing in the educational program?

3. Considering the limited funds at their disposal and the problems they have staffing schools for normal children, do you think that Catholic education is justified in branching out into the expensive and highly specialized field of educating the retarded, as Father Behrmann suggests?

4. After reading Sister Bernarda's article, do you think that any competent teacher should be able to work with the slow learner in a regular classroom, or should such children have specially trained teachers and be placed in special rooms?

5. With whom do you agree more, Father Campbell or Father Hynes? Why?

6. Explain briefly why and to what extent you do or do not agree with Dr. Odenwald's thesis. Identify what you regard as the strongest and weakest links in his argument.

7. What are some suggestions for providing for individual differences which are not brought out in this chapter?

Intelligence:
a post-progressive analysis

Robert B. Nordberg

Subsequent selections in this chapter deal with educational provisions for the mentally retarded, the slow learner, and the exceptionally bright student. That these three differ among themselves in something called intelligence is obvious enough, but the nature of intelligence is not obvious at all. Several definitions and theories have been advanced to explain what it is and how it works, but none is universally accepted even among Catholic educators and psychologists. In the following article, Dr. Nordberg, of Marquette University, reviews and criticizes some of these theories and defends his concept of what intelligence is.

Several issues of this journal could be filled by a bibliography of studies on intelligence done in this century. A more prudent writer than the present one might, therefore, confine himself to aspects of the subject narrow enough to fit into whatever obscure corners remain. Nevertheless, at a rather crucial time in American education, we are setting out to ask and answer: What is human intelligence and how does it work? We shall be limited chiefly to the standpoint of educational psychology.

Why does it matter? In education alone, it matters almost supremely. One view of intelligence implies that schools should help the learner fulfill his rational nature; another view implies they should provide him with vast quantities of specifics. One view leads to the search for systematic generalizations where they

Reprinted with permission from *The Catholic Educational Review*, 59:217–226, April, 1961.

241

are possible; the other would, for example, teach the pupil every mathematical combination he will ever use. As for method, one theory of intelligence is conducive to the memorize-and-repeat pattern; another leads to understand-and-apply. The problem of who should teach is at stake. Do gifted students need gifted teachers? Is it (as some say) dangerous and unhealthy for teachers to be brilliant? The writer has filled out many recommendation-forms for prospective teachers on which one is asked almost everything about the applicant except "How bright is he?" or "What does he know?"

One does not live very long without realizing that attitudes towards intellect and its operation are a function of the total personality, not simply of what one happens to know about the matter. Nor need one be especially perceptive to notice that phrases such as "academic standards" or "intellectual exercise" mean many things to many people. The quarrel over the respective claims of speculative and empirical knowledge goes back to Heraclitus and Parmenides, if not to that primeval Garden. On the philosophical front, varieties of empiricism have assaulted the intellect's claims in modern times. Positivists have denied the validity of any criterion of proof or meaning save empirical verification. Pragmatists have insisted that meaning can be found only in consequences, the meanings of which lie only in further consequences—so that the definitive significance of anything is, like the Holy Grail, always just beyond the next turn or hill.

Nobody disputes that pragmatism, for a long time, almost took over American education. It has become fashionable to say, though, that Professor John Dewey was misunderstood and "not to blame" for some excesses of "progressive education." This is probably true insofar as no one man is responsible for the temper of the times. One can also agree that most classroom teachers in the "progressive" tradition were probably neither aware of nor interested in the subtler theoretical twists and turns of Pierce, James, and Dewey. This is but to say that they faithfully carried out the pragmatic maxim: Disregard speculation. The writer disagrees with those who say that the teachers most faithful to "progressive" or "life-adjustment" tenets were not carrying out Dewey's basic philosophy. They were carrying it out splendidly, if only because so many teachers seem to be (strangely enough) a bit anti-intellectual at heart.

Psychology has been in the battle too. One might think that a science would not find itself split over an ancient quarrel. Here we see again how metaphysics is always coming through the back door if barred at the front. Edward L. Thorndike, who influenced educational psychology more than anybody else, started with materialist-atomist premises and ended with materialist-atomist conclusions. To him, intelligence was not a single thing, but the sum of a multitude of specific mental associations. This view fits well with his connectionist theory of learning.[1] Like most atomists, Thorndike gradually moved away from this extreme position, but he died without fundamentally repudiating it. Thurstone's multiple-factor

[1] Edward L. Thorndike, *Educational Psychology* (New York: Teachers College, Columbia University Press, 1903).

concept modified Thorndike, but is subject to mistinterpretation.[2] Some writers cite the identification of these various factors to deny that there is any G or general factor. This conclusion is both untrue and a *non sequitur*. Finally, one might cite "the flight from transfer," the excessive fear of generalizing, that has marked so much of contemporary thought and education. In short, much of the modern world has tried to bury intelligence. But it is hard to bury the living!

What Is It?

One can say what something "is" in the sense of defining a word or of defining a thing. We are here doing the latter. Intelligence is *a generalized capacity to abstract and symbolize*. We shall first cite empirical proofs of this definition, then a few philosophical ones.

Empirical proof that intelligence is general.—First, factor analysis of intelligence tests has clearly established a G-factor, rather clearly equivalent to general intelligence. This was established first by Spearman as displayed to a large degree in some functions and a lesser degree in others, and described by him as a combination of "neogenesis and abstraction." [3] Moore later showed a "super-G" based upon extracting a common factor from the G-factors of smaller groups.[4] Second, IQ typically correlates with various school subjects to approximately the degree that they require forming and expressing ideas. Science Research Associates did a factorial analysis of scores on tests in their SRA Achievement Series, Factor 1 involves something they stated to be involved in all the tests. "These skills, which are common to all cognitive-type tasks, are categorically labeled General Achievement and are assumed to be almost the same as skills that are measured by the general factor in intelligence tests." [5] This factor had its highest loadings on tests such as comprehension and vocabulary, its lowest on tests of auditory and visual discrimination. This pattern fits well with studies by Monaghan [6] and McManama [7] which show the G-factor expressed most directly in items involving analogies, definitions, fable-interpretation, or other highly verbalized skills.

Of course, intelligence cannot be "general" except in the sense that pertains to

2 L. L. Thurstone, *Primary Mental Abilities* ("Psychometric Monograph," No. 1; Chicago: University of Chicago Press, 1938).

3 Charles Spearman and L. Wynn Jones, *Human Ability; a Continuation of the Abilities of Man* (London: Macmillan Co., 1950), p. 69.

4 T. V. Moore, *Multiple Correlation and the Correlation Between General Factors* ("Studies in Psychology and Psychiatry,'" III, No. 2; Washington: Catholic University of America Press, 1933).

5 Louis P. Thorpe and others, *SRA Achievement Series—Technical Supplement* (Chicago: Science Research Associates, 1957), p. 24.

6 Edward A. Monaghan, *Major Factors in Cognition* ("Studies in Psychology and Psychiatry," III, No. 5; Washington: Catholic University of America Press, 1935), p. 36.

7 Sr. Maurice McManama, *A Genetic Study of the Cognitive General Factor in Intelligence* ("Studies in Psychology and Psychiatry," IV, No. 2; Washington: Catholic University of America Press, 1936), p. 26.

its nature. We cannot logically deny its generality because it does not extend to things quite other than itself. Yet, this has been a common line of criticism, as in the following:

> Most intelligence tests were primarily measures of verbal ability and, to a lesser extent, of the ability to handle numerical and other abstract and symbolical relations. Gradually psychologists came to realize that the term "intelligence" was a misnomer, since only certain aspects of intelligence were measured by such tests. To fill some of the major gaps left by intelligence tests, psychometrists began to develop tests of so-called special aptitudes, such as mechanical, clerical, artistic, and musical aptitude.[8]

Such things as musical and artistic aptitude are not intelligence, although they have some degree of correlation with it. To criticize intelligence tests for not measuring them or to imply that the tests are misnamed on that ground, is as pointless as saying that a scale is not a fair measure of one's weight because it ignores how tall one is. Intelligence is general in the sense of appearing in all manifestations of an intellectual order.

Empirical evidence of a capacity. It is basic to Thomistic thought that, between being and non-being, lies potentiality, or possibility to be. Various philosophies have bogged down by trying to reduce potentiality either to actuality or to nothing. Similarly, psychologists have often got confused about intelligence by trying to make it either "something" (in the sense of achievement, mental or overt) or into an arbitrary, man-made construct. It is neither; it is a capacity. Evidence and measurement of a capacity must always be indirect, since measurement and observation are material processes and need an actual and physical object. The remarkable constancy of the IQ when properly measured is a kind of indirect evidence of its status as a capacity, however.[9]

Empirical evidence of an abstractive capacity. Terman, in the time when empirical concepts of intelligence were crystallizing, wrote that "An individual is intelligent in proportion as he is able to carry on abstract thinking." [10] We have already encountered Spearman's work and conclusions. To abstract is to consider the bare nature of a thing, apart from all material and individuating conditions. As is shown clearly by the previously cited SRA correlations and by many others, intelligence tends to correlate with every mental endeavor to the extent that abstracting is involved.

Empirical evidence of a symbolizing capacity. A symbol is a material sign of a non-material idea. Language is thus the bridge between the sensory and intel-

[8] Anne Anastasi, "The Measurement of Abilities," *Journal of Counseling Psychology,* I (Fall, 1954), 164.

[9] Norman L. Munn, *Psychology—the Fundamentals of Human Adjustment* (Boston: Houghton Mifflin Co., 1946), pp. 417-422; Leona E. Tyler, *The Psychology of Human Differences* (New York: Appleton-Century-Crofts, Inc., 1956), pp. 80-85.

[10] Lewis M. Terman and others, "Intelligence and Its Measurement—a Symposium," *Journal of Educational Psychology,* XII (1921), 128.

lective sides of our nature. That is why brute animals cannot speak or write and angels do not need to. Language is a peculiarly human thing, even if we sometimes study and teach it as if it were purely an animal function.[11]

The symbolic character of intelligence is shown in its high correlations with arithmetic and in the fact that vocabulary is its best single index. Leona Tyler wrote that

> . . . vocabulary is an excellent indicator of *general* intelligence in children, as it correlates highly with most other types of intellectual activity. If a single test must be given to a child in order to ascertain the mental level at which he is functioning, a vocabulary test is more satisfactory than any other.[12]

This is generally admitted, and the high correlation of verbal items on IQ tests with the G-factor is well known. Yet, many authors criticize the tests for being "too verbal." This is a meaningless criticism, because intelligence is a very "verbal" thing!

An excellent illustration of the "anti-verbal" attitude is an article by Davis and Hess. This article criticizes intelligence tests for posing "academic" problems. In case this is not indictment enough, an appositive follows, "the kind which are taught in the average classroom." It is explained that such problems "do not stem from real-life situations at all, but from a highly traditional, unrealistic middle-class school culture." [13] (One can visualize John Dewey standing off-stage, applauding.) The article goes on to reveal that lower-class children "do not understand, and therefore cannot learn well, the teacher's culture." [14] Here is food for thought for those of us who thought you could learn only what you did *not* already know.

The authors did four years of research, but

> . . . there still was not a shred of statistically valid evidence that, on any range of problems, the lower occupational groups could do as well, in terms of absolute attainment, as the higher occupational groups. *So* we set up "experimental" individual and group tests. . . . [Italics mine.] [15]

The "so" seems to say, "therefore," i.e., "We were going to prove our hypothesis one way or another." A hypothesis *ad hoc* is later introduced to do just that. One might wonder, "What is behind all this? Why are the authors so confessedly reluctant to let the evidence speak for itself?" The closing passages give a clear answer: We are told that the intelligence of a bright child is apt to be under-

---

[11] R. B. Nordberg, "Levels of Communication in Reading," *Catholic Educational Review*, LIV (February, 1956), 92-100.

[12] Tyler, p. 92.

[13] Allison Davis and Robert Hess, "How Fair Is an IQ Test?" *Readings in Guidance*, ed. H. B. McDaniel (New York: Henry Holt and Co., 1959), p. 68.

[14] *Ibid.*, p. 68.

[15] *Ibid.*, p. 69.

estimated "if he does not show the middle-status traits of neatness, cooperation, docility, cleanliness, and eagerness for school tasks." [16] (Is there any IQ test that gives even half a point for any of these minor vices?)

Then we are told of "a responsibility for keeping open the routes of upward social movement, to the youth of the United States" so that those in the lower classes can join the middle classes, whose way of life the authors have been criticizing. "Opportunity for climbing the social and economic ladder is one of the genuinely democratic aspects of American life . . ."; [17] education is a chief means to this vertical mobility; intelligence is prerequisite for education. Therefore, one gathers, we are asked to change our concepts of intelligence in such a way that those at the foot of the socio-economic ladder are at least as bright as all other people. All very bewildering!

Intelligence, Meaning, Transfer

Intelligence is, then, as Gannon excellently summarizes it, "a hierarchical factor operating through all the manifestations of an intellectual order, but making its clearest appearance in tests requiring a combination of abstraction, verbal symbolization, and education of relations." [18] Meaning is, simply stated, the abstracted universal, existing as a concept in the mind. It is the product of the use of intelligence. Transfer is, simply stated, the application of meanings insofar as they fit situations. Here we have a beautiful and clear pattern: Intelligence is the power; meaning is the product of the power; transfer is the use of the product. Judd [19] and Orata [20] by emphasizing transfer through conscious generalization, were giving meaning its due, and, therefore, intelligence. Woodworth and Thorndike,[21] by denying transfer except through "identical components," were slighting meaning and intelligence.

It is possible to show philosophically that human intelligence is what empirical lines of inquiry also indicate it to be. We shall not labor the latter approach, for brevity's sake. Intellect in man is his power to grasp the non-material essences of things. From this viewpoint, intelligence can be called the operation of intellect. By its very nature, then, it is general in the sense earlier argued. Again, it is a

[16] *Ibid.,* p. 70.

[17] *Ibid.*

[18] Timothy J. Gannon, *Psychology—the Unity of Human Behavior* (Boston: Ginn and Co., 1954), p. 312.

[19] Charles H. Judd, "The Relation of Special Training to General Intelligence," *Educational Review,* XXXVI (June, 1908), 28-42.

[20] Pedro T. Orata, *The Theory of Identical Elements* (Columbus: Ohio State University Press, 1928); "Transfer of Training and Educational Pseudo-Science," *Mathematical Teacher* XXVIII (May, 1935), 265-289; "Recent Research Studies in Transfer of Training with Individuals for the Curriculum, Guidance and Personnel Work, *Journal of Education Research,* XXXV (October, 1941), 81-101.

[21] E. L. Thorndike and R. S. Woodworth, "The Influence of Improvement in One Mental Function upon the Efficiency of Other Functions," *Psychological Review,* VIII (1901), 247-261, 384-95, 553-64.

capacity in fundamentally the same sense in which intellect itself is such. Still again, as the operation of intellect, is could not escape being concerned with abstracting and symbolizing.

Intelligence in Classroom and Clinic

Some meanings are rational; some, arbitrary. Arbitrary meanings are those that, at least for a given learner at a given time, have no discernible "reason why." They just *are*. The alphabet, the mechanical aspects of our numbering system, a series of historical dates, are examples. Other meanings are rational: they can be anticipated, deduced, understood. Arbitrary meanings make few demands upon the intelligence; they simply have to be memorized. Too often, education is approached as if all meanings were arbitrary, as in tests of the sort where one merely has to recognize the "right" answer when it is presented in a multiple-choice context. Education should stress rational meanings wherever they are to be found as soon as any necessary foundation in arbitrary meanings has been laid. As Pius XII said,

> In order to study seriously, you must beware of the belief that the number of things learned is the fundamental element in building your educational edifice. What is necessary is not a great number of materials, but rather learning well, understanding profitably, and examining thoroughly everything that is necessary and useful.[22]

Contrast this with the viewpoint generally adopted by no less influential a group than the President's Commission on Higher Education. This group officially regretted "the present orientation of higher education toward verbal skills and intellectual interests," and suggested that the colleges and universities concentrate more on "many other aptitudes—such as social sensitivity and versatility, artistic ability, motor skill and dexterity, and mechanical aptitude and ingenuity." [23]

Fundamentally, a misconception of intelligence is behind the classroom approach that is seldom concerned with comprehension as tested by application or with the student's ability to organize and express what he knows. It would be hard to think of a less demanding or significant criterion of learning than "recognizing the right answer." Just as the cigarette industry has not felt motivated to stress research findings on cancer, so publishers of standardized tests can hardly be expected to lead the way in criticizing the conception of education as an intellectual bingo game, scored by electricity. But can't we, like the man in that cigarette ad, "think for ourselves"?

[22] Pius XII, "The Bases of Sound Education," Address to the Students of Rome. *The Pope Speaks,* IV (Summer, 1957), 14-20.
[23] President's Commission on Higher Education, *Higher Education for American Democracy* (New York: Harper and Brothers, 1947), p. 32.

Some approaches to the mentally gifted and retarded also bear the stamp of Thorndikean specificity. Terman's long and careful work on the generalized character of giftedness continues to be slighted.[24] Some authors discuss "the gifted" in terms of any achievement or aptitude in which one might be superior. They say that the gifted comprise a very small percent of the population, but their definition would make everyone gifted. Anybody is superior to somebody at something! The notion that it is unseemly for one person to be brighter than another "in a democracy" seems to rise again here. Therefore they offer this smörgasbord definition, after which they usually get down to business and talk about levels of intelligence. It is, indeed, the case, that some children can climb ropes, make baskets, or slash tires, with greater facility than others, but it hardly follows that the curriculum should stress things of this sort as much as, say, learning what justice is.

The mentally retarded are, likewise, talked about more in terms of peripheral or irrelevant features than in terms of their mental retardation. Such children may, in given cases, be asocial, love routine, be hard to discipline, and so forth. But why?: It is very hard for them to abstract and generalize. The expression "slow learner" is a good illustration of blinking at unpleasant facts. Those who learn faster usually learn better.

Intelligence and Future Educational Theory

We are pulling out of an era when American education was dominated by a concept of man as differing from the chimpanzee by (as one semanticist said) a quarter-inch of cortex. Man's knowledge, it followed, was not *qualitatively* different from that of the lowliest sensitive creature. This view fitted well with the concept of intelligence as a series of S-R associations, meanings as blind and contextually determined, and schooling as stamping in desired habits and stamping out undesired ones. Small wonder that intellectuals who sought a haven in teaching soon had their eyes opened! Catholic schools never went all the way with this anti-intellectual tradition, but they were inevitably contaminated by it to a degree.

What will happen now? The public has finally noticed what pragmatism is in education and has vigorously rejected it. What outlook will be next? We can hardly expect American education as a whole to adopt a Thomistic philosophy. Even though this philosophical system is capable of standing by itself and has important things to say about education, many people nevertheless can regard it in no way save as an appendage to Catholicism, which, in turn, they dismiss without a hearing. Nevertheless, many people are now realizing that the Catholic schools and colleges were much less de-intellectualized by positivist and pragmatist traditions than were most others, and they are impressed by this. We are in a

[24] Lewis M. Terman, "The Discovery and Encouragement of Exceptional Talent," *The American Psychologist,* IX (June, 1954), 221-230.

good position, therefore, to insure that some basic features of our educational philosophy are adopted in some places where Dewey and Company formerly reigned unchallenged. We can help towards this, and help to make sure that Catholic schools and colleges provide the leadership they ought to provide, by respecting in theory and practice the general nature of intelligence, and all its consequences.

Testing: measure or evaluate?

Sister Barbara Geoghegan, S.C.

*The preceding article just touches on the subject of
intelligence testing; the next one goes into the
matter in greater detail. After distinguishing
between measurement and evaluation, Sister
Barbara discusses some of the major problems in the
area of testing, describes what she considers to be a
good testing program, and offers teachers, school
administrators, and parents sound advice about the
proper use of tests and test results.*

. . . We in the schools are more cognizant today, I believe, of our need to
identify early the talents and abilities not only of our gifted, but of all pupils, in
order that every one of them may realize insofar as possible the talents with
which he is endowed, be they the biblical one, two, or ten. This, of course, we
have always sought to do to some extent. We have always used and will continue
to use judgments of teachers who daily experience evidences of the capacities of
their pupils. But such judgments can be made only after long and many observations, and we are people in a hurry. Here we should be in a hurry, for the earlier
we recognize strengths and weaknesses, and help to develop the first and to overcome the latter, the sooner we can bring the child to a realistic understanding of
self, and the more readily he can set up for himself honest and worthy ideals
toward which to strive.

Toward this purpose we have also used teacher-made or standardized tests,
either to substantiate or to aid the judgment of teachers. Today we find ourselves
overwhelmed by a plethora of tests whose name has become legion. This past
year, in the field of education alone, 122 million test booklets and answer sheets
were sold to the schools, enough to give three tests to every child at every level
of education in the United States. In addition, by the end of this year, the civil

Abridged and reprinted with permission from *The Catholic Educator*, 33:153 ff.,
October, 1962.

services will have administered about 5 million tests. The Armed Forces last year gave 135,000 qualification tests in addition to a number of special proficiency tests. In our own schools, on each of our principals' desks, there are brochures and flyers urging the use of some instrument or battery to measure accomplishment or achievement, or to predict future achievement, or for selective placement, or for some other educational purpose. All of which gives rise to many problems: some of them immediate and current, some of them perennial in the field of testing.

Before going further, let us consider for a minute the title of this article: *Testing: Measurement or Evaluation?* If this present acceleration of testing in our schools is to benefit our pupils, we must be quite sure that we know whether we are using tests as *instruments* of *measurement* or of *evaluation*.

To measure is to compare with a fixed standard or criterion, to estimate in comparison with something else. Measurement here would include the age-old processes of comparison with a criterion such as we exercise when we mark or grade student performance; testing of all sorts, from the teacher-made five-minute quiz to the ninety minute end-of-the-year final examination. To evaluate is to *fix the worth of, to estimate the force of*. Measurement asks *How much? How Many?* Evaluation asks *How Well?*

It is no accident that the courses in our college that used to be termed *Tests and Measurements* or *Educational Measurements* now are titled *Evaluation of Learning* or *Methods of Evaluation*, or some similar title. I *measure* fairly accurately, and even rigidly, John's ability to solve quadratic equations. I will find it more difficult, but also more important, to *evaluate* his ability to comprehend the theory of sets. I *measure* rather accurately Jane's status of knowledge of French vocabulary as learned from the high school text; her ability to conjugate the French irregular verbs; to translate the written page of a French novel. I will not so easily *evaluate* her fluency in speaking the language, her facility and correctness of pronunciation, her understanding of the spoken French word. To labor the point a bit further, a teacher may *measure* accurately by means of a printed test Jack's proof-reading ability as he identifies errors in punctuation, usage, and spelling in a series of graded exercises. With less ease will the teacher *evaluate* his ability to produce the written or the spoken word; to develop a thought logically, expressed not only in correct but also in clear incisive sentences free of clinchés and pedestrian phrases.

Evaluation, then, is a broader term than measurement. It has been said that evaluation is a warm term; measurement, a cold term. Perhaps for us as educators, evaluation is a *good* word; measurement should be a *bad* word.

Do the tests we use today measure, or do they evaluate? The answer may lie in the tests themselves, or it may lie in the use we make of them. There has been since World War II a growing movement to make tests instruments of evaluation rather than of measurement. Many of the older achievement tests, for instance, have been withdrawn from the market because they measured factual knowledge rather than understanding of basic concepts. These are being replaced by very different instruments. One of these is the ETS test in French, with its records and tapes and written exercises attempting to evaluate true goals of learning much more nearly than did the old Cooperative Test in French. So, too, with social studies, with English; instead of items aimed at disgorgement by the testee of memorized facts, we find those which would sound out the principles, the causes and motives, as well as the facts of history; appreciation and discrimination in literature, as well as ability to scan a verse or to identify an author. We are, in the newer instruments, nearer to global appraisal than we were twenty, ten, or even five years ago. The instruments are becoming more evaluative.

We said that tests may evaluate or measure, and we hasten to add, according to the way we use them. If we make of the best appraisal instrument a measurement device, using it rigidly and inflexibly, without regard to any other knowledge we have of this student, we are using it wrongly and we are abusing those whom we test with it.

This brings us again to the problems of testing in our schools, and it is within the framework of these concepts of measurement and evaluation that I would now like to approach these problems. There is a question we must ask first. *Why Test?* What are our purposes in using *this* test? in *this* school? at *this* time? with these pupils?

A testing program is justifiable, good and useful, in terms of its purposes. Only if the best program in the world is actually and really aimed at helping the student can we say that it is good. Justifiable purposes would be included under five general headings:

1. To determine the capacities, strengths, and weaknesses of the student in order that the student may know them, so that he may develop his capacities to the utmost and strengthen so far as he can, his weaknesses.

2. Therefore, to help him as he ascends the educational ladder to choose courses suitable *for him* and to perform to capacity in order to realize his potential in those courses.

3. To evaluate his progress by periodical tests of educational development.

4. To modify his educational plans in accordance with all data obtained from test results together with all other available information.

5. In the light of accumulated data, to evaluate the curriculum, the prevailing methods and techniques in the specific institution, in *this* school, serving the needs of *these* students, in *this* community. (This is not to say that testing programs determine curriculum and modus operandi; it is to say that the results of testing programs properly used can improve the services of the school to its particular population.)

Now, still within the framework of these concepts of measurement and evaluation, let us look at our particular present problems with regard to tests and testing programs. Their solutions are not general. Each school system, indeed, each school, must solve them in terms of their own situation and their own student body. Currently we have three groups of situations that cause us some perplexity. The first arise from emphasis on national and regional scholarship tests for high school juniors and seniors. We are encouraged to permit the top five per cent of our students to participate in these testing programs. The problem? Other pupils wish to participate also. Shall we let anyone who wishes and is willing to pay his dollar participate? Or shall we restrict participation? If we do restrict, where shall we put the cutting point?

In a recent guidance workshop a teacher blandly informed the group that her school does not participate in national testing programs at all, lest the school show a poor rating. Where is the obligation here? To protect the school? Or to make available the opportunity that these programs afford?

There is another problem. Suppose I have in my school eight students who place high. Five are chosen; three are not. How do I explain this to parents? We know that there is a quota established among private and public schools in making awards. How explain the quota? Or do we explain it at all?

Second among current problems are those arising from industry's preoccupation with tests as agents of selection and placement of employees. It would seem that for those of our young people going out into the business world, we have the obligation to give them experience with these instruments so that they are not paralyzed when they meet them in the employment office. This implies giving them the proper attitude toward tests—that tests are useful and helpful devices, not examinations to be approached in fear and trembling. This is a matter to be discussed later in this article.

Among current problems, we have a third group arising from placement and/or selection tests for incoming freshmen to college or to high school. Let us consider for a few minutes those tests used for high school freshmen. Shall we make our own tests or use standardized ones? If we use standardized tests, what ones shall we use? This much we know, that unless we are subscribing to a testing service, we may as well make up our minds to change the instruments annually. Alas, teachers are ambitious for their pupils, or for their own reputations, and it is not unknown that students are coached, and coached strenuously, in all the forms of a given achievement test.

In New York City, where the screening process is widespread, it was not unusual for one student to take as many as eight or ten entrance tests in as many different schools. Nine of the schools may carry him on their lists, thus preventing the entrance of nine other students deserving of a Catholic education. The answer has been to seek from a central agency a single test to be given all students of subscribing schools. The student names three schools of his choice to which the results are to be sent. Thus much duplication of effort is avoided, to say nothing of the wear and tear on the student, the teachers, and the school administrators.

Here again, we have the problem of measurement versus evaluation. Some high schools, and some colleges, will take only the top-ranking performers on these entrance tests, ignoring all other data. Others will consider previous achievement, extra-curricular activities, and the like. Who is to say that justice prevails when test scores alone are the criteria for admission? Our philosophy of education, not our *written*, but our *lived* philosophy, will be needed in the solution of this problem. As a well known educator has said in referring to the use of SCAT, "We do not screen, we weigh."

Finally, we come to the perennial, always-with-us problems of testing. First of these is a tendency toward over-emphasis on test results as the one or the major basis of selection and placement in grouping, in admissions, or in planning a course of study. Related to this problem and part of it is the over-reliance on an IQ derived from a single test as a predictor of a child's academic success.

Decision making with regard to the welfare of a child for his whole future is a very serious matter. Let us ask ourselves this, "Have we the right, on the basis of the results of a single test, to decide for this child that he will go into this or that course, or that he will be placed in this or that group?" Again, does a teacher act in justice when, on the basis of low performance in a semester examination by a student who has given day-by-day evidence of ability, she gives him a grade on the basis of the examination alone? This is of particular significance if class standing is affected so that the pupil may not enter the college or the high school of his choice, or the school which offers what he needs. This is measurement with vengeance; certainly it is anything but evaluation.

If we give a battery of tests to John Jones, can we, on the basis of these test results alone, pinpoint his scores on a scale as the final word in the question of his capacities and potential? To do so is to *measure*. But if in addition to test results, we have a file of his school-produced papers; samples of his daily performance; his past school record; then our conference with John and parents becomes an *evaluating* session, and is worth the energy we give to it.

Related to this problem, and part of it, is the over-reliance on an IQ derived from a single test as a predictor of academic success. College admissions officers express great concern over the records given in high schools in this regard. High school principals express equal concern when the records of those who apply to the ninth grade carry an IQ obtained perhaps in the fourth or the first grade, with no subsequent index of academic potential.

Think of the number of factors that may affect a child's performance on a single test: a headache, a heartache, perhaps, after a night lying in the dark listening to a parent's quarrel; the unwarm and unaccepting or unaccepted atmosphere in which he finds himself as he enters a new school, surrounded by strange companions and stranger teachers. And yet we all know cases in which high school freshmen have been placed arbitrarily into algebra or general math, or homemaking, or rapid-moving groups on the basis of a single so-called "intelligence" test given on the High-school day in the spring, or on the first day of school in the fall.

There is, too, the problem of proper use of test results by administrators, teachers, and guidance personnel. We have already touched upon the misuse of such results in grouping and placement. But what about using them to help the child? Or to help the teacher to understand the child? How many teachers have any idea of the appraised learning capacity of the pupils they meet daily? How many know the level at which these children read? Yet in many schools today are some such records which could be, should be, and probably are available in the files, gathering dust and turning yellow. This represents one of the mortal sins of the teaching profession. A very simple device that preserves the necessary secrecy in this matter of student's measured ability is a code which uses the letters F to O, ascribing 1 to F, 2 to G, and so on, with O standing as zero. With such a code, it is a simple matter for the teacher to inscribe in her record book the child's IQ as NO for 90, FFG as 112, and so on. The percentile rating might be listed in the same way.

Another problem is related to those already mentioned, and it is a touchy one—interpreting test results to parents, to students, and to the general public. What happens to a child if his over-anxious and over-ambitious parent is told that the child's learning potential is but average or that it is less than average? There can result severe parental rejection with far-reaching damage to the child. So what to do about it? It takes patience, deep understanding, and the enlightenment of the Holy Spirit to lead the parent to an understanding acceptance of the truth. And this truth goes back to the previous problem—our need for being quite sure of the truth which we interpret and of basing it on adequate evaluation. What happens to the child of superior ability, too immature to understand that his endowments are God's gifts to be valued and developed the better to serve Him, when he learns that he possesses superior learning ability?

How can the teacher counselor best handle the case of the ninth-grader whose verbal ability lies at about the tenth percentile, whose numerical ability is at best described as mediocre, but who wants to be a civil engineer? How can we help him arrive in all honesty at a true concept of self and to form a realistic self-ideal for him? How will a teacher best deal with the fifth-grader skilled at numerical calculation, but who reads at a second-grade level? How do we give a child of low ability a true self-image and yet not discourage him from all effort to learn? How do we handle the earnest well-meaning P.T.A. member who is disturbed beyond reason when he hears or reads the report of the December testing survey, demanding to know why the fourth grade mean reading score is only 4.1, three months behind the norm? (Perhaps *normal*, like *measurement*, should become a bad word for teachers.)

What about interpreting the IQ to our teachers? Here again we come back to the concept of measurement. No group instrument (and indeed no clinical instrument, administered by the best-trained psychologist available) can give us a fixed point so that we can say, "This child's score lies here on this scale." Let us take the so-called test of general intelligence, the Terman-McNemar. The manual for this test tells us that the standard error of measurement for the advanced form is 3.5. This standard error means that if today Bill rates an IQ of 110 on the advanced form of the Terman-McNemar, and if tomorrow it were possible to repeat the test, eliminating boredom and practice effect, the chances are two out of three that his IQ obtained the second time would not vary from yesterday's by more or less than 3.5. This means that 66 times out of 100, on a retest, his score would yield an IQ of 110 plus or minus 3.5 and that his true measure is likely somewhere between 106.5 and 113.5. But once out of three times it is possible that he might place somewhere along a line bounded by 2(3.5)—somewhere between 103 and 117. All of this we say when we state that Bill's Terman-McNemar IQ is 110.

On the California Tests of Mental Ability, the standard error of measurement for the primary form is 4.5. The chances are two out of three that a child's true measure lies somewhere between 97.5 and 107.5 if his index or IQ is 102. There is also some slight chance that it lies between 93 and 111. Similarly, in the case just mentioned, when a group's mean reading score is three months below that of the norm, the three month differential is well within the probable error of measurement and perhaps means nothing at all. The point is this: in interpreting intelligence test scores, that is, in assaying a child's capacity to learn, we must be careful not to resort to measurement, to a limited precisely fixed point on a given scale.

Finally we come to the problem of selecting proper instruments for the purposes of evaluating an individual's potential to learn, or in evaluating that which he has already learned. A related problem of what tests to use is that of when to use them.

We are convinced that a second mortal sin of testing is committed when we test too soon. How much reliance can we place on an IQ obtained in the second month of a child's formal school experience? Yet many testing programs call for a so-called "intelligence test" to be administered in October of the first grade. Think of the different situations from which these children come to school: some have been cherished, helped, read to, listened to, talked to, even pushed. Others have grown like Topsy, with little or no attention. Some have love and affection; some have had little of it. Some have grown up among older persons; others have had little companionship of any kind. Yet, when they are just becoming used to school life, some even just beginning to get over a truly traumatic experience of separation from home, we attempt to evaluate their learning potential by a series of common exercises for which many of them are just not ready.

It might be most enlightening and interesting for a teacher to administer such an instrument in October of the first grade, and its equivalent form in February. Repeated over three or four years, the difference in favor of the February testing would be surprising. The harm lies chiefly in the fact that these early-obtained IQ's are committed to a pupil's record as an index of ability to do school tasks, and stand there until the next testing period. In the meantime, a busy teacher sees the record, decides that this child gives little promise and therefore exerts her energies, which must be husbanded, toward youngsters that she feels will more likely profit by her efforts. The child who is starting school needs to be evaluated, but not by a so-called intelligence test at this early stage. A reading readiness test is the best answer at the beginning of a child's school life.

In the matter of selection of tests, too, we must exercise care. In the first place, we should exclude from our consideration those which claim to uncover for us all the child's potential in the area of verbal, numerical, spatial relations, and the like, and all this within a span of 45 minutes! No area of ability can be sufficiently sounded within a period of five or seven minutes, and tests which claim to do so are inherently unsound. In this matter, also, we would do best nowadays to investigate programs available through different agencies. Then we can compare within schools and between schools on some common basis. In selecting tests, for either a school or a system, we would do well to take a careful look at the facilities of the agencies for research and study; at the professional status of the personnel responsible for the program; at the services and interpretations available to the school which uses the program. We would do well to examine with care their brochures to determine whether there is evidence of professional restraint or of over-enthusiastic claims. Every person responsible for testing would do well to study the criteria established by the American Psychological Association Committee together with members of the Association for Educational Research, aimed at giving some kind of measuring rod for the tests we would like to use.

We do well, also, if we confine ourselves to those instruments which meet most of these carefully drawn-up criteria. We must consider, too, in seeking a testing service whether the service we are soliciting really meets our needs. If all our students go out to work immediately after high school, then the United States Employment tests would probably be more valuable than the College Entrance Board Tests.

If in our elementary schools we are using one program, while the high schools to which our students go are employing another, we might consider getting together to consider one sequential program that would give continuous measurement of growth, such as the STEP program (sequential tests of educational progress) in the fields of reading, writing, listening, numerical ability, and other areas. Similarly, the ITED's (Iowa Tests of Educational Development) at high school and early college level, together with the Iowa Tests of Basic Skills at the elementary level, give such a continuous and progressive type of evaluation.

There is a definite trend away from the single-index IQ to the multi-factor instrument which provides several indices of aptitude. Among these we would mention for high school and eighth grade use, the Differential Aptitude Tests; the SCAT; the older Psychological Examination of the ACE. These give some indication of abilities in verbal and numerical areas; the Differential Aptitude goes further, into English, spatial relationships, ability to think abstractly.

We might best serve teachers and pupils by combining both multi-factor and the old type that yield the single IQ. (Teachers still want the IQ, unfortunately, but the percentile ranks obtained from the multi-factor instruments are more readily used for counselling purposes.) Perhaps by using both we can come to de-condition our teachers from their IQ position and condition them to use more readily the multi-factor evaluation.

We began this article by referring to our obligation to locate and identify talent in our schools, for the primary reason that the individual's greatest happiness will be attained in actualizing the potential that is in him. This is not to depreciate the average and low ability pupil. Each has his own potential too, to be realized to the utmost possible degree so that he can best fill his place in this world and in the next.

It is our task as teachers to help him achieve a sound understanding of self, to form a realistic self-image and a worthy self-ideal. To do so we need to appraise his strengths and weaknesses; we need to *evaluate* him.

In this task of evaluation, tests have much to contribute. But tests will not serve education well if they are used by naive educational reformers as instruments of measurement with which to influence and control the movement of education. Only when they are part of the total process of evaluation are they valuable. With this type of evaluation, decision making is possible; motivation is possible.

Here is the value of testing programs for us—we can help youth to realize and develop the talents that are theirs, be those talents one, two, or ten, so that, having actualized the potential that is God's gift to them, they may receive at the final graduation the "scholarship" beyond all scholarships: "Well done, thou good and faithful servant."

The education of retarded children

Rev. Elmer H. Behrmann

Despite the financial and personnel limitations under which they operate, more and more Catholic school systems are taking an interest in the education of the mentally retarded. Father Behrmann, director of the Department of Special Education for the Archdiocese of St. Louis, discusses in the following article several aspects of the problem. He not only explains why retarded children should be given a Christian education, but suggests what and how they should be taught.

Montaigne has said that the most universal quality is diversity. Educationally speaking this universal diversity is expressed in the principle of individual differences. Our Divine Savior elaborated the principle of individual differences long ago when He related the parable of the talents, telling how to one man the Master gave five talents, to another two talents, and to a third man only one talent.[1]

There are those among our Catholic children of school age who in God's providence have been given only one talent. These are the children who are psychologically labelled "mentally retarded," "defective," or more kindly "exceptional." Those are the children who mentally will never mature, because somewhere along the line an unknown cause has stopped or slowed the normal growth of their intellectual faculties. Yet the pathetic tragedy of these children's lives, is not alone that they have been grievously deprived in the exercise of the one faculty which makes us human—namely, our reasoning power—but their misery is compounded when, because of the lack of proper educational facilities, they are denied even the opportunity to develop their lone talent. Is society by its lethargy in providing proper educational facilities burying the one talent of these

[1] Matthew xxv:15.

Reprinted with permission from *The Catholic Charities Review,* **45:8–14, March, 1961.**

children and exposing the handicapped child to the harsh confiscation of what little he does have? If so, then society must stand ready to plead guilty to a social injustice when the Lord shall come and demand a reckoning. Surely when the educational table for our normal children seems at times to be laden not only with the necessities of mental life, but also with its luxuries, is it too much to ask that more than a few crumbs fall the way of the less gifted child?

Mental retardation is a haunting problem which overshadows the lives of the loved ones of every exceptional child, to which no satisfactory natural answer can be given. There is only one explanation. One day a blind man was brought to Jesus Who healed him. Shortly someone asked Christ: "Master whose sin is it, this man's or his parents', that he should be born blind?" And the answer of Christ still enriches the meditation of all who have had or worked with handicapped children. It is their strength, not merely their consolation. "Neither hath this man sinned nor his parents, but that the works of God should be manifest in him." [2]

Is mental retardation something new, something peculiar to our stressful twentieth century? Human nature being what it is, it can reasonably be inferred that since the creation of man, the human race has had the problem of dealing with those among them who through disease, accident, inheritance or training were not endowed with the ability to learn, to adjust, or function in society as adequately as their neighbors.

In pre-Christian days, the lot of defective children usually was liquidation or indifference.[3] With the coming of Christ came also compassion and care for the poor, the lame, the blind, the demon possessed and the mentally afflicted. With Him came the Magna Carta for all deviates and unfortunate victims of society: "Thou shalt love the Lord thy God with thy whole heart and with thy whole soul and with thy whole mind . . . and thou shalt love thy neighbor as thyself." [4] This is the fundamental principle of Christ's social teachings, underscoring the fatherhood of God and the brotherhood of man in all human relations.

This new philosophy began to be applied during the middle ages particularly by the religious orders that voluntarily assumed the care of handicapped children. It is interesting to note that St. Nicholas, Bishop of Myra, initiated charitable efforts for the care and protection of the mentally defective as early as the fourth century. The beginnings of the program of institutional care can perhaps be traced to the thirteenth century when the first colony for the custodial care of the mentally defective was established in Belgium. In the middle of the seventeenth century a chateau in Paris, later known as the Bicetre, was used by St. Vincent de Paul and his Sisters of Charity, as a place of refuge for various unfortunates, the homeless, the outcast, and the bodily and mentally infirm.[5]

During the seventeenth and eighteenth centuries institutions for the deaf and

[2] John ix:3.
[3] Frampton, Merle *and* Gall, Elena (editors) *Special Education for the Exceptional*, Vol. I, p. 5, Boston, Porter-Sargent, 1955.
[4] Matthew xxii:37.
[5] Wallin, J. E., *Education of Mentally Handicapped Children*, p. 2, New York, Harper & Bros., 1955.

the mentally deficient and for other groups were established in Europe. During the nineteenth century we find the beginnings of the formal education of mentally defective children: Jean Itard, French philosopher and physician; Edward Seguin, French teacher and surgeon; Deteressa Maria Montessori, Italian physician and teacher; O. Decroly, Belgian physician; and Alfred Binet, French experimental psychologist, all made major contributions to the education of mentally defective children.[6]

First American School

The first residential institution in America to be especially established for the education of mental defectives was a private school opened by Dr. Hervey B. Wilbur in Barre, Mass., in July 1848.[7] In the years that followed States began to recognize their responsibilities, and by the middle of the century several state schools had been established. Special classes in local school systems did not become widely known until the early part of the twentieth century, although some classes had already been organized in a few large cities before 1900.[8]

Today classes for all types of exceptional children are well established departments of many public and private school systems. It was not until about the time of World War I that special education in local school districts made significant advancement. By this time compulsory school attendance had become widespread in the U. S. The school could no longer neglect children, and parents could no longer permit children to remain at home without official exemption from school attendance. Progress since the early twenties has been so rapid that by June 1952 all the States except Nevada, Montana, and the Territory of Hawaii had enacted some form of school legislation in the interest of one or more groups of handicapped children.[9]

Concerning Catholic special educational facilities, a survey [10] showed that at the time there were known to be 15 Catholic schools for the mentally retarded. By 1955 the number had risen to 54, including both school and day classes. Today the number of such facilities for Catholic retarded children is considerably greater, because all through the past 10 years a new life has been stirring in Catholic special education. A quickening interest has been born among Catholic religious and lay educators to do something constructive about this major problem. Most significant of all has been the establishment in 1953 of the Department of Special Education in the National Catholic Education Association, thus coordinating all

[6] Kirk, Samuel *and* Johnson, G. Orville, *Educating the Retarded Child:* pp. 70-84, Boston, Houghton Mifflin Co., 1951.

[7] Wallin, *op. cit.* p. 10.

[8] National Society for the Study of Education: Forty-Ninth Yearbook, Part II. *The Education of Exceptional Children,* Nelson B. Henry (ed.), p. 8, Chicago, The University of Chicago Press, 1950.

[9] Wallin, *op. cit.* p. 2.

[10] Behrmann, Rev. Elmer H., *The Organization of a Department of Special Education in the Archdiocese of St. Louis,* pp. 89-128. Unpublished Ph. D. Dissertation, Dept. of Education, St. Louis University, June 1952.

the previously unrelated activities in this field into one cohesive organized body. As a result Catholic special education has acquired status nationally; the learning problems of these handicapped children have been brought into intelligent focus, and their rights to share in the blessings of a Catholic education are finally beginning to be recognized.

Yet in spite of the tremendous advances that have been made in the U. S. relative to the education and care of all exceptional children, the cold embarrassing fact of the whole matter is that according to U. S. government statistics [11] approximately only one handicapped child in 10 is receiving the kind of an education, public or private, which will best develop his abilities to their maximum. Pathetically it can be asked: "And where are the other nine?"

Who Are the Retarded Children?

These are children of such incomplete mental development that they are unable to adapt themselves to the normal environment of their fellows in such a way as to maintain existence independently of supervision, control, or external support. They are usually characterized by intellectual inferiority and social incompetence and fall below a 70 I.Q.

Mental retardation stems from a variety of causes, which may be hereditary or acquired. Some of the commonest clinical types of retarded children are the brain damaged, the mongoloids, the convulsive, the epileptic, and those with various disorders such as cretins, the hydrocephalics, the microcephalics, etc. Mental retardation is essentially incurable, but its effects in a child can often be modified and ameliorated through indicated medical and educational facilities plus proper social training.

An astounding fact about retarded children who are so little understood or accepted by the general public, is that they amount to at least 2 or 3 per cent of the population, and constitute the largest single group of seriously handicapped children. There are 4,800,000 retarded children in the U.S. today; there are 330 retarded babies born every day in the U. S.; one in every four adults will have some connection with a retarded child; retarded children amount to more than twice the combined totals of children who are blind, afflicted with polio, cerebral palsy and rheumatic heart disease.[12]

Ordinarily for diagnostic purposes retarded children fall into three levels:

1. The totally dependent or low-grade defective child: theoretical 0 to 25 I. Q. These children comprise about 2 per cent of all mentally defective children.

2. The middle-grade defective child, usually called trainable: from 25 to ap-

---

[11] Martens, Elise H. Ch. V., *Statistics of Special School and Classes for Exceptional Children*, 1947-48. pp. 1-13. Biennial Survey of Education in the U. S. 1946-48. Washington, U. S. Gov. Printing Office, 1950.

[12] Sister Mary Theodore, O.S.F., *The Challenge of the Retarded Child*, p. 12. Milwaukee, The Bruce Publishing Co., 1959.

proximately 50 I. Q. These amount to about 13 per cent of all mentally defective children.

3. The high-grade defective, usually called the educable retarded child; from approximately 50 to 75 I. Q. These constitute about 85 per cent of all retarded children.

An educable child is one who profits from specialized academic and vocational instruction. Generally speaking he can be expected to achieve from a second to a fourth grade subject level by the age of 16. A trainable child has potentialities for learning self-care, social adjustment in the family and neighborhood, and economic usefulness in the home, residential school, or sheltered workshop. He will require some care, supervision, and economic support throughout his life. A totally dependent child will require care and complete supervision throughout his life, and is usually placed in an institution.

Why Should the Retarded Children Be Educated?

Many practical reasons could be adduced to justify the education of retarded children, such as the savings to taxpayers if these children need not be supported as adults in public institutions; the amount of taxes they too would contribute to the government from their earnings, etc.

Strangely enough, some people, even Catholic Americans, assume that the money and time spent on the educational and training of these children with learning potential, may be tolerated for reasons of pity, of community benevolence, but the question of human rights, dignity, and integrity do not seem to enter their minds. Fortunately Americans are maturing to the point where the rights of all minority groups are beginning to be recognized and respected. I submit that mentally retarded children have strict rights in social justice to an education or training suited to their capacities.

They enjoy first a natural right to have their one lonely little talent developed. God does not give powers of mind or body, even though limited, if He never intended their use, for this would make God do a foolish thing.

Secondly, they have a right to an education based on the American democratic principle that all men are equal before the law, equal in their right to learn, if not in their capacity to learn. James T. Adams has eloquently written:

> But there has also been the American dream, that dream of a land in which life would be better and richer and fuller for every man with opportunity for each according to his ability or achievement.[13]

Thirdly, they have a most clear Christian right to an education. With the birth of Christ there was introduced into education a new ideal and perspective,

[13] Adams, James T., *The Epic of America.* p. 404. Boston, Little, Brown and Co., 1932.

the ideal of the supernatural destiny of man. As Father McGucken, S.J., explains it:

> Every child born into this world is regarded as a child of Adam. Through the life, passion, death and resurrection of Christ, the Son of God, every one of the descendants of Adam can be restored to his rightful heritage as a child of God. The whole business of the Church is for this purpose, to give this new life to all the sons of men, to keep it alive and growing, bringing forth fruits. So too the education work of the Church is precisely for that purpose. Her whole educational aim is to restore the sons of Adam to their high position as children of God, citizens of the kingdom of God. The key of the Catholic system is the supernatural.[14]

You simply cannot understand the work of the Catholic Church on earth in any phase if you do not have a supernatural, other worldly point of view. St. Paul calls it the "foolishness of the cross."

> For the foolishness of God is wiser than men and the weakness of God is stronger than men . . . But the foolish things of the world has God chosen to put to shame the wise, and the weak things of the world has God chosen to put to shame the strong.[15]

Somehow the Catholic special education of Catholic retarded children seems to exemplify perfectly this other worldly point of view. This work seems good, right, and necessary, for it is the work of God. Christ spent His life among the handicapped dispensing His works of love. "It is not the healthy who need a physician," said He, "but they who are sick."[16]

What Type Educational Facility Can Be Supplied to Educate the Retarded?

Granting the rights of these children to a suitable education, what form of educational agency seems most appropriate? The answer to this question depends on local circumstances, a child's needs, and the educational philosophy which an administrator may hold.

There are first of all public residential institutions which most States maintain for the instruction and supervision of retarded children and adults, even on a life placement basis. There are also many private residential schools throughout the U. S., with varying admission policies and permanency of placement.

A more recent trend in the education of the retarded has been the establish-

---

[14] McGucken, William J., S.J., *The Philosophy of Catholic Education*, p. 16. New York, The America Press, n.d.
[15] I Cor. i:18-30.
[16] Matthew xviii:30.

ment of local community facilities, usually on a day basis. These facilities are either schools totally dedicated to instructing the retarded, or individual special classes localized within certain regular schools. This latter approach, i.e., special day classes, can be called the policy of integration wherein retarded children are taught separately but are brought into daily contact with normal children, with whom they must eventually adjust as adults if they are to be accepted into later community life.

Special day classes offer many advantages of economy, transportation, acceptance of retarded children in the social life of the school by the normal child, participation by retarded children in parish liturgical life, part-time placement in the normal classroom, etc. The classes can be flexibly located to accommodate population density, and offer usually a quick entry into this field for almost any diocesan school system. This form of integration offers normal children a wonderful opportunity to practice corporal and spiritual works of mercy. One crippled 14-year-old retarded boy who had never been to school before, was carried downstairs from a second floor apartment every morning, and lifted into a car by two students who volunteered for the task. In another instance some retarded children were doing so well that they were placed in a regular class for an hour or so each day. At the end of the year, they had become so popular the students asked permission for them to wear a cap and gown and go through the graduation ceremony with the regular class because "they're our friends."

Since it would not be realistic to assume that all Catholic retarded children would be sent to full-time Catholic special classes or schools where they might exist, then it becomes necessary to think of supplying Catholic instruction to Catholic retarded children in public special classes or schools. In this particular area the Confraternity of Christian Doctrine could be of invaluable assistance in setting up part-time instructional classes after school hours, or on the weekend by means of the various media recommended by the Confraternity.

In the full-time academic instruction of retarded children, the class load must remain small, preferably about 15. The classes should be ungraded, with each child working at his own level and speed. The instruction must be individualized as much as possible, and the curriculum should be adapted to the individual needs, interests and abilities of the children so as to promote fullest utilization of their potential.

What Should Retarded Children Be Taught?

The answer to this question depends on the purposes or objectives of a special education program for the retarded. It can be assumed that the education of the mentally retarded is not basically different in its aims from that of any other group of children. These aims are to teach the individual how to live better, both for this world and the next; to teach him to use all his capacities; to teach him to become a useful and contented member of society. The adjusted curriculum for mentally retarded children should foster wholesome growth in full measure for each child, and should never lose sight of the sound psychological principle that these children have the same fundamental needs for love, security, recognition and success that normal children have.

In our St. Louis Archdiocesan special educational program we strive to implement the following objectives:

1. Religious training to promote spiritual and moral growth.
2. Maximum adequacy in the essential academic subjects.
3. Development of social and personal skills to promote acceptable human relations.
4. A practical arts program including manual, vocational and work experience to develop maximum economic self-sufficiency.
5. Training in civic responsibility.[17]

We try to teach retarded children religion, to prepare them for first Holy Communion.[18] We teach them the basic academic subjects of reading, spelling, writing, and number work. We give them vocational training. We help them acquire emotional control and social maturity; we train them in every way possible to fit easily and happily into adult community living, and if possible to become employable in work suited to their abilities.

No school system is better than the quality of its teachers. Special education teachers must be qualified in heart and in mind if they are to satisfy the fundamental needs for love, security, recognition and success of the children under their care. They must be prepared to render service that often is over and above the call of duty, soothing away those tears, wiping untended noses, zipping zippers—being at once teacher, mother and nurse.

In the classrooms we use all sorts of audio-visual aids: film and slide projectors, radios, TVs, recorded lessons, earphones, and all the very latest instructional equipment especially designed to capture and hold the attention of retarded children many of whom are quite hyperactive and distractible. The alert teacher of these children will use every available means at her command to convey her instruction in the most concrete manner possible. Retarded children cannot absorb abstractions nor generalizations; they are "thing" minded, and new concepts must always be associated with some concrete "thing" e.g., "two and two equals four" is abstract, but "two apples plus two apples equals four apples" is concrete.

A detailed discussion about effective teaching procedures and special class management is beyond the scope of this paper. There are available many excellent resources to which the reader is referred for further elaboration of these areas.[19]

In our educational efforts for retarded children, we cannot point to any

---

[17] cf. *Curriculum Guide for Use in the Special Ungraded Classes for the Educable Mentally Retarded Child*. Published by the Department of Special Education, Archidiocese of St. Louis, 4472 Lindell Blvd., St. Louis 8, Mo., 1958.

[18] cf. *COME*, an illustrated First Communion Catechism of Minimum Requirements. Distributed by the School Sisters of Notre Dame, 5341 Emerson Ave., St. Louis 20, Mo., 1958.

[19] Kirk, Samuel *and* Johnson, G. Orville, *op. cit.*, cf. Bibliography pp. 361-417.

startling public transformations or dramatic success with these children. But often the most rewarding outcomes of a program can be the intangibles like love, peace of mind, and happiness—these not only for the children but also for the teachers and parents.

We have cases of our "graduates" who are working as aides in hospitals, and in ceramics in sheltered workshops, doing simple work in stores and supervisory work with younger children. A mongoloid boy with an I.Q. of 50 is doing very satisfactory work in his father's grocery store, after an intensive training period in our special school.

I think it would be wonderful for both the children and religion if some of the religious orders would think favorably of taking our higher grade retarded children into religious life as domestics, lay brothers, maintenance workers—wherever they might be needed for simpler routine work. Under supervision these youngsters would be faithful, satisfied workers, and in turn would enjoy the security of life offered by the various communities.

Conclusion

There stands off the shores of New York the thrilling Statue of Liberty, gift of the French people to the people of the U. S. Holding aloft the beacon light of liberty, it stands as the symbol of hope and happiness to the underprivileged and oppressed millions who have come to our shores.

It is sincerely to be hoped that through the suitable education of retarded children, America will all the more adequately meet the challenge of moulding a thoroughly Christian concept of civilization.

Teacher and the slow learner

Sister M. Bernarda, O.S.B.

*Not to be confused with the mentally retarded child
is the slow learner. The latter ordinarily is not
placed in a special school or even in a special room,
and it is debatable whether or not he should be.
Drawing on her extensive experience as a teacher at
every grade level from the elementary school through
the university, Sister Bernarda discusses some of the
special educational problems of the slow learner and
gives a number of specific suggestions for helping to
overcome them.*

In the three decades of my years of service in Catholic education, I have been privileged to see a remarkable transition in educational trends and methods. From all angles, significant changes and improvements have occurred and are continuing to occur. More and more we realize that the achievements in Catholic teaching have been consistently and positively implemented in every possible way. The subject and content matter, the technique of presentation, the achievements of pupils, the wholesome teacher-administration interest in individual children, have all received impetus toward more effective educational fulfillment. The school *is* meeting the demands of current educational needs; the Catholic school in particular is doing a singularly remarkable work. I have been privileged to be a part, a small part of this achievement in progress, and while there have been many discouraging features and numerous setbacks in the attainment of our goals, there have been also consoling and encouraging successes.

A Heartening Trend

One of the most heartening and Christian trends in education is the particularizing of the study of individual differences. It is an established fact that differences

Reprinted with permission from *The Catholic Educator*, 32:648–651, March, 1962.

exist among creatures. The supreme power of our Heavenly Father in the marvelous plan of creation is evidenced in the differentiations of nature. All about us in the glorious world in which we live, we see a confirmation of the Creator's ingenuity. The marvelous power of God is revealed on every page of life. Insect and plant life, animal and bird life, life in the massive waters that surround our glittering world—all living creatures sing the triumphant "Te Deum" in praise of God and of His Almighty Power.

Any educator knows that among men, too, there are variations of ability and differentiations in performance among the pupils in even one classroom. Any good standardized achievement test indicates this adequately; any interested and zealous teacher can prove this. Because these differences do exist among children, a significant classroom problem exists, and we have contrived to meet these variations in performance. In the traditional pattern of learning, the general situation in the school has been geared to the average child. Normally children enter school at a standard chronological age which varies, however, in the separate states. This pattern of trying to fit every child into the same mold, into the same groove, has had its limitations. Certainly, emotional problems can be created for both the fast and the slow learners.

The school cannot ignore these individual differences. It must attempt some solution, and one solution is suggested in homogeneous grouping. Not in every instance, however, can homogeneity be realized. In every school system there are large and small schools; rural and city schools; ungraded and consolidated schools. True homogenous grouping can be affected only in those schools with more than two rooms to a grade. Ability grouping has received a rejuvenation during the past few years. By its very nature it becomes controversial. Some educators believe it to be the only solution to educational needs; others are skeptical and will not accept it, pronouncing it undemocratic and unfair. The best judges in the plan, however, are those who work with it daily. Individually each child stands alone; each child must be given the opportunity to achieve at his own pace, both vertically and horizontally. Identification and placement of children in their respective groups is an important aspect of ability grouping. The academic status of children can best be determined by achievement tests.

Characteristics of the Slow Learner

During the decade of the 1940's great interest had been centered on the slow learner and the mentally retarded child. However, both extremes of exceptional children, the bright and the slow, are receiving attention during more recent years. This article will be confined to the slow learner in the classroom, and the first thing to be considered will be the characteristics of the slow learner. The slow child is identified because his basic ability falls below that of his group, or he may be classified as slow because his rate of learning is below that of the average. The slow learners form the highest intellectual group of retarded children, and they comprise about fifteen per cent of the school population. The average and the fast children in the classroom outstrip them. Usually they do the poorest work in the regular classrooms of heterogeneous grouping. Normally, they are like the average or bright children in their emotional, social, and physical and motor development. Even though they are retarded and cannot keep pace with the other children intellectually, they are not so poor that they cannot be assisted. These children are educable and while their deviations in ability be markedly poor by contrast with average or bright children, in their own group they are not intellectually impossible. Therefore, the slow child has a right to a program which will meet his educational needs.

Intelligence is one of the powers of the soul; a person's mental ability resides in the intellect. Since God created the intellect, God permits the difference. He alone created the differences. God permits that this particular child should have this particular intellect. Knowledge and remembrance of this will be sources of consolation to any teacher who stands daily before her slow learners in the classroom. The slow learner is frequently inattentive, because he possesses a short attention span. He is often discouraged by lack of success in his efforts, and he can become the object of the impatience of the teacher because he needs more time. He frequently misunderstands the assignment unless it is clearly explained by the teacher, and he knows exactly what he is to do. Recurrently, he is careless in the presentation of his work, and it lacks completeness and thoroughness, but with encouragement and guidance he can do better work. It is better to attempt a little well done, than to endeavor achieving a quantity. Qualitative goals rather than quantitative ones should be set by the teacher.

Repetition and Drills Necessary

Because his retentive powers are comparatively limited, he finds it difficult to retain essential points. Constant repetition and recurring drills are necessary in order to assist him to absorb even only fragments of the general principles. He lacks creativity, originality, and initiative, and he cannot work with abstractions. He lacks intellectual curiosity and resourcefulness and yet the imagination of this type of child can sometimes be surprising, as is evidenced on one occasion when a slow learner said to his teacher: "Sister, there are so many beautiful flowers in our garden. Some of them are so high they reach to heaven." And then, there is the story of the little boy Michael, in the low average first grade. The Sister was telling the story of the Annunciation and had just finished saying: "And God chose the Blessed Virgin to be His mother, because she was so good and holy, and God waited for her to say 'Yes,'" when suddenly, Michael called out: "Sister, I bet you if the Blessed Mother had said 'No,' God would have chosen *my* Mother, 'cause she's so good and so holy."

Frequently Inarticulate

The slow learner does not always have ability to distinguish between similarities and differences in objects—at least, he cannot always do this easily. His vocabulary is limited and because of this he is frequently inarticulate in the classroom. The percentage of speech defects among them is greater than among average children. Generally, these children possess the social traits of honesty, truthfulness, and sincerity. Physically, the slow learner frequently has poor muscular coordination and he becomes more easily fatigued. He displays a greater degree of dependability upon the teacher than does the average. He needs recognition and approval and he must attain success, because the sense of victory in one step is the only means of attaining success in the next step. As Brother Louis Faerber of the Society of Mary says: "A series of victories must be the goal for the slow learner and this is attained by success in easy things." After each success the degree of difficulty should be increased.

Needs to Participate

Each child needs the opportunity to participate on his own level of ability. Just as the average child cannot compete with the genius, so the slow child cannot compete with the average child. He can become frustrated, perhaps humiliated, when he sees those about him achieving what he attempts and cannot accomplish. He must be given every opportunity, therefore, to develop to his capacity and to achieve at the mental level given him by God.

The teacher's first step in meeting the slow learner in the classroom, in order to help him personally, is to develop attitudes of acceptance, sympathy, and understanding among the other children. It is generally recognized among educators that the development of social habits, attitudes, and emotions is equally as important as training in school subjects, and that this development must not be left to chance but must be definitely planned. An individual with an I.Q. of 80 requires a longer time and more repetitions to learn essentials than the individual with higher I.Q.'s, but he can learn them—perhaps modified, perhaps incompletely, but there are slow children who can do long division and fractions, who can diagram simple sentences, and who can write simple interesting letters.

It is important to discuss the teacher of the slow learner. With a teacher who gives her dedicated service in an atmosphere of love, these children are happy. The teacher must never forget the dignity of the child—his dignity as a child of God, no matter in what group he is placed. She needs at all times to see the whole person in the slow-learning pupil. He is primarily a person; he is a child of God; he is a person with important learning to achieve. He needs confidence in an adult who will help him grow toward his individual level to emotional and social maturity. The selection of the teacher for the slow learner is of paramount importance for success. Supervisors should be alert and watchful and should be observant of aptitudes for this kind of work. They should advise their Mother Superiors before the appointments of the school year as to the type of teacher needed for this special work. No teacher should be given slow learners unless this group appeals to her. She should be a competent, successful, experienced teacher. Only when she knows the work of any specific grade can she help the child profitably. If *all* teachers are asked to be Christlike, to be fair and impartial, if the qualifications for all teachers are high, then for the teacher of the slow learner they should be higher. She must be a teacher who is amiable, cheerful, lovable, and kind; *that* spirit which should exude from *every* teacher, must be more marked in her case. An aura of other worldness seems to surround the successful teacher of the slow learner. She is a teacher whose heart is expanding with the warmth of Christ's charity. She is filled with the sentiments of the compassionate Christ of the Gospels. "I have compassion on them." She must have spiritual depth, emotional stability, and insight that pierces the veil which hides the real beauty of the souls of the children entrusted to her by Almighty God. She must understand the nature of the child; she should know what it is to be a child. Francis Thompson eloquently described the child speaking of Shelley: He asked: "Know you what it is to be a child?" He answered his own question: ". . . it is to have a spirit yet streaming from the waters of baptism; it is to believe in love, to believe in loveliness to believe in belief; it is

> To see a world in a grain of sand,
> And a heaven in a wild flower,
> Hold infinity in the palm of your hand,
> And eternity in an hour.

It is to know not as yet that you are under the sentence of life; nor petition that it be commuted into death."

Humble and Tactful

The teacher of the slow learner is humble and tactful; she possesses a sense of humor. Mediocrity and indifference to ideals have no part in her life. She has a strong prayer life, and her own self-knowledge makes her aware of her own weaknesses, her own inability to cope with the problems of life without God's help. This teacher is not opinionated; she works cooperatively with her colleagues. She is loved not only by the children but by their parents, who see in her the embodiment of goodness and Christlike zeal. Her serenity, her friendliness, the warmth of her personality, draw her to others. The teacher of the slow learner is merciful with that mercy expounded in the beatitudes: "Blessed are the merciful for they shall obtain mercy." And Shakespeare's lines on mercy recalled from eighth grade days when memorization was the rule, are thoughts to consider:

> The quality of mercy is not strain'd,
> It droppeth as the gentle rain from heaven
> Upon the place beneath: it is twice blessed,
> It blesseth him that gives and him that takes.

If Our Lord promises to reward the cup of cold water given in His Name, how much more will He reward this priceless teacher whose heart expands with empathy and mercy? On Judgment Day He will say: "I was a slow learner, and you had compassion on me; I could not learn the tables, and you forgave me; I was not neat and thorough in my assignments and you tolerated me; I was restless and confused and you had faith in me; I forgot so easily the things I learned and you were patient with me; I read haltingly and slowly and yet you encouraged me; I was inattentive, but still you loved me."

Exude Kindness and Consideration

Ideally, the teacher should have great love for these children under her care. She must have a love and a zest for teaching itself. She must exude kindness and consideration for others with consistency and with impartial attitudes, and she must have firmness without being inflexible; she must be kind without being soft and indulgent. To reiterate: No teacher should be given a slow learner group unless she is a thoroughly dedicated, good teacher, unless she wants them. In addition to the kindness that must radiate from her, her very bearing, her voice, her expression, her eyes, must all bespeak love for this child. She must remember that every child cannot be perfected and she must face the fact that not every one is capable of the academic excellence normally expected of a regular class. She must be optimistic like the snail in a favorite story:

> Once cold morning during the last week of January, a snail started to climb a cherry tree. Two days later, a beetle stuck his head through a crack in the bark where he had been trying to keep warm. He called: "Hey, Buddy, there's no use going on higher. There are no cherries on this tree." The snail replied: "But there will be cherries when I get there."

Attitude of Optimism

The Gospel story, too, is analogous to an attitude of optimism. Teachers can be compared to laborers in the vineyard. Indeed the field is white with the harvest and teachers have been deputed by their superiors to be overseers in the vineyard. In story books, in fairy tales, overseers are ordinarily harsh and officious. But Catholic teachers should be more like the vine dresser in the Gospel. When the owner of the vineyard sought his advice about the fruit tree that was unyielding, the overseers was patient and understanding. "Sir," he said respectfully, "let it alone this year, till I dig around it—perhaps it may bear fruit." The Catholic religious and lay teacher must be forever patient and forbearing, waiting for the day when these little slow learners will bear fruit.

It would seem that the slow learner can best be helped in homogeneous grouping. He profits tremendously from this type of arrangement. The enrollment in the slow learning group should be comparatively smaller than in the groups of other levels. If there is not a well-established program and a good classroom routine, some of the children would tend to become potential discipline problems because of their higher proneness to emotional or social maladjustments. Extreme reticence, lack of confidence, even pronounced aggressiveness can be personality factors with which the teacher will need to cope.

Fears Ridicule

It must be remembered that the slow learner fears ridicule, and who does not? He cannot read or write coherently, and he is aware of this deficiency to a large degree. Sometimes these slow learners will do nothing simply because they fear to make a mistake. They can be sullen, immobile, impassive, inscrutable. The teacher should try to discover if the child has a flair for drawing or for lettering. If he displays violent temper on occasions, it cannot be corrected by the display of a greater temper by the teacher. Returning temper with more temper is not a means of reaching the child. Patient, individual instruction, the quiet voice of the teacher in such a situation, succeeds better—otherwise, she will ignite a blaze of rebellion.

The teacher should endeavor to minimize the child's personality shortcomings and should attempt to ease the tension that results from having his inadequacies disclosed. Each succeeding accomplishment no matter how trivial, is another stone added to the foundation of his self-confidence. It must not be forgotten that the very core of the emotional problem of these children is their mental retardation. Attitudes are all important. The attitude of the school itself—the attitude of the teachers in that school will help mold more Christian thinking toward the slow learners. Certainly the Catholic school's very purpose of existence, will be frustrated, if Christian thinking in the school is not the prevailing attitude. Faculty meetings, Parent-Teacher meetings, teacher-training courses must find a place in the preparation of teachers and faculty members for assisting the slow learner. Attention should be directed to the fact that intelligence is given by God —that God determines the amount of intelligence each individual is to possess; and that acceptance of His plan certainly ought to lessen the possibility of unkindness. Discussion about the child in the convent, or in the home, should always be done in a serious, professional, and charitable manner. These children with their foibles, their failures, should not be sport at recreation. They should not be held up as objects of ridicule. The dignity of the child must never be forgotten. Intelligence is excellent only insofar as it draws the creature nearer to God. The sane course for the teacher of the slow learner is to love her work, to play her part in the Catholic Church cheerfully, courageously, and with high trust in God. Above all, to be successful no matter in what field—whether with the slow, with the gifted, or with the average, or with the child on the elementary level or on the secondary level—whether in heterogeneous grouping or in homogeneous grouping, the teacher must know herself.

Curriculum Modified

The curriculum must be modified for adaptation to the slow learner. In schools where there are only two classes in homogeneous grouping, the second group—

the slow group, is more likely really to be heterogeneous. With three or more rooms of one grade, the distribution may be more finely drawn; therefore, more successful. The teacher of the slow learner group should have the ordinary course of study because of the average children she might have in her class, but will expect the very slowest in her group to absorb only minimum requirements. She must never forget that the children before her are not miniature adults, but *children*. It is not important that they retain a large store of knowledge of historical facts; it is not important that they know the exports and imports of countries; it is not important that they learn other extraneous matters of this nature, but it is vital that they derive satisfaction and enjoyment from the daily round of their duties and that they learn the basic knowledge of living. The impress of the character of a good teacher upon the child is a thing of priceless, of inestimable value. Confidence begets confidence; love begets love.

Special classes for the gifted?—yes!

Rev. Philip A. Campbell

**At the opposite pole from the mentally retarded and
the slow learner is the exceptionally bright child
about whom so much has been written in the post-
Sputnik era. One of the most widely argued questions
about the education of gifted children continues to
be whether or not they should be segregated from,
or taught along with, children of average mental
ability. Father Campbell believes that they should
be placed in separate classes. In the following article
he explains why.**

The problem of adequately meeting the educational needs of the gifted child is one which has ever perplexed those charged with that responsibility. A glance at the pages of history reveals that this is certainly not a new problem, yet the highly technical skills demanded of today's scientific leaders would seem to indicate that progress in achieving a solution to this problem is of great importance right now.

In order that any discussion or argument might proceed logically it is necessary first that terms be defined. There are several approaches to the definition of the gifted child, and Baker suggests that, "Even the term 'gifted' is undesirable in some respects since it suggests special privilege, which is not the real philosophy behind their education." [1] It will be seen when the criteria of identification are considered that high intelligence alone is not a sure criterion, but certainly high intelligence is one of the requisites. The regulations of the Pennsylvania State Council of Education,[2] to cite a local source, speak of the gifted as those of such superior mentality that adequate educational opportunity for them can be furnished only in special classes designed for their special needs. Paul Witty finds such definitions either unclear or too restrictive, for he states, "Perhaps it is desir-

Reprinted with permission from *The Catholic Educator*, 31:140 ff., October, 1960.

able to broaden our definition and to consider any child gifted whose performance, in a potentially valuable line of human activity, is consistently remarkable." [3] Because this definition would eliminate the truly gifted child who is (perhaps as a result of neglect on the part of educators) inclined to be lazy, it might be better to accept as safe in searching for a definition the regulations established, as quoted, by the Commonwealth of Pennsylvania. In general, it would seem that the definition must include not only the successful child, but also any child of superior intelligence who can be made to work in accord with his talents. Obviously, the means of identifying such children become more important than the definition which might be applied to them.

According to Helen Kleyle [4] the three basic means of recognizing the gifted child are standardized tests, teachers' judgments, and classroom performance. The combination of all three of these is necessary to the formation of an accurate decision. "It is generally agreed," she states, "that the gifted child should evidence an I.Q. of 130 upwards on the Stanford Binet or a similar intelligence test." [5] The teacher who has the child in class and has had the opportunity to observe carefully should be able to contribute some accurate information in this matter. The criterion of classroom performance can never be taken alone as a certain sign, but when combined with the other two criteria mentioned should give a fairly accurate indication of the presence or absence of the gifts required.

A desire for accuracy would also suggest that the children under consideration be given individual tests by the school's psychologist.

It is quite possible, of course, that a supposedly gifted child may not belong with other gifted children, or may not respond to whatever special treatment might be attempted despite all these precautions. In such a case he should be returned to the regular classroom and subjected to the normal procedures of other children. This presupposes the fact that special classes for the gifted are to be established, a fact which remains to be made in the succeeding words of this article. It is only regrettable that the talents of some gifted children must be wasted.

It is expected that the number of gifted children will be very small. The following statement of the Tri-State study is of interest in this regard:

> The number of children above average in intelligence will vary from community to community. The following statements are in terms of intelligence quotients on the 1937 revised Stanford Binet Scale, and do not apply to intelligence quotients from other tests. Intelligence quotients of 136 or higher appear in one percent of the general population.
>
> Intelligence quotients of 132 or higher appear in two percent of the general population.
>
> Intelligence quotients of 125 or higher appear in five percent of the general population. [6]

Despite this low rate of incidence, it is still most important that programs be designed to benefit the talents of these gifted children because it is from among these that the leaders of tomorrow will come. In the words of one text, "Failure to make provision for an educational program which will prove challenging to those pupils will result in waste not only to those immediately concerned but also to society in general." [7]

What attempts have been made thus far to help these children and to meet their educational demands is the material of the succeeding few paragraphs.

The history of the progress which has been made in this field of study covers a period of many years and has really not been very encouraging. Baker, to whose work reference has already been made, treats of the history of the movement, and it is to him that credit must be given for most of the facts here recorded.[8]

The names of great men of the past fill the pages of history books, of course, but it is not known that they were in the class designated by the established definition of the gifted child. It is certain that, with few exceptions, any special training they received was the result of individual effort and not the fruit of any organized program established for their peculiar talents.

Plato is supposed to have advocated the use of special tests to discover talented persons of his nation, and to train them in accord with their abilities was his aim. The practice of using enslaved Greeks to educate the children of Roman nobility is possibly a result of his efforts.

The most outstanding example of the selection of gifted persons for special tasks can be found in the rule of Suleiman, the Magnificent, ruler of the Ottoman Empire during the sixteenth century. He was solicitous in choosing the most promising youths of his nation and in providing them with special training. The fear, in his time, that he might conquer the word is sufficient commentary on the value of such a program.

In more recent times Hitler made use of similar practices in his campaign for world conquest. The early years of World War II bear testimony to the effectiveness of his interest in the gifted. Who is to say in this present era of confusion and concealment what means of selectivity are being employed by the Soviet Nation in its striving for world domination.

The modern period of classes for the gifted children in our own country began about 1920. At that time programs were begun in Cleveland, Los Angeles, and Rochester, New York. By 1930 only thirty of 762 cities over 10,000 population had any program for such children. The United States Office of Education revealed that in 1947–1948 fewer than 21,000 gifted children in the country were receiving special training, and ninety per cent of these were in New York City.

A Conference of Education for the Gifted was held in 1940 at Columbia University. At this meeting considerable credit was given to the American Association for Gifted Children. This association, according to Kleyle, "has done an outstanding service to American education by making educators aware of the imperative necessity of providing for the needs of the gifted child." [9]

The work of the past few years in this field has been a little more encouraging, though not outstanding. Programs are being conducted now in a number of American cities, Pittsburgh among them. The "Major-Work" program in Cleveland is possibly the best known attempt to work with the gifted, and to this project we must give consideration. A program is also being employed in the diocese of Pittsburgh at the present time which is intended to cope with the fast learning child and is, therefore, of some value to the gifted if not completely adequate for his needs. This, too, merits our consideration in this article.

The types of programs which have been established for the education of the gifted child are basically five in number: acceleration, segregation, ability groupings, selective curriculum, and general enrichment of the curriculum.

The gifted child quite naturally learns much faster than his normal classmates and has, as a result, often become a trouble-maker in the classroom. The procedure often resorted to in the past to cope with such a situation was acceleration or double promotion. In speaking of children whose I.Q.'s were found to be over 130, Commins states, "About 80% of the group were found to be accelerated in the elementary grades and to have graduated from high school about a year in advance of the normal age." [10] Although moderate acceleration could possibly not be of harm to the child, such a child has often been found to be lacking in social development as a result of this process. Because he is smaller in size than his intellectually equal but chronologically superior classmates this child is often left out of games demanding physical strength. The frustrating effects of such occurrences could have a deleterious bearing on the social development of the child.

The division of students in a school according to ability ratings is possible in a large school and is a step toward the selective curriculum. Because of the low percentage of gifted children in the average school this would usually result in a mixture of the gifted and the bright. The grouping of these children according to ability is certainly not going to curtail their speed of learning. Obviously, then, a curriculum must be provided which will meet the demands of their very fine talents. The time that they save must be utilized. In accord with this thought Witty states, ". . . the extra time should not be devoted to more of the same type of endeavor or to busy work." [11] With reference to these necessary adjustments he adds:

> The gifted child requires a curriculum adapted to his extremely rapid rate of learning. The gifted child needs a curriculum of diversified experiences to suit his many-sided interests and to produce well-rounded development. The gifted child requires a curriculum that will enable him gradually to attain social maturity.[12]

It would appear from these words that the mere provision of additional subjects to be taken is not the complete answer. This would amount, more or less, to a rapid accumulation of credits and earlier graduation, which has not been proven to be a real benefit to gifted students. In any event, even if this were the complete answer, it would be impossible in the smaller high school. Enrichment of the curriculum in both the large and small high school appears to be the only answer to the problem, unless segregation of the gifted will bring about the desired end. It is the intent of this article to show that segregation of the gifted, together with the enrichment of the curriculum, is the means most suited to the achievement of the desired end.

Segregation is the procedure employed in the City of Cleveland and elsewhere which separates the gifted children from normal children for a part of the day. This ordinarily involves transportation to a centrally located special school and then a return to variously located average schools. During their time in the special school they are given the opportunity to pursue a more intensive course than is available to them in their regular classrooms. They receive special instruction in art, music, language and literature, typewriting, research reports, book-reviewing and composition. The program seems directed primarily to the elementary grades, although Norris indicates that it also has application to the high school student when she states, "Today Cleveland has about 1,600 students enrolled in forty-two major-work and enrichment classes at the elementary, junior- and senior-high levels." [13] The dangers of such a program are possible conceit on the part of the pupils, overwork and social inability, according to Witty.[14] The attempt is made to avoid this evil in Cleveland by returning the children to their own classrooms for half of each day's work. Whether or not this attempt is successful is not known at this time, but Dr. Kleyle quotes the superintendent of schools in that city as saying:

> Cleveland has not had the disadvantage which comes from setting aside an entire school for the education of the gifted only, but rather has the advantage of the Major-Work Classes as an integral part of the regular school in which they are housed.[15]

Perhaps it might be inserted here almost parenthetically that the aims of Catholic education are being sadly neglected if it is necessary to become involved in elaborate transportation problems in order to inculcate the virtue of humility in those whose every ability and training should demand an appreciation of their gifts as being precisely what they are, gifts of God. This thought, however, shall be further pursued in the conclusion of this article.

In the field of secondary education the idea of segregation has been carried to what is thought its logical conclusion by the City of New York in its establishment of specialized schools for the gifted. This is possible, of course, only in a very large city where many gifted children are to be found. Concerning the success of this program, Morris Meister has thus expressed himself:

> Student selection on the basis of interest, ability, and terminal aims creates both a favorable learning situation and a democratically desirable social environment. The specialized high school provides many students with a purpose, which, for them, the general school lacks. The specialized high school provides many students with a curriculum which is consistent with the idea

of a well-rounded education. The specialized high school makes a better integration of the curriculum possible.[16]

Then, as if to answer the question of the advisability of such a program of specialized schools, this same gentleman adds that in the June, 1950 graduation class of one of these schools there were 391 boys and girls; 175 scholarships were made use of by this group in 125 colleges. These scholarships were valued at $200,000.[17] The reader need only compare the cost of a college education in 1950 to the cost of today to realize the monetary values here involved.

It is obvious that enrichment of the curriculum is a part of almost all of these programs, and by some, your author not included, enrichment is thought to be preferable to segregation. Baker, for example, has written that, "Enrichment provides many opportunities for gifted children without some of the possible disadvantages of acceleration or segregation." [18] This does not seem, however, to be at all in keeping with modern educational thinking. The small group of American men who are thought to be the best equipped physically, mentally, and emotionally to enter into outer space are very definitely separated from their inferiors and given special training. Everyone recognizes their abilities and no one seems to resent their segregation. In every classroom the children who are brighter and want to learn are clearly recognized not only by their teachers but also by their classmates as being such and are often a source of help in training slower students. Merely to give these children more difficult assignments is to distinguish them from others. Why not make the separation complete, place them in special classes, and give them the opportunity of competing with those who are of equal ability? The distinction exists; the differences are apparent. There is no value in attempting to pretend that the gifted child is normal. He is not normal. God has given him special gifts, and he should have the opportunity of developing those gifts. That opportunity can best be afforded him when he is placed in an atmosphere of learning and where there is competition to spur him on to greater intellectual activity. The child who excels in the field of athletics is made to know that he is different and is often given educational opportunities he doesn't desire simply that these abilities might be developed. The child who is intellectually gifted should also be given such opportunities. It is thought that his contribution to society will be somewhat greater.

Some of the greatest intellectuals of history have been men of profound humility. If segregation and the opportunity to grow in knowledge create in a person the tendency to act contrary to the norms of decent human society, then either his teachers have failed in their responsibility before Almighty God, or that person is not truly gifted in the sense of our definition. That is why such great care must be exercised in the selection of students to whom special training is to be given.

Educators who have studied the problems of the gifted child for many years are not in complete agreement as to the best definition of the creature. They do seem to agree in this, however, that he can best be identified by a combination of high intelligence, teacher recommendation of talent, and general success in academic work and standardized tests.

Although his existence has been suspected for many centuries, attempts to really do something about and for him seem to be mostly, with a few notable exceptions, the work of the educators of this century.

The results of their studies have led modern educators to attempt many means in an effort to meet the intellectual demands of these chosen few, so few, indeed, as to number less than three or four per cent of the world's population. Such ideas as ability groupings, selective curriculum, specialized schools, and others can be reduced to three major schools of thought; those of acceleration, enrichment of the curriculum, and segregation.

Acceleration must be rejected, for it tends to place a child in a class with those who are emotionally and physically his superiors, resulting in his being the object of either derision or rejection, neither of which can contribute to his intellectual progress.

Enrichment of the curriculum is certainly a part of the answer, for the mere addition of similar work, or "busy work," will only create monotony for the gifted child. By enrichment is meant the pursuit of special instruction in art, music, languages, book-reviewing, research work, typewriting, etc.

Enrichment, however, is only a part of the real answer which is segregation. As soon as the child in the normal classroom is set aside by being given such special assignments as those indicated above, he is being segregated. The segregation, then, should be completed. He should be separated completely from the normal, from even the fast learning child and given the opportunity to develop his abilities in the company of other children of the same age who are equally gifted. This is to enable him to utilize his gifts; this is to enable him to make his proper contribution to society; this is to enable him to answer God for the ten talents he has received; this is the task of Catholic education.

REFERENCES

1. Harry J. Baker, *Introduction to Exceptional Children* (New York: The Macmillan Company, 1953), p. 282.
2. Tri-State Area School Study Council, *Essential Special Provisions for Exceptional Children* (Pittsburgh: Tri-State Area School Study Council, 1955), p. 11.
3. Paul Witty, "The Gifted Child," *The Education Digest,* Vol XVIII (May, 1953), p. 10.
4. Helen M. Kleyle, "An Integrated Language Arts Program for the Gifted Child in the Intermediate Grades" (unpublished paper, The University of Pittsburgh, Pittsburgh, 1955), p. 2.
5. *Ibid.*
6. Tri-State Area Study, *op. cit.,* p. 3.
7. Paul B. Jacobson, William C. Reavis, and James D. Logsdon, *The Effective School Principal* (New York: Prentice-Hall, Inc., 1955), p. 409.
8. Baker, *op. cit.,* pp. 288-290.
9. Kleyle, *op. cit.,* p. 5.

10. W.D. Commins, *Educational Psychology* (New York: The Ronald Press Company, 1937), p. 188.
11. Witty, *op. cit.*, p. 11.
12. *Ibid.*, pp. 10-12.
13. Dorothy E. Norris, "Tailor-Made for High IQ's," *N.E.A. Journal,* Vol. 42 (May, 1953), p. 276.
14. Paul Witty, *The Gifted Child* (Boston: D. C. Heath and Company, 1951), p. 262.
15. Kleyle, *op. cit.*, p. 12.
16. Morris Meister, "What Provisions for the Education of Gifted Students?" *Bulletin of the National Association of Secondary School Principals,* Vol. 35 (April, 1951), pp. 33-34.
17. *Ibid.*
18. Baker, *op. cit.*, p. 291.

Special classes for the gifted?—no!

Rev. Harry G. Hynes

*In the following article, Father Hynes takes issue
with the judgments expressed in the preceding
selection and explains why he believes the best
interests of the gifted are served by educating them
in a regular classroom. In defending his position he
considers the problem of identifying the gifted and
of developing their potentialities. He concludes that
of the various possibilities so far proposed,
enrichment in a heterogeneous class is the best.*

Should we place our "gifted" students in special classes? This is a serious question that is of great concern today to all school administrators both public and parochial. After much consideration of the problem I am inclined to support the negative view. In arriving at this conclusion my analysis of the problem took into consideration the following points:

1. Who are the "gifted"?
2. How and when can we best discover them?
3. Once discovered, how can their potential best be realized?

Who Are the "Gifted"?

In using the term "gifted" we are referring naturally to that small percentage of students whom Almighty God has blessed with great intellectual ability. This group has always been of serious concern to educators who realize that it is their responsibility to actuate the tremendous potential of these students to the betterment of their fellow man and society in general. Certainly in the plan of the

Reprinted with permission from *The Catholic Educator*, 31:141–144, October, 1960.

Almighty, the prime reason for having given such a potential to so small a percentage of humans is that they are destined or called by God to lead those whom He has blessed with a lesser capacity. "To whom much is given, of him much will be expected." Consequently, Catholic educators are conscientiously concerned with the responsibility for the future that God has placed on these "gifted" students, as well as their own concomitant obligation to actuate fully the intellectual potential of these gifted students whose formal education has been delegated to the schools.

This problem of what we are doing for the gifted student has been under the educational microscope from the moment several years ago when Russia put Sputnik I into space. A hue and cry then arose across our land as to where were our American scientists. Why was it that Russia had scooped us in the Space Race? What were our schools doing in the training of scientists?

As a result of this hue and cry the schools of America, on the elementary, the secondary, as well as on the college and university levels, through Governors' Committees and other interested civic groups, turned the eye of introspection upon themselves to see wherein they had failed or were lacking. To this degree, the fact that Russia had beaten us to the punch was most salutary. Many in American education had become too complacent. We had accepted as fact that, just as America was the greatest industrial nation in the world, so too, ours must be the greatest educational system. I still believe our basic policies to be sound but there had crept in over the years certain points of weakness that this "post-Sputnik" furor had forced us to seek out, uncover, and admit. We are now on the way to eliminating much which had no rightful place in the school curriculum and have set about buttressing up many weaknesses that this introspective analysis helped to uncover.

One of the Weaknesses Uncovered

One of the weaknesses uncovered was in the area of that small group known as the "gifted," who have the God-given potential to be the scientists, the educators, the law-makers, and leaders of the future. Were our educational programs recognizing this group and sufficiently supplying for their needs? If not, why not? This is the problem that concerns us in this article.

When we use the term "gifted" in its strict technical denotation we refer only to about one per cent of our national school population. This one per cent has achieved a ranking somewhere in the area of an I.Q. of 200 or more. More generically even in educational circles the classification of "gifted students" is used to include also students who in a strictly technical denotation are referred to as "superior students." Anyone with an I.Q. between 130 and 150 is rated as "superior." Since the "gifted" student in the strict technical sense is a rare being in any particular school, we shall use the term for the purpose of this article to include also the superior student or anyone with an I.Q. factor of 130 or more.

How Best Discover the Gifted?

The simple answer to the question "When can we best discover the gifted?" is: As soon as possible. Too often these children have not been definitely identified until they have reached high school age. Much valuable time that could have been used on the elementary level especially in formation of habits of study and research has then already been wasted. This points up the need in every elementary school for a sound testing program directed by a teacher or supervisor who has had experience in guidance. All of us know that the I.Q. factor is not and cannot be the sole determinant in discovering the gifted student. A sound overall testing program must be used early on the elementary level.

In determining the gifted students, tests must take into consideration mental ability, aptitudes, and personality. Moreover, we know that intelligence favors no class distinction. Consequently, the development of culture-fair tests of problem-solving ability may prove to be an important development in seeking out hidden talent especially among those who are underprivileged economically. It is this latter group that constitutes the prime potential source of overlooked talent. Frequently, the concept of creativity and imaginative thinking will provide the first clue to the identification of a gifted child in the first grade or in kindergarten.

The idea that giftedness is synonymous with high achievement and that talent will give evidence of itself in the course of the regular school experiences no longer can be accepted. Recent studies have shown that many talented students are achieving below grade norms and that the discrepancy between actual and expected achievement is far greater for gifted children than it is for those of average ability.

How to Realize Potential

This brings us to the main point of our discussion. In days gone by, the "gifted" student in the elementary school, once discovered, was often permitted to "skip a grade." This technique, instead of helping the student, in many cases hurt him for life. In most cases, the physical, social and emotional maturity of the gifted child had not kept pace with his intellectual maturity and as a result he felt out of place socially and emotionally with his new classmates and all sorts of complexes were soon found to exist in his over-all makeup.

Acceleration has a definite place in planning the educational needs of the gifted child, but this type of acceleration, e.g., skipping a child from the third to the fifth grade is certainly not the answer.

Today, four kinds of programming for the gifted student are possible:

1. Retain the gifted student with his grade-mates and provide an enriched experience.

2. Place the gifted student in separate schools or classes.

3. Place the gifted student in some separate classes and retain him in some regular classes.

4. Accelerate the progress of the student by pushing him through the schools at a more rapid rate.

Number four of the above possibilities we have already commented on from a negative viewpoint. For the purposes of this article we are concerned primarily with number one and number two. I am supporting the program enunciated in number one above, as opposed to the program in number two, which would place the gifted student in special classes.

Reasons for Opposing Special Classes

My reasons in opposing special classes for the gifted are as follows, and I am referring primarily to the gifted student on the elementary level. Because of the greater maturity and the subsequent ability to adapt himself better to environment, I would not rule out special classes for the gifted child on the secondary level.

The gifted child must be given the opportunity of observing a variety of patterns in intellectual behavior. If he is to mature not only intellectually, but also socially and emotionally and to assume his role fully in society, he must be aware of intellectual levels other than that of his own. These he will readily become aware of if he is grouped heterogeneously rather than homogeneously in special classes.

In educating the gifted, three kinds of objectives are generally stated.

1. Stimulate the gifted student to do more precise *critical* thinking.

2. Stimulate him to do more *creative* thinking.

3. Develop in him traits of independence, perserverance, stability and responsibility.

It has been said that the gifted student is one who not only can do things that others cannot do, but can also do them faster. If such a pupil is *properly challenged and kept interested,* he becomes outstanding in all areas. This, then— challenging and keeping him interested—is the sum total of the three above-mentioned objectives.

Since the development of critical attitudes is important, to my mind heterogeneous grouping of the gifted and less-gifted provides the opportunity to both for evaluative judgment. It is necessary that the less-gifted become more aware of the fact that there is always more that they can know and that there is among their own chronological age group someone who can contribute that extra knowledge. Moreover, the gifted must acquire the ability to explain things to the less-gifted without an air of condescension and the less-gifted must acquire the ability to follow explanations and instructions without resentment. As we have stated above, the prime reason for which the Almighty has blessed this group with a greater talent must lie in the fact that he has destined them for leadership. Consequently, the gifted should be able to lead the less-gifted, whereas the less-gifted should learn to conform. Indeed, the gifted must achieve the high standards of judgment, respect these standards themselves, and teach them to the others. They must do as much as possible, because as the saying goes, "They have the brains." These character traits can be achieved most through heterogeneous grouping of the gifted with the less gifted.

But one may ask, in such a grouping how can the gifted be properly challenged and kept interested from an intellectual point of view?

The Answer Is Enrichment

Our response to such a question is that this can be readily accomplished by *enriching the school program for the gifted students.* Enrichment may be achieved as follows:

1. Inculcating in the student good study skills and work habits is enrichment in the highest degree and finest sense of the word. School conditions, especially in smaller schools where there are two grades to a classroom with but one teacher for both, may make it virtually impossible to have a formal program of instruction for the gifted student, but every classroom teacher should and can teach the student how to study most effectively and how to develop good work habits. The gifted student must be taught how to read with understanding, to report, to discuss, and to summarize what he has read; how to see the relationships between ideas; how to weigh evidence before expressing judgment; how to determine the reliability of facts; how to determine sound bases for reaching conclusions. Good work habits must include budgeting of time, keeping notebooks, collecting and using source material, use of the library—all of these are basic for any student but are particularly necessary for the gifted child.

2. Differentiating curriculum content and activities for the gifted pupil in the heterogeneous class. This can be in the form of special assignments which are challenging to the gifted pupils; or, having completed the regular assignment, the superior student may engage in extra activity, such as a report on a special phase of the assignment. There are unlimited possibilities in this type of enrichment, but it requires wide ingenuity on the part of the teacher, as well as a keen understanding of each pupil's needs, interests, and potentialities.

3. Extending the pupil's sphere of activity into the total school program and into the community. Pupils with talents in the fields of music, art, and drama, can develop and utilize these talents to a good advantage by contributing to the total school program. Allowing the pupil to perform in school assemblies, to exhibit his art work, to engage in extracurricular activities in line with his talents, such as radio, TV, talent shows, help him to achieve many worthwhile satisfactions and learnings.

Independent and Group Activities

4. Giving opportunities for independent and group activities. Opportunities for this form of enrichment can be many. The gifted student can be encouraged to use his talents in initiating an activity, such as the writing of an original play or operetta, or planning for a book or science fair, and then extending this independent activity into a group activity.

5. Developing known talents of pupils. Enrichment of the curriculum for the gifted pupil overlaps when specific instances are cited. Giving opportunities for initiating independent and group activities should also help to further the development of known talents of pupils. In addition, these students should be encouraged to pursue their talents in elective classes or in out-of-class activities. Clubs of all kinds offer enrichment in dramatics, in music, in art, in science, in literature, and in practically any field in which the student has a special interest.

6. Discovering unknown talents of pupils. Perhaps discovering unknown talents of pupils is the greatest challenge of all. Actually, a gifted pupil should and usually does all things well. Even without an elaborate testing program a good teacher quickly spots students of exceptional ability. Testing will confirm this, of course, but most teachers personally confirm their opinion of a student's ability by comparing their evaluation with that of other teachers. This evaluation is the report card. However, for those who appear to have no special talents, opportunities to explore new areas of experience—manual, recreative, and aesthetic—should be given them.

7. Training for leadership. All classes can train for leadership. Students appointed as chairmen are responsible for seeing that materials that are needed for committee work are on hand and that each member of the group is contributing and doing his share; for helping individuals where help is needed; for guiding and directing the course of committee work; for reporting upon the progress of committee work. Serving on the student council is another way to develop leadership.

8. Teaching community service and democratic attitudes. This form of enrichment can benefit all students, but gifted students should be taught community service by permitting them to head school drives, such as for the Red Cross, March of Dimes, Christmas Seals, the missions, for charity, for school improvement—the physical plant, equipment, etc. The opportunity to share in common undertakings and to learn the techniques of working well with others is a rewarding experience.

9. Encouraging normal development, because stress and strain would make brightness a penalty. At the present time there are an increasing number of schools throughout the United States planning programs for their talented students. The impetus toward special instruction for the gifted is now as strong as it once was for special teaching of the slow learner. Care should be taken lest en-

thusiasm run away with common sense and good judgment. A gifted student should be permitted to develop as normally as any other pupil in the school. Above all, his social training must not be neglected; he must mingle with many pupils of different abilities and talents. The social situation should closely approximate the situation he is likely to meet in adult life. He must not be allowed to pursue his studies and to develop his talents to the detriment of his health. Extracurricular activities will be of great value to the pupil who is inclined to do little outside of his regular class work. The gifted student must not be penalized for his superior intellect.

Keep Ultimate Aim Ever in Mind

The forms of enrichment already mentioned are but a few of the things that can be done to provide for the needs of the gifted student being educated in a heterogeneous group. However, one thing must always remain as a constant reminder to us as Catholic educators: The ultimate aim of education, as of life, cannot change with time, persons, or place, but must be formulated in terms of eternal values, which, of necessity are forever unchanged. Catholic educators are training children of God. That gifted student who is now your concern in second grade will one day be an adult called by God to use his special talents in one of three states of life—the religious, the married, or the single state. We need talented scientists, talented lawyers, legislators, etc. But we also need talented priests and Sisters for the future of God's Church. Certainly God in His providence has singled out some of these gifted students to work in His vineyard as priests, teaching Sisters, and Brothers. While we seek to discover the gifted student and provide a program that will realize his full potential, let it be our concern also as Catholic educators to encourage that potential not only in terms of the good of the individual and the good of society, but also in the light of the fact that God has destined the gifted student to lead others toward eternity either as a single person, a husband or wife, or in religion as a priest, a teaching Brother, or a teaching Sister.

Personality development versus academic achievement

Robert P. Odenwald

The author, a psychiatrist, questions the wisdom of placing such great emphasis on academic achievement in Catholic schools. He wonders if the schools do not have a higher objective, viz., teaching about God, and a broader one, viz., helping students achieve the fullness of their personality potential. He argues for the kind of school that concerns itself with the whole child, and not only with bright children, but slow learners as well. Broadly conceived, the school's purpose is to develop wholesome personality traits; the article contains some suggestions for school improvement in the direction of this purpose.

One might be inclined to argue that personality development is entirely compatible with academic achievement in our Catholic schools. Ideally this may be true, and certainly it should be true. But practically, I insist that there is a decided opposition between these two concepts. The Catholic ideal of personality of necessity is that of an ideal life, lived primarily for God, and directed constantly toward Christian perfection. I ask you to stop and think. Does academic achievement, held in such high regard in our schools, aim at such a goal? I doubt very much that it does.

First of all, let us define our terms. What do we mean by personality development? And what is the servitude to academic achievement which I condemn as a goal of Catholic education?

Reprinted with permission from *The Catholic Educational Review*, 53:229–237, April, 1955.

Your personality is your own; it distinguishes you from everyone else. No one else has or can have a personality like yours. Your personality is the "you" that we know. It is the sum of all your traits, your habitual way of behavior, your distinctive physical and mental qualities; it is your total response to your environment.

Personality is not born within you, it is something you acquire in a lifetime. It is colored and altered from time to time by your emotions, by sickness, by anything evil that befalls you. Luckily, this change in personality is usually temporary, and basically you are the "you" that has been graciously developing through the years. For our discussion here let us consider personality to include all the psychological traits or characteristics of an individual potentially or actually present, and which, let me emphasize this, are arranged according to some particular plan or philosophy of life.

In a philosophy of education other than that of our Catholic school system, it is conceivable that the ideal of personality development can be of a driving, determined, executive type of training that destroys whatever is in the way of achievement of "success." Does academic achievement of this present day aim at such a goal? Yes, I am sorry to say, it does; it is measured in terms of success only. In order to have a few excel, to be pointed out as "the best," the efforts of the teacher are directed toward the development of these few, while little heed is given to the less-talented pupils who trail along. This, then, is the problem that faces all educational systems, including the Catholic. Education should train its students to place spiritual values highest in their philosophy of life and at the same time prepare them to compete in a world where "success" is the catchword to more and greater success.

Note that I say this is not a problem for Catholic educators alone, for we firmly maintain that educators must all face the same question: Is education primarily concerned with the development of the human personality to its noblest possibilities, or is it primarily concerned with academic accomplishments? If achievement is the principal goal, then development of personal nobility becomes subservient to it.

Obligation to Develop the Whole Child

Who of us will not admit that theoretically it is the function of the school to develop the whole child, not merely his intellectual capacities? Many persons probably smugly believe that our Catholic schools are accomplishing this goal as well as can be expected. Of a few this may be true. But in the main, our Catholic philosophy of education is permeated with the idea that students must be egged on to excel. There is a simple psychologic explanation back of this attitude. For long, tedious years our Catholic schools have had to fight for their very existence, and they have had to continuously prove themselves of a quality in all ways equal to that of the public schools. Perhaps now the mechanism of overcompensation is at work in the minds of our Catholic teachers. They wish to prove that their schools are even better than non-religious schools, by producing pupils who can win contests of statewide or national scope. In this way their schools may be recognized as being superior.

I ask you, do brilliant accomplishments of a few exceptional students make the school a better school? Tell me, are its claims to worthiness so flimsy that the school must pick a chosen few to champion its cause?

Does not the superiority of our Catholic educational system rest principally on the fact that it teaches our children about God and about His commandments? Does it, or does it not, teach a way of life? Or do we support at considerable effort our own system of schools in order that our first-graders may be pushed to read a few more books than other first-graders, or that our eighth-graders may have a winner in the national spelling bee, or that one of our high school seniors may win a state oratorical contest? Surely, this is not why we pay once and then a second time in support of schools. The sacrifice of our added burden would then be a futile one. I do not claim for one moment that we should withdraw our students from such competitions, nor should we belittle or disdain their victories. It is the overemphasis on their desirability as a goal of education. We must ask ourselves, what is the cost to our children?

Let me make myself clear by citing a few examples illustrating the point I wish to make. Our Catholic schools are filled with students whose only interest in their studies seems to be the prominence they gain by sitting at table one instead of table five in the first grade, or being on the honor roll in the eighth grade. This is education that defeats its own purpose.

One of the first laws of the psychology of learning is that the student shall have the will to learn, the will to acquire knowledge of the subject matter, the will to assimilate it as his own. The will to be first in the class, is psychologically and pedagogically an inadequate motive for basic learning and for remembering for any length of time.

How often we read in the papers of some youth whose intellectual superiority has somehow soured! He is committed to a mental institution for safekeeping, or he is sentenced to the penitentiary for some unspeakable crime. You may say that we cannot place the blame on our educational system. But often we can. If development of personality is an aim of education, it will nurture those traits which best fit the individual to some standard of perfection. It will involve the development of a philosophy of life which can sustain the individual's continuous atttempt to attain the perfection of the ideal standard.

The Catholic school which prides itself on the intellectual prowess of its students and the worldly success of its graduates can scarcely be proud when some of these intellectual giants become drunken rowdies on their nights off campus, or when the successful graduates become known as "slick operators" in the business world. Fortunately, these are exceptions among our brighter students. What we are seeking to emphasize is that educational efforts should not be slanted toward the development of only the intellectually superior. It must be aimed at the personality development and learning of every individual pupil in the class.

Concern for Slow Learners

What happens to the less-talented persons who fail to uphold the glory of the school by shining forth as contest winners? We can not overlook the fact that in each school there are a few exceptionally bright pupils and a few who learn with difficulty. In between is the great number of average students, those with so-called normal intelligence. It is for this large group that the curriculum must be planned. They must be trained for the place they are to take in this competitive world.

We stand admiringly before a magnificent building which has just been completed. We feel a deep admiration for the great architect who planned the building and for the masterful contractor who accomplished its erection. They surely were men of exceptional powers. They had the ability to direct the many hands that reared the splendid edifice. But what of the men who did the actual work? Each had to have the particular ability for the work required of him. If we watched the building grow, we stood amazed at the solid masonry that went up before our eyes, at the maze of pipes running from floor to floor, at the intricate wiring being installed, and at the cleverness of the carpentry. Each bit of work had to be perfect. A flaw could be the cause of an expensive leak, a possible fire, an ultimate collapse of a wall. These workers are our average citizens, men who not only know their work but men whose personality development has made them take pride in doing an honest job. These are the men whose children we are educating toward good citizenship.

I asked a recent eighth-grade graduate of one of our Catholic schools how she liked the school. She shrugged her shoulders. "Okay, I guess, only we had contests in everything from the first grade all the way through the eighth. I got pretty sick of them." Of course she did, because they proved to her that she was a second-rater, a mediocre person with no excellent qualities and only a few average ones. Would you say that a Catholic education did all that it should to prepare her to meet the world as a young Christian woman full of the enthusiasm of living, and at the same time aware of her potentialities and her handicaps? You may glibly answer that perhaps there were the cold, hard facts and the girl simply had no talent. Then, it is you that are cold and hard. If this girl had been your daughter, sweet and cheerful, sympathetic and tender, you would deny that she was entirely without talent. Do you dare believe that of any human being? On what would you base your judgment? We all have read biographies of noted men who did poorly at school, excelled in their mathematics and flunked in English; stayed up all hours of the night working on an invention and failed in history. All of these are evidences of misjudgment on the part of the school, of teaching that was not geared to develop the talents of the individual.

Any educational system that stifles, belittles or degrades any of its students because they can not keep up with the seemingly intellectually gifted is doing a grave injustice to one of God's little ones and ignorance can be their only plea for forgiveness.

You may attempt to defend these errors of our educational system by lightly saying, "After all, the students are taught religion. It is hardly the fault of the school that they do not practice it better." You may think the same is true of personality development: "The school does what it can; it is hardly the fault of the school if its treatment doesn't take." What shall we say of a Catholic university which finds itself forced to dismiss students in the graduate courses for cheating, after those students had been in Catholic schools for over sixteen years? Would we say that such a Catholic school had placed its emphasis on personality development or upon academic achievement? Which must have seemed more important to those unfortunate students caught in the whirlpool of ceaseless competition?

We can not blindly claim that all the youths addicted to narcotics, that all juvenile delinquents come from schools where religion is not taught. Little children enter our schools, sweet and soft, ready to be moulded into fine Catholic citizens. Where have we failed in our duty to develop strong Christian personalities?

You can not but admit to yourselves that we do have a very real problem in our educational system. Certainly we can help to better this situation, even though we may not be able to completely solve the problem in our highly competitive American culture.

Some Suggestions for Improvement

The schools can do much to develop wholesome personality traits. Among the traits well suited to schoolroom training are: initiative, self-resourcefulness, persistence and creativeness; honesty, co-operativeness, social-mindedness and freedom from personal bias. If these and other worthy personality traits are to be fostered in the schoolroom, then we must look critically upon the general atmosphere of the school, the administration of school policy, the procedures of the individual classroom and of the school as a whole, all this from a mental-hygiene point of view. Mental-hygiene implications are met in all learning situations. Therefore mental-hygiene objectives have pertinence in every type of subject: history, science, shorthand, or any other subject, as well as in the extracurricular activities of student and teacher together.

One of the corrective measures which we would advocate for the improvement of schools is the careful training and selection of teachers in view of their attitude toward the role of teacher and in view of their own personality make-up. In general, emotional immaturity breeds its own kind, and the emotionally immature teacher can have a seriously harmful effect upon her pupils.

"The instructional activities should be individualized to meet the needs of the pupil," writes one of the foremost educators. This of course implies a great deal more individual attention to pupils. It necessitates a good psychological testing program. It means a great deal of remedial instruction. Curricular requirements would have to be modified to meet individual talents. All in all, this means a great deal more work for teachers and a great many more teachers to do the work. But, to all objections I can only say: Are the children worth helping, or should we be satisfied just to force the three R's down their throats and not really prepare them to live in our modern world? In a good school program each child would become a case study, an individual personality, perhaps with certain handicaps and with certain potentialities, in a unique environment. The school system would strive to help each child on the child's own terms and not on the general terms laid down by the school directors.

A crucial point in modern education, and one closely related to academic achievement, is the competitive marking system. To my mind this helps neither the brighter children nor the duller children. I think that one of its principal purposes may be to aid teachers to dominate their pupils and hold the threat of failure over their heads. For the bright students, the competitive marking system frequently means pride in false achievements, demands for recognition in all they do, love of competition for its own sake, and fear of those who threaten their standing. They may gain laurels far beyond their due on the basis of effort extended, and as a result they may become easily discouraged later on when life demands greater efforts and grants less rewards.

Overemphasis on intellectual achievement leads to distaste for school in those slower in learning. Unfortunately, it even encourages cheating among both the smart and the dull. As long as the teacher regards intellectual achievement as the sole test of the educative process, she will rely entirely on class competition and maintain a distressing hierarchy among her pupils.

The process of assigning grades is a bugaboo of the competitive system, causing undue emotional conflict among children. The pupils become "apple-polishers" from the first grade up through professional school, and they display their anxiety openly. Proper motivation for study is destroyed.

Therefore, for mental-hygiene reasons the wise teacher will eliminate as much as possible unwise competition among her pupils. Co-operation should be stressed in its place. Unless a feeling of co-operative effort is aroused, tension will arise. No child willingly falls behind his classmates, however much he pretends an indifference to failure. Approval is a basic need of everyone.

The child should be trained to compete only against himself, to better his own efforts, to develop his own potentialities, to accomplish the best of which he is capable. The parable of the talents has an ageless application in the field of education.

The school is an important center for training in social consciousness. When academic achievement is the only goal of the school, then only those who excel will come to feel that they have something to contribute to society. Too frequently the classroom is a field of favorites, where only the chosen ones are called upon to contribute anything of their own, either by doing little tasks for the teacher, or displaying the excellence of the class by their recitations when visitors are to be impressed. The more inadequate, the more insecure the teacher, the more she will need to exalt herself by "showing off" her better students and hiding the poorer ones by ignoring them. The less-gifted members of the class come to feel that they are mere bystanders, "leaners-on" of society, with no positive role to play in community activities. When a child is unfavorably compared with another, as in competitive school activities, his personal worth seems questioned. An emotionally mature teacher with a sound knowledge of mental hygiene will moderate the keen competition that so frequently motivates the school activities and will persuade the students to enter them in a spirit of co-operation and for the enjoyment and self-improvement they can receive from these joint activities.

The teacher and the school should provide an atmosphere of acceptance in which each pupil feels free to explore his environment and move toward the satisfaction of his needs without fear of humiliation. It is both impossible and undesirable for the teacher to shield the child from all failure. Rather, the teacher should strive to maintain an atmosphere wherein the child feels so secure and accepted that he can acknowledge failure and deal with it realistically and without panic.

To accept and approve all the child's acts would interfere with learning by keeping the child from recognizing the real consequences of his reactions. The teacher should accept the child as he is, but at the same time encourage him to improve constantly.

Conclusion

Society through its educational leaders should stop the emphasis being placed upon academic achievement as the only and principal goal of education. Rather, it should esteem the whole individual, aiming at maturation of his personality, his moral integrity and his willingness to share in community life and welfare. Academic achievement can never be a measuring rod of a happy, healthy personality. Many a youth who has had poor grades in school or who has even failed in school has become socially useful and adjusted when given the opportunity to prove his worth.

If we are to grow a free and democratic world, we can best nourish the tender seeds in the schoolroom. If personality development is the goal of education, society should and can find a satisfying place for everyone to contribute his share to the progress of the world. Society can not look to the intellectually superior for every accomplishment. The goal of every student should be to become a well-balanced Christian individual ready to assume a beneficial role in society, possessing within himself a mature personality that will bring him a virtuous and happy life.

part V

Problems and behavior
of adolescents

QUESTIONS TO GUIDE YOUR READING

1. *Are Sister Henrianna's generalizations about adolescents valid?*
Are they adequate? Has she omitted any significant points?
Does she make any points with which you disagree?

2. *Evaluate Sister Amatora's procedure in her study, "School*
Interests of Early Adolescents." Were any of her findings surprising to you?

3. *Evaluate the procedure used in Father Meissner's study.*
Which of his findings seem most important to you? Why?

4. *In what sense is Mr. Mahan using "philosophy" when he discusses*
the philosophy of adolescence?

5. *Do the articles in this chapter confirm or deny the statements*
often made that adults do not really understand adolescents
even though they think they do, and that adolescents have problems and
sometimes misbehave because they honestly do not know
what adults expect of them?

6. *Do you find anything in Father Bless's article that appears*
to be debatable? If so, explain.

Know your teen-ager

Sister M. Henrianna

One of the first principles of pedagogy is that the teacher know her pupils. Of all pupils, those in their early teens seem to be the most difficult for an adult to understand. More has been written about this age group, particularly in recent years, than any other. In the following article, Sister Henrianna in effect summarizes much of the literature on the subject. She discusses in nontechnical terms some of the more striking developmental characteristics of young adolescents and brings out the educational implications of their problems and needs.

In our modern age the junior high school child is a bewildered teen-ager struggling through a vital period of physical change and complex transitions which involve his body, mind, and personality. No longer a child and not yet accepted as an adult, he stands in great need of guidance and direction. Psychologists refer to this period of adolescence as one of the strategic points in the life of an individual, a period of "storm and stress" in which the person's character frequently takes its final form. The stage is set for the adult saint or sinner, the law-abiding citizen or the anti-social criminal. Today the teen-ager is very much in the spotlight. With tremendous energy and often with warped ideas he is demanding the attention of the adult world in no uncertain terms. The questions which baffle parents and teachers of today are: "How does the junior high school child think? What does he like? What are his interests? What are his emotions?" He is greatly in need of help: someone who will sympathize with his enthusiasms and frustrations; someone who will understand and forgive his inconsistencies; someone who will overlook his gigglings and his gripings.

Reprinted with permission from *The Catholic Educator*, 32:635 ff., March, 1962.

Importance Always Appreciated

The study of adolescence has been under scientific investigation only since the turn of the century, yet the human race has always appreciated the importance of adolescence and has recognized the significance of its development. Down through the history of mankind this is evidenced in the honor of the individual's passage from childhood to maturity. Saint Luke in relating the journey to Jerusalem for the feast of the Pasch specifically mentions Christ's age because of the importance the Jews affixed to that age. At the end of the twelfth year every Jewish boy, according to regulations set down by the rabbis, became " a son of the precept"; that is, he entered adulthood and was therefore subject to all prescriptions of the Mosaic Code such as fasting and making pilgrimages to the temple.[1] A Roman boy at the age of fourteen was acknowledged as a Roman citizen and was given the privilege of wearing the "toga virilis," the sign of manhood. In the age of chivalry a page at the age of fourteen became a squire with the privilege of accompanying a knight into battle in preparation for his own knighthood. Semicivilized peoples in Africa and Australia observe various ceremonies in recognition of the adolescence of both boys and girls. Indians in our Southwest continue their age old traditions of observing certain rites when an Indian girl reaches puberty in recognition of her potential motherhood in the propagation of their race. Among the Apache Indians an elaborate party is usually held at which, in the height of the festival, the young girl "makes her debut" with the implication that now she is eligible for marriage.

Two Periods of Adolescence

Some psychologists divide the adolescent years into two periods; namely, the early period or the early teens corresponding approximately to grades seven, eight and nine, and the later period or later teens. We are dealing here primarily with the early teen years. A general overall picture of the early adolescents placed into separate sex categories might be as follows: Girls like to study, dislike cheating, cry when hurt, are easily frightened, are kind to animals, do not stick to a hard job, do right even when not watched. Boys show the reverse of this pattern. But to get a deeper insight into the mind of the adolescent we must observe his behavior patterns at school, with his family circle, and in his social activities.

At school there may be a variety of behavior patterns. The typical adolescent is very critical of his teacher and is uninhibited in expressing his opinion to his friends. He seems to have an intuitive sense in judging the merits of the teacher. He admires good discipline and good teaching but is galled by the assertion of authority and is a proverbial griper when restricted by regulations. He is responsive under a teacher who is consistent, who stresses factual knowledge, permits pupil participation in class discussions, leads him to comprehend ideas in relation to one another, and develops initiative for thinking in an orderly and systematic fashion. All these factors inflate his ego and satisfy his drive for intellectual security. Teachers often derive deep satisfaction in meeting the challenge of dynamic eighth graders who become enthusiastic in class projects and assume a fine sense of responsibility. Much of the restlessness of the seventh grader has disappeared so that a definite progress can be recognized as the child moves toward the ninth grade.

More Phases to Consider

But there are more phases to consider. If the adolescent does not respect the teacher, or feels that he is disliked or is not accepted by his peers, he may become extremely aggressive either because of his own inexperience or due to overcompensation for the feeling of being unwanted. This attitude is not confined to boys although it is more common among them. Such a pupil will try to get away with things and frequently will get others to join him in a hostile group to play practical jokes on the teacher, usually with an undercurrent of belligerence. If he cannot identify himself with the group, if he feels unloved and unwanted, he is apt to become a real "problem child" resorting to all kinds of antics in the classroom and on the playground. Thus he satisfies the urge to gain attention or to feign the competence and security which he so deeply craves. In many instances the outwardly aggressive child, the bully, actually feels the deepest insecurity.

Determine Cause

The wise teacher realizes that every behavior reaction has a cause. Therefore she ought to make every effort to determine that cause in order to keep a balance between individual needs and group needs. The restless and belligerent teen-ager who may be the cause of ulcers and sleepless nights may be starving for legitimate attention and love, which is being denied him in his family circle. Not infrequently such cases occur in the upper socioeconomic bracket where keeping up with the Joneses takes precedence over family affection and attention. Perhaps the child suffers from a lack of friends at school or in his own neighborhood. These and innumerable other factors could cause feelings of failure and frustration. A teacher's friendliness or kind words of encouragement or conversation before or after class may give such a child enough confidence to reveal the cause of his abnormal behavior.

Many a behavior problem of teen-agers is a direct result of inability to read since this severe handicap stigmatizes the student as a failure among his classmates. A truly dedicated teacher will find the child's actual reading level, then motivate him to develop reading skills in order to achieve success. Conferring with parents and arranging for special help for such a student may save him from later disaster. However, academic progress should not be the sole criterion of success. Ability in any field of endeavor should be recognized in the teen-ager, whether it be singing, painting, hammering, gardening, or mopping a floor. There is a definite need in our world for these skills and for recognition of the dignity of work. If Johnny's failure to read can be balanced with his success in singing or with some task of responsibility, he will receive the normal recognition for successful achievement. Safety valves can reduce in teen-agers such pressures as nervous tensions, fear, or surplus energy. Often a hearty laugh with (never at) the pupils in the classroom will create an atmosphere of friendly acceptance and give them a true feeling of security.

Asserts Independence

The modern ninth grader all too frequently likes to assert his independence by living in a climate of anti-intellectualism. Although many students pursue their studies conscientiously, a goodly number actually fear social ostracism if they strive for academic excellence. Unfortunately school becomes important, not as a medium for acquiring knowledge, but merely as a source of friendships, which weigh so heavily in the life of a teen-ager, and a place for sharing activities such as sports, dances, and clubs. Ninth graders seem to despise English grammar, griping because "it doesn't make sense" and "it's useless." However, they do enjoy the broadening outlook of world affairs in social studies and are fascinated by the marvels of the solar system and the experimental part of science which at present is challenging adults and teen-agers alike. Find even one of our youngsters who is not ready to go to the moon!

Now let us take a glance at the adolescent in his home environment. Here he is the despair of his parents who are often more frustrated than he is. They are utterly aghast at the notions of their offspring and quite helpless in the face of the human dynamo who, in his struggle for independence from parental authority, questions decisions, is resentful of commands, is suspicious, even patronizing, even pitying his parents for their old-fashioned ideas regarding how modern youth should grow up. He is ready at all times to argue, for he knows all the answers! Boys, in their impatience to assert adulthood, may resort to smoking, gambling, bad language, and destroying property. Fortunately the average adolescent gradually outgrows these delinquent tendencies and adjusts himself to normal adult life. Dr. Paul Furfey made case studies of 168 boys in an eastern city, ranging in age from six to sixteen. Case 44 is most encouraging! Read it.[2]

Factors to Capitalize On

In their growth from grades seven to nine many teen-agers develop a stronger amount of willingness, proficiency, and responsibility in the chores around the home. Wise parents will capitalize on these factors. Both boys and girls do baby-sitting, chiefly to replenish their ever sagging pocketbooks, but boys especially enjoy handyman jobs such as repairing electric appliances, running errands, or caddying. Girls begin to take greater pride in cleaning their rooms, attempting a new recipe, making breakfast on week ends, and delving into sewing, music, and dancing. But please give them enough time for "talking things over" on the telephone!

Social Problems

Now let us take a closer look at the social problems of the adolescent. Because of the mysterious biological changes in growth the adolescent has lost his poise and nonchalance which he possessed at the age of ten and finds himself awkwardly self-conscious, averse to meeting guests of the family, often avoiding strangers, even walking blocks out of his way to avoid meeting the one person he most desires to see. Why? He is blocked with fears that his poor social adjustments will be exposed to ridicule. If at all inclined to be an introvert, the adolescent in this phase of adjustment to social environment can suffer agonizing moments of frustration. The adolescent is painfully sensitive in his intense desire for acceptance and social esteem.

A constant fear of being left out of the group compels adolescents to move in groups. An important fixture of their social life is the "hang-out," that delightful place where they can assert their independence without parental interference. Here they feel that deep inner security of "belonging to the crowd." Here they acquire the latest slang expressions, cultivate the arts of sophistication, discuss movies and TV, gripe about anything and anybody, shout the latest song hits, and admire the newest fads in hair-do's. The craving to gain prestige among their peers causes boys as well as girls to be the despair of their parents in monopolizing the bathrooms. Enchantingly oblivious of time they are busily engaged before the mirror primping up, going through antics of facial expressions, and experimenting with loud neckties, fancy skirts, and colored shoestrings. And every curl must be exactly in place! If mirrors could speak they would reveal the agonizing frustrations, the hopeful aspirations, and the deep satisfactions of these impatient youngsters who have not yet been accepted by their elders yet scorn the "kid-stuff" of yesteryear.

Patterns of Interests Differ

Due to the two levels of maturity the social patterns of interest differ somewhat in the two sexes. Seventh and eighth grade girls often seek the companionship of high school boys since girls mature approximately two years earlier than boys. While eighth grade girls may be deeply interested in the opposite sex, eighth grade boys may not yet have emerged from the bracket of woman-haters. Biological changes in these years cause youngsters to become very conscious of their sex; hence, they become aroused with great curiosity concerning the origin of life. With this problem many teen-agers suffer acute anxiety, hidden fears, and moral scruples. The sex attraction, a perfectly normal God-given drive, affects bewildered teen-agers with various degrees of intensity. Many girls become "boy-crazy," strive mightily to fall in love, use every charm within their power to attract the masculine sex, and feel frustrated if their drive to love and be loved is not fulfilled. Boys can always find an outlet in the world of sports. It must be understood that emotional experiences are not an evil in themselves but become destructive only when misused and abused. Hence training for mastery of the emotions is of vital importance. If management of the emotions has been a part of the child's training since childhood, then by the time of adolescence he should have acquired emotional control and stability, having learned to regulate fears, curb anger, moderate his affections, and control his imagination.

Associations with Opposite Sex

Associations with the opposite sex under wholesome and normal conditions is part of the development of youth; and, with the sanction and supervision of parents, it can provide our youth with enriching and joyous experiences. If our boys and girls have acquired through the grades the virtue of self-control and a correct, dignified, and reverent attitude toward sex, they will be capable of using their abundant energies toward legitimate and worthy enterprises. Social activities for our youth can bring about qualities of leadership and cooperation, develop a consciousness of social problems, stimulate a sense of responsibility, and inculcate a spirit of loyalty and dedication to a cause. Both Hitler and Mussolini recognized the potentialities of the adolescent in organizing their youth programs. It is the responsibility of parents and teachers to prepare the adolescent boy and girl to meet their emotional problems and to direct their responses into morally correct channels. Such guidance is most effective when given with sympathetic understanding and the example of self-control in their own daily lives.

Golden Age of Religious Development

Training in morality is of vital importance during adolescent growth for this period is the golden age of religious development. Many religious vocations germinate during this period. The inculcation of worthy ideals, the training of the will, and the formation of proper habits will result in good moral conduct. A religious environment both in the home and in the school, centered in a personal devotion to God and to our Blessed Mother, will steadily develop principles of right living, thinking, and acting. If the adolescent passes through this period in a normal way, the proper foundations for a wholesome adulthood are laid. The important lesson for the adolescent is to learn to adjust himself to the innumerable and complex problems of daily living in a truly Catholic spirit. If parents and teachers succeed in their task of understanding and guiding the adolescent, he will expand and flower into vigorous ideal Christian adulthood, and be a shining light to the Church and to his community.

NOTES

1. Rev. L. C. Fillion, *The Life of Christ* (Herder, 1945), V. I., p. 379.
2. Paul Furfey, The Growing Boy (Macmillan, 1939), pp. 138-139.

Understanding the adolescent

Raymond J. Steimel

When youth go through what psychologists call their most crucial period, there is special need for understanding. This selection makes no claim to definitiveness, but in it the author does deal with some of the important points that must be known and appreciated if adolescents are to be accorded social equity commensurate with their level of maturity. They may appear as the most exasperating, the most unpredictable, and the most inspiring segment of the population: the impact of each of these appearances will depend greatly on our insights into adolescent behavior.

Introduction

The American adolescent is almost unique in the history of the world. While the period of transition during which the teenager is neither child nor adult has obviously existed since the beginning of man, the special sociological and psychological climate in which the modern teenagers grows to maturity seems peculiar to this generation. To both teenagers and adults adolescence is a period filled with contradictions. It is a time of dependence and self-determination, a time of leisure and of intensive activity, a time of conformity and of rebellion, and a time of carefreeness and of responsibility.

The modern teenager might be described as:

A boy or girl whose energies are already sapped by the sheer process of physical growth, caught up in a whirl of school work and social activities in

Reprinted with permission from *Psychological Counseling of Adolescents*, The Catholic University of America Press, Washington, D.C., 1962, pp. 15–26.

and out of school, confronted by decisions which will affect his entire life, confused by the shifting attitudes of parents, teachers, and society in general, all of whom doubt him and his behavior—and bewildered by the complex and rapidly changing civilization into which he must soon fit, assuming all of the responsibilities of maturity.[1]

Adolescence—A Crucial Period

Due to the frenzy of activity, the confusion, and the drastic changes, both physical and psychological, that are taking place, there is very little time to make an adjustment or settle down before facing the serious business of planning one's life. Vocationally, these last years of high school hold a significance unparalleled in the development of the individual. It is then that they get their first real experience with the world of work. It is then that they develop their attitude toward money, employers, advanced education, and, last but not least, toward fellow workers and employers. They know they will soon have to make a vocational choice, and while many realize the significance of such a step, they do not know how to go about it. As a result, major decisions are sometimes made on the basis of immediate opportunity or emotional attachment with little regard to long-range planning. When years later they find themselves trapped in a job or college sequence in which there is neither hope for personal growth nor the realistic possibility of change, they are faced with the dilemma either of continuing in an unpleasant situation, or of starting over again. The price of a change is usually a significant decrease in salary, plus a delay of several years in the acquisition of life's goals. There is little doubt that the vocational decisions made in adolescence greatly influence the future course of one's life.

Psychologically, this period is of no less importance. No period in the development of the individual, except perhaps the first years of childhood, is more critical in the emotional and social adjustment of the person. For a child the adjustment is almost completely interwoven with that of the parents, particularly the mother. As an adolescent, however, the individual must learn for himself acceptable ways of interacting with his environment. Surveys indicate that the problem of relating to other people is one of the most pressing concerns of the teenager. His self-reliance, his attitude toward people, his ability to communicate and get along with others will depend more on his own resources than on his parents. It is during this period that the young man or woman begins to feel the full responsibility for his action. The inability to get work, the loss of a job, the failure in school have a very personal meaning. It is now I who have failed, I who did not make the grade. Whether they meet with success or failure, each individual is expected somehow to emerge from all these experiences with the kind of personality that will be an asset to him in his struggle through life.

There is no greater challenge to the American parent or teacher than to help the teenagers through these important years. If childhood is referred to as the years of formation, then adolescence might well be called the years of decision.

It is, however, in the very area of helping adolescents to make their decisions that most adults feel helpless. In 1957, Bill Davidson writing in *Collier's* wrote that "Never in our 180-year history has the United States been so aware of—or confused about—its teenagers." [2]

That we are aware of them is only natural. For it is during adolescence that the young boy or girl blossoms forth as the mature man or woman. It is also during this period that the previously rather drab or colorless personality takes on distinctive qualities which stamp it with the character of an individual person. It is likewise during this period that the last ties of parental dependence are severed and the young man or woman becomes a responsible agent in his own right. By and large, this is a pleasant kind of awareness. There is another kind of awareness that teenagers merit, however, which is not so pleasant. Their peculiarities in dress, make-up, and language, their indifference to the many expectations of society, and their disrespect for authority have a way of demanding attention whether we want to give it or not.

The confusion, however, that exists in the minds of many parents and teachers is another thing. Confusion under any circumstances is undesirable. Certainly, confusion in the matters of education and guidance of adolescents is cause for alarm. Only when this confusion is removed can we hope to come to grips with the real problem of adolescents. Above all else this demands an understanding of the adolescent and willingness to work with him.

The Need for Understanding

Perhaps the greatest need of the adolescent today is understanding, especially adult understanding. How often have we adults heard the complaint, "You just don't understand." Almost every survey that is made on adolescents indicates that many of them really want to be understood and would like to have the opportunity to discuss their problems with a sympathetic adult. Somehow they never seem to find the adult with whom they can talk freely.

One seventeen-year-old sums up his feelings in the following letter attached to a questionnaire.

> Most parents do try I think to understand us but it's not an easy thing to do. Teenagers seem to live in a world of their own. They want to be boss in everything. It takes an awful lot of patience and understanding to know how to cope with us. Most parents don't want to try this though. When a teenager feels that he is not being treated right or he's deeply misunderstood things are going to happen. An awful lot needs to be done with that problem. If parents tried to understand teenagers more they would get along much better. [3]

In spite of an expressed desire on the part of teenagers for help and understanding in solving their problems, very little effective assistance is being rendered. Somehow we adults have not been able to meet their challenge. It would be a gross misrepresentation to say that adults are not interested. Anyone who has worked with teenagers and parents can attest to the sincerity of most parents in seeking what is best for their children. While mistakes are made, they do not spring from lack of interest. Most parents are willing, even at great sacrifice to themselves, to do what is right for their children.

Teachers, on the other hand, are certainly no less interested. They entered the profession primarily to work with young people. Their training includes not only academic subjects but also courses in human relations, in psychology, and in sociology, in order to prepare themselves for this kind of work. What is more, many of them take additional courses in adolescent development or personal counseling in order to equip themselves better for the difficult task of teaching. In fact, most teachers feel that they have failed in their duty if, along with the intellectual stimulation, they cannot contribute to the personal betterment of the student.

The question of understanding others, particularly teenagers, goes beyond the desire to be of help to others or even beyond special training in the area of psychological counseling. It seems closely related to the attitudes one maintains toward them. This does not mean that the desire and training are superfluous, but that these qualities must be accompanied by appropriate personal characteristics if they are to be used. All the brilliance in the world plus the sincerest desire to be of help to people is of little value if the personal contact cannot be made.

Though most educators agree that there are specific personality characteristics needed to be a good teacher, no effective screening program has ever been devised to weed out the undesirable candidate. Certainly, the normal college sequence and regular teacher certification remove some poor candidates. Still, not every person who completes the requirements for certification has either the qualities or the personality to become an effective teacher, any more than do all those who pass the bar examination necessarily become good lawyers. The same can be said for any profession. Any teacher will tell you that more than knowledge and skill is needed for success in working with people, especially a group as sensitive and as critical as teenagers. While it is not possible to list or even to describe the necessary personal qualities needed to work effectively with people, it is possible to give *some* of the attitudes that are indispensable in this kind of work.

There seem to be two basic approaches to working with people. The first might be called *directive*. In this the parent or teacher sees himself as a mature individual who is in a position to let others profit from years of experience and training. The first step, then, in helping or counseling someone is to obtain as comprehensive an understanding of the problem as possible. Once this is done, the solution is easy. The experienced person makes the decision for the less experienced. To many adults this procedure is the most practical and scientific way to get the job done. Unfortunately, human problems can seldom be reduced to such simple terms. The fact that the teacher communicates the solution to the pupil does not mean that the problem has been solved for this individual. Knowledge is seldom an adequate stimulus for action. No one likes to be told what to do. To many boys and girls the advice of well-meaning parents and teachers is just so many words with very little appreciation or understanding of the important issues at stake. While it is true that they may have sought out the adult and even asked for his advice, this does not mean that they want it. What they want is understanding and the privilege of making up their own minds.

This leads to the second approach to working with the adolescent. Here the parent or teacher also sees the boy or girl as young and inexperienced, but, at the same time, sees him as an individual who vitally wants and needs to be a part of any decision that is made. Basically the adult is convinced that the adolescent in spite of his youth is capable of handling his own problem when given a chance. Essentially this is an attitude of confidence, optimism, and interest. Someone has described it as an "unconditional positive regard."

To be sure, these are extreme points of view; and there is a broad area between them. The question is, which approach most closely approximates our behavior in dealing with people, particularly adolescents? Are they considered helpless individuals who need to be led each step of the way or are they responsible young men and women, who need encouragement and understanding, yes, but who are capable of making their own decisions? Are we the kind who willingly listen to the problem and then give advice, or are we rather the rare teacher or parent who avoids whenever possible the need to tell others what to do and who prefers to let them do their own thinking and make their own decisions?

This approach the teacher has toward the job, this attitude he has toward people with whom he works, appears to be of primary importance in determining the effectiveness of his work. Proper attitudes create an atmosphere of mutual confidence and understanding. For this reason it is frequently referred to as the "understanding approach."

The understanding approach is characterized by three basic attitudes. The first of these is *acceptance*. Acceptance is a positive attitude. It regards the boy or girl as a person of worth, responsibility and dignity. It is an attitude by which the individual is accepted regardless of what he may or may not have done. It is characterized by a warm interest in the individual, by a sincere appreciation of the feelings and emotions involved in every circumstance, and by a respect for the individual that goes beyond any prejudice or personal resentment. Such acceptance cannot help but induce in the adolescent confidence in himself and in you.

The fact that we accept the adolescent does not mean that we advocate, approve, or even sympathize with his behavior or plans, but simply that we recognize his right to do his own thinking and determine his own course of action.

Acceptance is best communicated through careful listening to whatever the adolescent has to say. The art of listening is indispensable to a good counselor. It is basic to all understanding. Even in our everyday contacts with people we need to learn to listen more and talk less. Its effects often astonish even the trained counselor.

Some years ago there was an elderly woman in Chicago who ran an ad in the paper that she would listen to anybody's troubles for the fee of one dollar an hour.

The response was tremendous. People, old and young, came to her with their problems. She would listen attentively to each without saying a word. After a session with her, the clients reported that they were relieved and felt considerably better. Curious observers attempted to identify what special gift the woman had. After some investigation it was discovered that not only did she have no special training or preternatural power, but that the only qualification she had was that she was stone deaf and could not hear a single word that was said.

Listening alone, however, is seldom very productive; what is needed is interested, attentive listening.

Patterson states that:

> The basic, most universal, most important technique in counseling and psychotherapy is listening. Listening to what another has to say is a basic manifestation of interest and respect.
>
> To listen is perhaps the most difficult thing a student counselor has to learn. Not only must he avoid jumping in to direct the clients remarks, breaking in to ask questions, or attempting to demonstrate his competence or knowledge; he must be able to listen without preoccupation with his own attitudes, feelings or needs.[4]

It should be mentioned here that although there are times and places where direct injunctions are in place and even necessary, these instances are rare— probably much more rare than we are willing to admit. Being non-directive or understanding in our work with individuals or with groups is possible in far more instances than most of us realize. Both Snygg and Combs and Rogers in their respective books devote a special chapter to use of the understanding approach in the classroom setting. Good teachers and supervisors seem to allow for a maximum amount of self determination.

It is certainly safe to say that most of the adolescents who come to adults for advice already know what both the school and society expects of them. What they want is someone with whom they can talk, someone who will think with them, someone who will listen, and someone who will respect them.

The second basic attitude is *permissiveness*. In many ways this is very similar to acceptance. Permissiveness is essentially a nonjudgmental attitude which permits the student to state his case in whatever manner he chooses. He may express any feelings, thoughts, or desires that he thinks appropriate. By the same token, he may withhold whatever he chooses as well. There is no danger of reprisal, no danger of censure or even disapproval. The parent or teacher is not there to decide what is right or wrong, acceptable or unacceptable. This is left entirely up to the individual. The atmosphere is one of acceptance, permissiveness, and confidence. The underlying conviction is that very little, if anything, can be accomplished unless it is initiated by the individual who stands to profit or lose by the decision. From a boy's or girl's point of view, this permissiveness constitutes a recognition of his or her right to privacy of the information, a respect for him or her as an individual. It takes away from the discussion any fear of blame thus making it possible to discuss freely anything they choose. It often happens that the very fact that the teacher has the necessary patience and self-discipline to listen and to refrain from probing or making judgments instills in the young man or woman the confidence necessary to discuss and eventually to do something about his problem.

The third basic attitude is *confidence in the capacity of the individual for self-direction.* This does not mean that we expect the student to arrive at the most reasonable solution nor ever the most practical solution; but it does mean we expect him to come to a solution. Many others and better solutions exist, but the only one that has any real meaning or educational value at this time is the one that this person finds within his ability and motivational system.

At times it almost appears as though some adults are afraid to let the younger generation grow up and assume adult roles in society. At birth the child is in a state of complete helplessness. Unlike many of the other animals, it is completely at the mercy of its parents during the first years of its life. At birth also should begin the gradual shift of responsibility from the parent to the child. This process continues through childhood and adolescence and is ordinarily completed by the end of high school. The assumption is that during the years of maturation the balance of responsibility gradually passes from the parent to the child until finally in adolescence the young man or woman is fully prepared to assume an adult role in society. How complete this transfer of responsibility is or how well prepared the young man or woman is by the time of graduation will depend upon the nature of earlier experiences. Adolescents do not become mature by accident.

This tendency to direct the lives of others can constitute a very real temptation for the adult who feels he has had the relevant experiences. No two experiences are exactly the same. Even though the externals of the experience often appear identical this never guarantees that the individuals involved are affected identically. Besides, in the case of many adults these experiences are so out-of-date that they no longer hold much real significance for the teenager of today.

These attitudes of acceptance, permissiveness, and confidence in the ability of individuals to solve their own problems are sometimes referred to as "the internal frame of reference," or as Patterson prefers to call it "the understanding approach." It is an attitudinal set or almost a philosophy of life which determines our method of dealing with others. In practice it makes the task of the teacher or parent much simpler. No longer is he expected to be an expert in areas where he knows so very little; no longer is he expected to make decisions where he is not qualified. Rather, his job is to provide for each individual the kind of setting in which he will be encouraged and helped to make his own decisions. The teacher or counselor tries to perceive the world as the student perceives it, to judge it as he judges it, and to understand as completely as possible how the student feels about it.

This may sound as if the role of the teacher or parent in helping our youth has been reduced to that of a sounding board, a distinterested listener. Such is not the case. There is an art of listening. It takes both skill and self-discipline. It is this close attention to everything that is said, this serious attempt to understand the views of another, and this sincere reflection of feelings, that eventually engenders in the student a sense of self-assurance, confidence, and responsibility. Perhaps for the first time in his life the adolescent realizes that the one person who stands to profit or lose from any action he may choose to take is himself. He likewise soon realizes that he cannot expect an outsider to solve his problem or to take responsibility for him. The plan of action which emerges from such considerations will not only, as a rule, be in accord with accepted standards of behavior but will also have the advantage of being his own, a plan with which he will identify and a plan which he will work hard to execute.

Many adults are still hesitant to form a close, permissive relationship with adolescents since they apparently fear that this freedom will be abused. Maslow, however, considers this love for and respect for other human relationships and states that, "While they are powerful tools, they are not dangerous ones. We may expect that ordinarily we cannot hurt anybody by loving and respecting them." [5]

The goal is to offer the kind of help the individual can use. Not everyone will be able to take advice, but everyone will appreciate and profit from understanding and respect.

Conclusion

Some has described modern teenagers as the "most exasperating, the most unpredictable, and the most inspiring citizens in America." To the extent that they are unpredictable, there should be something that can be done about it. Unpredictability may be due to the fact that their behavior is so inconsistent and sporadic that it defies any kind of systematic analysis. If such is the case, the situation is hopeless and there is nothing that we can do about it. On the other hand, unpredictability may be due to the fact that we know so little about the needs, aspirations, and goals of the modern teenager that we have great difficulty in knowing what to expect of them. In that case there is something that can and should be done. Certainly, the studies like the one of Remmers and Radler, or sound books on adolescent psychology are great helps in learning more about adolescents. In other words, if we knew what to expect of them, they would no longer remain such a source of confusion to the older generation. While it is true that psychologists never expect to understand human behavior completely, they nevertheless are deeply convinced that the more that is known about a person, the better can one understand and predict his actions.

To the extent that these teenagers are the most *exasperating*, we are faced with a much more difficult problem. Unpredictability implies lack of knowledge; exasperation implies lack of understanding. This is not remedied solely by surveys or intensive studies. Rather it seems to be something that depends on the way we relate to other people. Attitudes of acceptance, permissiveness and confidence in the individual have proved effective in creating a relationship of mutual confidence, understanding, and self-direction. Acquisition of these attitudes depends to a large extent on just how convinced we are that we should respect the importance of the self-concept in others. If we can offer the proper atmosphere, we can go a long way toward giving these teenagers a chance to discuss their problems freely and to be understood.

To the extent that they are the most inspiring citizens in America today, I'm sure no one of us would find fault. It is a ray of hope in an otherwise dismal world. Indeed, it is their enthusiasm and optimism that make working with them so interesting and challenging.

The role of the adult, then, in working with them would seem to be, in the first place, to learn as much about them as he can, to do all in his power not only to understand them, but also to make them feel that they are understood and accepted, and finally to take a little hope and inspiration from the tremendous fund of energy and enthusiasm with which these young men and woman face these years of decision. If this energy can be directed through the proper guidance and understanding, then we adults and teachers can certainly set in action a tremendous power for good, and contribute our bid toward meeting the challange of today's youth.

NOTES

1. H. H. Remmers and D. H. Radler, *The American Teenager* (New York: Bobbs-Merrill Co., Inc., 1957), p. 50.
2. B. Davidson, "18,000,000 Teenagers Can't Be Wrong," *Collier's* (January 4, 1957.
3. Remmers, *op. cit.*, p. 86.
4. C. H. Patterson, *Counseling and Psychotherapy: Theory and Practice* (New York: Harper and Brothers, 1959), pp. 168-169.
5. A. H. Maslow, *Motivation and Personality* (New York: Harper and Brothers, 1954), p. 320.

The philosophy of adolescence

Thomas W. Mahan

*The article that follows develops two principal
points: the nature of and problems common to the
adolescent period and the philosophical and
psychological implications of these problems. The
underlying theme is supportive of the doctrine that
schools have a primary obligation of developing
social and personal adjustment among their
students. There are implications here affecting the
curriculum, the teacher, and the environment of
the school. All these, the author argues, must
proclaim their service to the youth of America.*

Scientific study of the adolescent has increased steadily since G. Stanley Hall published his work in 1904.[1] In spite of this growth of interest and study, the American high school has not as yet been able to adapt its program efficiently to meeting the needs of our teen-age youth. The purpose of the present paper is not to contradict the many scientific studies on adolescent problems and attitudes nor to replace them; it is, however, an attempt to get a more basic insight into adolescence and from this deeper view to evolve a more efficient educational methodology. As has been pointed out, the period of adolescence has grown considerably in the American cultural scene and gives promise of perhaps even greater extension.[2] Thus the need for considering this problem becomes ever more acute—and the need for relating scientific investigations to a sound philosophy of man ever more imperative. The hope of the author is that the present article may point the way for some to accomplish this task.

[1] G. Stanley Hall, *Adolescence.* New York: D. Appleton and Co., 1904.
[2] Luella Cole, *Psychology of Adolescence,* p. 3. New York: Rinehart and Co., 1949.

Reprinted with permission from The Catholic Educational Review, 50:589–560, November, 1952.

The Nature and Problems of Adolescence

Adolescence is more than a period of a few years, arbitrarily chosen as a subject for study. It is an epoch in every person's life, fraught with tensions and centered about one phenomenon and the various phases of that phenomenon. As a result, any intelligent treatment of a specific phase of adolescent life must be grasped as fitting into the over-all framework of the adolescent's "state of being." Many are inclined to identify this period of life with the onslaught of sexuality—the maturing of the sexual organs and the needed adjustment of the individual's life as a result of this. This, however, is a questionable view. It is the more questionable because it takes a part of reality and attempts to make it the whole of reality. Surely no one would deny that sexuality plays a prominent role in adolescence, but the prominence of its role, if the present writer's views be correct, is an effect and not a cause.

This is a subject demanding our attention if we are to work successfully with our high school pupils. It is a grave error to reduce their problems to the biological level in their root cause, and we shall never help the students to solve their problems so long as work is restricted to that level. The modern tendency to exaggerate the biological stems from the spirit of materialistic evolutionism that is still with us. But the cause of the adolescent's attitudes and behavior are much deeper than that. They stem from this awareness that he is a person—that he is an independent individual, equipped with powers of his own, and that he must face life as an independent person. As a child he saw himself as a part of reality. He blended into the objective world and was not set up in opposition to it. It is certainly true that the child is aware that he exists. He knows that *he* feels, that *he* plays. Yet he has not developed a consciousness of self. He does not reflect on the difference between the ego and the non-ego. He tends to look upon all objects as existing just as he exists. He plays the part of an airplane as well as a father, and just as realistically.

This attitude changes, imperceptibly at first, until it reaches the stage of adolescence. Then the youth sees the world as something outside of him and foreign to him. He senses his power and faculties and looks out at the world with adventure—and with fear. Now this realization of selfhood is accompanied by what is the main trait of adolescence—uncertainty. This is an expected consequence. The boy or girl at this time has seen his dream world of childhood ruined; he is faced with building a new one. He senses, but does not comprehend the meaning of his own existence and powers. He is tossing about on a sea churned by varied hopes and fears and he cannot decide in which direction to turn the rudder. From the metaphysical point of view we could expect no other reaction. Man is a finite and contingent being, one in whom there is a basic striving for an absolute accompanied by a fundamental sense of anxiety. Realizing his own incompleteness man still refuses to resign himself; he seeks for completion. How else could the adolescent seeing himself as contingent react? His uncertainty finds its roots in his very existence.

It is here that we have the key to a philosophy of adolescence. For many years now character education and personality development have claimed an ever larger larger role in the secondary school. Educators generally have recognized the problem in its overt manifestations, but that is not sufficient. Man's personality cannot be formed by giving it a superficial veneer. Our attempts to bring about mental, moral, physical, social and personal adjustment must begin with the recognition of this key factor: man is a creature filled with strivings and unsatisfied powers. He is then incomplete—not in the sense that he is lacking any essential quality, but in the sense that he is alone with himself and realizes that he has not lived up to his abilities and powers. He is seeking a union outside himself and only then will he rest.

The practical consequences of this reaching toward the fulfillment of personality and its resultant uncertainty are what attract our attention. It often seems to us that the most disastrous effect of his uncertainty is the casting aside of the absolute values of childhood and the substitution of relativism. We who have been brought up in a tradition of objective truth are especially prone to look upon this as a truly pathological symptom. Yet it is a very natural thing. The adolescent has lost faith in the world of his childhood, so why should he not lose faith in the props upon which it stood—his parents, his teachers, his priest, or minister? They are the prophets of the old world; he now looks for the prophets of the new. If you add to this the fact that the adolescent feels the independence resulting from the growth of his own abilities, you can see how the occurence of anything else would be abnormal. Thus authority and anything imposed from without is rejected. The old to him is fixed and limited because it belonged to a fixed and limited world—and even more important, the old is insincere because it was found in a deceptive world.

And this brings us to the paradox of adolescence. Authority is trampled underfoot, and yet security is needed. Uncertainty breeds insecurity, and the youth cannot stand insecurity. Then a new authority has to be set up—but not one imposed from without. Rather one freely accepted. Here is where radicalism reaps its harvest. A radical movement recognizes that an adolescent is in revolt, and it knows that he needs some straw upon which to hold, and these it offers him. It appeals to his independence and to his daring, and it wins many a wholehearted acceptance.

But the adolescent is not only daring—he is also afraid. He recognizes his own inconstancy. He fears that he cannot even trust himself. We often say that social adjustment is the major problem among high school students and this is, to a certain extent, true. The reason why there is so much truth in this is that the youth is revolting against his elders and feels out of place among them, and he also feels that he cannot assume the responsibility of social life because he is uncertain of himself. One day he sees things one way; the next day another way. Finding himself in this condition he recognizes the emptiness of his promises and fears the fickleness of his feelings. To avoid these becoming known he must withdraw from society. These again are but signs of man's incessant striving to rise above his own contingency. This fear of acting is a refusal to give oneself up to any other idol because of self-worship. And that is certainly a danger with the adolescent. Allowed to hide in his own shell, he may come to think that everything must be made subject to him and that he must reign. The man who is afraid to act lest he make a mistake is a proud man.

This paradoxical situation takes on another concrete form in the establishment of ideals or idols, and in daydreaming. An ideal is a value which has been established as a goal, and the ordinary method of attaining a goal is through action. But the adolescent shrinks from this road—he is afraid that he will fail. Hence, rather than fail, he withdraws from the world of reality and daydreams. Here again the uncertainty of the adolescent is vividly clear, as is his recognition of himself as a person. Otherwise, why should he establish a goal? Why would he fear failure? These are questions that cannot be answered in distortions of sex repressions. They are, of course, cases of repression and compensation. The thought of failure is banished; and the dream of success replaces actual success.

The prominence of sexuality at this stage of life has been mentioned, and it would be wrong to neglect it in this paper. What part then should we say is played by sexuality in the normal adolescent? We all know that maturity is accompanied by sensations and anxieties which are new to the youth. Just as he feels in awe at the aspect of his controlling his mind and will, just as he sees them as the makers of his new world, so he views the development of sexuality. These are facts that have received sufficient emphasis; I should like to stress another element in this occurrence. The youth has been forced to daydream in order to satisfy the needs of his uncertainty, but daydreams for the adolescent must have a relation to reality. He is not satisfied, as is the child, with fairy tales and wild imaginings. No, his daydreams are a substitute for reality and they must somehow approximate it. How better than through sex? The only reality over which we have complete control is ourselves, so we introduce ourselves into our dreams. And hence our sexual sensations and desires come into play because they are real and easily excited.[3]

The important fact to see in this is that often these dreams are not basically sexual. Sex is a form of compensation. We cannot give our dreams sufficient reality by thinking ourselves a success in the distant future so we make ourselves a success in a more down-to-earth manner where the possibility is not too remote. And I think that there is another factor we might consider here. Are all actual sexual aberrations among adolescents basically sexual? If you question such a deviate from moral standards, he will probably tell you that he could not help himself—he had to do it. And the fact of the matter is that he will believe that this is so. But how often is this necessity more a "necessity" to break with the old authority? How often does it stem much more from loneliness and uncertainty

[3] Rudolph Allers, *Character Education in Adolescence*, pp. 114-143. New York: Joseph F. Wagner Co., 1940.

than from actual sexual desire? I rather think that if properly studied we would find sex as much a compensation for more fundamental ills as Freud makes these other ills compensations for sex.

Philosophical and Psychological Implications

With this study of the characteristics of the adolescent we are prepared to place him in the classroom. Here all the tendencies we have described come into play. The adolescent sees himself forced to attend class; he feels that "truths" are being impersonally pumped into him. His natural action is revolt. Ordinarily this revolt is veiled by an outward appearance of doing what is expected. But it may be purely outward. His heart is not where his body is, and since he cannot be where he wills, he may look upon the school as a prison and the teacher as a taskmaster.

These are problems rooted in the concept of the school itself wherever compulsory education comes into play. They may be aggravated by external difficulties which also influence an adolescent's behavior. There is no question but that social environment will play a large part in a youngster's behavior. If the youth feels himself rejected and suppressed at home, the school may well afford the opportunity to release his resentment. If the social background of the adolescent is one of ignorance, filth, and general neglect, we may well expect that these elements will color his reaction to school.

The teacher, then, is faced with seemingly insurmountable difficulties. His is the task of shaping the personalities of his pupils, and to do this every possible means must be utilized. However, before an intelligent discussion of classroom methodology can be begun a clear understanding of the philosophical and the psychological principles involved must be ensured. The teacher cannot afford to be wrong—too much is at stake.

In education it is the human person, as an individual and as a member of society, who plays the major role. Recently much consideration has been given to the place of education in our society, and many objectives such as "education for democracy," or for freedom, or for tolerance have been elicited. But the vagueness of these concepts renders them useless. Man is not a more highly organized animal living on a social plane. His strivings, his basic insecurities are signs of a higher calling and a higher origin. It is here that Catholic education becomes the only truly realistic education.

First let us look at man from the viewpoint of the scientist. What can we fairly propose as the subject matter for experimental psychology? I do not expect that there would be much objection to the statement that "the fully conscious individual reaction" is its prime concern. Now any theory which can adequately explain this must do justice to the reaction and show the meaningfulness of the reaction. The psychologist calls a reaction meaningful when it is experientially accompanied by meaning. But the more interesting question here is whether or not there is one meaning which can explain all conscious reaction. For an example, let us consider the removal of a hand from a hot stove. We remove the hand because the sensation is unpleasant. Similarly, consideration of all our sensory reactions would show a striving for pleasure and away from pain. Raised to a higher level we may say that pursuit of happiness and flight from sorrow are common elements in all conscious activity.

Nor is this a mechanical reaction. That theory lingers on, but subsequent experimentation has shown its fallacy. Both Ach and Michotte at the beginning of this century showed by laboratory experiments that an active element originating from within the person was needed to explain the facts. Ach conceived of this as a release of energy, a "determining tendency" which, operating subconsciously, directed the completion of any resolution. There is, however, no basis for this theory. Rather the will does not release any energy; it merely directs the psychological processes. It is also important to realize that the will does not have despotic control over bodily activities. Psychology has shown that definite "traces" must be established in the nervous system, especially in muscular tissue, through instinctive reaction to stimuli before the will can command the activity.[4]

Thus experimental psychology itself must admit the existence of powers beyond the scope of scientific measurement. These powers are the ones that must be most considered in the development of human personality. Now that we have justified scientifically our assumption of the will, let us consider its workings more intimately.

Conscious striving demands that the person be aware of his goal. What is the lowest possible stage of such an experience? It would seem to be the condition wherein only the pleasurable stimulus is actually in consciousness. This is what we would call an "impulsive experience." This is what many would call instinct, but let us make a distinction here which I think is a valuable one. We shall restrict the use of the word instinct to signify a purposeful form of behavior, comparable to a deliberate action, yet adopted without insight. I mention this to clarify a point which will be recalled when we return to the adolescent. There is then only one instinct—the instinct to happiness—but this instinct is expressed in various manners and on various planes of activities, some of which are impulsive. But the essential unity of man is seen in the fact that all his strivings are for happiness. And the fact that he is always seeking happiness shows another fundamental fact—that man is not complete. He needs others in order to fulfill himself, and he must give himself to others in order to obtain this fulfillment.

There remains another further problem. What determines whether or not a man wills? We may answer that whenever there is an aim, a value, or a motive, will power is at work. Thus the determinant of the activity is the existence and strength of the motive. Anything that appears of value to the will can move it. Here is the foundation of the freedom of the will. Everything, insofar as it exists, is good, and any good can be desired. Thus the will can always choose any object —and it may choose not to will. However, we must not fall into the dangerous way of thinking that the will is strengthened by repeated activity. Rather it ap-

[4] Johannes Lindworsky, *Theoretical Psychology,* trans. Harry R. De Silva, pp. 131 f. St. Louis: B. Herder Book Co., 1932.

pears that the motive for that activity becomes enhanced by repetition and this makes subsequent actions easier.

We are now moving into a field of utmost importance to educators. Our earliest values stem from pleasant sensations, and even later intellectual values are increased by the addition of the feeling of pleasure. This brings out an important point. We tend to forget the fact that the objectively greater values are often not equated with the subjectively more desirable. Here we have to steer a course between Scylla and Charybdis. There are two dangers. We may strive to instill an objectively higher value into a pupil and incite nothing but stubbornness because it means nothing to him. But the other danger is equally as great. We must be careful not to train the will to turn to only the value with immediate reward. This is a factor of which naturalism ought to take account. Education must instill permanent life motives and these must have unchanging objects.

The surest guarantee of permanence is thought content, and this content assimilated into a complex set of attitudes which will help to ensure its presence. It should also be related to a situation, given practical applicability. But this does not mean that Goethe's dictum, "In the beginning was the deed," is to replace the Johannine statement, "In the beginning was the Word (or reason)." Action is to follow thought, not precede. The practical application flows from the theory, and thus the theory is all-important. Yet these objective values must be connected with immediate values discovered in the adolescent's mind. The educator must be especially careful not to make the learning of the new values arduous and pervert them into non-values. Purely external drilling and training is of no avail. We must reach the minds and wills of the pupils.

Let us now return to the adolescent. The proper development of his personality and thus the overcoming of his uncertainty can come only through the intellect and the will. These alone can securely serve as a foundation for his later life. Yet both these faculties are dynamic. They are always striving after the one object that will satisfy them, and are always falling short. The intellect desires truth, and intuitively it knows that each truth it exhausts is not sufficient—and yet each truth points to an absolute truth.

Yet this tendency of the intellect and will is not a sign of hopelessness. Rather it is a drive leading man along a path which perhaps he would not otherwise travel. Man cannot stifle his intellect; he can only abuse it. The same is true with the adolescent, and it is through these tendencies that we will develop the adolescent. However, our first move in dealing with the adolescent is to make him feel that he is wanted. There is a twofold tendency in love—the desire to possess and the desire to be possessed—and only in the fulfillment of both desires will all longing cease. This, to be sure, is only possible with God. In heaven, and there alone, will we be completely possessed and possess to our fullest ability. But here on earth, in a finite manner, a similar thing is possible. If the adolescent sees that we are giving ourselves to him in our love, friendship, and help, he ordinarily will reciprocate. Every man wants to be loved. A word of caution is needed here. Love must not be pictured as a sentimental thing. Love is something very real, and in its essence it is the giving of oneself. Thus it is something personal, and that is why our efforts at social reform have failed. This attempt to reach people through the impersonal agencies of social reconstruction can breed nothing other than a greediness for gifts and help. It is only the personal element and not the material that can transform. The American people in general and especially its more prominent citizens could well listen to Cicero's words, "For what is so absurd as to be swept away by many inanimate things, as by honor, glory, buildings, clothing, and physical beauty, and not at all to be moved by a living man endowed with virtue, by him who can either love, or return love." [5]

That is our first move. To become—not an authority—but a friend. This does not demand that we come down to the adolescent's level. By his very tendency to establish idols he is willing to have someone "over" him, so long as that someone is stripped of all the disconcerting elements. Until we have established this rapport with the adolescent, little is possible. Once this is established, we must open the mind of the pupil to truth, help him in the light of his present interests to establish new values for his entire life, and encourage him to meet reality. He is then seeing his instinctive tendency for happiness answered. Happiness is the solution to uncertainty. Withdrawal and aggression can never do more than veil the uncertainty. They are but poor disguises for an anxiety that gnaws ravenously at the very heart of man. If we can lead the adolescent to trust in us and to look up to us, then this uncertainty is lessened. There is someone he feels will understand. We have given him a value capable of achievement and thus given him the courage to face reality and meet temporary failure.

The objection that all this is theoretical is very just. It cannot be anything else, for any general law is theory. The application of the law in a concrete case must take into consideration innumerable modifying conditions—the first of which is the individual difference of the child. But the process must be the same. There must be the establishment of rapport between the students and the teacher. Then must come the stimulation of interest in study by appeal to the student's present interests leading to the enthronement of higher values. Only this process can justify our educational expenditures.

Conclusion

It is in this framework that an effective learning situation must be established. The high school has a primary obligation of developing social and personal adjustment among its students. However, there is a tendency to forget that the bases of all adjustment are to be found in man's truly human powers, the intellect and will. It is the will, the power of love, of loyalty, and of sacrifice, that must first be won by the teacher. The teacher is more than an intellectual guide; he must also be a personal inspiration. The classroom must lose its austerity and abstractiveness; it must proclaim its service to the youth of America.

[5] Marcus Tullius Cicero, *Laelius de Amicita*, sect. 49, p. 20. New York: Benj. H. Sanborn Co., 1937.

However, the process cannot stop with the will. The will directs the action of the intellect and the training of the will in this regard is the school's task. The student should see the goal he is working toward and should see his progress along the way. For too long a time we have been teaching skills without showing the functional purpose of the skills to the students. We have stated that it is the meaningfulness of the action that counts. No student is truly lazy or completely disinterested. His nature forbids him to be. He has a mind and a will that refuse to let him rest. We must capitalize on that restlessness and through that very restlessness bring about the easing of the student's insecurity—in other words accomplish his personality adjustment.

People must be able to think and judge, and that is our task. For this I think we must put aside our cliché of education for democracy and create a curriculum calculated to develop the mind and will. If we cannot give the pupil the revealed light of religion, can we not at least teach him to use the natural light of reason? Cannot history forget some of its facts and study recurring ideas and analyse them? Cannot literature see more than the style and show the depths of the struggle between good and evil, the worth of the human person, the person's craving for love and for God? Cannot the various languages somehow encourage the pupil to do more than learn tonight's vocabulary and lead him to study the culture and thought of these peoples? Cannot the sciences show the student both their wonders—and their limitations? These are worth-while challenges to the teacher; they are tasks which make him a source of strength to the world.

There is a final note that I should like to add. The school is not a rehabilitation hospital, and now and then we will meet the student, hardened probably by his social environment, who appears to be really evil. Most adolescents, rebels though they are, are lovable because they want to love and be loved. But once in a while there comes along the ruffian, uncouth and uncontrollable. Often the ordinary school cannot cope with him. He, too, has revolted and has probably despaired of ever attaining any worth-while goal. Yet somehow he must be a success—somewhere the *fieri sicut dei* bids him shout, *Non serviam*—and he chooses his path. For him we can but pray.

But above all the teacher must be human, and he must be able, even in discouragement, to sing that idealistic tone:

Mourir pour ce qu'on aime
C'est un trop doux effort. . . .

Some indications of sources of anxiety in adolescent boys

W. W. Meissner, S.J.

The next article also deals with the problems of adolescents, but is limited to a consideration of boys, whose fears, worries, feelings, and doubts are studied intensively. It is based on a questionnaire given to more than 1,200 male Catholic high school students in four Eastern states. Their responses indicate their feelings in and about eight areas. A detailed analysis and discussion of the responses is given, and comparisons between the boys at different age levels are made.

A. INTRODUCTION

In understanding the adolescent's outlook on life and its problems, it is helpful to have some indication of the problem areas which are sources of worry and anxiety for him. The forces which combine to create these anxiety areas are multiple and form a dynamically shifting constellation not only in terms of the adolescent's own development and maturation, but also in terms of the social and cultural context in which that growth occurs.

The importance of social class to the development of the adolescent's self-concept was pointed out by Klausner (7). He found a differential gradient in the self-concept in different socio-economic levels. In the upper levels greater self-aggression and psycho-social isolation was evident and in the lower levels greater insecurity combined with inferiority and aggression. Similar differences have been discovered in Gough's studies (5, 6) of status difference in high school seniors. Role-wishes have also been found to change significantly (1) from a con-

Reprinted with permission from *The Journal of Genetic Psychology*, 99:65–73, September, 1961.

cern with looks, stature, and mental capacity at the junior high school level to involvement in personal-social relations and social welfare at the high school level.

Over 15 years ago, Fleege (3) concluded his extensive investigation of the adolescent boy with a rating of the major problems which confronted the adolescent. His list, in order of decreasing frequency and intensity, included sex adjustment, decision in the matter of vocation, lack of understanding from older people, lack of social opportunities, financial difficulties and difficulties within the school setting. More recently, Gesell and his associates (4, pp. 341–343) summarized an intensive investigation of 165 teen-agers (including 83 boys) and listed the worries and fears of the respective age groups. The 14 year olds were worried about school, personal-social problems and to some extent world conditions. They are afraid of the dark, crowds, and to some extent of high places. Social fears began to manifest themselves in the form of fear of people, performing in public, and quarreling in the family. The 15 year olds are concerned chiefly about grades and homework as well as social acceptance. Their fears are somewhat greater than the 14 year olds but the content has changed little. The 16 year olds are worried about homework and examinations and their own futures. Worries of a more self-centered nature appear: appearance, character, personality problems. They have few fears, but those mentioned include new social situations and also fear of animals (snakes) and heights. These age groups correspond to the freshmen, sophomores, and juniors represented in the present study.

B. PROCEDURE AND RESULTS

The results presented in this study are drawn from a 217-item questionnaire which was administered to 1278 high school boys from nine different schools. The schools were private schools under Catholic direction and were scattered through the states of New York, New Jersey, Pennsylvania, and Maryland. The questionnaires were given in each instance with a standard set of instructions which were read to the subjects by the administrator. The test forms were sent to the respective administrators in sealed envelopes, were opened in the presence of the subjects, and immediately after completion of the test they were resealed and returned to the experimenter. The boys were selected according to classes from the school populations. As a group they represent the median range in academic achievement. The distribution according to years was as follows: 331 freshmen, 313 sophomores, 343 juniors, and 291 seniors. The age range of the total populations extended from 13 to 18 years. The average age of the freshmen was 14.3 years, the sophomores 15.2, the juniors 16.2, and the seniors 17.2. With the exception of the senior group, these age groups are roughly equivalent to the Gesell age groups. The boys were predominantly from a middle class family background.

For the purpose of this study, eight questions were selected from the questionnaire which present some indication of the problems or areas which give high school boys occasion for worry or anxiety. The questions were all free response items. For each question the responses were ranked in the order of frequency and a rank-order coefficient was computed between the rankings for respective years (2, pp. 165–167). The significance of the correlation was tested for each correlation (2, p. 167).

The questions selected as indicating areas of worry and anxiety were the following:

1. What are the things you worry about most?
2. What is your biggest personal problem or difficulty in life? (If you haven't any, write "None.")
3. What are the things you fear most? (If nothing, write "Nothing.")
4. What are the things you usually have doubts about?
5. When you feel sad and depressed or "down in the mouth," what generally causes this feeling?
6. When you feel lonely, what do you think are the causes?
7. Mention the difficulty or problem in your school life that puzzles you most. (If you haven't any, write "None.")
8. Please mention any problem of yours which has been omitted in these questions.

The results obtained from the preceding questions are contained in Table 1.

C. DISCUSSION

The results will be discussed in reference to the individual questions and then in reference to common response categories in the whole set of questions.

Question 1. The predominant causes of worry for these boys seem to center around the school and their relations to it. The family is also a consistent source of worry. Worries about sex show a numerical increase in juniors and seniors and a significant jump in rank between junior and senior year. An indicator of changing concerns is the jump in worries about their future lives from the lower to the upper classmen and the appearance in the upper classes of worry over the subject of vocation. The correlations between the years are all significant with the exception of that between the freshmen and the seniors. This would indicate a change in the patterns of worry and concern from the beginning to the end of the high school years.

Question 2. This question indicates that the great source of personal difficulty is sex. Many boys, especially from sophomore year on, manifest difficulties not only with their relationships with girls but also in personal sex habits. Masturbation is mentioned most often in second and third years of high school. School and family become less and less a source of difficulty as the boy matures. As in the previous question, there is a rise in concern with the future and with the problem of vocation. The latter seems to be a special problem for seniors. Interestingly enough, it seems that personal difficulties with parents is a problem for a few lower classmen, but after the sophomore year it is not mentioned at all. Low correlations between freshman year and the other years and a significant correlation among the other years would indicate that the most significant changes in personal problems occur soon after freshman year, i.e., around 14–15 years of age.

Question 3. Besides the "Nothing" response, the boys express a great fear of hell and an increasing fear of death. There is also an increase in the fear of failure and in the later years a fear of the future. The boys express a fear of God which seems to slacken among the juniors and seniors. A great many incidental

Table 1   Rank-order correlations for responses to eight questions

Response category	Ranking within years 1		2		3		4		Between years r	
Question 1:										
School	1	(206)†	1	(195)	1	(187)	1	(100)	1-2 =	0.84**
Family	2	(39)	2	(27)	2	(29)	4	(20)	1-3 =	0.61*
Sex	3	(11)	4	(9)	6	(17)	3	(23)	1-4 =	0.29
Money	4	(10)	4	(9)	4	(22)	5.5	(19)	2-3 =	0.82**
Popularity	5	(6)	4	(9)	5	(19)	5.5	(19)	2-4 =	0.75**
Hell	6	(5)			10	(2)	14	(1)	3-4=	0.84**
Future	7	(4)	6	(8)	3	(23)	2	(36)		
Religion	8.5	(3)	8.5	(3)	10	(2)	11.5	(2)		
Sin	10	(2)	7	(5)	7	(7)	8	(12)		
Vocation					8	(3)	7	(13)		
Question 2:										
None	1	(104)	3	(55)	2	(51)	2	(43)	1-2 =	0.22
School	2	(77)	2	(66)	3	(49)	7	(15)	1-3 =	0.58
Sex	3	(69)	1	(91)	1	(102)	1	(85)	1-4 =	−0.50
Family	4	(15)	7.5	(9)	7	(17)	9	(7)	2-3 =	0.83**
Sin	5	(14)	12.5	(3)	9.5	(7)	10	(6)	2-4 =	0.80**
Future	6	(12)	4	(18)	4.5	(30)	4	(30)	3-4 =	0.88**
Popularity	7	(9)	5	(16)	4.5	(30)	5	(19)		
Parents	8	(8)	9	(8)						
Vocation	9	(6)	6	(13)	6	(20)	3	(38)		
Personality			7.5	(9)	8	(14)	6	(17)		
Religion			14	(2)	9.5	(7)	12.5	(3)		
Question 3:										
Nothing	1	(123)	1	(91)	1	(85)	1	(85)	1-2 =	0.82**
Failing exams	2	(48)	3	(35)	3	(37)	8.5	(11)	1-3 =	0.52*
Hell	3	(35)	2	(41)	2	(54)	2	(42)	1-4 =	0.64*
Sin	4	(30)	8	(11)	5	(21)	6	(13)	2-3 =	0.62*
Sex	5	(14)	7	(12)	8	(15)	5	(19)	2-4 =	0.49
Death	6	(13)	4	(25)	4	(28)	3.5	(26)	3-4 =	0.66**
Unpopularity	7	(12)	6	(16)	6	(17)	8.5	(11)		
God	8	(9)	5	(18)	9	(13)	15	(2)		
Failure			9.5	(8)	7	(16)	3.5	(26)		
Future					10	(11)	7	(12)		

Response category	1		2		3		4		Between years r	
Question 4:										
Sex	1	(43)	1	(45)	2	(40)	2	(34)	1-2 =	0.71*
School	2	(23)	4.5	(16)	4	(13)	6	(7)	1-3 =	0.39
Sin	3.5	(14)	4.5	(16)	5.5	(12)	5	(8)	1-4 =	0.37
Religion	3.5	(14)	2	(24)	1	(47)	1	(47)	2-3 =	0.82*
Vocation	6	(6)	3	(18)	3	(30)	3	(31)	2-4 =	0.88**
Family	5	(7)	6.5	(5)	10	(1)	9	(2)	3-4 =	0.97**
Personality	7	(4)	8	(3)	8	(4)	8	(4)		
Popularity	8.5	(3)	6.5	(5)	7	(7)	7	(5)		
Future					5.5	(12)	4	(23)		
Question 5:										
School	1	(101)	1	(84)	1	(93)	2	(52)	1-2 =	0.90**
Disappointment	2	(40)	2	(27)	2	(54)	1	(68)	1-3 =	0.80**
Family problems	3	(15)	4	(17)	4	(19)	15.5	(3)	1-4 =	0.30
Unpopularity	5.5	(9)	6	(12)	8.5	(8)	9	(7)	2-3 =	0.77**
Sin	5.5	(9)	5	(13)	6	(12)	6	(11)	2-4 =	0.39
Sex	8	(7)	3	(22)	3	(31)	3	(22)	3-4 =	0.70**
Punishment	8	(7)	7	(11)	8.5	(8)	13	(4)		
Arguments	8	(7)	9	(8)	5	(15)	5	(12)		
Personality					12	(6)	7	(10)		
Question 6:										
Being alone	1	(31)	2	(25)	3	(24)	4	(17)	1-2 =	0.58*
Unpopular	3	(19)	1	(35)	1	(52)	1	(49)	1-3 =	0.01
Not seeing									1-4 =	—0.19
friends	4	(10)	6	(10)	11.5	(5)	6	(14)	2-3 =	0.56*
Different interest	6	(6)	10	(5)	6	(13)	7	(12)	2-4 =	0.69**
Self-pity	10.5	(4)	12	(4)	7	(9)	9.5	(5)	3-4 =	0.82**
Sex	14.5	(1)	5	(13)	2	(30)	3	(19)		
Personality			10	(5)	5	(14)	2	(21)		
Question 7:										
None	1	(183)	1	(141)	1	(130)	1	(116)	1-2 =	0.93**
Subjects	2	(87)	2	(87)	2	(106)	2	(69)	1-3 =	0.91*
Teacher	3	(13)	3	(17)	3	(30)	3	(23)	1-4 =	0.96**
Discipline	4	(7)	5.5	(7)	4.5	(9)	5	(8)	2-3 =	0.89**
Homework	5	(6)	4	(12)	6	(8)	6	(7)	2-4 =	0.67*
Popularity	6	(2)	5.5	(7)	4.5	(9)	8.5	(4)	3-4 =	0.82**
Personality			8	(3)	7.5	(7)	4	(14)		
Question 8:										
Sex	1	(25)	2	(26)	2	(41)	3	(15)	1-2 =	0.36
Studies	2	(17)	1	(29)	1	(60)	1	(40)	1-3 =	—0.46
Teachers	3	(12)	3.5	(10)	3	(22)	2	(32)	1-4 =	0.39
Popularity	4	(7)	10	(2)	10.5	(1)			2-3 =	0.81**
Vocation	6.5	(5)	5	(6)	6.5	(3)	7	(3)	2-4 =	0.47
Discipline	6.5	(5)	3.5	(10)	4	(13)	4	(14)	3-4 =	0.82**
Family problems			8	(3)	5	(10)	8.5	(1)		
Religion			6.5	(4)	6.5	(3)	5	(5)		
Personality			12	(1)	8.5	(2)	6	(4)		

* The correlation is significant at the 5 per cent level of confidence.

** The correlation is significant at the 1 per cent level of confidence.

† The number in parentheses represents the absolute number of responses in each category.

responses were given to this question which are not indicated on the table: fear of punishment, responsibility, loss of parents, height, parents, pain, snakes, etc. None were mentioned with any significant frequency. Low correlations indicate a tendency for patterns of fear to shift from year to year.

Question 4. Doubts are expressed primarily about sex and religion. Doubts about sex tend to decrease as the boys mature, but at the same time doubts about religion increase. Doubts about vocation are also increasingly manifested and, in the upper years, doubts about the future. These two categories are undoubtedly related. Doubts about school and family problems, however, decrease as the boy grows older. The significant changes here also tend to occur after freshman year as indicated by the low correlation between the rankings of this group and the other groups.

Question 5. A good many of the boys admit to feelings of sadness and depression and ascribe their depression mainly to their failures in school and to disappointment and frustration in general. A major cause of such depression is found in disappointing relations with girls, especially in the older boys. Family problems (financial, arguments with parents, etc.) are a consistent source of depression among the younger boys, but there is a significant drop in such problems among seniors. Unpopularity seems to become somewhat less of a problem as the boy grows older, although some juniors and seniors seem to become depressed about their own personality development. This seems to follow the pattern of self-centeredness described by Gesell. Arguments with friends, especially girl friends, are also listed as a source of depressed feelings. Low freshman-senior and sophomore-senior correlations suggest that patterns of depression tend to alter after sophomore year. This suggestion is reinforced by the high freshman-sophomore correlation.

Question 6. High on the list of causes of loneliness is unpopularity. There is an increased tendency in later years to look on loneliness as related to personal deficiencies (sensitivity, shyness, etc.) rather than the mere fact of being alone. Feelings of loneliness are increasingly related to sex. Boys tend to feel more and more left out of things as they grow older because they may not have a girl with whom they can engage in heterosexual social activities, i.e., dances and parties. There is a significant increase in this problem from freshman to sophomore year and another significant jump from there to the upper years. The upper years correlate highly indicating a certain degree of stabilization, as compared with the low correlations in the first two years. Freshman-junior and freshman-senior correlations are especially low indicating significant changes.

Question 7. There is a fairly high degree of agreement in the pattern of school problems in each of the years. The greatest source of difficulty seems to be the choice of subjects studied. The boys want to know why they have to study the subjects they do and what use these subjects will be for later life. Great dissatisfaction is also had with the teachers—usually not in general, but rather it seems that every boy has his problems with one or possibly more teachers. Discipline and homework, as might be expected, are constant sources of difficulty.

Question 8. The question asked about problems which had been omitted from the questionnaire, but almost all responses repeated problems previously handled. Sex is a major problem area, but it slackens off here in the upper years. More important than sex are the problems the boys have with their studies. This seems to become more and more of a problem in the later years. A prominent place is given here to religious problems and vocational difficulties. Religious problems especially seem to become of greater importance in later years. Discipline and teacher-relations are also prominent, seeming to indicate with studies a predominance of preoccupations centering around the school and its activities. Only the correlations between second and third and again between third and fourth years are significant. This would suggest a constantly shifting pattern of interests and concerns as the boy develops from year to year. The freshman-sophomore and freshman-junior correlations are the lowest. Again the pattern of alteration between earlier and later years is manifest.

The responses reveal certain common patterns which would seem to indicate general areas of worry, concern and anxiety. The more or less frequent responses which recur in a number of questions are the following:

The School

School problems are a consistent source of worry to the high school boy. Although it remains a high source of concern, school becomes less and less a major area of concern as the boy grows older and other interests develop. His fear of failure decreases and drops significantly in senior year. He progressively manifests less doubt about the things he is required to do in school. Failure in school work is a consistent source of depression. When asked to mention a personal problem, most boys responded with difficulties about the reasons for studying certain subjects, e.g., Latin, Modern Language, History, etc. The biggest school problems in the order of importance were subjects, teachers, and discipline.

Sex

Sex is a consistent source of worry, difficulties, fear and doubt. Many boys of high school age are just beginning to have heterosexual experiences and there are many things they do not know. Both in the form of heterosexual difficulties and of personal chastity, sex was listed as the major personal problem for sophomores, juniors, and seniors. Sex is not so much a source of fear as it is of doubt. Difficulty in getting along with girls is listed as a major cause of depression, as well as a source of feelings of loneliness, particularly for the older boys.

Popularity

This is a constant source of worry to the high school boy. It seems to become more frequent in the older boys when popularity takes on more social significance.

As a source of fear and doubt, unpopularity is not a primary, but a fairly consistent problem. Feelings of depression due to unpopularity seem to decrease as the boy matures, but unpopularity is given the first rank in sophomore, junior and senior years as a cause of loneliness. There may be some relation between the predominance of unpopularity and difficulties in relations with girls as sources of loneliness among the older boys.

Immorality and Religion

From the freshman to the senior year there is an increasing amount of worry about sin, but it does not constitute a major personal problem. A fair number, especially freshmen, express their fears about sin and their doubts about it. This seems to lessen as they grow older. Immoral actions are consistently a source of depression. Religion is a cause of worry rather infrequently and is mentioned as a personal problem by only a few upperclassmen. Fear of God is mentioned by a fair number in the earlier years but takes a significant drop among seniors. However, as a source of doubt, religion becomes more and more prominent until it is listed as the primary source of doubts for juniors and seniors.

Vocation and the Future

The future becomes more and more a source of worry for the growing boy until for the seniors it takes a place second only to the school. Worry about vocation is expressed by a few juniors and a few seniors. There is a steady increase in the numbers who find the future and the problem of vocational choice a major personal problem. Among seniors, the choice of vocation is second only to sex as a personal problem. A few of the older boys express fears about the future but many more have doubts about the future as well as about their vocation in life. A few seniors indicate that vocation is the most puzzling problem they have.

D. SUMMARY AND CONCLUSION

Eight free-response questions were selected from a questionnaire administered to 1278 high school boys. The questions were selected as indicators of sources of worry and anxiety for the high school boy. The responses were ranked for each question and a rank-order correlation computed between the respective rankings of the classes or years. The results indicate that the major sources of worry and anxiety for the high school boy of middle-class background are the school, sex, unpopularity, immoral activity, religion, vocation, and his future life. The significant changes between patterns of anxiety sources seem to occur primarily after the freshman year, with some significant changes (for depression and to a lesser extent fear) coming after the sophomore year.

REFERENCES

1. Cobb, H. V. Role-wishes and general wishes of children and adolescents. *Child Dev.*, 1954, **25**, 161-171.
2. Edwards, A. L. Statistical Analysis. New York: Rinehart, 1958.
3. Fleege, U. H. Self-Revelation of the Adolescent Boy. Milwaukee: Bruce, 1945,
4. Gesell, A., Ilg, F. L., & Ames, L. B. Youth: The Years from Ten to Sixteen. New York: Harper, 1956.
5. Gough, H. G. A new dimension of status: I. Development of a personality scale. *Amer. Sociol. Rev.*, 1948, **13**, 401-409.
6. ———. A new dimension of status: II. Relationship of the St scale to other variables. *Amer. Sociol. Rev.*, 1948, **13**, 534-537.
7. Klausner, S. Z. Social class and self-concept. *J. Soc. Psychol.*, 1953, **38**, 201-205.

School interests of early adolescents

Sister Mary Amatora, O.S.F.

*What subjects have most appeal to young
adolescents? What other aspects of school life do
they find most attractive? How do the sexes differ in
their school-related interests? To help answer
questions such as these, Sister Amatora surveyed
679 seventh- and eighth-grade pupils from ten
different states, using a procedure similar to that
employed in the study just reported. Detailed
analyses of her findings are presented in the
following article.*

A. INTRODUCTION

Though research in curricula has gained impetus in the past decade, few studies concerning interests of children and adolescents are related to it. Curricula are, for the most part, organized on the basis of adult-determined needs of pupils. In their efforts to provide what they believe to be the best for the child, educators seldom, if ever, give consideration to pupil interest.

Nonetheless, it is known that various factors in the school influence the pupil in many ways. McCandless and Castenada (11) found a relationship between anxiety and school achievement. Symonds (15) states that much of the incentive for learning comes from intrinsic interests in the activities themselves.

Fagin (5) is of the opinion that the schools should provide outlets for abilities and interests. He further states that frequently interests are neither developed nor guided along proper channels because of distorted concepts of students. Leach (9), in his study of intelligence levels and interest area choices, found persuasive interests ranking relatively low, outdoor area interests high, and computational area interests receiving the highest interest.

Reprinted with permission from *The Journal of Genetic Psychology*, 98:133–145, March, 1961.

334

In their study of the permanence of school interests, Sterrett and Davis (*14*) found that retention was influenced by the value of the objective thought. Tyler (*16*), comparing the interests of English and American school children, found correlations of about .8 between item percentages for the two groups; and correlations of .46 and .47 between the sexes for American and English groups respectively.

The phenomena of mass psychology in the classroom as investigated by Stauffer (*13*) indicates that repressive interference results in a loss of interest. On the other hand, Harris (*7*) shows how school interests are modified through enrichment of experiences and enlargement of environmental boundaries.

Analysis of interests in school subjects by Lentke (*10*) showed boys to be more interested in mathematics, physical education, and the sciences while girls preferred languages. Neither liked music nor citizenship. As they grew older, boys continued to select more science subjects than language subjects. Rudman (*12*), studying the informational needs and the reading interests of children in grades four through eight, found that the children are not necessarily interested in reading about the same things they want to ask about. He also found a shift in interest as children proceed from grade to grade.

Albrecht (*1*) found elementary pupils' lack of interest in achieving to be one cause for lowered achievement in school subjects. Interest, in its relationship to personality adjustment, also effects dropouts, as is revealed by Arnholter's (*2*) study. In an experimental study of children's attitudes toward school, Fitt (*6*) found economic status to be positively related to favorable school attitudes. In a study of children's interests in books, Carsley (*3*) found that for the majority of children, the home offered a better environment for private reading of books than school. May not school interests be a factor in these findings?

B. PURPOSE

Studies of school interests are usually based upon check lists, inventories, or questionnaires. The writer is of the opinion that an expression of true interest would be achieved more readily if the subjects were completely free to state their interests without suggestion or clue from a ready-made or printed form.

The present investigation of interests of boys and girls in early adolescence endeavors to tap the precise things connected with school life that most interest them. The writer hopes, by using free expression, that the subjects in the experiment will respond freely in order that the study may uncover aspects of young adolescents' interests in school not brought to light by the usual type of research.

C. METHOD

In order to achieve the purpose of the investigation, the use of current types of check lists, questionnaires, and inventories was ruled out. If boys and girls were to express their interests freely, they would have to be given but a single question, thus allowing the widest possible scope in their answers.

1. Subjects

As the study was directed to the young adolescent, it was decided to use a sample of seventh- and eighth-grade boys and girls from widely separated geographical areas. The 10 cooperating private schools in California, Indiana, Louisiana, Maine, Minnesota, Missouri, North Carolina, Pennsylvania, Texas, and Washington ranged in size from 127 to 956 pupils. Town or city in which they were located ranged in population from 2,000 to 800,000.

2. Procedure

A form letter explaining the nature of the research and directions to the children was sent to the principals of the participating schools. Using ordinary tablet paper, children were requested to give age, grade, sex, date, school, city, and state; and then to respond to the question: "What are three of your greatest interests connected with school life, in order of importance to you?"

D. ANALYSES OF DATA

After eliminating 12 papers because of incomplete data or illegibility, a total of 679 papers was available for analyses. These included replies from 192 eighth-grade boys, 149 seventh-grade boys, 181 eighth-grade girls, and 157 seventh-grade girls.

Median age for eighth-grade boys was 13.4 ± 0.4; for seventh-grade boys, $12.2 \pm .05$; for eighth-grade girls, 13.1 ± 0.6; for seventh-grade girls, 12.1 ± 0.4.

1. Analyses of Boys' Interest

An analysis of the boys' interests relative to school life is presented in Table 1. A brief inspection of this table reveals a somewhat diversified interest among the various activities connected with school life.

2. Degree of Choice in Interest

In order to differentiate degree of interest in the various interest categories, it was deemed advisable to analyze separately the data for first, second, and third choices of interest.

   a. First Choice of Interest. The first three columns of Table 1 indicate the first choice of interest for the boys in this study. A glance at the third column for total boys' interests shows the largest percentages of interests in four groups, namely, history, spelling, arithmetic, and sports. Collectively these account for

Table 1 School interests of 341 boys in early adolescence

Interest categories	First choice			Second choice			Third choice		
	Grade 8	Grade 7	Total	Grade 8	Grade 7	Total	Grade 8	Grade 7	Total
Arithmetic	13.6	6.4	10.0	7.2	2.2	4.7	10.9	0.7	5.9
Art	1.5	5.6	3.5	3.0	1.5	2.3	0.6	7.9	4.2
History	12.1	9.9	11.0	12.8	13.6	13.2	11.5	11.4	11.4
Civics	2.9	1.4	2.1	2.6	0.7	1.7	4.9	1.4	3.1
English	1.5	2.8	2.1	5.1	7.1	6.1	4.9	5.0	5.0
Geography	3.9	3.5	3.8	2.6	13.6	7.6	3.6	5.7	4.6
Languages	0.5	0.7	0.6	0.4	0.7	0.6	0.6	0.7	0.6
Music	0.5	2.8	1.6	0.8	3.6	2.2	1.2	2.1	1.6
Reading	3.9	4.2	4.0	8.1	5.7	6.9	8.6	6.5	7.5
Religion	4.9	8.5	6.8	5.5	5.0	5.3	3.6	10.0	6.8
Science	7.8	6.4	7.1	4.3	4.3	4.3	4.2	3.6	4.0
Social studies	0.5	1.4	1.0	3.0	2.1	2.6	0.6	1.5	1.0
Spelling	8.2	12.7	10.4	10.2	15.0	12.6	10.9	15.7	13.3
Shop	3.9	6.4	5.1	0.8	2.1	1.4	1.8	0.7	1.3
Library	1.4	1.4	1.4	2.6	0.7	1.6	1.2	1.4	1.3
Study period	1.9	2.1	2.0	1.3	1.4	1.3	1.2	0.7	0.9
Sports	13.6	6.3	10.0	9.8	5.7	7.7	7.4	5.7	6.5
Friends	1.4	1.4	1.4	2.1	0.7	1.4	1.8	2.1	2.0
Teachers	1.0	2.1	1.5	0.8	1.4	1.6	0.6	2.9	1.9
Lunch period	1.0	1.4	1.2	1.3	2.1	1.7	4.2	2.1	3.1
Recess period	3.4	4.2	3.9	3.8	3.6	3.7	3.0	3.6	3.3
Clubs	0.5	1.4	1.0	0.8	0.7	0.8	1.2	1.5	1.3
Activities	1.0	2.1	1.5	1.3	1.4	1.3	1.2	1.4	1.3
Miscellaneous	9.1	4.9	7.0	9.8	5.1	7.4	10.3	5.7	8.1
Total	100.0	100.0	100.0	100.0	100.0	100.0	100.0	100.0	100.0

more than 40 per cent of the first interests. Next highest interests are in science, 7.1 per cent; religion, 6.8 per cent; and shop 5.1 per cent.

b. Second Choice of Interest. Among the second choice of school interests of these boys one finds two categories emerging high: history, 13.2 per cent; and spelling, 12.6 per cent. Following this there is a considerable drop with lower ranks for sports, 7.7 per cent; geography, 7.6 per cent; reading, 6.9 per cent; and English, 6.1 per cent. Here one finds geography and English emerging in higher percentages than in first choices while arithmetic, religion, science, and shop have dropped to considerably lower percentages. Could the cause here be similar to that indicated by Khan (8) wherein he found pupils disliking geography because it was taught in an uninteresting manner?

c. Third Choice of Interest. The last column of Table 1 indicates third choice of interest pertaining to school life among the seventh- and eighth-grade boys. Standing out in this column among highest-ranking third interests are spelling, 13.3 per cent, and history, 11.4 per cent. One becomes immediately aware of the fact that these two subjects were among the highest in all choices of interest. A total of 36.3 per cent of all the boys in this study listed spelling as either their first, second, or third interest; and 35.6 per cent listed history as their first, second, or third interest. Thus, one finds approximately three-fourths of the boys in the study expressing an interest in history and spelling. Next highest ranking categories among third interests are reading, 7.5 per cent; religion, 6.8 per cent; sports, 6.5 per cent; arithmetic, 5.9 per cent; and English, 5.0 per cent. Percentages of students expressing interest in the other categories are all considerably smaller.

3. Grade-level Similarities and Differences

Further study of Table 1 reveals some similarities and differences between the boys of the seventh and of the eighth grades. It is principally in the non-academic items that one finds similarities in percentages for both groups. The two grade levels are most alike in amount of interest in study and library, in intermissions and in teachers and friends.

In arithmetic, one finds in all three choices of interest a considerable increase in the eighth grade over the seventh grade, with percentages of 13.6, 7.2, and 10.9 respectively for the eighth-grade boys and percentages of 6.4, 2.2, and 0.7 for the seventh-grade boys. Grade-level differences in the same direction are second largest for sports. Here one finds 13.6 per cent, 9.8 per cent, and 7.4 per cent of the eighth-grade boys listing this as their first, second, and third choices respectively; whereas one finds 6.3 per cent, 5.7 per cent, and 5.7 per cent of the seventh-grade boys indicating this item as their first, second, and third choices of interest.

Two other areas of interest indicating grade-level differences, though smaller, are science and civics. While more eighth graders than seventh graders are interested in these two areas, both differences are small.

Grade-level differences favoring seventh-grade boys are apparent in a number of areas. Largest differences occur in spelling, geography, and shop. In these one finds approximately twice as many seventh graders as eighth graders listing one or other of these items among their first, second, or third choices. Other areas of interest claiming the attention of more seventh graders than eighth graders are religion, social studies, English, music, and art. In these areas one finds about 25 per cent more seventh graders than eighth graders listing an item.

In the remaining three subject-matter areas, namely history, languages, and reading, one finds approximately the same distribution of items listed among seventh- as among eighth-grade boys.

4. Composite Interest Areas

For a further analysis of boys' interests, individual item categories were grouped in their respective areas. Thus, one readily perceives from Table 2 the general areas which claim a preponderance of interests of these early-adolescent boys.

A first glance at this table reveals a real interest in science and mathematics among eighth-grade boys. Among seventh-grade boys, interest in this area is considerably less. When one looks at the columns for total interests, one finds the areas for social studies and literature and languages high. Among first choices of interests, differences in the three top-ranking areas are not great; but in the second and third choices of interests, one finds a great increase in the latter two areas. If one considers all items listed by all boys, whether in first, second, or third choice, one finds a total of 63.5 per cent expressing an interest in social studies and a total of 69.8 per cent expressing an interest in literature and languages. This corroborates the findings of Chase (4) in whose experiment boys also had high ranks in these areas. Other subject-matter areas claim but small percentages comparatively. These are the areas of religion, music, art, and shop, claiming totals of 18.8 per cent; 15.5 per cent; and 7.9 per cent, respectively in the combined three choices of interest.

Ranking fourth highest is the area including various items classified as sports, activities, and clubs. These claim a total of 31.6 per cent when all three choices are combined. Items listed under activities included such as programs, plays, field trips and the like. Clubs included such items listed as Boy Scouts, group meetings, etc. All items listed in this area pertained to these activities held at or in connection with the school.

Other areas of interest listed by these young adolescents may be somewhat surprising. Yet, the study did indicate the preference of some boys for study and library periods and for others, the intermission periods including both the recess and the lunch period. Just why these should be more interesting to the boys than the subject-matter areas is a question worth further investigation. Surprisingly enough, small percentages in all grades and in all three choices were more interested in persons, either teacher or friends, than in school learning.

Items listed by these boys in fewer frequencies were grouped as miscel-

Table 2 Composite interest areas of boys

Interest areas	First choice			Second choice			Third choice		
	Grade 8	Grade 7	Total	Grade 8	Grade 7	Total	Grade 8	Grade 7	Total
Math and science	21.4	12.8	17.1	11.5	6.5	9.0	15.1	4.3	9.7
Social studies	19.4	16.2	17.8	21.0	30.0	25.5	20.6	20.0	20.2
Literature and languages	14.1	20.4	17.2	23.8	28.5	26.1	24.0	27.9	26.5
Shop	3.9	6.4	5.2	0.8	2.1	1.4	1.8	0.7	1.3
Art and music	2.0	8.4	5.2	3.8	5.1	4.4	1.8	10.0	5.9
Religion	4.9	8.5	6.7	5.5	5.0	5.3	3.6	10.0	6.8
Study and library	3.3	3.5	3.4	3.9	2.1	3.0	2.4	2.1	2.2
Intermissions	4.4	5.6	5.0	5.1	5.7	5.4	7.2	5.7	6.5
Sports, clubs and activities	15.1	9.8	12.5	11.9	7.8	9.9	9.8	8.6	9.2
Friends and teachers	2.4	3.5	2.9	2.9	2.1	2.5	2.4	5.0	3.7
Miscellaneous	9.1	4.9	7.0	9.8	5.1	7.5	10.3	5.7	8.0
Total	100.0	100.0	100.0	100.0	100.0	100.0	100.0	100.0	100.0

laneous. These were such items as hobbies, patrol boy duty, last bell, altar boy, school grounds, movies, courtesy lessons, maps, writing, rules, and monitoring.

5. Analyses of Girls' Interests

Analyses of girls' interests in school activities is presented in Table 3. Herein one finds the various categories of interest practically the same as those found in the study of boys' interests.

6. Degree of Choice in Interest

By comparing the totals given in Columns 3, 6 and 9 of Table 3, one can readily perceive the degree of choice given the various interest areas by the girls in the present study. Examination of these columns portrays some differences from first to second choice and again from second to third choice.

   a. First Choice of Interest. The highest-ranking interest among the girls is quite obviously interest in arithmetic, with 14.6 per cent of all the girls listing this item as their first interest. Second and third interests, considerably lower than arithmetic, are religion, represented by 10.6 per cent; and spelling, 9.4 per cent. The fourth highest interest category is that of sports, claiming a total of 8.0 per cent of all girls. Next in rank are reading, with 7.5 per cent; history, 5.3 per cent; music, 4.8 per cent; and art, 4.1 per cent.

   b. Second Choice of Interest. Several changes are noted in the figures of Column 6 representing the total of the girls' second interests. Highest ranking among these is spelling, claiming 13.4 per cent of all girls. Next in rank is arithmetic, with 10.1 per cent. Following these in order of rank are: religion, 8.7 per cent; English, 8.2 per cent; reading, 7.4 per cent; and sports, 6.5 per cent. Other areas showing a lesser degree of interest among the girls include art, 5.7 per cent; history, 4.4 per cent; science, 4.3 per cent; and music, 3.1 per cent.

   c. Third Choice of Interest. The third choices of interests as indicated by the girls in this study are again quite different in rank order from both the first and the second interests. As given in the last column on Table 3, the highest ranking third interest is reading, 10.1 per cent. Subjects closely following this are arithmetic, 8.8 per cent; spelling, 8.8 per cent; history, 8.2 per cent; religion, 7.7 per cent; and English, 7.1 per cent. Other areas of interest, considerably smaller, include music, 5.1 per cent; sports, 4.8 per cent; art, 4.1 per cent; and science, 3.2 per cent.

7. Grade-level Similarities and Differences

A comparison of the percentages for seventh- and eighth-grade girls reveals a number of similarities and differences. At a glance one notes in all six columns

Table 3 School interests of 338 girls in early adolescence

Interest categories	First choice			Second choice			Third choice		
	Grade 8	Grade 7	Total	Grade 8	Grade 7	Total	Grade 8	Grade 7	Total
Arithmetic	13.0	16.5	14.6	8.0	12.1	10.1	8.4	11.1	8.8
Art	2.3	5.9	4.1	4.7	6.7	5.7	3.1	5.0	4.1
History	4.2	6.5	5.3	3.8	4.9	4.4	6.3	9.9	8.2
Civics	3.3	1.1	2.2	3.8	1.2	2.5	2.1	1.9	2.1
English	5.1	1.1	3.1	8.5	7.9	8.2	5.8	8.0	7.1
Geography	0.5	1.1	0.8	2.4	2.4	2.4	1.1	2.5	1.9
Languages	4.2	1.2	2.7	0.5	0.7	0.6	1.6	0.6	1.2
Music	3.7	5.9	4.8	1.9	4.2	3.1	5.8	4.3	5.1
Reading	7.4	7.6	7.5	5.1	9.7	7.4	13.6	6.2	10.1
Religion	10.9	9.4	10.6	7.0	10.3	8.7	7.8	7.4	7.7
Science	1.4	2.3	1.8	5.6	3.1	4.3	3.7	2.5	3.2
Social studies	2.0	1.2	1.6	0.9	1.8	1.3	0.5	1.2	0.9
Spelling	8.8	10.0	9.4	14.1	12.7	13.4	4.7	14.8	8.8
Library	2.8	1.2	2.0	2.4	0.6	1.5	4.2	0.6	2.5
Study period	0.9	1.8	1.3	1.4	1.2	1.3	0.5	1.2	0.9
Sports	8.4	7.7	8.0	10.7	2.4	6.5	5.2	4.3	4.8
Friends	1.4	1.2	1.3	1.4	1.2	1.3	2.6	3.1	2.9
Teachers	2.3	2.9	2.6	0.9	1.2	1.0	3.7	3.7	3.7
Lunch period	0.5	0.6	0.5	1.4	1.2	1.3	2.6	0.6	1.7
Recess period	3.3	7.1	5.2	2.8	2.4	2.6	2.1	1.8	2.0
Clubs	3.3	1.2	2.2	2.4	0.6	1.5	1.5	0.6	1.1
Activities	1.4	1.2	1.3	2.3	2.4	2.4	3.1	4.3	3.8
Miscellaneous	8.9	5.3	7.1	8.0	9.1	8.5	10.0	4.4	7.4
Total	100.0	100.0	100.0	100.0	100.0	100.0	100.0	100.0	100.0

that most of the higher ranking areas are similar for both grade levels; likewise are grade-level similarities noted in areas having least interest.

Several areas of interest show larger percentages among eighth-grade girls than among seventh-grade girls. The former show a greater degree of interest in the areas of English, languages, civics and sports. One finds approximately twice as many, or more, eighth-grade girls listing one of these areas as their first, second, or third interest as seventh-grade girls.

The direction of difference is the opposite for other areas of interest. More seventh-grade girls than eighth-grade girls are interested in arithmetic, history, geography, science, art, spelling, and music. In these areas, for all three choices of interests combined, one finds from 10 to 30 per cent more seventh-grade girls than eighth-grade girls.

For two areas of interest, namely religion and reading, one finds very little grade-level difference.

8. Composite Interest Areas

Individual items of interest expressed by girls were grouped in their respective areas. These are presented in Table 4, which reveals a preponderance of interest in the area of literature and languages with 22.7 per cent as total first choice; 29.6 per cent, second choice; and 27.6 per cent, third choice. Thus, in all three choices of interest, a total of 79.9 per cent of different girls in the study listed an item in this general area in their free expression of school interests.

Though the percentages in all cases are somewhat smaller, interest in science and mathematics ranks second among the girls in both grades and for most choices. Among first choices of interest, religion ranks third with 10.2 per cent but falls to fifth rank in second and third choices.

In the first choice of interest, social studies area and music and art area rank fourth and fifth respectively with 9.9 per cent and 8.9 per cent of the girls indicating these areas. In second and in third choices, social studies rises to third rank and music and art area rises to fourth place.

A number of girls expressed interest in non-subject-matter areas. Among these the general area including clubs, sports and activities ranks highest with 11.6 per cent of the girls expressing this as their first choice of interest; another 10.4 per cent, as their second choice; and still another 9.5 per cent, as their third choice. Grade-level differences are also apparent here in that more eighth-grade girls expressed this interest that did seventh-grade girls.

Another group of girls found their chief school interest in people at school, including teachers and friends. This claims a total of 12.7 per cent of the girls in all three choices of interest. A slightly larger group of girls expressed their chief interest at school as the times of intermissions, including both the lunch hour and the recess period. Items of interest listed under miscellaneous include: writing, clothes, newspapers, piano, stories, home economics, vocations, and walks.

Table 4 Composite interest areas of girls

Interest areas	First choice			Second choice			Third choice		
	Grade 8	Grade 7	Total	Grade 8	Grade 7	Total	Grade 8	Grade 7	Total
Math and science	14.4	18.8	16.6	13.6	15.2	14.4	12.1	13.6	12.9
Social studies	10.0	9.9	9.9	10.9	10.3	10.6	10.0	15.5	12.8
Literature and languages	25.5	19.9	22.7	28.2	31.0	29.6	25.7	29.6	27.6
Art and music	6.0	11.8	8.9	6.6	10.9	8.8	8.9	9.3	9.1
Religion	10.9	9.4	10.2	7.0	10.3	8.7	7.8	7.4	7.6
Study and library	3.7	3.0	3.3	3.8	1.8	2.8	4.7	1.8	3.3
Intermissions	3.8	7.7	5.8	4.2	3.6	3.9	4.7	2.4	3.5
Sports, clubs and activities	13.1	10.1	11.6	15.4	5.4	10.4	9.8	9.2	9.5
Friends and teachers	3.7	4.1	3.9	2.3	2.4	2.3	6.3	6.8	6.5
Miscellaneous	8.9	5.3	7.1	8.0	9.1	8.5	10.0	4.4	7.2
Total	100.0	100.0	100.0	100.0	100.0	100.0	100.0	100.0	100.0

E. SUMMARY

A study of the school interests of 679 young adolescents from widely separated geographical regions of the United States was carried out in an experiment designed to elicit their true interests by giving them complete freedom in their expression of school-related interests. Tabulation of all items was made separately for sex and for grade level. Data were analyzed for each group according to (*a*) degree of choice in each interest category, (*b*) grade-level similarities and differences, and (*c*) composite interest areas.

REFERENCES

1. Albrecht, K. Wesensbild einer grosstadtischen Volksschulklasse von vierzehn-jahrigen Jungen. *Prax. Kinderpsychol. Kinderpsychiat.*, 1955, **1**, 24-26.
2. Arnholter, E. G. School persistence and personality factors. *Person. Guid. J.*, 1956, **35**, 107-109.
3. Carsley, J. D. The interests of children in books. *Brit. J. Educ. Psychol.*, 1957, **27**, 13-23.
4. Chase, W. L. Subject preferences of fifth-grade children. *Elem. Sch. J.*, 1949, **50**, 204-211.
5. Fagin, B. Guiding the vocational interests of the child. *Education*, 1953, **74**, 171-179.
6. Fitt, A. B. An experimental study of children's attitude to school in Auckland, N. Z. *Brit. J. Educ. Psychol.*, 1956, **26**, 25-30.
7. Harris, D. B. How children learn interests, motives, and attitudes. *In* Henry, N. B., *49th yearbook NSSE, Part I*, 129-155.
8. Khan, M. H. Attitude of the pupils toward geography. *J. Educ. Psychol.*, 1950, **8**, 153-157.
9. Leach, K. W. Intelligence levels and corresponding interest area choices of ninth grade pupils in thirteen Michigan schools, *J. Exp. Educ.*, 1954, **22**, 369-383.
10. Lentke, H. M. Eine Erhebung an hoheren Schulen uber das Interesse an den Schulfachern, insbesondere an der Biologie. *Psychol. Beitr.*, 1956, **2**, 308-326.
11. McCandless, B. R., & Castenada, A. Anxiety in children, school achievement, and intelligence. *Child Devel.*, 1956, **27**, 379-382.
12. Rudman, H. C. The informational needs and reading interest of children in grades IV through VIII. *Elem. Sch. J.*, 1955, **55**, 502-512.
13. Stauffer, E. Massenpsychologische Phanomene in der schule. *Heilpadag. Werkbl.*, 1954, **23**, 238-244.
14. Sterrett, M. D., Davis, R. A. The performance of school learning; a review of studies. *Educ. Adm. Superv.*, 1954, **40**, 449-460.
15. Symonds, P. M. What education has to learn from psychology. *Teach. Coll. Rec.*, 1955, **56**, 277-285.
16. Tyler, L. E. Comparison of interests of English and American school children. *J. Genet. Psych.*, 1956, **88**, 175-181.

Role of the school in the religious formation of youth

Willem Bless, S.J.

In this selection the author treats of the important issue of responsibility in education and the respective roles of the Church, the family, and the state in the formation of youth. In his discussion he shows how the school completes the educational task for these agencies and explains the source of its competence for helping children become adult and independent. In Father Bless's view Catholic education is possible only in a Catholic school where a commitment is made to direct and indirect religious formation. Yet despite an unequivocal allegiance to religious objectives, secular teaching and education are recognized as having an autonomous value, which should be emphasized as completely as possible in Catholic schools.

We know the influence exercised by the Christian family and the parish on the religious formation of youth. I therefore propose to talk about the role of the school and youth movements in the matter. I shall chiefly deal with the task incumbent on the school. Most of the considerations apply equally to youth movements, *suo modo.*

We will divide the subject into two parts: 1. The school's competence; 2. Religious formation proper to the school.

Reprinted with permission from *Lumen Vitae*, 12:99–112, March, 1957.

I. THE SCHOOL'S COMPETENCE

In order to define the task of the school as regards religious formation, we must first give an exact idea of the school as an educative milieu, and start with a few fundamental principles. Education consists of helping the child to become adult and independent. At birth, the human being is entirely dependent on his surroundings in order to live and develop. He is born a member of human society and the latter must help him to become adult and independent.

On Whom Lies the Responsibility of Education?

There are three necessary societies, distinct, although bound together in a harmonious whole, in the midst of which the child of Catholic parents is born: Holy Church, the Catholic family and the State. The Church has the supremacy in education, for she has received the supreme doctrinal authority from her Divine Founder. Her mission is to make Revelation known to all men and to lead them to a Christian moral life. Thanks to the sacraments given her by Christ, she has the power to transmit the divine life to men. Every human being is born again in her "in spirit and in truth."

That is why the Church, as much by reason of her origin as by the exercise of her educative mission, is independent of all temporal authority, which implies that she is equally sovereign in the choice of the means, necessary, or merely useful, for accomplishing this mission. It is precisely because the life of divine grace penetrates the whole of human life and also surpasses all purely human authority that the Church, as a supernatural community, occupies this eminence.

When we want to determine the educative role of parents, we must be careful not to consider them and the Church as opposing factors. It is not enough to say that the parents are the immediate educators of the child, as their function of paternity and maternity gives them this inalienable right, and then to limit this right to the secular sphere alone. As a matter of fact, it is in their quality of members of the Church that they have become parents. It is in the Sacrament of Marriage, in the heart of the Church of God, that they obtain the grace and strength to bring up their children as Catholics: before anything else they are the delegates invested by the Church with the power to educate their children in the sacred sphere as well. The rights of Catholic parents and of the Church are not in any way opposed, but on the contrary are exercised "in the framework of the Church." Parents are titulars of the Church's right to educate, and it is only insofar as these parents neglect their duty or have to be guided in its accomplishment, that the Church and they become opposing elements. There was a time— which, in many countries is not perhaps entirely past—when Catholic parents were scarcely aware of this educative task in the heart of the Church, and when the Church's hierarchy had to oppose them more than ought to have been the case. In her activity in schools and youth movements for instance, the Church was unavoidably giving the impression that she had too little respect for the rights of Catholic parents. At that period the laity accepted this sacerdotal authority without protest. Nowadays the laity are beginning to be aware of their role in the Church and it is therefore time to seek and establish a just balance in the educational sphere. This can only be a benefit to the whole Christian community.

At birth, the child is also part of a nation, a particular political community; the State has therefore also a right to educate, this right belonging to it in virtue of its duty to serve the general temporal interest, and also because the motherland is the country in which the child has been born. The child's education is not incumbent on the State by reason of the same principles as those invoked by the Church or family. The latter have this right, in fact, because they transmit life itself. It is none the less true that the State has its own rights and duties in the matter of education. The State has to make the child into a good patriot, which in our day means: a good citizen of the world. The State has therefore not only the right to cultivate the civic virtues and community sense, but also the obligation to watch over the intellectual, moral and physical development of its citizens, with regard to the circumstances of our period and the requirements of the general interest. The parents who, as members of a particular political community, bring children into the world, are qualified before all others to bestow upon them this civic education. Moreover, the State has the duty to protect and encourage the education given by the Church and the parents. It should defend the child against the family "when the parents' work is inadequate, physically or morally, in consequence of disregard of their duty, incapacity or unworthiness" (Pius XI in his encyclical *"Divini Illius Magistri"*).

What Place Has the School in All This?

Having thus described in principle the task of Church, family, and State, we now turn to that of the school. The school is an auxiliary institution, created by the Church, family and State for the fulfilment of their duties as educators. We should emphasize the fact that in the beginning the school was created on the initiative of the family and Church long before the State thought about it.

Each of these three has its own rights with regard to the school.

The Church and Catholic parents demand that the school should help them to educate their children in a *Catholic* manner. That is why both reject the school called neutral or laicising, from which religious education is excluded. "Such a school is also practically impossible, for in reality it becomes a school which is hostile to religion." (Pius XI). It is also quite insufficient to complete neutral education by a religion course.

Catholic education is only possible in the Catholic school, that is to say, a school in which the teachers, curriculum and textbooks are impregnated with the Catholic spirit. Religion should be, in such schools, the base and crown of all the teaching.

Just as the life of grace ought to regulate the whole natural life, in spite of the laws proper to the latter, so the Catholic conception of life should be the 'final' norm of all the secular branches of learning. That does not mean that secular subjects must be 'Christianized,' which would confer upon them a sacred character quite out of keeping with their secular nature. But the secular subjects should be taught in such a way that, while they retain their autonomy they fit into the general framework inspired by the final, sacred, norm. We would even go so far as to state that secular subjects only reach their full temporal significance, their most harmonious development, when taught in this spirit. No exclusive supernaturalism, nor independent naturalism! We shall return to this.

Let us remark, in this connection, that the school is more than a continuation of the family, and that in this sense it does not depend solely on the parents. The family is an imperfect community which has to be completed by the whole Christian community if it is to achieve its work of education. This is a task which the Christian community has entrusted to the schoolteachers it has trained. An experienced teacher has to enlarge beyond the limits of each individual family the Christian culture started by the parents. The Catholic parents must therefore help in education. The family and school should complete one another, be integrated in each other. But the parents are not, as a rule, qualified to run the school themselves. In Holland, parents, encouraged and guided by the religious authorities, are now starting more and more "parents' committees," which give parents the opportunity to co-operate in the education of their children.

The hierarchical authorities of the Church can conveniently entrust the practical organization of the Catholic school to Catholic teachers and parents, recognizing them as their delegates, fulfilling their task in the framework of the Church. The doctrinal authority of the Church should finally lay down the norms and eventually intervene in cases of default on the part of the delegates, teachers or parents. But in all normal cases, the Catholic laity ought to be left the greatest possible independence in the practical organization of the school.

In secular education—in which, as we have seen, the State has its rights— we reach the same conclusions by analogy. There also, the family is an imperfect community, which has to be completed by the whole national community if it is to carry out its educative task. There also, experienced teachers have to raise and develop the national culture and that of other nations beyond the limits of the family taken individually. The parents have also their word to say. But by its nature, this education is incumbent upon teachers who are competent in the matter. This will be increasingly the case as the child grows and approaches maturity. The State also should consider experienced teachers and parents as its own delegates with a view to the formation of good patriots. It should define the final norms and eventually intervene if its delegates are in default. But in normal cases, it should leave the greatest possible independence to teachers and parents in the practical organization of their education. This leads us to the real subject of this address: the religious formation proper to the school.

In the religious formation which the school is called upon to bestow, we may distinguish *direct religious formation:* the sacred formation of the pupils, and *indirect religious formation:* secular formation.

A few words first as to the school milieu, the foundation of both formations.

The milieu is a complex collection of circumstances influencing the child. An old neglected building, uninhabitable premises, out of date equipment, dirty benches, etc., do not encourage the creation of a sound and airy milieu, so indispensable if the child is to breathe freely, both physically and in the matter of religious instruction. The great care taken nowadays in the construction of the modern school constitutes an incontestable progress, on condition that the atmosphere is not troubled by an excess of modern pragmatism.

But the spiritual atmosphere, created in the school by the teacher, is of even greater importance. The growing child is much more influenced by the manner of life suggested to him than by the doctrine taught. He tries instinctively to identify himself with the adults who are helping him to mature. For this, it is indispensable that the teachers should themselves be openhearted Christians, persons worthy of being imitated. Their limits and failings are part of their individuality, and the child will not be much harmed by them, so long as the fundamentally Christian attitude of his teachers is not lacking. We think that the essential condition for the child's identification with his teacher is not so much in the intellectual plane as in the affective. The child must be approached with love, he must be certain that he can display his affection in all security; a disinterested love should surround the child, especially at school. It is precisely because the school is an educational institution tending essentially to the communication of intellectual knowledge, that this auxiliary institution should not, at any price, lose sight in its educative work of the affective life of the child. Love is the fundamental law of Christianity and also of Christian education. Whatever the extent of the child's eventual knowledge, his education is a failure if he has not learnt to love and does not know himself to be loved.

II. RELIGIOUS FORMATION PROPER TO THE SCHOOL

The school should not only teach the child the contents of Revelation, but also ensure that he receive a real initiation: doctrine ought to be presented to him as a reality with which he himself wills to be imbued. Doctrine should attract the child to Christian life.

1. The Religion Course

It is not our object here to deal with teaching methods; we shall consider the religion course only as a factor in the milieu. Religious instruction ought to be given in quite a different manner from secular lessons, for, in fact, the subject matter is totally different. We appeal to different qualities in the child. In secular studies, the child has to learn what the teacher knows himself and what his mind can grasp. The child expects to make the master's knowledge his own. He trusts him, has faith in him, but he will himself be able to penetrate the knowledge thus transmitted to him. The subject of this knowledge is a real object, assimilable by the human intellect.

In the religion course, on the contrary, the child has to be taught knowledge of quite another order. The teacher neither understands nor penetrates what he is communicating, but he believes in revelation. He bears witness to a divine knowledge surpassing human intelligence as such; this knowledge is not intelligible either for teacher or pupil, except in the light of faith.

For the purely natural intellect, the content of our Faith is absolutely incomprehensible and surpasses the strength and norms of our understanding—but in the light of faith, this content appears to us "as in a clouded mirror." Only in Heaven will this content be seen "facie ad faciem." The religion lesson does not deal with problems which can be solved. It communicates mysteries which are articles of faith. The atmosphere of the lessons depends on the teacher's devotional attitude, witnessing to his faith in Revelation, which ought to obtain the pupil's adhesion to faith. A knowledge of the articles of faith which is not accompanied by a total surrender to that faith can only be a material and not formal knowledge of the mysteries.

The attitude of the religion teacher is therefore entirely other than that of the teacher of secular subjects. The preacher ought to obtain attentive silence from his audience when he talks of the things of faith: the mysteries ought to remain intact during, and even after, his exposition.

A mystery speaks not only to the intellect, but to the whole human being with all his faculties. To present the system, doctrine, theory, does not convey its full reality; a mystery is a revelation of the concrete action of God in human life and calls for a response on the part of the human person.

The word of God accompanies its action and sheds light on it. "To accept as true all God has revealed, exclusively on the authority of God Himself" is a definition of faith which can be taken as being purely 'authoritative.' God is then the imperative norm.

We prefer to define faith as a personal surrender of man to God, Who reveals Himself in the most personal way possible, and this surrender implies the total acceptance of Revelation. God is then the Eternal Being revealing Himself personally to us and not requiring anything else of us than free self-surrender. It is this that makes Revelation the Good News of God.

May we add in passing that the religion course given in this spirit responds admirably to the psychological needs of modern youth. Youth of today is protesting against the exclusively intellectual and pragmatical tendency of their elders. They consider us as having petty minds, refusing to give up our faith for purely formal motives, but with a personality too narrow to expand in a free and personal surrender to the God Who reveals Himself to us. They think our moral attitude pitiful and far too pragmatic. As a result, we have become anxiety-ridden, which is the last thing that they themselves desire to be. For instance, an older girl writes: "If our teachers realized better the background in which we live, they would take greater care to prevent our faith from foundering; our catechisms are all right, but they are not made to fit into real life; religious instruction is only a section of its own among all the other subjects taught us, whereas Christian education should be a synthesis in which the divine predominates" (*Lumen Vitae,* VI (1951), p. 398). This denotes an intense desire for the veritable liberating atmosphere of religion. The mystery, presented judiciously, is also a psychological liberation, because it creates a personal relationship between God and man. A personalizing religious instruction is a great support for the pupils and helps them to acquire a balanced maturity. Religious instruction is a holy activity, and because of that the religious teaching of a layman must be supplemented by religious instruction from a priest. By virtue of his priesthood, he has the best right to preach Revelation. Close cooperation between priest and teacher is indispensable. It is also greatly to be recommended that the lessons should take place in appropriate premises, which contribute to the creation of a religious atmosphere. Religious instruction given in the Catholic school is no doubt a step forward, but the classroom in which all the lessons are given is not a holy place like the church. Should it not be suggested that a special place be reserved for religious instruction in order to create that 'holy' atmosphere which would distinguish this subject from all others?

Would it not also greatly profit the religious atmosphere and mystical character of religious instruction if there were far *greater unity in the systematic, biblical and liturgical lessons?* The mysteries take place as *historical* events. The historical evolution of God's action among us will therefore be the starting point, the foundation of our religious teaching, with of course the discernment which God bestows by the doctrinal authority of the Church and the sacred science of theology.

A systematic exposition of revelation, separated from the biblical events, necessarily gives those without scientific training the impression of an abstract doctrine or theory. Are not our religious textbooks too often *compendia theologiae dogmaticae?*

If our religious instruction were inspired more by the Bible it would become more concrete and more personal. The Bible is in itself universally human and therefore accessible to all. By reason of its intuitive thought it suits more particularly the contents of the mystery of salvation. We thus return to the method employed by the Church in the beginning in her catechesis: "Our starting point is no longer a doctrine or a theory which can be more or less 'illustrated' or applied. On the contrary, we start from the concrete economy of salvation, revealed by events and by symbols given by God and explained in a coherent doctrine" (Colomb in *Catéchistes,* 1951). A mystery is not an act of God in the past, but a revelation of God continually renewed to all men and for all time. That is why each mystery can take place anew, be celebrated in a total gift of faith by every man, in particular on the feasts instituted by the Church. If we succeed in presenting a mystery in this biblical manner, we shall find it easier to link our instruction to the liturgical celebration of the mysteries of the Faith. The development of catechesis is strongly directed towards this liturgical conception, that is, that personal surrender to the mysteries exacts their symbolical celebration in the liturgy. The Church leads us by these symbols to the mysteries of God. The Mystery of salvation takes place *now.* Under symbolic signs, liturgical celebration makes surrender to faith effective and thus comes as a transition between the intellectual explanation and life: preaching is incomplete without the liturgy.

This is why we think that our religious instruction should be linked to the liturgical celebration of the mysteries of faith and be a preparation for them. Without in any way neglecting a systematic exposition of all the mysteries, it seems desirable that the catechism should be entirely integrated in the framework of the liturgical year.

Speaking of a biblical catechesis, the necessity of integration in the liturgical year becomes evident, because the liturgy derives almost exclusively from biblical sources. By preference, it employs the harmony of the two Testaments as a means of preaching, as well as the symbolism of historical realities, types of future achievement in Heaven. Biblical catechism renders the student sensitive to symbols.

The religion course should also be especially careful about the pedagogy of prayer. The Bible is the best prayerbook to teach the child to pray in the spirit of the Church: each lesson should result in prayer, surrender in faith to the mystery is accomplished in prayer. The development of the subject taught is not possible without the pupil's entire personal activity. This personal activity is not a superfluous luxury, not a pleasant supplement to be added when the children have been impregnated with the whole of the doctrine, but a means of interesting the whole personality of the subject. As a result of our oral teaching, the children have more or less assimilated the doctrine, but this assimilation is far from complete. What they have heard cannot penetrate into them except by their personal activity. "We can think with our hands in our pockets." The child thinks with his hands, his whole body. Personal activity cannot take the place of religious instruction, or interfere with the attentive application of the pupils. But pictures, drawing, singing, modelling, interviews, the search for the solution of speculative problems, ought not to be absent from good religious instruction, on condition that they are in their right place.

2. *Living Initiation*

The school ought also, *suo modo*, to ensure an initiation into life side by side with the religious instruction. It ought to prepare the pupils for the great feasts of the Church. Preparation for First Confession and Communion and Confirmation should not consist in a series of technical instructions but in an initiation to the life of the Church in all its fulness. Although confession and mass at school are not the ideal of cooperation between family and school—it is above all the duty of the family to insist on it—religious instruction should nonetheless advise frequent confession and communion and teach the children to live in the exercise of these Catholic practices. The doctrine of Revelation should be lived in the midst of the school community; Christian charity should be practiced with school companions as much as with others. The idea of the apostolate, the missionary idea, should be put into practice there. There are many opportunities for truly Christian teachers to impregnate school life with the real *sensus catholicus* without undue exaggeration, which might cause the pupils later on, not only to throw off this forced yoke, but perhaps faith itself. Much tact is needed in order not to irritate children from non-Catholic or simply less fervent homes: the opportunities always depend on the actual situation.

A very good way of making contact about religious formation between school and parents more intimate is what are called *"parents' evenings."*

Once or twice in the year the school arranges evening gatherings for the parents of all the pupils or for those of one particular class. The school invites the parents and the children take part by means of some recitations, music, etc. An experienced speaker talks to the parents on a subject connected with education and the cooperation of parents and school, such as: Religious education in the family, Cathechism at home, Preparation for confession and communion, Prayer and examination of conscience, the religious education of adolescents, How ought we to initiate our children?

After this introduction the speaker and the parents discuss together various questions and attempt to solve them.

Our Catechetical Centre has already organized a thousand evenings of this sort. In order to help the parents to question their children on Christian doctrine and lead the children to talk about religion, we publish each year a leaflet giving the exact questions of the catechism which the children have to learn by heart each week. These are distributed to the parents at the beginning of each new school year. More than 30,000 parents take part in this scheme in Holland.

These questions on the catechism and religious conversations are not only good for the children, but also a valuable way of bringing parents back into touch with Revelation.

3. Indirect Religious Formation

After having described the school's direct religious formation, we must now deal with indirect religious formation: secular teaching.

In his encyclical on education, Pope Pius XI declares that a school does not deserve the name 'Catholic' unless the whole of the teaching, the teachers, curricula and textbooks, are impregnated with the Catholic spirit. We mentioned this at the beginning of our introduction. Let us now be more precise.

The whole of creation is marked by the redemptive work of God. Every human action in this creation is a cooperation between nature and grace. They are, on the contrary, opposed to one another in sin. In many human activities, the redemptive work of God is accomplished incognito, God acting anonymously. These are the cryto-Christian activities of the profane. There is no doubt that the whole of creation is impregnated with the work of divine redemption. Nothing escapes grace. The whole creation is under the divine influence, but this cooperation between God and men is only explicitly revealed in sacred activities. It remains hidden in secular activities. We are deliberately not speaking of natural or supernatural activities, in order not to fall into an abstract conceptual opposition.

If therefore the nature of secular activities resides in a hidden cooperation between God and men, it is misconstruing the value of the secular if we try to bestow upon it a public or sacred character, as though that were an absolute condition for the secular to acquire any kind of value.

Secular teaching and education have for the Catholic their own autonomous value which should be brought out as completely as possible in Catholic schools.

It cannot be denied that we Catholics show such negligence in secular education that we do not appear to recognize its value at all. Good Catholic education also requires complete secular culture and formation. The child ought to know the cultural and artistic history of his nation and also, at the present time, the culture of many other nations in order to become a good "citizen of the world." An excellent Catholic teacher asked me recently what he ought to do to become a good 'Catholic' master. I knew that he occupied himself a great deal with Church activities, but that he rather neglected the teaching of his own subject. I replied, "You cannot do better than to teach your subject as well as possible." He was very disappointed, for in his estimation, that had nothing to do with being "a Catholic teacher."

I knew quite well that my answer was incomplete, but it gave the essential point. The Catholic school ought to be able to compete with the non-confessional in all secular subjects. Our Catholic pupils have as much right as the others to the best methods and a thorough secular formation.

But should we not add an element which would satisfy the desires of the Church?

Much is now being said of 'christianizing' secular things. The meaning is that the secular ought to obtain its value from its integration into the sacred order of things. We think that this Christianization of secular subjects ought to be condemned, because it fails to recognize sufficiently the value of these subjects. There is no Catholic arithmetic, gymnastics, chemistry or biology. Anyone who thinks to make our schools Catholic schools in this way will be disappointed by the result. He will form supernaturalistic men, whose "one way" education supplies its own condemnation. What then did the Pope mean by "The Catholic spirit in teachers, curricula and textbooks?" Having stated what he did not mean, we will now try to elucidate the phrase.

Every action of man in creation implies, we said, a cooperation between nature and grace. Every human act emanates from a conception of life and is finally determined by the relationship existing between man and God. No activity escapes this truth. None can be considered as being neutral. In secular activity, this conception of life is the background on which the secular subject stands out. The activity is no less secular, but this background takes away from the secular its own limits and directs it towards the total development of concrete human life. In the order of nature and grace what is secular in itself requires this background, which gives its relative value the position due to it. Without this background, the secular tries to impose itself as something in itself absolute and not limited.

If this background is Christian, the secular possesses an implicitly Christian value. In this way the secular is in itself implicitly religious and a Catholic education requires this indirectly religious formation.

Secular subjects should be treated as such. Their strength lies there. But they should stand against the background of a Christian conception of life. There is a constant interplay between nature and grace in life. If secular subjects expressly demand this background of conception of life, it should be supplied, not in order to christianize secular subjects, but to do justice to their own relative value. It will sometimes be indispensable to insist on this point when teaching history, geography, biology. In many other branches of secular learning this "conception of Christian life" will have to remain as far as possible a 'background.' The more the positive value of the implicitly Christian secular subject is emphasized, the more chances there are of teaching it without danger. Should the religious formation at school therefore be confined to religious instruction and other holy activities? We reply that a distinction must be made between direct and indirect religious formation. The latter is given by secular formation in which the religious side remains in the background and renders justice to the value proper to the secular. These direct and indirect religious formations constantly meet in concrete human life and, in their profound essence, are indissolubly bound to one another. That is why a school is Catholic only if this Catholic mentality remains in the background of the secular instruction, and determines finally its ultimate sense.

Apply this to another sphere: the religious or moral life of the pupils. This application will illustrate our thought.

In virtue of the grace of baptism, the Christian is entirely orientated towards God. This orientation cannot be constantly actual and conscious. It is impossible and thus unreasonable to want to make the pupils act only in virtue of exclusively supernatural motives. The human being in his daily life ought even to act chiefly from natural motives: such a thing is obvious; a well brought up girl acts thus; that is sporting; a well brought up boy does not do that; be helpful; help one another, etc. There are implicitly Christian motives which have their own value, motives on which it is well to insist from time to time, especially during religious lessons. But in daily life, supernatural motives ought not to be stressed too often and too exclusively, or the pupils will have the impression that they ought to do all sorts of things for the intrinsic motive: "That is the will of God." On the other hand, it is preferable to show the pupils how God has expressed His holy will precisely in the complete collection of circumstances in which He has placed them. To integrate themselves as Christians in this structure, to respect the 'natural' relationships, that is doing the will of God, living Christian lives.

We have indicated the duty of the Catholic school in the matter of religious formation, the ideal which all of us ought to pursue together.

It will not be possible to realize this ideal in non-Catholic schools. Religion can be taught in them as an isolated subject, but the school will not be for all that, as an educative institution, "dominated by the Catholic spirit." A Catholic teacher can all the same reach better implicitly Christian results in a non-Catholic school than a non-Catholic teacher, on condition that he understands his duty.

Everything has not been said about the role of secular branches of learning with regard to religious formation. It is indeed very often a fact that secular subjects are not taught in an implicitly Christian spirit. No account is taken of the norms given above, and an absolute value is given to the secular.

In the course of recent years serious study has been given to this relationship between the secular and the religious in teaching. It is still too soon to tell the result. Healthy Catholic milieux ought to make prudent experiments and attempt to determine the value of the secular with regard to the religious, rather than make drastic reforms.

The duty of the Catholic school and teacher as regards religious formation is of primary importance today. Parents, alas, often fail in their duties. That is why the school, as an auxiliary educative institution, is all the more indispensable. Fortunately, there are still many men and women, religious or not, wishing to devote their lives to religious formation of youth, sometimes even for very modest remuneration. Insofar as they are equal to their task, they will train a new generation of Christians, journeying with Christ to the Father Who is in Heaven.

part vi

Education for values

QUESTIONS TO GUIDE YOUR READING

1. What are the main differences between the "old" and the "new" catechetics? Which do you prefer? Why?

2. Is moral education possible without religious instruction? Is religious instruction possible without moral education?

3. In what ways are Mr. Ball's and Father Henle's recommendations alike, and how do they differ?

4. Which of Father Stanton's reasons for Catholic lack of interest in social problems seems most reasonable to you? Why?

5. What are some assumptions in Father Twomey's article? Do you agree or disagree with them? Why?

6. What is your reaction to Father Hagmaier's statement that "the Catholic school has too often usurped the obligations which belong first and foremost to the parents"?

Up-to-date catechetics

Thomas F. Stransky, C.S.P

*One of the most significant movements in this
Ecumenical period has been the so-called
"catechetical revival," an attempt to strengthen and
generally improve religious education. A leading
figure in this movement has been Father Johannes
Hofinger, S.J., who organized a conference in
Eichstaett, West Germany, of leading Catholic
scholars from all parts of the world to discuss the
problem of teaching Christian doctrine more
effectively. The following article is based on an
interview with Father Hofinger by Father Stransky,
a Paulist priest who has worked in the Secretariat
of Christian Unity in Rome.*

What brought about the recent catechetical "revival"?

As long as children were living in deeply religious families and breathing the
air of a strongly Christian environment, "traditional" catechetical instruction was
thought to be adequate. It systematized in questions and answers what children
were already living—a Christian life in a Christian environment. Its tone was
almost exclusively intellectual and abstract.

The catechetical revival began about fifty years ago in central Europe. There,
particularly in formerly "Catholic" cities such as Munich and Vienna, the Church
was witnessing a new phenomenon. Thousands of children were stepping from
homes where religion was weak into a society which was rapidly becoming de-
Christianized. Many ceased to practice the faith.

A closer look at the religious instruction being given revealed serious faults.
At the end of the eighteenth century the state had made elementary school at-

Reprinted with permission from *The Catholic World*, 192:94–101, November,
1960.

tendance compulsory and hence religion had become another "school" subject. The emphasis in religious instruction was no longer on faith and life but on doctrine and knowledge. Worse yet, both doctrine and method were tainted with a popular, enlightened rationalism which replaced the truths of revelation with a religion of reason, turning religion itself into a mere handmaid of morality.

The problem gradually became clear. The more the religious milieu broke down, the more it became necessary to instill *personal conviction* in the pupils. Catechesis had to do more than instruct minds; it had to form solid apostolic Christians.

This is the central idea behind the catechetical revival: we must "convert" children totally to Christ, and this first "conversion" must last throughout their lives.

Do you think that this kind of crisis in education is a local problem—or do you find that similar if not identical problems exist every place in the world?

Obviously the problems of religious instruction are not confined to central Europe. I have traveled around the world seven times. Recently I was in the United States; soon I will be going to South Africa. The more I travel and the more people I meet, the more I am convinced that what is most lacking in catechetics today is neither good will nor interest on the part of teachers, but an intelligent appreciation of the basic principles and methods of proclaiming God's word so that it can achieve the effect God wants. And I know that this isn't just my own opinion. There was almost universal agreement about this at the International Study Week on Mission Catechetics held this summer at Eichstaett, Germany.

With the breakdown of religious traditions and the spread of materialism and Communism, the old distinction between "mission lands" and other countries is disappearing. Although the situation may differ somewhat from place to place, the basic problem is the same in Europe and Africa, Japan and the United States, South America and India. The catechetical movement is gradually becoming world-wide, and interest in up-to-date catechetics is growing.

What was the significance of the recent Eichstaett meeting?

For the first time, internationally known catechetical scholars and missionaries came together to pool their knowledge and experience in the catechetical movement in an attempt to adapt catechetics to the missionary needs of the Church today. To complain about old catechisms and old methods would have been easy; we wanted a positive program. By intensive teamwork, we drew up and approved unanimously a set of principles for catechesis, guides for catechists and suggestions for writing new catechisms and religious textbooks.

What is the general trend in modern catechesis?

We can never achieve success in our teaching apostolate by a mere increase in catechetical activity. A reform is needed which combines the findings of modern psychology and the conclusions of the so-called "kerygmatic revival." That word *kerygmatic* frightens most people. It shows that the revival stresses the content of teaching rather than method and techniques. The Greek *kerygma* means "message" and in the New Testament *kerygma* means specifically the Good News of Salvation that Christ preached and commissioned His Church to proclaim.

How can we impart to the pupil not mere knowledge of formulas but a consciousness of a reality? How can our catechesis introduce the student to this Christian message (*kerygma*) expressed in the synthetic ordering of doctrines, in the Bible and in liturgical worship? What is the best order of presentation and what doctrine should be emphasized if catechesis is to be of greatest profit to people today, to develop and confirm a real Christian life in them and form faithful disciples of Christ who give witness to Him? In presenting the whole *kerygma,* what should we emphasize? These are the questions we tried to answer at Eichstaett.

But haven't we always been teaching religion in this "kerygmatic" way?
I don't think so. Read the older catechisms and teachers' manuals.

One of the reasons for the large number of fallen-aways today has undoubtedly been the inadequacy of the faulty religious instruction which they received.

So much of our catechetical instruction has been but a summary, or watering-down, of scientific theology. Now I by no means disparage theology; I was once a professor of dogma. It's just that theological science has a very different purpose from catechetics. Theology is a disciplined and detailed contemplation of God's revelation, taught primarily from the viewpoint of truth, without considering too much its value for life. Catechetics treats the same doctrine from a different standpoint, as a good, as a value for the person, as a doctrine for living. In most cases Christ's word can be a power to mold lives only if it is identified and experienced as the one and only worth-while thing in life. It's not enough that our children know their faith, they must also see its unity, its beauty, and experience its warmth. This cannot be achieved by intellectual techniques of instruction alone. The catechism that just lists doctrines may attain thoroughness, accuracy and clarity, but is it an organic unit that brings out that God has Good News for us? We know many details and dispensable fragments, but find it hard to see the core of a message which God says surpasses by far what the heart of man can think of or hope for.

One of "The Basic Principles of Modern Catechetics" agreed upon at Eichstaett calls for systematic teaching: the systematic presentation of the Faith has its roots in the Creeds and the preaching of the early Christian proclamation, and has derived its organic development from the authoritative teaching of the Church through the ages. The catechism gives the learner spiritual insights into the relationship between the faith and Christian life and enables him to cope with the questions of the day as an articulate Christian and to express his faith to those who inquire about it.

But, as we often heard at Eichstaett, let's emphasize the inner core of God's revelation, so that the details or borderlines of revelation are seen as secondary.

What is this inner core?

We tried to outline the basic content of catechesis in the Eichstaett principles.

Our Gospel is nothing else than Christ introducing us into the intimacy of God: "No man comes to the Father except by Me" (*John*, 14:6).

Catechesis is Christ-centered, because there is no aid given us on the way leading to the Father which has not its center in Christ and does not actively share in His mission "to save that which was lost" (*Luke*, 19:10). Through Christ we know about the Father and receive the Good News about His Kingdom. By His death, resurrection and ascension, Christ saves us from our sins. He works in us through the Holy Spirit and leads us toward that day when He will judge all men and bring the world to its final perfection. Christ continues to live and act and complete His Father's work in His Church, especially through His sacraments. He teaches, directs, sanctifies His own by means of His representatives. The commandments, flowing from His Great Commandment of Love, are not merely divine directives but our loving response to Christ's divine love—living out the implications of His sacraments.

A dogma, then, has greater or less consequence in our catechesis in the measure that it expresses a more or less significant aspect of this Mystery of Christ. As Father Domenico Grasso, S.J., of the Roman Gregorian University explained at Eichstaett, grace will have more importance than sin, sanctifying grace more than actual grace, the Holy Spirit more than Our Lady, the Resurrection of Christ more than His childhood, the mystical aspect of the Church more than its juridical, the Church's liturgy more than private devotions, baptism more than penance, the Eucharist more than the Last Anointing, the Bible more than any other book.

You see that our modern catechetics is incorporating the conclusions of the biblical and liturgical movements.

What has the biblical movement contributed to modern catechetics?

The Bible must be given a prominent place in catechetical teaching because it is God's own inspired Book. This doesn't mean doing what some "revised" question-and-answer catechisms have done—merely adding scripture texts as a kind of divine support.

The basic method of all catechesis is to teach the way God has given His revelation: God performs some concrete event which radiates and reveals a doctrine that would move men's hearts to live according to it. For example, in the Old Testament God intervened in history at Sinai when He fulfilled His earlier promises and freely chose Israel as His people. The biblical *events* thereafter remind the Israelites what God has done for men. They dwelt on the doctrine of God's loving concern for His Chosen People to prepare a way for the world's Messiah. God chose them as His own and binds them to Himself. This initial action of God awakens a response of love and gratitude and unworthiness, and binds the people to remain deeply faithful to Him by keeping His commandments. Event—truth—action. God is the best modern Pedagogue!

The biblical movement has brought out more clearly the organic unity of the whole Bible, not a disconnected series of interesting stories or moral demands, but a history of salvation through which and in which God has chosen to save us. Once again, the Bible finds its center in Christ, for it relates the role of Christ in the Father's whole historical plan: how God prepared for Christ's coming in the New Testament, how His coming brought about our salvation and reunion, and how Christ continues to communicate Himself through a Chosen People, animated by the Holy Spirit, until He returns as the Lord of Glory. It is through the Bible, then, that we learn God's pattern of working His plan of salvation in time and space.

Do you use the Bible then as part of catechetical instruction?

Yes. Modern catechetics no longer uses the Bible as an accessory, a supplementary proof of the doctrine or a mere study of the historical background to revelation. In certain recent textbooks, the biblical quotations come no longer at the end but have become the very departure for a catechetical lesson. One of the Eichstaett recommendations is that younger students possess a book of Bible "extracts" which contain passages from the historical books, psalms, prophetical writings, Gospels, epistles and the Apocalypse. Explanatory sections clarify the connection of one extract to another, and point out what bearing the passage has on God's plan of salvation. With such a preparation, by adolescence everyone should possess his own complete New Testament, to be used as a source and reference book during catechism classes. If a child is trained to read God's Book in a prayerful and reverent manner, it can become, as it should, his lifelong vade mecum.

What has the liturgical movement contributed to modern catechetics?

A recital of past biblical events does not suffice for good catechesis because God *continues* to intervene in history, especially in the Mass and the sacraments. By taking part in the Liturgy, the Christian enters into the stream of grace God set aflow at the creation of the world. Liturgical catechesis, then, completes the work of biblical catechesis and the necessary presentation of doctrine.

We debase the Liturgy if we consider its primary purpose catechetical. It is primarily directed to the worship of God; we pray what we know. Catechesis leads "the royal priesthood" (*I Peter*, 2:9) into the Liturgy so that we can fully join the community in its divine worship and know what we are praying.

At the same time, the Liturgy contains a wealth of instructive power. In the course of the Church's liturgical years, we have summarized the story of salvation: it speaks of Christ in those who prefigured Him, in His teaching and life, His miracles, death and resurrection; it tells of Christ living in the saints of the past and in us today. The Liturgy also teaches us through the texts, mainly from the Bible, that are read and sung by the Church. The sound pedagogical principles of "the intuitive process" and "learning by doing" are used in the Liturgy. The rites with their words and gestures, poetry and music, indeed help make the Christian message enter into more than the mind. (We must make children aware of this.)

Here I may mention a practical conclusion reached at Eichstaett: "In order that the Liturgy may produce its due catechetical effect, it should display its intrinsic excellence by means of its intelligibility, beauty and clarity. Only thus can its full catechetical value be exploited. But we cannot do this unless certain reforms are introduced." Some suggestions, for example, centered on having the whole Mass of the Catechumens in the vernacular.

Can we revive easily our old catechisms which have not integrated the aims of modern catechetics?

We had to face this question honestly at Eichstaett, since so much time, money and talent depend on the answer. We agreed that new catechisms cannot just add a few more questions, scriptural quotations and liturgical directives. The Eichstaett conclusion reads: "The mere revision or modification of former textbooks or catechisms which were not drawn up according to the principles of the catechetical renewal cannot produce a good work which fulfills the basic demands of catechetics."

Complete revisions are found, for example, in the new German catechism and the recent syllabus for the Archdiocese of Bombay. (The introduction of the latter speaks of a refusal to copy "old catechisms" and of making "a drastic rearrangement" of doctrine.)

A catechism is only a tool, so we can't stress too much the intellectual and spiritual formation of the catechist himself. The ideal catechism, neverthless, is a guide. More than a list of questions and answers, it must guide both the teacher and pupil in the three pedagogical steps of seeing, thinking and doing. Thus, we desire a lesson-form catechism that moves from the concrete to the doctrine and to life, organically centered around our life in Christ, and introducing one into the Bible and into the Liturgy. The questions and answers which come at the *end* of the whole lesson merely summarize and make precise the contents of the lesson.

Is this method understressing the importance of memory work?

A popular accusation based on misunderstanding. Memory comes from God, not the devil, and the whole man must be won for God. That includes the memory. However, modern catechetics supplies a sound pedagogical principle: never memorize anything that is not first clearly understood, "assimilation before memory." How false the method: have the children memorize as much as they can, so that they have a storehouse of matter to be tapped later in life when they can understand. We can easily distort the joyful character of the Christian message by creating anxieties accompanying an exaggerated number of little-understood formulas to be learned by heart and by attendance at class, which can often become a dry exegesis of an official catechism's questions and answers. All the new textbooks have a reasonable number of answers that can be easily understood at the *end* of the learning process. I may mention, in addition to questions and answers, appropriate texts from the Bible and the Liturgy as well as prayers should also be memorized.

Can the United States make a contribution to the catechetical movement?

I have traveled much in the United States and have given 30–40 hour courses in catechetics at Notre Dame, the University of Portland, the University of San Francisco and St. Louis University. (This is the same basic course I give in Africa, the Philippines, India and Australia.)

Nowhere have I seen a more interested and generous laity who not only support your "miraculous" school system, but are ready to help the Church, especially in instructing the many Catholics in public schools. And the already solid religious knowledge and practice of so many American Catholics is certainly due largely to the self-sacrificing teaching sisters. In short, in no country have I discovered more virtuous and energetic catechists willing to be trained in modern catechetics. Good work is being done, but can you improve it?

At present the catechetical movement in the U. S. A. is not as advanced as in the lands north of the Alps, where it is in tune with the biblical and liturgical revivals. Frankly, there is a great disproportion between the potential and the actual number of first-class catechetical specialists and thinkers who can form these catechists to take part in the catechetical movement.

This disproportion is gradually decreasing. The sisters especially are demanding even a better special training for themselves. I may mention that many of the shortcomings may stem from an inadequate training of many priests in modern catechetics. The United States has the potential to make a large and important contribution to the modern catechetical movement if it would guide the enthusiastic catechists—priests, sisters, laity—with the principles outlined at Eichstaett. The mere recognition that there is a weakness in the catechetical training of seminarians is already the beginning of progress.

On the possibility of moral education

Charles F. Donovan, S.J.

*Some Catholic educators, as well as some educators
of other religious faiths and some of no faith
whatever, are agreed that the school cannot "teach
morality" and that it would not be the school's
function to attempt to do so if it were possible.
Father Donovan takes issue with this point of view
in the article that follows, maintaining that moral
principles and values can and should be taught in
any kind of school regardless of its religious
affiliation or lack thereof. Father Donovan is the
Academic Vice-president of Boston College.*

One of the paradoxes of contemporary education is the fact that friends of morality and of moral education seem unsure or even negative as regards the role of the school in moral education. Whether they are associated with secular or expressly religious schools seems to make little difference. Spokesmen for both kinds of school, though personally committed to a moral or even a religious interpretation of life, have advanced theories concerning moral education that curtail the influence of the school as contrasted with the role that schools, both public and church-related, have presumed to exercise in the past.

The thinking of such theorists seems to be dominated by two major considerations. First, morality cannot be taught and hence is not a proper concern of institutions essentially devoted to teaching. Secondly, schools are agencies for the development of intellect. Truth, not goodness, is the object of the intellect. So morality cannot be a direct business of schools, as schools.

Two such diverse thinkers as Maritain and Dewey may be cited as apparently giving substance to the first contention. Maritain says, ". . . because it [the school] deals essentially with that which can be taught, it refers to the education and formation of intelligence more than of the will." [1] In his little treatise, *Moral*

Reprinted with permission from *Educational Theory*, 12:184–186, July, 1962.

Principles in Education, Dewey challenges the value of teaching "about morality," comparing it with the presentation of literally dry lectures about swimming.[2] Many others have scouted the value of a catechetical, learn-and-recite method of moral education. It has been pointed out that just as the devil can quote scripture, a delinquent child, with heart uncontrite, can correctly recite the decalogue.

What this case adds up to is that moral learning is not the same as propositional learning, that morality as a personal code of conduct cannot be learned with the same facile detachment as a theorem in geometry or as the geography of Central America. But some have ignored the analogy between moral and intellectual learning and, whereas Dewey would say morals cannot be learned as can the Greek alphabet, there has been a tendency to drop the analogue and simply say, morality cannot be learned. The pointing up of the distinction between moral and merely academic learning has been necessary, but it has led to a negativism if not despair regarding moral education. It seems only common sense to conclude that what cannot be taught has no place in a school.

The second line of reasoning stems from the conviction, very strong in western culture, that schools have to do with intellects, with truth, whereas holiness, probity, moral ideals are someone else's business. Says Mark Van Doren: "The conscious business of education is with the intellect." [3] A contemporary Dominican educator contends, "The proper and immediate end of the school is the inculcation of the intellectual virtues." [4] Even a great religious figure like Cardinal Newman held that liberal education makes not the Christian but the gentleman, a person morally neutral who can as readily be a profligate as he can be a saint.[5]

Few would deny that intellectual excellence is a primary concern of education, but when it is made the exclusive concern, it is logical to consider morality as academically irrelevant. Some of the intellectualists attempt to soften the severity of their doctrine by teaching that while intelligence is the object of schools, morality may be the object of those who run schools, and so morality may be bootlegged onto a campus or into school precincts by administrators as an extra-curricular adjunct of education.

But is such pussyfooting or surrender necessary? Is this defeatist attitude taken by the teaching profession regarding other non-intellectual values it holds dear? Far from it. Teachers of history would indignantly reject the suggestion that their task is to teach only facts; that a historian's attitude, a commitment to the objective weighing of historical evidence, since it is moral, is outside their province. Teachers of the arts would consider themselves to have failed were they to communicate to their students no more than a catalogue-competence. The California Institute of Technology and the Bronx School of Science surely do not regard the imparting of the scientific spirit and dedication to experimental evidence as something extracurricular. To them this spirit, this dedication is more important than any particular formula or datum of science. It is the heart of the matter. It belongs in the classroom. It is the professor's direct concern.

In a perceptive essay the American philosopher Theodore Greene points out that in every major area of learning there are critically important matters that cannot strictly be taught.[6] The philosopher cannot "teach" a passion for clear and consistent thinking, the professor of language cannot "teach" a feel for or love of language and its precise use, the scientist cannot "teach" respect for fact and hatred of error, illusion and evasion, the historian cannot "teach" a lively realization of the evils of provincialism and the value of more embracing and catholic perspectives.

Is Greene counseling despair? Quite the contrary. While he asserts that these all-important attitudes cannot be directly communicated by conventional instruction, he maintains that they can be cultivated in the young by indirection—by example, inspiration, and contagion. This he calls one of the pardoxes of education: ". . . what is most important can be achieved only by indirection, and what can be achieved directly is, in the last analysis, merely a means, not an end in itself. The teacher's total responsibility is, on this analysis, *not* fully discharged in his formal instruction; far more important than all his knowledge and skill is his character, or his basic attitudes, his scale of values, and his philosophy of life." [7]

If aesthetic appreciation, linguistic sensitivity, passion for truth, and respect for fact are not to be declared educationally out-of-bounds as being non-teachable, why should ethical responsibility be so dismissed? Why are values and attitudes concerning poems and social systems and experimental data relevant in the classroom while values and attitudes concerning one's personal moral conduct are deemed irrelevant?

There is a difference, of course, in that the former values are essentially related to definite academic subjects (scientific objectivity is tied to science teaching, etc.), whereas one may ask what academic subject, unless an isolated course in ethics or, perhaps, religion, has as a necessary concomitant moral values? But the point here is not to indicate what teachers or what disciplines should consider themselves responsible for the "teaching" of morality, but simply to question the validity of arguments that have been advanced against the appropriateness or possibility of teaching morality in schools. Many circumstances such as the sentiment of a community or the control of an institution may affect or preclude moral teaching in a school. This paper is concerned only with the theoretical possibility of moral education, disregarding practical circumstances.

The case against those who would banish moral education from classrooms as (a) not being possible, and/or (b) not being intellectual and hence not suitable may be summed up thus. First, if moral education is impossible, that is, pedagogically impossible, in the school, it is impossible anywhere else. If the effort to make young men and women better persons is to be discouraged in schools on the ground that the mere communication of precepts does not alter anyone's character, then it should be discouraged as futile elsewhere, because the same liability would burden moral teaching in the home or Sunday school. If on the other hand moral formation is said to be possible outside of school through the inculcation of ideals and values, through morally wholesome examples and atmosphere, and by the presentation, as Whitehead suggested, of the habitual vision of greatness, then surely in some measure the same thing is possible and desirable within the school, and, indeed, within the classroom.

Secondly, if non-propositional learning—attitudes, values, commitments, enthusiasms—are appropriate and important objectives of teachers of science, history, philosophy and other subjects, why should moral values and commitments be deemed educationally inappropriate? The fact that a teacher of moral values cannot guarantee "conversion" or inner conformity is no bar. Neither can the teacher of scientific method, of historical research, of philosophical reflection, or even of aesthetic appreciation. None of these teachers can be sure that even if their students master the "content" of their courses, they also have assumed a new mental character and henceforth will think like scientists, historians, philosophers, or artists. This is perhaps the highest challenge and reward of teaching: to produce a lasting change in the mental or moral *character* of one's students. Success is not automatic; but even occasional success is worth the effort.

If the foregoing analysis is correct, it would follow that teachers—at any level and in any kind of school—who are moved to work for the moral formation of youth should not be discouraged by either the alleged impossibility or academic impropriety of the endeavor.

REFERENCES

1. Jacques Maritain, "Thomist Views on Education," in *Modern Philosophies and Education,* Fifty-fourth Yearbook of the National Society for the Study of Education, Part I (Chicago: University of Chicago Press, 1955), p. 63.
2. John Dewey, *Moral Principles in Education* (Boston: Houghton Mifflin Co., 1909), p. 2.
3. Mark Van Doren, *Liberal Education* (New York: Henry Holt and Co., 1942), p. 62.
4. Rev. Thomas C. Donlan, O. P., *Theology and Education* (Dubuque: William Brown Co., 1952), p. 58.
5. Cf. Section 9, Discourse V, "Knowledge Its Own End" in Newman's *Idea of a University.*
6. Theodore M. Greene, "A Liberal Christian Idealist Philosophy of Education," in *Modern Philosophies and Education,* Fifty-fourth Yearbook of the N.S.S.E., Part I (Chicago: University of Chicago Press, 1955), pp. 122–123.
7. *Ibid.,* p. 124.

Dilemmas of the prayer decision

Robert J. Henle, S.J.

When the Supreme Court declared unconstitutional
the requirement that an officially composed,
nonsectarian prayer be recited in public schools, the
reaction of many Catholics was decidely critical. In
the following article, the Academic Vice-president
of St. Louis University explains why he agrees with
the Court's decision, but then goes on to explore the
problem of preventing secularism from becoming a
kind of national religion. In this article he is, of
course, primarily concerned with the nation's public
schools.

In the 1961-62 term, the Supreme Court was faced with a case[1] brought to it on complaint of several parents in the Union Free School District No. 9, New Hyde Park, New York, alleging, in effect, that the State Board of Regents and the School Board in authorizing and ordering the use of a prayer in the public schools of that district were in violation of the disestablishment clause of the First Amendment.

The decision of the Court was delivered in a majority opinion written by Justice Black. Concurring with this opinion were Chief Justice Warren, Justice Brennan, Justice Clark, and Justice Harlan. Justice Douglas concurred in the decision but presented a separate opinion. Finally, a dissenting opinion was written by Justice Stewart.

Let us examine the majority opinion. First, the facts. The Board of Regents of the State of New York, a state agency, as the Court said, with "broad supervisory, executive, and legislative powers over the state's public-school system," recommended that each public-school day should commence with an "Act of

[1] *Engel* v. *Vitale,* 370 U.S. 421 (1962).

Reprinted with permission from *Social Order*, 13:32–48, March, 1963.

Reverence to God." [2] The wording: "Almighty God, we acknowledge our dependence upon thee, and we beg thy blessings upon us, our parents, our teachers, and our country," was a nonsectarian one and agreed upon by representatives of the major faiths. The use of this prayer was part of a "program to further religious beliefs." [3]

Among other things, the Regents advocated teaching the public-school children "that Almighty God is their Creator, and that by Him they have been endowed with their inalienable rights of life, liberty, and the pursuit of happiness." [4]

The Board of Education had "directed the school district's principal to cause the . . . prayer to be said in the presence of a teacher at the beginning of each school day."

The Supreme Court called attention to two facts on which its decision rested. First, that the formula recited aloud was simply and per se a prayer—a religious act, an act of reverence to God. The Court noted that no exception had been taken to this, that all parties admitted that the formula and the act in question were, in the strictest possible sense, a direct religious act and that there was no other aspect or intent present. That this strict and narrow reading of the fact was essential to the case is expressly confirmed by a footnote appended to the majority opinion:

> There is of course nothing in the decision reached here that is inconsistent with the fact that school children and others are officially encouraged to express love for our country by reciting historical documents such as the Declaration of Independence which contain references to the Deity, or by singing officially espoused anthems which include the composer's professions of faith in a Supreme Being. . . .

The case before the Court was not that of a song which, while primarily patriotic, may in some stanzas contain references to God or to religious beliefs, or that of the reading of a public or political document which alludes to God. The act in the case was simply and solely a religious act. It was a prayer. It was meant to be a prayer. It was recommended and ordered as a prayer.

The second fact is that this religious formula was devised by, recommended by, and ordered by government officials. The Court noted that the Board of Education was "acting in its *official capacity* under *state* law," that the Board of Regents was "a *governmental* agency created by the *state* constitution." (Italics added.) Further, while it was not expressly so stated, it must be understood that the teachers were included among the government officials and were representatives, simply and solely, of the state, of government.

Given these facts (1) that the act is simply and solely a religious act, that its

[2] Resolution taken at meeting of November 30, 1951, of the New York Board of Regents.
[3] Allegation of the petitioners as quoted by the Court.
[4] Resolution of November 30, 1951.

formula is simply and solely an expression of religious belief and attitude and (2) that the prayer was adopted and ordered by government officials acting in their official capacity, the majority opinion stated the Court's holding as follows:

> . . . we think that the constitutional prohibition against laws respecting an establishment of religion must at least mean that in this country it is not part of the business of government to compose official prayers for any group of the American people to recite as part of a religious program carried on by government.

And further on:

> The New York laws officially prescribing the Regents' prayer are inconsistent with both the purposes of the establishment clause and with the establishment clause itself.

Justice Black therefore concurred with petitioners' contention that the action of New York stands in violation of the constitutional prohibition of establishment. It was not on a showing of coercion, not, therefore, on a violation of the religious liberty clause, that this opinion rests. Justice Black took note, however, that in any such case there is some measure of coercion because actually the teacher's influence, the influence of the majority, the prestige of government and of the school, are put back of a set formula of prayer.

Based on Logic and Law

In the light of the factual situation that the Court decision was concerned solely with an act, directly and immediately religious, and that this act was as such adopted, imposed, and administered by agents of government, I can see no way in logic or law to escape the conclusion to which the Supreme Court came.

There was no new principle of constitutional law developed in the majority opinion. The broad principle invoked was, of course, the prohibition of establishment of religion, but it was here applied to a very narrowly limited and specific case. The footnote to the majority opinion made it clear that this decision is to be construed in a very strict sense. Justice Black distinguished the prayer from "The Star-Spangled Banner." Though a stanza of this song is in fact an expression of religious belief, it is seen as incidental to the primary patriotic intent of the song and of Congress in establishing the song as our national anthem.

It would appear that some of the adverse critics of the decision have overlooked the narrow ground covered and the strict interpretation of the facts by the Court. In his dissenting opinion, for instance, Justice Stewart, at least three times, spoke as though the Court were saying that people who wanted to pray could not be allowed to pray. He wrote: ". . . I cannot see how an 'official religion' is established by letting those who want to say a prayer say it." Again: ". . . we deal here with . . . whether school children who want to begin their day by joining in prayer must be prohibited from doing so."

It appears to me that the case as described by Justice Stewart would in principle be quite a different case from that before the Court. Justice Black and his colleagues did not say that school children may not say a prayer if they want to. They said that it is no business of government officials to compose and approve a prayer for any body of Americans to say under official government auspices.

Again, I agree with Justice Black that it makes no difference how small or insignificant this particular violation may be. The fact that the act in question is quite a diluted kind of prayer makes no difference. As a matter of principle, any encroachment upon religion by the state should be immediately opposed in the name of the First Amendment. Hence, in my opinion, the action of the Supreme Court was an action based upon clear principle, sound logic, and the given facts.

Repercussions to Court Decision

The announcement of this decision brought a storm of criticism and counter-criticism and of widely divergent comments, some of which seemed to consist of nothing more than exclamations of joy or sorrow. This reaction emphasized that there is great confusion of both the intellectual and emotional levels relative to the relationship of religion to the state, to the separation of church and state, and to the meaning of the First Amendment.

Although there is not a common view on these matters, some talk as though there is a simple clear-cut American or traditional doctrine on this point which can be applied like a standard rule to each individual case. Such people usually appeal to the wall of separation between church and state. Nothing, however, has served more to obfuscate discussion and to create the illusion of a doctrine of absolute and clear-cut separation between state and religion than the reiteration of the wall-of-separation metaphor.

What does a "wall" separate? Activities or people or things that can be put in space? Two plots of ground can be walled off. A wall can be put between two people or between two nations. But what kind of a "wall" can be put between the citizen and the churchgoer who is one person, or between the legal and religious aspects of the marriage ceremony? I submit that the use of this metaphor makes clear discussion impossible. No metaphor can be turned into a legal or logical principle, and this metaphor has proved extraordinarily inept for this purpose. Authorities on constitutional law have pointed out the difficulties and dangers inherent in trying to make logical or legal use of this extraconstitutional metaphor.[5]

The wall metaphor was first used by President Jefferson in a letter to the Baptists of Danbury, Connecticut, in 1801. A section of his letter containing the

---

[5] *E.g.*, Arthur E. Sutherland, Jr., professor of law, Harvard, "Due Process and Disestablishment," *Selected Essays in Constitutional Law*. Harvard Law Review Association, Cambridge, 1952, pp. 1310-1311; Paul G. Kauper, "Church and State: Cooperative Separatism," *Michigan Law Review*, Vol. 60, No. 1 (November 1961), pp. 6-7.

metaphor was quoted by Chief Justice Waite in *Reynolds* v. *United States* (October 1878), but in more recent decisions the metaphor itself has become part of the text of Court opinions, and popularly, has become a slogan of those who, either through deliberate policy or through misconception, advocate in effect an absolute separation of state and religion. One of the merits of Justice Stewart's dissenting opinion is a strong protest against the use of this metaphor in a legal context.[6]

Justice Black repeated this metaphor in the majority opinion, but, I think I discern a rhetorical trick in his use of it. Instead of simply repeating the phrase, he prefixed a neat modifier to it: "The *constitutional* wall of separation between church and state." (Italics added.) If this is taken seriously, the wall must now be interpreted by the constitutional doctrine, not the Constitution by the metaphor of the wall. I suggest that this reverses the explanatory function of the metaphor, and if carried out rigorously, will finally eliminate the metaphor from critical discussion.

Let us return to the case in question. The holding of the Court rested on two assumptions of fact: (1) that the act in question was simply, solely, and per se a religious act and (2) that the act was adopted, enjoined, and administered by officials and agencies of the state as such. In this assumption, the teacher and the school constitute simply, solely, and per se an agency of government, an arm of the political state.

Historical Development of U.S. Schools

Bearing these facts in mind, let us consider some of the history of our schools. The schools of the United States were originally thought of as belonging to the communities in which they were located. In many cases they were simply started by communities or by groups of parents. They were not thought of as being organized, managed by, or dependent upon some official at the national capital or even at the state capital. When pioneers settled the west, groups would send east for a teacher and set up a school by informal local agreement. These schools mirrored their communities. The manners and mores, the religious beliefs, the ideals of the family circle were identical with those of the schools. There was, for the most part, thorough mutual reinforcement. These schools were religious schools, reflecting again the predominant or common faith of the particular community. In the early period the schools were in effect Protestant schools. As long as local communities and sections of the country remained fairly homogeneous, this situation presented no problems and certainly suggested no great legal issues.[7]

---

[6] Justice Stewart wrote: "Moreover, I think that the Court's task in this as in all areas of constitutional adjudication is not responsibly aided by the uncritical invocation of metaphors like the 'wall of separation,' a phrase nowhere to be found in the Constitution."

[7] It should be remembered that the First Amendment did not apply to the states until after the adoption and the judicial interpretation (*Gitlow* v. *New York*, 268 U.S. 652, in 1925, and subsequent cases) of the Fourteenth Amendment (1868).

As the pluralism of our society grew more pronounced by increasing mobility and communication as well as by immigration, the schools began to experience the tensions and pressures of religious diversity. First, it was a kind of Protestant pluralism resulting in a movement to eject "sectarianism" from the schools. But the schools remained essentially Protestant. When the flood of immigration poured a mass of Irish, Italian, and central European Catholics into our country and especially into our large cities, new pressures developed. The Protestant Bible was read in school; Protestant prayers were said; Protestant ministers were often, officially or unofficially, school officers. After fighting and fleeing from English Protestantism, the Irish Catholics wanted no part of this situation. And so, there were a series of incidents, of arguments, and of court cases, the result of which was to reduce the Protestant character of the public school. And the Catholic Church, to avoid the Protestantism and the secularism of the public schools, as well as to provide a full religious education, as the Catholic conscience demands, adopted the policy of establishing a separate school system.

Where the numbers of Jews increased, the same pressures and legal actions were repeated but aimed at reducing the *Christian* character and tone of the public schools. And now similar pressures have built up to remove all theistic or even deistic influences from the public schools, as the Ethical Culturists and other secularists find them still too religious.

It is true that in many parts of the country, where communities are still predominantly of one religion, the public schools are in effect religious schools. The State of Mississippi still *requires* the reading of the Bible (Protestant version) in the public schools.[8] Some years ago a directive was sent out from the State Office of Education, instructing teachers how to comment on the daily Bible reading. This was a thoroughly Protestant document and could just as well have been sent to Baptist Sunday-school teachers.

Such a condition becomes intolerable in a community made up of all varieties of Protestants, of Roman Catholics, of every type of Jew, of agnostics, atheists, and Ethical Culturists. What sort of a public school can serve such a community? What sort of common denominator of belief or of prayer could be acceptable— quite aside from the constitutional issue—to the members of such community? [9]

In the perspective of this kind of problem, the public school is losing its identity as a creature of a given community and is being viewed more and more as an agency of the political state solely and simply. In the majority opinion in the Prayer decision, the teacher, along with the Regents of the School Board, is an official of government and does not directly represent the parents of the com-

[8] It is noteworthy that *twenty* states entered the Prayer case on behalf of the New York Regents.

[9] The petitioners in the Prayer case objected to the Regents' prayer as containing articles of belief repugnant to their consciences. From another quarter, a Lutheran group objected that Christ's name had been deliberately omitted to mollify non-Christian elements and that the prayer therefore was in fact a denial of faith and a blasphemy. I sympathize with both sides as well as with the good intentions of those who tried to devise an acceptable common prayer.

munity. This conception of school and of teacher is one of the basic assumptions of the majority opinion. Like the state itself, the teacher and the school must be neutral, and in fact negatively secular.

The Political State and the Social Community

In order to understand this situation, another digression is necessary. The only way we can *simultaneously* maintain a viable and genuine pluralism and a religiously neutral state is to maintain a distinction between the state and the social community of which the state is the political and legal structure. If we go back to pre-Christian days, we find both in pagan society and in Jewish society that community and state, religion and law, are all one. The Jewish state, the city state, the empire, are all the whole community, the arbiter of religion as well as of other matters.

The Christian distinction between church and state already introduces a basic distinction within human society, and this distinction becomes sharper and more necessary when a society becomes, like ours, one of vast and unprecedented pluralism. Here in the United States we have a pluralistic society which nonetheless has only one system of law and one government, in which this one government is neither identified with any of the groups that constitute the pluralistic society nor hostile to them. This I believe is really a new thing in political experience.[10]

In the majority opinion in the *Everson* case, which was likewise written by Justice Black, there is a paragraph which constitutional lawyers say is one of the most explicit and detailed statements in the literature of the Court regarding the meaning of the nonestablishment clause of the First Amendment:

> The 'establishment of religion' clause of the First Amendment means at least this: Neither a state nor the Federal Government can set up a church. Neither can pass laws which aid one religion, aid all religions, or prefer one religion over another. Neither can force nor influence a person to go to or to remain away from church against his will or force him to profess a belief or disbelief in any religion. No person can be punished for entertaining or professing religious beliefs or disbeliefs, for church attendance or nonattendance. No tax in any amount, large or small, can be levied to support any religious activities or institutions, whatever they may be called, or whatever form they may adopt to teach or practice religion. Neither a state nor the Federal Government can, openly or secretly, participate in the affairs of any religious organizations or groups and vice versa. In the words of Jefferson, the clause against establishment of religion by law was intended to erect 'a wall of separation between church and state.' [11]

[10] The limited pluralism of medieval society (Christians and Jews), of India, and now of Spanish Morocco, was handled by having a pluralism of legal systems and a set of subsocieties.

[11] *Everson* v. *Board of Education*, 330 U.S. 1, 15-16 (1947).

This paragraph has since been quoted over and over again, without qualification, as being the doctrine of the First Amendment. But this interpretation has been repeatedly and severely criticized by students of constitutional law as containing a novel extension unwarranted by history, political experience, actual practice, or constitutional law.[12] Moreover, it can confidently be asserted that, in both its original context as well as in its reaffirmations, it was a dictum and not a holding.

However, I do not wish to press either of these points here. In fact, I am quite satisfied with the paragraph provided it is properly interpreted according to original context. The text states flatly that the Government can give no aid of any kind, under any pretext, to any religious, or for that matter, antireligious group. Yet, *in the same opinion,* the Court admits that subsidized transportation aids the Catholic Church and yet *rules such subsidy constitutional!* If the paragraph were in itself an adequate statement of the relevant constitutional principles and of the Court's views, the Court would be involved in a hopeless self-contradiction. Only the introduction of the qualifying principles from the rest of the opinion makes the decision of the Court intelligible and gives an adequate presentation of the constitutional principle. I submit, therefore, that the paragraph in question should never be quoted without reference to the one immediately following. For therein the doctrine of "no aid" is properly balanced and qualified.

We must consider the New Jersey statute in accordance with the foregoing limitations imposed by the First Amendment. But we must not strike that State statute down if it is within the State's constitutional power even though it approaches the verge of that power. . . . New Jersey cannot, consistently with the 'establishment of religion' clause of the First Amendment, contribute tax-raised funds to the support of an institution which teaches the tenets and faith of any church. On the other hand, other language of the Amendment commands that New Jersey cannot hamper its citizens in the free exercise of their own religion. Consequently, it cannot exclude individual Catholics, Lutherans, Mohammedans, Baptists, Jews, Methodists, nonbelievers, Presbyterians, or the members of any other faith, *because of their faith, or lack of it,* from receiving the benefits of public-welfare legislation. While we do not mean to intimate that a state could not provide transportation only to children attending public schools, we must be careful, in protecting the citizens of New Jersey against state-established churches, *to be sure that we do not inadvertently prohibit New Jersey from extending its general state law benefits to all citizens without regard to their religious belief. . . .* (Italics added.)
. . . cutting off church schools from these services, so separate and so indisputably marked off from the religious function, would make it far more difficult for the schools to operate. But such is obviously not the purpose of the

---

[12] *E.g.,* Edward S. Corwin, "The Supreme Court as a National School Board," *Law and Contemporary Problems,* Vol. 14 (Winter 1949), pp. 3-22; Kauper, *op. cit.,* pp. 8-9.

First Amendment. That Amendment requires the state to be neutral in its relations with groups of religious believers and nonbelievers; it does not require the state to be their adversary. State power is no more to be used so as to handicap religions than it is to favor them.

If we were to isolate the first paragraph without the qualifications expressly stated by the Court itself, not only would we have to say that the New Jersey transportation subsidy is unconstitutional, but we would have to agree with the extreme and novel views of Justice Douglas in his concurring opinion in the Prayer decision. We would have to go down the line of an almost endless list of practices and cancel them out: the chaplains of the armed forces; grants to Baptist, Methodist, and Catholic hospitals; tax exemptions for churches; the right to incorporate religious bodies; police and fire protection for churches, etc. All these practices would fall under an unqualified and general prohibition of aid to religion. One can only conclude with Professor Kauper that in this paragraph, "It is clear . . . that either the Court was painting with too broad a brush in condemning all aid to religion or was using the term in a special way that needed further clarification." [13]

Otherwise, the Court's interpretation of the establishment clause would have destroyed the religious-liberty clause and established at least negative religious tests for common-welfare benefits.

Absolute Separation Impossible

We are faced, then, with a situation in which church and state, government and religion, interact, overlap, and cooperate in what Professor Kauper calls "cooperative separatism." We do not have and cannot have the hard and fast separation suggested by the wall metaphor. If we must have a metaphor, it would be more accurate to think of a living organism within which there is another organism enclosed in a membrane which separates and distinguishes but permits osmosis in both directions.

We have recognized—along with the classic Christian tradition—a distinction between church and state, between religion and civil law, between religion and politics. But in the reality of human affairs, it is not possible to practice religion or maintain a church except within the framework of the legal system of some political state. Hence, if we are not to have a persecuting state, if we are to preserve religious liberty, there must be established formal interrelationship between church and state, between religious and legal structures.

The wall-of-separation has been a very satisfying metaphor for those who wish to make the separation between church and state absolute, without any accommodation or cooperation. Absolute separation of this kind is possible only when the state is *positively secularist*, when it is a persecuting state. Absolute sep-

---

[13] Kauper, *op. cit.*, p. 9.

aration is the condition of a persecuting political society which suppresses all overt religious organization and activity. Most Americans who have talked about separation as being absolute in our tradition have not thought out what absolute separation would mean or what it has meant historically. It would mean that religious bodies could not incorporate, could not own property, could not claim the protection of laws, let alone common-welfare benefits. Ministers of religion would not be recognized as professional men. There would be a wall high and impregnable with no peepholes, no cracks for communication, too high for messages to be tossed over. The metaphor and the absolutist doctrine become absurd when carefully examined. *Separation* like *union* is not a single-meaning term. At its absolute extreme, *separation* means persecution, with only the state left. *Union,* at its fullest meaning, denotes a situation in which church and state have so merged that each has lost its identity.

But this is not and has not been the situation in the United States. Absolute separation is inconsistent with our traditions, our present practices, and a multitude of other constitutional, legal and social precedents. As Dr. Katz, former Dean of the Law School at Chicago University, has said: ". . . the separation required by the Constitution is the separation which is compatible with religious liberty." [14] The state must be neutral; it cannot be indifferent to and it must not be hostile to religion.

The terms *separation of church and state* and *union of church and state* do not define two simple and contradictory positions; they rather represent the opposite ends of a continuum within which a balanced solution must be found. Absolute separation and absolute union are both destructive of religion, and neither can be justified in the American tradition or within the framework of our principles. *For the problem in our country is to find concrete solutions which balance state neutrality, religious liberty, the rights of minorities, and other relevant principles.* Our solution to the dichotomy of pluralism-in-unity and liberty demands a distinction between community and state.[15]

The crux of the matter is to establish the appropriate relationships between the political components and the religious pluralism of the community. There are many examples in American political and legal experience of ingenious solutions to the problems of these interrelationships.

Interrelations of Church and State

One of these is marriage. After the rise of the secular state in Europe—especially when that state was positively secular—there was a constant struggle between church and state over the business of the marriage ceremony. It is incredible how much bitter wrangling went on over this matter—doubly incredible to us Amer-

14 Wilber G. Katz, "The Freedom to Believe," *The Atlantic Monthly* (October 1953), p. 67.

15 Kauper defines the state in this context as "the politically arranged community with its monopoly of coercive power." *Op. cit.,* p. 14.

icans, because we have arrived at a very satisfactory solution to the problem. We require a civil license for marriage; we require an official civil recording of the marriage; but the essential rite of marriage, which occurs between the license and the official record, lies open to determination according to the consciences and wishes of the contracting parties. They select the rabbi, minister, priest, or justice of the peace because he is a rabbi, minister, priest, or justice of the peace. They choose a religious ceremony or a nonreligious ceremony because it is a religious or a nonreligious ceremony. And it is not simply that the state leaves them free to make this choice; the state *ratifies* their choice and makes the rabbi, minister, or priest in effect an *officer of the state*, the official in charge, whose signature on the civil document certifies the marriage to the civil records office.

The marriage ceremony, then, is an overlap in the concrete where a simple act has both a religious and a civil aspect, where a single person is both a religious and a civil official. This arrangement, it seems to me, exemplifies the best of balanced solutions. There is the fullest liberty for religion and nonreligion; the state appropriately recognizes the pluralism of its community and yet is neither indifferent nor hostile to religion or nonreligion.

At this point, I wish to use the distinction between state and community in order to deal with another aspect of the whole problem. Justice Stewart, in his dissenting opinion, argued that to outlaw the Regents' prayer was to deny our children "the opportunity of sharing in the spiritual heritage of our nation"; he speaks of the "religious traditions of our people" and summarizes his thesis by quoting the Court itself: "We are a religious people whose institutions presuppose a Supreme Being." [16]

The Regents themselves had appealed to the same spiritual and religious traditions. There is no doubt that these traditions exist; that they are asserted even in official documents like the Declaration of Independence; that, despite the strength of current secularism and the many moral evils existing in our society, our people are very largely and strongly religious and predominantly Christian. But, it seems to me that our political principles and the logic of our constitutional law force us to attribute this spiritual heritage and this religious character to the American *community*, not to the American *state* as such. The American state as such is neither religious nor nonreligious, neither Christian nor Jewish, neither theist nor atheist. This, in turn, forces us to recognize an ambiguity in the term *American*. There is an American spiritual heritage; it is the heritage of the people and of the community, not an official heritage of the American state. *Americanism*, insofar as it relates to our political and legal forms, insofar as it describes strictly the status of our people as citizens, must be a religiously neutral term, negatively secular.

In the light of these distinctions and principles, several other important positions become clear. There cannot be an official American ideology, if *American* is understood as describing our political state and if *ideology* is understood to be

[16] *Zorach* v. *Clauson*, 343 U.S. 306, 313 (1952).

an ultimate set of principles, values, and beliefs. If *Americanism* simply refers to our common political creed, we agree on certain second-level principles like the due-process requirement, religious disestablishment, etc. But the ultimate bases upon which these second-level principles rest are determined varyingly according to the diverse religious and ideological convictions of our pluralistic community. Thus, we may agree on the need to eliminate segregation, but the Catholic will justify this need by appealing to the universal Fatherhood of God and Christ's command of supernatural charity; the pragmatist will appeal to a criterion of social progress and workability; and so on, through all the variations of belief within the community.

There are, indeed, some for whom these second-level principles are ultimate; who have no beliefs or conceptions beyond them. But this kind of absolutizing of political principles must be distinguished from official Americanism.

Negatively v. Positively Secular

Throughout this discussion, I have frequently used the expressions *negatively secular* and *positively secular*. It is now time to sharpen their meaning. Secularism is here taken as being opposed to traditional religion; it admits of no revelation, no values beyond this world. A positive secularism excludes all these because it denies them and holds its own values to be all values. Positive secularism is, therefore, an ultimate position that stands in opposition to Catholicism, Protestantism, and traditional Judaism. Hence, when a state is positively secular, it is the equivalent, politically and ideologically, of an established religion. Every other form of religion becomes incompatible with the state so concerned.

I have called the American political state secular because it is separated from, distinct from, and neutral toward religion. Since, however, it is neither indifferent nor hostile to religion, it is negatively secular. By contrast, the Third French Republic was positively secular. It declared itself, on principle, a secular state, and in effect, outlawed religion. It positively excluded and denied religion. From this positive secularism, the negative secularism of the American system can be and must be clearly distinguished.

This distinction is of capital importance. To blur or erase it would lead to the establishment of secularism as an official religion. Within the pluralism of our community, secularism as a set of ultimate values must stand alongside the more clearly recognized religions. The state is neutral as respects believer and nonbeliever—Christians, Jews, atheists, and secularists. Positive secularism is, in effect, a *theological* position and as such must not be allowed to become a principle of government. Negative secularism is a *political*, not a *theological*, position and as such must be clearly distinguished from positive secularism.

On the same principles, it is clear that the state cannot enforce an ideology. The separation and neutrality of the state leave it defenseless at the level of ultimate principles. Subversive ideas cannot as such be made the object of legal action, political coercion, or police repression. This point has been well understood by our courts, and their adherence to these principles has brought upon them criticism from well-meaning citizens who are alarmed at their "soft" treatment of Communists. But the state, with its "monopoly of coercive power," can defend itself only against overt acts, not against ideas.[17] If it is true that, "We are a religious people *whose institutions presuppose a Supreme Being*" (italics added),[18] the courts cannot protect our institutions in their presupposition but only in their actual existence and structure.

This does not, of course, mean that we, as a people, are ideologically defenseless. The community and most of the groups within it can and do carry on study, teaching, and discussion in matters philosophical and theological. It is upon those who have firm and sound convictions that the ultimate defense, even of our political and legal institutions, must rest. There is no reason, provided all necessary safeguards are set up, why the state cannot support and cooperate in such activities. In effect, it is now doing so through the academic freedom allowed professors in state-supported universities and through the legal status given religious education, etc.

This defense of our institutions by the teaching of their religious presupposition was one of the aims proposed for themselves by the New York Regents. In their resolution of November 30, 1951 (the prayer resolution), they said, in part:

> Belief in and dependence upon Almighty God was the very cornerstone upon which our Founding Fathers builded. Our State Constitution opens with these solemn words: 'We, the people of the State of New York, grateful to Almighty God for our freedom, in order to secure these blessings, do establish this Constitution. . . .' [19]
>
> . . . In our opinion, the securing of the peace and safety of our country and our State against such dangers points to the essentiality of teaching our children, as set forth in the Declaration of Independence, that Almighty God is their Creator. . . .

In the light of this additional discussion, one can agree wholeheartedly with the substance of these statements of the Regents and agree at the same time with Justice Black that the indicated religious activities and (at least implicit) religious instruction cannot be carried on by persons who are *simply and solely agents of the state (government)* and acting *as such.* One can agree that Communist ideology is a dire threat to all our ideals and yet also agree with the courts in maintaining that we cannot proscribe ideas as such but only overt acts or incitement to them.

[17] *Yates* v. *United States*, 354 U.S. 298 (1957).

[18] *Zorach* v. *Clauson*, 343 U.S. 306, 313 and quoted by Justice Stewart in his dissenting opinion.

[19] It should be noted that this opening statement of the Constitution is made by the *people* not by the *state* of New York.

Application to Public Education

The public school, which began as the creature of the community when the community was homogeneous, has been forced, by pressure of increasing pluralism within the community itself, to separate from the community and assume the same stance as the state, namely a neutral and negatively secular one. Minority elements within the community have used not only local pressure but the coercion of law, state and Federal, to move the public school from sectarianism, to common-denominator Protestantism, to common-denominator Christianity, and finally to complete negative secularism. This internal movement has been strengthened by the increasing application of the Federal Constitution to the states.

In the United States we now have a negatively secular state as the legal and political organization of the community—a community plural and diversified in, among other things, religious positions. This community, however, can claim a spiritual heritage that overwhelmingly represents (even in its avowed atheists and secularists) the attitudes, values, and beliefs of the Judeo-Christian tradition. No wall of separation, solid and unbreachable, can be run up between this community and the political state.

The end product of the pressures of historical development and of religious pluralism is a public-school system which is becoming negatively secular in the strict sense—a common school which is common only negatively and which no longer truly reflects the society, pluralistic in the extreme, of which it is theoretically the common school.

But the real problem we now confront is this: Is education, as a total process in the concrete, the sort of thing that *can* be made negatively secular without *thereby becoming positively secular?*

In the efforts to make the public school as neutral as the state itself, law and logic have assimilated it simply to government, and this means the progressive exclusion of activities, doctrines, books, persons, and values of a religious nature from the public school. It means that school officials and teachers are viewed legally as simply officers of government and not as agents also of a social community, carrying out a delegation of parental functions.

Can such a neutralized school, exclusively viewed as an agency of government, truly claim to mirror, represent, and serve the actual pluralism of our society? Can education in the concrete be negatively secular? Or is it in the nature of the case that education, reduced by negation and exclusion to secularism, must become, in fact, *positively* secular? If so, we are put in the paradoxical position that our negatively secular state can provide only positively secular education and that, therefore, it can support only a public-school system which more and more satisfies only the secularist minority of our people or those who view religion as separable from general education, as a concern which can and should be taken care of at home or in church.

If this argument is sound, we are approaching a situation in which positive secularism, through the public-school system, will be equivalently an established national religion, supported by the prestige, power, and money of government in opposition to religion and religious education.

On the one hand, therefore, it is clear that any operation determined and administrated solely by government officers as such must maintain a strict negative secularism—a complete religious (and ideological) neutrality. On the other hand, we have a society in which religious (and ideological) convictions, organizations, activities, and purposes are both diverse and immanent, so that in the concrete, no hard and sharp line can be drawn between all that is religious and all that is not religious. The maintenance of the negative secularism of government is an essential condition of religious liberty within a pluralistic society. This alone, however, is inadequate. As soon as government enters those areas of concrete activity wherein religion is an important immanent factor, the effort to maintain the negative secularism of government becomes an effort to secularize society positively and to this extent government, itself, becomes an anti-religious and hostile force. A solution must be found to this dilemma; otherwise that which in government is an essential condition of religious liberty becomes, in the concrete, a destroyer thereof. Such a solution has been found in regard to marriage, the chaplains' corps, adoptions, aid to hospitals and health centers, etc.

But have we solved the dilemma in the matter of education? No one can deny that we have found some excellent partial solutions. One of the most fundamental is the legal status given religious and private schools, in that their students satisfy the compulsory school laws. Likewise, in many areas of higher education solutions analogous to that of the marriage arrangement have been found, *e.g.,* the GI Bill of Rights, the grant and contract policies of government agencies, etc. In the matter of auxiliary benefits (school lunches, bus transportation, etc.), a similar solution has been found. The National Science Foundation has a distinguished record of cooperation in a way compatible both with the negative secularism and with the nondiscriminatory obligations of government. If the intent is to provide support for sound research in physics, it is certainly outside the right of government to even ask whether the principal investigator is Jew, Catholic, Protestant, Buddhist, or whether his institution is a Buddhist temple, Baptist college, or Catholic university.

The key to the solution in many cases is to set up a cooperative situation in which government is one party and in which the openness of government to free determination by individual citizens is clearly recognized. Thus, the intent of government in the GI Bill was to provide education for all those eligible; the determination of programs and institutions was left to the individual. In this way government respected fully the educational freedom and the religious freedom of the GIs without compromising its negative secularism. It did pay tuition to Baptist and Catholic colleges, to nonsectarian schools, to Jewish and Christian theological seminaries, but the determination was not that of the government but of the individual. It was an admirable solution, in accord with tradition, precedent, and constitutional principle as well as with fairness and good sense. I can conceive of no worse way to face this problem than through a new constitutional amendment. We need no new organic laws and no new constitutional principles; we need imaginative and fair-minded cooperative solutions in the light of existing laws and precedents.

In other words, despite some excellent solutions in higher education, we have not yet found a thoroughgoing solution in the general field of education. The multiplication of completely independent school systems (public, Catholic, Protestant, Jewish), with public financing pitted against the effort of religious educators, with little or no intersystem cooperation and the danger of a diversity which may totally destroy the efficiency and any common character in our education, does not now appear to be a final viable solution. New thinking and open thinking is needed.

It was not the purpose of this paper to offer concrete proposals. I have tried to analyze basic principles and to clarify the conceptual distinctions which are necessary to dissipate the confusion which the controversies over the Prayer decision have revealed and which must be used in working out practical (perhaps multiple) solutions. It is essential, therefore, that all of us put aside prejudice, simplistic formulae, and absolutistic slogans and cooperate in solving the very real problems of maintaining religion and religious values in our pluralistic society.

Religion in education: a basis for consensus

William B. Ball

Like the author of the preceding article, Mr. Ball is
very much interested in the Supreme Court's
decisions regarding the constitutionality of prayer
and the teaching of religion in the public schools.
Reviewing some of these decisions, he finds in them
a basis for agreement among those who hold
contrasting views on the subject of religion's place in
the schools that serve a pluralistic society.

As we move deeper into 1963, it is apparent that the question of religion in the schools now tops all American Church-State issues in explosive importance. In the field of legislation, Catholics are firming up their ranks to ward off the mortal threat to church-related schools which they see posed by Administration proposals for aid to education. In the courts, major Jewish and secularist groups are waging an ardent battle to remove religious practices from public school life. The vast Protestant community—united in its opposition to Catholics on the Federal-aid question—is badly splintered on Bible-reading, baccalaureates and a host of other school practices, once as unquestioned as they were Protestant. For a time when ecumenicism and brotherhood are so much in the air, an immense amount of interfaith shin-kicking is taking place on the ground.

There is also evident in all groups a growing willingness to explore together possible ways out of the religion-in-education difficulties, and a dawning fear that failure to find some solutions to these largely civil issues may disappoint all hopes for better understanding upon matters essentially religious. But the ways out must be paths which each major group will feel it can take with dignity, and with security for the rights which it believes to be involved. And certain it is that a

Reprinted with permission from *America*, the National Catholic Weekly Review, 920 Broadway, New York, N.Y., 10010, 108:528–532, April 20, 1963.

substantial segment of our population, freshly armed with the Supreme Court's pronouncements in the school-prayer case, will not renounce its stated opposition to all forms of theistic religious practices in the public schools. Equally certain is the determination of the parents of six million children in Catholic schools to see that the latter schools continue to exist—with government aid, if necessary.

These realities, unpleasant to contemplate, will not be winked away. Pooh-poohing the expressed fears of others or attacking their suspected motives will only stimulate, not moderate, the tensions related to these realities. Jewish Americans have been made more, not less, united and militant by the suggestion that their expressed concern for religious freedom in the schools is façade rather than fact, and that behind that façade lies the hidden purpose to drive religion from the land. And, perhaps, nothing has so galvanized Catholic sentiment of late than the inference that behind Catholic efforts on behalf of parochial schools lurks a long-range aim to crowd out the religious freedom of others. In a land where all religious groups are now minority groups, most are showing willingness to engage in the give-and-take of open discussion and criticism; but none any longer feels it can afford to suffer the accusation of group conspiracy.

If pejoratives and motive-labeling have not served to quiet the contenders, have less offensive means been proposed? Less offensive, perhaps, but equally futile are a host of educational nostrums and constitutional placebos now making headlines. So, for example, amendment of the First Amendment is being urged—seemingly without regard to the considerable legal complexities which (speaking at least of the several amendments thus far proposed) would be entailed.

While such violent therapy promises little solution to the great religion-in-education problems, just as little is promised by another alternative, the "teach about" proposition. According to this idea, the public schools, while not permitted to teach religion, can teach *about* religion as a part of culture and of history. But to the many who really want religion *as religion* in the public schools, "teach about" may not prove fair play. On the other hand, if it satisfies these, others will likely say that "teaching about" has become "preaching about," and litigations will ensue.

Simplistic solutions such as these will not relieve widespread concern for education, for freedom and for religion, which are at the heart of the controversy. Amendment has, however, at least the virtue of pointing to constitutional law as the prime area for the working out of whatever solutions may be achievable. John F. Malloy, writing in AMERICA (6/10/61) suggested with humor (but not with tongue in cheek) that our present Church-State problems, especially Federal aid, had been needlessly complicated by lawyers. While members of the legal profession can accept this jibe with characteristic humility, it would be quite another thing to agree that the contending factions, "left to themselves" and unencumbered by constitutional concerns, would somehow happily resolve their differences respecting religion in education. In the American scheme of things, issues such as these are necessarily seen in their relationship to the Constitution, which remains, it must be kept in mind, our best expression of civil consensus.

I believe that we have at hand the makings for basic community agreement on the education-freedom-religion relationship, or at least for providing justification for a truce. These "makings" are to be found where, perhaps, few today believe them to lie: in judicial statements by the U. S. Supreme Court.

Many will doubtless greet with howls of outrage the suggestion that Supreme Court pronouncements can be looked to as any sort of basis for concord among the intensely contending groups. Regardless of any consensus said to be expressed originally in the religion clauses of the Constitution, is it not the court which has rendered those clauses confusing at best, and, at worst, articles of secularism? Some will sharply remind us that it is the Supreme Court which only last summer banished prayer from public schools, while others will ridicule any attempt to find any sort of harmony in the court's decisions, especially considering the mass of dicta, the shifting of positions by individual justices over the years and the exquisite qualifications with which many doctrinal expressions by the court have been elaborated.

Bearing all this in mind, there is still good reason to look into Supreme Court decisions for a possible basis for consensus in the religion-in-education controversy. For one thing, the court's decisions do represent, until changed, the sole legally authoritative interpretation of the fundamental law of the land. Like them or not, they are realities which we must face. Again, in spite of its notable failings, the court is an institution of great eminence in the country, its prestige being relatively little weakened by justified criticism often directed against it. Moreover, it is true that the court has, over the course of the years, dealt with great public problems relating to religion and education.

Perhaps there is some point, then, in attempting to see, in their essences, these problems with which the court has dealt and to see, in ultimate terms, the results at which it has arrived. This search for a viable basis for consensus involves ignoring much of the fanciful rhetoric, homemade history and "advanced" (circa 1912) philosophic views which appear in some of the more recent decisions. It also implies, at least on the part of lawyers, a willingness to overlook some recent procedural extravagances upon the part of the court—such as its record of hasty willingness to accord standing to sue, in some religion cases, to persons who have suffered no real injury. Finally, it is not to be assumed that the court itself has fully realized the conclusions about religion-in-education questions to which some of its decisions inevitably lead.

Constitutional scholars appear to agree that Supreme Court decisions now render clear two major principles concerning religion in education: first, public education may not include official promotion of religion; second, public objectives in education may be achieved in institutions which sponsor particular religious or philosophic views.

The first principle is solidly established by the decisions of the court in the *McCollum* case, in 1948, which voided programs of formal religious *instruction* on public school premises, and in the *Engel* case, in 1962, which barred officially sponsored *religious exercises and practices*. Both had been prefigured by the decision of the court, in 1942, exempting a member of Jehovah's Witnesses from a public school flag-salute practice. In the latter case, *West Virginia State Board of Education v. Barnette,* the court had laid it down in unmistakably plain terms that public education was not to serve as a transmission belt for any ideology. Justice Frankfurter, lone dissenter in the case, eloquently argued the constitutionality of the flag-salute statute; he judged that to hold otherwise would be to effect "the subordination of general civil authority of the state to sectarian scruples." But the religious concerns of the objecting parents in the case were rated more highly by the majority, which pronounced anathema upon State inculcations of orthodoxies in the public schools, even in matters not patently "religious." "If there is any fixed star in our constitutional constellation," said Justice Jackson, "it is that no official, high or petty, can prescribe what shall be orthodox in politics, nationalism, religion or other matters of opinion. . . ."

Vexation over the success of a flimsy case in *Engel,* and fears respecting the possible ultimate implications of the decision, must not obscure our focus upon the basic principle which it shares commonly with the *McCollum* and *Barnette* cases: government is barred, in the educational process, from prescribing orthodoxies—by which the court appeared to mean all values respecting religion, nation, politics and probably general outlook and ethics. This principle, in turn, rests upon a principle even more basic: a constitutionally protected right of the child to be free from religious and philosophic impositions by the state which conflict with his own religion or philosophy.

Almost four decades ago, the court dealt with a maximum effort upon the part of government to establish official orthodoxies in education: the Oregon statute requiring all children to attend public schools. The campaign to bring this about had harshly inveighed against pluralism in education with phrases, strangely echoed in 1963, such as: "Mix the children. . . . Mix those with prejudices in the public school melting pot for a few years while their minds are plastic, and finally bring out the finished product—a true American."

Happily, the court was not favorably impressed by Oregon's proposal to manufacture true Americans and declared, in *Pierce v. Society of Sisters,* that the statute was unconstitutional. Much has been made of the *Pierce* decision for its implications respecting parental rights and the right of separate education in church-related schools, but the ultimate meaning of *Pierce* is its vindication of the foregoing principle of freedom in learning. In *Pierce,* the court declared that the Constitution barred "any general power of the state to standardize its children by forcing them to accept instruction from public school teachers only." The language about standardization went to the matter of *minds* and to freedom of mind from inculcation of values rejected by conscience.

The suggestion that the court has ousted from the public schools more than theistic religious inculcations will, I fear, be rejected before being considered. Theist critics of the court, on the one hand, and ebullient secularists, on the other, have for some time been loudly chanting in striking unison: "The court has now thrown religion out of public education." Each group will tell you that it means, of course, practices, instruction, etc., relating to belief in God. But the court has not limited its banishments to matters connected with belief in God. *Barnette* went well beyond this, as we have seen. And the *McCollum* and *Engel* decisions must also be read as going beyond this. This is because the court, in 1961, told us that the term "religion," as used in the Constitution, comprised very much more than theism. With this new definition of religion by the court, the freedom-in-learning principle is rendered complete.

The case was *Torcaso v. Watkins,* and it involved the refusal by the State of Maryland to issue a commission as notary public to Roy A. Torcaso because of his unwillingness to declare a belief in God, as required by the Maryland Constitution. Torcaso appealed ultimately to the U. S. Supreme Court, and the court declared that the Maryland Constitution violated his rights as a "believer" and as one having a "faith" which was entitled to "free exercise." He had, said the court, a "religion," although not a religion based upon belief in God. The court proceeded to say that the term "religion" must be understood to include such bodies of belief as "ethical culture, secular humanism, and others."

Whatever may have been the surprise of declared nonbeliever Roy A. Torcaso when he found himself escorted into the tents of the believers by the Justices, the constitutional surprise which the decision imports has not yet fully caught up with many who have damned, and many who have praised, the court's ruling on school prayers. The implications of the *Torcaso* case for public education are very broad. Fitting in perfectly with other vindications by the court of the freedom-in-learning concept, the *Torcaso* decision underscores the critical importance of Philosophy, of the individual's world outlook, his beliefs, his "way of life"—all of which the court lumped together in its open-ended definition of "religion." The court thus created a juridical base for what had been recognized by many as a philosophic fact: that no system of educating the young is philosophically neutral, and that philosophy, whether expressed or implied, is of the highest significance in education.

One could fairly assert that there is no real neutrality in the public school in which theistic religion is simply banned. This nonneutrality is vividly emphasized in new and widespread programing in inter-group relations, now being purposefully advanced as a substitute for the old God-centered ethical core. Though these programs are well-intentioned, they are, nevertheless, generally inculcatory in purpose and method. Their very point is to prescribe conduct. These prescriptions rest upon philosophical underpinnings, and the occasionally mystical character of these underpinnings does not render them "neutral."

If a child is taught that he should have a certain social attitude because of the "fellowship of man" or because "this is what democracy wants of us," let it not be said that these reasons are somehow "neutral." To the contrary, these reasons are what they are meant to be: ultimate governors of conduct, points of recourse when the mandated attitudes are challenged, that which is in the moral bank to back up the check drawn in favor of a social precept.

While, strictly speaking, it is the mandate of the *Barnette* and *Engel* decisions that all of *this* religion, too, be purged from public education, it must remain for the future to disclose whether litigants, following the example of the plaintiffs in *Engel*, will demand its banishment. For the millions who desire a God-centered education for their children, the desire for peace may outweigh the strict demands of legal logic, and enough satisfaction may be accorded them through general and effective recognition of the second major principle which the Supreme Court has laid down with respect to religion in education—namely, that public objectives in education may be achieved in institutions which sponsor particular religious or philosophic views. This principle was achieved by the court in its decisions in the *Cochran* and *Everson* cases, which spell out two vitally important recognitions. First, these decisions recognize the obvious fact that public moneys may support the achieving of public objectives in education and that such objectives are, in fact, achieved not only in State institutions but also in non-State institutions. Secondly, these decisions complement the freedom-in-learning principle because they render economically possible the providing of education in institutions which comport with conscientious choice. In the latter respect, the close relationship of *Cochran-Everson* to the *Pierce* case, with its warnings against "standardizing" children, is striking.

Objections are presently being strongly urged against the view that public funds can be used to support the teaching of "secular" subjects where such teaching permeates these subjects with "religion." But, as has already been noted by Charles M. Whelan, S.J. ("Textbooks and the Constitution." Aм. 6/ 16/ 62), the legal test in any such case is not whether the public support renders conscientious choice a practical thing but whether, with the permeation, the essential secular learning is achieved. Moreover, when the matter of value-inculcations in public schools is considered, it becomes readily apparent that permeation is no monopoly of the church-related school.

Education, Chief Justice Warren told us in the *Desegregation Cases,* is "the very foundation of good citizenship." The court moreover stated that, in the matter of education, policies of the past may need to be repudiated. "We cannot turn the clock back," said the court, stressing the desirability that our educational clocks be set to keep time with the time's needs. The question of religion in education, like the question of education according to race, must not be permitted to remain fixed in concepts which the prejudices of an earlier day dictated.

Yet, in the case of religion in education, the fixation is mainly in the popular mind and is no *necessary* product of the decisions of our highest court. I have tried to show that decisions of the court respecting religion in education must be read as a harmonious whole, simultaneously protecting freedom in education and vindicating public support for such education as lies within the competence of the state to promote. Under such reading, a parent may choose for his child a school where no reverence is ever paid the name of God, where the child may be totally free of theistic influences and pressures and thoroughly indoctrinated in "democratic ethics." And such school may be publicly aided. But, also under such reading, a like freedom is recognized for other citizens and a like status for other schools. Public funds, under this view, are used to support the specific secular education provided by all schools meeting reasonable state requirements.

According to this view, given us by the court, the state, while renouncing any pretensions as a dictator of religion, becomes a handmaiden of education. The great practical benefit of consensus upon this view will be fuller realization of democracy and a larger prospect of peace.

Formation of Christian social leaders

Edward S. Stanton, S.J.

*Perhaps the two charges most commonly leveled
against Catholic education (by its friends) are,
first, that so small a number of Catholic graduates
are dedicating themselves to the intellectual life
and, second, that so few of them are actively
concerned with the social problems of the day. The
two, of course, cannot be separated except in theory,
but it is with the latter that Father Stanton is
primarily concerned in the article that follows. He
offers three reasons for the social inactivity of
Catholic high school graduates and a few suggestions
for developing their social consciousness.*

Early in our Lord's public life He made a trip down to Jerusalem and on that occasion found business being carried on as usual in the various courts of the temple. Caught up with zeal for His Father's house and justly indignant at the desecration of this holy place, He tied together some rope He found there and, swinging this cord, He worked His way down through the tables and stalls, over-turning some, brushing merchandise off others, calling on all to leave. He spoke as one having authority, not as the Scribes and Pharisees. From this point forward the hypocritical leaders of the Jews tried to trap Jesus in His speech. As the Gospel says, they frequently "tested Him" before His apostles and friends. One such test that was put to Christ was the sly question: "Master, is it lawful to pay tribute to Caesar?" The Master's answer: "Render to Caesar the things that are Caesar's and to God the things that are God's." [1]

It has been my observation, especially in recent years, that our Catholic

[1] Mark 12:14-17.

Reprinted with permission from *The Catholic Educational Review*, 60:433–441, October, 1962.

schools and colleges do extremely well in teaching our young people their duties towards God and the Church; on the other hand, we have failed in many instances to impress upon them a sense of responsibility to "render to Caesar the things that are Caesar's." To satisfy his obligations to Caesar, a Catholic must be devoted to the general well-being of his neighborhood, his city, his state, his country, and the whole wide world. This means concern for, and an apostolate to, society in general and not merely to individual members of a small segment of society. It means the racial problem of the South is *his* problem, the moral tone of radio and television is *his* to maintain; the fact that there are rich nations and poor nations should so trouble *him* that he will read Lady Barbara Ward Jackson's latest book on this subject.

In this area of living we can learn much from other religious groups in this country. The Jewish people, for instance, who firmly believe that the Messianic Age is yet to come, are today working hard for the sort of world they want. Protestants put us to shame with their generous labors in behalf of the underprivileged of the general community; they have more than their share of workers in local Red Cross units and similar agencies. This may be because in this country, at least in the past, their approach to religion seems to have been more social than doctrinal.

In the Church of Rome Popes, especially of the last hundred years, have given much guidance and encouragement to participate in collective, enlightened, and methodical enterprises, to modify the mentality of their environment, to influence ways of living and acting, to obtain a reformation in the structures of society, so that, not only individuals but moreover society itself becomes what it should be, according to the principles of social order and Christian morality. However, if one looks around a parish, a city, or a diocese for young Catholic social leaders, he will, I fear, find only a few who have taken the words of the Popes seriously. Why is this so? Because we, their teachers, have not been sufficiently clear and positive in teaching them to think and act socially. This is not to say that there are not many young graduates of Catholic high schools who have left all to follow Christ in the seminary or the convent. Certainly many young nurses have volunteered for assignments in difficult posts; many young teachers are giving two and three years of their lives to the needy in Alaska, Alabama, Jamaica; many former students of ours are model husbands and wives and enlightened parents of five, eight, and ten children.

Weakness of Negative Approach

Many young Catholics who have undertaken action in behalf of society at large have, unfortunately, gone about it in a rather negative way. They know the books they should not read, the movies they should not see, the TV ads and shows they find offensive, the magazines they want removed from drug stores, and the Communists they want to see deported or imprisoned. All of this, of course, has its place. But the question still remains: "How many of our young high-school and college graduates ambition taking positions where they radically affect the very structures of society?" How many, for instance, are taking up careers in Hollywood, on Broadway, on TV? How many are writing popular songs and modern plays? How many are serving as editors of *Seventeen, Ingenue,* or *Harper's?* How many are members of the State Department? How many are serving the country and the world as members of the Peace Corps? How many have gone into basic research in the Brookhaven laboratories? Aside from the President[*] (and he was not exposed to the Catholic educational system), how many have achieved prominence in public life on the national scene?

Enough sociological surveys have been made to say, without fear of contradiction, that American Catholics do not have proportional representation in many of these key fields of influence. The question now arises: "Why do we not have more young Christian social leaders?" Three explanations might be offered. The first is that our young Catholic people are not aware of the social problems. The second is that money is still the root of much evil. And the third is that they are too timid.

Unawareness of Problems

Let us consider the first cause for their lack of involvement in social problems: their unawareness of the existence of problems in some instances and of their scope in others. Here there seems to be a very definite link between a lack of Catholic leadership in the social and political fields and the relative absence of a vigorous intellectual life in our Catholic schools and colleges. Leading Catholic intellectuals like Bishop Wright, Monsignor Ellis, Father Ong, and Father Weigel have analyzed this situation with great perceptiveness. One answer to the comments these men made a few years ago was a resounding objection to their simple utterance. This was silly. We should try to find truth in their statements and try to use the truth for the betterment of our schools.

We will be in a better position to correct what is wrong and promote what is good, once we have clarified our ideas of what we mean by the intellectual life. Doctor Thomas O'Dea in his excellent book on this subject, *The American Catholic Dilemma,* gives an interesting definition of intellectuals which he borrows from Father Walter Ong. He says intellectuals are "those men and women whose main interest is the advancement of knowledge, or the clarification of cultural issues and public problems." [2] One who reads this definition closely will see that a division is suggested here between intellectuals of the *first* order and intellectuals of the *second* order. Intellectuals of the first order are, according to this definition, concerned with the furthering of knowledge. Now in order to pursue the intellectual life on this level, first, one must be possessed of a very keen and penetrating mind, and second, one must live in circumstances of health, nervous con-

[*] [John F. Kennedy.]

[2] Thomas F. O'Dea, *American Catholic Dilemma* (New York: Sheed and Ward, 1958), p. 22.

stitution, and financial security which make possible the search for knowledge for its own sake. Clearly, only a very small percentage of our students can realistically plan to live as intellectuals in this rarified atmosphere. On this level intellectuals push forward the frontiers of knowledge by deep and exhaustive research. This is the class of intellectuals where we as Catholics would group together such men as Jacques Maritain, Étienne Gilson, Christopher Dawson, Gustave Weigel, and Karl Rahner.

According to our definition, intellectuals of the second order are those who are "concerned with the clarification of cultural issues and public problems." All Catholic high-school and college teachers and a very large proportion of their students can and should ambition living an intellectual life on this level. It may well be that because we have thought of the intellectual life too exclusively in terms of the first type, we have not achieved more success in promoting the intellectual life on the second level in our religious communities and in our schools and colleges. Either "cultural issues and public problems are to be clarified" by Catholics who have studied the mind of the Church, or their solution will be arrived at by those who don't know the Church's plan for a Christian social order. Father John Considine, M.M., after a recent visit to South America, quoted a Catholic Bishop who is concerned about the social situation in his country. The Bishop said: "Great social changes are coming about in our country; they will take place either with or without the Church. If without—*against* the Church."

Concern for Cash

The second explanation for a lack of social action on the part of Catholic high-school graduates is money or materialism. The desire for money exerts a harmful influence on Catholic high-school students in two different ways: (1) it inordinately engrosses their attention; (2) once money is acquired it inclines its owner to be identified with the world he should be striving to change.

A large proportion of our young people are taking jobs because, as they say, they "have to, in order to help the family." If one takes the time to examine just how serious is this need for more money one finds, often enough, that the parents of the children we teach in school are living far above their means. They buy on credit, they ambition living in the sort of house that is described on TV ads and in modern magazines, not in the house they should realistically plan to make their home. Many parents are victimized by the soft sell of Madison Avenue.

To counterbalance this influence at home our students need a vigorous and challenging spiritual program presented to them in closed retreats, in up-to-date religion classes, and in extracurricular spiritual training programs. All too often in our Catholic high schools the students hear far more about the temptations they have to face from concupiscence of the flesh, than they hear about temptations which derive from concupiscence of the eyes and the pride of life, with the result that girls fill their closets and bureau drawers with enough dresses to clothe all the children in a mountain village in Bolivia. As sophomores, boys go to work with a rather strong sense of obligation to the family; they plan to pay their way through college. By senior year many of them drive to school in their own cars and two nights a week take their girl friends out to drive-ins and the "tower of pizza."

The world of ideas and the challenge to study in order to bring a solution to the cultural issues and public problems of the day escape them, "leave them cold." Would it be an exaggeration to say that many, if not most, of our Catholic high-school graduates leave school without buying *on their own*, say, ten books which will offer them a fuller view of the world and the problems about them. While they are not keeping up with the world of ideas they *are* keeping up with the world of styles. Last year, after traveling to forty American cities to lecture, Mr. Douglas Hyde summed up his most recent impressions of the Church in this country, saying: "The fundamental heresy of American Catholics is that they are trying desperately to keep up with the Joneses." This turns out to be an expensive, an absorbing, a distracting, a frustrating and quite unchristian occupation.

"Blessed are the poor in spirit, for theirs is the kingdom of heaven," our Lord told us early in His public life.[3] Note that He did not say (although it is included) theirs *will be* but theirs *is* the kingdom of heaven. When Christians strive too hard to be accepted by this world they find themselves weighted down with worries and material concerns, and they do not enjoy the freedom of the children of God. They are not at home in the kingdom of God. And this is the second bad effect of an inordinate desire for money: people are not detached. If one is not detached from the world he cannot stand off from it and see how feverishly sick it is. Only detached Christians will be ready to pull up their shallow roots and go to another part of the world to help other people solve their problems. Authorities in Washington want one volunteer from each parish in the country for PAVLA. How many have gone so far from your school? Only detached people will shrug off apathy and develop in their souls sympathy for the negroes, for the divorced, for those who have no sense of orientation towards God—or, for that matter, towards any human person outside of their family.

Timidity of the Young

A third reason for little, if any, social action among many of our Catholic high-school graduates is timidity. Young people are constantly plagued by what we call "human respect." If a girl goes to Mass every day someone will remark: "She's going to the convent!" and that is the kiss of unpopularity. If a boy does not have a steady girl friend, questions are asked: "Where has he been? What is he? A square?" If they are truly dependent on their parents through an obedient spirit, their companions will try to embarrass them out of this attitude. And, brave and composed as they try to appear, our young people are often seriously upset by their timidities.

[3] Matthew 5:3.

There are many reasons for this, as Father Andrew Greeley points out in his book, *Strangers in the House*.[4] One basic explanation is the general sense of insecurity that all young people must work their way through in the process of growing up. Another might be that they have not mastered, either at home or in school, the art of writing or the art of talking. Then again, and most of all in this instance, timidity is a lack of Christian courage, an unwillingness to bear witness to Christ and to the Church. Inasmuch as they have not put on the mind of Christ, inasmuch as they have not familiarized themselves with the mind of the Church in relation to the semipagan world about them, and especially inasmuch as they have not disciplined their souls by a regular routine of spiritual exercises, they are unwilling to endure persecution. Unmindful of St. Paul's warning that "all those who will live holy lives in Christ Jesus will suffer persecution," they do not see the place of misunderstanding, unpopularity, and a lack of social acceptance in their lives.

It is a hard doctrine we must preach to them; it is the doctrine of redemption through suffering. God the Father chose death on the Cross for His only begotten Son. Christ, in turn, warns His followers: "If anyone wishes to come after me, let him deny himself, and take up his cross daily, and follow me." [5] "If they have persecuted me, they will persecute you also." [6] Redemption, passively looked at, as the theologians say, was accomplished by Christ's death on Calvary. Redemption of the whole world in this year of grace, Redemption actively looked at, will be carried out by other Christs, His brothers and sisters by adoption, who must themselves be crucified to the world, men and women to whom the world itself is crucified. There is no easy way for us to bring redemption to the world of 1962. Now this deep mystery of our faith will be clearly perceived in the soul's depths only by those Christians who bow their heads and bend their knees in prayer, who frequently, even daily, lift their minds and hearts to God. Regular spiritual reading will help to make this clear to our students; the lives of the Saints will give them courage and show them how to live a full Christian life; frequent use of the Sacraments will bring it about that the God-life takes fuller possession of their souls. Liturgy and contemplation are the best preparation for an active and effective apostolate to a world that does not know or understand Christ or His Mother, and therefore will not know or love or serve Them.

Suggestions for Action

Now, in conclusion, a few suggestions are offered. The point has been made that the Church wants Christian social leaders—thousands of them to bring to the world Christian views of how people should think and act. There are not as many social apostles as there should be. The reason is that students in our high schools are unaware of social problems because their instructors are unaware.

4 Andrew Greeley, *Strangers in the House* (New York: Sheed and Ward, 1961).
5 Luke 9:23.
6 John 15:20.

Solution (1) Read *America, Commonweal,* or *Ave Maria* every week. (2) Read *The Catholic World, Jubilee,* and *Worship* every month. (3) Read books on the life of a Christian in the world. (4) Buy fifty manila folders and start saving articles which deal with social issues and public problems—on art, business, communications, community, communism, delinquency and so on. This world is yours to save and sanctify through the young people whose minds you enlighten, whose hearts you set on fire.

The second explanation for a lack of commitment on the part of students to the problems of a Christian Social Order is that money ties them down to this world, keeps them from being detached; with the result that they are looking for comfort and do not want to be discontented by thinking of the spiritual and temporal lot of the "have-nots." Wherefore, teachers must live and talk much about the blessedness of the "poor in spirit." Teach them to relish the wisdom of St. John of the Cross' remark, "He who has set his heart on nothing finds fulness everywhere." Teach them to do without.

Finally, timidity inclines our young people to settle for security and keeps them from involving themselves in the structures of a society whose many pressures plague them. Deeply desirous of being emancipated from the world of childhood and of being accepted in the world of adults, they assume the pose of "conformity," hoping this will be the only price they must pay for maturity.

Part of their training in Christian courage is natural; part is supernatural. Secret longings for leadership will languish and die if young people are not trained in the techniques of writing and speaking. If they cannot communicate, they cannot lead. "Good example is not enough today—if it ever was enough," said Pius XI. Excellent dramatic societies, debating, and current events clubs have their place here.

When many teachers and administrators talk about and make provision for the "gifted student," they have in mind those who achieved high ratings in IQ and achievement tests. It seems only proper that programs be set up and promoted for those who are more richly endowed with gifts of heart and soul as well as of mind. Highly competent persons should be placed in charge of the Catholic leadership programs in our schools and colleges, whether these be the Legion of Mary, Young Christian Students, or the Sodality of Our Lady. Through these programs many young Catholic social leaders will be formed. In the world of politics, foreign service, the arts, the fields of communication, basic research and the professions, the Christian view of life and death will be presented, for the most part, by those who have been trained to leadership. In our competitive world people with training in leadership have an edge over others. It is our role to give our more promising students this edge.

Social formation:
the forgotten imperative

Louis J. Twomey, S.J.

In the next article, Father Twomey pulls no punches in criticizing Catholic educators, among others, for having failed to contribute as significantly as they could and should to the Christian reconstruction of society. His criticism, though blunt, is constructive. He suggests what must be done in Catholic education to foster students' social awareness and overcome their apathy toward others in the world around them. Father Twomey is director of the Institute of Industrial Relations at Loyola University in New Orleans.

"In my lifetime the issue would most probably be resolved one way or the other (in favor of) Christianity or communism. . . . The job, I felt, was first and foremost to get Christians moving, not just because they were anti-Communist but because they had been made to see that their actions . . . would decide the course of history for centuries ahead."

Thus spoke one of the Catholic world's most distinguished laymen, Douglas Hyde. He made the statement in 1950, two years after his conversion from twenty years of top-rank leadership in the British Communist party (cf. *I Believed,* G. P. Putnam's Sons, New York, 1950, p. 805).

All available evidence today points to the urgency of taking at face value Hyde's ten-year-old summing up of the supreme crisis of our times. It is the purpose of this paper to examine whether we Catholics, and specifically we Catholic educators, are caught up in any such sense of urgency.

By the nature of their commitment, Catholics are anti-Communist. But many,

An address to the College and University Department of the Southern Regional Unit of the National Catholic Educational Association, Memphis, Tenn., November 28, 1960. Reprinted with Father Twomey's permission.

402

perhaps even most, are purely negative in their confrontation with communism. They seem unwilling to admit that communism is an effect, not a cause; that the worldwide, and now the spatial threat of communism would never have been possible had it not been for the religious, political, economic and social failures of the West. By the West, I mean that grouping of nations whose guiding principles are derived, professionally at least, from Judeo-Christian teachings.

It is these failures of the West which have created the conditions in which communism took root on November 7, 1917, and thereafter flourished as no other movement in history, not excluding Christianity. For communism is dynamic negativism. It is rushing to fill the voids created in men's souls as well as their stomachs by the unwillingness or inability of so-called Christian nations to measure up to their profession. It should be obvious, then, that communism will be withstood and eventually rolled back not merely by damning it, but by the dedicated implementation of the imperatives of Christian justice and Christian charity.

But this approach will become actual only when we Catholics, and particularly we Catholic educators, have the humility to admit our own large share of responsibility for communism. In this regard let me suggest by way of a series of questions some possible leads to what, in my opinion, is a long overdue examination of conscience.

Why in the minds of uncounted millions of little people everywhere is the Church conceived in the image of the upper classes only?

Why is it that the God-Man was born in a stable, lived ten-elevenths of His life in what by modern standards was a rude shack in the Galilean hills? Why in His public life did the birds of the air have their nests and the foxes of the fields their holes, but the Son of Man had not whereon to lay His head? Why did He die deserted on a Cross? Why was He buried in a stranger's tomb? And yet, of the divine agency He founded to perpetuate His redemptive mission on earth, very many of the poor and downtrodden will reiterate what they are now saying in the back streets of our cities, and in the back countries of the world: "You preach a very fine-sounding doctrine, but only the Socialists and the Communists are doing something to improve our condition."

How is it that Pius XI in 1925 could say to that tremendous social apostle and founder of the Young Christian Workers, Monsignor Joseph Cardijn: "The greatest scandal of the 19th century was the loss of the workers to the Church" (cf. *Challenge to Action,* ed. by Rev. Eugene Langdale, Fides Publishers, Chicago, 1955, p. 11). Why has the Church yet to recover from this scandal?

How explain the fact that in the Western world, communism has made its deepest inroads in those nations with Catholic foundations and traditions? I refer to Italy with the largest Communist party outside of Soviet Russia and Red China; to France with the strongest Communist party in the free world and where less than two per cent of the workers are practicing Catholics; to Spain, which tore itself apart on this issue of communism from 1936 to 1939 in one of the bloodiest of civil wars, and to most of the republics in Latin America where communism is an imminent threat.

Where were the priests and the nuns and the educated laity during the agonizing decades when the little people of Cuba were either forgotten or deplorably ground down as virtual slaves for the rich land owners, the cattle ranchers, the American corporations, and for the well-scrubbed, well-heeled elite in Havana? Why was it left to a wild man like Fidel Castro to capture the imagination of, in his language, "the humble people," to win their loyalty, and then stand by the side of Nikita Khrushchev to hold out to them his perverted type of salvation?

Why among the newly-emerging African nations does the Church find itself in a precarious situation mainly in areas formerly the colonial possessions of countries with Catholic culture? And this after decades of missionary effort.

But it is easy to spotlight the real or imaginary sins of others. To turn the light in on ourselves is quite a different matter. And yet who of us can deny the serious deficiencies in our own record? In the perspective, for example, of the cold, calculated overriding of the God-given rights of our Negro fellow citizens, what American can rightly question the tragic truth of the indictment of former Secretary of State, John Foster Dulles, that "racial discrimination in the United States is our greatest national scandal and our most dangerous international hazard"?

What American Catholic can deny that so many Catholic schools on every level of the educational hierarchy will accept atheists, agnostics, Protestants and Jews who are white, but not even the most highly qualified Catholics who are Negro?

How explain that very many Catholic hospitals receive white patients, however complex their ethnic composition, but not Negro patients, however grave their ailment?

Why is it that, although Negroes may be members of so-called "white" parishes, they are rarely allowed to participate in integral parochial life?

How account for the dismal truth that graduates of our Catholic schools are, by and large, as racially prejudiced as those who have been educated in secular institutions?

Is it any wonder that our Faith in the United States, and particularly in the South, is viewed as a white man's religion? Yes, members of other races may belong but only on terms set by the white man.

And in other fields of human relations, the picture is hardly more encouraging. Why is it, for instance, that very many graduates of our Catholic schools, priests and religious included, have what almost amounts to an instinctive prejudice against organized labor and seemingly accept the proposition that labor unions are somehow inherently suspect and a threat to "the great American way of doing business"? How the laboring masses were lost to the Church in Europe and Latin America becomes less puzzling as we examine the lack of interest in and sometimes the positive antagonism towards the organized labor movement in the United States on the part of large numbers of priests and religious and laymen, most of whom are descendants of the banana peddlers, the ditch diggers, the railroad workers, and the coal miners of a generation or two ago. We only delude ourselves if we believe that thus the Church can be ingratiated with the American workingman.

And in still another vastly important field, that of international relations, we discover large numbers of Catholics who look with suspicion, not to say hostility, on any effort to build up a world order that would demand the slightest surrendering of absolute sovereignty on the part of the United States. How can they maintain this rigid isolationism in the face of the often repeated pleadings of Pope Pius XII, the greatest and most genuine of all internationalists? It was he who said: "Nothing is more in conformity with the traditional doctrine of the Church . . . [than] an effective political organization of the world" (cf. address to the Fourth Congress of the World Movement for World Federal Government, April 6(1951). Again, how can a not inconsiderable number of prominent Catholic newspapers and editors, priests and religious, laymen and laywomen keep up a constant harassment of the United Nations Educational, Scientific and Cultural Organization? And this despite the fact that our present Holy Father has often praised Unesco and maintains permanent observers there. Moreover, the president of Unesco is an outstanding Catholic lay apostle, Vittorino Veronese. "Every Catholic," says Veronese, "can feel perfectly at home in the work of Unesco. Its goals do not in any way conflict with our Faith."

This brief and certainly incomplete probing into our deficiencies is a painful process. Assuredly, I do not relish it. But, in my opinion, it is necessary if we would come to know something of the reasons why within forty-three years communism has extended its land-spread to almost one-third of the earth's surface and its tyranny over 37 of every 100 of the earth's population. It will also give us an insight into the shoreless tragedy of why millions of the racially and economically exploited look elsewhere for deliverance than to the institution founded by the poor Christ. Moreover, through this probing, we can, if only we will, alert ourselves and our students to the demands of "the revolution of rising expectations" in the Far East, the Near East, the continent of Africa, Latin America and even here at home. Upon the outcome of this revolution will depend the survival of all that we have known and loved.

We have been proposing blunt questions. And we believe that, however distasteful, these questions must have honest answers especially from us who carry the heavy responsibility of getting young men and women ready to live the full Christian life in the fateful 1960's. We render the Church and ourselves no good service if we attempt to evade such answers through some sort of escapist rationalization. I submit the following considerations at least as the raw material, so to speak, out of which we can construct realistic answers.

But before proceeding, I should like to protest that in what I have said and in what I am about to say I have no intention whatever of disparaging the magnificent work that has been done and is being done in the elementary grades, in the high schools, colleges and universities of our Catholic educational system throughout the United States.

No amount of constructive criticism dims the glory which the dedicated educational efforts of our bishops, priests, brothers, nuns, laymen and laywomen have richly merited. But we cannot rest satisfied with what we have accomplished. Our contention is, therefore, that in humbly acknowledging our deficiencies, we not only do not discount the great achievements of the past, but rather we prepare ourselves for even greater achievements in the future.

It is in this spirit that I now turn in a search for appropriate answers to the inquiries submitted above.

Traditionally in the Catholic sense, education has been taken to mean that process of instruction, study and research whereby the spiritual, moral, intellectual and physical faculties of the student are so developed as to enable him to achieve that kind of success in time which will assure his success in eternity.

On the face of it, this is a very broad definition. There are few perhaps who would quarrel with it. As stated, it is at least an indication of why the Church makes such tremendous sacrifices to maintain a school system. But when we go beyond generalities, and begin to explore implications, we head into difficulties. The implication we have chiefly in mind is that education is "the harmonious development of *the whole man.*" We certainly agree. But we do take issue with those whose interpretation of "the whole man" has the practical result of so narrowing the objective of education as in fact not to train the whole man but only a part, and thus to fall considerably short of his harmonious development.

What does the term, "whole man," mean? In the first place, all will agree that it includes the individual nature of man. Man is an individual, separate and distinct from every other person and thing, with rights and obligations which attach to him individually and personally.

No one familiar with Catholic education can doubt that it is doing an altogether superior job in training students how to be good individuals and good family members. In so doing Catholic educators, administrators and classroom teachers are making a contribution to God and country of incalculable importance.

But the "whole man" is something yet more than man as an individual person or a member of a family. He is *by nature* destined to work out his salvation within that complex framework of relationships established in the religious, political, economic and cultural institutions which make up what we call society. In other words, man as God made him is not only an individual, but a social being as well. Hence, any system of education which neglects formally and specifically to train its students how to exercise their rights and fulfill their obligations as members of society can hardly lay claim to "the harmonious development of *the whole man.*" However thorough may be his training as an individual and family member, the student is not educated in the full-rounded sense unless he is likewise trained to take his place fittingly and effectively in the several social environments of which he is to become a part.

We sincerely believe that Catholic education has gone far, very far indeed, in getting men and women ready to evaluate the things of time in the perspective of eternity and to live accordingly. But, as we see it, it has gone far enough. Until we are willing to recognize social formation as a functional and integral part of the educational process, we will continue to turn out graduates who, although they may be exemplary individuals and family members, will never come to know the true richness of the Faith as it applies not only to personal and family living, but to the right ordering of political, economic and social life.

Under our present handicap of failing to make social formation a principal objective in our several curricula, we cannot hope that later on our graduates will be able to make any significant contribution to the Christian reconstruction of society which all the modern Popes, from Leo XIII down to and including our present Holy Father, have said is a dire necessity. Graduates of Catholic schools have not been conspicuous in their willingness to give of their time and energy in answering what St. Pius X said is the great need of our times: "Action!" Action is that great apostolate "to which Catholic Action should be specially devoted, namely, the practical solution of the social question according to Christian principles." (cf. *A Symposium on the Life and Work of Pope Pius X*, pub. by the Confraternity of Christian Doctrine, N.C.W.C., Washington, 1946, p. 126).

Our alumni for the most part are ill-equipped to fill the role of the layman as outlined by Pius X. And still worse, there are some at least who are even ill-disposed to acknowledge the competency of the Church to interpose her authority except in matters strictly dogmatic. Thus they subject themselves to the stinging rebuke of Pius XII when, in addressing the First World Congress of the Lay Apostolate, October 14, 1951, he congratulated the delegates on their "resistance to that noxious tendency which exists even among Catholics and which would like to confine the Church to those questions said to be 'purely religious'—not that pains are taken to know exactly what is meant by that phrase. Provided the Church keeps to the sanctuary and the sacristy, and slothfully lets humanity struggle outdoors in its distress and needs, no more is asked of her." (cf. the *Catholic Mind*, February, 1952, p. 120).

But in all fairness it can be asked: on whom the greater blame? On our graduates, or on ourselves, their teachers? We can hardly expect them to be alert to the principles and practices of the papal social encyclicals, if in their formative years, these documents were unexplored territory.

By 1931, communism had engulfed the whole of Eurasian Russia, and this within less than fourteen years. Faced with the appalling progress of communism toward "the forcible overthrow of all existing social conditions," (*Communist Manifesto*, concluding section), Pius XI on May 15 of that year issued what some consider the most important non-dogmatic pronouncement by a Pope since the Protestant Revolt in the early 16th century. I refer, of course, to the encyclical "On Reconstructing the Social Order" (*Quadragesimo Anno*). Let me cite just one passage from this encyclical: ". . . Unless utmost efforts are made without delay to put them [Christian social principles] into effect, let no one persuade himself that public order, peace, and the tranquillity of human society can be effectively defended against the agitators of revolution." (*op. cit. #62*). But who listened to the old man of the Vatican? It is no exaggeration to say, not even we Catholic educators.

Again, this same Pontiff on March 19, 1937, pleaded with the Catholic world in his encyclical "On Atheistic Communism" (*Divini Redemptoris*): "If the manner of acting of some Catholics in the socio-economic field has left much to be desired, this has often come about because they have not known and pondered sufficiently the teaching of the Sovereign Pontiffs on these questions. Therefore, it is of the utmost importance to foster in all classes of society an intensive program of social education adapted to the varying needs of intellectual culture. . . ." (*op. cit.* #55).

It is now over twenty-nine years since *Quadragesimo Anno* and twenty-three since *Divini Redemptoris*. And as of this moment communism completely dominates almost one billion people in vast stretches of every continent with no end in sight to its threat to upturn "the existing social and political order of things." (*Communist Manifesto*). This is one measure of the extent to which "the agitators of revolution" have perverted "public order, peace and the tranquillity of human society."

How do we account for the discrepancy between papal injunctions and our failure to respond? The answer, it seems to me, is that we ourselves are not convinced that the social formation of our students is an indispensable part of the harmonious development of the whole man. In turn, we haven't passed on social consciousness to our students because we are ourselves not socially conscious. And unless we recognize social formation as integrally associated with the educational process, we will never develop appropriate techniques to make the regular curriculum the medium of social formation nor will we be adequately preparing our students for the turbulent life of the 1960's.

In this regard, I am aware that the situation has improved. Yet, in my experience, it is still true that the average graduate of a Catholic high school or college has often times never heard of *Rerum Novarum, Quadragesimo Anno,* or *Divini Redemptoris,* much less studied their contents and made them his own.

At no time in the past was there the necessity as of today for a Catholic to resist the indifferentism of a society, which in the main has forgotten Christ. To do this, he needs the strong antidote of integral Catholicism, which can and does pronounce authoritatively in economic and social matters and not alone in matters dogmatic and spiritual. But if he is not supplied with this antidote in his Catholic schooling, there is slight chance, as experience amply proves, that later on he will accept it, if ever he comes to know it.

In all this we are not asking for wooden uniformity among Catholics and assuredly not for push-button robots. But it does seem that Catholic men and women nurtured in the same spiritual and intellectual environment should be able to agree at least on the essentials. And one of the essentials is that the Church has "the right and the duty to pronounce with supreme authority upon social and economic matters" (cf. *Quadragesimo Anno,* #41). But without this vision of a Church committed to "the duty of disseminating and intrepreting the whole moral law . . . in the universal order of purposes" (loc. cit. #41-42), what solid ground is there for unity among American Catholics on those issues upon which pivot the fate of the world?

In our almost exclusive emphasis on private and family morality, we are seriously neglecting social morality. As a result, we are promoting "Compartmentalized Catholicism." And compartmentalized Catholicism is part-time Catholicism —part-time in the sense that those infected with it restrict in practice at least the influence of the Faith to certain "Compartments" of their lives.

Unnumbered products of Catholic schools fit the description. We are sending them out pretty much to shift for themselves in the political, economic, and social spheres of human living. In this shifting, as surveys show, these graduates place themselves in that category of behavior patterns dictated by the pressures of their occupational and social environment. In other words, in formulating their attitudes toward the secular aspects of life, they are little affected by what the Church in her political and social philosophy has to say. And thus out of a compartmentalized view of their Faith, these Catholics with appalling ease conform their thought and action to an institutional framework reflecting a secularistic, not to say, a neopagan viewpoint.

One of the most frightening examples of conformism is the number of graduates, even of our colleges and universities, who say the question of interracial justice and charity is a political and social matter and therefore no concern of the Church. Accordingly, many of them publicly defied ecclesiastical authority in its condemnation of compulsory segregation. Others take membership in and assume leadership of such organization as the White Citizens Councils. Still others, in our State legislatures, enter into a shameful conspiracy to use the majesty of the law as an instrument of oppression to undermine the God-given human rights of the Negro.

This and other types of conformism constitute, as we see it, the most serious weakness of the Church in the United States. And there is real tragedy in this weakness. We say this in the conviction that the world is almost literally dying for the lack of what the Catholic Church has. But the Church can never administer her saving balm to a world it is not reaching. And this world is made up of that vast institutional complex in which men play politics, pass, execute and adjudicate laws; provide medical services; plead before a court; design bridges; operate banks; run businesses; belong to labor unions and management associations; set fashions; produce stage, movie and TV entertainment; drive trucks, dig ditches; live in suburbia or overcrowded cities; are employed, unemployed, underemployed or overemployed; are members of the power elite or of racially and religiously persecuted minorities.

This is the world with all its institutions, good, bad and horrible, which the Church must sanctify with the principles and practices of Christ. But as an indispensable condition for this, her laymen and laywomen must be inspired with the dedication and generosity to accept the sacrifices necessary to buck the tide of secularism and to resist the temptation to easy conformity.

The development of such a laity, however, is a forlorn hope as long as priests from our pulpits and the religious and lay people in our classrooms persist in giving the impression that being a good individual, a good son or daughter, a good husband or wife, a good father or mother, is all that makes up being a good Catholic.

The Church desperately needs "transmission belts" among the laity to carry her message to the world. But this system of communication cannot be built on anything less than an understanding of integral Catholicism, Catholicism as an all-pervading way of life. But this kind of Catholicism cannot be put across to the vast majority of Catholics if the social teachings of the Church are by-passed in our schools and pulpits.

The failure of the Catholic educational system adequately to develop the social nature of its students has had disheartening effects. It creates serious and at times scandalous disagreements among Catholics. Catholic unity is thus impaired and the effectiveness of the Church in applying sound social principles to the solution of the fearful problems of today's world undermined. It makes for "private interpretation" in moral matters, which can grow into a chronic disease in the American Church. It sets loose, as we have already observed, our Catholic-educated men in the world of the professions, banking, business, labor and even the priesthood without firm moral directives to guide them in their socio-economic relations. It encourages an aping of the expected behavior patterns of the prosperous middle class. And in this lurks the danger of the Church's being alienated even in the United States from the working classes.

There can be little doubt that to think with the Church is to think socially. But for this, students in Catholic schools at all levels must be systematically trained not only in the what, but also in the how, of the Church's social teachings. Because this emphasis has generally been lacking in our Catholic curricula, we are not developing the kind of knowledgeable, zealous laity without whom the impact of the Church on the modern world is severely circumscribed. The great challenge for us Catholic educators, as I believe, is to work out an effective methodology of incorporating social formation into "the harmonious development" of our students. In this way only can we make our full contribution to mankind's desperate cry for peace with justice.

I can conclude in no better way than by sharing with you a stirring passage from the address to the Second World Congress of the Lay Apostolate held in Rome, October 5, through 13, 1957, by Joseph Folliet, Vice-Chairman of the "Semaines Sociales in France":

> Our time is one of Catholicity. Speeded by the bewildering progress of communications and required by interdependence in economic and cultural life, the world seeks unity through struggle and strife, blood and tears. But physical unity does not mean unity of rights, still less unity of spirit. At every moment, an inexpiable war may call everything into question and, for centuries, stop the human caravan on its way. The unification of the world calls

for universality of consciences. The Catholic Church alone can inspire this universality of conscience; the Church is above nations, races, civilizations, cultures; the Church is universal in fact and in right, in space and in time. Far from repudiating any of the original features that mark out nations and civilizations, the Church is above them all and unites them all. Catholicism is the appointed religion for a time marked for universality.

. . . In a world which, for the first time in history, is tending towards unity, Catholicism provides an ideal and an experience of universality. This, therefore, is what our time expects from the Catholic Church and what it has a right to expect from us, in the very name of the Catholicism we profess. For us, it is the time of total and full Catholicism.

In the terrible crisis of today, mankind waits for the Church, waits for us.

Please God, mankind will not wait in vain. For then the fortress will have been betrayed by those whose sworn duty it was to defend it.

The parent is the primary teacher

George Hagmaier, C.S.P.

*In the next article, Father Hagmaier makes an
important distinction between Catholic schooling
and Catholic education: The former is only a small
part of the latter. Education in the broader sense
begins and continues in the home; the parents are
the child's first and most influential teachers. If they
do not lay the proper foundations and cooperate
with school authorities, there is little that any school
or teacher can do for or with their children. Father
Hagmaier, the coauthor with Rev. Robert Gleason,
S.J., of* Counseling the Catholic, *is associate director
of the Paulist Institute for Religious Research.*

The crisis in Catholic education is far more complex than it appears. There is
today great danger that the financial aspects of maintaining our Catholic school
system will obscure an even more desperate and pressing need—a careful re-
evaluation of the rights and responsibilities invested in the Catholic parent.

Too many of our people today hold the pervasive and damaging notion that
Catholic *schooling* is the same as Catholic *education*. The significance of "total
education" extends far beyond the classroom. The school, it is true, makes certain
specific and invaluable contributions to the formation of the mature and intelligent Christian. We are at the moment giving understandable attention to the
critical needs of our schools. There is a danger, however, that we are giving far
too little attention to what happens *before* the child enters the classroom, and to
the maturing process that should continue, once formal school has ended.

The family circle is the child's first and most important school, and parents
are the world's most influential teachers. More and more scholarly evidence from
pedagogues and psychologists confirms the intuition of the poet: "Childhood
shows the man, as morning shows the day." The importance of early learning ex-

Reprinted with permission from *The Catholic World*, 195:20–25, April, 1962.

periences in the home must not be minimized. It is in the home that lifetime attitudes are formed, discipline is developed, intellectual curiosity is enkindled, lasting values are built and religious beliefs and motives are fostered. It is as difficult for a good school to compensate for a poor family life, as it is for a mediocre school to cancel out a wholesome home background.

The indifference of so many parents and teachers to the importance of the home in the education of the young is a most disturbing aspect of the Catholic scene today. Too many parents are content to leave the religious and moral training of their children to the nuns, brothers and priests—and some religious teachers seem all too willing to take on such responsibilities. In blunt terms, the Catholic school has too often usurped the obligations which belong first and foremost to the parents.

Catholic parents must be reassured that they can be informed and effective educators of their children. Why is it that so many parents seem to panic at the prospect of fulfilling their basic duties effectively? Is it because in so many instances the school has been trying to do what the home should be doing? Are our parents out of practice? Mothers and fathers should teach the young child his prayers, should give simple instructions in the basic teachings of the Church. It is the parent who should by word, and even more importantly, by example, lay the groundwork for the moral training of the child. The parent should feel quite capable of preparing his youngster for his first confession, first Communion and Confirmation. In fact, mother and father, rather than the child, might well be examined by the parish clergy regarding their competence to instruct in these matters.

Further, the parents, not the school, should supervise their children's Mass obligations, should accompany them frequently to the confessional and the Communion rail. The willingness of parents to allow the school to herd their youngsters by classes to these sacramental activities is evidence that they fail to see the value of *family* participation in the liturgy.

Hitler, Freud and the Jesuits have all been quoted to the effect: "Give me a child until he is seven and then do with him what you will." There is much truth in this dictum. The basic attitudes toward God, morality and the sacraments are absorbed by the child in the bosom of his family, and become fairly well jelled at an early age. Hence, the importance of solid, healthy parental attitudes toward religion and the spiritual life.

Where does the youngster acquire his first notion about what his Heavenly Father is like? From his relationship with his own father. If the head of the household is remote, autocratic, arbitrary and vindictive, it will be very difficult for a young son or daughter to imagine that God the Father is loving, compassionate, solicitous and forgiving. If an insecure mother portrays the Almighty as a policeman, a sort of divine baby-sitter who watches and disapproves even when she's not there, it is likely that her child will develop essentially anxious and fearful, rather than trusting and hopeful, spiritual attitudes.

The parents' views of the spiritual life will have much to do with the way a child responds to his Christian heritage. If parents regard membership in the Church primarily as a confining, legalistic commitment, then it is not surprising to find their offspring unable to go beyond a ritualistic, compulsive, "magical" and uninspired practice of their faith.

Because young people are by nature impetuous and undisciplined it is a real temptation for parents to use religion as a "club" to constrain mischief and compel conformity. Certainly there must come to every child a growing awareness of the meaning of "right" and "wrong" in terms of religious and moral values. But a mature and upright moral conscience can be formed only with the greatest delicacy, and it is fatal if tentative experiments in independence are too early and too readily identified with sin and disobedience.

Above all, too much stress upon the "do's" and "don'ts," too many external pietistic religious observances can come between the child and Christ, and can obscure the youngster's active incorporation into His living Mystical Body. Surely the Jesus who "suffered little children to come to Him" did not regale his enthusiastic young adorers with finger-shaking admonitions, dry catechetical formulae and long devotions of wearying monotony.

Parents have a glorious opportunity to bring their children to a loving, welcoming Christ—a divine Friend who overlooks a sketchy sign of the cross, a wobbly genuflection, a whispered giggle in His house, or a clumsily folded pair of little hands. Mother and father can lead their children to the *real* Christ by their own loving acknowledgment of Him. A spontaneous prayer life, a reverent recognition of the presence of Christ in each other, a persistent awareness of God's glorious creations in the world of nature, a sensitivity to His presence in the midst of the Christian community, a positive asceticism which regards the human body as a desirable and gratifying object of God's handiwork—the enduring impact of such obviously holy and rewarding parental convictions can do more to bring the young child to a real, meaningful, personal involvement with the person of Christ than a lifetime of sermons, catechism classes, spiritual reading and routine devotions.

A distortion of an old scholastic principle has led to the all-too-pervasive conviction that "practice makes perfect." Parents and teachers still cling to the notion that a repetition of "good" acts is bound to insure the formation of good habits. This axiom is valid only when the individual is *properly motivated.* The *whole* person must be moved; the heart as well as the mind must be touched. This is true in matters of religious belief and observance; it is particularly true of the *sacramental life* of the young Christian.

It is not enough to tell a child that the sacraments—especially Penance and the Eucharist—are good. He must *experience* their goodness, and he must see their goodness at work in others, especially in his parents. If regular confession and frequent Communion are to be a joy and not a chore, it is vitally important that each of these sacramental experiences becomes a true encounter with Christ. The young child must be led away from agonizing and petty scrutinies of his little psyche, and toward a conscious and confident fellowship with his loving Lord.

All these attitudes can be most effectively instilled—and indeed sustained—

by the enlightened and devoted Catholic home. Our understandable concern for the preservation of our Catholic school system has perhaps misled some Catholics into believing that the physical presence of their child in a Catholic classroom is a guarantee of future religious excellence. Again, we must remind ourselves that there are limits to the effectiveness of any educational system. There is just so much we can do well.

Overcrowded classrooms, inadequate facilities, shortages of guidance personnel, hastily trained religious teachers, underpaid lay staffs—these are sometimes as characteristic of the Catholic school as they are of the public schools. We can well ask: How adequately can we teach the Catholic life and safeguard the faith under such circumstances?

Granting the acute crisis in our *Catholic* schools, the Church in America faces an even greater challenge. The challenge can be dramatized by this simple statistic: the *majority* of our American Catholic young people are not enrolled in Catholic schools, as of now. The obligation of the Church to provide for the religious education of *all* her children has led the hierarchy, clergy and laity to give more and more attention to methods of instruction and training outside the formal school setting. In many cases these experiments are still in embryo. But there is increasing evidence that fresh and novel techniques can be quite successful.

Catholic educators, who are seeking both to revitalize our Catholic schools and to establish more effective training programs outside the school, feel that the following viewpoints need to be stressed.

(1) Parents must be helped to acknowledge and to carry out their responsibilities as primary educators of their children with confidence and joy. They can be prepared for these duties by more practical, down-to-earth courses in marriage and family life in our high schools and colleges. Too few of our Catholic schools concentrate on practical training along these lines. All too often such courses in family living are lumped with the fringe curriculum, along with basket-weaving, driver training, social dancing, etc.

More parishes are providing family-living programs for parents, especially for the young couple. Seminarians are being trained in more formal ways to supervise Cana, pre-Cana and Christian Family Movement activities. Diocesan Family Life bureaus are better staffed with full-time, trained personnel who are supervising the mushrooming demands of their localities.

(2) Many more parishes are making use of the professional people in the community to provide an even broader program of educational "self-help" through lectures, workshops, reading programs and discussion groups. The Confraternity of Christian Doctrine is being implemented as never before, and a great deal more money and time and more professionally trained people are becoming a part of the parish instruction program or participating in released-time activities. There is still, however, a glaring imbalance in the amount of funds assigned the established Catholic school, as compared with the piddling sums and skeleton staffs set aside to educate the majority of our young people who are not in parochial schools. As our population grows, we must come more and more to see the parish itself, rather than the parish school, as the center of Catholic education.

(3) We must also encourage our Catholic people to show greater interest in the public schools. Not only is this our responsibility as citizens, but vibrant Catholic parish life will want to concern itself with every educational enterprise affecting the community. Many of our best Catholic teachers, and more and more of our Catholic children—over half at present—are part of the public school system. For this reason alone, public education should have our sympathetic interest. And Catholics everywhere should work to dispel a somewhat pervasive impression that there is something shameful or sinister about the neighborhood public school. It is high time that we make special efforts to bring the public school, its faculty, student body and parent organization into the orbit of our Catholic community.

(4) Finally, we need far more intensive parent-teacher co-operation in our Catholic schools. The school is, after all, an extension of the home, and the religious teacher is a stand-in for the parent. It is important that the parent and the teacher understand each other. The day is past when the only services that teachers risk asking of parents are to raise money, run school bazaars, measure uniforms, baby-sit and chauffeur student groups to museums. More and more parents today are well educated themselves, and quite capable of contributing their views about curriculum changes, homework, school discipline, social affairs and religious practices.

A properly run parent-teacher's organization with good, two-way communication, can provide the necessarily isolated nun or brother with a "real-life view" of the pressures, conflicts and challenges within the modern home. All too often teachers who have entered the religious life at the end of their senior high school year know less about family life than the youngsters they have in class.

An important implication of the pluralistic society in which we live is that many important human concerns have become fragmented and unrelated. Education—broadly, that learning process which goes on from the cradle to the grave—is beleaguered by the evils of our disjointed society. Critics of the Catholic school are dead wrong when they speak of parochial education as dangerously divisive. The Catholic school has been and can continue to be an indispensable fountainhead for the preservation and dissemination of spiritual truths vital to our people and to our country.

What should concern us, however, is the danger that we might misread the role that the Catholic school can best fulfill—that we will expect, indeed demand, of the Catholic teacher certain educational tasks which belong properly to the parents and the home. We are hearing these days that the golden age of the Catholic laity is at hand. The Catholic layman is becoming more and more involved as an active participant in the liturgy. He is more sacrament-minded, more concerned with vibrant parish activities centered around his family, more adept at the new catechetics, more keenly interested in adult education.

It is time, then, that our intelligent and zealous Catholic lay people join their priestly leaders in a thoughtful and intensive examination of how, in the face of increasing difficulty, we can best insure a deep, meaningful, lasting religious education for *every* Catholic child—in or out of the Catholic school.

part vii

Discipline and counseling

QUESTIONS TO GUIDE YOUR READING

1. *Are there any major points connected with discipline which you consider to be important that Father D'Alonzo does not at least touch upon in his article? How do you think he would deal with these points?*

2. *Do you agree with Dr. Cottle that there are five common elements in counseling? Explain your agreement or disagreement.*

3. *Under what conditions is it permissible or advisable for a counselor to divulge information to parents or school officers?*

4. *Do you accept Dr. Nordberg's thesis that there is such a thing as Christian counseling? Is there such a thing as Christian discipline?*

5. *Is it fair to the client if the counselor allows his own values to intrude in the counseling situation? Explain and defend your answer.*

6. *With whom are you more inclined to agree, Father O'Brien or Dr. Lee? Do you think Dr. Nordberg is more in agreement with Father O'Brien or Dr. Lee?*

What is discipline?

Rev. Alfred D'Alonzo, C.S.C.

As a number of surveys have shown, one of the major problems of teachers—not only of beginning teachers, but of experienced veterans as well—is discipline. Before discussing the "how" of this problem, it is necessary to consider first the "what" and the "why." In the following article, Father D'Alonzo does just this. He explains what discipline is and what its purposes in the classroom are. Then he discusses some direct and indirect means of discipline, and some principles he has found to be of value.

In all communities established by man there is an essential need for law and order. This is true because law embraces those regulations in virtue of which one is led to perform certain actions and is restricted from the performance of others. Without such measures a community would eventually cease to exist. Chaos and disorder would reign and the civic structure would collapse because of internal dissension and decadence. Hence, there would be no communal life for gregarious man unless certain persons were vested with authority and the prerogative to command and govern. Once these men are placed in charge of the direction of the community, they have a right to be obeyed for the sake of the common good. To insure the survival of the society, a rational ordering of things concerning the common good is essential. Therefore, laws are imperative for the existence of the society and its culture.

If any infractions of the law are detected, the custodian of the law has the duty of imposing censures. This he does because the common good has been infringed upon; and also, to correct the culprit and to discourage future infractions.

Reprinted with permission from *The Catholic Educator*, 31:550 ff., March, 1961.

Same Principles Apply to School

In the perfect societies of the family and the Church, there are authoritative hierarchies with definite laws geared towards achieving their specific goals. If the members of these communities refuse to obey regulations, penalties could be imposed. Although the school is an auxiliary society, these same principles are in practice. School government is necessary because the school, as an educational institution, has been established to satisfy certain human needs. Therefore, right order is demanded if this institution is to achieve the needs and desires which nurtured it. If such were not the case then bedlam would reign, disorganization would be apparent, and confusion would result. Nothing would be conducive to intellectual development. Valuable time would be consumed in admonishing rather than in teaching. To provide for the intellectual growth of students, peace and quiet are needed; and in order to secure peace and quiet, discipline is a requisite.

But what is discipline? An element frequently incorporated in the definition in some form or other is *control*. Control, along with submissiveness, is stressed again and again by a majority of authors. And these are the features of discipline which have been handed down from generation to generation, from teacher to teacher. The chief means used to secure control and submission have been the rod and the whip. Throughout history these "teaching aids" have played a prominent part in the education of youth.

None of the schools of antiquity ever dreamed of teaching without tears; the slogan of the ancients was: no progress without painful efforts! Even in the days of intellectual enlightenment, the motto of the schoolmen was indicative of their teaching methods: *Qui Parcit Virgae Odit Filium!*

The use of the rod by the school masters of yesteryear did not solve problems, but rather created them. True, it managed to get the boys quiet *hic et nunc*, but did the rod insure lasting results? Would the boys be induced to act better in the future? Would they voluntarily attempt to act well? Often, not; only when the rod was raised to strike would the students react in a favorable manner. The old adage of spare the rod and spoil the child has left much to be desired.

In reaction to this type of discipline a school of modern educationalists advocated a laissez-faire policy. This policy gave free reign to the child and afforded him opportunities to give vent to his inhibitions. Liberty was sanctioned to the point of abuse. The whim of the child dictated classroom matter. Discussions descended to debates. Direction fell from the hands of the teacher. Instead of improving the situation, these advanced ideas only added more fuel to the fire which threatened to devour the school.

Re-evaluation of Practices Needed

After viewing these extremes, I am of the firm conviction that a revision of policies and a re-evaluation of practices pertaining to discipline are urgently needed. Definitions and goals of discipline have been too vague too long. Obviously, there is need for a comprehensive study of this matter. Because of my experience in handling disciplinary problems, I do have some suggestions for the reader's consideration. If a teacher were to heed these recommendations, he would be aiding the student to find himself, to know himself, and to help himself.

However, before any means can be determined to cope with this problem of discipline, it is first necessary that the end of discipline be clearly stated. This is indispensable because the end must be set down prior to taking steps required for its achievement. One must know where to go before he decides how to get there. Just what is desired of discipline? What part should it play in the educational program? These are the crucial questions one must answer before discussing specific corrective procedures.

End Is Twofold

I believe the end of discipline is twofold. The immediate or proximate end is the maintenance of a healthy learning atmosphere in the school, and the ultimate end is self-mastery or self-control by means of which a student strives after those things which are good or which will lead to integrity and moral excellence. Our concern will be with the ultimate end. No matter what the constituent element of discipline comprise—assuming responsibilities, obeying intelligently, thwarting impulses or restraining behavior—the ultimate concern of disciplines can be stated succinctly: how can one make a student good?

Philosophers, following the sagacious doctrines of St. Thomas, teach that this task is impossible; each man must make himself good. But St. Thomas also states that man, because he is a social being, requires the aid and guidance of his fellow man in order to perfect his human faculties. This is done through teaching. Inasmuch as teaching is a cooperative art, it utilizes the assistance of human beings to help develop his mind and acquire knowledge. If virtue is to be acquired, then knowledge must be sought. Before one can desire something, he must know it or know about it. Students have this capacity to know because God endowed human beings with an intellect which seeks the truth and a will which strives after the good. By reason of their rational natures, students possess, at least in potency, a longing for the truth. Therefore, students should be presented with truth and their intellects should be developed to appreciate the truth. In this manner, students will be motivated toward the truth and also the good which is intrinsically contained in the truth.

Knowledge Will Not Make a Student Good

Ordinarily the more one knows about a subject, the more he likes it and desires to possess it. However, we cannot infallibly state that knowledge will make a student good. *De facto* this is not true. When a student is taught about the virtues—their proper object and their values—he then possesses speculative knowledge. As long as this knowledge is only in the intellect, it is not a moral virtue. A virtue, according to St. Thomas, is a good quality or habit of the mind by which one lives righteously and according to which one cannot act badly. Virtue, because it is a good habit, makes one skillful in doing well that for which he has a capacity. Action, then, is the ultimate end of virtue because virtue tends to perfect the potencies of the soul. This means that definite acts must be performed in order that one become virtuous.

Consequently, a student must bridge the gap between the speculative and the practical orders before he can develop virtue, and this is done by prudence. By directing the practical intellect to do the right things, at the right time, and for the right reason, the virtue of prudence perfects the practical intellect. Therefore, a student must acquire this virtue of prudence in order to be good. Prudence is the key which will unlock all the other doors; it is the moving force which will direct a person toward the good. However, prudence cannot be taught nor can it be imposed by another from on high. It is developed through the successive repetition of good acts and good judgments. By these repeated acts the habit of prudence is formed.

Cultivate Prudence as First Step

It is imperative, then, that prudence be cultivated in the student as the first step on the path of goodness. But how can this be accomplished? Father W. J. Buehler in his book, *The Role of Prudence in Education,* answers this question. Only personal experience can contribute directly to the growth of prudence. The only way to get experience in prudence is by living prudently, and that takes time. Consequently, prudence does not characterize youthful actions because, as an acquired virtue, it is the result of repeated acts which require the experience that can only come with time.

Therefore, it is possible to presume that most of the students in secondary schools lack maturity, and, consequently, they cannot see the good aspects in certain acts. As a result, their wills are not drawn toward the good. Despite the fact that a student's intellect is in possession of the truth, he is unable to appreciate the truth unless he has the necessary prudence. The issue seems circular in shape. The student must desire to do those things which are good, but in order for him to pursue the good, he must know about it. But even knowledge cannot infallibly assure that a student will seek the goodness in certain actions or accept the goodness of certain regulations. To do this, he must possess prudence. However, such a trait comes from a repetition of good selections, judgments, and acts which implies that prudence is not a virtue typical of youth.

There Is a Solution

Nevertheless, there is a solution to this dilemma. Students must be assisted in forming habits which will induce them to seek those things which they know are right and good. In this manner they will be creating a prudential climate within which they will think, act, and speak—an atmosphere which cultivates the virtue of prudence and insures proper discipline.

The first step along this path is to induce the student to act in conformity with regulations on the authority of another. The experience and prudence of an elder can help the youth to form right judgments. In this manner the intrinsic goodness of an act is assured on the authority of another. This authoritative guidance serves to motivate the student to act. With the help of the teacher or guide, the student will be able to recognize that which is good; and when confronted by a set of similar circumstances, the student will be able to elicit acts directed toward the good.

Win Confidence of Students

For some teachers this procedure of direction may be difficult to achieve; nonetheless, they should certainly try. If a teacher is successful in winning the confidence of the students, then obedience will follow without questions asked. When an inferior has complete confidence in the ability of a superior, obedience follows promptly and willingly. The same may be said of a student if he has confidence in his teachers. This confidence is often built on the student's observations of the prudent actions of the teacher, of his respect for law and authority, of his good judgment, of his methodical approach to problems, and of his warm understanding of youth. In this way the student sees in the life of the teacher those many good qualities which the student has been asked to make part of his own life. Consequently, the teacher can direct the student towards moral excellence not only by his words, but also by his good example.

To assist the student in the development of good judgment and the acquisition of prudence, the teacher has another means, and this is coercion. Although coercion should be the last means selected to motivate a student, it can be used legitimately. The right to use coercive measures in order to assure conformity to the laws belongs to the authority of the state, the Church, and the family. The teacher, as a member of the auxiliary society, the school, is entrusted with the parental prerogative to use coercion. According to moralists, the teacher possesses the delegated authority of the parents. Despite this fact, teachers are cautioned to use coercion only as a last measure because of possible negative repercussions.

Although these methods and procedures may not be infallible, they certainly can be helpful in developing youth. It must be remembered that a student is a free agent; he can choose to act or not. Sometimes, despite cogent arguments, good example, and even brute force, a student cannot be reached. In such a situation the teacher should not give up all hope. The student can still be helped through the mysterious workings of prayer and divine grace.

Indirect Methods

In addition to these suggestions which aim directly at reaching the ultimate end of discipline, we should also consider those practices which achieve the goals of discipline through indirect methods. In high school this is often necessary because the immature mind of the student must be led to self-mastery by means of a number of intermediary steps. Youth must be led to appreciate good habits and be encouraged to cultivate them if they are to be effective. The manner or means by which this is done must vary because of individual differences.

There are, however, certain positive principles of discipline which, because they are fundamental, may be efficacious. One of these basic principles is suggestion. Suggestion is a process by which a series of associated ideas follow one another. The notions of cleanliness, neatness, right order, and responsibility can be transmitted by the appearance of the classroom or the sight of the school building. If the school is dirty, run down, in need of paint and repair, and if the furniture is old and initialed, how can the administrator expect the students to be orderly and neat? Everything around them suggests just the opposite.

Imitation

Allied to the principle of suggestion is that of imitation. Man is prone to imitate. By applying this principle in the classroom, students should be influenced toward the good. If the teacher is a model of virtue some of his good qualities will rub off on the students. If the teacher is neat and clean in appearance, the students will adopt his good taste and good example. If the teacher respects the rights of others and is fair and just, the students will be influenced to act in like manner. Consciously or unconsciously, students imitate and copy the patterns set down by the teacher. By using both imitation and suggestion properly, the teacher will have at his command powerful devices which greatly contribute to meaningful discipline.

Another positive principle of discipline is approval. Students, as well as adults, want to belong; they want to comply and to be accepted. Recognition is important for an adolescent because it puts the stamp of approval on his work and increases its value. Psychologically, praise and recognition dispose the student to attempt to uproot his faults. The student realizes that he must remove those qualities which would mark him as disrespectful, disorderly, or defiant. In this way he tries to comply with good order. On the other hand, if a student has no chance to earn legitimate recognition, he may seek the praise of other students by defying authority.

Compassion

Compassion is also a helpful principle in achieving the ends of discipline. A youngster's behavior may be affected by his family conditions, by the breaking up of a home, by friction in the home, or by parental neglect. All or each of these can cause a child to feel isolated and alone. In these instances the child is slighted because the parents are taken up with their own selfish interests. The result is that he feels he does not belong; he is a stranger in his own home. A great deal of uncertainty and mental anguish flow from this lack of affection and from this parental rejection. A sense of insecurity envelopes such a student and he becomes preoccupied with fears about family stability. If there is a lack of love and a lack of attention at home, the student may attempt to satisfy these needs in evil ways. Such a student may return to normalcy by means of compassion.

Understanding

Another principle which could be very beneficial in attaining the goals of discipline is understanding. In order for the teacher to guide the student in developing good habits and avoiding disciplinary pitfalls, the teacher should remember that the high school student is undergoing a physiological and psychological development which has a tremendous impact on him. The student is growing up. Physically he is approaching or has attained bodily maturity, despite the fact that the mental maturity may lag. A teen-ager is sometimes disturbed about the control of this new urge he finds within himself. And yet it gives him a sense of power and independence. He needs guidance and direction, but will not ask for it. The adolescent strives to manage his own life, to decide for himself what he should do and not do. He will look upon the commands and rules of adults as unjustified interferences with his newly-found liberties and capacities, and for this reason he will develop an oppositional state of mind.

A youngster during this period of adolescence is also troubled by another inner conflict, that of the dual standards of behavior and morals, one for him and the other for adults. If something is judged wrong or bad for him and good for adults, he sees a conflict. The youth is told one thing and he observes another in practice. Such a state of affairs confuses an adolescent and causes him to reject rules and regulations imposed on him by authority, whether these be for his own good or for the good of the community. During this period of growth and development the student needs a friend, one who sympathizes with him and is in a position to counsel the student because of an understanding of the problem of youth.

It is my hope that these words may assist the teacher to understand and appreciate, not only what is going on in the classroom, but also within the student.

In this manner the teacher will be able to avoid classroom disorders by foreseeing them and contribute by his wisdom and understanding to the optimum growth of the student. By applying the principles cited, the teacher will be able to assist the student to form a healthy mental attitude toward school life, school activities, and school goals. Then, by constantly striving after the good, the student will pursue good and wholesome ways of acting. When he has reached this lofty plateau, surveillance will be curtailed and regulations reduced, because the ultimate end of discipline—self-mastery—will have been reached.

Some common elements in counseling

William C. Cottle

*Regardless of a counselor's preferences for directive
or nondirective therapy, the counseling situation will
still revolve about common elements. Dr. Cottle
lists five elements which he believes form part of
any counseling process: rapport between counselor
and client, communication and understanding,
knowledge of the "tools" of counseling, changes in
the client, and a structure in which counseling may
proceed. A recognition of common elements may
reduce the friction among techniques of counseling.*

Most articles in the literature about counseling have enumerated the merits of one system while criticizing all the other systems that have been developed. Much time and space have been wasted trying to show that one system of counseling is better than another. It is the purpose of this paper to discuss the elements which appear to be common to all systems of counseling and, therefore, the techniques which are essential to all counselors in their work with clients.

Whether it is called rapport or "a warm, permissive atmosphere," every counselor has to develop a counseling relationship with the client. Such a relationship must be based on *mutual* trust and respect between the counselor and the client. On the part of the client this involves a willingness to change and confidence in the counselor's ability to help bring about such change. This willingness to change includes a knowledge that something is unsatisfactory and a desire to do something about it. It is frequently called readiness for counseling and is at least partially dependent on the amount of anxiety present in the client. Counseling readiness on the part of the client is essential before progress in counseling

Reprinted with permission from the *Personnel and Guidance Journal*, 32:4–8, September, 1953.

can occur. Without it there is nothing forcing the client to work toward changing his behavior.

The counseling relationship on the part of the counselor means acceptance of the client as he is and treating him as a person worthy of respect. The counselor must recognize that the client needs to do the things he does in order to maintain himself as a person. It is a rare client who deliberately does things at odds with society; he does them because they are the only solution he sees to his momentary problems. Therefore it is up to the counselor to help him arrive at a place where he is free to make choices more in harmony with the aims of society. It is up to the counselor to help the client develop more alternative solutions to his problems. This can only be achieved in an atmosphere of mutual trust and respect.

Another phase of the counselor's attempt to develop a relationship with the client is the growth of the client's capacity to solve his own problems. The experienced counselor readily admits that most clients are better able to solve a problem than would usually be expected. They often know more about their attitude toward and reaction to their environment than anyone else ever could know. This is difficult for many educators to accept because they are so used to being the best informed person in an area and therefore the person with the answer. This capacity of the client to solve his own problems, however, is the essence of our belief in democracy and is also the essence of a sound counseling relationship. It permits the client and counselor to share the responsibilities of the counseling interviews.

A third phase of the counseling relationship is the development of an atmosphere of frankness and honesty. To the client this is a feeling that in this interview there is no longer the necessity to hide from others or from himself. He can examine his plans, goals, and values in an atmosphere free from criticism and fear. To the counselor it is a recognition that these matters being discussed are the property of the client and he is entitled to know as much about them as he can tolerate and use at a given time. The counselor hopes eventually to reflect or present all information needed, but he does this in terms of what he estimates the client can use constructively. The counselor tries to prevent a situation where the client feels so threatened he cannot function.

This control of threat in the interview is a major function of the counselor. His training and experience should be such that he can judge the amount of threat the client can handle and take steps to minimize this through acceptance and reflection of client statements. The acceptance of client statements in a matter of fact manner frequently minimizes their threat to the client. So also the choice of the proper words in reflecting meaning back to a client or in phrasing other counselor-talk will minimize or increase the threat to the client. It is at this point that the judgment of the counselor greatly affects the progress of the case.

These factors combine to create what is called the counseling relationship. They are based primarily upon understandings and attitudes of the counselor and the client. These in turn are communicated in various ways. It is this element of communication in the counseling interview which becomes the second major topic of consideration as a common element in counseling.

The term "communication" is used here, rather than semantics, in order to emphasize that there are many ways of expressing meaning between two or more individuals. Communication includes not only words and their meaning, but posture, gestures, voice inflection, and facial expression. Unless attention is called to them, it is highly possible to overlook these ordinary ways of expressing meaning. Failure of typescripts and tape recordings to express in full what transpires in a counseling interview is caused by their inability to present these monoral expressions of meaning.

The shrug of the shoulders may say, "What difference does it make?" The crinkled nose may be saying, "I don't like that kind of thing." The relaxed position of the body may say, "I can sit back and take it easy, too"; while leaning forward in a position of more tension may indicate, "I'm interested, go on and tell me more." There are many ways to express meaning with a minimum of words. The counselor must not only be aware of them and use them, he must know how the client is interpreting them. This constant check on meanings abstracted by the client is one of the most difficult aspects of counseling. It is also one of the most necessary conditions of good counseling.

This skill in communication which the counselor must develop is a two-way skill. It is one where meaning is expressed to the client and where the client's meaning is readily understood. On an oral basis it requires that the counselor be a person of many vocabularies or vocabulary levels. The counselor must be able to use the language of his client to express meanings, rather than the counselor's own vocabulary. In the counseling interview the counselor must adapt to the vocabulary of the client as the chameleon changes color to match his surroundings. He must do this to make it easier for the client to grasp meanings and in order to understand what the client is trying to express.

Lindgren points out that general semantics as a tool in counseling permits us to determine the life values of the client. He says that although we have been accustomed to evaluating people in terms of a norm or average, we must also determine how they depart from this norm as an individual difference. Lindgren emphasizes that this combination of knowledge of the individual attitude of the client and of research data about normative behavior helps the counselor empathize with the client. This means that the counselor must be able to separate denotative or factual elements from connotative or symbolic elements in a client's speech. He must know that a client frequently thinks of occupations in terms of symbolic "signal reactions." He notes the area where these emotionally charged words exist and avoids them in the interview. The counselor cannot discuss the job of the airline hostess in an unemotional setting with the high school junior who is just "dying" to have such a job.

Thus in many ways the counselor communicates to the client and interprets what the client conveys to the counselor. In all of this the main concern is with the meanings being communicated rather than the actual words or gestures used. This is related to a third common element.

The Counselor's Knowledge about People

This third element common to counseling interviews is the breadth and depth of knowledge about people attained by the successful counselor. Such knowledge begins with a liking for people and for sharing experiences with them. It includes experiences in living at all walks of life. It means the scientific knowledge of people acquired through academic courses in the social sciences as well as the practical or applied knowledge acquired from group activity in work and play, from reading, movies, radio, or television. The greater the fund of insightful experiences with people the counselor has acquired, the more apt he is to be able to understand what a client tries to tell in the interview. The richer the counselor's background in all walks of life, the easier and more accurately he perceives the content and meaning of what the client tries to tell him. This background promotes greater empathy with the client. It permits the counselor to look out on the world from the client's eyes without the emotional involvement of the client himself. As a client once said, "Our talking here in an interview is like reading two books on the same subject." By this he expressed his feeling that his perception and that of the counselor were similar, yet sufficiently different that he was able to gain a different perspective.

This background of training acquired by the counselor includes sufficient experience with abnormals to be able to identify abnormalities encountered in counseling and to know whether to attempt treatment or to refer. It involves experience in using biographical data and other recorded data from all pertinent sources. It necessitates that the counselor be able to identify the client's ability to evaluate himself. Is this client's evaluation of self near the evaluation placed on him by society? Can the counselor help the client to change his self-appraisal? Are the client's goals and values mature, self-satisfying, and socially acceptable? These are some of the questions the counselor must be ready to ask and answer out of his background acquired for counseling.

Two other techniques the counselor must acquire as part of his background are the ability to handle pauses in the interview and a knowledge of when and how to terminate an interview. Pauses in an interview can be caused by the client's need to think through a phase of his problem that has just occurred to him. They can produce much valuable insight into behavior. At this point the counselor needs only to know that the client is comfortable and busy, then he waits for the client to break the pause. If, however, the client seems restless and ill-at-ease, it may be a sign that he needs help from the counselor. In this case it may be necessary for the counselor to break the pause in some fashion.

To say that a counselor needs to know when and how to terminate an interview sounds simple, but it is a difficult technique to master. The easiest way is to restrict all counseling interviews to a maximum of one class period. Thus the client knows as the period ends that he must leave and he usually takes responsibility for doing this. In some instances however, the client will be so engrossed in discussing his situation that he loses all sense of time. Here the counselor will need to break in to terminate the interview. In some extreme cases the counselor will need to rise, grasp the client by the arm, and escort him to the door as he discusses with him matters terminating the interview. It is highly convenient to have the receptionist announce the next appointment as another means of terminating an interview.

The Client's Change in Feelings

A fourth common element in the counseling interview is the change in feelings expressed by the client as he progresses in the interviews. Whether they are "vocational" interviews or "therapeutic" interviews (if they can be differentiated), the feelings expressed at the beginning are usually those of confusion, uncertainty, and negation. As the client progresses in the interviews his growth is accompanied by an expression of feeling which changes from a majority of negative statements to those of an ambivalent nature. From a statement like, "I hate my mother because I think she is a mean woman," to one like, "I don't like the way my mother forces me to do things, but maybe she has to make me do them." Continued growth begins to produce a preponderance of positive statements such as "I can understand now how my mother would feel left out of the things my father and I do, and resent it. Probably we're to blame for the way she acts." Usually this change from negative to ambivalent to positive feelings expressed in the interviews can be used as an indicator of the progress of the case when checked against overt changes in the behavior and in the appearance of the client.

The insight which accompanies a changed attitude toward his own behavior on the part of the client plays a part in the change from negative to positive statements of feeling. This insight is the broadened understanding of why the client behaves in this fashion. He understands the reasons why he has been behaving in such a manner and usually finds that there is no longer a need to maintain such behavior patterns; or that he now knows behavior patterns which will accomplish the same thing in a manner more suitable to him at present. Thus his changed attitudes toward his behavior will actually result in changed behavior. He no longer has the need to hide from himself or from society, thus he can use all his effort in constructive work rather than using the majority of his effort to maintain an outmoded form of behavior. This permits him to be more efficient as a better adjusted person.

A fifth common element in counseling is the structuring that takes place. This may consist of an explanation of procedures to be followed during aptitude testing. Such an explanation usually includes efforts to show how the counselor integrates information from records, personal data forms, interviews, and testing to present as complete a picture of the client as possible. It may also include a description of the processes whereby the client contributes to this pool of information. Such matters discussed here may involve how and when he reports for testing, what he does with his personal data form, how he makes future interview appointments, and so forth.

Most structuring concerning the limitations to be observed in counseling interviews is probably just as effective if it is implied rather than spelled out for the client. This will have to be governed by the rapidity with which the client gains insights during the interview. Some clients who are seriously disturbed may not gain insight very fast. For such persons the counselor may need to be quite specific about the procedures and limitations of the interview. On the other hand, such clients may become more disturbed at overt structuring. Actually, there is probably no need to be concerned over whether the structuring is overt or implied. It will have to depend on the counselor's judgment about how the client is being affected in each case. As a general rule counselors feel they are doing a smoother job if the structuring occurs as a natural outgrowth of other phases of the interview.

Summary

In summary then, this paper has considered five elements which appear to be quite common in all systems of counseling. Enumeration of these elements is a part of any attempt to integrate various systems of counseling and develop a common body of counseling theory. The first common element is the relationship developed between the counselor and the client. It is based on an attitude of mutual respect and confidence, counseling readiness, acceptance of the client as a worthy person, faith in the client's capacity to grow, an atmosphere of frankness and honesty, and minimizing the amount of threat in the interview.

The second common element discussed is the way in which the counselor and the client communicate in an interview. It was emphasized that meanings are more important here than surface statements and that communication includes much more than the spoken word. This is why no medium except motion pictures or television can present a complete picture of the counseling interview.

A third common element considered is the breadth and depth of knowledge which the counselor brings to his work. This includes not only the tools and techniques of counseling learned in formal courses, but also the informal study of people during the counselor's leisure and work activities.

A fourth common element is the change in feelings and attitudes which accompanies the progress of a client in interviews. The successful counseling process is accompanied by a change in attitudes toward his own behavior on the part of the client and consequent change from expression of a preponderance of negative feelings to a preponderance of positive feelings. The amount of insight present is a useful measure of the success of the counseling.

The fifth and last common element that was discussed here is the structuring or the limits which are developed to determine how the counseling will proceed.

These are the factors which seem to appear in all systems of counseling. They are the elements which identify the successful counselor whether he is directive, nondirective, or eclectic.

Is there Christian counseling?

Robert B. Nordberg

*In the field of nondirective counseling, the
"pioneering genius," as Professor Nordberg calls
him, is Carl Rogers. In the selection that follows,
Professor Nordberg critically examines some of
Rogers's views in the light of relevant Christian
principles. He also sets forth and defends his
argument that there can and should be a system of
counseling which is legitimately Christian.*

In 1958, the writer proposed a conception of counseling as being not so much
nondirective as noncoercive, nonthreatening.[1] This was not done from desire to
add to the already unnecessarily large vocabulary of the field, nor with any presumption of suggesting a new school of thought. Rather, it was an allegation of
what most "client-centered" or Rogerian counselors actually do, and a proposal
of an outlook that would fit better with their practices than does the typical non-
directivist's epistemology.

Certain questions about this conception have arisen repeatedly in classes,
correspondence, and so forth. The present article will attempt to answer them and
also to face a continuing paradox of Catholics in counseling: Most of our discussions center around the theories of Professor Carl R. Rogers. In one way this is
fitting. Rogers has been the pioneering genius in the field, beyond doubt. At the
level of techniques and descriptive psychology, we are deeply in his debt. In
another way, however, it is frustrating to be obliged to return continually to his
naturalism as against our supernaturalism, his phenomenology as against our
qualified dualism, and his somewhat vague relativism as against our critical

---

[1] R. B. Nordberg, "Counseling: Non-Directive or Non-Coercive?" *Catholic Educational Review*, LVI, No. 1 (January, 1958), 40-44.

Reprinted with permission from *The Catholic Educational Review*, **61:1–6,**
January, 1963.

realism.[2] Is it not possible to build the theory of counseling on a more positive basis, rather than simply reacting to another school of thought? Is not our own theological and philosophical heritage rich and valid enough that it can combine with clinical data in a synthesis that makes its own case, independently of what anyone else happens to be saying? We should look much more to our own intellectual riches before hopping on every existentialist, Zen-ish, phenomenological, or beatnik band wagon that comes rolling along.

Two Views To Be Avoided

Christian doctrine combines with classical philosophy to teach about man that he is a thinking, choosing creature. When such a creature has problems (all the time), how does he solve them? He learns. What is necessary to learning? Two things, basically: the intelligence and the intelligible—the mind that knows and the world that it knows. A teacher or counselor provides neither of those. Counseling is cure by talk. What does this talk accomplish? The client must already understand the meanings of the words or they will convey nothing to him. A teacher or counselor—or writer, even—can, however, by use of language, point to new relationships among elements the student already "knows."

Even then, these relationships must be grasped by the learner. A fundamental fact for counseling, for all communicating, is that *one person cannot think for another.* It often happens, though—especially when ego-involved problems that go deep and have lasted long are at stake—that one does not do much successful thinking without help from another rational being. There are, therefore, two views of counseling to be avoided. The first is that the counselor can manufacture the solution and simply "place" it in the client's head. The second is that the client can do the job by himself. It is the relationship between the two persons that produces the new insights, learning, adjustment, in the counselee. He is, moreover, the most direct cause of these changes, simply because everyone must, in the last analysis, think, learn, act, adjust, for himself.

The main consequence of all this for the counselor is that he must, if he wishes to be effective, work through his client's intelligence and will. And what does this entail? There is a certain total mental set of the client at the outset: all of his knowledge, attitudes, interests, values. This may be thought of as a sort of quantum, a set of blocks that can be arranged into a bigger, better tower. This fits well with Rogers' statement, "Genuine insight includes the positive choice of more satisfying goals"; [3] with Leona Tyler's statement, "The first thing the client needs to achieve is a sense of the general direction he wishes to go, the

[2] These positions are not only "his" but, in general, those of the widely accepted viewpoint that he represents, and in which he has been a leader. Philosophically, this is phenomenology; psychologically, it is permissiveness.

[3] Carl R. Rogers, *Counseling and Psychotherapy—Newer Concepts in Practice* (Boston: Houghton Mifflin Co., 1942), p. 208.

purposes that the decision he makes must serve for him"; [4] with Porter's reminder that "psychotherapy is a process which occurs within the client—not the counselor"; [5] and with many other such injunctions from counselors who regard themselves as client-centered.

Here, nevertheless, is where the philosophical realist must take issue with the Rogerian school, whose adherents insist that the only defensible goals in counseling are those the client chooses for himself, and that this is *why* they are defensible. We can agree heartily that, if he does not choose them, they will not operate in his life, but we cannot agree that their objective merit depends to the slightest degree upon whether he chooses them or not. The writer's earlier treatment of counseling as noncoercive (rather than nondirective) was an attempt to salvage Rogerian techniques within a framework of epistemological realism.[6]

Two Conditions of the Counselee

Now, if all so far is correct, there are two conditions of the counselee with which we must be concerned. The first, X, is his intellectual-psychological state when counseling begins. The second, Y (usually delineated only within a broad latitude), is the hypothetical intellectual-psychological state in which the counselor wants the client to be before the job can be regarded as completed. The challenge is to *help* the client—remember, *he* ultimately does it—to get from X to Y. The "You can't get there from here" attitude cannot be taken by the counselor. X *must* be the point of departure. The counselor may believe, perhaps rightly, that X is a very poor formulation of the student's problem, maybe even not the "real" problem. Nevertheless, because X *is* the student's formulation, it must be used. The only place he can travel from is where he is.

How do you get the client from X to Y? He gets there by a series of rational steps. This suggestion of reasoning may scandalize some voluntarist psychologists. Certainly it would be a rare, albeit interesting, client who would cure himself by producing a series of connected syllogisms. Nevertheless, the client is, in a broad sense, reasoning. He is ordering his thoughts, building them into new patterns. With feelings of self-esteem or self-rejection involved, this may be a very painful process for the counselee. He may try all sorts of unconsciously mediated delays, confusions, and evasions. The counselor needs, therefore, to keep him gently on the track and headed for the station, but the steam that moves the engine must be generated within itself. The opposite of good counseling is also, and not accidentally, the opposite of a good teaching approach: a "because I say so" attitude in the counselor or teacher. It is imperative that the client see every point for himself.

[4] Leona E. Tyler, *The Work of the Counselor* (2d ed.; New York: Appleton-Century-Crofts, 1961), p. 195.
[5] E. H. Porter, Jr., *An Introduction to Therapeutic Counseling* (Boston: Houghton Mifflin Co., 1950), p. 61.
[6] Nordberg, *Catholic Educational Review*, LVI, No. 1, 40-44.

The phrase "client-centered counseling" seems unobjectionable, understood in this sense of working through the client's intelligence and will. Notice the simplicity and clarity of the case for client-centeredness that almost builds itself from the Christian view of man's nature. We can deduce in a rather direct and lucid way what has been evolved among secularists in counseling through dozens of experiments and tons of literature and is still possessed by them only in a very loose, descriptive and rather confused way.

Since our arguments apply mostly to teaching as well, and since most formal teaching is and doubtless should be highly "directive," it would seem that our argument from man's nature and concerning the causality of the client's adjustments does not demonstrate the need for the counselor to avoid expressing opinions and asking questions. This is true. The question of how best to move from X to Y, in teaching or in counseling, depends upon the "subject-matter." It is the earlier-cited element of ego-involvement, of psychological threat, that calls for such counselor-responses as reflection and support. "Emotional upset or the need for defensive behavior by the individual can preclude or prevent learning." [7] Most academic exercises involve no such threat to the self-concept, whereas the insights at the end of the counselee's road may well require some painful surgery on the self-concept. This simple psychological fact, not any sceptical theory of knowledge, is the real reason why we cannot "just tell" the client what to do, how to feel, what to believe. The importance of acceptance of the client depends almost entirely upon this factor of putting him at ease. Again, however, the philosophical realist must accept the sinner but not, in the long run, the sin. Professor Rogers wrote in a letter:

> People who try out a client-centered orientation in their work tend gradually to develop a deep confidence in the ability of the person, as he admits all his experience to awareness, to make his own choices, to be his own guide, even in matters of the most profound importance. I did not know whether this complete freedom would be compatible with a Roman Catholic view, since it seemed to imply that the individual was his own deepest authority.[8]

Rogers was quite right. A premise that "anything goes" if it pleases the client is not compatible with Catholic thought, although we must remember that the counselor's concern with objective norms should be more strategic than tactical. In the same letter, Rogers warned of the danger of accepting a pseudo-Rogerian position. The approach I have suggested is Rogerian in procedures and tactics, objectivist (and therefore non-Rogerian) in philosophy. Whether this is "pseudo" depends upon the viewpoint of one's evaluation, and the position in question might be an emancipation rather than a "danger."

Let the Christian humanist derive the theologico-philosophical facets of his

[7] Edward C. Glanz and Ernest B. Walston, *An Introduction to Personal Adjustment* (Boston: Allyn and Bacon, Inc., 1958), p. 28.
[8] C. R. Rogers, letter to Mr. William H. Schenk; May 8, 1953.

own theory of counseling from his own heritage rather than chasing after the vagaries and anti-intellectualism of phenomenology, Zen Buddhism, and the other contemporary visitors to psychology's heterogeneous garden. Why should we exchange a precious pearl for a bit of gaudy costume-jewelry!

Two Questions about Noncoercive Approach

The question that has come up most often about "noncoercive" counseling is: What do you do if you have been using nondirective responses for quite a while and the student seems no nearer to any insights. Do you then "just tell" him? My answer is that it doesn't matter much what you do in such cases. What you had best do is chalk up a failure, which everyone must do now and again. It may make you feel better to "just tell" at that point, but most counselors will doubtless agree that the chances of your making much impression on the client's future behavior this way are very small. The fact that the reflective technique has "gotten nowhere" may argue that the counselor has been more directive and less reflective than he supposes. It may also mean that the problem is so deeply ego-involved for the client that there simply is not going to be any progress short of psychiatric referral, and perhaps not even then.

Another frequent question has been whether the "noncoercive" approach proposes to distinguish material from formal sin in the client for counseling purposes. This question was excellently treated in a study by Father Lawrence Breedlove.[9] Still another question has been whether the counselor's moral, aesthetic and logical obligations are discharged simply by a negative approach—not encouraging the "bad"—or whether he has a positive obligation to steer towards specific "goods." This was very well treated by Anselment in another study.[10]

When one visits high schools, public and private, often the chief feeling about their guidance programs is that they have become routinized, or always were. The mechanical and obvious are taken care of, the forms are filled out, each student is seen by the counselor twice a year and walks back to class wondering what the interview was about and for. But incipient neuroses, psychoses, and character disorders develop to and beyond the danger point before they are detected. This, of course, can occur under any philosophy of counseling. Surely, however, a Christian holism, entailing a deep sense of what the student ultimately is and why he exists, ought to be conducive to a more inspired approach. And there *can* be, in a legitimate sense—such has been our argument—Christian counseling!

[9] Lawrence Breedlove, "Non-Directive Counseling and Material Sin" (unpublished Master's thesis, Department of Education, The Catholic University of America, 1959).

[10] Joseph Anselment, "Counseling in the Light of Factors Limiting Free Choice" (unpublished Master's thesis, Department of Education, The Catholic University of America, 1961).

The limits of confidentiality

Alexander A. Schneiders

*A much-discussed and much-misunderstood problem
—the one of confidentiality—is examined in this
article. The author essays to set the limits of
confidentiality: Is it ever permissible for a counselor
to relay information to school administrators or
parents? Answers to the question of confidentiality
must be given clearly and unequivocally, for the
foundation of client confidence rests upon them.*

Everyone engaged in counseling or psychotherapy agrees that the person to whom personal or confidential material is entrusted is bound by certain definite principles of secrecy or confidentiality. The information imparted comes under the heading of the *entrusted secret*—information revealed under the condition that it be kept secret. This condition need not be explicitly defined, since it is understood from the nature of the relationship between counselor and client. There is in effect an implicit contractual relationship which imposes the obligation of confidentiality, and the professional secret is a special and rigorous type of entrusted secret, which imposes on the counselor a serious moral and social obligation to guard it very carefully.

This obligation varies with the nature of the information imparted and the effect that revealing it would have on the client. The obligation is most serious when such revelation would do serious harm to the client, damage his reputation, or cause him undue embarrassment. Confidentiality ceases to exist when the information given is common knowledge or does not possess the quality of secrecy.

Rules and Exceptions

Granting the validity of such rules, there are situations in which it would be difficult if not imprudent to enforce them. If confidentiality were an absolute, and

Reprinted with permission from the *Personnel and Guidance Journal*, 41:252–254, November, 1963.

the imparting of the information were regarded as a violation of the rights of the counselee at all times, it would be exceedingly difficult for counselors to fulfill their functions; and it would be equally difficult for administrators to be of adequate help to students. In other words, there are certain actual *limits* to confidentiality that must be recognized if the counselor is to accomplish his tasks. Actually, there are two questions here. To what extent must we limit ourselves in the use of information imparted in counseling, and, to what extent must we resist encroachment on confidentiality? It is the first question that we are most concerned with here.

These two questions raise a number of others. If there are limits to confidentiality, or if confidentiality is relative rather than absolute, under what circumstances should information be withheld or transmitted? Also, we must determine what kind of information can be released and to whom it can be given. Is the counselor obligated to reveal the limits of confidentiality to a client before he accepts any information? There is also the problem of determining priority of allegiance, since the counselor owes some allegiance to the institution as well as to the client. The same holds true with regard to the parents of the client. Finally, is the obligation of confidentiality lessened when the information is used for instruction, publication, or staff conference?

Let us consider briefly some possible uses of confidential material. Considering first the intramural situation, there are a number of persons who may become involved in the relaying of information, including faculty advisors, deans, counseling staff, counsulting psychiatrists, and persons involved in the staff conference. Also, such information might be useful to research programs or publications, or to reports requested by various persons or committees interested in the client. In each instance, communication of confidential material may be unavoidable, necessary, or even professionally desirable.

Counselors must determine also what rights parents have to certain information regarding their children. Sometimes the parent alone can contribute effectively to the solution of a particular problem and the counselor must determine which responsibility takes precedence. In still other extra-mural situations reports to agencies or outside persons might become necessary, or the counselor may be required to give testimony because a civil court refuses to recognize his right to privileged communication. Detailing these possible uses of confidential material does not imply that it should be used in this way. In some instances, as with the staff psychiatrist, it may be perfectly ethical to communicate an entrusted secret, whereas in others there is a great deal of disagreement as to what is permissible. In all instances the basic rights of the counselee and the principles of confidentiality must be carefully safeguarded.

Obviously the limits of confidentiality will be influenced by the kinds of material involved. It is common practice to communicate certain materials to faculty advisors, deans, and similar personnel, and just as common to withhold other material. Thus a high school record or college board test results might be shared with the faculty advisor, whereas interview material is often securely guarded.

In general, the practice seems to be that personal and objective data, including objective test data, may be guardedly communicated to responsible persons; whereas the more intimate and confidential material of the interview is communicated only to carefully selected persons, and often only under the condition of a written release from the counselee. Thus it is important to distinguish the possible uses of material as well as the types of communicable material. The limits of confidentiality have to be adapted also to the characteristics of different situations. A university counseling center does not function in the same way as a psychological clinic, nor does a clinic function in the same way as a social service agency. General principles of confidentiality always apply regardless of setting but specific uses of material vary from one setting to another.

Principles and Their Application

From these observations certain principles of confidentiality and communication emerge quite clearly. (1) The obligation of confidentiality is relative rather than absolute since there are conditions which can alter it. (2) Confidentiality depends on the nature of the material so that material which is already public or can easily become so is not bound by confidentiality in the same way as is the entrusted secret. (3) Material that is harmless does not bind the counselor to confidentiality. (4) The material that is necessary for a counselor or an agency to function effectively is often released from the bonds of confidentiality. (5) Confidentiality is always conditioned by the intrinsic rights of the counselee to his integrity and reputation, to the secret, and to resist unjust aggression. Such rights can be protected by the counselor even against the law. (6) Confidentiality is limited also by the rights of the counselor to preserve his own reputation and integrity, to resist harm or aggression, and to preserve privileged communication. (7) Confidentiality is determined and limited by the rights of an innocent third party and by the rights of the community.

These seven principles are general in nature and have to be interpreted for each situation. The rights of the counselor have to be scrupulously defined as do the rights of an innocent third party. Also the principle of the common versus the individual good has to be spelled out carefully, in order to preserve the rights of the counselee. In each instance a set of norms has to be worked out in order to define the exact limits of confidentiality.

While such norms cannot be defined adequately here, there are several principles that can be noted. For example, as long as the client retains the right to a secret, it must be kept even though harm befalls an innocent party. When this right is forfeited the obligation ceases to exist. The obligation of secrecy lapses when (1) the common welfare demands revelation, (2) the secret is invalid, (3) there is unjust aggression, (4) the client gives consent, or (5) there is publication of the secret. Care must be taken with point number four when there is joint ownership of a secret to see that consent is obtained from all persons involved. In addition, the revelation of confidential material is permitted when to do so would prevent serious harm to the client, the assumption being that the client himself would give permission in order to prevent harm to himself. An innocent third party may be protected by the revelation of confidential material, but only when the client is an unjust aggressor. If the common welfare demands keeping the secret, it must be kept even in the face of grave danger.

Certain rules must be followed in communicating material. The professional secret may be revealed only to the extent necessary to meet the situation effectively, and it may be revealed only to the person or persons who have a strict right to the information. When a secret is lawfully revealed, the recipients are placed under the obligation of the entrusted secret. Such communication ordinarily should be carefully controlled by the written consent of the client. When all of these principles are carefully observed, the counselor should not find it too difficult to apply the limits of confidentiality in a sensible manner and to arrive at a good judgment concerning the communication of confidential material.

Discipline and counseling: are they incompatible?

Rev. Thaddeus J. O'Brien, O.Carm.

In some schools, particularly Catholic high schools, the counselor and the disciplinarian are one and the same person. When this is the case, does the student perceive that person in such a way as to endanger their counseling relationship? Father O'Brien thinks not. He bases his conclusion, at least in part, on an experiment involving senior girls and their counselors in two Chicago area public high schools. The experiment and Father O'Brien's views on the compatibility of discipline and counseling are discussed in the next selection, which is based on an address he gave at a convention of the American Personnel and Guidance Association.

Do high school students perceive a counselor with an *authoritative* role as being, by that fact, more *authoritarian* than a counselor who has no such role? What follows will be an attempt to answer that question, or at least suggest the direction in which the answer may be found.

The term "role" is here used in Getzel-Guba sense: "a set of complementary expectations involving the actor (that is, the individual considered in abstraction from his personality and roles) in his interaction with other individuals." [1] The role, then, is a complexus of complementary behaviors, a series of tasks to be met which create a certain impression with other individuals.

Reprinted with permission from *The Catholic Counselor*, 7:3–9, Autumn, 1962.

Role and Personality

The importance of the definition lies in the distinction that "role" is seen as something quite apart from personality. The role is like a mask inserted between a man and the world outside him. A man wears his role very much as the Greek actor wore the *persona* (the mask) through which he spoke his lines in a play.

There is a real danger that the *persona,* the role, be mistaken for the person. Even the actor himself could make this mistake. A manager in a big firm, for example, could become so used to commanding subordinates that he would continue to command, even when away from his work. He could order his wife and children. His role might then be conceived as engrafted onto his personality and affect other aspects of his life.

There is also real danger that the counselor with an authoritative role could actually become authoritarian. The concern here, however, is not basically with the counselor but with the student's perception of the counselor. For the sake of simplicity, therefore, it will be assumed that the counselor is able to separate his role from his true personality. The question is: can the student make this separation? Or, put another way, does a counselor's authoritative mask so affect a student's perception of him as to be a block to the establishment of a counseling relationship?

Authoritative

Note the use of "authoritative role" and not "authoritarian role." The reason can be found in the meaning of the words. "Authoritative" means possessing authority, entitled to obedience and respect. "Authoritarian," on the other hand, means one who is favorable to the principle of authority. In the former word, authority seems to stand apart, to be detached from the person; in the latter word, authority seems to cling to the person, to be an outlook, a judgement—and it may even denote an adjunct of personality. The word "authoritative" is more consistent with the concept of role.

Concretely, "authoritative" is taken to imply the possession of disciplinary power. In the school it would mean the power (and often the necessity) to assign tasks, detention, suspensions—even to expel a student if circumstances warrant it. By the same token, it could mean the power to bestow institutional rewards on pupils. The authoritative role, then, is a particular set of complementary expectations brought about by a counselor's possessing power of authority, power which can be punitive and which demands obedience and respect from the students.

By student perceptions is meant the way a student sees a counselor, the impact of a counselor on a student in their interactions. Does the student see a given counselor as warm, friendly, understanding, or cold and forbidding? And if a student sees a counselor as uninviting, can this be attributed to an authoritative role which the counselor inhabits? The adolescent, of course, is at a period in life when he is trying to establish independence. Authority does not set well with many adolescents even when it is from God. The problem being probed here is how does a student feel about confiding in someone who has the power to punish him?

Positive Perceptions

As a direct offshoot of the basic question, a second poses itself: is it possible for someone holding this threatening power of authority to establish an atmosphere of confidence in which ease-of-expression on the part of the client is possible? This is really a question of counseling effectiveness. Can a counselor so separate himself from his role that the student sees this and responds to the counselor apart from the authoritative role? Or is it possible that the role is actually an aid to counseling effectiveness, that the student places a positive rather than a negative value on the authoritative role of the counselor?

To test the basic question two counselors and the preceptions students demonstrated toward them were studied. One counselor had an authoritative role coupled with the task of counseling; the other had no disciplinary power whatsoever.

Two suburban public high schools cooperated in this study. The two schools are located in communities of similar size and population dispersion. Both communities are suburbs of the Greater Chicago Area. The counselors cooperating in the study both worked with senior girls. The authoritative counselor, in addition to her counseling tasks, had the duty of handling tardiness, suspensions, and disciplinary action of every kind. The non-authoritative counselor had no disciplinary power whatsoever. While she was kept informed on problem students and was consulted by the dean in particular cases, actual discipline was out of her hands.

Attitude Scaling

The experimental design was simple. An authoritarianism scale was used. In each school thirty students took the test along with their counselor. After a certain time lapse, the test was re-administered, this time to the students alone. At this second testing, although the same instrument was used, the instructions were different: students were directed to answer the questions as they felt their counselor would answer them. They were to put themselves in her place and then reply to the questionnaire.

The instrument employed was basically that developed by Webster, Sanford, and Freedman.[2] With the exception of ten questions dealing with religious conviction, and simplification of language in two questions, this test was used verbatim.

Two advantages were seen in the use of this test:

1. Since the test is fairly recent and since it is not one of the standard tests in the field, it was reasoned that there would be less likelihood of the counselor knowing what the answers *should* be.

2. The test was standardized on freshman college girls. The present subjects, seniors in high school, were considered in many ways to be similar to such a group.

Knowledge of Duties

In addition to the test, several questionnaires were administered to the students. It was hoped that from the answers to these questionnaires supplementary information on the students might be obtained. The type of information sought was the student's ideas as to the range of areas in the counselor's duties; the subjects the student was currently pursuing; the relationship over and above the counseling relationship the student had with the counselor; student opinion as to whether the counselor had been any special help to the student, and if so, in what way.

Students were known to the investigator only by numbers assigned them by their counselor. It was intended that anonymity might encourage a more frank response to questions.

It was reasoned that the two testings were necessary. The first test would provide some idea about the characteristics of the girls in the sample. It served as a check to see whether the two samples were similar in temperament. The first test also served as a further control. Since it was assumed that a person with an authoritarian personality will see others as being more authoritarian than they really are, if a student obtained a high authoritarian score that fact might account for the student's high rating of her counselor. The second testing was, of course, the core of the study, since it yielded a measure of the extent to which the student found the counselor to be authoritarian.

Research Results

The tests were administered at the two schools in March and April of 1961. Twenty-eight seniors were present for both testing days in the authoritative school; thirty-one in the non-authoritative school.

In summary, the following results were evident:

1. The scores of the two counselors were low, indicating a low authoritarian factor. The prime authoritative difference between the counselors was their difference in role. One had authoritative tasks, the other did not.

2. The two groups of students were similar as to courses pursued, and mean score on the pretest (self-rating with respect to authoritarianism). Students in both the authoritative school and the non-authoritative school were practically the same. The similarity between two groups therefore was a constant against which the differences in perceptions of the counselor (if any appeared) should have stood out in bold relief.

3. When the students took the test as if they were the counselor, the mean score in both schools tended to be *lower* than the students had rated themselves. (The mean on test #1 for the authoritative school was 79.17; for test #2 it was 76.21. In the non-authoritative school the mean on test #1 was 80.77; for test #2 it was 78.38.) Both groups of students saw the counselor as lower in authoritarian traits than they saw themselves. Moreover, the differences between schools with respect to student self-perceptions and perceptions of their counselor were minimal. The two groups of girls did not see the counselors differently.

Role Dominance

In the face of the foregoing what can be said? First of all, it appears that the students in the authoritative school did not have perceptions of their counselor different from those held by the girls in the non-authoritative school. Hence, it does not seem that the discipline role in the authoritative school proved to be an influence upon student perceptions of their counselor.

Would it be true to say that all students would see the two counselors in the same way? The data do not warrant such a statement. The groups tested were all seniors in high school. They were either seventeen or eighteen years old. A reasonable level of maturity might be supposed in such a group. It is a question whether the results would have been the same given a less mature group. A boy or girl in early adolescence might have presented a much different picture. Conflicts with authority usually reach their peak in a boy or girl of thirteen, but the slackening-off period does not come immediately after that.[3] The point is that a boy's or girl's place in adolescent development might make a difference in the perception of authority. Generalization outside the age bracket of late adolescence might be dangerous.

Question of Secrecy

Can it be said then that, given a mature adolescent, there is no reason for separating counseling and discipline? Again, to say such a thing would mean blinding oneself to some very real problems. The most obvious of these is the time factor: discipline and counseling in the normal large American high school are each full-time jobs. To burden one person with both tasks, in normal circumstances, would be to demand too much.

There is also the question of professional secrecy. In the counseling interview a counselor might receive confidential information calling for strong disciplinary action. Burdened with the responsibilities of discipline and guidance, the counselor would find himself in a very perplexing situation. It is not inconceivable that the counselor might be torn between his duty to the community and his duty to the individual who rendered this confidence.

In the questionnaire given to the students in the authoritative school the girls were asked to give reasons why the counselor should or should not have disciplinary power. The majority of the students felt that the two tasks should go together. One may say, of course, that since these students knew no other system it might be expected that they would feel this way. Nevertheless, a study of their reasoning shows that they felt very real benefits accrue to them because disciplinary power resides in their counselor. One student wrote: "I don't think there is any practical reason to separate the duties." Another said, "I believe that discipline and guidance go together. Our counselor knows the person much better and can help to a greater extent." Others wrote in similar fashion: "There wouldn't be much success with students unless there was discipline involved." "She knows you and your past better than most people in the school and can tell what you deserve."

Advantages

These comments cover student reasoning on the point. The girls touched several distinct advantages to the combination of guidance and discipline.

In fact, they indicated something that has been largely overlooked by counselors—the possibility of discipline *as* being *supportive* to the student's perception of the counselor, not simply non-detrimental. Many of these girls felt that the combination of tasks gives the counselor a more complete picture of the student; it aids the counselor by giving a broader framework upon which to hang suggestions and counsel. Following the same line of reasoning it can be seen that if disciplinary duties can be hamstrung by knowledge received in the counseling interview, the reverse can also be true. There are countless times when a knowledge of the student's inner life—family situation, personal problems, companions —could bring about a much more just handling of violation of school rules.

One cannot help wondering whether the reason why many counselors have such strong feelings about keeping discipline and guidance separate is the way in which the tasks are thrust upon them in their everyday school situation. A teacher, for example, will send a student to the counselor because the student was misbehaving in class. The boy or girl will come in bearing a note: "Do something with this child!" The boy or girl enters the counseling interview with feelings of hostility toward the teacher and with considerable confusion about the counselor's role. Normally, the student has no reason for linking discipline and his counselor. And yet the student knows that he has been sent to the counselor for some type of disciplining. Since the student has no disciplinary expectations for the counselor, the whole situation just does not make sense.

Penalty and Respect

However, if the counselor has a disciplinary role, much of the above problem disappears. The student is in a situation where he expects discipline and guidance, from one person. The student knows that the counselor has the power to make a penal judgment but also the student understands that, as a counselor, this man or woman respects him as a person. The student might well speak more confidently in his own defense knowing that the counselor is able not only to listen and sympathize but also that he is able to do something if the youth's complaint is just.

It seems to have been largely overlooked by many counselors that it is impossible to escape authority entirely. The counselor must, in fact, stand for authority. Any counselor who has successfully segregated himself from all authority and who has further indicated this to the students committed to his care, does serious injury to these students. To attempt to reject or entirely to separate oneself from authority leaves the student with the impression that there is something wrong with it. Such a false notion can do great injury to young minds. Discipline is a normal adjunct of life. It is not only inescapable; it is necessary. The counselor cannot separate himself from discipline if he is actually going to help a child develop into a healthy-minded individual. As Berdie puts it:

> Counselors who have warned us of difficulty, and even impossibility, of relating counseling and discipline seldom have concerned themselves with the meaning of the latter term. Discipline according to the dictionary means 'to educate; to develop by instruction and exercise; to teach, to order and correct the operation of, as one's talents or faculties; to train in self-control and obedience; to give standards.' How can one deny the discipline role of any counselor, and equally important, how can one discipline without counseling? The dilemma properly concerns the nature of the organization of a counseling program rather than only its function.[4]

Fusion of Tasks

It seems that, in this question of setting authority in its proper perspective, the fusion of counseling and discipline has great dividends to offer.

A short paper of this kind finds more questions than answers. The potentialities for further work in this area are overwhelming, and it is hoped that further explorations into the field are not too far off. Until studies of wider scope come to light, however, this study serves some purpose. The basic question of the paper has been answered negatively: students studied did not perceive the authoritative counselor as being more authoritarian than the other counselor. Because of the real limitations of the study, but a single generalization can be safely maintained; *it is an oversimplification to say that discipline and counseling are incompatible.* If nothing else has been proved, this statement in itself will be of interest and importance to the guidance profession.

REFERENCES

1. J. W. Getzels and E. G. Guba, "Role Conflict and Personality," *Journal of Personality,* 1955, 24, p. 74.
2. Harold Webster, Nevitt Sanford, and Mervin Freedman, "A New Instrument for Studying Authoritarianism in Personality," *Journal of Psychology,* 1955, 40, pp. 73-84.
3. Elizabeth B. Hurlock, *Developmental Psychology.* N. Y.: McGraw-Hill Co., 1959, p. 246. See especially Chapters VII and IX for a more complete picture of the differences between early and late adolescence.
4. Ralph Berdie. "Counseling Principles and Presumptions," *Journal of Counseling Psychology,* 1959, 6, p. 181.

Counseling versus discipline: another view

James Michael Lee

*In the next article, Dr. Lee maintains that counseling
and discipline are such distinct functions that the
same person cannot perform them both
simultaneously. A disciplinarian might give counsel,
he says, but does not do counseling. In the course
of his paper, he sets forth his views on the nature of
counseling and the role of the counselor.*

In the autumn, 1962 issue of the *Catholic Counselor* Father Thaddeus J. O'Brien, O. Carm., reported a study which had as its main thesis the proposition that discipline is not detrimental to counseling but indeed is supportive of it. This assertion is an important one because it touches not only upon the existential relationship between counselor and client, but also touches upon the de facto situation in many public and most Catholic secondary schools, viz., that the counseling and disciplinary functions are united in a single person. If such a thesis is valid, then much of the professional thinking about secondary school guidance is incorrect and much of the practice in secondary school guidance situations is correct.

A main feature of that presentation argues in effect that *role* and *personality* are always operationally separated. On theoretical grounds, there would appear to be considerable doubt about this thesis. In the literature, role has come to be closely associated with *expectation*. Thus, for example, the school position of counselor is a role, and with this role there are automatically evoked certain expectations in the pupils even before the counselor ever walks into his counseling office on the first day of the term.

Reprinted with permission from *The Catholic Counselor*, 7:114–118, Spring, 1963.

But the cardinal point is that expectation does not arise from role only; nor does interaction between counselor and client affect the client's perception of the counselor solely or even primarily in terms of counselor role.

The client perceives the counselor not primarily in terms of role, but in terms of what that particular counselor is in the existential order, i.e., the total personality and behavior matrix of the counselor. Two counselors in a school may have precisely the same role, but the student perceptions of these counselors will be far more conditioned by the different personalities and behaviors of these counselors than by their specific role.

Personality Matrix

Indeed a particular teacher may be selected by the student to counsel him about personal and vocational problems. The pupil comes to that teacher with the expectation of finding a trusted, nonthreatening friend who will help him solve his problem. This perception arose not from the teacher's role—which is thought of as being chiefly instructional—but from that particular teacher's personality and behavior matrix.

Strang (*12*, p. 121) has noted in this connection that a counselor's reputation is probably the most important single factor in contributing to the success of his work. This reputation is not so much *role-derived* as *personality-derived*, or else everyone having the formally designated counselor role would be perceived by the students in the exact same manner. Pupil expectations then, like their perceptions, seem to derive far more from personality than from role.

The more the personality of the counselor (or anyone else for that matter) is known by the students, the less important will be his *formal role* in their eyes; the less the personality is known, the more important becomes the formal role.

This whole preamble is not to minimize the existence or effect of role, but rather to view it in its proper place.

Eternal Power

But what is this personality and behavior matrix of the counselor which the client encounters? Certainly it is a matrix which is conditioned by his role or set of roles. If it were not so conditioned or influenced, the roles would be inoperative, and Father O'Brien's original question would be without meaning. But disciplinary role implies a *punitive power*. This power is of necessity external, exclusively directive, and threatening. It is external because it is imposed upon the student by the administrative authorities. It is exclusively directive because it spells out in precise terms what these authorities wish the student to do or undo. It is threatening because of its essence, punishment must be threatening to a person.

Therefore it may be concluded that if the counselor who is also charged with being a disciplinary arm of the administration is performing both roles effectively, he must be both: (1) external, exclusively directive, and threatening; and (2) internal, not exclusively directive, and nonthreatening. Certainly there is no counselor, however directivist, who would advocate that a counselor should be the first of these. Thus Williamson, regarded by many as being the most celebrated champion of the directivist school, has shown in his recent writings that directivism would not support the first set of roles.

On the basis of the foregoing analysis the implications that role can be operational or existentially separated from personality, that the students primarily perceive roles at once rather than personalities, and that the same person can exercise two conflicting roles would appear to be in question. Indeed the empirical study, probably did not measure *role* perception but rather *personality* perception.

Role versus Personality

If the disciplinarian's role is punitive, what is the counselor's role as interpreted by the present writer? Probably the best reply is that he has no specific role. He is ambivalent, a person through whom the stream of existence courses, one whose role or mask is not in any way clear or distinct so that the personality of the interacting client is not determined to any large measure by the etched, clearly perceived role of the counselor. In a recent statement on this counselor neutrality, Rogers (9, p. 417) has noted: "I hypothesize that personal growth is facilitated when the counselor is what he is, when in the relationship with his client he is genuine and without 'front' or facade, openly being the feelings and attitudes which at that moment are flowing in him." This concept will be discussed later; suffice it to say here the disciplinarian without a definite role would be no disciplinarian. Hence the incompatibility of discipline with counseling.

From comments at the beginning of Father O'Brien's report, it appears that there is a chance that the *personalities* of the counselors masked their roles, and so what occurred was not pupils' perceptions of the *roles* (which the investigation sought) but of the *personalities*. The fact that both counselors had low authoritarian levels adds fuel to this possibility. It is quite possible and indeed perhaps probable that these pupils had rarely or never perceived much separation of the counseling and disciplinary roles. Hence it was perfectly natural for them to respond as they did. Their apperceptive mass may therefore have forced a verification of the hypothesis. Nor can this be explained by pupil comments, for pupil comments, after all, are verbalizations of what they responded to in the test, and are just as much conditioned by the very apperceptive and existential forces which caused them to respond as they did to the instrument.

There have been few empirical investigations on this phase of education. One of the best of such studies, that of Kounin and Gump, seems to have reached an opposite position. These researchers (6) concluded that pupils who have punitive teachers "manifest more aggression in their misconducts, are more unsettled and conflicted about their misconduct in school, and are less concerned with school-unique values" than pupils who have non-punitive teachers.

Self Discipline

Discipline can mean and indeed has meant many things to many educators, as Sheviakov and Redl (*10*) have noted. Throughout most of his report, Father O'Brien equates discipline with punitive measures and the power to exercise these punitive measures. Toward the end of the article, he makes discipline synonymous with education and the inculcation of self-discipline. Now there is a vast difference between punitive discipline and self-discipline. In another place (*7*) the present writer has summarized the research investigation on this question, with the conclusion that punitive discipline is injurious to the inculcation of self-discipline in the pupil. Certainly all discipline, whether punitive discipline or self-discipline should be guidance-minded. Strang (*13*) has emphasized for many years that discipline can and should be primarily a guidance vehicle. To Strang as well as to most counseling theorists and guidance workers, discipline is not necessarily punitive, nor is it solely punitive.

There is an implication that it has been school counselors in the field who have strong positive feelings about keeping counseling and discipline separate because by effecting such a separation these guidance workers will avoid to some extent at least, the common difficulty of having misbehavior cases of all sorts thrust upon them. These counselors seem to wish to eliminate the common impression that the guidance specialist is the miracle man in the school. However, it has been the theorists, not the practitioners, who have most stressed this separation. It is interesting to note in this connection that in the index of Father Charles Curran's important book, *Counseling in Catholic Life and Education,* there is no listing for discipline. On the other hand, Hill and Green's survey (*4*) of guidance counselors in public schools showed that some of those persons thought that disciplinary responsibilities should be part of their function.

Fusion of Functions

Indeed the fusion of disciplinary and counseling functions is particularly common in Catholic high schools. Father Philip L. Stack's nationwide investigation (*11*) of guidance practices in Catholic secondary schools disclosed that in nearly two-thirds of the Catholic high schools surveyed, the disciplinary and guidance functions were performed by the same person. A study (*3*) by Harris of over 100 Catholic high schools in New York State revealed that in nearly two-thirds of these schools the counseling services were given not by a guidance specialist but by the school principal.

In the hands of less informed Catholic educators, this proposition may be the trumpet upon which an apologia for the wisdom of present policies will be played for the benefit of the parents, teachers and lay public. The present writer's review (*7*, Chapter 4) of the pertinent research on discipline concluded that administrators are almost exclusively interested in external misbehaviors of pupils, while mental hygienists are of the opinion that the internal, psychoemotional conflicts are more serious.

A current research project by the present writer suggests that there are very few administrators in the diocesan superintendents' office which have been given any concrete assistance in terms of guidance materials to secondary schools or to guidance specialists in developing their guidance programs. Therefore it remains for the Catholic guidance and counseling theorists and practitioners not to condone or in any way abet the current unfortunate state of affairs, but rather to more clearly and openly state the case for counseling *qua* counseling rather than a diluted or disguised form of discipline.

Problem: Priest-Counselor

A special problem of the interrelationship of counseling and discipline is that of the priest-counselor. Of this unique problem, Father Charles F. Donovan, S.J. has written: "Many Catholic personnel workers are themselves vowed to obedience, or they work in a milieu where obedience is a primary virtue. It is all too easy to transfer the superior-subject relationship of the religious community to the school situation, and covertly assume the role of superior to whom unquestioning obedience is owed by the students."

In another direction, does the disciplinary power which a priest has by virtue of his office impede his counseling role? Or do the merciful and ministerial roles of the priest compensate for his authoritativeness?

The problem of religious obedience and counseling raised by Father Donovan is currently being explored by a Holy Cross priest working toward his doctorate in education at the University of Notre Dame. While his particular area of interest is the possible conflict between the religious life and being a university administrator, nonetheless his research has great implications for the religious priest as a guidance worker.

The second direction of the problem was discussed by Hagmaier and Gleason. These clerics (2) concluded that the priest-counselor is primarily a listener. Certainly a disciplinarian cannot be *primarily* a listener; he must be a doer, an enforcer. This creates a role conflict in a priest, who is properly habituated to spiritual command.

Even clerical garb creates of itself an authoritative role perception which is conceived of by many Catholics as commanding, disciplinary, and not one-of-us. This is why the priest-workers laid down the soutane in their plunging into the milieu, and why some priests engaged in depth therapy in our own country do not wear clerical attire in their encounters with their clients.

A Catholic psychologist of note is even now engaged in empirical research on the question of whether the clerical or religious role *in se* has an effect on the visual perception of Catholics. Thus the discussion has once again returned to its earlier axis, viz. the relationship between role and personality, the primacy of personality, and the conditioning effect of role.

Non-directivism

Certainly any connotation of punitive discipline has no place within the framework of non-directivism. Most counseling theorists writing today seem to have incorporated enough non-directivism into their thinking so that only the extreme directivists could possibly hold such a proposition. Even Nordberg, whose position as a counseling theorist might be described as "conservative," eschews alignment with directivism (8). Though he avoids non-directivism, he clearly favors a theory and practice which he terms "non-coercive." But any sort of punitive discipline is ipso facto coercive.

Of the many underpinnings of non-directivism, five may be identified as illustrative of the incompatibility of discipline and counseling from the point of view of this theory: (1) The counselor realizes that he does not know the answer. A disciplinarian knows the correct answer, the appropriate behavior, else how would he be able to know what to punish, whom to punish, or how to punish? (2) The counselor does not judge a client to be right or wrong, but reflects feeling and withholds judgment. But punishment is the enactment of a judgment. (3) There is a completely permissive, nonthreatening atmosphere in the counseling interview. Discipline of its nature is threatening to the pupil, and thus destroys permissiveness, the openness of the client, the free offering of his being to another. (4) The counselor does little talking. Punishment, if administered properly and constructively, requires that the punisher not only spell out fully the details of the punishment but also the reason for the punishment and finally give an admonition to the pupil to avoid future misbehavior. (5) The client releases hostility, discharges guilt feelings and gradually perceives the solution for himself. Indeed a pupil is usually punished precisely for releasing hostility; to do it in front of the person who is to discipline him would only convince the disciplinarian of the merits of the punishment—it might even motivate him to increase the punishment.

Unique Experience

What are some of the essentials of a counseling situation which make it a unique type of experience? And are these essentials compatible with discipline in the punitive sense of this term? The first essential of a counseling situation is that it be a liberating learning experience. In his brilliant essay, Father Adrian L. van Kaam, C.S.Sp., has described the counseling situation from the viewpoint of an existential psychologist (5): "Counseling is essentially a process of making-free, a humanizing of the person who has lost his freedom in sectors of his existence where he can no longer transcend his life situation by giving meaning to it."

Does punitive discipline effect an existential manumission from the psychological and emotional chain which binds certain aspects of the client's being? Does it freely permit the person himself to effect this manumission? In a counseling situation a person learns to become himself. In a punitive disciplinary situation, the person is told what to do, or even at times what to become.

The second essential of a counseling situation is that it effect a deep personal relationship between the counselor and the client. In Father van Kaam's words: "People learn to hide the personal world in which they live in order to protect themselves from being misunderstood, humiliated, condemned or abused."

Without a deep permissive personal relationship, the client will have the moat of his psychological and existential defense systems wholly or partially filled, and the portcullis to his being will never be raised. The fear of disapproval and condemnation is to Father van Kaam one of the greatest barriers to a deep personal relationship. From such a relationship flows permissiveness. But punitive discipline is of its nature a disapproving act, a condemnatory act, a humiliating act (for the pupil); therefore discipline seems incompatible with counseling.

It would seem from this discussion that if the counselor does stand for authority, he is no longer a counselor. A counselor must be *praeter auctoritatem*, else a permissive, open counseling climate cannot ensue.

The third essential of a counseling situation is that it promote pupil self-direction. The pupil must come to the insight either by himself (non-directivist), or be guided to develop the insight by the counselor (directivist). However he should not be *told* the insight, or what is worse, have the insight presented to him in a punitive package, which is what is done in a disciplinary interview. *Punishment* is externally administered, and as such is not *intrinsically* promotive of self-direction. Discipline seems therefore incompatible with counseling.

The fourth essential of a counseling situation is that it be exploratory. A disciplinary situation is conducive to pupil exploration only in the way in which he can seek to avert the punishment, or attempt to please the disciplinarian by mouthing things which the disciplinarian would like to hear, e.g., how the pupil will mend his ways. But counseling exploration is of a different order—it is projecting one's existence into new areas of reality, of savoring these new areas, of trying to determine whether his existence and the new realities will mesh harmoniously. It is an expansion of being.

The projecting of one's existence demands a positively toned psychoemotional climate, and is impossible in a situation which is threatening or even neutral. The engine of one's existence—projection—needs a warm climate to function properly; it will fail to start or will immediately stall if the icy winds of threat blow on it. Discipline is such an icy wind, and so is incompatible with counseling.

To sum up in a brief sentence, a "counselor" who is also a disciplinarian may give counsel, but he does not do counseling.

REFERENCES

1. Charles F. Donovan, Christian humanism and Catholic guidance. *Readings for Catholic counselors*, 2nd ed.
2. George Hagmaier, C.S.P. and Robert Gleason, S.J., *Counseling the Catholic.* New York: Sheed and Ward, 1959.
3. Philip Harris, O.S.F., Organizing the counseling program. *Counseling in the secondary school*, ed. Stafford, C.S.V., Washington: Catholic University of America Press, 1960.
4. George E. Hill and Donald A. Green, The selection, preparation, and professionalization of guidance and personal workers. *Review of educational research*, XXX, Apr. 1960.
5. Adrian L. van Kaam, C.S.Sp., Counseling from the viewpoint of existential psychology. *Harvard educational review*, XXXII, Fall, 1962.
6. Jacob S. Kounin and Paul V. Gump, The comparative influences of punitive and nonpunitive teachers upon children's conceptions of misconduct. *J. educ. Psychol.*, LII, Feb. 1961.
7. James Michael Lee, *Principles and methods of secondary education.* Chpt. XIV, Guiding and counseling the secondary school student and Chpt. XV, discipline, New York: McGraw-Hill, 1963.
8. Robert B. Nordberg, Counseling: non-directive or non-coercive. *Catholic educational review.* LVI, Jan. 1958.
9. Carl Rogers, The interpersonal relationship: the core of guidance. *Harvard educational review*, XXXII, Fall, 1962.
10. George V. Sheviakov and Fritz Redl, *Discipline for today's children and youth.* rev. Association for Supervision and Curriculum Development, National Education Association, Richardson, Washington: 1956.
11. Philip L. Stack, *A national study of the guidance services in Catholic secondary schools.* Washington: Catholic University of America Press, 1958.
12. Ruth Strang, *Counseling techniques in college and secondary school*, Rev. New York: Harper, 1959.
13. Ruth Strang, *The role of the teacher in personnel work*, 4th ed. New York: Bureau of Publications, Teacher's College, Columbia University, 1953.

Some ethical and scientific values in the counseling psychotherapeutic process

Rev. Charles A. Curran

In this article Father Curran examines the client's personal pursuit of values in client-centered therapy. This strangly complex phenomenon embraces, according to the author, values on different levels: inner values, ultimate values, and the rediscovery of values. Yet, basic to all of this is the formation of a value system, a point dealt with here also.

The English essayist, G. K. Chesterton [1], once described a young man who left England on a journey of discovery. He was determined to discover by himself a perfect country and there settle and raise a family. He went from city to city, from civilization to civilization, from the most primitive to the most developed, in a difficult and thorough search. Finally, across a sea he came to an unknown shore and found there if not a perfect setting, one that was the most satisfying. And as he explored, in delight, his newly found land, he climbed a hill to look at a new landscape and there saw off in a distance, the gleaming towers of the cathedrals and buildings of London. He had found by long and arduous pursuit, what he had, in a way, always known and loved.

The counseling psychotherapeutic process is, as I have seen it, a search for values but not in the usual sense of this phrase. It is rather, an adventurous and thrilling personal pursuit, in an independent and sometimes seemingly dangerous way, of values which are uniquely new and personal for the client. As the therapeutic process moves forward, one of the most consistent things I have observed

Reprinted with permission from the *Personnel and Guidance Journal*, 39:15–20, September, 1960.

is the increasing anxiety of the client, particularly the younger client, to safeguard his newly acquired cache of self-determined values and to resist forcibly the counselor or anyone else trying to impose, even surreptitiously, values from the outside.

But the astonishing thing here is, as Chesterton's analogy suggests, that this intensely jealous and often fiercely independent pursuit does not necessarily produce social rebellion or philosophical and theological anarchy. Rather, the opposite seems most often to happen. When the client, with deep personal integrity and security, probes himself in the searching and sincere profundity of his relationship with the counselor, he retraces the basic steps by which civilization and society itself has, in some way, been formed. Or to put it another way, he surprisingly finds, in this absolutely personal pursuit, many of the basic values that are most fundamental to our whole Western Civilization and often shared in varying forms by all civilized society if these societies are really understood. Here, it seems to me, with a strange twist and in a way G. Stanley Hall and others of his time would perhaps never have dreamed, we have "ontogeny recapitulates phylogeny."

In this paper, therefore, I would like to discuss (1) the client's personal pursuit of values in client-centered therapy particularly as I have observed it in clients, and some things this seems to imply, and (2) how this is related in some ways to the philosophical and theological value systems of Western Civilization.

A Greater Rationality

Rogers has recently said, describing his observations of this same therapeutic process, the following:

> I have little sympathy with the rather prevalent concept that man is basically irrational, and that his impulses, if not controlled, will lead to destruction of others and self. Man's behavior is exquisitely rational, moving with subtle and ordered complexity toward the goals his organism is endeavoring to achieve. The tragedy for most of us is that our defenses keep us from being aware of this rationality, so that consciously we are moving in one direction while organismically we are moving in another [5, p. 202].

A major factor in personal conflict and unhappiness, as Aristotle pointed out, is this fact: that a person can seek an apparent good which satisfies one or the other of his needs but which is actually contrary to the over-all reasonable good of his whole person. Problems arise apparently because an individual's craving for particular personal, emotional, or sensual satisfactions are leading him away from the reasonable goals which he ultimately seeks. A man is, therefore, capable of a most complex self-deception. He can allow himself to be misled by particular urges to objects and goals which he knows will not really satisfy him nor ultimately be good for him.

For a number of years now we have been doing research on this process of the shifting perception of motivating personal values in the client's counseling awareness. It invariably involves a shift in focus and an increasingly broader realization of all the factors involved in a situation or personal relationship. This in turn results in a changing perception of what is really good and thus his choices and actions change. We have discussed this research elsewhere [3] but to illustrate this, may we consider excerpts from a second interview and contrast it with the insight stage of the tenth interview with the same person [3].

These data were drawn from a series of interviews of a married woman in a serious infatuation with another man. In the second interview the only thing she considers beyond herself and John is one brief phrase: "I've got people that I don't want to hurt either." In the whole of the first and second interviews the above statement represents the only expression of consideration for any factors or persons except herself and John. However, if we contrast this limited viewpoint with the insight stage of the tenth interview, we have a striking change in perception. The superimposed image of John and herself has given away to quite a different picture of the whole situation.

> When John and I were together it just sorta pushed everything into the background . . . But you just can't turn aside and say, "Well, I'm going back to where I was"—even though I, if I really wanted to—I couldn't do that. It's hard to give up John after all the good times we've had and the things we've done, but when you stop and think what could have happened why you see things different. (Long pause) . . . but I know even now, just by not seeing John, I'm better physically and spiritually too . . . Yes, the way it was before I wasn't really happy, it was just a state of conflict and misery and fear of being found out and thinking of the kids and all—no, it really wasn't happy, even when it seemed most enjoyable . . . There's no happiness in it. You're always under a constant strain. (Pause) I'll lose a lot in a worldly way but I'll gain too. I would gain more than I would lose spiritually.

Observe here the perceptual language in the phrase, "When John and I were together it just sorta pushed everything into the background," suggesting the superimposed image of "John and I" blocked out the over-all awareness of her responsibilities to her husband, family, and God. The second phrase, "But when you stop and think what could have happened why you see things different," suggests that the thinking process of the counseling interviews also brought about a different self-perception. When we analyze what is the difference in these perceptions, it seems to be the removal of the superimposed, narrowed focus on "John and I" for the broad reality awareness of the responsibilities to husband, children, and God. Now, even though giving up John is a severe sacrifice when she focuses on the pleasure that John brought her, she sees herself to be better off physically and spiritually, when her perceptions are clearly on the total field of responsibilities, as distinct from John [3].

Stated in goal-directed language, this viewpoint would suggest that the super-imposed image is itself an apparent good and that the self tends to move towards this apparent good until its perceptions are broadened and the reasoning and insightful process of the personality, in this case brought about through counseling, brings out from the background the real good, the total perceptual field. This puts into its proper perceptual organization the immediate good, which in this case, came from the relationship with John. When the immediate good is measured against the total perceptual field of all values involved, the self chooses and moves towards the relationship of husband, children, and God in the total perceptual field, as the real good, and rejects the apparent good which previously was a narrow focus on "John and I."

Toward Inner Values

We see too in these insight excerpts and this description of the therapy process, a goal-directed and self-responsible morality. That is to say, we are not dealing here with some type of built-in Kantian "categorical imperative" which can be variously explained by the effects of social mores or early conditioning and learning of cultural attitudes or the imposition of family attitude or some other type of code. All these things may in fact be operating in the client in the counseling relationship and probably are operating, but the peculiar quality that the therapeutic process seems to reveal is an inner capacity where, by holding up inadequate and ultimately unsatisfactory goals, I can stimulate myself to want these goals and to project on them much more meaning than they really have. Evil then comes in the degree to which I am responsible for such self-deception and for the impulsive yielding to emotions or basic drives which cause me to seek these disproportionate goals.

Obviously, there is a wide variety of degrees of responsibility in such matters and while certain objective factors—such as legal or theological codes may determine—doubtless enter here, there is at the same time almost always a strong factor which only the person himself at the deepest level of his self-understanding —best acquired through counseling—would only know and be able to reveal.

We see in the therapy process therefore, an inner value system which is yet objectively effective in producing a better operational fulfillment and achievement. Operational reality, by implication, has apparently some kind of reasonable substructure, granting all its apparent disorder, into which the client's own reasonable process penetrates. The therapy process, as we see it, ultimately facilitates not only a more reasonable integration and control of the personality but also somehow a better, more adequate way of living. This pursuit of a basic reasonableness in the midst of widespread disorder, which the counseling therapy process implies, is what joins its implications to our whole legal, social, philosophical, and theological tradition in one of its most ancient Judaeo-Greek-Christian forms.

Let us pursue further what happens philosophically in the client's therapeutic process. It seems to me one way of illustrating what happens might be symbolized by a triangle. The client begins at the point, with unique and personal events, situations, feelings, and reactions that seem peculiarly to happen only to him. Slowly he moves down to the discovery that others share many of these things— that he is not as different or unique as he thought. He begins to adapt himself to others and to learn from others but in a way most interestingly personal and self-determined. In counseling, where the counselor struggles to understand him and thus he is helped to understand himself, he studies and investigates himself in an intense search which the counselor's responses keep objective and in a sense impersonal.

The Discerning Listener

In our focus on the release and emotional oneness and commitment of the counseling relationship, we have perhaps somewhat overlooked the degree of value that the counselor's accurate understanding and verbalization adds to the client's clarification and objectification of himself. In a recent research project we have been having clients comment on their reactions to the interview a few minutes after it is over. One of the most consistent comments is the way the counselor's response helped them to understand what, in a complex and often emotionally involved way, they had just said. The following illustrates this:

> I've never been listened to so well—no one before ever cared so much about what I was saying. I have confidence in speaking. Even if what I say is stupid or foolish, I am not made to feel stupid or foolish myself. I trust the counselor to hold what I say and not to let it slip or become blurred. In such a situation I can react to myself and my own thoughts and feelings much as I might react to those of someone else. There is an objectivity about the counselor's responses that is freeing.

Another person said:

> When I finished last time I thought I was too confused to say anything more. Then, as I heard your responses, I somehow understood what I had said and it seemed very easy to say something further. I didn't sound really as foolish or stupid as I thought. I began to become understandable to myself.

But this reasonable objectivity about oneself in counseling is the exact opposite of a cold analysis. On the contrary, it is only possible to a maximum degree in a profound relationship of mutually deep commitment. It is a commitment made possible by a love on the counselor's part which Greek and Medieval philosophers called *amor benevolentiae*—a love that concerns only the other and his good. This they contrasted with *amor concupiscentiae* where the person was seeking some self-determined return from the other. But in the commitment of mutual love of *amor benevolentiae,* the counselor is not only a catalytic agent of emotions, he is at the same time and even more essentially a warm, understanding, auxiliary reasoning power.

Toward Ultimate Values

Where does this mutual process of client reasonable self-search lead? It leads, it seems to me, down the triangle to issues and values that are increasingly more universal and more ultimate. It can lead—it does not always—to the most ultimate question of all, the meaning of life itself and to a struggle with all these final anxieties which in the traditional language of Western Civilization one would have to call philosophically metaphysical and theological.

But even when the basic and most universal issues of life, symbolized by the broad base of the triangle, are not questioned by the client, they seem contained and implied in the values by which he questions and changes more immediate personal situations. Some years ago Rogers wrote, discussing a case, that insight tends to move through the "difficult and painful . . . not for its immediate but for its longtime satisfaction" [*4, p. 210*].

This awareness might be carried to ultimate conclusions. The analysis of the counseling process demonstrates that increased insight and a broader understanding of his personal values, aims, and purposes enable a person to direct himself towards and eventually to reach, more ultimate goals that are more permanently satisfying. But no transient, material thing can, upon analysis, produce the permanent security, peace, and lasting happiness that each one seeks. The fear of loss is the other side of every human possession and security. This kind of evaluation should logically lead a person to seek a final and ultimate Good, which will be a permanent source of happiness.

Each man seems therefore to be in a state of both being and becoming for which no transient goal or value—however immediately satisfying—can offer any final long-time fulfillment. We seem to have implied here a profound core existential anxiety in man—an essential dissatisfaction to which Augustine's famous remark was applied: "Oh God, Thou hast made us for Thyself Alone and our hearts are ever restless until they rest in Thee." This being and becoming would be then, something both unique and yet shared by all mankind and, I believe, by God.

A Task in Freedom

But it is not only this pursuit of values that are ultimately the most universal and perduringly rewarding that relate the counseling psychotherapeutic process to the pursuit of values well-known in the tradition of Western Civilization. It is also in the more immediate values which the process of change in itself contains.

The counseling psychotherapeutic process at its best facilitates a person's own reasonableness, literally frees him to be more reasonable when he is enslaved by conflicting, emotional, instinctive, or somatic urges. This greater state of reasonableness not only enables him to study himself in an unthreatened and non-defensive way and to accept and use all he learns about himself, but it also makes him capable of a more adequate judgment of his own immediate or ultimate life goals and better means to them. Finally, this counseling psychotherapeutic process seems to do a third thing. It integrates the person's whole psychosomatic self so that he is now also able—often to his amazement—to do with surprising ease, what he now knows he should do and wants to do.

We have here an illustration in which a client discusses deep positive changes in himself:

> . . . and yet, frankly, it hasn't been at the expense of much consciousness on my part. Does this happen? I just don't know . . . I just don't want to be naive and say that this change has to be due to what we have done at this table. But I know that it is the *greatest* cause for the change. There may be other factors like my work, a change in Marie, and so on, that help to make me more agreeable, too. I'm not perfect or a new person but my temperament has been of fewer moods and less apartness. The changes have been obvious to Marie, too, and she tells me so . . .
>
> Yep, that's it. The same personality with greater control and more integrated function . . .
>
> And the role that you played did it.
>
> If you had said to me to quit browbeating my wife, or to stop this, or to stop that, it would have been a useless attempt. I think that technique would have completely failed. Instead I've brought these things out time and again, time and again. The fruits of these discussions are that I'm better and that the cure has been effortless on my part. I'm not perfect or anything, but I've been so much better, and it's noticeable to others especially Marie [6, pp. 243–262].

This, perhaps surprisingly, is very similar to, if not the exact process that Aristotle and many of the ancients and medievalists considered the prudential process. Prudence was considered an incommunicable ability that could be acquired ultimately only by oneself. It could not as such, be taught. The first stage of this prudential process was the self-investigation and inquiry which was called counsel. But this is not seeking counsel from another, as it later implied, but rather taking counsel with oneself, sometimes with the help of another. From this concept apparently came our modern word, "counseling."

This first stage led then to the second prudential stage which involved a double judgment—the rejection of past reactions, operations, and plans and the development of new and more adequate personal solutions. The third prudential stage followed from this and was the self-command stage which brought order and integration into the emotions, impulses, and bodily functions so that a prudent man could carry out what he judged to be according to his own reasonableness.

Values Rediscovered

What I mean to say here in this discussion of the values of the therapeutic process as they relate to our civilization might be best illustrated by an incident reported in the Korean War. There was great difficulty in the soft mucky terrain and the huge modern tanks were bogging down in the mud. But in one section the soldiers found a path, overgrown with bushes and not used for many years apparently, which actually held up even the largest tanks and trucks and immeasurably facilitated their movements. When they investigated the history of this valuable passageway they learned it was at least a thousand years old constructed by hand in some very ancient now forgotten dynasty.

This exactly illustrates something of my astonishment in the dawning realization that many of the things this counseling process is revealing about human nature in a fresh and dramatic way, are yet not so completely new but that some of the ancient philosophical conceptions of Aristotle's Ethics and what used to be called the Cardinal Virtues can yet hold this powerful modern and new psychological movement. To be sure, much underbrush and debris have gathered here, that must be swept away. Much misunderstanding, confusion, and misinterpretation of ancient ethical and characterological terms like prudence, temperance, fortitude, and humility must be carefully clarified and adapted to all that we now profoundly know of the therapeutic process. But I am convinced that there is yet much that could be helpful to us, even now, like the ancient road in Korea. There is evidence, I believe, that would join these new psychotherapeutic discoveries to the ancient ethical tradition and value scheme of our Western Civilization, without in any sense warping the meaning and usefulness of either. But we must be willing to drop our own historical stereotypes and, perhaps, even ancient prejudices and seek to understand these conceptions with something of the freshness and clarity they really had for the men of much earlier times. By this I do not mean necessarily any return to some basic theological or philosophical unity, however desirable this may or may not be. I rather mean the common ethical concepts which in fact we all more or less accept by implicit observation in Western democratic society and which most of us want to preserve for ourselves and our children. But we accept these values too implicitly perhaps, and we are in danger of chopping at the roots of the tree or letting someone else chop at these roots and eventually jeopardize the tree, while we yet enjoy and treasure its fruits. We need to seek, perhaps, not only personal integration but to see that this can also be in some way an integration with the whole civilization that produced us. We need to know not only our relationship to our parents, family, and immediate environment but also to those older peoples who thoughts and values have affected us with equal, if unknown, potency.

What then, finally, would be the personal values involved for us if we could do this—as the ancient Korean road proved so valuable to the movement of the modern tanks? Basically, I think it would do two things. It would free us from the more recent, probably Kantian, ethical concept that all personal values must be imposed from without which has come not to mean either by parents, society, or even more threatening and dangerous, by the state. It would restore again the possibility of starting out, like Chesterton's traveler, on a thrilling personal pursuit of oneself in a fierce and independent search for reasonable self-values and yet allow that one would ultimately come by this process, not to violent rebellion and anarchy, but to ancient and secure traditional values. These values have helped to carry through many centuries the burden of human hearts and, I think, can still help this burden.

Secondly, this would restore our own sense of belonging to the civilization that produced most of us and is basically responsible for our whole democratic tradition. It would make a place for education in values which in no way would impinge on a man's freedom to be unsparingly honest and sincere with himself in his own self-determined pursuit, through counseling psychotherapy, or by other educational and social means. This kind of personal pursuit the Greeks and Medievalists would have called, with a meaning strange to our modern ears, the seeking of humility. But by this word they would not have meant a fawning, inferior, "Uriah Heep" sort of thing, the "umble" man, but something very clean, dignified, and positive. This concept of humility has been defined as "the reasonable pursuit of one's own excellence." Such a definition, it seems to me, gives in one phrase about as good a statement as anything we have to delineate a core therapeutic concept and basic value scheme. This could be equally applicable to counseling, psychotherapy, education, and society itself without in any way doing violence to society and the rights of others and yet at the same time without distorting or warping the person's profound and deep need of personal integrity, responsibility, and basic independence.

REFERENCES

1. Chesterton, G. K. *Orthodoxy,* New York: Lane, 1918.
2. Curran, C. A. The counseling relationship and some religious factors. *J. Counsel, Psychol.,* 1959, 6, No. 4, 266–270.
3. Curran, C. A. Some preliminary perception experiments related to insight in counseling therapy. In Bier, William (Ed.), *Perception.* New York: Fordham University, 1957.
4. Rogers, C. R. *Counseling and psychotherapy.* Boston: Houghton Mifflin, 1942.
5. Rogers, C. R. A note on "The Nature of Man" *J. Counsel. Psychol.,* 1957, 4, No. 3, 202.
6. Snyder, W. U. *Casebook of non-directive counseling.* New York: Houghton Mifflin, 1947.

part viii

New directions
in teaching and learning

1. What do you consider to be the principal advantages of
(a) the ungraded classroom, (b) the Montessori method, (c) programed
instruction, (d) shared time?

2. What do you regard as the main weakness or shortcoming of each
of the four above-mentioned procedures?

3. Weighing the advantages and limitations of each, explains why
you are strongly for, mildly for, neutral toward, mildly against,
or strongly against each of these four innovations.

4. Evaluate any one of the "new directions" discussed in this
chapter as a means of providing what you would accept as a
distinctively Catholic education. If you are unable to, explain why.

5. What, really, is meant by integration of theology and other subjects?
Why should Father Whalen want to integrate theology with mathematics
and science?

Shared time:
the Pittsburgh area's experiment

John G. Deedy, Jr.

One of the most noteworthy proposals advanced to help solve the financial problems of private schools is that of "shared time." As yet, this proposal has not been acted upon to any great extent, but where it has been tried, it has aroused considerable interest and little if any serious opposition. The plan in operation is being watched carefully by Catholic educators as well as public school officials because of the great differences it might eventually make in both of their fields. Mr. Deedy, editor of the Pittsburgh Catholic, explains how "shared time" works in one of the first localities to try it.

The Pittsburgh area's experiment in shared-time education—described by national news media as the pilot program which moves shared time substantially beyond the talking phase—has passed its freshman year mid-terms with straight A's.

From superintendents to students, there are the highest grades for the program under which 23 students from St. Thomas' District High School in Braddock, Pennsylvania, received part of their education at St. Thomas' and part at Forbes Trail Area Technical School in Monroeville, Pennsylvania, seven miles distant.

Begun last September* after long months of consultation and preparation, the program is being watched carefully—and for good reason. Shared time represents what many educators believe is the solution to the constitutional dilemmas sur-

* [1962.]

Reprinted with permission from *Ave Maria*, 97:5–9, March 2, 1963.

rounding government aid to education. Catholics particularly are watching, for shared time could mean the answer to the problems of expense, accommodations and teachers in the Catholic school system.

What shared time means to church, community and student is immediately obvious from a glance at the St. Thomas'-Forbes Trail relationship. Forbes Trail is a school designed to educate talented youth in technological and scientific subjects; it is a specialized type of education which requires costly equipment and highly trained teachers. St. Thomas' is a medium-sized average Catholic high school of limited budget and desk space, serving children of working-class families, the majority of them steelworkers.

St. Thomas', naturally, can afford so much; Forbes Trail can afford enormously more. Its sources of income are the federal, state and county (Allegheny) governments—the county source being the 22 school districts from which Forbes Trail draws its pupils. In a day when technological skills are so important Forbes Trail furnishes the youngsters with an education which enables him upon graduation to step into fields where, till now, postgraduate study would have been demanded. Likewise, it equips him with skills to take advantage of new employment in expanding fields of science and technology.

Under the St. Thomas'-Forbes Trial arrangement, the 23 students from St. Thomas' take courses such as marketing, chemistry, computer programs and maintenance, engineering and automotive technician, at Forbes Trail; then they return to their home school for Christian doctrine, social studies, English, mathematics, typing, etc. They are at Forbes Trail from 7:30 to 10:30 a.m., and at St. Thomas' from 11 a.m. to 3:15 p.m. Travel between the two schools is via public-school bus and, so as not to violate statutes relating to the transportation (rather nontransportation) of nonpublic-school students, the terminal for departure and arrival is a public school, a 10-minute walk from St. Thomas'.

And the arrangement is working beautifully.

"At this point, the experiment has progressed far beyond expectations," comments Msgr. John B. McDowell, superintendent of schools for the Diocese of Pittsburgh. "All those dire predictions about shared time haven't materialized at all."

The headmaster of St. Thomas', Father Leo G. Henry, bears this out. "Basically the program is fine and there are no real problems," Father Henry declares. "There were some administrative problems at the beginning, but they did not prove insurmountable. . . . About the only thing we have to watch is that we do not make any general announcements to the student body before 11 o'clock, else we miss the 23 boys and girls who are at Forbes Trail."

The director of Forbes Trail, Mr. Francis J. Brown, also minimizes difficulties. "There are certain administrative problems that crop up out of variations in schedule, but we have these problems anyway," he remarks. "Remember, we're dealing with 22 schools districts and 10 different high schools. St. Thomas' High is just one among others."

An important point to note is that at Forbes Trail all pupils show on the rolls as students of the school district in which they are domiciled; they do not appear as students from St. Thomas' High or Braddock High or any other school. "The pupils from St. Thomas' High are not parochial-school students to us," Mr. Brown stresses. "They're students from a particular school district." However, the students' marks are mailed by Forbes Trail to St. Thomas', and at St. Thomas' they are entered on the student's report card. "Forbes Trail does not issue report cards, and all marks are sent to the high school from which the student comes." Mr. Brown comments.

Mr. Brown was asked if there were any faculty problems, any built-in resentments about accepting students from St. Thomas' High into Forbes Trail, even though the formalities of the public-school educational code had been met. "Absolutely not!" Mr. Brown answered. "We're worried about education. Children need the education we're in business to impart; we see that they get it. They're the sons and daughters of taxpayers, and this school is set up for taxpayers' children. They're entitled to the education; they need it; our sole concern is that it's available to them."

Was there any acceptance problem among the students themselves? "No, my experience is that children get along well together," Mr. Brown stated.

The students themselves support this view. Sally Miller, a St. Thomas' senior from North Braddock, and Fred Seng, a St. Thomas' junior from Wilmerding, report that they and their 21 "share-time colleagues" feel perfectly at home at Forbes Trail. "We didn't even have to make any adjustment as best I can recall," Fred smiles. "It's not much different socially from St. Thomas'," Sally chimes in.

Father Henry speaks enthusiastically about co-operation on the administrative level between the two schools. "We're on a first-name basis, and if anything comes up that requires talking out we just reach for the phone," he says.

Msgr. McDowell adds that "the mechanics of shared time to this point are so good that we'd like to enlarge the program next year. This is our determination. We'd also like to include more schools in the program, but this depends a lot on whether the public-school districts are willing to finance it."

Msgr. McDowell, who was described recently by a national news service as the "chief Catholic supporter" of shared-time education, points to a division of subjects on the basis of value content as a first principle of shared time. Not surprisingly, it is the division which is the basis for the St. Thomas'-Forbes Trail program, minor variations allowed.

"As one views the gamut of school subjects, it becomes evident that certain subjects are more involved with and concerned with values than others," Msgr. McDowell explains. His theory is that so-called value-content subjects be taken in the parochial school and those subjects less bound up with philosophical objectives in the public school.

He classifies value-content subjects as Christian doctrine, guidance, social studies, fine arts, science and English. In the other group he lists languages, mathematics, the practical arts, commercial subjects, safety and physical education.

As for the science variation, Msgr. McDowell comments that "while concerned with values because of interpretations required and because of certain moral and spiritual guides which are inherent, it is still concerned with values in a less direct way."

As might be presumed, education in science is viewed by Msgr. McDowell as one of the strong reasons for pushing shared time. "Right now our science laboratory equipment is comparable to that of the public school (excluding schools like Forbes Trail, of course), but we are working at a handicap here. We're forced to borrow funds for our labs under the NDEA [National Defense Education Act]; the public school gets them for the asking. Thus we're at a disadvantage to begin with, and this disadvantage will become the more pronounced as science becomes more and more sophisticated and science education more and more expensive."

Msgr. McDowell sees this financial disadvantage at work in other areas of education as well, notably in the fine arts and in languages. "Our bands and orchestra programs are good in our high schools," he relates, "but I'd like to see these programs starting at the elementary level. However, we're faced again with expense—both for teachers and instrumentation. The last is especially costly. And as for languages, we can afford but few language laboratories; the public schools, again, get theirs for the asking."

One of the great benefits for parochial schools in shared time, according to Msgr. McDowell, is the technological training which is made available to the parochial-school students. His reasoning sheds more light on the St. Thomas'-Forbes Trail arrangement.

"Between 38 and 40 per cent of our children go on to college and another 20 per cent into post-high but noncollege programs," he states. "This means that 40 per cent leave high school for the labor market. Now let's face it: It's pretty tough for this group to get a job today without technological training. Yet our schools cannot afford to provide for the technological-type education which the 40 per cent needs. At the same time these students have to compete in the world. So shared time is a bonanza in this respect; for under shared time they will be getting the best and the most up-to-date."

Msgr. McDowell sees numerous advantages in shared time, and he sees these as multifaceted, applying to Church, state and citizenry. He itemizes six advantages that could redound from a broadly national shared-time system:

(1) It would give the parochial school the opportunity to educate effectively all its children. (At the moment only about 50 per cent of Catholic children who apply to Catholic schools are being accepted. Under a carefully programed shared-time schedule, the number could be doubled, one group being taught in the parochial school while the other was at the public, and vice versa.)

(2) It would assure the community and Catholic parents, in this case, that all these children were receiving in major part a religiously oriented education.

(3) It would create new opportunities to achieve a better working relationship between public and private-school officials and, therefore, as fringe benefits it

would eliminate many of the charges that Catholic schools were dropping undesirable students; that they were not melting with the community at the school level; that they were divisive.

(4) It would offer the American community an opportunity to maintain private and parochial education through substantial aid given directly to the student and to the public school and, therefore, avoid the distressing conflict of aid to religion debates.

(5) It would lessen the tax burden on the total community because it would involve the full use of all existing school buildings and teaching personnel.

(6) It would make it possible for the Catholic community to do more at every level, because shared time would eliminate the excessive cost of erecting gymnasiums, language, mathematics and commercial facilities, and perhaps even cafeterias.

As for the disadvantages of shared time, Msgr. McDowell does not view them as terribly serious. (Incidentally, he dismisses as a canard the argument that shared time weakens the public school. "Actually, it should strengthen the public school by winning for it wider support, especially in large Catholic communities," he says.)

With regard to disadvantages, Msgr. McDowell sees the possibility of repercussions from elements of the Catholic community and from the professional Catholic educator who feels that a full Catholic program is still the ideal; he sees the problem of co-ordination of schedules and, possibly, some transportation difficulties; he sees potential problems of records, grading and administrative matters.

But these worries—if, indeed, that is the word—are apart from the St. Thomas'-Forbes Trail experience—though it must be kept in mind that this experience is limited and experimental.

"I've had not one kickback, not one complaining phone call on the St. Thomas'-Forbes Trail program," assures Msgr. McDowell, "and this is amazing. For no matter what program we institute ourselves, no matter how simple and innocent it may be, we'll get dozens of calls. But here we have a half-year under our belt, and not one complaint!"

Nor has Father Henry at St. Thomas'. "The children are happy and the parents pleased," he declares.

Does all this mean that shared time is proven?

No one will go so far as to say yes to this question. All agree that the experiment is exciting and interesting and novel. But no one has uncrossed his fingers yet.

The integration of theology, science, and mathematics

Rev. John P. Whalen

**Curricular integration usually strikes a note of
sympathy among educators, especially Catholic
educators, for they are almost naturally inclined to
accept the doctrine of the unity of knowledge. Here
the author argues for integration, particularly in
the areas of knowledge covered in the article's title,
but maintains that integration is most likely achieved
by keeping these fields distinct and pursuing them
with intensity. Does there seem to be a paradox
here?**

In a very interesting article which appeared recently in *Thought*, Father Costanzo wrote:

> Either you do or do not hold that all of man every moment of his life is religious, that there is no human endeavor which may insulate itself against the all-pervading loving dominion of God. To educate is to develop an individual to be what he is meant to be—by God. Religious training at home and religious instruction in church and synagogue, and a purely secular education in godless moral and spiritual values are simply not complementary.[1]

The significance of this rather compelling declaration for nonreligious education is obvious. It seems, however, that it might indicate something of a conflict or at least an area of obscurity even within the circles and confines of Catholic education.

[1] Joseph F. Costanzo, "Religion in Public School Education," *Thought*, XXXI (Summer, 1956), 237.

Reprinted with permission from *The Catholic Educational Review*, 55:464–479, October, 1957.

Catholic education has as its avowed purpose to educate the individual, as a member of Christ's Mystical Body, to be what he is meant to be by God. To do this, it must employ methods that are in some ways similar to and in some ways dissimilar to those employed in non-Catholic education. It uses similar teaching methods, similar curricula, similar courses, and so forth; and yet we like to feel that Catholic education produces a product quite different from the product of other kinds of education. We like to feel this way because the Church is expending literally millions of dollars to set the stage and cut the dies for the production of such products, and we would not like to think that the investment of so much money, not to speak of the dedicatory efforts of thousands of consecrated religious, is in vain.

Yet, what is the specific difference between Catholic and non-Catholic education? What is there about Catholic schools that makes them more unlike public schools than Catholic swimming pools are unlike public swimming pools? The obvious answer is probably duplex: the religion courses and the spirit of discipline that pervades Catholic education. One sometimes wonders whether there is an automatic transfer of training from the one hour of religion (among seven hours of the school day) to the rest of the curriculum, just as one wonders whether the discipline that makes for orderly classes and prohibits violent breaches of the moral code or the code of etiquette is one that comes from an inner conviction on the part of the student or rather one that is imposed from the outside and can be forgotten almost as soon as it is discontinued. If one could believe St. Thomas Aquinas, that we become in some way what we know, it would seem that to achieve that inner integration that is so necessary for the mature Christian, it is necessary to achieve some inner integration in the intellectual and volitional diet by which the Christian is to grow. *Man ist was er isst*—more so intellectually than in the way this pithy statement was originally used.

It is not impossible to arrive at some integration between the teachings of Christ's Church and the social sciences since both have the same man for their object, man as a member of society, a member of the family, as a member of the state, and as an individual. It is possible, it seems, to achieve some integration between religion and the languages, depending upon the literature studied, because in literature it is possible to find man's ideas about himself, about the nature of life, and about his relationship to God, all of which can be used to produce at once a good linguist and a good Catholic. However, when it comes to a consideration of the physical, biological and mathematical sciences, which have for their objects the study of matter and in their formal objects preclude the study of non-material reality, how is it possible to bring about an integration of these pursuits with the teaching of religion? Is it possible to leave off consideration of God for the hour of chemistry, physics, or biology? Are these studies human endeavors which may insulate themselves against the all-pervading loving dominion of God? If we feel that they are, we have no further problem; but to the extent that the problem is so resolved, to that extent we are not really Christian.

We are faced with a problem which is quite basic to Catholic education. It is a problem that is quite profound in its ramifications and we may reasonably expect that the solution of it is not superficial. We are faced by the traditional conflict between science and religion, a conflict which has been overworked considerably through the years by scientific writers who have had little patience with theologians and by theologians who have had little patience with scientists. At the heart of the problem through the years there appears a basic misunderstanding of the theological approach to truth by scientists and of the scientific approach to truth by theologians. It seems that four solutions to the problem have been advanced —all of which have been exploited and all of which are unsatisfactory: (1) repudiate theology; (2) repudiate science; (3) make science subordinate to theology; (4) make theology subordinate to science. It would not be untrue to say that most of the writing on the relationship of science to religion and vice versa could be classified under one of these attempts to solve a problem that is, probably, more basic than any of the solutions offered for it.

Source of Science-Theology Conflict

There should be, one would expect, a fifth possible solution that might be called the solution of integration without repudiation or subordination. If the problem is to be solved satisfactorily, it would seem that it should take into account the nature of man and of his powers of knowing, which powers constructed the sciences in question. The nature of reality as we know it should be taken into account as well, since this is the stuff of which the sciences in question are composed. This solution should consider the methods which man uses to arrive at truth about reality, which methods are based both on the specific aspect of reality under consideration and the nature of man's knowing powers. Finally, this solution should sum up and put into order the information arrived at. It would then be possible to look with the eye of objectivity at the position and importance of the various aspects of reality as we know it, and, therefore, at the position and importance of the various sciences which expose these aspects of reality for us. In this problem, as in most things in human life, integration comes only by individual efforts; it cannot be accomplished for us. Integration must take place in a person because only the person has sufficient resiliency and sufficient subtlety to be able to construct a unity from the manifold of reality.

It should be said that it is the conviction, not only of Catholic educators but of men in general, that there can be no conflict between truths. If there be areas of obscurity in the study of reality, this fact is to be expected. Depending upon the basic principles with which a person begins his examination of reality, given a rigid consistency in applying these principles to an area of obscurity, there will necessarily be differing conclusions about the nature of the obscurity. It is of the nature of reality, fraught with what might be called natural mysteries and multifarious problems, and of the nature of mind, which is not perfect nor immediate in coming to conclusions, that there be differing schools of thought about difficult concepts. However, if a person is not beset by an intellectually provincial spirit, if he is open to truth, if he is sensitive to new insights and humble enough to accept them, from whatever quarter, there is no essential reason why there cannot be a resolution of difficulties.

Much of the difficulty that has resulted from the attempts to come to some common grounds between science and religion has arisen not from the denial of scientific truth by theologians nor of theological truth by scientists, but by the intrinsic difficulty the mind of man has in the act of synthesis. Ours seems to be an age of analysis. It is necessary to analyze things to understand them because it is not possible to study the parts of the things without some division; but it is also equally necessary to synthesize the elements of our analysis again before the whole of truth can be arrived at. The first act of understanding is one of analysis; the second, one of synthesis. We seem to stop at the analysis. We have differentiated reality almost out of existence; it is time that we integrate it.

Integration through Distinctiveness

And yet, how is this integration to be accomplished with reference to religion and the natural sciences? The natural sciences, mathematics, and religion are distinct sciences and must remain such if they would not destroy each other. There can be no intrinsic overlapping such as seeing a triangle as a symbol of the Trinity in mathematics, or a circle as the Eternity of God. Such practice is childish. There can be no such thing as a chapter of a science book entitled: "The Atomic Age: Proof of God's Existence." Such practice is pietistic. But, if mathematics arrives at truth, and if science arrives at truth, and if theology arrives at truth, and if truth is one, and if truth is a reflection of the True, which is just another way of saying God, then there must be some way to tie all the loose ends together. This must be done not to prove anything; not to develop an atomic-age apologetic, but simply to fulfill our vocations as seekers after truth.

It is just as senseless to teach religion during mathematics class as it is to teach mathematics during religion class. Religion, science, and mathematics are, and must remain, specifically distinct disciplines because they have specifically distinct ends, methods, and lights. If it is the nature of these sciences to be distinct, then whatever integration of them is possible must come about by fulfilling their natures. And so, we arrive at the rather paradoxical view that it is specifically in their distinction that they can be intelligently integrated.

If it is their nature to be distinct, possibly it would be wise to come to some conclusions about their natures. The sciences under consideration, natural science, mathematics, and theology, are all constructs of the human mind. It is true that one of them, theology, takes its inception from a source that is not only different from the human mind, but even vastly superior to it. But the actual organization and inner logic of all the sciences do nothing but reflect the organization and inner logic of the mind turned on reality. If there is a basic consistency in any of the human sciences, it is because there is a basic consistency in the human mind and in the reality upon which it focuses.

To the extent, therefore, that the human mind (which is basically the same for scientist, mathematician, and theologian) focuses on reality (which should be considered the same by all thinkers), there will be an essential element of similarity in the construction of all possible valid human sciences. But, to the extent that the human intellect is facile and can turn itself to different considerations at different levels of reality, and to the extent that objective reality is a manifold and gives a basis in reality for differing considerations, there will be an essential element of dissimilarity in any possible valid human science. We should reasonably expect, then, that human sciences will be analagous to one another.

We have running through the whole of human science two elements: the first, mind; the second, reality. Depending on the relative proportion of each in a mixture, we have differing sciences, differing bodies of knowledge, each constructed by mind acting on reality. The methods employed in each science must be tailored by the requirements of the aspect of reality which mind is considering. If sciences have objects that are really distinct, they must by the same token have methods that are really distinct. Since method is particularized by object, the consistent application of method on object should result in truth. There is no guarantee for, and almost a presumption against, arriving at truth by the application of the method of one science on the object of another. Consequently, just as each science must be kept distinct to be valid, so too, method, to be valid, must be applied only within the confines of the science for which it was designed.

Different Objects, Methods, and Lights

Theology, science and mathematics differ in their objects, in *what* they study. Theology studies God and the relationship that exists between God and man. The object of natural science is the symbolic explanation of the material world. The object of mathematics is the study of the extension of matter, the study of the accident of quantity as belonging to real, material being.

Because of differing objects, these studies must employ different methods. The method of theology or the theological method is the use of the powers of induction and deduction on propositions to which the mind gives assent by faith. Its method is historico-logical; it constructs a human science built on divine revelation. The natural sciences, because of the nature of the object of their study, use a method that is quite different from the theological method. The scientific method consists of the observation of phenomena, the classification of phenomena, the formulation of hypotheses to explain the interrelationships of phenomena, the testing of such hypotheses under controlled conditions, the prediction of future behavior of material things on the basis of hypotheses, the testing of such predictions for universality of application, and finally the summing up of several hypotheses so tested into broad general principles called laws. In mathematics the method again is different. Mathematics concerns itself with the symbolic representation of the extension of a material being, the examination of the quality or inequality of the representative symbols, the examination of the variation of one symbol with the variation of another or other such symbolic representations of reality, the substitution of equivalents for original symbols, and the application of the law of equivalence to determine new relationships.

Not only do theology, the natural sciences, and mathematics differ in their objects and in their methods, they also differ in the light they bring to bear on reality. Theology is constructed by the mind using the light of faith to originate the science and the light of reason to organize it. The natural sciences use the light of reason alone to come to a knowledge of reality or at least to represent reality symbolically, and to organize it into a well-defined, ordered body of knowledge. Mathematics, too, uses the light of reason exclusively and, like the natural sciences, not only does not make use of the light of faith, but cannot make use of it without certainly failing to achieve its object.

Operationalism, Tool of Natural Science

On the basis of the foregoing, it must be said that the natural sciences stop at the symbolic representation of the operations of material reality. It is interesting that physics takes as its start the property of inertia. Inertia is a property characteristic of matter and is universal in that all matter is characterized by inertia. Recent work in physics, especially by Einstein, has shown that energy also is characterized by inertia. Consequently, there is some basic similarity between matter and energy, which similarity, carried to its theoretical limits, predicted at least a theoretical convertibility of the one into the other. Our own day has seen the practical consequences of this theoretical convertibility. The point is, however, that we are still very far from discovering the nature of material reality even though we know quite well how it behaves under controlled conditions.

The progress of physics in the last hundred years is based largely on the work of Newton in his vast generalizations characterizing all matter as possessive of inertia. And yet, to characterize matter as possessing inertia and defining it in terms of inertia is like characterizing a human being as being lazy and defining him in terms of his laziness. We can do a great deal with a man if we know he is lazy but not nearly so much as we could do if we really knew what he is. Even with the progress of the natural sciences, we feel that while we have seen, classified and represented facets of the "personality" of matter, we have never been formally introduced to it.

Since we have not yet, and some feel will never, come to understand the basic stuff of matter, it is a very natural temptation to define matter not by what it is but by what it does. In the light of the scientific method, this procedure is not readily to be condemned; it is capable of shedding much light on otherwise obscure corners of things. Operationalism, as such an outlook is called, while it contains within itself the seeds of its own destruction, can make valuable contributions to the physical sciences. Indeed, it seemed almost to be necessary to formulate such a procedure after the Einsteinian $e = mc^2$ rocked physics on its heels and said that matter is not matter but something that acts like it, and energy is not energy but something that acts like it, and the two are convertible. Matter is not a *something* which behaves in a certain way under certain conditions; matter is rather to be considered as the behavior of another *something* which eludes our grip. The same is to be said of energy. And so, the study of matter and energy is really the study of behavior, or better, of operations; operationalism, with its operational definitions, seems almost called for in physical science.

It is when other scientists, with the inferiority complex that comes with giving one's allegiance to new sciences which have not really taken form, begin to use in their studies a procedure that belongs specifically to established physical sciences, that the use of such a procedure is no guarantee of new knowledge, and more than this, might even lead to erroneous conclusions. Such is the present condition, it may be said parenthetically, of the social scientist using operationalism as an investigative tool. In spite of the materialist, operationalism is no more called for in psychology, for example, than introspection is called for in atomic physics. The same could be said, a fortiori, of education. The way to become scientific and to make a contribution to science, is not to imitate procedures of a field of study which everyone recognizes as scientific, but to give oneself to the inner logic of one's own investigations and employ procedures which this inner logic demands. It would seem that if modern sociology, psychology, and education need some form of apologia to justify themselves as sciences, it would be better for sociologists, psychologists, and educators to be extremely competent in their own fields rather than low candle-power physical chemists.

Deduction, Proper to Mathematics

Much the same can be said of the analysis of the nature of mathematics as was said of the nature of the natural sciences, with the exception that while induction is possible, valid and necessary in the physical sciences, it has no place whatever in the mathematical sciences. There are mathematical proofs called "Proofs by Induction" but this term is really a misnomer. These proofs should be called rather proofs by recurrent reasoning, based on two considerations: (1) the realization that if a proof is true of one member of a sequence, its truth for the next member of the sequence follows by a logical necessity; (2) the recognition of the proof as true for the first member of the sequence. This type of "induction" is not induction at all but rather the application of the Principal of Recurrence of Pascal, deductively, to a sequence. Mathematics is perhaps the most deductive of all sciences. For that reason, there is a rigidity about mathematics that is found nowhere else except perhaps in formal logic.

Theology is largely deductive; but the principles from which its deductions are made are so numerous and complex that it is not possible to feel the same restraints of reason that are present in mathematics. Once the relatively few axioms of mathematics are stated and accepted as representative of reality, the entire body of present-day mathematics can be deduced from them by the consistent application of the principles of reasoning, the same principles that are studied in formal logic.

Almost as soon as one indulges himself in the abstractions of mathematics, however, and as soon as he submits to the compelling exactness of the science, he divorces himself from the reality of material being. There is nothing in nature that is perfectly triangular, nor anything that corresponds perfectly to a cubic equation. There is not only no material being that can be represented by the Greek letter *Pi*, but the numerical value of *Pi* is such that its value cannot be marked off on an ideal number scale.

Limitations of Mathematical and Scientific Knowledge

Neither natural science alone, nor mathematics alone, nor, it seems, the wedding of the two satisfies man's desire to know the true nature of material reality, and neither, separately nor together, makes any claim to examine anything but the material world. It is interesting, as a case in point, to mention the ideal gas laws, which are derived from mathematics, as applied to gas behavior. It has been found, much to the discouragement of scientists, that the ideal gas laws are indeed ideal on paper, but they cannot be applied with complete accuracy to any known real gas. There have been several attempts, accordingly, to modify the ideal gas laws and bring them into correspondence with the experimentally known behavior of gases. There have been at least four outstanding empirical equations that take the ideal gas laws and add something here, as a guess, and subtract something there, as another guess, and hope that they meet with more consistent applicability than the original mathematically deduced laws. The four outstanding attempts mentioned are the Van der Waals Equation of State, the Kammerlingh Onnes Equation of State, the Berthelot Equation, and the Beattie-Bridgeman Equation of State. Neither the ideal gas laws, nor any of these four other equations of state, is a true symbolic representation of the nature of gaseous reality, nor even of its behavior. We are really no closer to coming to grips with material reality after knowing these equations, indeed less close, than we are to feeling pain after having said the word.

Both science and mathematics presume that there is order in the world. They have even demonstrated this within limits. Both are psychologically realistic; they feel that it is worth thinking about their objects because such thought can be carried on with a consistency which is not illusory. And yet, both, taken together with combined forces, have thus far been able to demonstrate only how material reality behaves under certain conditions. Neither has come to any definite conclusions about what reality is. Neither has come to any definite conclusions that would satisfy man's desire to know what a thing is. The result is that there should arise in the minds of the students of both mathematics and science a rather essential question mark: what and why? The realization that these questions cannot be answered by the sciences that create them sets the stage psychologically for another science.

Theology Completes Mathematics and Science

Theology begins where the natural sciences and mathematics leave off. Theology begins with the questions "what" and "why" and makes as its object their solution. Theology is of its nature more inclusive than the other sciences and must include the natural sciences and mathematics in its method, but cannot be included in them. The proper objects of theology are man, God, and the efforts of man to get to God. God is pure spirit; man is a combination of spirit and matter, and thus theology must concern itself not only with the domain of matter, which is the only concern of the natural sciences, but with spirit as well. Its object is thus much wider.

The possibilities for theology to present an explanation of the universe in which we find ourself are much greater than are the possibilities for the other sciences to do so, since theology, from its better point of vantage, is capable of seeing where matter fits into the scheme of things, where spirit fits into the scheme of things, and what the connection is between them. It is in the relationships of things to each other that there is meaning, and, consequently, truth. A thing must be seen in context in order to be seen properly. Certainly the study of individual things or even of an entire area of reality cannot produce real knowledge if the individual things or the area of reality are not seen in relation to all the rest of reality; it is impossible to make value judgments about the relative worth of things otherwise.

Because of the intimate connection between all things created, and because, as theology would say, they all have their own part to play in the manifestation of the glory of God, there can be no integration of knowledge on a valid and permanent basis without at the same time a fulfillment of our intellectual and volitional vocation of giving glory to God. If, by some inclusive overview, some universal *Weltanschauung*, we could determine with precision not only the nature of created reality, but the precise relationship it has to uncreated reality, we would have an integrated knowledge of the world in which we live. If such an overview formed the basis of our educational system, we would have an integrated educational system.

There can be no integration without a center of reference. This center of reference must be one to which all other things that in any way affect our lives are, or can be, referred. Such a point of attribution cannot, obviously, be an organic chemical upon which we are doing research, nor a classical mathematical problem, nor, if we would be whole beings, a position for which we are ambitious. Sometimes we make this center of our lives a person, only to be terribly disillusioned when the very center of our integrated conscious life proves to be destructible.

The center of life, as the center of education, must be something or someone undeniably permanent and immovable if we would not build upon sand. If the recognition of individual things must center about something to which they all belong or in which they all share in some way, then the integration of these individual things, the search of education, concerns this center. If in the true knowledge of the nature of created things we recognize their proper place in the manifestation of the glory of God, and at the very same instant fulfill our own vocation of giving glory to God by the proper and sacred use of these created things, the center of our integration should be something or some one through whom, and with whom, and in whom God receives all honor and glory.

Three Significant Factors of Integration

If one were to make a super-synthesis, and run the risk that all syntheses run, that of oversimplification, it might not be too incorrect to say that essentially only three things exist that have real significance: God, man, and the distance that separates them. It is interesting that there is a science, or several, of man; there is a science of God; but there is no science of the distance between them. For every thinking man, these three concepts form, consciously or unconsciously, a fairly basic problem in his psychological life. God, as we know Him, even from nature, is a supreme being who gives impetus to the motion in the world without Himself being moved by another. He is characterized by an intelligence that is overpowering; He is the cause of all things, and, by a stretch of our rational powers, we can say that we can discover by our own powers that He is a creator. Even from the natural sciences, astronomy, botany, zoology, and the others, we can arrive at a concept of God which we are sometimes almost afraid to formulate consciously.

Then we look at ourselves by comparison. We know our weaknesses, our fatigue, our failures in attempting to do what is right, our limitations, our smallness when compared to other people we know, and our overwhelming smallness when we realize that we are just one among an approximate billion and a half human beings like ourselves who are now living on earth. When we further realize that earth is a very mediocre planet in the solar system which is a very mediocre system in the universe, we are at times so appalled that instead of being humbled either we fail again to formulate the concept or we get discouraged.

If we could study man without being haunted by the comparison we are almost forced to make between man and God, or if we could just study God without allowing the study to pass the walls of the academic and enter the realm of the personal, we would be quite content. However, always rising from the back of our minds is the spectre of comparison: God exists, we exist, there must be an integration of the two, and yet the gap between us and God is limitless, and we are powerless to bridge it. This is a definite, basic problem since the existence of God and the existence of man as two facts must be faced up to and given some solution.

Three False Solutions of the God-Man Relationship

There are three solutions that are at once obvious: (1) deny the existence of God either directly in so many words, or, what is more common, by ignoring His existence; (2) deny man's existence is one of two ways: by denying the existence of his body or of his soul; (3) admit the existence of both God and man but deny that there is an infinite distance between them.

If one is an atheist, and denies God's existence, there is no problem to him in the relations of man to God. However, the life of man being what it is, there is a void created by such a denial that can be filled only by something equally psychologically important. This becomes for some political statism; for others, scientism; for still others, mathematicism; for others yet, psychologism, and so on. For Christians, such a view is not only incorrect, it is myopic. It is bourgeois and dull. It immediately divorces from one's consideration an infinite area of reality and by the same token colors the remaining rather small areas of reality to such an extent that Christians feel they cannot be observed and studied objectively. Atheism is certainly a way to solve a basic problem of human life, but the solution breeds other problems that are equally basic and imbalances that are equally disturbing.

Another solution to the same problem is to deny that there is a difference, and thus, a distance between God and man. The results of this solution are, in theory, in practice or both, to identify man and God. There is no distance between man and God: pantheism. There is some bridgeable distance between them: the traditional theory of the superman which formed the basis not only of Naziism but also of Communism. Man can, by his own power, supersede himself; the race can become divinized. In its less drastic forms, such a solution to the problems of man and God result in misguided philanthrophy, humanitarianism, push-buttonism, making earth heaven with the tacit denial of anything of importance other than earth. This solution to the problem, Christians will admit, is facile and even attractive at times, but essentially unworthy.

The third obvious solution to the dilemma is to deny the existence of man as we know him. It is rather silly to deny his existence totally, and so some deny the existence of his soul, others that of his body. Those who deny the existence of man's body are the traditional philosophical idealists with their religious analogues, the Christian scientists, spiritists, astrologists, and the like. The spirit is unlimited by matter, and to that extent boundless. If this be so, the distance between God and man, if indeed the adherents of this solution are not at the same time atheists, becomes bridgeable. Whether we actually bridge it or not is relatively unimportant for the solution to the problem; the essential thing is that it *can* be bridged by our own power. The sciences which study man's body of course, suffer considerably from this solution to the problem. Such things as medicine, anatomy, physiology, and the like become not only invalid but useless for those who adhere to this solution to the problem.

Probably in our age, the most prevalent solution of the God-man relations is denial of the existence of man's soul, both academically and practically in daily life. This tendency, in its grossest form, is materialism, the overt denial of the existence of the soul such as was made by men like Watson. Our age, however, is somewhat more genteel than ages past. We take a dim view of such an unequivocal denial of man's soul. We use today more subtle means to accomplish the same objective. Without actually drawing an honest conclusion about it, we act as though the only things that exist are those things which can be measured, weighed, and so on. We apply, consciously or not, with complete abandon, the methods of the physical sciences to non-material reality. We know the methods of physical science to be valid in the physical sciences. When they fail to achieve results in the sphere of the non-material, we perpetrate the solipsism of not distinguishing method and object. We feel that there are only two things that can be done: deny the validity of the method of physical sciences (which we cannot do because of its accomplishments) or deny the existence of non-material reality (which we can do, and which some do). Actually the distinction to be made is that the method of physical science is valid for its object; but its results in fields that are apart from its object will not only be of questionable value, but a priori are practically certain to be useless.

Materialism, however, whatever form it assumes, whether blatant or refined, offers a facile solution to man's basic problem, of his relations to God. If only man's body exists, and if man's body disintegrates with death, there is nothing left after death and no need to consider any relations between God and man; if there are any, they are impertinent.

Christ, the Only Safe Bridge

It is the belief of Christians both that God exists and man exists, and that there is a distance between the two that a life of striving cannot of itself bridge. The denial of any aspect of reality results in a lack of perspective and a categorization of life which are destructive of the fulfillment that all men long for. Christians feel that a bridging of the distance between God and man is not only possible, but exists, and that that bridge is Christ who is at once God and man, and who in Himself unites the two aspects of all reality, the created and the uncreated. It is unnecessary to deny the existence of God, or to resort to pantheism, or to become a materialist or an idealist. It is necessary only to become Christian.

While it is impossible to superimpose methods, objects or lights in the various areas of intellectual examination without confusion or, what is worse, error, it is equally impossible to separate the study of created reality from uncreated reality without achieving the same results. Without theology there cannot be a fully informed science or mathematics. There can be no integration of knowledge without the fulfillment of the individual. The fulfillment of the individual is impossible without the fulfillment of his vocation and this is to give honor and glory to God which can be accomplished only through Him through whom and with whom and in whom is all honor and glory, Christ. Education, as life, for the Christian must be Christocentric to be integrated.

> There he made his lodging in a cave; and all at once the Lord's word came to him, Elias, what dost thou here? Why, he answered, I am all jealousy for the honor of the Lord God of hosts; see how the sons of Israel have forsaken thy covenant, thrown down thy altars and put thy prophets to the sword. Of these, I only am left, and now my life too, is forfeit. Then word came to him to go out and stand there in the Lord's presence; the Lord God Himself would

pass by. A wind there was, rude and boisterous, that shook the mountains and broke the rocks in pieces before the Lord, but the Lord was not in the wind. And after the wind, an earthquake, but the Lord was not in the earthquake. And after the earthquake a fire, but the Lord was not in the fire. And after the fire, the whisper of a gentle wind. Elias, when he heard it wrapped his face in his mantle, and went out to stand at the cave door.[2]

God was not in the earthquake, nor the wind, nor the fire, but in the whisper of a gentle wind. God is not known through science or mathematics, but through a super-science, in the body of truth that comes from all science, a little from here and a little from there—in the integration that can never be accomplished except in the innermost soul of man in quiet, and in gentleness after a long time of seeking after the truth. It comes to him as the whisper of a gentle wind which can be easily overlooked, easily drowned out by the blast of a bomb or the roar of a jet engine, or even the click of a push button. Truth can be found totally only by making a plunge at the end of reason into faith. Integration can be affected only in the individual because only the individual is versatile enough to be moulded by all aspects of truth into a unified whole. Integration cannot be accomplished by a course called Integration 101. It comes gradually, gently, to each person and by the efforts of each person, whose way has been prepared by the direction and the integrated lives of those who teach him or influence him in any way.

Integration can be accomplished only by keeping the fields of theology, mathematics, and natural sciences specifically distinct and pursuing them with intensity to set the ground work for the value judgment the individual must make about God and man.

[2] III Kings, 19:9-13 (Knox version).

The ungraded primary

Rt. Rev. Msgr. James E. Hoflich

In order to help provide for differences in mental ability among their students, particularly during the first few years of schooling, several schools have been experimenting with various forms of ungraded or nongraded classrooms. Although the plan itself is not really new, the great current interest in it is. Among the first school systems to try the ungraded arrangement on a large scale was that of the St. Louis Archdiocese. In the next article, Monsignor Hoflich explains and evaluates the ungraded program as it operates there.

In 1953 all of the elementary schools of the Archdiocese of St. Louis were "Ungraded" in the Primary. The purpose of this action, of course, was one phase of a long-range program for the improvement of instruction. A specific study to determine why so many children left the primary grades without satisfactorily acquiring the basic reading skills brought to light the following information:

1. Many children are too immature when they enter the first grade.
2. The policy of social promotion carries with it many evils.

On the basis of these findings we made the following changes:

New Entrance Date

We advanced the entrance date. Children must be six years of age by September 15 to be admitted into the first year primary.

The child will learn only when he is *ready* to learn. Many factors enter into the child's readiness for learning. His physical, emotional, and social maturity as

Abridged and reprinted with permission from the *National Catholic Education Association Bulletin,* 52:9 ff., November, 1960.

well as his chronological age are very important. To attempt to teach any specific learning skill before a child is ready for it is a *waste of time and effort* on the part of both teacher and pupil. Recent studies confirm the wisdom of the new age regulation.

Reorganized Primary Based on Levels of Achievement

In September 1953, we determined definite levels of achievement based on the sequential development of skills. The content of the levels is precisely the same as that formerly taught in the first three grades. The essential difference is this: *levels* are defined in terms of skills which the child has and can show that he has; the term *grade* gives no assurance as to which skills he has achieved. Another significant difference is the rate of learning and the time spent in the various content areas. The teacher is not pressured to cover prescribed subject matter within a certain period of time. She adapts procedures and subject matter to the abilities of the children, and she adjusts the speed of the program to the children within the groups, always recognizing progress whether fast or slow. This eliminates hazy half-knowledge, pushing and straining to meet grade standards. The teacher's responsibility is to keep each child moving along as fast as he is capable of achieving success. Social promotion and chronological age placement are thus abolished in favor of continuous progress and growth.

The sequential reading skills must be presented and taught to the child by the classroom teacher. Interest is a vital factor in teaching these skills, but in order to maintain interest in the basic text it is necessary to keep the child from reading ahead. It is for this reason that the child is not permitted to take his reader home until it has been completed. Parents can best assist the teacher by reading aloud to their children and by encouraging them to read library books.

Flexibility

No reference is made to the terms "First Grade," "Second Grade," or "Third Grade." The program allows for easy shifting from group to group or room to room. The child is placed in the group where he can work most effectively. His progress is considered *satisfactory* if he is doing all he is capable of doing. The *time* required to complete a particular level or the *room* in which he completes it are not important factors.

Appraisal of Pupil's Progress

Effective teaching with proper adjustment to individual needs requires continuous appraisal of progress. At the end of each level a test is administered to the children within the group to determine whether they have successfully achieved the required specific skills before they are advanced to the next level. Results of these tests are recorded on a cumulative Individual Progress Record. A diagnostic study of the strengths and weaknesses of each child, based on the test summary sheet, prevents the evil of advancing children without knowing definitely whether they are or are not ready. Our objective is to have each child work to the best of his ability.

Parents are informed of the child's progress through periodic conferences as well as report cards which are issued six times during the school year.

Time Spent in the Primary

The minimum time a child spends in the primary department is three years; the maximum time is four years. Rapid learners are given an enriched program to continue building reading power. A few gifted and mature pupils may be able to complete Level H before the required three years. In this event these pupils will be privileged to start the fourth grade reader while remaining in the primary unit. Slow learners are given sufficient time to achieve the required skills according to their rate of learning. They are not retarded; they are not failed. The following September the next teacher continues on the page where the child left off in June.

Schools where the ungraded primary has been functioning over a period of years report a surprising low percentage of children actually requiring a four-year program—approximately 5 per cent. Contrast this with the reported 15 per cent to 20 per cent failure pattern common throughout the country! . . .

Acceleration

Since the Parish School Board adopted a minimum starting age of six years by September 15 for the primary, some children will be approximately seven years old when they enter primary. Therefore, at the end of the primary a small group of these older pupils may be able to go directly to the fifth grade teacher's room. There may also be a small number of younger pupils who will be eligible for acceleration. The accelerated pupils will not skip a grade. The pupil's Individual Progress Record will indicate where the fifth grade teacher is to continue the reading instruction.

A standardized test, recommended by the School Office, is to be administered to all primary pupils who have completed Level H by June of the third year primary. The tests are to be administered and scored by the principal or some person delegated by her. The teacher of the pupils may *not* give the tests. The achievement on the standardized test for pupils who are nine years and six months or older in June must be 5.0 in reading and 5.0 in arithmetic. Children younger than this will be required to achieve a score of 7.0 in reading and 5.0 in arithmetic. The primary faculty and the principal are to confer as to the elgibility of the pupils to be accelerated. . . .

An Evaluation of the Ungraded Primary in the Archdiocese of St. Louis

. . . According to Archdiocesan records, hundreds of children have been benefiting from the flexibility of grouping as provided in the ungraded primary. In a traditionally graded school, some of these children would have been stifled in their intellectual development; others would have been pushed and pulled beyond their intellectual capacity.

Children who were given the advantage of the modified acceleration plan are reported doing well—their performance compares favorably with that of their non-accelerated companions in whatever grade they might be. Children who took four years in the primary are able to do fourth grade work much more efficiently because they were not thrust into too challenging a situation, too soon.

In all of this, the alert teacher knows the difference between letting the child progress at his own rate and letting a child take life too easy. And—taking life too easy for one child might mean straining to the utmost for another. There is another factor to consider also—if a superior child decides to take life easy, he might seem to be making life easier for his teacher who does not have to keep him "going," but—remember there is that obligation to keep each child working to *his* capacity. I grant that this is not easy, but the day will come when "Your children will rise up and call you blessed" for having helped them develop their potentialities to the utmost.

What factors are necessary for any ungraded primary to function successfully? First of all, the creation of levels of skills to be mastered by the pupils should make teachers more acutely aware of just what to teach at each level, thus making teaching more purposeful with very definite and specific objectives of instruction. Second, the removal of rigid grade barriers enables the teacher to teach the child at his own level, but the teacher must also free herself from any notion that she is a "first grade," "second grade," or "third grade," teacher. The mere removal of the label from the classroom door does not suffice—there must be, on the part of the teacher, a complete conversion to the doctrine of developmental teaching, of pacing teaching to the child's rate of growth and development.

To stand at one's classroom door with a glint in one's eyes proclaiming to the world: "I am a Second Grade Teacher and teach only second grade material—all who enter here *must* be reading a second grade book" is proclaiming an extremely narrow and dim view of the overwhelming facts of research in child growth and development. What you should be is a *Primary Teacher*—that all-embracing individual who accepts and teaches a child at the level at which he is.

Intra-room and inter-room flexibility is an essential means of adjusting pupil progress. A three-year study was conducted in a large elementary school of the Saint Louis Archdiocese, during which time a group of children was carefully followed during its progress through the ungraded primary. The children assigned to Room A were the rapid learners, those in Room B the average learners, while those in Room C were the slow learners.

The teaching of a class of slow learners is a difficult task—one that challenges the ingenuity and patience of a teacher, but one that can be extremely rewarding for the teacher who has a loving understanding of the many problems confronting the slow learners. These teachers bring a near sparkle into the lives of these less-gifted children who have to plod along at a slow rate, but who can and *do* experience success under proper teacher-guidance. These teachers do yeoman service to our children who have been less endowed. It must be recognized that whatever intellectual gifts children possess, be they great or small, are God-given; all the child can do, all the teacher can do, is work with what these God-given gifts are.

No teacher can, however, do justice to a slow-learning group if she has an overcrowded classroom. Parallel teachers with the more rapid and average learners surely realize that they should have the larger number of children, thereby lessening the classroom load of the teacher with the slow-learning children.

Teachers of the slow-learning group will probably agree with the bulk of research evidence which indicates that heterogeneous classes often prove fatal to slow learners, since these pupils find it impossible to compete with gifted pupils and tend continually to be thrust back farther and farther into a consciousness of their own failure. Sometime it is claimed that pupils of higher ability give slow learners a standard to strive for. The fact remains, however, that since the basic mental equipment for achieving such standards is lacking in slow learners, it is neither fair nor an inducement to their learning to have them enter into competition which foredooms them to failure.

Remember this: if a child works up to his own ability, he really "rings the bell"; and you, the teacher, the parents, and the child himself should be equally proud and satisfied.

The success of any ungraded primary program is realized completely when all the teachers in the primary division of a school form a closely knit unit and there is much professional interchange of ideas and cooperation on pupils' progress. As a teacher of children in the primary division of a school, rather than a teacher of first, second, or third grade material, the teacher's own professional growth as an educator is inevitable. *All* children in the primary division become *our* children, and the primary school becomes a happier place for teachers to teach and for children to learn.

Montessori and Catholic principles

Aubert J. Clark, O.F.M. Conv.

*The educational theories and methods of Maria
Montessori were known to well-informed American
educators since the latter part of the nineteenth
century, but they were not implemented to any
considerable degree in this country until a few
years after her death in 1952. Since then, they have
become extremely popular, especially, as Father
Clark points out, among young Catholic parents. In
the following article, Father Clark compares the
Montessori method with traditional Catholic views
on the nature of the child, the role of the family and
the teacher, and the place of training for social
development.*

Recently the United States has witnessed a rather remarkable and widespread
interest in the teaching methods of Dr. Maria Montessori (1869–1952). Whatever the explanation, so many American parents and educators have been inquir-
ing about Montessori that their questions have served as a catalyst to promote
comment. Both popular and scholarly magazines, as well as newspapers,[1] have
printed articles; *Time* magazine has devoted a part of its education section to the
best known proponent of the revival, Mrs. Nancy M. Rambusch, and her school,
Whitby School (opened 1958);[2] Mrs. Rambusch has appeared on television to

[1] Cf. E. M. Standing, "Montessori and Rational Psychology, *Dominicana*, XLVI
(Fall, 1961), 228-234; J. A. Morris, "Can Our Children Learn Faster," *Saturday Evening
Post*, November 18, 1961, 17-24; and *The Catholic Transcript* (Hartford), June 8,
1961, p. 10.

[2] "Education," *Time*, May 12, 1961, p. 63.

Abridged and reprinted with permission from *The Catholic Educational Review*,
60:73–81, February, 1961.

explain her interest in Montessori, and has conducted a demonstration program at the annual convention of the National Catholic Educational Association.

Montessori schools exist or are planned for in Los Angeles, Washington, Boston, Philadelphia, Cleveland, Chicago, and many other areas. Although there seems no special reason for it,[3] the revival has been concentrated largely in Catholic circles and among young married couples of the upper-middle and middle class. St. Aidan's School of Washington, D.C., might serve as a typical example of the current techniques of organization. About twenty-five young couples and a few of their friends organized an association, which is now incorporated. They invited speakers with a knowledge of the Montessori method to address them. Convinced of the worth of what they heard and read, they arranged for the use of a building on the grounds of Dunbarton College, secured (with some difficulty) the services of a trained Montessori teacher, collected the necessary money and materials, and opened St. Aidan's School on January 8, 1962. A remarkable example of lay initiative and the lay apostolate!

Since most of the St. Aidan's group and so many of the people at present involved in the Montessori revival are Catholics, it might be profitable to point out areas where it seems that an investigation of the Montessori doctrine in the light of Catholic principles could be of interest and assistance. A vast literature devoted to explanation and comment on the method as such already exists, and Montessori's psychology has been examined by Standing in the light of Thomistic teaching. Hence, we shall limit our effort to a more general attempt to ascertain the degree to which the Montessori method harmonizes with a Catholic view of the nature of the child, the role of the family and teacher, and the place of training for social development. A selected bibliography of works by and about Maria Montessori is appended for those who desire to carry the investigation further.

Lack of Philosophical Preciseness

Like so many educational reformers who developed and propagated personal systems or methods, Dr. Maria Montessori never left a single, systematized account of the principles behind her methodology. This lack has been subject to some criticism by historians of education,[4] and one has concluded that Montessori was "an indifferent philosopher," [5] whose teaching procedures often contradicted or had no discernible relation to her general principles. Certainly there are special problems for the Catholic seeking to discover the relationship of Montessori to his traditional Aristotelian-Thomistic philosophy.

[3] The Montessori method is used with apparent success in schools connected with many religions. India is one of the centers of current Montessori work and finds her techniques quite compatible with Brahmanism, Mohammedanism, and Buddhism. Montessori schools are part of the public school system of the Borough of Acton, London, and were fairly common in China before the Communist takeover.

[4] R. Freeman Butts, *A Cultural History of Western Education* (New York: McGraw-Hill Book Co., 1955), p. 406.

[5] Luella Cole, *A History of Education: Socrates to Montessori* (New York: Rinehart & Co., 1950), p. 572.

One major difficulty, as always, is terminology. One is inclined to feel that much of Montessori's method is her personal intuition and shrewd common sense based on observation and expert diagnosis, but not expressed in precise philosophical terms. This may be seen in *The Absorbent Mind*,[6] one of her last works, whose French title is a bit more revealing, *L'Esprit Absorbant de L'enfant*.[7] Herein Montessori attempts to describe the mind of the child which is full of mystery, which is quite different from that of adults, and which has a nature and workings admittedly not yet fully understood. Throughout the book she uses phrases and sentences which are both obscure and confusing to the scholastically-trained mind, and which seem to have equally little relation to any other system of philosophy. For example, what does it mean to say that "the newly-born infant must possess a different type of mind from ours, endowed with different powers"[8] or to say that in the first months of his existence, before he is able to move, "the child takes in the whole of his environment by means of the absorbent power of his unconscious mind"?[9] Similarly, Montessori's use of certain phrases leads to some confusion. One is doubtful of the possible meaning to be given to such expressions as "create" in the phrase, the child "creates" his own mind; or "incarnation," in the phrase, "progressive incarnation" used to describe the development of the child.[10] This is not to say that such expressions cannot be or have not been explained satisfactorily by Montessori or her disciples, but to illustrate the difficulties facing anyone who attempts to extract from Montessori a precise set of philosophical ideas or principles which can be held up to the more well-known statements of Catholic philosophy and principles.

On the Nature of the Child

Granted this difficulty, we turn to a consideration of Montessori's opinion on the nature and dignity of the individual child. Certainly this is of fundamental importance; no educator can afford to neglect a clear conception of the nature of man and what it means to be an individual. All Catholic philosophers would agree on the simple assertion of the catechism that man is a creature composed of body and soul and made to the image and likeness of God. All would agree that, though we have much in common with the animal, we are decidedly different, conscious of the spirit within us that enables us to live beyond the pale of the beast and to look forward to an eternal life. All would agree on the traditional Catholic affirmation of the inherent personal dignity of the individual.

---

[6] Maria Montessori, *The Absorbent Mind*, trans. Claude Clermont (Adyar, India: Theosophical Publishing House, 1959).

[7] Maria Montessori, *L'esprit Absorbant de L'enfant*, trans. Georgette Bernard (Bruges: Desclee de Brouwer, 1959).

[8] *Ibid.*, p. 24.

[9] *Ibid.*, p. 24.

[10] E. Mortimer Standing, *Maria Montessori* (Fresno, Calif.: Academy Library Guild, 1957), pp. 90, 91, and *passim*.

There seems little doubt that Maria Montessori is definitely in accord on these basic principles. Her stand on basic Aristotelian and Thomistic psychology has been explained at length by E. Mortimer Standing.[11] She was particularly concerned with expressing her concern for the dignity of man, that is, for her, the child. One of her most persistent themes was a devastating criticism of parents and adults who treat children as insignificant. Montessori felt that the dignity of man lay in his spiritual qualities and began at birth. She attacked those who treated the child as "a little thing, an empty thing without importance," [12] and talked of a need for a completely new attitude towards the infant. She was particularly critical of Americans.[13] Her program for the training of a Montessori directress made respect for the inherent dignity of the child, even the smallest child, a prominent element, and she often expressed a desire that every mother be especially trained in this regard.[14]

It seems fair, then, to conclude that Montessori stands in harmony with the basic principles of Catholic philosophy on the nature of the child and the dignity of the individual—concepts of the greatest importance in any theory of education. But the individual is not to be considered alone; from the moment of his birth he is ordinarily a member of the family unit. And Catholics hold that there are certain rights and responsibilities of the family in education.

On the Role of the Parent

That the family enjoys the fundamental right to educate is a principle dear to the hearts of Catholics and too familiar to need elaboration here. Equally well known are the corresponding duties of parents to provide for the total welfare of their offspring, to assure proper physical nurture, spiritual development and intellectual training suitable to the society in which the children are to develop. As one might expect, Montessori presumes the traditional priority of the family, particularly from the child's infancy to about the age of three. She is not too explicit on this point, but it can be safely assumed in the light of the general tenor of her works and her proposals for the education of mothers.

After this fundamental agreement, however, it seems that Montessori and the family tend to part company. Her long-time associate and official biographer did not even deem it necessary to include the terms, "family," "home," "parents," "father," or "mother" in his index; [15] and although Montessori's own works are generally not indexed, one cannot but notice the lack of reference to the family.

11 *Ibid.*, 71-148, and *loc. cit., passim.*

12 Maria Montessori, *Reconstruction in Education* (Madras; India: Theosophical Publishing House, 1948), p. 2.

13 Maria Montessori, "Mother and Child," *Journal of Proceedings for the National Education Association of the United States* (1915), p. 1128.

14 She had a program for "Mother's Helpers" which has not received much attention and was never developed sufficiently to be a factor of major importance.

15 Standing, pp. 350-354.

Montessori was quite stringent in her criticism of parents' treatment of their children, considering the average parent rather like a misguided zealot who admittedly desires good for his child and acts out of love, but in reality causes great harm. According to Montessori, the best thing that parents can do is to refrain from interfering in this great work whereby the child himself creates the man. Rather coldly, she argues that mothers have lost the instinct to guide their offspring and that science must instruct mothers in a new education.[16]

Montessori seems rather weak on the subject of parental authority moreover, and the role of the parent as a moral guide. It appears that she tends to underemphasize the role of parental and maternal authority when she remarks that "the adult by his continuous supervision, by his uninterrupted advice, by his dictatorial attitude, disturbs and thwarts the development of the child." [17] It is true that she has spoken in support of parental authority,[18] but she does not seem to give an adequate definition or explanation of such authority, nor a clear idea of its origin, nature and limits. It seems that it would be possible to interpret Montessori's teaching in such a way as seriously to diminish the role of the parent. Further clarification of this point is evidently needed.

On the Role of the Teacher

Montessori's conception of parental authority relates also to the role of the teacher *in loco parentis*. Here we feel that Montessori departs sharply from the traditional concept of a teacher, who is spoken of in Montessori terms as exercising "the role of the teacher as non-mother." Always aware that basically the child must do his own learning, we have generally thought of the teacher as one who is a guide, who takes a thoroughly active part in the learning process, who fulfills certain professional norms, who plans the subject matter to be covered and decides upon the order and manner of presentation—in short, who plays a role quite different from that of a Montessori directress.

Even from the purely secular point of view, Cole comments on the difficulty common to all educators who desire to emphasize the freedom of the child. Since they are committed to a type of unforced learning, they automatically exclude any form of didactic teaching and find, after a while, that children's interests and spontaneous activities are not in themselves enough for schoolwork.[19] Their problem is not what happens, but what fails to happen. It is then that the traditional teacher would step in and play her usual role. One is not sure where Montessori would stand in this instance.

[16] Maria Montessori, *Education for a New World* (Madras, India: Kalakshetra Publications, 1948), p. 27.

[17] Maria Montessori, *The Child* (Madras, India: Theosophical Publishing House, 1948), p. 11.

[18] Montessori, *The Absorbent Mind*, pp. 14-15.

[19] Cole, p. 574.

On the Social Development of the Child

Finally, we turn to an ambiguous area which appears to present a problem for which neither Montessori nor her disciples have found a satisfactory solution, that is, the area of the social development of the child. That this was a problem for Montessori in her lifetime is evidenced by her last book, *The Absorbent Mind*, which was in part intended to answer her critics, and where she says:

> Teachers who use direct methods cannot understand how social behavior is fostered in a Montessori school. They think it offers scholastic material but not social material. They say, "If the child does everything on his own, what becomes of social life?" [20]

That it is still a problem for her disciples is shown by the lead article of a recent publication of the Association Montessori de France. "Première question: Si les enfants dans les écoles Montessori travaillent plus individuellement que collectivement, comment peuvent-ils se préparer à la vie sociale?" [21]

It would seem that Montessorians realize the need for a type of education which would equip the child for social living, for citizenship, and for life in the national and international world. That Catholics agree on the need for such education is evident from a glance at any authoritative work. The problem lies chiefly in the accusation that the Montessori method stifles such socially-oriented education. The charges usually center around contentions that: (a) her method involves work which is almost entirely on an individual basis with little group instruction or joint projects, and (b) the notion of citizenship and/or patriotism barely figures in the vast total literature authored by Maria Montessori.[22] As far as the latter point is concerned, Montessori seems to have favored the idea of a community of nations and looked to a larger goal.[23] Since we do not desire here to become involved in the issue of nationalism versus internationalism,[24] we shall center our attention on the first point.

There is little doubt that the Montessori method tends largely to individual instruction, and in the current popular accounts of the new Montessori schools in the United States this point is emphasized. The freedom of the child to work alone on the particular apparatus which at the moment appeals to him is an integral part of the methodology. Mrs. Rambusch explains it:

[20] Montessori, *The Absorbent Mind*, p. 224.

[21] Association Montessori de France, *Bulletin*, No. 28 (Mars, 1960), I.

[22] As far as one can see, except for a statement that patriotism can best be taught between the ages of twelve and eighteen, Montessori does not consider this notion any further.

[23] Montessori favored "a universal movement for human reconstruction" which would not be limited "to any one nation or to any particular political trend." Cf. *The Formation of Man* (Madras, India: Theosophical Publishing House, 1955), p. 13.

[24] Cf. Sr. Joan Bland, "Teaching International Relations," *Bulletin of the National Catholic Educational Association*, LVII (February, 1961), 16-24.

The "prepared environment," the role of the teacher as non-mother, and the emphasis, in the child's early years, on work, and that individual work, are distinctive features of Montessori's approach to learning. As Piaget after her, Montessori recognized that the young child's unequal struggle for self-affirmation precludes his entering into groups. A child under the age of eight rarely "constellates" in groups larger than three children. The cherished American dictum of the "felt needs of the group" becomes meaningless when applied to young children. The felt needs in the classrooms of young children are invariably those of the teacher. The Froebelian kindergarten, as is its American counterpart, was completely group oriented. . . . The Montessori classroom is not.[25]

Group projects or games do not seem to be an integral part of the system (though they exist at Whitby School), nor does the curriculum structure involve any planned program of an orderly or cyclical nature designed to acquaint the child gradually with the society in which he lives. It seems to be a serious defect that over the course of her very long life Montessori never drew up any more than a vague proposal for a curriculum plan, since this reduces her contribution largely to what is essentially a neutral methodology.

Montessori, as we have noted, recognized the problem. She answered her critics by pointing out that in her schools a community spirit was fostered by the exercises of practical life, by training in courtesy, by mixing different ages in ungraded groups,[26] by having the older pupils help the younger,[27] by interesting all in each others' work, and by concluding from observation that children tend to turn spontaneously to the companionship of others after a period of individual work. In principle, Montessori stated that she recognized the need for children to associate in community activity,[28] and fully supported all the usual values attributed to education for social development.[29] In fact, she held that it was easier for the child to adapt quickly to the tensions of our modern, pluralistic society.[30] On paper, there is no question but that Montessori had an important place for education in social living.

Yet, precisely how this was carried out in her practical methodology has been the subject of some concern. In a Montessori school, as in any other, there is in practice much social interplay. And there seems to be little doubt that, when she herself taught, in her hands the most simple exercise could become the experi-

[25] Nancy M. Rambusch, "The Montessori Approach to Learning," *Ibid.*, LVIII (August, 1961), 321.
[26] Montessori deserves credit as one of the earliest initiators of the ungraded primary class.
[27] Cf. Montessori, *The Absorbent Mind*, p. 225 ff.
[28] Maria Montessori, *To Educate the Human Potential* (Madras, India: Kalakshetra Publications, 1956), p. 6.
[29] Maria Montessori, *The Advanced Montessori Method* (New York: Frederick A. Stokes Co., 1917), I, p. 98.
[30] *Ibid.*, 337.

ence of a lifetime. But this was a personal charism. The problem is whether or not *the system* provides for such experiences in any structured plan to be used by a less talented directress. The answer is still ambiguous, and ought to be the subject of further objective study.

Conclusion

We have noted briefly one area where Dr. Maria Montessori appears to be in complete accord with traditional Catholic principles, one area where she appears to have departed somewhat, and a third area where there is a certain amount of ambiguity. We hope that the problems and issues which we have raised will stimulate, not partisan defense or attack, but further scholarly study on the part of those interested in the current revival of a remarkable theory.

Programed instruction

Sister Mary Nora, S.S.N.D.

*Programed learning may prove to be one of the
most significant educational developments of the
1960s, if not one of the most revolutionary
innovations in the entire history of education. Or it
may, as some of its critics have maintained, prove to
be little more than a fad, which will soon pass into
oblivion. Without attempting to predict what the
role of programed instruction will be in the
schools of the future, Sister Mary Nora believes that
Catholic school administrators should participate in
the determination of that role. To do so, they must
be informed about the subject. The purpose of the
following article is to foster an understanding of, and
stimulate interest in, education via automation.*

Since education is directed toward an automated age, today's administrator, acting in his role of educational interpreter, is frequently asked by parents, teachers, and boards of education, "What is programed instruction?"

Programed instruction is a combination of the Socratic method of teaching by question and "the Cartesian method of breaking down course materials into small pieces arranged in a hierarchic order." [1] The program presents the individual with questions and answers, problems to be solved, or exercises to be worked independently at his own rate of speed. There is some type of feedback or correction so the student knows his progress at each step and receives a cue

[1] Charles I. Foltz, *The World of Teaching Machines* (Washington: Electronic Teaching Laboratories, 1961), p. 3.

Abridged and reprinted with permission from the *National Catholic Education Association Bulletin*, 58:8–20, May, 1962.

for correcting his errors. Three characteristics differentiate programed instruction from most audio-visual media:

> First, continuous active student response is required, providing explicit practice and testing of each step of what is to be learned.
> Second, a basis is provided for informing the student with minimal delay whether each response he makes is correct, leading him directly or indirectly to correction of his errors.
> Third, the student proceeds on an individual basis at his own rate—faster students romping through an instructional sequence very rapidly, slower students being tutored as slowly as necessary, with indefinite patience to meet their special needs.[2]

In the early 1920's, S. L. Pressey of Ohio State University advocated that teachers be freed for their professional duties and pleaded that clerical work be not categorized as an instructor's function. With this in mind "he developed an apparatus which taught, tested, and informed the student as to the correctness of his answers." [3] Little attention was focused on his research at that time.

Technological progress coupled with B. F. Skinner's investigations into the learning processes triggered interest in the teaching machine.

> . . . his machine would teach rather than test, and it would teach by presenting questions in such a way that the child would always (or almost always) produce the correct answer. Reinforcement of the answer would "shape" the child's behavior, adding this "response" to his "repertoire," and he would learn arithmetic or spelling. . . .[4]

Norman Crowder of the Western Design Division of United States Industries and Sidney L. Pressey lead a vocal minority in opposing Skinner's method of programing. They maintain that presentation of larger logical units explaining some principle in its entirety is more effective than breaking down a program into minutiae. Skinner is a proponent of the constructed response while the multiple-choice answer is characteristic of the Crowder program.[5]

In the hope that teaching machines would be a panacea for all educational deficiencies, specialists, machines, literature, and programs mushroomed until today the market is flooded with material ranging from excellent to worthless. Surrounded by these pressures the administrator must keep an open mind buttressed by solid knowledge, must be discriminating, and yet provide the necessary

[2] A. A. Lumsdaine, "Teaching Machines and Self-Instructional Materials," *Audio-Visual Communication Review* (Vol. VII, No. 3, Summer, 1959), p. 164.

[3] Nelda B. Ikenberry, "Teaching Machines," *Elementary English* (Vol. XXXVIII, No. 6, October, 1961), p. 395.

[4] Martin Mayer, *The Schools* (New York: Harper and Brothers, 1961), p. 396.

[5] Foltz, *op. cit.*, p. 16.

leadership in the use of any teaching aid which has a significant role in achieving curriculum goals.

Perhaps the most eloquent and urgent call for such leadership has been made by J. Bernard Everett, assistant superintendent in Newton, Massachusetts:

> It seems to be increasingly evident, therefore, that the major responsibility for the future of programed learning rests primarily with public-school educators like myself. We cannot afford to wait for the academic scholars, the professors of education, or our professional associates to tell us what to do. We must take the initiative, for if we don't it will be seized by others less qualified than we are to decide what should happen in the schools.[6]

Questions persist and the administrator is confronted with queries such as:

1. Will P. I. replace the teacher?
2. Does P. I. depend on teaching machines?
3. How can P. I. best be used?
4. Should P. I. attempt to teach the entire course?
5. How do we know P. I. will work?
6. Why isn't P. I. just another workbook?
7. What about tests and experiments? [7]

The purpose of this paper is to explore answers which some researchers and administrators have given to these questions as programed instruction moved from the laboratory phase into the field testing stage.

The administrator can remind the interrogators that "teachers were not displaced by books, motion pictures, or television." [8] "But just as the introduction of the printed book stimulated rather than reduced the demand for teachers, so should other technological advantages." [9] Good teachers have always been among the first to welcome any new device or material which would help them to become more proficient in their art. It appears that programed instruction, with or without machines, will facilitate and supplement the efforts of the teacher freeing him "from many of his routine tasks, to make his work more satisfying and more effective by giving him more opportunity to teach better informed students and more time to spend with individual students." [10] Perhaps programed books and teaching machines may transmit factual knowledge, concepts, and skills with a higher degree of efficiency than a teacher, but the warmth, understanding, and

---

[6] Kenneth Komoski, "What Are the Schools Doing?" *NEA Journal* (Vol. L, No. 8, November, 1961), p. 28.

[7] Ohmer Milton and Leonard J. West, *Programed Instruction—What It is and How It Works* (Chicago: Harcourt, Brace and World, Inc., November, 1961, pp. 27-30.

[8] Forrest E. Conner, "What Should an Administrator's Attitude Be?" *NEA Journal* (Vol. L, No. 8, November, 1961), p. 26.

[9] *Programed Instruction in Books and Teaching Machines,* McGraw-Hill Book Co.

[10] Leslie P. Greenhill and Alexander Frazier, "Technology in Education," *NEA Journal* (Vol. XLIX, No. 6, September, 1960), p. 72.

inspiration which a teacher gives is a dimension in education which no machine can supply.

However, to the harassed administrator plagued by the problems of teacher shortage and crowded classrooms, programed instruction may be a boon.

From current literature on the subject the administrator is aware that machines are not the only devices designed for self-instruction.

Glaser, Homme, and Evans are among those who have developed simple methods which retain some of the key features of their more elaborate counterparts. These educators have employed responses-and-correction sequences provided by a special, nonconventional form of "programmed" question-and-answer book.[11]

From a financial point of view these are desirable. It should be noted that they lack the fun and features of stimulus control devices which have a strong appeal. This type is neither self-scoring nor cheat proof.

Mechanical devices of many sorts have been used in American education for over a half-century. Teachers have used flash cards, phonic wheels and word ladders, display racks, projection lanterns, the flash meter, tacistoscopes and other devices. "Various types of practice exercises and workbooks that were introduced a quarter-century and more ago embodied the principles found in some of the new teaching machines and in programmed learning." [12]

Auto-instructional devices have a wide technological range and cost from a portable $19.85 model to a $6,500 complex IBM-type.[13]

This range includes no machine at all—for example, merely a set of cards in a cardboard or plastic case, or a mimeographed sheet; a write-in (constructed response) machine; a machine using slides and tape; a multi-choice machine; a film machine; and a machine using a combination of microfilm and motion pictures; and a set of machines electronically tied in with a television broadcast.[14]

The administrator can investigate, examine, evaluate, select, and use any type of programed instruction which his budget will allow.

Opinions as to the most effective way in which to use programed instruction are as numerous as administrators, teachers, and researchers. Perhaps the results of experimentation in programed instruction will indicate that certain individuals learn faster and better with one type of programing used in a particular way

---

[11] A. A. Lumsdaine, *op. cit., The Education Digest,* (Vol. XXV, No. 4, December, 1959), pp. 3-4.

[12] Arthur I. Gates, "News and Comment—Teaching Machines in Perspective," *The Elementary School Journal* (Vol. LXII, No. 1, October, 1961), p. 1.

[13] Ikenberry, *op. cit.*

[14] James D. Finn and Elinor Richardson, "The Principal Faces the New Technology," *The National Elementary Principal* (Vol. XL, No. 4, January, 1961), p. 21.

while others are more successful with a different program following the same method.

Some proponents of programed learning believe that the program and the classroom should dovetail, one complementing the other. Still others feel that the program should be so written as to operate almost entirely independently of any instruction by the teacher, who would be free for individual conferences with the students.[15]

Since programed instruction runs the gamut of simple factual materials to complicated enrichment programs for the gifted, and programed textbooks are portable, the assignments could be given for completion in a regular class period or at home. The child works individually at his own speed, motivated by the enjoyment of continuing success as the program unfolds step by step so it would be difficult to name any one best way to use programed instruction.[16]

Whether electrically or manually operated, whether holes are punched, buttons pushed, or statements written, there are basic principles common to all machines.

A program is taken from the library by the student and is inserted in the machine. It consists of thirty or forty statements and questions each of which develops in very small steps the topic being studied. The programed material which has been placed in the machine is reviewed at least twice by the student. If his responses are 100% correct each time, then he may move on to the next lesson and insert a new programme. When he errs, his mistakes are recorded and the particular question comes back until he gets the correct solution. The number of errors he makes in total and for each question are also recorded for his satisfaction and for the teacher's information.[17]

What the teacher does with this information underscores her value as a teacher.

Some programed instruction has been designed to teach an entire course. At Hamilton College, John Blyth and John Jacobson programed a freshman course in logic which they tested. They reported many advantages and no disadvantages.[18]

Eastman Kodak prepared and tested a 70-item course for its employees on how to read the punchings on IBM data cards. The company was amazed to

[15] Foltz, *op. cit.*, p. 5.

[16] Roy E. Larsen *et al.* "Efficient Use of Teachers' Time and Talent," *Decade of Experiment 1951-1961* (New York: The Fund for the Advancement of Education, April, 1961), p. 63.

[17] Hector Trout, "Push Button Teaching Is Here!" *The Saskatchewan Bulletin* (Vol. XXVII, No. 4, April, 1961), p. 23.

[18] Foltz, *op. cit.*, p. 9.

find that in a very short time the employees mastered a technique which had previously resisted their best teaching efforts.[19]

In the "Appendix A" of *The World of Teaching Machines* there are fifty-three annotated academic programs listed.[20]

It is obvious to any educator that the machine is only as good as the program fed to it and that the machine has limitations. "It may have more patience than a teacher, but when an answer is wrong, it can't talk the problem through with the user and help him gain the insight needed to move forward with understanding." [21] Skinner points out:

The machine itself, of course, does not teach. It simply brings the student into contact with the person who composed the material it presents. It is a labor-saving device because it can bring one programmer into contact with an indefinite number of students. This may suggest mass production, but the effect upon each student is surprisingly like that of a private tutor.[22]

The findings of an opinion poll based on a four per cent proportional sampling of 16,000 school administrators in continental United States which brought a forty-two per cent response indicates that although self-teaching devices and programed instructional materials will be used increasingly in the schools, they will supplement rather than replace textbooks in the future.[23]

To those who ask, "How do we know that programed instruction will work?" the administrator can answer prosaically, "We won't unless we try it."

Studies at Harvard (Skinner and James Holland), the New York Collegiate School (Komoski) and in the Roanoke, Virginia (Dr. Allan Calvin) and Western Pennsylvania public school systems (Lumsdaine and Klaus of the American Institute of Research) indicate that learning time is decreased on the average of 50 per cent. Several of these programs have been tested for periods of a year or more. The results may be considered statistically accurate and free from any "novelty effect." [24]

Viewed against the backdrop of the current knowledge of the nature of learning, programed instruction appears to measure up to the important following principles:

19 *Ibid.*
20 *Ibid.*, pp. 71-76.
21 Frazier, *op. cit.*, p. 73.
22 A. A. Lumsdaine, "The Development of Teaching Machines and Programmed Self-Instruction," *New Teaching Aids for the American Classroom* (Stanford: The Institute for Communication Research, 1960), p. 146.
23 "Use of Teaching Machines Will Grow, But They Won't Replace Textbooks," *The Nation's Schools* (Vol. LXVIII, No. 6, December, 1961), p. 60.
24 Foltz, *op. cit.*, p. 7.

1. The active participation of the student must be enlisted at each step along the way.

2. The material must be arranged and presented in a rational and cumulative sequence.

3. Swift and effective tutorial appraisal must reply to each step the student masters.[25]

The effectiveness of any machine will depend upon how well the material is organized for presentation. It has long been the pattern of administrators to maintain an educational smörgasbord of media. Tested and effective programs will have their place to be chosen according to the needs of the individual student.

In reply to whose who observe a similarity between programed learning and workbooks, the administrator might point out that "a program is a self-contained sequence of instructional items which can be presented to individual students under controlled conditions. It is designed specifically to teach material and is repeatedly tested and revised until it gives consistent and acceptable results. The items in a standard workbook provide practice on material taught elsewhere. A workbook is not designed to do a teaching job." [26]

Many teachers will recall their own pioneering days when they planned and organized material which they duplicated and distributed to the various groups in the class. This resembled programed instruction material and differed from the regular type of workbook material in many instances.

Lloyd E. Homme maintains "the only really definitive test of the difference between a workbook and a program is, in the final analysis, the differences in the effects they have on student behavior." [27] It would be an interesting point of research to find the similarities between the two.

There are more than one hundred programs underway at the present time. Colleges, universities, foundations, government agencies, and the United States Navy and Air Force have all done extensive work in testing and experimentation, and yet programed instruction is still in its infancy.[28]

In the spring of 1960 some 3,000 self-tutoring frames were used in book form by fifteen high schools in the Pittsburgh area. Comparing the performance of this group with the control group which did not use the self-tutoring materials for the physics course, "the test results demonstrated that the use of the material made a significant contribution to the student's achievement." [29]

[25] Donald A. Cook, "Programmed Learning: A Revolution in Instruction," *Newsletter Graduate Faculties* (Columbia University, November, 1960) p. 2.

[26] Wells Hively, "Inside Opinion," *Programed Instruction* (Vol. I, No. 3, December, 1961), p. 1.

[27] Lloyd E. Homme, "Inside Opinion," *Programed Instruction* (Vol. I, No. 3, December, 1961), p. 2.

[28] Foltz, *op. cit.*, pp. 1-12.

[29] A. A. Lumsdaine, "Teaching Machines and Auto-Instructional Programs," *Educational Leadership* (Vol. XVIII, No. 5, February, 1961), p. 277.

The Carnegie Foundation issued a $50,000 grant to Robert J. Weiss and Edward J. Green of Dartmouth to carry on a three-year experiment with machine teaching to be conducted on the graduate level. To date the experiment indicates that students can proceed at their own rate, that examinations and testing are a rewarding and learning experience, and that the fear of falling behind relieves much anxiety otherwise experienced by many individuals.[30]

A similar experiment is being carried out at Dartmouth on the undergraduate level in the German Department under Hans W. Weber and Herbert R. Sensenig. It is reported that the students indicated a favorable reception of the machine teaching, but they preferred to use class time for discussion and student-teacher contact and do the machine programs for homework supplement.[31] . . .

Our present intelligence and aptitude tests will need redesigning in order to measure performance on the teaching machines. The types of learning difficulties that are revealed in operating "the teaching machines will not lend themselves to diagnosis by means of the presently available psychological tests." [32]

In spite of the cooperative efforts of researchers and administrators the latter is faced with the futurama of administrative implications resultant from technological development. One can envision a different type of school construction with the learning laboratory equipped with teaching machines, closed circuit T.V., the library, and science laboratories at the heart of the school; the classrooms located in the wings of the building; the office wired for electronic recording devices; the lecture rooms designed for group work to strengthen weaknesses. The personnel of the future schools boast of programmers, master teachers, technicians, guidance counselors, psychologists, clerks, electricians, maintenance men, and statisticians all working cooperatively for efficient teaching. The cost of buildings, equipment, and salaries will mount.[33]

The programing process is difficult, time-consuming, and expensive. A good program requires the service of a course specialist, a psychologist with knowledge of programing techniques and some knowledge of the course material, and often special technical personnel. Estimates for the original cost of a program for a single term of work run as high as $175,000. In preparing a physics program of the Skinnerian type it was found that it took between one half to three quarters of an hour of professional work per item. Between 30,000 and 40,000 items were necessary for the full term's course and a total of 1,500 professional man-hours of work were required.

Non-Skinnerian programing is expensive also. The branching programs, although they cover more ground in each step, require so many extra branch-

[30] "A Search for a Faster and Better Way to Learn," *Dartmouth Alumni Magazine Reprint,* January, 1961.
[31] *Ibid.*
[32] Arthur R. Jensen, "Teaching Machines and Individual Differences," *Automated Teaching Bulletin* (Vol. I, No. 3, Summer, 1960), p. 13.
[33] Trout, *op. cit.,* pp. 24-25.

ing items that the cost of preparation is as high or higher than Skinnerian programs.[34]

Even after all these problems are solved and all the answers to the questions raised in this paper given, the administrator will be challenged with a continuing volley of inquires.

What becomes of people whose function in the business world is displaced by machines? How does man adjust to a society where many of the tasks which he considered the unique province of human intelligence are performed faster and better by machines, whose impulses for action approach the speed of light as compared to the neural impulses with their relatively low 220 miles per second passage? How do we impress upon our children the importance of free will when confronted with machines which, at first glance, seem to have the element of free choice? To quote M. I. T. President Julius Stratton, "The world into which we were born is gone: we have little or no idea of the world into which our children will grow to maturity. It is this rate of change, even more than the change itself, that I see as the dominant factor of our time." [35]

It seems imperative that Catholic administrators get in on the ground floor so that they will be in a position of influence and make their voices heard in "shaping the philosophy of the age of the machine." [36] Whatever may be the thinking of any administrator in the field of programed instruction he must answer this provocative question, "Will we abandon the field to the programists or guide our children to the knowledge of the compatability of science with a belief in God?" [37]

[34] Foltz, *op. cit.*, p. 26.
[35] E. W. Brotherton, "Teaching Automation on the Secondary Level," *Catholic Business Education Review* (Vol. XII, No. 4, June, 1961), p. 42.
[36] *Ibid.*, p. 43.
[37] *Ibid.*

A team-teaching program in history

Brother Norbert Brockman, S.C.

*In order to make the best possible use of their
teachers and at the same time give their students the
richest possible opportunities to learn, a number of
schools have experimented with team teaching.
Brother Norbert Brockman, a Professor of Political
Science at the University of Dayton, would
encourage more schools to do so. In the next article,
he describes a team-teaching program at a
Covington, Kentucky, Catholic high school for boys.*

Among the newer approaches to teaching that have developed in recent years,
one of the most fruitful and promising is that of team teaching. Although teaching teams have been established on a number of bases in various situations, the
essential characteristics are the same: two or more persons undertake to teach a
variable group, that is, one which can vary in size from day to day and from one
learning situation to another.

During the past school year, the author was head of the Social Studies Department at Covington Catholic High School, a medium-sized boys' high school
in Northern Kentucky. The purpose of this article is to describe the team program
for freshman world history which was used there and to answer the question that
the participants so often were asked about the program: Does it *really* work?
The article should, as well, answer some other practical questions regarding
scheduling, class preparation, and student activities. As will be obvious, the author is convinced of the usefulness of team teaching not only for the large, multi-
sectional high school, but also for the smaller, more restricted one.

Specific Goals, Plans

Without spending much time in theorizing, it should be remarked that it is very
important to appreciate the advantages of the team method. Unless the teachers

Reprinted with permission from *The Catholic Educator*, 33:817 ff., May, 1963.

involved have specific goals in mind and specific plans for using the team approach to solve them, team teaching will not be able to contribute vitally to the educational program of the school. In Covington, the goal was a need to offer enriched learning opportunities for talented students in a school too small to have an honors class. At the same time, and most important, it was strongly felt that the good, but not brilliant youngsters deserved the opportunity and challenge of more and better work than a single teacher could possibly prepare in an ordinary situation.

Student Group and Staff

A teaching team need not follow any rigid pattern, although it includes a master teacher who coordinates and directs the program. Two teams, in English and Spanish, were described by a panel from Chaminade High School, Dayton, Ohio, at the 1962 meeting of the National Catholic Education Association. One team was composed entirely of experienced teachers; the other had several teachers and two teachers' aides. The possibilities are quite varied. In Covington, the team consisted of the author as director and two student teachers, who used the experience to fulfill their university and state requirements for student teaching. In addition we had the cooperation of an excellent librarian, which is a key consideration.

The students were high-school freshmen. There were sixty-seven in the group, ranging in ability from those with very high academic ability to the very average. Although there were no slow learners taking part, about six of the students could be classified as poor students due to poor motivation for study. Class size was determined simply by grouping two of our normal classes together, and could have been much larger without undue difficulty. The class was divided into eight groups of eight or nine students each, the grouping being based on ability and previous performance. Since the program was started only after the school year had begun, this sorting out of students was not difficult. In a program starting with the beginning of the school year, this would probably wait for a few weeks, at least.

Facilities

The program made use of several classrooms for small group activities. The main center of work, however, was a large room seating seventy-five students, used during the rest of the school day as a study hall. The front wall was painted a flat white for use instead of a movie screen for visual aids. A portable stage with a blackboard and desk ordinarily sat in front of this wall.

The students had the use of the library during the class period. Usually the boys from the history program were the only students present. The librarian, who had a copy of the printed program, supervised the readings and made himself generally available for library assistance.

Each student had a textbook and kept a notebook. The teachers kept a file of standardized tests, special assignments, and maps. Along with wall maps, these were the only materials used. There is, of course, opportunity here for greater variety.

The Program

The program was based on a distribution of activities. Lectures alternated with group discussions, audio-visual demonstrations, library periods, and supervised activities. Each team member acted as discussion leader for one or more of the small groups mentioned above. That teacher also corrected all assignments and other papers for each boy in his groups. It was felt that this system would give the students a greater feeling of consistency. All papers were returned after grading, usually with comments.

The lectures were given to the entire class together. Each of the three team members presented the material for the topics on which he was most competent, although the largest number were given by the director of the program. Each lecture was usually discussed by the teachers before class, and some effort was made to have a unity of interpretation of the material. The English Department tested the students with the S.R.A. Reading Laboratory exercises on note-taking, and found them generally superior. After a short while, we stopped checking student notebooks because the youngsters had discovered that good notes were essential to good marks, and did not slack off. In several cases the teacher presented a lecture according to a prepared outline, a copy of which was given to each student. We discovered that with an outline, the students took poorer and less complete notes than otherwise, and we abandoned this practice. The teachers stressed strong organization to help in note-taking. Questions were not discouraged during the lectures, but were not very frequent, due perhaps to the fact of the size of the group.

Organized on Two-week Units

The program was organized on two-week units, and every two weeks each group had a period for a discussion on a topic for which they had prepared. Each topic was broken down with several questions which the students could look up. In addition, they had a brief list of suggested readings which they were to investigate during their library periods. For most boys, this was their first contact with critical reading. A few had to be shown what the index to their textbook was for when they began. Soon, however, they became adept at using the library materials so that they would have something to contribute in the discussion. The discussions were graded, and since each group had been chosen by ability, general participation was no problem. Since the questions accompanying the discussion topic were quite specific, the students could usually find the material without assistance, although the librarian was always available for help. About one week before a group had a discussion scheduled, we tried to give it a period in the library to prepare.

Periodically, the entire group assembled in the lecture hall for an audio-visual demonstration. This was never done for entertainment purposes, and was always followed up with an assignment on the material covered. Using an opaque projector, we had a demonstration on Renaissance art, and another on medieval architecture. A tape recorder was used to present a series of readings and musical selections on the Romantic Movement. Whenever possible, we tried to show the relation of cultural history to the political and economic events being studied. A larger school, with an art teacher, for example, would be able to exploit this more fully than we were. Being in a small city with a limited library collection, we were not able to obtain movies that we thought of enough value to use, and so we limited their use to one film, on the Second World War period. Again, a larger school in a larger city would have greater opportunities along these lines.

Other Groups Occupied

The question naturally arises as to what the groups not having discussions or library research periods were doing. On an ordinary day, two groups would be in discussion periods, and one in the library. The others, under the supervision of the remaining member of the team, remained in the lecture hall to work on various activities. Since the lectures tended to be concerned with broad issues in history, although detail was not lacking, the students were responsible for filling in the details through these supervised activities. This proved itself simple and effective. Using their notes and textbooks, each boy was to complete one of a variety of papers prepared for the day's lesson. Some of these were charts which the student had to complete, such as one asking for the names, discoveries, and nationalities of the major explorers of the Sixteenth Century. A set of standardized tests, *not* written for our textbook, were also used. The boys could usually complete the objective-style material within one fifty-five minute period. Periodically, we sprang a surprise test to see if this method was getting results, and we found that generally, the students were learning factual material very satisfactorily.

The periods of supervised work were used to return previous student assignments, and this gave the teacher the opportunity to talk over with some students particular problems he had in finding material, in expressing ideas in essay tests, etc. These periods were also used for administering tests and book-reports, and in reviewing material with the poorer students, who would be placed in the back of the hall for that purpose.

Covington Catholic High School operates on the nine-week quarter system. In one nine-week period, the following activities occupied each group: lecture presentations, 24 periods; discussions, 4; library periods, 2; audio-visual demonstrations, 2; book report, 1; tests, 4; supervised activities, 7.

A Typical Unit

In order to show the operation of the program, the schedule of a typical unit of material is given below. Each nine weeks, a full schedule was given each student, so that he could plan his work.

Monday, lecture: "Causes of the Protestant Revolt."

Tuesday, discussion, Groups D & E. Library, Group A. Others worked out a project on the major Protestant reformers and their theories.

Wednesday, lecture: The Theology and Ideas of the Early Protestants."

Thursday, discussion, G & H. Library, B. Groups A, D, & E did the project done by the others on Tuesday; C & F (the advanced groups) had a special assignment.

Friday, lecture: "The Religious Wars and Catholic Reformation."

Monday, lecture: "The Rise of Bourbon France."

Tuesday, discussions, A & C. Library, D. Test, others.

Wednesday, discussions, F & B. Library, E. Test, A,C,D, G & H had special work (review for G, a group of poorer students).

Thursday, Washington's Birthday, holiday.

Friday, lecture: "The Continental Dynasties."

Of the five lectures given in this period, the director of the program gave two, and the others were presented by the student teachers. The students had three homework assignments in the period besides the preparation for their discussions. Two of the assignments were maps, one on the religious conflict and another on the continental powers of the Seventeenth Century. The third assignment was taken from a series of essay questions given out at the beginning of the quarter as part of the outline. This assignment was concerned with the Catholic Reform and the Council of Trent. In addition, the students were preparing a biographical sketch on a person from this general period, chosen by themselves. This was due the week after this unit (Henry VIII proved a very popular subject!).

Discussion Topic

The discussion topic during these two weeks was the beliefs of the early Protestants. Two chapters of Philip Hughes' *A Popular History of the Reformation* and three documentary selections from Thomas Neill's *Building of the Human City* were suggested on the outline. In addition, the history reserve shelf in the library contained three volumes of readings from Church history, six textbooks other than those we were using in class, and about a dozen books that were pertinent. Because of the obvious lack of background of freshmen, only Catholic sources were used.

The discussion questions were as follows:

1) What did Luther mean by "justification by faith"?

2) What is predestination? What is the Protestant notion of this? What is the Catholic idea?

3) What did the Protestants think of the sacraments? How did Luther and others disagree on the Eucharist?

4) What abuses existed in the Church at this time? Did the Protestant Revolt solve any of these problems?

5) What changes did the Council of Trent bring about?

6) Why was the faith of the common people weak at this time?

7) Do you think that Protestantism shares the same ideas today as its early founders had?

Besides preparing by reading and studying their own notes from the lectures, the freshman religion teacher gave some time to the matter of this discussion, especially question two.

One question is notable by its absence—there is no mention of the Protestant doctrine of Original Sin. Each discussion had such a missing question, to test the thoroughness of the students' preparation. In five discussions, the question came up spontaneously, which was, to say the least, a gratifying surprise to the teachers. In two groups, the subject had to be introduced, but the students had made themselves familiar with it. In only one group were they totally unaware that the Protestants had had anything to say on the subject. In short, we were quite satisfied that the students were doing the suggested readings, and more.

The facet of the team approach that strikes the teacher accustomed to the traditional classroom situation is its great flexibility. Personal contact with the students is accentuated rather than lessened, and it is possible to do so many more things. Possibly because of the greater variety of activities and the greater personal attention, the students were pleased with the program. Grades improved noticeably, especially among the poorly motivated students. In other schools and other situations, needless to say, almost endless variations can be played on this theme of draining every opportunity of its educational value.

The constant change of activities does tend to have the students lose contact with their standing in the course. "How am I doing?" was a constant question. We tried to answer it regularly by evaluation with each boy during the periods of supervised activities.

Our experience (and other team programs have had the same) was that the quality of the explanations and lectures was far better under this system. Each teacher had more time to prepare, he had as well the stimulation of discussions with the other members of the team, and the stimulus of having several teachers sitting in on his lectures.

One final consideration: team teaching is new and attractive. While it eases up on some of the work of teaching, by spreading out the correcting chores, for instance, it does not emancipate the teacher from work. Preparation is a demanding task. The teacher who wants to stay a chapter ahead of the students will be lost. He will find himself forced to think through problems in a way he may not have in a long time. The teacher will find that team teaching produces an eagerness in his students that he never suspected was there. At the same time he cannot become beguiled by the experimental nature of the program. It fits into the school's total educational plan only if there are clear goals in mind. In short, it has to produce results. The author is convinced that it does.